2015-2016 EDITION

AMERICAN GOVERNMENT AND POLITICS TODAY

The Essentials

Barbara A. Bardes
University of Cincinnati

Mack C. Shelley II
Iowa State University

Steffen W. Schmidt
Iowa State University

CENGAGE
Learning·

Australia • Brazil • Mexico • Singapore • United Kingdom • United States

CENGAGE
Learning·

American Government and Politics Today: The Essentials, 2015–2016 Edition

Barbara A. Bardes
Mack C. Shelley II
Steffen W. Schmidt

Product Team Manager: Carolyn Merrill

Senior Content Developers:
Rebecca Green, Anais Wheeler

Associate Content Developer:
Amy Bither

Product Assistant: Abigail Hess

Senior Media Developer:
Laura Hildebrand

Marketing Manager: Valerie Hartman

Senior Content Project Manager:
Ann Borman

Senior Art Director: Linda May

Manufacturing Planner: Fola Orekoya

Intellectual Property Analyst:
Alexandra Ricciardi

Intellectual Property Project Manager:
Betsy Hathaway

Production Service & Compositor:
Lachina Publishing Services

Interior and Cover Designer:
Studio Montage

Cover Image credit: Vote bumper
sticker: Jeffrey Coolidge/Photodisc/
Getty Images; woman using digital
tablet: Alejandro Rivera/Getty
Images

Interior Design credits: 2014 Elections:
©iStockphoto.com/manley099;
Beyond Our Borders: Leroy Francis/
hemis.fr/Getty Images; Which Side
Are You On? White Packert/The
Image Bank/Getty Images; How
You Can Make a Difference: John
Burdumy/Moment/Getty Images

For product information and technology assistance, contact us at
Cengage Learning Customer & Sales Support, 1-800-354-9706

For permission to use material from this text or product,
submit all requests online at **cengage.com/permissions**
Further permissions questions can be emailed to
permissionrequest@cengage.com

Library of Congress Control Number: 2014953623

ISBN-13: 978-1-285-85315-4

ISBN-10: 1-285-85315-6

Text Only ISBN: 978-1-285-85886-9

Cengage Learning
20 Channel Center Street
Boston, MA 02210
USA

Cengage Learning is a leading provider of customized learning solutions with
office locations around the globe, including Singapore, the United Kingdom,
Australia, Mexico, Brazil, and Japan. Locate your local office at **www.cengage
.com/global.**

Cengage Learning products are represented in Canada by Nelson Education, Ltd.

To learn more about Cengage Learning Solutions, visit **www.cengage.com.**

Purchase any of our products at your local college store or at our preferred
online store **www.cengagebrain.com.**

Printed in the United States of America
Print Number: 01   Print Year: 2014

Brief Contents

Contents

MindTap™

1. To get started, navigate to: www.cengagebrain.com and select "Register a Product".

A new screen will appear prompting you to add a Course Key. A Course Key is a code given to you by your instructor - this is the first of two codes you will need to access MindTap. Every student in your course section should have the same Course Key.

2. Enter the Course Key and click "Register".

If you are accessing MindTap through your school's Learning Management System such as BlackBoard or Desire2Learn, you may be redirected to use your Course Key/Access Code there. Follow the prompts you are given and feel free to contact support if you need assistance.

3. Confirm your course information above, and proceed to the log in portion below.

If you have a CengageBrain username and password, enter it under "Returning Students" and click "Login". If this is your first time, register under "New Students" and click "Create a New Account".

4. Now that you are logged in, you can access the course for free by selecting "Start Free Trial" for 20 days, or enter in your Access Code.

Your Access Code is unique to you and acts as payment for MindTap. You may have received it with your book or purchased separately in the bookstore or at **CengageBrain.com**. Enter it and click "Register".

NEED HELP?

For CengageBrain Support: Login to **Support.Cengage.com**. Call **866-994-2427** or access our **24/7 Student Chat!**
Or access the **First Day of School PowerPoint Presentation** found at cengagebrain.com.

to Instructors...

The fundamental theme of *American Government and Politics Today: The Essentials, 2015–2016 Edition* continues to be **the importance of participating in active citizenship, emphasizing critical thinking about political issues, and encouraging students to take action and become involved in the political process.** Whether the topic is health care reform implementation, Supreme Court rulings, or taxation, we constantly strive to involve students in the analysis. Our goal is to make sure that politics is not just an abstract process, but a very human enterprise. We emphasize how different outcomes can affect students' civil rights and liberties, employment opportunities, and economic welfare. To make sure students understand the link between themselves and the subject matter they are reading, new *Why Should You Care about . . . ?* features grab students' attention while they are reading the materials. We further encourage interaction with the political system by ending each chapter with a feature titled *How You Can Make a Difference*, which shows students how to become politically involved and why it is important that they do so. *Which Side Are You On?* features challenge students to find the connection between a current controversy and their personal positions. And to help students think critically about the world around them and spark discussion in your classroom, we pose **questions for critical analysis** with every boxed feature, table, chart, exhibit, and photo.

New to This Edition

We have made numerous changes to this volume for the 2015–2016 Edition. We have rewritten the text as necessary, added many new features, and updated the book to reflect the events of the past two years. For a detailed list of changes, please contact your Cengage learning consultant.

- Because we know that students respond to up-to-date information about political events, we incorporate compelling, thought-provoking current examples throughout. We also include the results of the November 2014 elections and analyze how these results will affect political processes at all levels of government. In each **new *2014 Elections*** feature, we place the election results in the context of the chapter's subject matter.

- The 2015–2016 Edition now includes **a separate Chapter 10 on *The Media*.** Because the new media have become so important, we felt it necessary to devote an entire chapter to this topic. We look at content providers and aggregators. We look at the importance of media in campaigns. We examine the importance of blogs versus magazines and discuss political blog sites and their biases. Net neutrality is an important topic in this chapter. Finally, we examine the influences and biases of talk radio.

- **More demographics material** is included throughout, particularly in Chapter 1, which presents material on positive and negative trends, such as unemployment and inequality on the one hand, and falling crime and teen pregnancy rates on the other.

- **Major updates to the content** have been made with respect to public opinion, interest groups, modern political parties, social media in politics, and the Obama legacy. The chapters on Domestic and Economic Policy and Foreign Policy have been completely updated and modernized. The text reflects the current events that most interest you and your students, including recent Supreme Court rulings and state legislation on same-sex marriage, marijuana, and the administration of Obamacare; privacy and recent NSA revelation coverage; current civil rights issues; foreign policy coverage of Syria and Ukraine; and more!

MindTap

MindTap is here to simplify your workload as an instructor, organize and immediately grade your students' assignments, and allow you to customize your course as you see fit. Through deep-seated integration with your Learning Management System (LMS), grades are easily exported and analytics are pulled with just the click of a button. MindTap provides you with a platform to easily add in current events videos and RSS feeds from national or local news sources. Looking to incorporate more recent and late-breaking news into the course? Add in our KnowNow American Government Blog link for weekly updated news coverage and pedagogy.

Sincerely,
Barbara A. Bardes, Mack C. Shelley II, Steffen W. Schmidt

to Students...

Many of the congressional races in the 2014 elections appeared crucial. Would the Republicans retain control of the House and perhaps regain control of the Senate? As it turned out, the Republicans indeed gained control of the Senate. Following the Louisiana runoffs, their margin was 54 seats to 46 for the Democrats. The Republicans improved their margin in the House by 15 seats and did very well in state races. In short, 2014 was a Republican year.

You'll learn about all of these developments and more in the 2015–2016 Edition of *American Government and Politics Today: The Essentials*.

Our hope is that this book inspires you to join the exciting process of being an active, informed citizen. Your American Government course and the material you'll read within will give you the knowledge you'll need to understand our political system and develop well-informed opinions on the current issues and controversies you'll encounter in your daily life. We strive to highlight how American government and politics directly affect you in every chapter. We also suggest easy ways that you can take action in your community and become involved in the political process.

Special Features

- *Take Action: A Guide to Political Participation* is filled with resources and suggestions to help students stay informed and get involved in the political process.

- Thought-provoking *What If . . . ?, Beyond Our Borders*, and *Did You Know?* features help you understand key concepts and current events as well as develop a more informed and global perspective.

- New *Why You Should Care about . . . ?* marginal features demonstrate why the topic at hand directly affects you and matters in your life.

- *Which Side Are You On?* sections challenge you to take a stand on controversial issues.

- *How You Can Make a Difference* features conclude each chapter with ways in which you can become actively involved in American politics.

- *2014 Elections* features highlight the important impact of the 2014 midterm elections and include an analysis of the campaigns and election results.

- **Critical-thinking questions** now accompany all boxed features, figures, tables, and photo captions, helping you apply and analyze the information presented.

- **Learning Outcomes** appear in each chapter opener, correlate to each major section to help you target your reading, and are revisited in each **Chapter Summary** and end-of-chapter **Quiz** to help you assess your comprehension and master the book's key concepts. Every chapter also concludes with **key terms** and a list of **additional print and media resources**. And the book is now seamlessly integrated with **MindTap**, with marginal icons throughout directing you to a variety of online interactive activities that will help you test yourself on the book's Learning Outcomes.

The Benefits of Using MindTap

For you as a student, the benefits of using MindTap with this book are endless. With automatically graded practice quizzes and activities, an easily navigated learning path, and an interactive eBook, you will be able to test yourself inside and outside of the classroom with ease. The accessibility of current events coupled with interactive media makes the content fun and engaging. On your computer, phone, or tablet, MindTap is there when you need it, giving you easy access to flashcards, quizzes, readings, and assignments.

Sincerely,
Barbara A. Bardes, Mack C. Shelley II, Steffen W. Schmidt

Resources

Students

Access your American Government and Politics Today: The Essentials *resources by visiting* **www.cengagebrain.com/shop/isbn/9781285853154**

If you purchased MindTap or CourseReader access with your book, enter your access code and click "**Register.**" You can also purchase the book's resources here separately through the "**Study Tools**" tab, or access the free companion Web site through the "**Free Materials**" tab.

Instructors

Access your American Government and Politics Today: The Essentials *resources via* **www.cengage.com/login**.

Log in using your Cengage Learning single sign-on username and password, or create a new instructor account by clicking on "**New Faculty User**" and following the instructions.

American Government and Politics Today: The Essentials, 2015–2016 Edition—*Text Only Edition*

ISBN: 978-1-285-85886-9

This copy of the book does not come bundled with MindTap.

MindTap for *American Government and Politics Today: The Essentials, 2015–2016 Edition*

Instant Access Code: 978-1-305-07847-5

Printed Access Card: 978-1-285-85885-2

MindTap for American Government is a fully online, personalized learning experience built upon Cengage Learning content. MindTap combines student learning tools—readings, multimedia, activities, and assessments—into a singular Learning Path that guides students through their course. Through a wealth of activities written to learning outcomes, it provides students with ample opportunities to check themselves for understanding, while also providing faculty and students alike with a clear way to measure and assess student progress. Faculty can use MindTap as a turnkey solution or customize by adding YouTube videos, RSS feeds, or their own documents directly within the eBook or within each chapter's Learning Path. The product can be used fully online with its interactive eBook for *American Government and Politics Today: The Essentials*, or in conjunction with the printed text.

Instructor Companion Web Site for *American Government and Politics Today: The Essentials, 2015–2016 Edition*

ISBN: 978-1-285-86550-8

This Instructor Companion Web site is an all-in-one multimedia online resource for class preparation, presentation, and testing. Accessible through **cengage.com/login** with your faculty account, you will find available for download: book-specific Microsoft® Power-Point® presentations; a Test Bank compatible with multiple learning management systems; an Instructor's Manual; Microsoft® PowerPoint® Image Slides; and a JPEG Image Library.

The Test Bank, offered in Blackboard, Moodle, Desire2Learn, Canvas, and Angel formats, contains Learning Objective–specific multiple-choice and essay questions for each chapter. Import the test bank into your Learning Management System to edit and manage questions and to create tests.

The Instructor's Manual contains chapter-specific learning objectives, an outline, key terms with definitions, and a chapter summary. Additionally, the Instructor's Manual features a critical-thinking question, lecture-launching suggestion, and an in-class activity for each learning objective.

The Microsoft® PowerPoint® presentations are ready-to-use, visual outlines of each chapter. These presentations are easily customized for your lectures and are offered along with chapter-specific Microsoft® PowerPoint® Image Slides and JPEG Image Libraries. Access the Instructor Companion Web site at **www.cengage.com/login**.

Student Companion Web Site for *American Government and Politics Today: The Essentials, 2015–2016 Edition*

ISBN: 978-1-285-86549-2

This free companion Web site for *American Government and Politics Today: The Essentials, 2015–2016 Edition* is accessible through **cengagebrain.com** and allows students access to chapter-specific interactive learning tools including flashcards, quizzes, glossaries, and more.

Cognero for *American Government and Politics Today: The Essentials, 2015–2016 Edition*

ISBN: 978-1-305-08124-6

Cengage Learning Testing Powered by Cognero is a flexible, online system that allows you to author, edit, and manage test bank content from multiple Cengage Learning solutions, create multiple test versions in an instant, and deliver tests from your LMS, your classroom, or wherever you want. The test bank for *American Government and Politics Today: The Essentials* contains Learning Objective–specific multiple-choice and essay questions for each chapter.

CourseReader

CourseReader for American Government

CourseReader 0-30 Instant Access Code: 978-1-111-47997-8
CourseReader 0-30 Printed Access Card: 978-1-111-47995-4

CourseReader: American Government allows instructors to create your reader, your way, in just minutes. This affordable, fully customizable online reader provides access to thousands of permissions-cleared readings, articles, primary sources, and audio and video selections from the regularly updated Gale research library database. This easy-to-use solution allows you to search for and select just the material you want for your courses. Each selection opens with a descriptive introduction to provide context and concludes with critical-thinking and multiple-choice questions to reinforce key points. CourseReader is loaded with convenient tools like highlighting, printing, note-taking, and downloadable PDFs and MP3 audio files for each reading. CourseReader is the perfect complement to any political science course. It can be bundled with your current textbook, sold alone, or integrated into your learning management system. CourseReader 0-30 allows access to up to 30 selections in the reader. Contact your Cengage learning consultant for details. Students should only purchase CourseReader if assigned by their instructor.

Election 2014 Supplement

ISBN: 978-1-305-50018-1

Written by John Clark and Brian Schaffner, this booklet addresses the 2014 campaigns and elections, with real-time analysis and references.

Acknowledgments

In preparing this 2015–2016 edition of *American Government and Politics Today: The Essentials*, we were the beneficiaries of the expert guidance of a skilled and dedicated team of publishers and editors. We have benefited greatly from the supervision and encouragement given by our Product Team Manager Carolyn Merrill. Rebecca Green, our Senior Content Developer, deserves our thanks for her efforts in coordinating reviews and in many other aspects of project development. We are especially appreciative of the photo research that she undertook for us. We are grateful to our Senior Content Project Manager Ann Borman for her ability to make this project as smooth running and as perfect as is humanly possible.

Our gratitude goes to all of those who worked on the various supplements offered with this text, especially the test bank author, Scott Wallace from Indiana University-Purdue University Indianapolis; the Instructor's Manual author, Tamra Ortgies-Young from Georgia Perimeter College; and Associate Content Developer Amy Bither and Senior Media Developer Laura Hildebrand. We would also like to thank Marketing Manager Valerie Hartman for her tremendous efforts in marketing the text and Product Assistant Abigail Hess for her contributions to this project. We are indebted to Lachina Publishing Services for the accurate and timely composition of this text. Their ability to generate the pages for this text quickly and accurately made it possible for us to meet our ambitious printing schedule.

Many other people helped during the research and editorial stages of this edition. Gregory Scott provided excellent editorial and research assistance from the outset of the project to the end. Susan Bradley's copyediting and Kristi Wiswell's proofreading skills contributed greatly to the book. Roxie Lee served as a coordinator for the flow of manuscript and pages with all of their corrections. We thank her profusely. We also thank Sue Jasin of K&M Consulting for her contributions to the smooth running of the project.

Any errors remain our own. We welcome comments from instructors and students alike. Suggestions that we have received in the past have helped us to improve this text and to adapt it to the changing needs of instructors and students.

Reviewers

We would also like to thank the instructors who have contributed their valuable feedback through reviews of this text:

Pat Andrews, *West Valley College*

Marcos Arandia, *North Lake College*

Sherman Brewer, Jr., *Rutgers University, Newark*

Martyn de Bruyn, *Northeastern Illinois University*

Ann Clemmer, *University of Arkansas at Little Rock*

Beatriz Cuartas, *El Paso Community College*

Jodi Empol, *Montgomery County Community College*

Crystal Garrett, *Georgia Perimeter College, Dunwoody*

Joseph Georges, *El Camino College*

Jack Goodyear, *Dallas Baptist University*

Willie Hamilton, *Mt. San Jacinto College*

Matthew Hansel, *McHenry County College*

Joanne Hopkins-Lucia, *Baker College of Clinton Township*

Frank Ibe, *Wayne County Community College*

Roger Jordan, *Baker College of Flint*

Jon Kelly, *West Valley College*

Thomas R. Kemp, *University of Arkansas at Little Rock*

Kevin Kniess, *Lakeland College*

Linda Lien, *Westwood College, Los Angeles*

Jan McCauley, *Tyler Junior College*

James Mitchell, *California State University, Northridge*

Eric Nobles, *Atlanta Metropolitan College*

Tamra Ortgies-Young, *Georgia Perimeter College*

Lisa Perez-Nichols, *Austin Community College*

William Parent, *San Jacinto College, Central Campus*

Travis N. Ridout, *Washington State University*

Ron Robinson, *Schoolcraft College*

Steven R. Rolnick, *Western Connecticut State University*

Margaret E. Scranton, *University of Arkansas at Little Rock*

Shyam Sriram, *Georgia Perimeter College*

Judy Tobler, *NorthWest Arkansas Community College*

June Trudel, *California State University, San Marcos*

Scott Wallace, *Indiana University-Purdue University Indianapolis*

Robert Whitaker, *Hudson Valley Community College*

About the Authors

Barbara A. Bardes

Barbara A. Bardes is professor emerita of political science and former dean of Raymond Walters College at the University of Cincinnati. She received her B.A. and M.A. from Kent State University. After completing her Ph.D. at the University of Cincinnati, she held faculty positions at Mississippi State University and Loyola University in Chicago. She returned to Cincinnati, her hometown, as a college administrator. She has also worked as a political consultant and directed polling for a research center.

Bardes has written articles on public opinion and foreign policy and on women and politics. She has authored *Thinking about Public Policy; Declarations of Independence: Women and Political Power in Nineteenth-Century American Fiction;* and *Public Opinion: Measuring the American Mind* (with Robert W. Oldendick).

Bardes's home is located in a very small hamlet in Kentucky called Rabbit Hash, famous for its 150-year-old general store. Her hobbies include traveling, gardening, needlework, and antique collecting.

Mack C. Shelley II

Mack C. Shelley II is professor of political science and statistics at Iowa State University. After receiving his bachelor's degree from American University in Washington, D.C., he completed graduate studies at the University of Wisconsin–Madison, where he received a master's degree in economics and a Ph.D. in political science. He taught for two years at Mississippi State University before arriving at Iowa State in 1979.

Shelley has published numerous articles, books, and monographs on public policy. From 1993 to 2002, he served as elected co-editor of the *Policy Studies Journal.* His published books include *The Permanent Majority: The Conservative Coalition in the United States Congress; Biotechnology and the Research Enterprise* (with William F. Woodman and Brian J. Reichel); *American Public Policy: The Contemporary Agenda* (with Steven G. Koven and Bert E. Swanson); *Redefining Family Policy: Implications for the 21st Century* (with Joyce M. Mercier and Steven Garasky); and *Quality Research in Literacy and Science Education: International Perspectives and Gold Standards* (with Larry Yore and Brian Hand).

His leisure time includes traveling, working with students, and playing with the family dog and cats.

Steffen W. Schmidt

Steffen W. Schmidt is professor of political science at Iowa State University. He grew up in Colombia, South America, and studied in Colombia, Switzerland, and France. He obtained his Ph.D. in public law and government from Columbia University in New York.

Schmidt has published 14 books and more than 130 journal articles. He is also the recipient of numerous prestigious teaching prizes, including the Amoco Award for Lifetime Career Achievement in Teaching and the Teacher of the Year award. He is a pioneer in the design, production, and delivery of Internet courses and a founding member of the American Political Science Association's section on Computers and Multimedia. He is known as "Dr. Politics" for his extensive commentary on U.S. politics in U.S. and international media. He is a weekly blogger for Gannett and comments on CNN en Español and Univision. He is the Chief Political and International Correspondent of the Internet magazine InsiderIowa.com.

Schmidt likes to snow ski, ride hunter jumper horses, race sailboats, and scuba dive.

Career Opportunities: Political Science

Introduction

It is no secret that college graduates are facing one of the toughest job markets in the past fifty years. Despite this challenge, those with a college degree have done much better than those without since the 2008 recession. One of the most important decisions a student has to make is the choice of a major; many consider future job possibilities when making that call. A political science degree is incredibly useful for a successful career in many different fields, from lawyer to policy advocate, pollster to humanitarian worker. Employer surveys reveal that the skills that most employers value in successful employees—critical thinking, analytical reasoning, and clarity of verbal and written communication—are precisely the tools that political science courses should be helping you develop. This brief guide is intended to help spark ideas for what kinds of careers you might pursue with a political science degree and the types of activities you can engage in now to help you secure one of those positions after graduation.

Careers in Political Science

LAW AND CRIMINAL JUSTICE

Do you find that your favorite parts of your political science classes are those that deal with the Constitution, the legal system, and the courts? Then a career in law and criminal justice might be right for you. Traditional jobs in the field range from lawyer or judge to police or parole officer. Since 9/11, there has also been tremendous growth in the area of homeland security, which includes jobs in mission support, immigration, and travel security, as well as prevention and response.

PUBLIC ADMINISTRATION

The many offices of the federal government combined represent one of the largest employers in the United States. Flip to the bureaucracy chapter of this textbook and consider that each federal department, agency, and bureau you see looks to political science majors for future employees. A partial list of such agencies would include the Department of Education, the Department of Health and Human Services, and the Federal Trade Commission. There are also thousands of staffers who work for members of Congress or the Congressional Budget Office, many of whom were political science majors in college. This does not even begin to account for the multitude of similar jobs in state and local governments that you might consider as well.

CAMPAIGNS, ELECTIONS, AND POLLING

Are campaigns and elections the most exciting part of political science for you? Then you might consider a career in the growing industry based around political campaigns. From volunteering and interning to consulting, marketing, and fundraising, there are many opportunities for those who enjoy the competitive and high-stakes electoral arena. For those looking for careers that combine political knowledge with statistical skills, there are careers in public opinion polling. Pollsters work for independent national organizations such as Gallup and YouGov, or as part of news operations and campaigns. For those who are interested in survey methodology there are also a wide variety of non-political career opportunities in marketing and survey design.

INTEREST GROUPS, INTERNATIONAL AND NONGOVERNMENTAL ORGANIZATIONS

Is there a cause that you are especially passionate about? If so, there is a good chance that there are interest groups out there that are working hard to see some progress made on similar issues. Many of the positions that one might find in for-profit companies also exist in their non-profit interest group and nongovernmental organization counterparts, including lobbying and high-level strategizing. Do not forget that there are also quite a few major international organizations—such as the United Nations, the World Health Organization, and the International Monetary Fund—where a degree in political science could be put to good use. While competition for those jobs tends to be fierce, your interest and knowledge about politics and policy will give you an advantage.

FOREIGN SERVICE

Does a career in diplomacy and foreign affairs, complete with the opportunity to live and work abroad, sound exciting for you? Tens of thousands of people work for the State Department, both in Washington, D.C., and in consulates throughout the world. They represent the diplomatic interests of the United States abroad. Entrance into the Foreign Service follows a very specific process, starting with the Foreign Service Officers Test—an exam given three times a year that includes sections on American government, history, economics, and world affairs. Being a political science major is a significant help in taking the FSOT.

GRADUATE SCHOOL

While not a career, graduate school may be the appropriate next step for you after completing your undergraduate degree. Following the academic route, being awarded a Ph.D. or Master's degree in political science could open additional doors to a career in academia, as well as many of the professions mentioned earlier. If a career as a researcher in political science interests you, you should speak with your advisors about continuing your education.

Preparing While Still on Campus

INTERNSHIPS

One of the most useful steps you can take while still on campus is to visit your college's career center in regard to an internship in your field of interest. Not only does it give you a chance to experience life in the political science realm, it can lead to job opportunities later down the road and add experience to your resume.

SKILLS

In addition to your political science classes, there are a few skills any number of which will prove useful as a complement to your degree:

Writing: Like anything else, writing improves with practice. Writing is one of those skills that is applicable regardless of where your career might take you. Virtually every occupation relies on an ability to write cleanly, concisely, and persuasively.

Public Speaking: An oft-quoted 1977 survey showed that public speaking was the most commonly cited fear among respondents. And yet oral communication is a vital tool in the modern economy. You can practice this skill in a formal class setting or through extracurricular activities that get you in front of a group.

Quantitative Analysis: As the Internet aids in the collection of massive amounts of information, the nation is facing a drastic shortage of people with basic statistical skills to interpret and use this data. A political science degree can go hand-in-hand with courses in introductory statistics.

Foreign Language: One skill that often helps a student or future employee stand out in a crowded job market is the ability to communicate in a language other than English. Solidify or set the foundation for your verbal and written foreign language communication skills while in school.

STUDENT LEADERSHIP

One attribute that many employers look for is "leadership potential," which can be quite tricky to indicate on a resume or cover letter. What can help is a demonstrated record of involvement in clubs and organizations, preferably in a leadership role. While many people think immediately of student government, most student clubs allow you the opportunity to demonstrate your leadership skills.

Conclusion

Hopefully, reading this has sparked some ideas on potential future careers. As a next step, visit your college's career placement office, which is a great place to further explore what you have read here. You might also visit your college's alumni office to connect with graduates who are working in your field of interest. Political science opens the door to a lot of exciting careers; have fun exploring the possibilities!

TAKE ACTION

A Guide to Political Participation

It's easy to think of politics as a spectator sport—something that politicians do, pundits analyze, and citizens watch. But there are many ways to get engaged with politics, to interact with the political world and participate in it, and even to effect change.

GET INFORMED

Find Out Where You Fit and What You Know

- You already have some opinions about a variety of political issues. Do you have a sense of where your views place you on the political map? Get a feel for your ideological leanings by taking *The World's Smallest Political Quiz*: **www.theadvocates.org/quiz/**.

- Which Founder Are You? The National Constitutional Center can help you with that. Go to **constitutioncenter .org/foundersquiz/** to discover which Founding Father's personality most resembles your own.

- The U.S. Constitution is an important part of the context in which American politics takes place. Do you know what the Constitution says? Take the *Constitution I.Q. Quiz*: **www.constitutionfacts.com/**. Was your score higher than the national average?

- At the National Constitution Center, you can explore the interactive Constitution and learn more about the provisions in that document: **constitutioncenter .org/**.

© Zurijeta/Shutterstock

- Find out what those who want to become U.S. citizens have to do—and what they have to know. Go to the U.S. Citizenship and Immigration Services Web site at **www.uscis.gov/**. What is involved in applying for citizenship? Take the *Naturalization Self-Test*. How did you do?

Think about How Your Political Views Have Been Shaped

- Giving some thought to how agents of political socialization—your family, your schools, and your peers, for example—have contributed to your political beliefs and attitudes may help you understand why others might *not* share your views on politics. Have some conversations with people in your classes or in your residence hall about the people, institutions, and experiences that influenced the way they view the political world.

- Now explore how your views on political issues compare with those of a majority of Americans. There are a number of good polling sites that report public opinion on a range of topics.

  o The Pew Research Center for the People & the Press conducts monthly polls on politics and policy issues: **www.people-press.org/**.

  o Public Agenda reports poll data and material on major issues: **publicagenda.org/**.

  o The results of recent polls and an archive of past polls can be found at Gallup: **www.gallup.com/**.

  o The Roper Center for Public Opinion Research is a leading archive of data from surveys of public opinion: **www.ropercenter.uconn.edu/**.

  o PollingReport organizes public opinion data from various sources by keyword: **pollingreport.com/**.

News

Keep up with news—print and broadcast. Remember that different news organizations (or media brands) will report the same information in different ways. Don't avoid certain news sources because you think you might not agree with the way they report the news. It's just as important to know how people are talking about issues as it is to know about the issues themselves.

- One of the best ways to get to the source of the news is to get your information from the same place that journalists do. Often they take their cues or are alerted to news events by news agencies like the nonprofit cooperative Associated Press: **ap.org/**.

- Installing a few key apps on your phone or tablet can make all the difference in being informed. Try downloading the Associated Press (AP) app for short updates from news around the world, as they happen. There are tons of other great political apps—some that are fairly polarized, others that are neutral, and still others that are just plain silly.

Blogs

The blogosphere affords views of politics that may be presented differently than the way the mainstream media do it.

- **Shortformblog.com** provides snippets of news and information from the White House and around the world in small, digestible amounts.

Social Media

Staying connected can be as simple as following local, national, or international politics on social media. President Barack Obama, Senator Elizabeth Warren, House Speaker John Boehner, and even the White House have Instagram accounts worth following. Most politicians and political outlets are also on Twitter and Facebook.

Check the Data

- It's not always easy to figure out if what newsmakers are saying is accurate. Politifact, a project of the Tampa Bay Times, is a good place to go to get the facts: **www.politifact.com/**. Check out the Truth-O-Meter, and get it on your smartphone or tablet.

- A project of the Annenberg Public Policy Center, **www.factcheck.org/** is a nonpartisan, nonprofit "consumer advocate" for voters that monitors the factual accuracy of what political players are saying in TV ads, speeches, and interviews.

Keep Up during Election Season

- Project Vote Smart offers information on elections and candidates: **votesmart.org/**.

- Nate Silver's FiveThirtyEight features election analysis, in addition to covering sports and economics: **www.fivethirtyeight.com/**.

- Stay connected to the horse-race aspect of electoral politics by tracking election polls. There are many good sources:

  o For a comprehensive collection of election polls, go to the RealClearPolitics Web site: **realclearpolitics.com/polls/**. RealClearPolitics is a good source for other political news and opinions as well.

  o Polls for U.S. federal elections, including state-by-state polls, can be found at **electoral-vote.com/**.

  o HuffPost Pollster publishes pre-election poll results combined into interactive charts: **elections.huffingtonpost.com/pollster/**. During presidential elections, additional maps and electoral vote counts can be found at HuffPost Politics Election Dashboard.

  o Interactive electoral vote maps are available at 270 to Win: **www.270towin.com/**.

- If you have the opportunity, attend a speech by a candidate you're interested in.

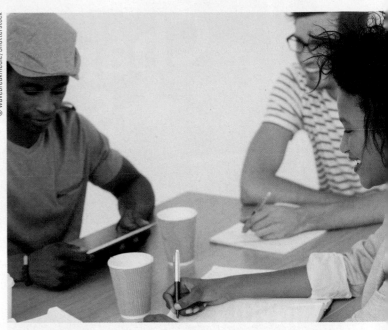

Monitor Money and Influence in Politics

The Center for Responsive Politics Web site is an excellent source for information about who's contributing what amounts to which candidates: **www.opensecrets.org/**. You can also use the lobbying database to identify the top lobbying firms, the agencies most frequently lobbied, and the industries that spend the most on lobbying activities.

Connect with Congress

You can, of course, learn a lot about what's going on in Congress from the Web sites of the House of Representatives and the Senate: **www.house.gov/** and **www.senate.gov/**. Look up the names and contact information for the senators and the representative from your area. If you want your voice to be heard, simply phone or e-mail your senators or your representative. Your chances of influencing your members of Congress will be greater if you can convince others, including your friends and family members, to do likewise. Members of Congress do listen to their constituents and often do act in response to their constituents' wishes. Indeed, next to voting, contacting those who represent you in Congress is probably the most effective way to influence government decision making.

Check GovTrack to find out where your representative and senators fall on the leadership and ideology charts, as well as their most recently sponsored bills and votes on legislation: **www.govtrack.us/**.

GET INVOLVED

Take an Interest in Your Community—However You Define It. Offer to Help.

Every community—large or small—can use energetic people willing to help where there is a need. Local nonprofit agencies serving the homeless, or battered women, or troubled teens often welcome volunteers who are willing to pitch in. You can learn a lot about the public policies that focus on social services while doing some good for others.

The Internet also has abundant resources about nonprofits and charities and how you can get involved:

- **Idealist.org** is a great place to find organizations and events that are looking for employees, interns, and volunteers. Filter by type and area of focus (women, disaster relief, animals, etc.) to find a cause that fits you.

- **Tinyspark.org** is a watchdog for nonprofits and charity organizations. It highlights individuals and groups that are doing good things in communities and around the globe and checks on those who may not be doing as much good as you'd think. Tinyspark also has a podcast.

- **Charitynavigator.org** is another tool for checking on charities. It reports on charities in terms of how much of their donations go to the cause, which charities are in the red, which are worth promoting, and the like—it's kind of like *opensecrets.org* for charities.

Design Your Own Ways to Take Action

- Are there people on your campus who, because of disability or recent injury, need someone to help carry belongings, open doors, or push wheelchairs? Start a network to match those who need assistance and those who want to help.

- Do you want to raise awareness about an issue? Is there a cause that you think needs attention? Talk with friends. Find out if they share your concerns. Turn your discussions into a blog. Create videos of events you think are newsworthy and share them online. Sign or start a petition.

Join a Group on Campus

You see flyers promoting groups and recruiting members posted all over campus—in the student center, in the residence halls, in classroom buildings. Chances are, there's a group organized around something you're interested in or care about.

Maybe it's an organization that works to bring clean water to remote parts of the world. Perhaps it's an organization that works to foster tolerance on campus. The American Civil Liberties Union may have a chapter on your campus. The American Red Cross may be there, too. You'll find College Republicans, College Democrats, groups organized around race or culture, groups that go on alternative spring break trips to give direct service to communities in need, service organizations of all kinds, groups that serve to create community among culturally underrepresented students, and groups that care about the environment. The list goes on and on.

If you have an interest that isn't represented by the groups on your campus, start your own. Your college or university has an office of campus life (or something similar) that can help you navigate the process for establishing a student organization.

Remember, too, that there are hundreds of political interest groups with national reach. Check out their Web sites to see if you want to join.

Vote (But First You Have to Register)

- You can learn about the laws governing voting in your state—and all of the others—by going to the Web site of the National Conference of State Legislatures and its link to Voter Identification Requirements: **www .ncsl.org/research/elections-and-campaigns /voter-id/**.

- Register: Enter "register to vote in [your state]" in a search engine. The office in your state that administers voting and elections (in some states it's the office of the secretary of state, in others it might be the State Board of Elections) will have a Web site that outlines the steps you will need to follow. If you need to vote absentee, you'll find out how to do that here, too.

- If you want to view a sample ballot to familiarize yourself with what you'll be looking at when you go to the polls, you will probably be able to view one online. Just enter "sample ballot" in a search engine. Your local election board, the League of Women Voters, or your district library often post a sample ballot online.

- Vote: Familiarize yourself with the candidates and issues before you go to the polls. If you'd like to influence the way things are done in your community, state, or Washington, D.C., you can do so by helping to elect state and local officials, a president, and members of Congress whose views you endorse and who you think would do a good job of running the government. Make sure you know the location and hours for your polling place.

© LHF Graphics/Shutterstock.com

© franckreporter/iStockphoto.com

Support a Political Party

Getting involved in political parties is as simple as going to the polls and casting your vote for the candidate of one of the major parties—or of a third party. You can also consider becoming a delegate to a party convention. Depending on the state, parties may hold conventions by U.S. House district, by county, or by state legislative district. In many states, the lowest-level conventions are open to anyone who shows up. Voting rights at a convention, however, may be restricted to those who are elected as precinct delegates in a party primary.

In much of the country, precinct delegate slots go unfilled. If this is true in your area, you can become a precinct delegate with a simple write-in campaign, writing in your own name and persuading a handful of friends or neighbors to write you in as well. Whether you attend a convention as a voting delegate or as a guest, you'll have a firsthand look at how politics operates. You'll hear debates on resolutions. You might participate in electing delegates to higher-level conventions—perhaps even the national convention if it is a presidential election year.

Work for a Campaign

Candidates welcome energetic volunteers. So do groups that are supporting (or opposing) ballot measures. While sometimes tiring and frustrating, working in campaign politics can also be exhilarating and very rewarding.

Find the contact information for a campaign you're interested in on its Web site and inquire about volunteer opportunities. Volunteers can assemble mailings, answer the telephone, or make calls to encourage voters to support their candidate or cause. Even if you have little free time or are not comfortable talking to strangers, most campaigns can find a way for you to participate.

Be Part of Campus Media

Do you have a nose for news and do you write well? Try reporting for the university newspaper. Work your way up to an editor's position. If broadcast media are your thing, get involved with your college radio station or go on air on campus TV.

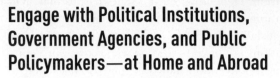

© baur/Shutterstock

Engage with Political Institutions, Government Agencies, and Public Policymakers—at Home and Abroad

- **Visit the government Web sites for your state and community and learn about your representatives.** Contact them with your thoughts on the matters that are important to you. Attend a city council meeting. You can find date, location, and agenda information on the Web site for your city. And if you're passionate about a local issue, you can even sign up to speak.

- **Check to see if internships or volunteer opportunities are available close to home.** Your U.S. representatives have district offices—one may be in the town in which you live. Your U.S. senators also have offices in various locations around the state. If you plan to be in Washington, D.C., and want to visit Capitol Hill, you can book a tour in advance through your senators' or representative's offices. That's where you get gallery passes, too.

- **Spend some time in Washington, D.C.** Many colleges and universities have established internship programs with government agencies and institutions. Some have semester-long programs that will bring you into contact with policymakers in Congress and in the bureaucracy, with journalists, and with a variety of other prominent newsmakers. Politics and government come alive, and the contacts you make while participating in such programs can often lead to jobs after graduation.

- **If you're interested in the Supreme Court** and you're planning a trip to Washington, try to watch oral arguments. Go to the Court's Web site to access the link for oral arguments: **www.supremecourt.gov/**. You'll find the argument calendar and a visitor's guide. (The secret is to get in line early.)

- **Become a virtual tourist.** If you can't make it to Washington, D.C., for a semester-long program or even a few days, take the U.S. Capitol Virtual Tour: **www.senate.gov/vtour/**.

- **You can take a virtual tour of the Supreme Court** at the Web site of the Oyez Project at IIT Chicago-Kent College of Law: **www.oyez.org/**. And you can listen to Supreme Court oral arguments wherever you are. Go to the Oyez site and check out ISCOTUSnow.

- **Check with the study-abroad office** at your college or university. Studying abroad is a great way to expand your horizons and to get a feel for different cultures and the global nature of politics and the economy. There are programs that will take you almost anywhere in the world.

- **Participate in the Model UN Club** on your campus (or start a Model UN Club if there isn't one). By participating in Model UN, you will become aware of international issues and conflicts and recognize the role that the United Nations can play in forging collective responses to global concerns. Model UN conferences are simulations of a session of the United Nations; your work as part of a country's UN delegation will give you hands-on experience in diplomacy.

GET INFORMED.
GET CONNECTED.
GET INVOLVED.

© Rommel Canlas/Shutterstock

The Democratic Republic

Penn State fans hold up an American flag during the game between Penn State's Nittany Lions and the Navy Midshipmen in State College, Pennsylvania.
Rob Carr/Getty Images

The five Learning Outcomes below are designed to help improve your understanding of this chapter. After reading this chapter, you should be able to:

- **Learning Outcome 1:** Define the terms *politics, government, order, liberty, authority*, and *legitimacy*.
- **Learning Outcome 2:** Distinguish the major features of direct democracy and representative democracy, and describe majoritarianism, elite theory, and pluralism.
- **Learning Outcome 3:** Summarize the conflicts that can occur between the principles of liberty and order, and between those of liberty and equality.
- **Learning Outcome 4:** Discuss conservatism, liberalism, and other popular American ideological positions.
- **Learning Outcome 5:** Explain how a changing American population and other social trends may affect the future of our nation.

(▶) **WATCH & LEARN** MindTap for American Government

Watch a brief "What Do You Know?" video summarizing The Democratic Republic.

We Had No Bill of Rights?

BACKGROUND

You know that you have the right to speak freely about the government without fear of being arrested for what you say. You have probably heard of the right to bear arms. These rights come from the Bill of Rights, the first ten amendments to the U.S. Constitution. Because of these amendments, the government may not pass laws that limit freedom of speech, religion, and many other freedoms. You will learn more about the civil liberties guaranteed by the Bill of Rights in Chapter 4.

The Bill of Rights is built into the founding document that guides our government. As a result, it commands a certain reverence. Merely by its existence, it can dissuade citizens and government leaders from impairing the civil liberties of fellow Americans.

WHAT IF WE HAD NO BILL OF RIGHTS?

Because the Bill of Rights protects our fundamental liberties, some people jump to the conclusion that, without it, we would have no rights. Consider, though, that almost all state constitutions enumerate many of the same rights. It is true that if the rights of the people were not written into state and national constitutions, these rights would be entirely dependent on the political process—on elections and on laws passed by the U.S. Congress and state legislatures. Popular rights would still be safe. Unpopular ones would be in danger.

THE RIGHT TO BEAR ARMS

Take as an example the Second Amendment, which guarantees to citizens the right to bear arms. If the Bill of Rights did not exist, would it mean that individuals would be unable to keep firearms in their homes? Probably not. Few localities in the United States have tried to ban handguns completely. Almost all states have gun laws that are far more permissive than they have to be under the Constitution. Indeed, it was not until 2008 and 2010 that the highest court in the land, the Supreme Court, even addressed this issue. The Court ruled that complete bans on possessing handguns are unconstitutional.

THE RIGHTS OF CRIMINAL DEFENDANTS

According to the Sixth Amendment, accused individuals have the right to a speedy and public trial. Also, according to the Fifth Amendment, no accused "shall be compelled in any criminal case to be a witness against himself, nor be deprived of life, liberty, or property, without due process of law." These rules protect people who are accused of crimes. Certainly, without the Bill of Rights, we could imagine many more restrictions on the rights of criminal defendants. Why? Because those accused of crimes are

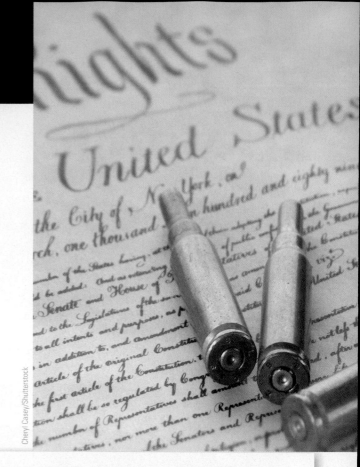

The Second Amendment to the U.S. Constitution, which protects the right to bear arms, is part of the Bill of Rights.

not a popular group of people. Many of the protections now given to criminal defendants would probably not exist if there were no Bill of Rights.

FREE SPEECH

Without the Bill of Rights, we would probably see many more laws restricting political contributions and advertising. We could expect laws against violent video games and pornography on the Internet. In contrast, given current popular attitudes, it is unlikely that "subversive" speech would be greatly restricted. Most Americans and their elected representatives support the right to denounce the government.

For Critical Analysis

1. The Fifth Amendment guarantees that no one can lose her or his liberty or property without due process. Yet, during World War II, we imprisoned tens of thousands of Japanese American citizens, based solely upon their race. Could that happen today to some other group of citizens, such as Muslim Americans? Why or why not?

2. Which of the rights mentioned in this feature do you think are the most important? Why?

Politics, for many people, is the "great game"—better than soccer, better than chess. Scores may be tallied only every two years, at elections, but the play continues at all times. The game, furthermore, is played for high stakes. Politics can affect what you spend. It can determine what you can legally do in your spare time. (The *What If . . .* feature that opened this chapter examined some of the ways in which your freedoms might be restricted if the Bill of Rights did not exist.) In worst-case circumstances, politics can even threaten your life.

Few topics are so entertaining as politics—and so important. How did the great game turn out in the elections held on November 4, 2014? We address that question in the *2014 Elections* feature that follows.

In our democratic republic, citizens play an important role by voting. Although voting is extremely important, it is only one of the ways that citizens can exercise their political influence. Americans can also join a political organization or interest group, stage a protest, or donate funds to a political campaign or cause. There are countless ways to become involved. Informed participation begins with knowledge, however, and this text aims to provide you with a strong foundation in American government and politics. We hope that this book helps introduce you to a lifetime of political awareness and activity.

Politics and Government

What is politics? **Politics** can be understood as the process of resolving conflicts and deciding, as political scientist Harold Lasswell put it in his classic definition, "who gets what, when, and how."[1] More specifically, politics is the struggle over power or influence within organizations or informal groups that can grant benefits or privileges.

We can identify many such groups and organizations. In families, all members may meet to decide on values, priorities, and actions. In every community that makes decisions through formal or informal rules, politics exists. For example, when a church decides to construct a new building or hire a new minister, the decision is made politically. Politics can be found in schools, social groups, and any other organized collection of individuals. Of all the organizations that are controlled by political activity, however, the most important is the government.

What is the government? Certainly, it is an **institution**—that is, an ongoing organization that performs certain functions for society and that has a life separate from the lives of the individuals who are part of it at any given moment in time. The **government** can be defined as an institution within which decisions are made that resolve conflicts and allocate benefits and privileges. The government is also the preeminent institution within society because it has the ultimate authority for making these decisions.

Government Is Everywhere

The government is even more important than politics. Many people largely ignore politics, but it is impossible to ignore government. It is everywhere, like the water you drink and the air you breathe. Both air and water, by the way, are subject to government pollution standards. The food you eat comes from an agricultural industry that is heavily regulated and subsidized by the government. Step outside your residence, and almost immediately you will walk down a government-owned street or drive on a government-owned highway.

From Your Birth. The county government records your birth. Your toys, crib, and baby food must meet government safety standards. After a few years, you'll start school, and

LISTEN & LEARN
MindTap™ for American Government

Access Read Speaker to listen to Chapter 1.

■ **Learning Outcome 1:** Define the terms *politics*, *government*, *order*, *liberty*, *authority*, and *legitimacy*.

Politics
The process of resolving conflicts and deciding "who gets what, when, and how." More specifically, politics is the struggle over power or influence within organizations or informal groups that can grant benefits or privileges.

Institution
An ongoing organization that performs certain functions for society.

Government
The preeminent institution within society in which decisions are made that resolve conflicts and allocate benefits and privileges. It is unique because it has the ultimate authority for making these decisions.

---

1. Harold Lasswell, *Politics: Who Gets What, When, and How* (Gloucester, Mass.: Peter Smith Publisher, 1990; originally published in 1936).

86 percent of all children attend public—which is to say, government—schools. Some children attend private schools or are home schooled, but their education must also meet government standards. Public school students spend many hours in an environment designed and managed by teachers and other government employees. If you get into trouble, you'll meet government employees you'd rather not see: the police, court employees, or even jail staff.

Why Should You Care?

Americans, for the most part, take our democracy for granted. We assume that our leaders, including the president, will uphold our democratic traditions. Nonetheless, the history of other nations has shown that even elected leaders can chip away at or destroy a nation's democratic system. For examples, try searching the Internet to investigate the state of democracy in Hungary, Russia, Sri Lanka, Ukraine, or Venezuela.

Throughout Your Life. Most young people look forward eagerly to receiving their government-issued driver's license. Many join the military on graduating from high school, and for those who do, every minute of the next several years will be 100 percent government issue. (That's why we call soldiers "GIs.") A majority of young adults attend college at some point, and if you are reading this textbook, you are probably one of them. Many private colleges and universities exist, but 73 percent of all college students attend public institutions. Even most private universities are heavily dependent on government support.

In nearly all states, you began paying sales taxes from the moment you had your own funds to spend. Some of those funds are made up of currency issued by the government. When you enter the workforce, you'll begin paying payroll and income taxes to the government. If, like most people, you are an employee, government regulations will set many of your working conditions. You might even work for the government itself—16 percent of employees do. If you are unfortunate enough to lose a job or fall into poverty, government programs will lend you a hand.

2014 Elections

The Outcome of the Elections

The year 2014 was a good one for the Republicans—by many measures, exceptionally so. After the Louisiana runoff elections in December, they were expected to hold the U.S. Senate by a margin of 54 to 46, a swing of nine seats. In the House, the Republicans did even better. A swing of 15 seats left them with an estimated total of 249, as opposed to 186 for the Democrats. House Democrats had not recovered from the sweeping Republican victory in 2010, and they were now down seven seats from where they stood after 2010. The result was the largest Republican House majority since the elections of 1928. It is true historically that the president's party often takes a beating six years into the president's term of office. By that time,

presidents may have outworn their welcome and become unpopular. Republicans sought to make Democratic President Barack Obama the issue, and in general they succeeded.

Republicans also did well at the state level. They picked up governorships in normally Democratic states such as Illinois, Maryland, and Massachusetts. They also took control of the largest number of state legislative bodies that they had held in generations. Despite these Republican gains, progressive ballot proposals did well. Four states raised their minimum wage, including conservative ones such as Arkansas and South Dakota. Alaska, Oregon, and the District of Columbia legalized the recreational use of marijuana.

To Your Death. Later in life, you may have health problems. Even before President Barack Obama's health-care plan went into effect on January 1, 2014, the federal government was already providing half of all the nation's health-care spending. Much of that spending came, and continues to come, from the federal Medicare program, which funds health care for almost everyone over the age of sixty-five. At that point in your life, you'll probably receive Social Security, the national government's pension plan that covers most employees. Eventually, the county government will record your death, and a government judge will oversee the distribution of your assets to your heirs.

Why Is Government Necessary?

Perhaps the best way to assess the need for government is to examine circumstances in which government, as we normally understand it, does not exist. What happens when multiple groups compete with one another for power within a society? There are places around the world where such circumstances exist. A current example is the nation of Syria, which is located in the Middle East. From 2000 on, the dictator Bashar al-Assad held absolute power in that nation. In 2011, a chain of peaceful protests led to an army crackdown, which in turn led to an armed rebellion. The central government lost control of large parts of the country, and rather than maintaining order, its forces repeatedly massacred civilians in contested areas. For their part, the rebels were not united—some were extreme Islamist militants, and others were more moderate. By 2013, rebels were not only fighting the government, but each other. Throughout much of Syria, law and order had broken down completely. By 2015, more than 150,000 people had been killed, and millions had been driven from their homes.

Fighting in Syria has destroyed entire residential districts. Here, Syrians search for survivors amidst the rubble following an airstrike in Aleppo in 2013. Two children were among at least 13 people killed. *How would we describe what is happening in Syria?*

Order
A state of peace and security. Maintaining order by protecting members of society from violence and criminal activity is one of the oldest purposes of government.

Liberty
The greatest freedom of the individual that is consistent with the freedom of other individuals in the society.

Authority
The right and power of a government or other entity to enforce its decisions.

Legitimacy
Popular acceptance of the right and power of a government or other entity to exercise authority.

As the example of Syria shows, one of the original purposes of government is the maintenance of security, or **order.** By keeping the peace, a government protects its people from violence at the hands of private or foreign armies and criminals. If order is not present, it is not possible for the government to provide any of the other benefits that people expect from it. Order is a political value to which we will return later in this chapter.

Limiting Government Power

A complete collapse of order and security, as seen in Syria, is actually an uncommon event. Much more common is the reverse—too much government control. In 2014, the human rights organization Freedom House judged that forty-eight of the world's countries were "not free." These nations contain 35 percent of the world's population. Such countries may be controlled by individual kings or dictators. Saudi Arabia's king Abdullah bin Abdulaziz and North Korea's dictator Kim Jong-un are obvious examples. Alternatively, a political party, such as the Communist Party of China, may monopolize all the levers of power. The military may rule, as has been true in Burma (also called Myanmar) until recently.

In all of these examples, the individual or group running the country cannot be removed by legal means. Freedom of speech and the right to a fair trial are typically absent. Dictatorial governments often torture or execute their opponents. Such regimes may also suppress freedom of religion. Revolution, whether violent or nonviolent, is often the only way to change the government.

In short, protection from the violence of domestic criminals or foreign armies is not enough. Citizens also need protection from abuses of power by their own government. To protect the liberties of the people, it is necessary to limit the powers of the government.

Liberty—the greatest freedom of the individual consistent with the freedom of other individuals—is a second major political value, along with order. We discuss this value in more detail later in this chapter.

Authority and Legitimacy

Every government must have **authority**—that is, the right and power to enforce its decisions. Ultimately, the government's authority rests on its control of the armed forces and the police. Few people in the United States, however, base their day-to-day activities on fear of the government's enforcement powers. Most people, most of the time, obey the law because this is what they have always done. Also, if they did not obey the law, they would face the disapproval of friends and family. Consider an example: Do you avoid injuring your friends or stealing their possessions because you are afraid of the police—or because if you undertook these actions, you no longer would have friends?

Under normal circumstances, the government's authority has broad popular support. People accept the government's right to establish rules and laws. When authority is broadly accepted, we say that it has **legitimacy.** Authority without legitimacy is a recipe for trouble.

Events in several Arab nations in 2011 and 2012 serve as an example. The dictators who ruled Egypt, Libya, and Tunisia had been in power for decades. All three dictators had some popular support when they first gained power. None of these nations had a tradition of democracy, and so it was possible for undemocratic rulers to enjoy a degree of legitimacy. After years of oppressive behavior, these regimes slowly lost that legitimacy. The rulers survived only because they were willing to employ violence against any opposition. In Egypt and Tunisia, the end came when soldiers refused to use force against massive demonstrations. Having lost all legitimacy, the rulers of these two countries lost their authority as well. The downfall and death of the dictator Muammar Qaddafi in Libya, however, came only after

did you know?
Chinese Communist leader Mao Zedong (1893–1976) once said, "Political power grows out of the barrel of a gun."

a seven-month civil war. (Unfortunately, Egypt's shaky new democracy collapsed in 2013 when the army seized power.)

Democracy and Other Forms of Government

The different types of government can be classified according to which person or group of people controls society through the government.

Types of Government

At one extreme is a society governed by a **totalitarian regime.** In such a political system, a small group of leaders or a single individual—a dictator—makes all decisions for the society. Every aspect of political, social, and economic life is controlled by the government. The power of the ruler is total (thus, the term *totalitarianism*).

A second type of system is authoritarian government. **Authoritarianism** differs from totalitarianism in that only the government itself is fully controlled by the ruler. Social and economic institutions, such as churches, businesses, and labor unions, exist that are not under the government's control.

Many of our terms for describing the distribution of political power are derived from the ancient Greeks, who were the first Western people to study politics systematically. One form of rule was known as **aristocracy,** literally meaning "rule by the best." In practice, this meant rule by wealthy members of ancient families. Another term from the Greeks is **theocracy,** which literally means "rule by God" (or the gods). In practice, theocracy means rule by self-appointed religious leaders. Iran is a rare example of a country in which supreme power is in the hands of a religious leader, the Grand Ayatollah Ali Khamenei. One of the most straightforward Greek terms is **oligarchy,** which simply means "rule by a few."

Anarchy is a term derived from a Greek word meaning the absence of government. Advocates of anarchy envision a world in which each individual makes his or her own rules for behavior. In reality, the absence of government typically results in rule by competing armed factions, many of which are indistinguishable from gangsters. This is the state of affairs in Syria, which we described earlier.

Finally, the Greek term for rule by the people was **democracy.** Within the limits of their culture, some of the Greek city-states operated as democracies. Today, in much of the world, the people will not grant legitimacy to a government unless it is based on democracy.

Direct Democracy as a Model

The Athenian system of government in ancient Greece is usually considered the purest model for **direct democracy** because the citizens of that community debated and voted directly on all laws, even those put forward by the ruling council of the city. The most important feature of Athenian democracy was that the **legislature** was composed of all of the citizens. (Women, resident foreigners, and slaves, however, were excluded because they were not citizens.) This form of government required a high level of participation from every citizen. That participation was seen as benefiting the individual and the city-state. The Athenians believed that although a high level of participation might lead to instability in government, citizens, if informed about the issues, could be trusted to make wise decisions.

Direct democracy also has been practiced at the local level in Switzerland and, in the United States, in New England town meetings. At these town meetings, which may

■ Learning Outcome 2: Distinguish the major features of direct democracy and representative democracy, and describe majoritarianism, elite theory, and pluralism.

Totalitarian Regime
A form of government that controls all aspects of the political, social, and economic life of a nation.

Authoritarianism
A type of regime in which only the government itself is fully controlled by the ruler. Social and economic institutions exist that are not under the government's control.

Aristocracy
"Rule by the best"; in reality, rule by members of the upper class.

Theocracy
"Rule by God," or the gods; in practice, rule by religious leaders, typically self-appointed.

Oligarchy
"Rule by a few."

Anarchy
The condition of no government.

Democracy
A system of government in which political authority is vested in the people. The term is derived from the Greek words *demos* ("the people") and *kratos* ("authority").

Direct Democracy
A system of government in which political decisions are made by the people directly, rather than by their elected representatives; probably attained most easily in small political communities.

Legislature
A governmental body primarily responsible for the making of laws.

These Woodbury, Vermont, residents cast their ballots after a town meeting. They voted on the school budget and sales taxes. *What type of political system does the town meeting best represent?*

include all of the voters who live in the town, important decisions—such as levying taxes, hiring city officials, and deciding local ordinances—are made by majority vote. Some states provide a modern adaptation of direct democracy for their citizens. In these states, representative democracy is supplemented by the **initiative** or the **referendum.** Both processes enable the people to vote directly on laws or constitutional amendments. The **recall** process, which is available in many states, allows the people to vote to remove an official from state office before his or her term has expired.

The Dangers of Direct Democracy

Although they were aware of the Athenian model, the framers of the U.S. Constitution were opposed to such a system. Democracy was considered to be dangerous and a source of instability. But in the 1700s and 1800s, the idea of government based on the *consent of the people* gained increasing popularity. Such a government was the main aspiration of the American Revolution in 1775, the French Revolution in 1789, and many subsequent revolutions. At the time of the American Revolution, however, the masses were still considered to be too uneducated to govern themselves. The masses were too prone to the influence of demagogues (political leaders who manipulate popular prejudices), and too likely to subordinate minority rights to the tyranny of the majority.

James Madison, while defending the new scheme of government set forth in the U.S. Constitution, warned of the problems inherent in a "pure democracy":

> *A common passion or interest will, in almost every case, be felt by a majority of the whole . . . and there is nothing to check the inducements to sacrifice the weaker party or an obnoxious individual. Hence it is that such democracies have ever been spectacles of turbulence and contention, and have ever been found incompatible with personal security or the rights of property; and have in general been as short in their lives as they have been violent in their deaths.*[2]

Like other politicians of his time, Madison feared that pure, or direct, democracy would deteriorate into mob rule. What would keep the majority of the people, if given direct decision-making power, from abusing the rights of those in the minority?

A Democratic Republic

The framers of the U.S. Constitution chose to craft a **republic,** meaning a government in which sovereign power rests with the people, rather than with a king or a monarch. A republic is based on **popular sovereignty.** To Americans of the 1700s, the idea of a republic also meant a government based on common beliefs and virtues that would be fostered within small communities. The rulers were to be amateurs—good citizens who would take turns representing their fellow citizens.

Initiative
A procedure by which voters can propose a law or a constitutional amendment.

Referendum
An electoral device whereby legislative or constitutional measures are referred by the legislature to the voters for approval or disapproval.

Recall
A procedure allowing the people to vote to dismiss an elected official from state office before his or her term has expired.

Republic
A form of government in which sovereign power rests with the people, rather than with a king or a monarch.

Popular Sovereignty
The concept that ultimate political authority is based on the will of the people.

2. James Madison, in Alexander Hamilton, James Madison, and John Jay, *The Federalist Papers,* No. 10 (New York: Mentor Books, 1964), p. 81. See Appendix C of this textbook.

The U.S. Constitution created a form of republican government that we now call a **democratic republic.** The people hold the ultimate power over the government through the election process, but all national policy decisions are made by elected officials. For the founders, even this distance between the people and the government was not sufficient. The Constitution made sure that the Senate and the president would not be elected by a direct vote of the people. Senators were chosen by state legislatures, although a later constitutional amendment allowed for the direct election of senators. The founders also established an *electoral college* to choose the president, in the hope—soon frustrated— that such a body would prevent voters from ultimately making the choice.

Despite its limits, the new American system was unique in the amount of power it granted to the ordinary citizen. Over the course of the following two centuries, democratic values became more and more popular, at first in Western nations and then throughout the rest of the world. The spread of democratic principles gave rise to another name for our system of government—**representative democracy.** The term *representative democracy* has almost the same meaning as *democratic republic,* with one exception. Recall that in a republic, not only are the people sovereign, but there is no king. What if a nation develops into a democracy but preserves the monarchy as a largely ceremonial institution? That is exactly what happened in Britain. The British, who have long cherished their kings and queens, found the term *democratic republic* unacceptable. A republic, after all, meant there could be no monarch. The British therefore described their system as a representative democracy instead.

Principles of Democratic Government. All representative democracies rest on the rule of the people as expressed through the election of government officials. In the 1790s in the United States, only free white males were able to vote, and in some states they had to be property owners as well. Women in many states did not receive the right to vote in national elections until 1920, and the right to vote was not secured in all states by African Americans until the 1960s. Today, **universal suffrage** is the rule.

Because everyone's vote counts equally, the only way to make fair decisions is by some form of *majority* will. But to ensure that **majority rule** does not become oppressive, modern democracies also provide guarantees of minority rights. If political minorities were not protected, the majority might violate the fundamental rights of members of certain groups—especially groups that are unpopular or dissimilar to the majority population, such as racial minorities.

To guarantee the continued existence of a representative democracy, there must be free, competitive elections. Thus, the opposition always has the opportunity to win elective office. For such elections to be totally open, freedom of the press and speech must be preserved so that opposition candidates can present their criticisms of the government to the people.

Democratic Republic
A republic in which representatives elected by the people make and enforce laws and policies.

Representative Democracy
A form of government in which representatives elected by the people make and enforce laws and policies; may retain the monarchy in a ceremonial role.

Universal Suffrage
The right of all adults to vote for their government representatives.

Majority Rule
A basic principle of democracy asserting that the greatest number of citizens in any political unit should select officials and determine policies.

CONNECT WITH YOUR CLASSMATES
MindTap™ for American Government

Access The Democratic Republic Forum: Discussion–Rule of Law and the Constitution

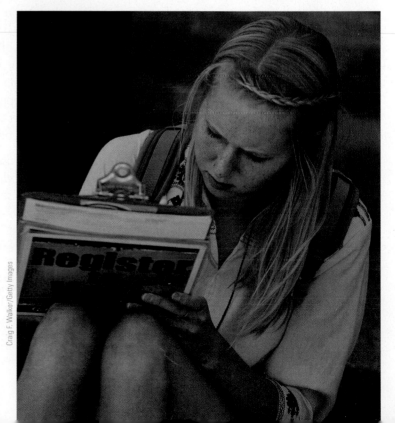

A University of Colorado student updates her address during a voter registration drive in Boulder, Colorado. *What do we call the form of government created by our Constitution?*

Craig F. Walker/Getty Images

Limited Government
A government with powers that are limited either through a written document or through widely shared beliefs.

Majoritarianism
A political theory holding that, in a democracy, the government ought to do what the majority of the people want.

Elite Theory
A perspective holding that society is ruled by a small number of people who hold the ultimate power to further their self-interests.

Constitutional Democracy. Another key feature of Western representative democracy is that it is based on the principle of **limited government.** Not only is the government dependent on popular sovereignty, but the powers of the government are also clearly limited, either through a written document or through widely shared beliefs. The U.S. Constitution sets down the fundamental structure of the government and the limits to its activities. Such limits are intended to prevent political decisions based on the whims or ambitions of individuals in government rather than on constitutional principles.

What Kind of Democracy Do We Have?

Political scientists have developed a number of theories about American democracy, including *majoritarianism, elite theory,* and *pluralism.* Advocates of these theories use them to describe American democracy either as it actually is or as they believe it should be.

Some scholars argue that none of these three theories, which we discuss next, fully describes the workings of American democracy. These experts say that each theory captures a part of the true reality but that we need all three theories to gain a full understanding of American politics.

Democracy for Everyone. Many people believe that, in a democracy, the government ought to do what the majority of the people want. This simple proposition is the heart of majoritarian theory. As a theory of what democracy should be like, **majoritarianism** is popular among both political scientists and ordinary citizens. Many scholars, however, consider majoritarianism to provide a surprisingly poor description of how U.S. democracy actually works. They point to the low level of turnout for elections. Polling data have shown that many Americans are neither particularly interested in politics nor well informed. Few are able to name the persons running for Congress in their districts, and even fewer can discuss the candidates' positions.

Why Should You Care?

In any democracy, citizens must remain vigilant. A lot is at stake—our way of life in particular. How do you stay vigilant? One way is to stay informed about what's going on in government. Staying informed is a lot easier today than it was, say, a hundred years ago. Newspapers and news magazines are everywhere. Perhaps more importantly, the Internet allows you to stay in constant touch with what your government is doing. There are blogs galore of all political stripes that you can check out.

Democracy for the Few. If ordinary citizens are not really making policy decisions with their votes, who is? One theory suggests that elites really govern the United States. **Elite theory** holds that society is ruled by a small number of people who exercise power to further their self-interests. American democracy, in other words, is a sham democracy. Few people today believe it is a good idea for the country to be run by a privileged minority. In the past, however, many people believed that it was appropriate for the country to be governed by an elite. Consider the words of Alexander Hamilton, one of the framers of the Constitution:

All communities divide themselves into the few and the many. The first are the rich and the wellborn, the other the mass of the people. . . . The people are turbulent and changing; they seldom judge or determine right. Give therefore to the first class a distinct, permanent share in the government. They will check the unsteadiness of the second, and as they cannot receive any advantage by a change, they therefore will ever maintain good government.[3]

Some versions of elite theory posit a small, cohesive elite class that makes almost all the important decisions for the nation,[4] whereas others suggest that voters choose among

3. Alexander Hamilton, "Speech in the Constitutional Convention on a Plan of Government," in Joanne B. Freeman, ed., *Writings* (New York: Library of America, 2001).
4. Michael Parenti, *Democracy for the Few,* 9th ed. (Belmont, Calif.: Wadsworth Publishing, 2010).

competing elites. Many Americans agree with simple versions of elite theory. Some believe that the top 1 percent of income earners—especially those who work in the finance industry—have too much power. For others, the elite is the federal government itself.

Democracy for Groups. A different school of thought holds that our form of democracy is based on group interests. Even if the average citizen cannot keep up with political issues or cast a deciding vote in any election, the individual's interests will be protected by groups that represent her or him.

Theorists who subscribe to **pluralism** see politics as a struggle among groups to gain benefits for their members. Given the structure of the American political system, group conflicts tend to be settled by compromise and accommodation. Because there are a multitude of interests, no one group can dominate the political process. Furthermore, because most individuals have more than one interest, conflict among groups need not divide the nation into hostile camps.

Many political scientists believe that pluralism works very well as a descriptive theory. As a theory of how democracy *should* function, however, pluralism has problems. Poor citizens are rarely members of interest groups. At the same time, rich citizens are often overrepresented. As political scientist E. E. Schattschneider once observed, "The flaw in the pluralist heaven is that the heavenly chorus sings with a strong upper-class accent."[5] There are also serious doubts as to whether group decision making always reflects the best interests of the nation.

Indeed, critics see a danger that groups may grow so powerful that all policies become compromises crafted to satisfy the interests of the largest groups. The interests of the public as a whole, then, are not considered. Critics of pluralism have suggested that a democratic system can be almost paralyzed by the struggle among interest groups. We will discuss interest groups at greater length in Chapter 7.

Fundamental Values

The writers of the U.S. Constitution believed that the structures they had created would provide for both popular sovereignty and a stable political system. They also believed that the nation would be sustained by its **political culture**—the patterned set of ideas, values, and ways of thinking about government and politics that characterized its people.

Even today, there is considerable consensus among American citizens about certain concepts—including the rights to liberty, equality, and property—that are deemed to be basic to the U.S. political system. Given that the vast majority of Americans are descendants of immigrants having diverse cultural and political backgrounds, how can we account for this consensus? Primarily, it is the result of **political socialization**—the process by which political beliefs and values are transmitted to new immigrants and to our children. The two most important sources of political socialization are the family and the educational system. (See Chapter 6 for a more detailed discussion of the political socialization process.)

The most fundamental concepts of the American political culture are those of the dominant culture. The term *dominant culture* refers to the values, customs, and language established by the groups that traditionally have controlled politics and government in a society. The dominant culture in the United States has its roots in Western European civilization. From that civilization, American politics inherited a bias toward individualism, private property, and Judeo-Christian ethics.

Pluralism
A theory that views politics as a conflict among interest groups. Political decision making is characterized by compromise and accommodation.

Political Culture
A patterned set of ideas, values, and ways of thinking about government and politics that characterize a people.

Political Socialization
The process by which political beliefs and values are transmitted to new immigrants and to our children. The family and the educational system are the most important sources of the political socialization process.

■ **Learning Outcome 3:** Summarize the conflicts that can occur between the principles of liberty and order, and between those of liberty and equality.

5. E. E. Schattschneider, *The Semi-Sovereign People* (Hinsdale, Ill.: The Dryden Press, 1975; originally published in 1960).

Civil Liberties

Those personal freedoms, including freedom of religion and freedom of speech, that are protected for all individuals. Civil liberties restrain the government from taking certain actions against individuals.

Bill of Rights

The first ten amendments to the U.S. Constitution.

Liberty versus Order

In the United States, our **civil liberties** include religious freedom—both the right to practice whatever religion we choose and the right to be free from any state-imposed religion. Our civil liberties also include freedom of speech—the right to express our opinions freely on all matters, including government actions. Freedom of speech is perhaps one of our most prized liberties, because a democracy could not endure without it. These and many other basic guarantees of liberty are found in the **Bill of Rights,** the first ten amendments to the Constitution, which we described in the *What If . . .* feature at the beginning of this chapter. Americans are often more protective of their civil liberties than are citizens of other democratic countries, a point that we discuss in this chapter's *Beyond Our Borders* feature that follows.

Liberty, however, is not the only value widely held by Americans. A substantial portion of the American electorate believes that certain kinds of liberty threaten the traditional social order. The right to privacy is a particularly controversial liberty. The United States Supreme Court has held that the right to privacy can be derived from other rights that are explicitly stated in the Bill of Rights. The Supreme Court has also held that under the right to privacy, the government cannot ban either abortion[6] or private homosexual behavior by consenting adults.[7] Some Americans believe that such rights threaten the sanctity of the

---

6. *Roe v. Wade,* 410 U.S. 113 (1973).
7. *Lawrence v. Texas,* 539 U.S. 558 (2003).

Beyond Our Borders

How Other Democratic Countries Restrict Civil Liberties

Americans tend to value civil freedoms more than the people of most other democratic countries do. Americans, in particular, prize freedom of speech. Not all democratic countries value it so highly. In Germany, for example, it is illegal to display the swastika, the emblem adopted by the Nazis. Swastikas cannot be affixed to plastic models of World War II–era aircraft. It is even a crime to give a Nazi-style straight-arm salute. Recently, a German sculptor got into serious trouble by crafting a satirical statue of a garden gnome giving such a salute. The German constitution gives the government the power to ban organizations that threaten the democratic order.

Finally, if you are on German soil and you want—even for historical purposes—to purchase a copy of Hitler's autobiography and political statement, *Mein Kampf (My Struggle),* you'll have to get it from another country via the Internet. The German state of Bavaria, which owns the rights to the book, has blocked reprints of *Mein Kampf* in Germany.

Most Americans are concerned about crime. Many Americans, however, would be even more concerned about possible injustices if they learned that 99.8 percent of all criminal prosecutions resulted in a conviction. Yet that is exactly what happens in democratic Japan. In that country, suspects can be held for up to twenty-three days before they are charged. The high conviction rate in Japan stems from a high confession rate. Those who are detained have no access to defense lawyers and no idea how long interrogation sessions will last. The Japanese constitution guarantees detainees the right to remain silent, but few Japanese citizens who are arrested are able to take advantage of that right. In several recent cases, innocent people have been browbeaten into making false confessions that are almost impossible to retract.

For Critical Analysis

Why would Germany continue to criminalize Nazi symbols more than seventy years after the end of World War II?

family and the general cultural commitment to moral behavior. Of course, others disagree with this point of view.

Security is another issue that follows from the principle of order. When Americans have felt particularly fearful or vulnerable, the government has emphasized national security over civil liberties. Such was the case after the Japanese attack on Pearl Harbor in 1941, which plunged the United States into World War II. Thousands of Japanese Americans were arrested and held in internment camps, based on the assumption that their loyalty to this country was in question. More recently, the terrorist attacks on the World Trade Center and the Pentagon on September 11, 2001, renewed calls for greater security at the expense of some civil liberties.

Bob Adelman/Corbis

One of the most fundamental rights Americans have is the right to vote. Here, African Americans in Camden, Alabama, vote for the first time after passage of the 1965 Voting Rights Act. *Does voting affect political socialization?*

Equality versus Liberty

The Declaration of Independence states, "All men are created equal." The proper meaning of *equality,* however, has been disputed by Americans since the Revolution.[8] Much of American history—and, indeed, world history—is the story of how the value of **equality**—the idea that all people are of equal worth—has been extended and elaborated.

First, the right to vote was granted to all adult white males, regardless of whether they owned property. The Civil War (1861–1865) resulted in the end of slavery and established that, in principle at least, all citizens were equal before the law. The civil rights movement of the 1950s and 1960s sought to make that promise of equality a reality for African Americans. Other movements have sought equality for additional racial and ethnic groups, for women, for persons with disabilities, and for gay men and lesbians. We discuss many of these movements in Chapter 5.

Although many people believe that we have a way yet to go in obtaining full equality for all of these groups, we clearly have come a long way already. No American in the nineteenth century could have imagined that the 2008 Democratic presidential primary elections would be closely fought contests between an African American man (Illinois senator Barack Obama) and a white woman (New York senator Hillary Rodham Clinton). The idea that same-sex marriage could even be open to debate would have been mind-boggling as well.

Promoting equality often requires limiting the right to treat people unequally. In this sense, equality and liberty are conflicting values. Today, the right to deny equal treatment to members of a particular race has very few defenders. Yet as recently as fifty years ago, this right was a cultural norm.

did you know?

The words "under God" were added to the Pledge of Allegiance only in 1954. The change was made during the Cold War, when the United States faced off against communist nations that were officially atheist.

COMPARE WITH YOUR PEERS
MindTap for American Government

Access The Democratic Republic Forum: Polling Activity–Defining Marriage in California

Equality
As a political value, the idea that all people are of equal worth.

---

8. Gary B. Nash, *The Unknown American Revolution: The Unruly Birth of Democracy and the Struggle to Create America* (New York: Viking, 2005); and Alfred F. Young, ed., *Beyond the American Revolution: Explorations in the History of American Radicalism* (DeKalb: Northern Illinois University Press, 1993).

This same-sex couple married in Washington state in 2012. *What, if anything, does the Bill of Rights say about this topic?*

Economic Equality. Equal treatment regardless of race, religion, gender, or other characteristics is a popular value today. Equal opportunity for individuals to develop their talents and skills is also a value with substantial support. Equality of economic status, however, is a controversial value.

For much of history, the idea that the government could do anything about the division of society between rich and poor was not something about which people even thought. Most people assumed that such an effort was either impossible or undesirable. This assumption began to lose its force in the 1800s. As a result of the growing wealth of the Western world and a visible increase in the ability of government to take on large projects, some people began to advocate the value of universal equality, or egalitarianism. Some radicals dreamed of a revolutionary transformation of society that would establish an egalitarian system—that is, a system in which wealth and power were redistributed more equally.

Many others rejected this vision but still came to endorse the values of eliminating poverty and at least reducing the degree of economic inequality in society. Antipoverty advocates believed then and believe now that such a program could prevent much suffering. In addition, they believed that reducing economic inequality would promote fairness and enhance the moral tone of society generally.

Property Rights and Capitalism. The value of reducing economic inequality is in conflict with the right to **property.** This is because reducing economic inequality typically involves the transfer of property (usually in the form of tax dollars) from some people to others. For many people, liberty and property are closely entwined. Our capitalist system is based on private property rights. Under **capitalism,** property consists not only of personal possessions but also of wealth-creating assets such as farms and factories. The investor-owned corporation is in many ways the preeminent capitalist institution. The funds invested by the owners of a corporation are known as *capital*—hence, the very name of the system. Capitalism is also typically characterized by considerable freedom to make binding contracts and by relatively unconstrained markets for goods, services, and investments.

Property—especially wealth-creating property—can be seen as giving its owner political power and the liberty to do whatever he or she wants. At the same time, the ownership of property immediately creates inequality in society. The desire to own property, however, is so widespread among all classes of Americans that radical egalitarian movements have had a difficult time securing a wide following in this country.

The Proper Size of Government

Opposition to "big government" has been a constant theme in American politics. Indeed, the belief that government is overreaching dates back to the years before the American Revolution. Tensions over the size and scope of government have plagued Americans ever since. Citizens often express contradictory opinions on the size of government and the role that it should play in their lives. Those who complain about the

Property

Anything that is or may be subject to ownership. As conceived by the political philosopher John Locke, the right to property is a natural right superior to human law (laws made by government).

Capitalism

An economic system characterized by the private ownership of wealth-creating assets, free markets, and freedom of contract.

amount of taxes that they pay each year may also worry about the lack of funds for teachers in the local schools.

Americans tend to oppose "big government" in principle even as they endorse its benefits. Indeed, American politics in the twenty-first century can be described largely in terms of ambivalence about big government.

Big Government and the Great Recession. In September 2008, a financial meltdown threatened the entire world economy with collapse. The incumbent president, Republican George W. Bush, was widely—if perhaps unfairly—blamed for the disaster. Many conservatives believed that Big Government must have been responsible. They argued that legislation to promote borrowing by low-income individuals helped trigger the meltdown. Others pointed out, however, that these low-income policies dated from the 1970s. These observers contended that the irresponsible lending at the heart of the crisis was mostly undertaken by private-sector bankers.

In any event, Americans demanded government action to save the economy, yet most programs aimed at accomplishing that goal were widely disliked. In particular, a bailout of banks and other financial institutions proved very unpopular.

In November 2008, the voters handed Democrat Barack Obama a solid victory in the presidential elections, and Democrats won large margins in the U.S. House of Representatives and the Senate. The new administration took major actions in an attempt to combat the recession in 2009, including an $800 billion stimulus package and the rescue of the automobile companies General Motors and Chrysler. Conservatives quickly grew alarmed at the new government activism. For example, they saw the auto bailouts as really a bailout of the unions.

One result was the Tea Party, a grass-roots conservative movement first organized in April of that year. Long-time conservative leaders soon established national groups that also adopted the Tea Party label—the name refers to anti-tax protests in the years leading up to the American Revolution. In March 2010, Congress and President Obama approved a major health-care initiative that had no direct connection to fighting the recession. For many, this act completed the picture of big government out of control. In November 2010, voters swung heavily to the Republicans, granting them control of the U.S. House.

Republican Overreach. With government divided between the parties, many observers predicted political deadlock. In fact, Congress passed less legislation than at any time in sixty-five years. A symbol of the impasse was the 2011 attempt by Republicans in the House to use a periodically scheduled raise in the federal government's debt ceiling to force cuts in spending. House Republicans also called for major tax rate cuts, tough restrictions to future funding for Medicaid, and privatization of Medicare for anyone currently under the age of fifty-five. By 2012, for many independents, concern over Democratic affection for government was now counterbalanced by fears that

> ### did you know?
> United States military spending is 39 percent of all military spending in the world—we spend as much as the next eleven countries put together.

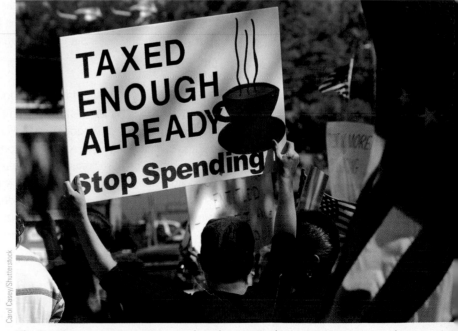

Carol Casey/Shutterstock

The Tea Party movement is not a political party. Rather, its supporters want less taxation and a scaled-down federal government. *How successful has the Tea Party been in recent years?*

Ideology
A comprehensive set of beliefs about the nature of people and about the role of an institution or government.

Conservatism
A set of beliefs that includes a limited role for the national government in helping individuals, support for traditional ideals and life choices, and a cautious response to change.

Conservative Movement
An American movement in the 1950s that provided a comprehensive ideological framework for conservative politics.

the Republicans might cut valued social programs. (We discuss some of the Republican arguments—and Democratic counter-arguments—in the *Which Side Are You On?* feature that follows.)

In the 2012 elections, despite continuing economic troubles, President Obama was reelected and the Democrats posted modest gains in the U.S. House and Senate. These relatively inconclusive elections did nothing to resolve the ongoing conflict over the proper size of government. Indeed, two events in 2013 underscored the importance of the debate. For the first sixteen days of October, House Republicans forced a partial shutdown of the federal government in an unsuccessful attempt to repeal the health-care reforms, now nicknamed *Obamacare*. Popular reaction to this step was very negative.

The Obamacare Web Site. Even as parts of the government were shutting down, Obamacare's online insurance "exchanges" were opening up. The exchanges were meant to help those who did not have employer or government-provided health-care insurance coverage to buy such plans from private companies. Initially, however, the online exchanges were a disaster. Two months passed before people could even use the site to sign up, and serious additional problems continued for some time thereafter. This management fiasco provided plenty of ammunition to those who argue that big government is typically incompetent.

Political Ideologies

A political **ideology** is a closely linked set of beliefs about politics. The concept of *ideology* is often misunderstood. Many people think that only individuals whose beliefs lie well out on one or the other end of the political spectrum have an ideology—in other words, people with moderate positions are not ideological. Actually, almost everyone who has political opinions can be said to have an ideology. Some people may have difficulty in explaining the principles that underlie their opinions, but the principles are there nonetheless. To give one example: a belief in moderation is itself an ideological principle.

Political ideologies offer people well-organized theories that propose goals for society and the means by which those goals can be achieved. At the core of every political ideology is a set of guiding values. The two ideologies most commonly referred to in discussions of American politics are *conservatism* and *liberalism*.

■ **Learning Outcome 4:**
Discuss conservatism, liberalism, and other popular American ideological positions.

Conservatism

Over the years, those who favored the ideology of **conservatism** have sought to conserve traditional practices and institutions. In that sense, conservatism is as old as politics itself. In America, limited government is a key tradition. For much of our history, limited government has included major restrictions on government's ability to interfere with business. In the past, enterprises were largely free to act as they pleased in the marketplace and in managing their employees. Government regulation of business increased greatly in the 1930s, as Democratic president Franklin D. Roosevelt (1933–1945) initiated a series of massive interventions in the economy in an attempt to counter the effects of the Great Depression. Many conservatives consider the Roosevelt administration to be a time when America took a wrong turn.

Modern Conservatism. It was in the 1950s, however, that American conservatism took its modern shape. The **conservative movement** that arose in that decade provided the age-old conservative impulse with a fully worked-out ideology. The new movement first demonstrated its strength in 1964, when Senator Barry Goldwater of Arizona was nominated as the Republican presidential candidate. Goldwater lost badly to Democrat

Which Side Are You On?

Does Entitlement Spending Corrupt Us?

The federal government provides benefits to certain individuals and families. Many of these benefits are called *entitlements* because you are entitled to receive them if you meet specific requirements. If you meet certain age and previous earnings requirements, you can receive a monthly Social Security check. In the event that you lose your job, you may be entitled to unemployment benefits for a certain number of weeks. If your family income is below a certain level, you are typically entitled benefits from the Supplemental Nutrition Assistance Program (SNAP, formerly called food stamps).

In recent years, federal entitlement spending has ballooned. Indeed, big government has gotten bigger in large part because Americans are receiving more entitlement payments every year. At all levels combined, government spending now has a value equivalent to about 37.6 percent of total national income. Some have argued that large-scale entitlement spending is corrupting us.

The More You Give People, the Less They'll Want to Work

Conservatives point out that entitlement transfers—adjusted for rising prices and population growth—are now more than seven times what they were in 1960. (In part, this is because major programs such as Medicare and Medicaid were first created in the 1960s.) Currently, almost half of Americans live in a household that receives at least one government benefit. If you count tax deductions, almost every household receives benefits.

Consider SNAP benefits. In 2007, 26 million Americans received them. By 2014, about 47 million Americans received them. The same story applies to Social Security disability payments. Four million people received disability checks in 1988. Today, there are more than eight million. Those are only some of many similar examples.

Fewer people are now in the labor force and those who are work fewer hours per year. Since 2000, the labor force participation rate has fallen continuously, even during boom times. Many believe that increased entitlement benefits have reduced people's desire to join the labor force. In other words, entitlements corrupt.

Entitlements Are a Necessary Part of the Social Contract

While the statistics presented above are accurate, political progressives do not accept the conclusions drawn. They say that with an aging society, we should expect to pay more for Social Security. The same is true for government-financed health care. Health-care expenses are not only driven up by larger numbers of the elderly, but by increasingly expensive (and effective) medical procedures.

Contrary to what some have argued, Americans are not divided between "makers" and "takers." At various times in our lives, we are all takers and almost all of us are makers. As President Obama said in his second inaugural address, "The commitments we make to each other—through Medicare, and Medicaid, and Social Security—these things do not sap our initiative; they strengthen us. They do not make us a nation of takers; they free us to take the risks that make this country great."

Americans believe in hard work just as much as they always have. The Pew Social Mobility Project sampled Americans on what is essential for getting ahead. More than 90 percent responded "hard work," and almost 90 percent answered "ambition." That doesn't sound like corruption, does it?

For Critical Analysis

Who ultimately pays for entitlement programs?

Lyndon Johnson, but from that time forward *movement conservatives* have occupied a crucial position in the Republican Party.

Conservative Values. American conservatives generally place a high value on the principle of order. This includes support for patriotism and traditional ideals. As a result, conservatives typically oppose such social innovations as same-sex marriage. Conservatives strongly endorse liberty, but they generally define it as freedom from government support of nontraditional ideals such as gay rights or as freedom from government interference in business.

Why Should You Care?

To learn more about how government works, consider local legislative bodies. They can have a direct impact on your life. For example, city councils typically oversee the police department, and the behavior of the police is a matter of interest, even if you live on campus. If you live off campus, local authorities are responsible for an even greater number of issues that affect you directly. Are there items that your local sanitation department refuses to pick up? You might be able to change its policies by talking with your councilperson.

Conservatives believe that the private sector probably can outperform the government in almost any activity. Therefore, they usually oppose initiatives that would increase the role of the government in the economy, such as President Obama's health-care reforms. Conservatives place a relatively low value on equality. Believing that individuals and families are primarily responsible for their own well-being, they typically oppose high levels of antipoverty spending and government expenditures to stimulate the economy, favoring tax-rate cuts instead.

Liberalism

The term **liberalism** stems from the word *liberty* and originally meant "free from prejudice in favor of traditional opinions and established institutions." Liberals have always been skeptical of the influence of religion in politics, but in the nineteenth century they were skeptical of government as well. From the time of Democratic presidents Woodrow Wilson (1913–1921) and Franklin D. Roosevelt, however, American liberals increasingly sought to use the power of government for nontraditional ends. Their goals included support for organized labor and for the poor. New programs instituted by the Roosevelt administration included Social Security and unemployment insurance.

Modern Liberalism. American liberalism took its modern form in the 1960s. Liberals rallied to the civil rights movement, which sought to obtain equal rights for African Americans. As the feminist movement grew in importance, liberals supported it as well. Liberals won new federal health-care programs such as Medicare and Medicaid, and the promotion of such programs became a key component of liberal politics. Finally, liberals reacted more negatively to U.S. participation in the Vietnam War (1965–1975) than did other Americans, and for years thereafter liberalism was associated with skepticism about the use of U.S. military forces abroad.

Liberal Values. Those who favor liberalism place a high value on social and economic equality. As we have seen, liberals champion the rights of minority group members and favor substantial antipoverty spending. In the recent health-care policy debates, liberals strongly endorsed the principle that all citizens should have access to "affordable" insurance. In contrast to conservatives, liberals often support government intervention in the economy. They believe that capitalism works best when the government curbs capitalism's excesses through regulation. Like conservatives, liberals place a high value on liberty, but they tend to view it as the freedom to live one's life according to one's own values. Liberals, therefore, usually support gay rights, often including the right to same-sex marriage. Liberals are an influential force within the Democratic Party.

The Traditional Political Spectrum

A traditional method of comparing political ideologies is to arrange them on a continuum from left to right, based primarily on how much power the government should exercise to promote economic equality. Table 1–1 that follows shows how ideologies can be arrayed in a traditional political spectrum. In addition to liberalism and conservatism, this example includes the ideologies of socialism and libertarianism.

Socialism falls on the left side of the spectrum.[9] Socialists play a minor role in the American political arena, although socialist parties and movements have been important

Liberalism

A set of beliefs that includes the advocacy of positive government action to improve the welfare of individuals, support for civil rights, and tolerance for political and social change.

Socialism

A political ideology based on strong support for economic and social equality. Socialists traditionally envisioned a society in which major businesses were taken over by the government or by employee cooperatives.

9. The terms *left* and *right* in the traditional political spectrum originated during the French Revolution, when revolutionary deputies to the Legislative Assembly sat to the left of the assembly president and conservative deputies sat to the right.

Table 1–1 ▸ **The Traditional Political Spectrum**
Which of these platforms are likely to be popular? Why?

	Socialism	Liberalism	Conservatism	Libertarianism
How much power should the government have over the economy?	Active government control over major economic sectors.	Positive government action in the economy.	Positive government action to support capitalism.	Almost no regulation over the economy.
What should the government promote?	Economic equality, community.	Economic security, equal opportunity, social liberty.	Economic liberty, morality, social order.	Total economic and social liberty.

in other countries around the world. In the past, socialists typically advocated replacing investor ownership of major businesses with either government ownership or ownership by employee cooperatives. Socialists believed that such steps would break the power of the very rich and lead to an egalitarian society. In more recent times, socialists in Western Europe have advocated more limited programs that redistribute income.

On the right side of the spectrum is **libertarianism,** a philosophy of skepticism toward most government activities. Libertarians strongly support property rights and typically oppose regulation of the economy and redistribution of income. Libertarians support *laissez-faire* capitalism. (*Laissez faire* is French for "let it be.") Libertarians also tend to oppose government attempts to regulate personal behavior and promote moral values.

Problems with the Traditional Political Spectrum

Many political scientists believe that the traditional left-to-right spectrum is not sufficiently complete. Take the example of libertarians. In Table 1–1 above, libertarians are placed to the right of conservatives. If the only question is how much power the government should have over the economy, this is where they belong. Libertarians, however, strongly advocate freedom in social matters. They oppose government action to promote traditional moral values, although such action is often favored by other groups on the political right. Their strong support for cultural freedoms seems to align them more closely with modern liberals than with conservatives.

Liberalism is often described as an ideology that supports "big government." If the objective is to promote equality, the description has some validity. In the moral sphere, however, conservatives tend to support more government regulation of social values and moral decisions than do liberals. Thus, conservatives tend to oppose gay rights legislation and propose stronger curbs on pornography. Liberals usually show greater tolerance for alternative life choices and oppose government attempts to regulate personal behavior and morals.

A Four-Cornered Ideological Grid

For a more sophisticated breakdown of recent American popular ideologies, many scholars use a four-cornered grid, as shown in Figure 1–1 that follows. The grid includes four possible ideologies. Each quadrant contains a substantial portion of the American electorate. Individual voters may fall anywhere on the grid, depending on the strength of their beliefs about economic and cultural issues.

Economic Liberals, Cultural Conservatives. Note that there is no generally accepted term for persons in the lower-left position, which we have labeled "economic liberals, cultural conservatives." Some scholars have used terms such as *populist* to describe this

did you know?
A poll of New York University students revealed that one-fifth of them would give up their vote in the next election for an iPhone and that half of them would renounce their vote permanently for $1 million.

Libertarianism
A political ideology based on skepticism or opposition toward most government activities.

Figure 1–1 ▸   **A Four-Cornered Ideological Grid**

In this grid, the colored squares represent four different political ideologies. The vertical choices range from cultural order to cultural liberty. The horizontal choices range from economic equality to economic liberty. *Why, in your opinion, have conservatives been so successful in making* liberal *an unpopular label?*

point of view, but these terms can be misleading. *Populism* more accurately refers to a hostility toward political, economic, or cultural elites, and it can be combined with a variety of political positions.

Individuals who are economic liberals and cultural conservatives tend to support government action both to promote the values of economic equality and fairness and to defend traditional values, such as the family and marriage. These individuals may describe themselves as conservative or moderate. They may vote for a Republican candidate, based on their conservative values. Alternatively, they may be Democrats due to their support for economic liberalism. Many of these Democrats are African Americans or members of other minority groups.

Libertarians. As a position on the four-cornered grid, *libertarians* does not represent the small Libertarian Party, which has only a minor role in the American political arena. Rather, libertarians more typically support the Republican Party. Economically successful individuals are more likely than members of other groups to hold libertarian opinions.

***Liberal* versus *Progressive*.** Even though all four ideologies are popular, the various labels we have used in the four-cornered grid are not equally favored. Voters are much more likely to describe themselves as conservative than as liberal. In the political battles of the last several decades, the conservative movement has consistently made *liberal* a term of abuse, and they have succeeded in devaluing the term among much of the public. Indeed, few politicians today willingly describe themselves as liberal, and many liberals prefer to describe themselves as **progressive** instead. This term dates back to the years before World War I (1914–1918), when it referred to advocates of reform in both of the major political parties. Public opinion polls suggest that *progressive* is a relatively popular label.

Progressive
A popular alternative to the term *liberal*.

Demonstrators march through downtown Boston. The marchers were opposed to the nation's growing student debt burden. *Which groups might support the demands of these students?*

How You Can Make a Difference

If you want to affect our democracy, you have to learn first-hand how a democratic government works. The easiest way is to attend a session of a local legislative body.

- To do so, look up the phone number of the city hall or county building on the Internet. Call the clerk of your local council or city commission. Find out when the next city council or county board meeting is.

- If you live in a state capital such as Baton Rouge, Louisiana, or Santa Fe, New Mexico, you can view a meeting of the state legislature instead.

- In many communities, city council meetings and county board meetings can be seen on public-access TV channels.

- Before attending a business session of the local council or commission, try to find out how the members are elected. Are the members chosen by the "at-large" method of election, so that each member represents the whole community? Or are they chosen by specific geographic districts or wards? What are the responsibilities of this body?

- When you visit, keep in mind the theory of representative democracy. The commissioners or council members are elected to represent their constituents. Observe how often the members refer to their constituents or to the special needs of their communities.

- Listen for sources of conflict. If, for example, there is a debate over a zoning proposal that involves the issue of land use, try to figure out why some members oppose the proposal.

- If you want to follow up on your visit, try to get a brief interview with one of the members of the council or board. In general, legislators are very willing to talk to students, particularly students who also are voters.

- Ask the member how he or she sees the job of representative. How can the wishes of constituents be identified? How does the representative balance the needs of the particular ward or district that she or he represents with the good of the entire community?

- You can also write to many legislators via e-mail.

Key Terms

anarchy 7	elite theory 10	liberty 6	property 14
aristocracy 7	equality 13	limited government 10	recall 8
authoritarianism 7	government 3	majoritarianism 10	referendum 8
authority 6	Hispanic 23	majority rule 9	representative democracy 9
Bill of Rights 12	ideology 16	oligarchy 7	republic 8
capitalism 14	initiative 8	order 6	socialism 18
civil liberties 12	institution 3	pluralism 11	theocracy 7
conservatism 16	Latino 23	political culture 11	total fertility rate 22
conservative movement 16	legislature 7	political socialization 11	totalitarian regime 7
democracy 7	legitimacy 6	politics 3	universal suffrage 9
democratic republic 9	liberalism 18	popular sovereignty 8	
direct democracy 7	libertarianism 19	progressive 20	

Chapter Summary

Learning Outcome 1 Politics is the process by which people decide which members of society receive certain benefits or privileges and which members do not. It is the struggle over power or influence within institutions or organizations that can grant benefits or privileges. Government is an institution within which decisions are made that resolve conflicts and allocate benefits and privileges. It is the predominant institution within society because it has the ultimate decision-making authority.

Two fundamental political values are order, which includes security against violence, and liberty, the greatest freedom of the individual consistent with the freedom of other individuals. To be effective, government authority must be backed by legitimacy.

Learning Outcome 2 Many of our terms for describing forms of government came from the ancient Greeks. In a direct democracy, such as in ancient Athens, the people themselves make the important political decisions. The United States is a democratic republic, also called a representative democracy, in which the people elect representatives to make the decisions. Theories of American democracy include majoritarianism, in which the government does what the majority wants; elite theory, in which the real power lies with one or more elite groups; and pluralism, in which organized interest groups contend for power.

Learning Outcome 3 Fundamental American values include liberty, order, equality, and property. Not all of these values are

fully compatible. The value of order often competes with civil liberties, and economic equality competes with property rights.

Learning Outcome 4 Popular political ideologies can be arrayed from left (liberal) to right (conservative). We can also analyze economic liberalism and conservatism separately from cultural liberalism and conservatism.

Learning Outcome 5 Population growth in the United States is slowing. By 2050, it is estimated that non-Latino whites will be a minority of the total population. Despite concerns about inequality and unemployment, many social indicators, such as crime rates, have improved in recent years.

Master the concept of The Democratic Republic with MindTap™ *for American Government*

REVIEW MindTap™ **for American Government**
Access Key Term Flashcards for Chapter 1.

STAY CURRENT MindTap™ **for American Government**
Access the KnowNow blog and customized RSS for updates on current events.

TEST YOURSELF MindTap™ **for American Government**
Take the Wrap It Up Quiz for Chapter 1.

STAY FOCUSED MindTap™ **for American Government**
Complete the Focus Activities for The Democratic Republic.

Additional Resources

The Web has become a vehicle to improve your understanding of any academic subject. A word of caution about political sites: not all of them care about accuracy. Many are interested only in providing ammunition for use in debates, regardless of whether the statements are true or not. You will need to use judgment when surfing the Web for political resources.

Online Resources

- For information on the federal government and its programs, go to **USA.gov**, which provides access to all federal government offices and agencies.
- To find out more about conservative politics in the United States, try **www.facebook.com/nationalreview**. You'll see posts by the staff of *National Review*, a conservative magazine.
- To learn more about liberal politics, visit **twitter.com/thenation**. You'll see tweets by the staff of *The Nation*, a liberal publication.
- Consider Wikipedia, the giant online encyclopedia written by volunteers. You might consult the Wiki article at **en.wikipedia.org/wiki /Political_ideologies_in_the_United_States**. Note that while the quality of Wiki articles is usually high, the site is occasionally attacked by vandals who insert false material into articles. Such false information is usually detected and deleted quickly, however.
- The Web is a good place to learn about political science as a profession. Try visiting the site of the American Political Science Association at **www.apsanet.org**.

Books

Fukuyama, Francis. *The Origins of Political Order: From Prehuman Times to the French Revolution.* New York: Farrar, Straus and Giroux, 2011. Fukuyama, a well-known political theorist, analyzes key features of the modern state. These include freedom from family and tribal allegiances, adherence to the rule of law, and political accountability.

Kenworthy, Lane. *Social Democratic America.* New York: Oxford University Press, 2014. Kenworthy is a political science professor at the University of Arizona. He makes the liberal case that a more active government can improve opportunity, security, and living standards for most Americans.

Skocpol, Theda, and Vanessa Williamson. *The Tea Party and the Remaking of Republican Conservatism.* New York: Oxford University Press, 2012. Skocpol is a political science professor at Harvard, and Williamson is her research assistant. Their account of the Tea Party movement is based on many personal interviews with activists.

Video

American Feud: A History of Conservatives and Liberals—Directed by Richard Hall, this 2008 documentary explores popular American ideologies through interviews with leading political commentators.

The Other Side of Immigration—This highly acclaimed 2010 documentary seeks to understand why so many Mexicans wish to come to the United States by interviewing both immigrants and those who are left behind in Mexico.

Quiz

Multiple Choice and Fill-Ins

Learning Outcome 1 Define the terms *politics, government, order, liberty, authority,* and *legitimacy.*

1. When citizens of a nation do not enjoy liberty, the government frequently will:
    a. abolish the right to a fair trial.
    b. provide government funds to churches.
    c. hold regular elections.

2. When authority is broadly accepted, we say that it has _____.

Learning Outcome 2 Distinguish the major features of direct democracy and representative democracy, and describe majoritarianism, elite theory, and pluralism.

3. A democratic republic is based on all of the following principles except:
    a. popular sovereignty.
    b. majority rule.
    c. unlimited government.

4. _____ theory describes our democratic system in terms of competition among groups.

Learning Outcome 3 Summarize the conflicts that can occur between the principles of liberty and order, and between those of liberty and equality.

5. A major theme of American politics during the twenty-first century has been:
    a. arguments over whether all citizens should have the right to vote.
    b. controversies over the proper size of government.
    c. disputes as to whether the government should assume the ownership of major banks.

6. Under _____, property consists not only of personal possessions but of wealth-creating assets.

Learning Outcome 4 Discuss conservatism, liberalism, and other popular American ideological positions.

7. Popular American ideologies include:
    a. conservatism, liberalism, and libertarianism.
    b. conservatism, liberalism, and socialism.
    c. communism, liberalism, and libertarianism.

8. A common term that has come to replace liberalism in current American politics is _____.

Learning Outcome 5 Explain how a changing American population and other social trends may affect the future of our nation.

9. Currently, most immigrants come from:
    a. Europe.
    b. Africa.
    c. Latin America (especially Mexico) and Asia.

10. In terms of race, Latinos _____.

Essay Questions

1. In Australia and Belgium, citizens are legally required to vote in elections. Would such a requirement be a good idea in the United States? What changes might take place if such a rule were in effect?

2. In your own life, what factors have contributed to your political socialization? To what extent were your political values shaped by your family, by school experiences, by friends, and by the media?

The Constitution

2

A student views the original Constitution at the National Archives in Washington, D.C. In a survey, Americans named the Declaration of Independence and the Constitution as the two documents that have most influenced the United States.
Brendan Smialowski/Getty Images

The five Learning Outcomes below are designed to help improve your understanding of this chapter. After reading this chapter, you should be able to:

- **Learning Outcome 1:** Explain how the colonial experience prepared Americans for independence, the restrictions that Britain placed on the colonies, and the American response.

- **Learning Outcome 2:** Describe the significance of the Declaration of Independence and the Articles of Confederation, as well as the weaknesses of the Articles.

- **Learning Outcome 3:** Discuss the most important compromises reached at the Constitutional Convention and the basic structure of the resulting government.

- **Learning Outcome 4:** Summarize the arguments in favor of and the arguments against adopting the Constitution, and explain why the Bill of Rights was adopted.

- **Learning Outcome 5:** Describe the process of amending the Constitution and the informal ways in which Constitutional interpretation has changed over time.

▶ **WATCH & LEARN** MindTap® for American Government
Watch a brief "What Do You Know?" video summarizing The Constitution.

What If...

Congress Chose the President?

James Madison (1751–1836) has been called the "master builder of the Constitution."

BACKGROUND

In Chapter 1, in the section "A Democratic Republic," we observed that the authors of the U.S. Constitution sought to keep the people from choosing the president through an *electoral college*. The various states choose *electors,* and then the electors choose the president. In short order, however, most would-be electors were publicly pledged to specific presidential hopefuls. The scheme to keep the public from picking the president therefore failed.

A second goal of the electoral college was a success, however—it kept the choice of the president out of the hands of Congress. This arrangement was a major part of James Madison's plan to divide the powers of government among multiple branches. Today, most Americans would consider it an infringement of their rights if Congress, not the voters, chose the chief executive. In many democratic countries, however, the legislature does exactly that. Such nations have parliamentary systems. Almost all European nations have such a system.

In a *parliamentary system,* the people in each district elect one or more members of parliament. Often, voters can choose among candidates from several parties. Following the election, the largest party or coalition of parties names an executive team—the cabinet—led by a prime minister, premier, or chancellor. The cabinet takes office when it wins a vote in the lower house of parliament. If at any point the prime minister and cabinet lose the support of the lower house, they are out. If an alternative coalition cannot be formed, an election is called on short notice. Would the American system have looked like this if the founders had let Congress pick the president?

WHAT IF CONGRESS CHOSE THE PRESIDENT?

If the founders had based the Constitution on one of the initial proposals at the Constitutional Convention, such as the Virginia Plan, the United States might have ended up with a parliamentary system. These initial proposals called for an executive elected by Congress.

It is also possible, however, that the U.S. system would have been somewhat different. It was not clear, under the Virginia Plan, whether if Congress elected the executive, Congress would also have the power to remove the executive by any measure short of impeachment and conviction. What if Congress elected a president who did not serve at the pleasure of the legislature as a prime minister does? If that were so, then following a midterm election (when members of Congress are elected, but not the president), the chief executive and the majority in the legislature could be of different parties. That is not possible under a parliamentary system.

EFFECTIVE VERSUS LIMITED GOVERNMENT

Under a parliamentary system, the executive and the majority in the legislature must be of the same party (or coalition of parties). As a result, the executive has little difficulty in passing its preferred programs. A parliamentary majority has few restraints on what it can do—a state of affairs known as *effective government.* The American system, with multiple points at which various powers can block action, is more likely to result in *limited government.*

A united Congress and president could exercise power in ways that are currently unusual. In fact, for a time during the first two years of the Obama administration, Congress and the president were united in this fashion. Such circumstances are rare in the United States, however. Even under a semi-parliamentary system in which Congress could not easily remove the president from office, such circumstances would be commonplace.

For Critical Analysis

1. How might your vote for the U.S. House of Representatives change if you knew that you were simultaneously voting for a national executive leader?

2. If the House always chose the executive, what effect would that have on the role of the U.S. Senate?

We the People of the United States, in Order to form a more perfect Union, establish Justice, insure domestic Tranquility, provide for the common defence, promote the general Welfare, and secure the Blessings of Liberty to ourselves and our Posterity, do ordain and establish this Constitution for the United States of America.

Every schoolchild in America has at one time or another been exposed to these famous words from the Preamble to the U.S. Constitution. The document itself is remarkable. The U.S. Constitution, compared with others in the fifty states and in the world, is relatively short. Because amending it is difficult, it also has relatively few amendments. The Constitution has remained largely intact for more than two hundred years. To a great extent, this is because the principles set forth in the Constitution are sufficiently broad that they can be adapted to meet the needs of a changing society.

How and why the U.S. Constitution was created is a story that has been told and retold. It is worth repeating, because knowing the historical and political context in which this country's governmental machinery was formed is essential to understanding American government and politics today. The Constitution did not result just from creative thinking. Many of its provisions were grounded in the political philosophy of the time.

The delegates to the Constitutional Convention in 1787 brought with them two important sets of influences: their political culture and their political experience. In the years between the first settlements in the New World and the writing of the Constitution, Americans had developed a political philosophy about how people should be governed and had tried out several forms of government. These experiences gave the founders the tools with which they constructed the Constitution—a document that was unique in the world both then and now, as you can see from this chapter's opening *What If . . .* feature.

The Colonial Background

In 1607, a company chartered by the English government sent a group of settlers to establish a trading post, Jamestown, in what is now Virginia. Jamestown was the first permanent English colony in the Americas. The king of England gave the backers of this colony a charter granting them "full power and authority" to make laws "for the good and welfare" of the settlement. The colonists at Jamestown instituted a **representative assembly,** a legislature composed of individuals who represented the population, thus setting a precedent in government that was to be observed in later colonial adventures.

Separatists, the *Mayflower*, and the Compact

The first New England colony was established in 1620. A group made up in large part of extreme Separatists, who wished to break with the Church of England, came over on the ship *Mayflower* to the New World, landing at Plymouth (Massachusetts). Before going onshore, the adult males—women were not considered to have any political status—drew up the Mayflower Compact, which was signed by forty-one of the forty-four men aboard the ship on November 21, 1620.

The reason for the compact was obvious. This group was outside the jurisdiction of the Virginia Company of London, which had chartered its settlement. The Separatist leaders feared that some of the *Mayflower* passengers might conclude that they were no longer under any obligations of civil obedience. Therefore, some form of public authority was imperative. As William Bradford (one of the Separatist leaders) recalled in his accounts, there were "discontented and mutinous speeches that some of the strangers

■ **Learning Outcome 1:**
Explain how the colonial experience prepared Americans for independence, the restrictions that Britain placed on the colonies, and the American response.

Representative Assembly
A legislature composed of individuals who represent the population.

[non-Separatists] amongst them had let fall from them in the ship; That when they came ashore they would use their owne libertie; for none had power to command them."[1]

The Significance of the Compact. The compact was not a constitution. It was a political statement in which the signers agreed to create and submit to the authority of a government, pending the receipt of a royal charter. The Mayflower Compact's historical and political significance is twofold: it depended on the consent of the affected individuals, and it served as a prototype for similar compacts in American history.

By the time of the American Revolution, the compact was well on its way toward achieving mythic status. In 1802, John Quincy Adams, son of the second American president, spoke these words at a founders' day celebration in Plymouth: "This is perhaps the only instance in human history of that positive, original social compact, which speculative philosophers have imagined as the only legitimate source of government."[2]

Pilgrim Beliefs. Although the Plymouth settlers—later called the Pilgrims—committed themselves to self-government, in other ways their political ideas were not those that are prevalent today. The new community was a religious colony. Separation of church and state and most of our modern civil liberties were alien to the settlers' thinking. By the time the U.S. Constitution was written, the nation's leaders had a very different vision of the relationship between religion and government. We look at some of the founders' beliefs in this chapter's *Which Side Are You On?* feature that follows.

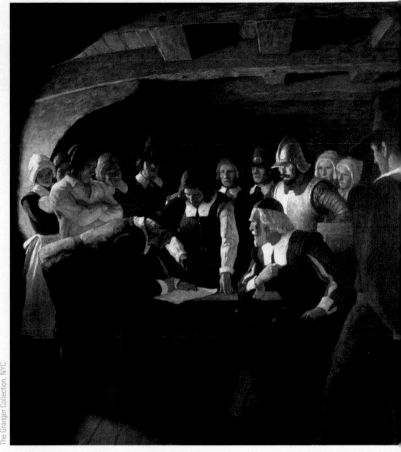

The Granger Collection, NYC

In 1620, the Mayflower Compact was signed by almost all of the men aboard the *Mayflower* just before they disembarked at Plymouth, Massachusetts. *Was it a constitution? Why or why not?*

More Colonies, More Government

Another outpost in New England was set up by the Massachusetts Bay Colony in 1630. Then followed Rhode Island, Connecticut, New Hampshire, and others. By 1732, the last of the thirteen colonies, Georgia, was established. During the colonial period, Americans developed a concept of limited government, which followed from the establishment of the first colonies under Crown charters. Theoretically, London governed the colonies. In practice, owing partly to the colonies' distance from London, the colonists exercised a large measure of self-government.

The colonists were able to make their own laws—for example, the Fundamental Orders of Connecticut in 1639. The Massachusetts Body of Liberties in 1641 supported the protection of individual rights. In 1682, the Frame of Government of Pennsylvania was passed. Along with the Pennsylvania Charter of Privileges of 1701, it foreshadowed our modern Constitution and Bill of Rights. All of this legislation enabled the colonists to acquire crucial political experience. After independence was declared in 1776, the states quickly set up their own new constitutions.

---

1. Nathaniel Philbrick, *Mayflower: A Story of Courage, Community, and War* (New York: Penguin, 2007), p. 37.
2. Ibid., p. 352. Today, the Mayflower Separatists are frequently referred to as the Pilgrims, but that name did not come into common use until two centuries after the colony was founded.

Which Side Are You On?

Should the United States Be a Christian Nation?

Christianity utterly permeated the world of the first English settlers in America. The oldest colonial documents are filled with endorsements of Christianity. Regular church attendance was often mandatory. Nine of the colonies had churches that were established by law.

The Declaration of Independence, however, makes no reference to Christ. The word *God* does not appear in the Constitution. By 1790, officially established churches were found only in Connecticut and Massachusetts, and the Congregational Church in Massachusetts had drifted so far from its Puritan origins that many of its members no longer accepted the divinity of Jesus. That is, they belonged to *Unitarian* congregations. One result of this development was that in the national elections of 1796 and 1800, neither major party fielded a presidential candidate who was, by modern definition, a Christian. John Adams, Unitarian, squared off against Thomas Jefferson, freethinker.

These facts raise the question: Just how Christian were the founders? More to the point, did the founders intend the United States to be a "Christian nation"? Scholars and school boards often differ on these issues.

One Nation, Under God

Christian conservatives point out that numerous American leaders throughout history have characterized the country as a Christian nation, beginning with John Jay, the first chief justice of the United States Supreme Court. The revolutionaries of 1776 often viewed the struggle in religious terms. Quite a few believed that God had a special plan for America to serve as an example to the world. The overwhelming majority of the colonists considered themselves Christians. Today, 78 percent of Americans identify themselves as such. If the term *Christian nation* merely identifies the beliefs of the majority, it is undeniably an accurate label.

To Christian conservatives who would like to change what is taught in the schools, however, the term means much more. They contend that American law is based on the laws of Moses as

set down in the Bible. They also believe that America's divine mission is not just an opinion held by many people—it should be taught as literal truth. Finally, this group, like many other Christian conservatives, argues that "freedom *of* religion does not mean freedom *from* religion." The language of the First Amendment means only that the national government should not prefer one church to another.

Church and Government Must Not Mix

Mainstream scholars disagree with the previous arguments, often vehemently. For example, Steven K. Green, a professor at Willamette University in Oregon, has searched for American court cases that reference the laws of Moses. He found none.

Ultimately, opponents say, to argue that the founders were not serious about the separation of church and state is to ignore the plain language of the Constitution. True, most of the authors of the Constitution were Christians, but the founders were also steeped in *Enlightenment rationalism*. Enlightenment figures such as England's John Locke (1632–1704), France's Voltaire (1694–1778), and Scotland's Adam Smith (1723–1790) emphasized reason and individualism rather than tradition. Enlightenment rationalism also rejected "enthusiasm" in religion. *Enthusiasm* referred to the spirit that allowed Protestant and Catholic Europeans to kill one another in the name of God over a period of two centuries. For the founders, mixing church and government was indeed a recipe for trouble.

For Critical Analysis

Today, candidates for president clearly benefit when they use religious language and when they are comfortable discussing their faith. Is this at all troubling? Why or why not?

British Restrictions and Colonial Reactions

The conflict between Britain and the American colonies, which ultimately led to the Revolutionary War, began in the 1760s when the British government decided to raise revenues by imposing taxes on the American colonies. Policy advisers to Britain's King George III, who ascended the throne in 1760, decided that it was only logical to require the American colonists to help pay the costs of Britain's defending them during the French and Indian War (1754–1763). The colonists, who had grown accustomed to a large degree of self-government and independence from the British Crown, viewed the matter differently.

In 1764, the British Parliament passed the Sugar Act, which imposed a tax that many colonists were unwilling to pay. Further regulatory legislation was to come. In 1765, Parliament passed the Stamp Act, providing for internal taxation of legal documents and even newspapers—or, as the colonists' Stamp Act Congress, assembled in 1765, called it, "taxation without representation." The colonists boycotted the purchase of English commodities in return.

The success of the boycott (the Stamp Act was repealed a year later) generated a feeling of unity within the colonies. The British, however, continued to try to raise revenues in the colonies. When Parliament passed duties on glass, lead, paint, and other items in 1767, the colonists again boycotted British goods. The colonists' fury over taxation climaxed in the Boston Tea Party: colonists dressed as Mohawk Indians dumped almost 350 chests of British tea into Boston Harbor as a gesture of tax protest. In retaliation, Parliament passed the Coercive Acts (the "Intolerable Acts") in 1774, which closed Boston Harbor and placed the government of Massachusetts under direct British control. The colonists were outraged—and they responded.

did you know?

The celebration of King George III's birthday on June 4 gave rise to the custom of summer fireworks, and after 1776, the celebration was rebranded and moved to the 4th of July.

The First Continental Congress

New York, Pennsylvania, and Rhode Island proposed the convening of a colonial gathering, or congress. The Massachusetts House of Representatives requested that all colonies hold conventions to select delegates to be sent to Philadelphia for such a congress.

The First Continental Congress was held at Carpenter's Hall in Philadelphia on September 5, 1774. It was a gathering of delegates from twelve of the thirteen colonies (delegates from Georgia did not attend until 1775). At that meeting, there was little talk of independence. The congress passed a resolution requesting that the colonies send a petition to King George III expressing their grievances. Resolutions were also passed requiring that the colonies raise their own troops and boycott British trade. The British government condemned the congress's actions, treating them as open acts of rebellion.

The Second Continental Congress

By the time the Second Continental Congress met in May 1775 (all of the colonies were represented this time), fighting already had broken out between the British and the colonists. One of the main actions of the Second Continental Congress was to establish an army. It did this by declaring the militia that had gathered around Boston an army and naming George Washington as commander in chief. Congressional participants still attempted to reach a peaceful settlement with the British Parliament. One declaration of the congress stated explicitly that "we have not raised armies with ambitious designs of separating from Great Britain, and establishing independent states." But by the beginning of 1776, military encounters had become increasingly frequent.

Painting by William Robinson/The Crown Estate/The Bridgeman Art Library International

King George III (1738–1820) was king of Great Britain and Ireland from 1760 until his death in 1820. Under George III, the British Parliament attempted to tax the American colonies. Ultimately, the colonies, exasperated at repeated attempts at taxation, proclaimed their independence on July 4, 1776. *Why would Britain attempt to tax the colonists?*

Milestones in Early U.S. Political History

1607 Jamestown established; Virginia Company lands settlers.

1620 Mayflower Compact signed.

1630 Massachusetts Bay Colony set up.

1639 Fundamental Orders of Connecticut adopted.

1641 Massachusetts Body of Liberties adopted.

1682 Pennsylvania Frame of Government passed.

1701 Pennsylvania Charter of Privileges written.

1732 Last of the thirteen colonies (Georgia) established.

1756 French and Indian War begins.

1765 Stamp Act; Stamp Act Congress meets.

1774 First Continental Congress.

1775 Second Continental Congress; Revolutionary War begins.

1776 Declaration of Independence signed.

1777 Articles of Confederation drafted.

1781 Last state (Maryland) signs Articles of Confederation.

1783 "Critical period" in U.S. history begins; weak national government until 1789.

1786 Shays' Rebellion.

1787 Constitutional Convention.

1788 Ratification of Constitution.

1791 Ratification of Bill of Rights.

Public debate was acrimonious. Then Thomas Paine's *Common Sense* appeared in Philadelphia bookstores. The pamphlet was a colonial best seller. (To do relatively as well today, a book would have to sell between 9 million and 11 million copies in its first year of publication.) Many agreed that Paine did make common sense when he argued that

> *a government of our own is our natural right: and when a man seriously reflects on the precariousness* [instability, unpredictability] *of human affairs, he will become convinced, that it is infinitely wiser and safer, to form a constitution of our own in a cool and deliberate manner, while we have it in our power, than to trust such an interesting event to time and chance.* [3]

Paine further argued that "nothing can settle our affairs so expeditiously as an open and determined declaration for Independence." [4]

Students of Paine's pamphlet point out that his arguments were not new—they were common in tavern debates throughout the land. Rather, it was the near poetry of his words—which were at the same time as plain as the alphabet—that struck his readers.

An Independent Confederation

On April 6, 1776, the Second Continental Congress voted for free trade at all American ports with all countries except Britain. This act could be interpreted as an implicit declaration of independence. The next month, the congress suggested that each of the colonies establish state governments unconnected to Britain. Finally, in July, the colonists declared their independence from Britain.

The Resolution for Independence

On July 2, the Resolution for Independence was adopted by the Second Continental Congress:

> RESOLVED, That these United Colonies are, and of right ought to be, free and independent States, that they are absolved from allegiance to the British Crown, and that all political connection between them and the state of Great Britain is, and ought to be, totally dissolved.

In June 1776, Thomas Jefferson already was writing drafts of the Declaration of Independence. When the Resolution for Independence was adopted on July 2, Jefferson argued that a declaration clearly putting forth the causes that compelled the colonies to separate from Britain was necessary. The Second Continental Congress assigned the task to him.

July 4, 1776—The Declaration of Independence

Jefferson's version of the Declaration was amended to gain unanimous acceptance (for example, his condemnation of the slave trade was eliminated to satisfy Georgia and North Carolina), but the bulk of it was passed intact on July 4, 1776. On July 19, the modified draft became "the unanimous declaration of the thirteen United States of America." On August 2, it was signed by the members of the Second Continental Congress.

Universal Truths. The Declaration of Independence has become one of the world's most famous and significant documents. The words opening the second paragraph of the Declaration indicate why this is so:

---

3. *The Political Writings of Thomas Paine*, Vol. 1 (Boston: J. P. Mendum Investigator Office, 1870), p. 46.
4. *Ibid.*, p. 54.

We hold these Truths to be self-evident, that all Men are created equal, that they are endowed by their Creator with certain unalienable Rights, that among these are Life, Liberty, and the Pursuit of Happiness—That to secure these Rights, Governments are instituted among Men, deriving their just Powers from the Consent of the Governed, that whenever any Form of Government becomes destructive of these Ends, it is the Right of the People to alter or abolish it, and to institute new Government.

Natural Rights and Social Contracts. The statement that "all Men are created equal" and have **natural rights** ("unalienable Rights"), including the rights to "Life, Liberty, and the Pursuit of Happiness," was revolutionary at that time. Its use by Jefferson reveals the influence of the English philosopher John Locke (1632–1704), whose writings were familiar to educated American colonists, including Jefferson. In his *Two Treatises of Government,* published in 1690, Locke had argued that all people possess certain natural rights, including the rights to life, liberty, and property. This claim was not inconsistent with English legal traditions.

Locke went on to argue, however, that the primary purpose of government was to protect these rights. Furthermore, government was established by the people through a **social contract**—an agreement among the people to form a government and abide by its rules. As you read earlier, such contracts, or compacts, were not new to Americans. The Mayflower Compact was the first of several documents that established governments or governing rules based on the consent of the governed.

After setting forth these basic principles of government, the Declaration of Independence goes on to justify the colonists' revolt against Britain. Much of the remainder of the document is a list of what "He" (King George III) had done to deprive the colonists of their rights. (See Appendix A at the end of this book for the complete text of the Declaration of Independence.)

■ **Learning Outcome 2:**
Describe the significance of the Declaration of Independence and the Articles of Confederation, as well as the weaknesses of the Articles.

Natural Rights
Rights held to be inherent in natural law, not dependent on governments. John Locke stated that natural law, being superior to human law, specifies certain rights of "life, liberty, and property." These rights, altered to become "life, liberty, and the pursuit of happiness," are asserted in the Declaration of Independence.

Social Contract
A voluntary agreement among individuals to secure their rights and welfare by creating a government and abiding by its rules.

The Significance of the Declaration. The concepts of equality, natural rights, and government established through a social contract were to have a lasting impact on American life. The Declaration of Independence set forth ideals that have since become a fundamental part of our national identity. The Declaration also became a model for use by other nations around the world.

Certainly, most Americans are familiar with the beginning words of the Declaration. Yet, as Harvard historian David Armitage noted in his study of the Declaration of Independence in the international context,[5] few Americans ponder the obvious question: What did these assertions in the Declaration have to do with independence? Clearly, independence could have been declared without these words. Even as late as 1857, Abraham Lincoln admitted, "The assertion that 'all men are created equal' was of no practical use in effecting our separation from Great Britain; and it was placed in the Declaration, not for that, but for future use."[6]

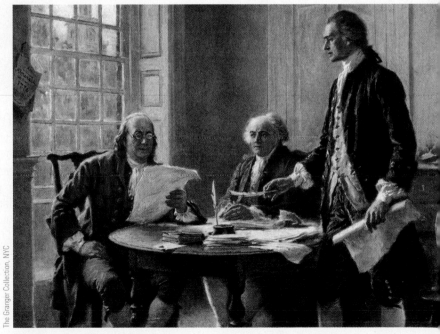

The Granger Collection, NYC

Benjamin Franklin (left) sits with John Adams while Thomas Jefferson looks on during a meeting outside the Second Continental Congress. *What important document came out of that congress?*

---

5.   David Armitage, *The Declaration of Independence: A Global History* (Cambridge, Mass.: Harvard University Press, 2007).
6.   As cited in Armitage, *The Declaration of Independence,* p. 26.

Essentially, the immediate significance of the Declaration of Independence, in 1776, was that it established the legitimacy of the new nation in the eyes of foreign governments, as well as in the eyes of the colonists themselves. What the new nation needed most were supplies for its armies and a commitment of foreign military aid. Unless it appeared to the world as a political entity separate and independent from Britain, no foreign government would enter into an agreement with its leaders. In fact, foreign support was crucial to the success of the revolution, as you will discover in the *Beyond Our Borders* feature that follows.

The Rise of Republicanism

Although the colonists had formally declared independence from Britain, the fight to gain actual independence continued for five more years, until the British general Charles Cornwallis surrendered at Yorktown in 1781. In 1783, after Britain formally recognized the independent status of the United States in the Treaty of Paris, Washington disbanded the army. During these years of military struggles, the states faced the additional challenge of creating a system of self-government for an independent United States.

Some colonists had demanded that independence be preceded by the formation of a strong central government. But others, who called themselves Republicans (not to be confused with today's Republican Party), were against a strong central government. They opposed monarchy, executive authority, and almost any form of restraint on the power of local groups.

Beyond Our Borders

France's Role in Defeating the British

By the summer of 1781, after six years of war, the American army was struggling. The British occupied New York City. In the South, a British army led by General Cornwallis had captured Charleston in South Carolina and Richmond in Virginia. Cornwallis was now headed toward Chesapeake Bay.

Washington, who was camped outside of New York City, had lost battle after battle. Still, he was never forced to surrender—after each loss, he retreated. In July 1781, a French expeditionary force linked up with Washington's army in New York, doubling the strength of the revolutionary forces. In August, the combined armies marched south to attack Cornwallis.

The Battle of Yorktown

In September, the French navy defeated the British navy in Chesapeake Bay, and the French were temporarily in control of the seas. In October, American and French forces defeated the British army at Yorktown, Virginia. Unable to retreat by sea, Cornwallis was forced to surrender. When the news reached London, the British prime minister resigned in disgrace.

A True World War

The war began as an American fight for independence. By the 1780s, however, it had turned into a global conflict. France, the Netherlands, and Spain were also at war with Britain. Battles took place in Gibraltar, India, Ireland, and the West Indies. Fighting in so many places, the British concluded that it would be impossible to replace Cornwallis's army and continue the war with the Americans. In September 1783, the British signed the Treaty of Paris granting independence to the United States.

For Critical Analysis

What might have happened if the British had ever been able to force Washington to surrender?

These Republicans, although not organized as a political party, were still a major political force from 1776 to 1780. Indeed, they almost prevented victory over the British by their unwillingness to cooperate with any central authority. During this time, all of the states adopted written constitutions. Eleven of the constitutions were completely new. Two of them—those of Connecticut and Rhode Island—were old royal charters with minor modifications. Republican sentiment led to increased power for the state legislatures. In Georgia and Pennsylvania, **unicameral** (one-body) **legislatures** were unchecked by executive or judicial authority. In almost all states, the legislature was predominant.

The Articles of Confederation: Our First Form of Government

The fear of a powerful central government led to the passage of the Articles of Confederation, which created a weak central government. The term **confederation** is important. It means a voluntary association of independent **states,** in which the member states agree to only limited restraints on their freedom of action. As a result, confederations seldom have an effective executive authority.

In June 1776, the Second Continental Congress began the process of composing what would become the Articles of Confederation. The final draft of the Articles was completed by November 15, 1777. It was not until March 1, 1781, however, that the last state, Maryland, agreed to ratify the Articles. Well before the final ratification of the Articles, however, many of them were implemented: the Continental Congress and the thirteen states conducted American military, economic, and political affairs according to the standards and the form specified by the Articles.[7]

The Articles Establish a Government. Under the Articles, the thirteen original colonies, now states, established on March 1, 1781, a government of the states—the Congress of the Confederation. The congress was a unicameral assembly of so-called ambassadors from each state, with each state possessing a single vote. Each year, the congress would choose one of its members as the president of the congress (that is, the presiding officer), but the Articles did not provide for a president of the United States.

The congress was authorized in Article X to appoint an executive committee of the states "to execute in the recess of Congress, such of the powers of Congress as the United States, in Congress assembled, by the consent of nine [of the thirteen] states, shall from time to time think expedient to vest with them." The congress was also allowed to appoint other committees and civil officers necessary for managing the general affairs of the United States. In addition, the congress could regulate foreign affairs and establish coinage and weights and measures. But it lacked an independent, direct source of revenue and the necessary executive machinery to enforce its decisions throughout the land. Article II of the Articles of Confederation guaranteed that each state would retain its sovereignty. Figure 2–1 that follows illustrates the structure of the government under the Articles of Confederation. Table 2–1 that follows summarizes the powers—and the lack of powers—of congress under the Articles of Confederation.

Accomplishments under the Articles. The new government had some accomplishments during its eight years of existence under the Articles of Confederation. Certain states' claims to western lands were settled. Maryland had objected to the claims of the Carolinas, Connecticut, Georgia, Massachusetts, New York, and Virginia. It was only after these states

Unicameral Legislature
A legislature with only one legislative chamber, as opposed to a bicameral (two-chamber) legislature, such as the U.S. Congress. Today, Nebraska is the only state in the Union with a unicameral legislature.

Confederation
A political system in which states or regional governments retain ultimate authority except for those powers they expressly delegate to a central government; a voluntary association of independent states, in which the member states agree to limited restraints on their freedom of action.

State
A group of people occupying a specific area and organized under one government. It may either be a nation or a subunit of a nation.

---

7. Keith L. Dougherty, *Collective Action under the Articles of Confederation* (New York: Cambridge University Press, 2006).

consented to give up their land claims to the United States as a whole that Maryland signed the Articles of Confederation. Another accomplishment under the Articles was the passage of the Northwest Ordinance of 1787, which established a basic pattern of government for new territories north of the Ohio River. All in all, the Articles represented the first real pooling of resources by the American states.

Weaknesses of the Articles. In spite of these accomplishments, the Articles of Confederation had many defects. Although congress had the legal right to declare war and to conduct foreign policy, it did not have the right to demand revenues from the states. It could only ask for them. Additionally, the actions of congress required the consent of nine states. Any amendments to the Articles required the unanimous consent of the congress and confirmation by every state legislature. Furthermore, the Articles did not create a national system of courts.

Basically, the functioning of the government under the Articles depended on the goodwill of the states. Article III simply established a "league of friendship" among the states—no national government was intended.

Probably the most fundamental weakness of the Articles, and the most basic cause of their eventual replacement by the Constitution, was the lack of power to raise funds for the militia. The Articles contained no language giving congress coercive power to raise revenue (by levying taxes) to provide adequate support for the military forces controlled by congress. Due to a lack of resources, the Continental Congress was forced to disband the army after the Revolutionary War, even in the face of serious Spanish and British military threats.

Figure 2–1 ▶
The Confederal Government Structure under the Articles of Confederation

Why would a state send multiple ambassadors if it only had one vote?

Congress
Congress had one house. Each state had two to seven members, but only one vote. The exercise of most powers required approval of at least nine states. Amendments to the Articles required the consent of *all* the states.

↓

Committee of the States
A committee of representatives from all the states was empowered to act in the name of Congress between sessions.

↓

Officers
Congress appointed officers to do some of the executive work.

↓

The States

Table 2–1 ▶   Powers of the Congress of the Confederation
Why would states be reluctant to forward taxes to the Confederation?

Congress Had Power to	Congress Lacked Power to
• Declare war and make peace. • Enter into treaties and alliances. • Establish and control armed forces. • Requisition men and revenues from states. • Regulate coinage. • Borrow funds and issue bills of credit. • Fix uniform standards of weight and measurement. • Create admiralty courts. • Create a postal system. • Regulate Indian affairs. • Guarantee citizens of each state the rights and privileges of citizens in the several states when in another state. • Adjudicate disputes between states on state petition.	• Provide for effective treaty-making power and control foreign relations—it could not compel states to respect treaties. • Compel states to meet military quotas—it could not draft soldiers. • Regulate interstate and foreign commerce—it left each state free to tax imports from other states. • Collect taxes directly from the people—it had to rely on states to collect and forward taxes. • Compel states to pay their share of government costs. • Provide and maintain a sound monetary system or issue paper money—this was left up to the states, and the paper currencies in circulation differed tremendously in value.

Shays' Rebellion and the Need to Revise the Articles. Because of the weaknesses of the Articles of Confederation, the central government could do little to maintain peace and order in the new nation. The states bickered among themselves and increasingly taxed each other's goods. By 1784, the country faced a serious economic depression. Banks were calling in old loans and refusing to make new ones. People who could not pay their debts were often thrown into prison.

In August 1786, mobs of musket-bearing farmers led by former revolutionary captain Daniel Shays seized county courthouses and disrupted the trials of debtors in Springfield, Massachusetts. Shays and his men then launched an attack on the federal arsenal at Springfield, but they were repulsed. Shays' Rebellion demonstrated that the central government could not protect the citizenry from armed rebellion or provide adequately for the public welfare. The rebellion spurred the nation's political leaders to action.

The minutemen were members of a colonial militia that was ready to fight the British at a moment's notice. *Why did the Continental Congress later turn the militia into an army?*

The Constitutional Convention

The Virginia legislature called for a meeting of all the states to be held at Annapolis, Maryland, on September 11, 1786—ostensibly to discuss commercial problems only. It was evident to those in attendance (including Alexander Hamilton and James Madison) that the national government had serious weaknesses that had to be addressed if it was to survive. Among the important problems to be solved were the relationship between the states and the central government, the powers of the national legislature, the need for executive leadership, and the establishment of policies for economic stability.

The result of this meeting was a petition to the Continental Congress for a general convention to meet in Philadelphia in May 1787 "to consider the exigencies of the union." Congress approved the convention in February 1787. When those who favored a weak central government realized that the Philadelphia meeting would in fact take place, they endorsed the convention. They made sure, however, that the convention would be summoned "for the sole and express purpose of revising the Articles of Confederation." Those in favor of a stronger national government had different ideas.

The designated date for the opening of the convention at Philadelphia, now known as the Constitutional Convention, was May 14, 1787. Few of the delegates had actually arrived in Philadelphia by that time, however, so the opening was delayed. The Convention formally began in the East Room of the Pennsylvania State House on May 25.[8] Fifty-five of the seventy-four delegates chosen for the convention actually attended. (Of those fifty-five, only about forty played active roles at the convention.) Rhode Island was the only state that refused to send delegates.

■ **Learning Outcome 3:** Discuss the most important compromises reached at the Constitutional Convention and the basic structure of the resulting government.

Who Were the Delegates?

Who were the fifty-five delegates to the Constitutional Convention? They certainly did not represent a cross section of American society in the 1700s. Indeed, most were members of the upper class. Consider the following facts:

1. Thirty-three were members of the legal profession.
2. Three were physicians.

did you know?

James Madison was the only delegate to attend every meeting of the Constitutional Convention.

---

8. The State House was later named Independence Hall. This was the same room in which the Declaration of Independence had been signed eleven years earlier.

Alexander Hamilton (shown in an 1804 portrait) was among those who wanted a monarchy.

3. Almost 50 percent were college graduates.
4. Seven were former chief executives of their respective states.
5. Six were owners of large plantations.
6. Eight were important businesspersons.

They were also relatively young by today's standards: James Madison was thirty-six, Alexander Hamilton was only thirty-two, and Jonathan Dayton of New Jersey was twenty-six. The venerable Benjamin Franklin, however, was eighty-one and had to be carried in on a portable chair borne by four prisoners from a local jail. Not counting Franklin, the average age was just over forty-two.

The Working Environment

The conditions under which the delegates worked for 115 days were far from ideal and were made even worse by the necessity of maintaining total secrecy. The framers of the Constitution believed that if public debate took place on particular positions, delegates would have a more difficult time compromising or backing down to reach agreement. Consequently, the windows were usually shut in the East Room of the State House. Summer quickly arrived, and the air became humid and hot by noon of each day. The delegates did, however, have a nearby tavern and inn to which they retired each evening—the Indian Queen. It became the informal headquarters of the delegates.

Factions among the Delegates

We know much about the proceedings at the convention because James Madison kept a daily, detailed personal journal. A majority of the delegates were strong nationalists—they wanted a central government with real power, unlike the central government under the Articles of Confederation. George Washington and Benjamin Franklin were among those who sought a stronger government.

Among the nationalists, some—including Alexander Hamilton—went so far as to support monarchy. Another important group of nationalists was of a more republican stripe. Led by James Madison of Virginia and James Wilson of Pennsylvania, these republican nationalists wanted a central government founded on popular support.

Many of the other delegates from Connecticut, Delaware, Maryland, New Hampshire, and New Jersey were concerned about only one thing—claims to western lands. As long as those lands became the common property of all of the states, these delegates were willing to support a central government.

Finally, there was a group of delegates who were totally against a national authority. Two of the three delegates from New York quit the convention when they saw the nationalist direction of its proceedings.

Politicking and Compromises

The debates at the convention started on the first day. James Madison had spent months reviewing European political theory. When his Virginia delegation arrived ahead of most of the others, it got to work immediately. By the time George Washington opened the convention, Governor Edmund Randolph of Virginia was prepared to present fifteen resolutions proposing fundamental changes to the nation's government. In retrospect, this was a masterful stroke on the part of the Virginia delegation. It set the agenda for the remainder of the convention—even though, in principle, the delegates had been sent to Philadelphia for the sole purpose of amending the Articles of Confederation.

did you know?

The word *democracy* does not appear once in the U.S. Constitution.

The Virginia Plan. Randolph's fifteen resolutions proposed an entirely new national government under a constitution. Basically, it called for the following:

1. A **bicameral** (two-chamber) **legislature,** with the lower chamber chosen by the people and the smaller upper chamber chosen by the lower chamber from nominees selected by state legislatures. The number of representatives would be proportional to a state's population, thus favoring the large states. The legislature could void any state laws.
2. The creation of an unspecified national executive, elected by the legislature.
3. The creation of a national judiciary, appointed by the legislature.

It did not take long for the smaller states to realize they would fare poorly under the Virginia Plan, which would enable Massachusetts, Pennsylvania, and Virginia to form a majority in the national legislature. The debate on the plan dragged on for a number of weeks. It was time for the small states to come up with their own plan.

The New Jersey Plan. On June 15, William Paterson of New Jersey offered an alternative plan. After all, argued Paterson, under the Articles of Confederation all states had equality. Therefore, the convention had no power to change this arrangement. He proposed the following:

1. The fundamental principle of the Articles of Confederation—one state, one vote— would be retained.
2. Congress would be able to regulate trade and impose taxes.
3. All acts of Congress would be the supreme law of the land.
4. Several people would be elected by Congress to form an executive office.
5. The executive office would appoint a Supreme Court.

Basically, the New Jersey Plan was simply an amendment of the Articles of Confederation. Its only notable feature was its reference to the **supremacy doctrine,** which was later included in the Constitution.

Bicameral Legislature
A legislature made up of two parts, called chambers. The U.S. Congress, composed of the House of Representatives and the Senate, is a bicameral legislature.

Supremacy Doctrine
A doctrine that asserts the priority of national law over state laws. This principle is stated in Article VI of the Constitution, which provides that the Constitution, the laws passed by the national government under its constitutional powers, and all treaties constitute the supreme law of the land.

George Washington presided over the Constitutional Convention of 1787. *Why might he have been chosen for this position?*

Great Compromise

The compromise between the New Jersey and Virginia Plans that created one chamber of the Congress based on population and one chamber representing each state equally; also called the Connecticut Compromise.

The "Great Compromise." The delegates were at an impasse. Most wanted a strong national government and were unwilling even to consider the New Jersey Plan. But when the Virginia Plan was brought up again, the small states threatened to leave. It was not until July 16 that a compromise was achieved. Roger Sherman of Connecticut proposed the following:

1. A bicameral legislature in which the lower chamber, the House of Representatives, would be apportioned according to the number of free inhabitants in each state, plus three-fifths of the slaves.
2. An upper chamber, the Senate, which would have two members from each state elected by the state legislatures.

This plan, known as the **Great Compromise** (it is also called the Connecticut Compromise because of the role of the Connecticut delegates in the proposal), broke the deadlock. It did exact a political price, however, because it permitted each state to have equal representation in the Senate. Having two senators represent each state diluted the voting power of citizens living in more heavily populated states and gave the smaller states disproportionate political power. But the Connecticut Compromise resolved the controversy between small and large states. In addition, the Senate would act as a check on the House, which many feared would be dominated by the masses and excessively responsive to them.

The Three-Fifths Compromise. The Great Compromise also settled another major issue—how to deal with slaves in the representational scheme. Slavery was still legal in several northern states, but it was concentrated in the South. Many delegates were opposed to slavery and wanted it banned entirely in the United States. Charles Pinckney of South Carolina led strong southern opposition to a ban on slavery. Furthermore, the South wanted slaves to be counted along with free persons in determining representation in Congress. Delegates from the northern states objected. Sherman's three-fifths proposal was a compromise between northerners who did not want the slaves counted at all and southerners who wanted them counted in the same way as free whites. Actually, Sherman's Connecticut Plan spoke of three-fifths of "all other persons" (and that is the language of the Constitution itself). It is not hard to figure out, though, who those other persons were.

The three-fifths rule meant that the House of Representatives and the electoral college would be apportioned in part on the basis of *property*—specifically, property in slaves. Modern commentators have referred to the three-fifths rule as valuing African Americans only three-fifths as much as whites. Actually, the additional southern representatives elected because of the three-fifths rule did not represent the slaves at all. Rather, these extra representatives were a gift to the slave owners—the additional representatives enhanced the power of the South in Congress.

Why Should You Care about . . .

The Constitution?

The laws of the nation have a direct impact on your life, and none more so than the Constitution—the supreme law of the land. The most important issues in society are often settled by the Constitution. For example, for the first seventy-five years of the republic, the Constitution implicitly protected the institution of slavery. If the Constitution had never been changed by an amendment, the process of abolishing slavery would have been much different and might have involved revolutionary measures.

The Slave Trade and the Future of Slavery. The three-fifths compromise did not completely settle the slavery issue. There was also the question of the slave trade. Eventually, the delegates agreed that Congress could not ban the importation of slaves until after 1808.

The compromise meant that the matter of slavery itself was never addressed directly. The South won twenty years of unrestricted slave trade and a requirement that escaped slaves in free states be returned to their owners in slave states.

Clearly, many delegates, including slave owners such as George Washington and James Madison, had serious objections to slavery. Why, then, did they allow slavery to continue? Historians have long maintained that the framers had no choice—that without a slavery compromise, the delegates from the South would have abandoned the convention. Indeed, this was the fear of a number of antislavery delegates to the convention. Madison, for example, said, "Great as the evil is, a dismemberment of the Union would be even worse."[9]

A number of historians have made an additional point. Many American leaders believed that slavery would die out naturally. These leaders assumed that in the long run, slave labor could not compete with the labor of free citizens. This assumption turned out to be incorrect.

Other Issues. The South also worried that the northern majority in Congress would pass legislation unfavorable to its economic interests. Because the South depended on agricultural exports, it feared the imposition of export taxes. In return for acceding to the northern demand that Congress be able to regulate commerce among the states and with other nations, the South obtained a promise that export taxes would not be imposed. As a result, the United States is among the few countries that do not tax their exports.

There were other disagreements. The delegates could not decide whether to establish only a Supreme Court or to create lower courts as well. They deferred the issue by mandating a Supreme Court and allowing Congress to establish lower courts. They also disagreed over whether the president or the Senate would choose the Supreme Court justices. A compromise was reached with the agreement that the president would nominate the justices and the Senate would confirm the nominations.

These compromises, as well as others, resulted from the recognition that if one group of states refused to ratify the Constitution, it was doomed.

Working toward Final Agreement

The Connecticut Compromise was reached by mid-July. The makeup of the executive branch and the judiciary, however, was left unsettled. The remaining work of the convention was turned over to a five-man Committee of Detail, which presented a rough draft of the Constitution on August 6. It made the executive and judicial branches subordinate to the legislative branch.

The Madisonian Model—Separation of Powers. The major issue of **separation of powers** had not yet been resolved. The delegates were concerned with structuring the government to prevent the imposition of tyranny, either by the majority or by a minority. It was Madison who proposed a governmental scheme—sometimes called the **Madisonian model**—to achieve this: the executive, legislative, and judicial powers of government were to be separated so that no one branch had enough power to dominate the others. The separation of powers was by function, as well as by personnel, with Congress passing laws, the president enforcing and administering laws, and the courts interpreting laws in individual circumstances.

Each of the three branches of government would be independent of the others, but they would have to cooperate to govern. According to Madison, in *Federalist Paper* No. 51 (see Appendix B), "the great security against a gradual concentration of the several powers in the same

Separation of Powers
The principle of dividing governmental powers among different branches of government.

Madisonian Model
A structure of government proposed by James Madison in which the powers of the government are separated into three branches: executive, legislative, and judicial.

did you know?
Neither John Adams nor Thomas Jefferson attended the Constitutional Convention. Adams was serving as the U.S. ambassador to Britain, and Jefferson was our ambassador to France.

---

9. Speech before the Virginia ratifying convention on June 17, 1788, as cited in Bruno Leone, ed., *The Creation of the Constitution* (San Diego: Greenhaven Press, 1995), p. 159.

COMPARE WITH YOUR PEERS
MindTap™ for American Government

Access The Constitution Forum: Polling Activity—Raising the Debt Ceiling

department consists in giving to those who administer each department the necessary constitutional means and personal motives to resist encroachments of the others."

The Madisonian Model—Checks and Balances. The "constitutional means" Madison referred to is a system of **checks and balances** through which each branch of the government can check the actions of the others. For example, Congress can enact laws, but the president has veto power over congressional acts. The Supreme Court has the power to declare acts of Congress and of the executive branch unconstitutional, but the president appoints the justices of the Supreme Court, with the advice and consent of the Senate. (The Supreme Court's power to declare acts unconstitutional was not mentioned in the Constitution, although arguably the framers assumed that the Court would have this power—see the discussion of *judicial review* later in this chapter.) Figure 2–2 that follows outlines these checks and balances.

Madison's ideas of separation of powers and checks and balances were not new. Indeed, the influential French political thinker Baron de Montesquieu (1689–1755) had explored these concepts in his book *The Spirit of the Laws*, published in 1748. Montesquieu not only discussed the "three sorts of powers" (executive, legislative, and judicial) that were necessarily exercised by any government but also gave examples of how, in some nations, certain checks on these powers had arisen and had been effective in preventing tyranny.

Figure 2–2 ▶ Checks and Balances

The major checks and balances among the three branches are illustrated here. The U.S. Constitution does not mention some of these checks, such as judicial review—the power of the courts to declare federal or state acts unconstitutional—and the president's ability to refuse to enforce judicial decisions or congressional legislation. Checks and balances can be thought of as a confrontation of powers or responsibilities. Each branch checks the actions of another. Two branches in conflict have powers that can result in balances or stalemates, requiring one branch to give in or both to reach a compromise. *Which result is more likely?*

- The Supreme Court can declare presidential actions unconstitutional.
- The president nominates federal judges.
- The president can refuse to enforce the Court's decisions.
- The president grants pardons.

THE JUDICIARY

- The Supreme Court can declare congressional laws unconstitutional.
- Congress can rewrite legislation to circumvent the Court's decisions.
- The Senate confirms federal judges.
- Congress determines the number of judges.

- The president proposes laws and can veto congressional legislation.
- The president makes treaties and executive agreements and issues executive orders.
- The president can refuse, and has refused, to enforce congressional legislation.
- The president can call special sessions of Congress.

- Congress makes legislation and can override a presidential veto of legislation.
- Congress can impeach and remove a president.
- The Senate must confirm presidential appointments and consent to the treaties negotiated by the president based on a two-thirds concurrence.
- Congress has the power of the purse and provides funds for the president's programs.

THE PRESIDENCY

THE CONGRESS

The Development of the Madisonian Model. In the years since the Constitution was ratified, the checks and balances built into it have evolved into a sometimes complex give-and-take among the branches of government. Generally, for nearly every check that one branch has over another, the branch that has been checked has found a way of getting around it. For example, suppose that the president checks Congress by vetoing a bill. Congress can override the presidential veto by a two-thirds vote. Additionally, Congress holds the "power of the purse." If it disagrees with a program endorsed by the executive branch, it can simply refuse to appropriate the funds necessary to operate that program. Similarly, the president can impose a countercheck on Congress if the Senate refuses to confirm a presidential appointment, such as a judicial appointment. The president can simply wait until Congress is in recess and then make what is called a "recess appointment," which does not require the Senate's immediate approval.

The Executive. Some delegates favored a plural executive made up of a committee. This idea was abandoned in favor of a single chief executive. Some argued that Congress should choose the executive. To make the presidency completely independent of the proposed Congress, however, an **electoral college** was adopted. As we explained in this chapter's opening *What If . . .* feature, the voters of the various states choose electors, and then the electors actually choose the president. The number of electors in each state is equal to the number of each state's U.S. representatives and senators added together. In addition, the Twenty-third Amendment to the Constitution now gives the District of Columbia the same number of electors as the least populous state.

The founders hoped that through this system, the president would be elected by prominent citizens, not ordinary voters. In fact, for some years after the Constitution was adopted, electors in about half the states were chosen by the state legislature, not directly by the voters. Even in those states, however, the organization of political parties from 1796 on gave ordinary voters some input into choosing the president. A vote for a party's state legislative candidate, after all, was also a way to support that party's presidential candidate. By 1832, the South Carolina legislature was the only one still choosing electors.

The Final Document

On September 17, 1787, the Constitution was approved by thirty-nine delegates. Of the fifty-five who had attended originally, only forty-two remained. Three delegates refused to sign the Constitution. Others disapproved of at least parts of it but signed anyway to begin the ratification debate.

The Constitution that was to be ratified established the following fundamental principles:

1. Popular sovereignty, or control by the people.
2. A republican government in which the people choose representatives to make decisions for them.
3. Limited government with written laws, in contrast to the powerful British government against which the colonists had rebelled.
4. Separation of powers, with checks and balances among branches to prevent any one branch from gaining too much power.
5. A federal system that allows for states' rights, because the states feared too much centralized control.

A Federal System. You will read about federalism in detail in Chapter 3. Suffice it to say here that in the **federal system** established by the founders, sovereign powers—ruling powers—were divided between the states and the national government. The Constitution expressly granted certain powers to the national government.

Electoral College
A group of persons called electors selected by the voters in each state and the District of Columbia (D.C.). This group officially elects the president and vice president of the United States.

Federal System
A system of government in which power is divided between a central government and regional, or subdivisional, governments. Each level must have some domain in which its policies are dominant and some genuine political or constitutional guarantee of its authority.

did you know?

The nation's population was 4 million when the Constitution was signed. (It is now about 320 million.) Philadelphia, with 40,000 residents, was our largest city.

Ratification
Formal approval.

Federalist
The name given to one who was in favor of the adoption of the U.S. Constitution and the creation of a federal union with a strong central government.

Anti-Federalist
An individual who opposed the ratification of the new Constitution in 1787. The Anti-Federalists were opposed to a strong central government.

■ **Learning Outcome 4:** Summarize the arguments in favor of and the arguments against adopting the Constitution, and explain why the Bill of Rights was adopted.

For example, the national government was given the power to regulate commerce among the states. The Constitution also declared that the president is the nation's chief executive and the commander in chief of the armed forces. Additionally, the Constitution made it clear that laws made by the national government take priority over conflicting state laws. At the same time, the Constitution provided for extensive states' rights, including the right to control commerce within state borders and to exercise those governing powers that were not delegated to the national government.

A Novel Form of Government. The federal system created by the founders was a novel form of government at that time—no other country in the world had such a system. It was invented by the founders as a compromise solution to the controversy over whether the states or the central government should have ultimate sovereignty. As you will read in Chapter 3, the debate over where the line should be drawn between states' rights and the powers of the national government has characterized American politics ever since. The founders did not go into detail about where this line should be drawn, thus leaving it up to elected officials and judges to divine the correct constitutional balance.

The Difficult Road to Ratification

The founders knew that **ratification** of the Constitution was far from certain. Indeed, because it was almost guaranteed that many state legislatures would not ratify it, the delegates agreed that each state should hold a special convention. Elected delegates to these conventions would discuss and vote on the Constitution. Further departing from the Articles of Confederation, the delegates agreed that as soon as nine states (rather than all thirteen) approved the Constitution, it would take effect, and Congress could begin to organize the new government.

The Federalists Push for Ratification

The two opposing forces in the battle over ratification were the Federalists and the Anti-Federalists. The **Federalists**—those in favor of a strong central government and the new Constitution—had an advantage over their opponents, called the **Anti-Federalists,** who wanted to prevent the Constitution as drafted from being ratified. In the first place, the Federalists had assumed a positive name, leaving their opposition the negative label of *Anti*-Federalist.[10] More important, the Federalists had attended the Constitutional Convention and knew of all the deliberations that had taken place. Their opponents had no such knowledge, because those deliberations had not been open to the public. Thus, the Anti-Federalists were at a disadvantage in terms of information about the document. The Federalists also had time, power, and wealth on their side. Communications were slow. Those who had access to the best communications were Federalists—mostly wealthy bankers, lawyers, plantation owners, and merchants living in urban areas, where communications were better. The Federalist campaign was organized relatively quickly and effectively to elect Federalists as delegates to the state ratifying conventions.

The Anti-Federalists, however, had at least one strong point in their favor: they stood for the status quo. In general, the greater burden is always placed on those advocating change.

10. There is some irony here. At the Constitutional Convention, those opposed to a strong central government pushed for a federal system because such a system would allow the states to retain some of their sovereign rights (see Chapter 3). The label *Anti-Federalists* thus contradicted their essential views.

The *Federalist Papers*. In New York, opponents of the Constitution were quick to attack it. Alexander Hamilton answered their attacks under a pseudonym in newspaper columns and secured two collaborators—John Jay and James Madison. In a very short time, those three political figures wrote a series of eighty-five essays in defense of the Constitution and of a republican form of government.

These widely read essays, called the *Federalist Papers,* appeared in New York newspapers from October 1787 to August 1788 and were reprinted in the newspapers of other states. Although we do not know for certain who wrote every one, it is apparent that Hamilton was responsible for about two-thirds of the essays. These included the most important ones interpreting the Constitution, explaining the various powers of the three branches, and presenting a theory of *judicial review*—to be discussed later in this chapter. Madison's *Federalist Paper* No. 10 (see Appendix B), however, is considered a classic in political theory. It deals with the nature of groups—or factions, as he called them. We discuss the ways in which groups influence our government in Chapter 7. In spite of the rapidity with which the *Federalist Papers* were written, they are considered by many to be perhaps the best example of political theorizing ever produced in the United States.[11]

The Anti-Federalist Response. The Anti-Federalists used such pseudonyms as Montezuma and Philadelphiensis in their replies. Many of their attacks on the Constitution were also brilliant. The Anti-Federalists claimed that the Constitution was written by aristocrats and would lead to aristocratic tyranny. More important, the Anti-Federalists believed that the Constitution would create an overbearing and overburdening central government hostile to personal liberty. (The Constitution said nothing about freedom of the press, freedom of religion, or any other individual liberty.) They wanted to include a list of guaranteed liberties, or a bill of rights. Finally, the Anti-Federalists decried the weakened power of the states.[12]

The Anti-Federalists cannot be dismissed as unpatriotic extremists. They included such patriots as Patrick Henry and Samuel Adams. They were arguing what had been the most prevalent view in that era. This view derived from the French political philosopher Montesquieu, who, as mentioned earlier, was an influential political theorist. Montesquieu believed that a republic was possible only in a relatively small society governed by direct democracy or by a large legislature with small districts. The Madisonian view favoring a large republic, particularly as expressed in *Federalist Papers* No. 10 and No. 51 (see Appendix B), was actually an exceptional view in those years. Indeed, some researchers believe it was mainly the bitter experiences with the Articles of Confederation, rather than Madison's arguments, that persuaded the state conventions to ratify the Constitution.

Patrick Henry (1736–1799). A revolutionary-era leader, Henry was a member of the Continental Congress and twice governor of Virginia. He and other Anti-Federalists opposed the new Constitution. *What kinds of arguments did the Anti-Federalists make?*

11. Some scholars believe that the *Federalist Papers* played only a minor role in securing ratification of the Constitution. Even if this is true, they still have lasting value as an authoritative explanation of the Constitution.
12. Herbert J. Storing edited seven volumes of Anti-Federalist writings and released them in 1981 as *The Anti-Federalist*. Political science professor Murray Dry has prepared a more manageable, one-volume version of this collection: Herbert J. Storing, ed., *The Anti-Federalist: An Abridgment of the Complete Anti-Federalist* (Chicago: University of Chicago Press, 2006).

The March to the Finish

The struggle for ratification continued. Strong majorities were procured in Connecticut, Delaware, Georgia, New Jersey, and Pennsylvania. After a bitter struggle in Massachusetts, that state ratified the Constitution by a narrow margin on February 6, 1788. By the spring, Maryland and South Carolina had ratified by sizable majorities. Then on June 21 of that year, New Hampshire became the ninth state to ratify the Constitution. Although the Constitution was formally in effect, this meant little without Virginia and New York. Virginia ratified it a few days later, but New York did not join in for another month (see Table 2–2 that follows).

Did the Majority of Americans Support the Constitution?

In 1913, historian Charles Beard published *An Economic Interpretation of the Constitution of the United States*.[13] This book launched a debate that has continued ever since—the debate over whether the Constitution was supported by a majority of Americans.

Beard's Thesis. Beard argued that the Constitution had been produced primarily by wealthy property owners who desired a stronger government able to protect their property rights. Beard also claimed that the Constitution had been imposed by undemocratic methods. He pointed out that there was never any popular vote on whether to hold a constitutional convention in the first place. Furthermore, even if such a vote had been taken, state laws generally restricted voting rights to property-owning white males.

State Ratifying Conventions. The delegates to the various state ratifying conventions had been selected by only 150,000 of the nation's approximately 4 million total inhabitants. That does not seem very democratic—at least not by today's standards. Some historians have suggested that if a Gallup poll could have been taken at that time, the Anti-Federalists would probably have outnumbered the Federalists. Much has also been made of the various machinations used by the Federalists to ensure the Constitution's ratification, including the purchase of at least one printing press to prevent the publication of Anti-Federalist sentiments.

Support Was Probably Widespread. Many small farmers feared that the Constitution would result in oppressive domination by a wealthy elite. Still, the perception that a strong central government was necessary to keep order and protect the public welfare appears to have been widespread among all classes, rich and poor alike. No doubt an effective national government would benefit the wealthy, as Beard argued. Yet it could help workers and small farmers as well. After all, the economic and political crisis that the nation faced in the 1780s fell even harder on the poor than on the rich.

Further, although the need for strong government was a major argument in favor of adopting the Constitution, even the Federalists sought to craft a limited government. Compared with constitutions adopted by other

David Sipress, *The New Yorker* Collection/The Cartoon Bank

"Now, should we add something at the end about how wise we are and therefore nothing in here should ever be changed?"

---

13. Charles A. Beard, *An Economic Interpretation of the Constitution of the United States* (New York: Macmillan, 1913; New York: Free Press, 1986).

Table 2–2 ▶ **Ratification of the Constitution**

What might have happened if Rhode Island had never joined the Union?

State	Date	Vote For–Against
Delaware	Dec. 7, 1787	30–0
Pennsylvania	Dec. 12, 1787	43–23
New Jersey	Dec. 18, 1787	38–0
Georgia	Jan. 2, 1788	26–0
Connecticut	Jan. 9, 1788	128–40
Massachusetts	Feb. 6, 1788	187–168
Maryland	Apr. 28, 1788	63–11
South Carolina	May 23, 1788	149–73
New Hampshire	June 21, 1788	57–46
Virginia	June 25, 1788	89–79
New York	July 26, 1788	30–27
North Carolina	Nov. 21, 1789*	194–77
Rhode Island	May 29, 1790	34–32

*Ratification was initially defeated on August 4, 1788, by a vote of 84–184.

nations in later years, the U.S. Constitution, through its checks and balances, favors limited government over "energetic" government to a marked degree.

The Bill of Rights

The U.S. Constitution would not have been ratified in several important states if the Federalists had not assured the states that amendments to the Constitution would be passed to protect individual liberties against incursions by the national government. Many of the recommendations of the state ratifying conventions included specific rights that were considered later by James Madison as he labored to draft what became the Bill of Rights. (We introduced the Bill of Rights in the *What If . . .* feature that opened Chapter 1.)

A "Bill of Limits." Although called the Bill of Rights, the first ten amendments to the Constitution essentially were a "bill of limits," because the amendments limited the powers of the national government over the rights and liberties of individuals.

Ironically, a year earlier Madison had told Jefferson, "I have never thought the omission [of the Bill of Rights] a material defect" of the Constitution. Jefferson's enthusiasm for a bill of rights apparently influenced Madison, however.

Was a Bill of Rights Necessary? Many framers thought that it was dangerous to enumerate specific civil liberties in a bill of rights. Future governments might assume that rights that were not listed did not exist. (This concern was addressed in the Bill of Rights itself by the Ninth Amendment.)

did you know?
One delegate to the Constitutional Convention proposed limiting the nation's peacetime army to 5,000 soldiers. George Washington sarcastically agreed, provided that the proposal be amended to say that no invading army could number more than 3,000.

Also, the Constitution already listed certain rights. The original document prohibits *bills of attainder*—laws that impose punishment on named individuals without trial. The original Constitution also bars *ex post facto* laws, which make an act illegal only after it has already happened. A trial by jury is required in federal criminal cases. Finally, individuals may not be jailed without due process of law. A judge can demand to know why a particular person is in custody (the demand is called a *writ of habeas corpus*). If no proper explanation is given, the judge can order the individual's release.

Madison Drafts the Bill.   Madison had to cull through more than two hundred state recommendations. It was no small task, and in retrospect he chose remarkably well. One of the rights appropriate for constitutional protection that he left out was equal protection under the laws—but that was not commonly regarded as a basic right at that time. Not until 1868 was the Constitution amended to guarantee that no state shall deny equal protection to any person.

The final number of amendments that Madison and a specially appointed committee came up with was seventeen. Congress tightened the language somewhat and eliminated five of the amendments. Of the remaining twelve, two—dealing with the apportionment of representatives and the compensation of the members of Congress—were not ratified immediately by the states. Eventually, Supreme Court decisions led to reform of the apportionment process. The amendment on the compensation of members of Congress was ratified 203 years later—in 1992![14]

Adoption of the Bill of Rights.   On December 15, 1791, the national Bill of Rights was adopted when Virginia agreed to ratify the ten amendments. On ratification, the Bill of Rights became part of the U.S. Constitution. The basic structure of American government had already been established. Now the fundamental rights and liberties of individuals were protected, at least in theory, at the national level. The proposed amendment that Madison characterized as "the most valuable amendment in the whole lot"—which would have prohibited the states from infringing on the freedoms of conscience, press, and jury trial—had been eliminated by the Senate. Thus, the Bill of Rights as adopted did not limit state power, and individual citizens had to rely on the guarantees contained in a particular state constitution or state bill of rights. The country had to wait until the violence of the Civil War before significant limitations on state power in the form of the Fourteenth Amendment became part of the national Constitution.

Why Should You Care about . . .

The Constitution?

Since the passage of the Fourteenth Amendment in 1868, the Constitution has defined who is a citizen and who is entitled to the protections the Constitution provides. Constitutional provisions define our liberties. The First Amendment protects our freedom of speech more thoroughly than do the laws of many other nations. As another example, few other countries have constitutional provisions governing the right to own firearms (the Second Amendment). Disputes involving these rights are among the most fundamental issues we face.

■ **Learning Outcome 5:** Describe the process of amending the Constitution and the informal ways in which Constitutional interpretation has changed over time.

Altering the Constitution

As amended, the U.S. Constitution consists of about seven thousand words. It is shorter than any state constitution except that of Vermont. The federal Constitution is short because the founders intended it to be only a framework for the new government, to be interpreted by succeeding generations. One of the reasons it has remained short is that

---

14. For perspectives on these events, see Richard E. Labunski, *James Madison and the Struggle for the Bill of Rights* (New York: Oxford University Press, 2008); and Steven Waldman, *Founding Faith: How Our Founding Fathers Forged a Radical New Approach to Religious Liberty* (New York: Random House Trade Paperbacks, 2009).

the formal amending procedure does not allow for changes to be made easily. Article V of the Constitution outlines the ways in which amendments may be proposed and ratified (see Figure 2–3 that follows).

The Formal Amendment Process

Two formal methods of proposing an amendment to the Constitution are available: (1) a two-thirds vote in each chamber of Congress or (2) a national convention that is called by Congress at the request of two-thirds of the state legislatures. This second method has never been used.

Ratification can occur by one of two methods: (1) by a positive vote in three-fourths of the legislatures of the various states or (2) by special conventions called in the states and a positive vote in three-fourths of them. The second method has been used only once, to repeal Prohibition (the ban on the production and sale of alcoholic beverages). That situation was exceptional—it involved an amendment (the Twenty-first) to repeal another amendment (the Eighteenth, which had created Prohibition). State conventions were necessary for repeal of the Eighteenth Amendment because prohibitionist forces were in control of the legislatures in many states where a majority of the population actually supported repeal. (Note that Congress determines the method of ratification to be used by all states for each proposed constitutional amendment.)

Many Amendments Proposed, Few Accepted. Congress has considered more than eleven thousand amendments to the Constitution. Only thirty-three amendments have been submitted to the states after having been approved by the required two-thirds vote in each chamber of Congress, and only twenty-seven have been ratified—see Table 2–3 that follows. (The full, annotated text of the U.S. Constitution, including its amendments, is presented in a special appendix at the end of this chapter.) It should be clear that

> **did you know?**
> The Constitution explicitly says that no amendment can alter the equal representation of the states in the Senate. This is the only such "entrenched" provision in the document.

Figure 2–3 ▸ **The Formal Constitutional Amending Procedure**

There are two ways of proposing amendments to the U.S. Constitution and two ways of ratifying proposed amendments. Among the four possibilities, the usual route has been proposal by Congress and ratification by state legislatures. *What could happen if Congress were to call a convention?*

PROPOSING AMENDMENTS

EITHER . . . By a two-thirds vote in both chambers of Congress . . .

OR . . . By a national convention called by Congress at the request of two-thirds of the states.

RATIFYING AMENDMENTS

EITHER . . . By the legislatures of three-fourths of the states . . .

OR . . . By conventions in three-fourths of the states.

➡ Typical (used for all except one amendment)
➡ Used only once (Twenty-first Amendment)
➡ Never used

the amendment process is much more difficult than a graphic depiction such as Figure 2–3 above can indicate. Because of competing social and economic interests, the requirement that two-thirds of both the House and the Senate approve the amendments is hard to achieve.

After an amendment has been approved by Congress, the process becomes even more arduous. Three-fourths of the state legislatures must approve the amendment. Only those amendments that have wide popular support across parties and in all regions of the country are likely to be approved.

Why was the amendment process made so difficult? The framers feared that a simple amendment process could lead to a tyranny of the majority, which could pass amendments to oppress disfavored individuals and groups. The cumbersome amendment process does not seem to stem the number of amendments that are proposed

Table 2–3 ▸ Amendments to the Constitution
Why so few?

Amendment	Subject	Year Adopted	Time Required for Ratification
1st–10th	The Bill of Rights	1791	2 years, 2 months, 20 days
11th	Immunity of states from certain suits	1795	11 months, 3 days
12th	Changes in electoral college procedure	1804	6 months, 3 days
13th	Prohibition of slavery	1865	10 months, 3 days
14th	Citizenship, due process, and equal protection	1868	2 years, 26 days
15th	No denial of vote because of race, color, or previous condition of servitude	1870	11 months, 8 days
16th	Power of Congress to tax income	1913	3 years, 6 months, 22 days
17th	Direct election of U.S. senators	1913	10 months, 26 days
18th	National (liquor) prohibition	1919	1 year, 29 days
19th	Women's right to vote	1920	1 year, 2 months, 14 days
20th	Change of dates for congressional and presidential terms	1933	10 months, 21 days
21st	Repeal of the Eighteenth Amendment	1933	9 months, 15 days
22d	Limit on presidential tenure	1951	3 years, 11 months, 3 days
23d	District of Columbia electoral vote	1961	9 months, 13 days
24th	Prohibition of tax payment as a qualification to vote in federal elections	1964	1 year, 4 months, 9 days
25th	Procedures for determining presidential disability and presidential succession and for filling a vice-presidential vacancy	1967	1 year, 7 months, 4 days
26th	Prohibition of setting the minimum voting age above eighteen in any election	1971	3 months, 7 days
27th	Prohibition of Congress's voting itself a raise or cut in pay that takes effect before the next election	1992	203 years

in Congress, however, particularly in recent years. Proposing an amendment that will never pass is an effective way for a legislator to engage in "grandstanding," that is, showing off.

Time Limits on Ratification. The framers of the Constitution specified no time limit on the ratification process. The Supreme Court has held that Congress can specify a time for ratification as long as it is "reasonable." Since 1919, most proposed amendments have included a requirement that ratification be obtained within seven years. This was the case with the proposed Equal Rights Amendment, which sought to guarantee equal rights for women. When three-fourths of the states had not ratified it in the allotted seven years, however, Congress extended the limit by an additional three years and three months. That extension expired on June 30, 1982, and the amendment still had not been ratified.

The National Convention Provision. The Constitution provides that a national convention requested by the legislatures of two-thirds of the states can propose a constitutional amendment. Congress has received approximately 400 convention applications since the Constitution was ratified—every state has applied at least once. Fewer than 20 applications were submitted during the Constitution's first hundred years, but more than 150 have been filed in the past two decades. No national convention has been held since 1787, and many national political and judicial leaders are uneasy about the prospect of convening a body that conceivably could do what the Constitutional Convention did—create a new form of government.

Informal Methods of Constitutional Change

Looking at the sparse number of formal constitutional amendments gives us an incomplete view of constitutional change. The brevity and ambiguity of the original document have permitted great alterations in the Constitution by way of varying interpretations over time. As the United States grew, both in population and in territory, new social and political realities emerged. Congress, presidents, and the courts found it necessary to interpret

Shown here are the most important documents relating to our system of government—the Declaration of Independence, the Constitution, and the Bill of Rights. *Which one outlines the amendment process?*

the Constitution's provisions in light of these new realities. The Constitution has proved to be a remarkably flexible document, adapting itself time and again to new events and concerns.

Congressional Legislation. The Constitution gives Congress broad powers to carry out its duties as the nation's legislative body. For example, Article I, Section 8, of the Constitution gives Congress the power to regulate foreign and interstate commerce. Although there is no clear definition of foreign commerce or interstate commerce in the Constitution, Congress has cited the *commerce clause* as the basis for passing thousands of laws.

In addition, Congress has frequently delegated to federal agencies the legislative power to write regulations. These regulations become law unless challenged in the court system. Nowhere does the Constitution outline this delegation of legislative authority.

Presidential Actions. Even though the Constitution does not expressly authorize the president to propose bills or even budgets to Congress,[15] presidents since the time of Woodrow Wilson (1913–1921) have proposed hundreds of bills to Congress each year that are introduced by the president's supporters in Congress. Presidents have also relied on their Article II authority as commander in chief of the nation's armed forces to send American troops abroad into combat, although the Constitution provides that Congress has the power to declare war.

Presidents have also conducted foreign affairs by the use of *executive agreements,* which are legally binding understandings reached between the president and a foreign head of state. The Constitution does not mention such agreements.

Judicial Review. Another way that the Constitution adapts to new developments is through judicial review. **Judicial review** refers to the power of U.S. courts to examine the constitutionality of actions undertaken by the legislative and executive branches of government. A state court, for example, may rule that a statute enacted by the state legislature violates the state constitution. Federal courts (and ultimately, the United States Supreme Court) may rule unconstitutional not only acts of Congress and decisions of the national executive branch, but also state statutes, state executive actions, and even provisions of state constitutions.

The Constitution does not specifically mention the power of judicial review. Those in attendance at the Constitutional Convention, however, probably expected that the courts would have some authority to review the legality of acts by the executive and legislative branches, because, under the common law tradition inherited from England, courts exercised this authority. Indeed, Alexander Hamilton, in *Federalist Paper* No. 78 (see Appendix B), explicitly outlined the concept of judicial review. In 1803, the Supreme Court claimed this power for itself in *Marbury v. Madison,*[16] in which the Court ruled that a particular provision of an act of Congress was unconstitutional.

Through the process of judicial review, the Supreme Court adapts the Constitution to modern situations and changing values. For example, it ruled in 1896 that

Judicial Review
The power of the Supreme
Court and other courts to
examine and possibly declare
unconstitutional federal or
state laws and other acts of
government.

---

15. Note, though, that the Constitution, in Article II, Section 3, does state that the president "shall from time to time . . . recommend to [Congress's] Consideration such Measures as he shall judge necessary and expedient." Some scholars interpret this phrase to mean that the president has the constitutional authority to propose bills and budgets to Congress for consideration.
16. 5 U.S. 137 (1803). See Chapter 14 for a further discussion of the *Marbury v. Madison* case.

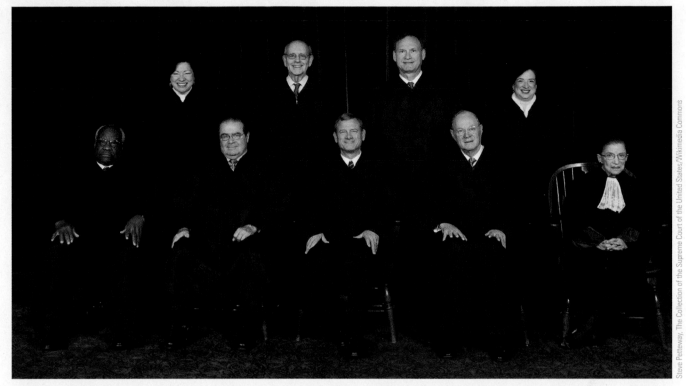

U.S. Supreme Court justices are (first row, left to right) Justice Clarence Thomas, Justice Antonin Scalia, Chief Justice John Roberts, Justice Anthony M. Kennedy, Justice Ruth Bader Ginsburg, (second row, left to right) Justice Sonia Sotomayor, Justice Stephen G. Breyer, Justice Samuel Alito, Justice Elena Kagan.

"separate-but-equal" public facilities for African Americans were constitutional. By 1954, however, the times had changed, and the Court reversed that decision.[17] Woodrow Wilson summarized the Court's work when he described it as "a constitutional convention in continuous session." Basically, the law is what the Supreme Court says it is at any point in time.

Interpretation, Custom, and Usage. Changes in ways of doing political business have also led to the reinterpretation of the Constitution. For example, the Constitution does not mention political parties, yet these "extraconstitutional" organizations make the nominations for offices, run the campaigns, organize the members of Congress, and in fact change the election system from time to time.

In many ways, the Constitution has been adapted from a document serving the needs of a small, rural republic to one that provides a framework of government for an industrial giant with vast geographic, natural, and human resources.

17. *Brown v. Board of Education of Topeka*, 347 U.S. 483 (1954).

How You Can Make a Difference

- At the time of this writing, national coalitions of interest groups support or oppose a number of constitutional amendments. One hotly debated proposal would create a constitutional requirement to balance the federal budget. In late 2011, a constitutional amendment to do just that failed in both the U.S. House and the Senate. The measure would have required a three-fifths majority in both chambers of Congress to approve any future deficit spending.

- If such an amendment sounds like a good idea to you, there are a variety of organizations you might investigate. These include Americans for a Balanced Budget Amendment at www.balanceourbudget.com.

- Other Americans have different concerns. In 2010, the Supreme Court struck down a wide range of campaign finance laws in *Citizens United v. Federal Election Commission*.[18] One result of this ruling was the "super PACs" that flooded television networks with attack advertisements during the 2012 elections. Often funded by very wealthy individuals, super PACs can spend as much as they want, provided that they do not openly coordinate their activities with a candidate's campaign.

- A proposed constitutional amendment would overturn the *Citizens United* ruling. If getting the money out of politics is of interest to you, you can examine activist groups that support this amendment. They include Democracy Is for People at www.democracyisforpeople.org.

Key Terms

Anti-Federalist 46	Federalist 46	natural rights 35	social contract 35
bicameral legislature 41	federal system 45	ratification 46	state 37
checks and balances 44	Great Compromise 42	representative	supremacy doctrine 41
confederation 37	judicial review 54	assembly 30	unicameral legislature 37
electoral college 45	Madisonian model 43	separation of powers 43	

Chapter Summary

Learning Outcome 1 The first permanent English colonies were established at Jamestown in 1607 and Plymouth in 1620. The Mayflower Compact created the first formal government in New England.

In the 1760s, the British began to impose a series of taxes and legislative acts on their increasingly independent-minded colonies. The colonists responded with protests and boycotts of British products. Representatives of the colonies formed the First Continental Congress in 1774. The Second Continental Congress established an army in 1775 to defend the colonists against attacks by British soldiers.

Learning Outcome 2 On July 4, 1776, the Second Continental Congress approved the Declaration of Independence. Perhaps the most revolutionary aspects of the Declaration were its statements that people have natural rights to life, liberty, and the pursuit of happiness; that governments derive their power from the consent of the governed; and that people have a right to overthrow oppressive governments.

During the Revolutionary War, the states signed the Articles of Confederation, creating a weak central government with few powers. The Articles proved to be unworkable because the national government had no way to ensure compliance by the states with such measures as securing tax revenues.

Learning Outcome 3 Dissatisfaction with the Articles of Confederation prompted the call for a convention at Philadelphia in 1787. Delegates focused on creating a constitution for a new form of government. The Virginia Plan, which favored the larger states, and the New Jersey Plan, which favored smaller ones, did not garner sufficient support. A compromise offered by Connecticut provided for a bicameral legislature and thus resolved the large-state/small-state controversy. The final version of the Constitution provided for the separation of powers, checks and balances, and a federal form of government.

---

18. 558 U.S. 310 (2010).

Learning Outcome 4 Fears of a strong central government prompted the addition of the Bill of Rights to the Constitution. The Bill of Rights, which includes the freedoms of religion, speech, and assembly, was initially applied only to the federal government, but amendments to the Constitution following the Civil War were interpreted to ensure that the Bill of Rights would apply to the states as well.

Learning Outcome 5 An amendment to the Constitution may be proposed either by a two-thirds vote in each chamber of Congress or by a national convention called by Congress at the request of two-thirds of the state legislatures. Ratification can occur either by the approval of three-fourths of the legislatures of the states or by special conventions called in the states for the purpose of ratifying the amendment and approval by three-fourths of these conventions. Informal methods of constitutional change include reinterpretation through congressional legislation, presidential actions, and judicial review.

Master the concept of The Constitution with MindTap™ *for American Government*

 REVIEW MindTap™ **for American Government**
Access Key Term Flashcards for Chapter 2.

 TEST YOURSELF MindTap™ **for American Government**
Take the Wrap It Up Quiz for Chapter 2.

 STAY CURRENT MindTap™ **for American Government**
Access the KnowNow blog and customized RSS for updates on current events.

 STAY FOCUSED MindTap™ **for American Government**
Complete the Focus Activities for The Constitution.

Additional Resources

Today, you can find many important documents from the founding period online, including descriptions of events leading up to the American Revolution, the Articles of Confederation, notes on the Constitutional Convention, the Federalists' writings, and the Anti-Federalists' responses.

Online Resources

- The National Constitution Center, at constitutioncenter.org, provides a variety of information on the document in an entertaining format.
- Several universities maintain online commentaries and document collections relevant to the Constitution. Cornell provides a detailed commentary on the Constitution at www.law.cornell.edu/anncon.
- Project Gutenberg offers a vast, free online collection of works that are no longer under copyright protection. For a copy of *The Federalist Papers* in any of several formats, go to www.gutenberg.org/ebooks/1404. For a collection of anti-federalist papers, see www.the-federalistpapers.org/anti-federalist-papers.
- You can get a free annotated copy of the Constitution and related documents as an app for your Android smart phone at https://play.google.com/store/apps?hl=en. The site offers *The Federalist Papers* for free as well. If you have an iPhone, you can find similar apps at Apple's App Store, but you'll probably have to cough up $0.99 for *The Federalist Papers*.
- The American Civil Liberties Union (ACLU) is the nation's leading civil liberties advocacy group. If you "friend" the ACLU on Facebook at www.facebook.com/aclu.nationwide, you'll get a regular stream of updates on efforts to protect the rights guaranteed by the Constitution.

Books

Maier, Pauline. *Ratification: The People Debate the Constitution, 1787–1788.* New York: Simon & Schuster, 2011. Maier, a professor at M.I.T., charts the Constitution's uncertain course toward ratification.

Taylor, Alan. *Colonial America: A Very Short Introduction.* New York: Oxford University Press, 2012. As with any series, the Very Short Introductions differ in quality, but this Oxford University project has scored hits. Taylor, a history professor at U.C. Davis, contrasts the English colonies with those of other nations to reveal what was truly distinctive about the English enterprise.

Wood, Gordon S. *The Idea of America: Reflections on the Birth of the United States.* New York: Penguin Press, 2011. Wood, a Brown professor, may be the most prominent living scholar of the revolutionary era. This collection of essays summarizes his life's work. Wood emphasizes the radicalism of the American Revolution, which truly did result in an entirely new conception of politics.

Video

John Adams—A widely admired 2008 HBO miniseries on John Adams and his wife, Abigail Adams, and other prominent Americans of the revolutionary period. The series is largely based on David McCullough's book, *John Adams.*

Thomas Jefferson—A 1996 documentary by acclaimed director Ken Burns. The film covers Jefferson's entire life, including his writing of the Declaration of Independence, his presidency, and his later years in Virginia. Historians and writers interviewed include Daniel Boorstin, Garry Wills, Gore Vidal, and John Hope Franklin.

Quiz

Multiple Choice and Fill-Ins

Learning Outcome 1 Explain how the colonial experience prepared Americans for independence, the restrictions that Britain placed on the colonies, and the American response.

1. When the First Continental Congress convened in 1774, the British government:
   a. welcomed the advice offered by the colonists.
   b. agreed to allow the colonies to form a separate government.
   c. treated the meeting as an act of rebellion.

2. In 1620, the members of New England's first colony signed the _____ _____ at Plymouth (Massachusetts).

Learning Outcome 2 Describe the significance of the Declaration of Independence and the Articles of Confederation, as well as the weaknesses of the Articles.

3. A major defect in the Articles of Confederation was:
   a. the lack of power to raise funds for military forces.
   b. the lack of treaty-making power.
   c. the inability to easily communicate with citizens.

4. The Declaration of Independence established as unalienable rights those of life, _____, and the pursuit of happiness.

Learning Outcome 3 Discuss the most important compromises reached at the Constitutional Convention and the basic structure of the resulting government.

5. Which of the following fundamental principles was not established by the Constitution of 1787?
   a. popular sovereignty, or control by the people.
   b. limited government with written laws.
   c. a system in which the central government had complete power over the states.

6. When no branch of government—executive, legislative, or judicial—is able to dominate the others, we call this the _____ of powers.

Learning Outcome 4 Summarize the arguments in favor of and the arguments against adopting the Constitution, and explain why the Bill of Rights was adopted.

7. The major drafter of the Bill of Rights was:
   a. Washington.
   b. Jefferson.
   c. Madison.

8. Those who opposed the ratification of the Constitution were called _____.

Learning Outcome 5 Describe the process of amending the Constitution and the informal ways in which Constitutional interpretation has changed over time.

9. The reason the U.S. Constitution has so few amendments is that:
   a. the formal amendment process is exceedingly difficult.
   b. the Constitution was written so well that it hasn't needed to be amended.
   c. Congress doesn't have time to consider new amendments.

10. When an amendment to the Constitution is proposed by a two-thirds vote in both the Senate and the House and is sent to the state legislatures, then _____ of the states must approve it if it is to be adopted.

Essay Questions

1. Consider what might have happened if Georgia and the Carolinas had stayed out of the Union because of a desire to protect slavery. What would subsequent American history have been like? Would the eventual freedom of the slaves have been delayed—or advanced?

2. A result of the Great Compromise is that representation in the Senate dramatically departs from the one-person, one-vote rule. The 38 million people who live in California elect two senators, as do the half-million people living in Wyoming. What political results, do you think, might occur when the citizens of small states are much better represented than the citizens of large ones? Do you see any signs that your predictions have actually come true?

Answers to multiple-choice questions: 1. c, 2. Mayflower Compact, 3. a, 4. liberty, 5. c, 6. separation, 7. c, 8. Anti-Federalists, 9. a, 10. three-fourths.

APPENDIX TO CHAPTER 2
THE CONSTITUTION OF THE UNITED STATES*

The Preamble
We the People of the United States, in Order to form a more perfect Union, establish Justice, insure domestic Tranquility, provide for the common defence, promote the general Welfare, and secure the Blessings of Liberty to ourselves and our Posterity, do ordain and establish this Constitution for the United States of America.

The Preamble declares that "We the People" are the authority for the Constitution (unlike the Articles of Confederation, which derived their authority from the states). The Preamble also sets out the purposes of the Constitution.

ARTICLE I. (Legislative Branch)

The first part of the Constitution, Article I, deals with the organization and powers of the lawmaking branch of the national government, the Congress.

Section 1. Legislative Powers
All legislative Powers herein granted shall be vested in a Congress of the United States, which shall consist of a Senate and House of Representatives.

Section 2. House of Representatives
Clause 1: Composition and Election of Members. The House of Representatives shall be composed of Members chosen every second Year by the People of the several States, and the Electors in each State shall have the Qualifications requisite for Electors of the most numerous Branch of the State Legislature.

Each state has the power to decide who may vote for members of Congress. Within each state, those who may vote for state legislators may also vote for members of the House of Representatives (and, under the Seventeenth Amendment, for U.S. senators). When the Constitution was written, nearly all states limited voting rights to white male property owners or taxpayers at least twenty-one years old. Subsequent amendments granted voting power to African American men, all women, and everyone at least eighteen years old.

Clause 2: Qualifications. No Person shall be a Representative who shall not have attained to the Age of twenty five Years, and been seven Years a Citizen of the United States, and who shall not, when elected, be an Inhabitant of that State in which he shall be chosen.

Each member of the House must be at least twenty-five years old, a citizen of the United States for at least seven years, and a resident of the state in which she or he is elected.

Clause 3: Apportionment of Representatives and Direct Taxes. Representatives [and direct Taxes][1] shall be apportioned among the several States which may be included within this Union, according to their respective Numbers [which shall be determined by adding to the whole Number of free Persons, including those bound to Service for a Term of Years, and excluding Indians not taxed, three fifths of all other Persons].[2] The actual Enumeration shall be made within three Years after the first Meeting of the Congress of the United States, and within every subsequent Term of ten Years, in such Manner as they shall by Law direct. The Number of Representatives shall not exceed one for every thirty Thousand, but each State shall have at Least one Representative; and until such enumeration shall be made, the State of New Hampshire shall be entitled to chuse three, Massachusetts eight, Rhode Island and Providence Plantations one, Connecticut five, New York six, New Jersey four, Pennsylvania eight, Delaware one, Maryland six, Virginia ten, North Carolina five, South Carolina five, and Georgia three.

A state's representation in the House is based on the size of its population. Population is counted in each decade's census, after which Congress reapportions House seats. Since early in the twentieth century, the number of seats has been limited to 435.

Clause 4: Vacancies. When vacancies happen in the Representation from any State, the Executive Authority thereof shall issue Writs of Election to fill such Vacancies.

The "Executive Authority" is the state's governor. When a vacancy occurs in the House, the governor calls a special election to fill it.

Clause 5: Officers and Impeachment. The House of Representatives shall chuse their Speaker and other Officers; and shall have the sole Power of Impeachment.

The power to impeach is the power to accuse. In this case, it is the power to accuse members of the executive or judicial branch of wrongdoing or abuse of power. Once a bill of impeachment is issued, the Senate holds the trial.

Section 3. The Senate
Clause 1: Term and Number of Members. The Senate of the United States shall be composed of two Senators from each State [chosen by the Legislature thereof],[3] for six Years; and each Senator shall have one Vote.

---

* The spelling, capitalization, and punctuation of the original have been retained here. Brackets indicate passages that have been altered by amendments to the Constitution. We have added article titles (in parentheses), section titles, and clause designations. We have also inserted annotations in blue italic type.

1. Modified by the Sixteenth Amendment.
2. Modified by the Fourteenth Amendment.
3. Repealed by the Seventeenth Amendment.

Every state has two senators, each of whom serves for six years and has one vote in the upper chamber. Since the Seventeenth Amendment was passed in 1913, all senators have been elected directly by voters of the state during the regular election.

Clause 2: Classification of Senators. Immediately after they shall be assembled in Consequence of the first Election, they shall be divided as equally as may be into three Classes. The Seats of the Senators of the first Class shall be vacated at the Expiration of the second Year, of the second Class at the Expiration of the fourth Year, and of the third Class at the Expiration of the sixth Year, so that one third may be chosen every second Year; [and if Vacancies happen by Resignation, or otherwise, during the Recess of the Legislature of any State, the Executive thereof may make temporary Appointments until the next Meeting of the Legislature, which shall then fill such Vacancies].[4]

One-third of the Senate's seats are open to election every two years (in contrast, all members of the House are elected simultaneously).

Clause 3: Qualifications. No Person shall be a Senator who shall not have attained to the Age of thirty Years, and been nine Years a Citizen of the United States, and who shall not, when elected, be an Inhabitant of that State for which he shall be chosen.

Every senator must be at least thirty years old, a citizen of the United States for a minimum of nine years, and a resident of the state in which he or she is elected.

Clause 4: The Role of the Vice President. The Vice President of the United States shall be President of the Senate, but shall have no Vote, unless they be equally divided.

The vice president presides over meetings of the Senate but cannot vote unless there is a tie. The Constitution gives no other official duties to the vice president.

Clause 5: Other Officers. The Senate shall chuse their other Officers, and also a President pro tempore, in the Absence of the Vice President, or when he shall exercise the Office of President of the United States.

The Senate votes for one of its members to preside when the vice president is absent. This person is usually called the president pro tempore because of the temporary nature of the position.

Clause 6: Impeachment Trials. The Senate shall have the sole Power to try all Impeachments. When sitting for that Purpose, they shall be on Oath or Affirmation. When the President of the United States is tried, the Chief Justice shall preside: And no Person shall be convicted without the Concurrence of two thirds of the Members present.

The Senate conducts trials of officials that the House impeaches. The Senate sits as a jury, with the vice president presiding if the president is not on trial.

Clause 7: Penalties for Conviction. Judgment in Cases of Impeachment shall not extend further than to removal from Office, and disqualification to hold and enjoy any Office of honor, Trust, or Profit under the United States: but the Party convicted shall nevertheless be liable and subject to Indictment, Trial, Judgment, and Punishment, according to Law.

On conviction of impeachment charges, the Senate can only force an official to leave office and prevent him or her from holding another office in the federal government. The individual, however, can still be tried in a regular court.

Section 4. Congressional Elections: Times, Manner, and Places

Clause 1: Elections. The Times, Places and Manner of holding Elections for Senators and Representatives, shall be prescribed in each State by the Legislature thereof; but the Congress may at any time by Law make or alter such Regulations, except as to the Places of chusing Senators.

Congress set the Tuesday after the first Monday in November in even-numbered years as the date for congressional elections. In states with more than one seat in the House, Congress requires that representatives be elected from districts within each state. Under the Seventeenth Amendment, senators are elected at the same places as other officials.

Clause 2: Sessions of Congress. [The Congress shall assemble at least once in every Year, and such Meeting shall be on the first Monday in December, unless they shall by Law appoint a different Day.][5]

Congress has to meet every year at least once. The regular session now begins at noon on January 3 of each year, subsequent to the Twentieth Amendment, unless Congress passes a law to fix a different date. Congress stays in session until its members vote to adjourn. Additionally, the president may call a special session.

Section 5. Powers and Duties of the Houses

Clause 1: Admitting Members and Quorum. Each House shall be the Judge of the Elections, Returns, and Qualifications of its own Members, and a Majority of each shall constitute a Quorum to do Business; but a smaller Number may adjourn from day to day, and may be authorized to compel the Attendance of absent Members, in such Manner, and under such Penalties as each House may provide.

Each chamber may exclude or refuse to seat a member-elect.
The quorum rule requires that 218 members of the House and 51 members of the Senate be present to conduct business. This rule normally is not enforced in the handling of routine matters.

Clause 2: Rules and Discipline of Members. Each House may determine the Rules of its Proceedings, punish its Members for disorderly Behaviour, and, with the Concurrence of two thirds, expel a Member.

---

4. Modified by the Seventeenth Amendment.

5. Changed by the Twentieth Amendment.

The House and the Senate may adopt their own rules to guide their proceedings. Each may also discipline its members for conduct that is deemed unacceptable. No member may be expelled without a two-thirds majority vote in favor of expulsion.

Clause 3: Keeping a Record. Each House shall keep a Journal of its Proceedings, and from time to time publish the same, excepting such Parts as may in their Judgment require Secrecy; and the Yeas and Nays of the Members of either House on any question shall, at the Desire of one fifth of those Present, be entered on the Journal.

The journals of the two chambers are published at the end of each session of Congress.

Clause 4: Adjournment. Neither House, during the Session of Congress, shall, without the Consent of the other, adjourn for more than three days, nor to any other Place than that in which the two Houses shall be sitting.

Congress has the power to determine when and where to meet, provided, however, that both chambers meet in the same city. Neither chamber may recess for more than three days without the consent of the other.

Section 6. Rights of Members
Clause 1: Compensation and Privileges. The Senators and Representatives shall receive a Compensation for their services, to be ascertained by Law, and paid out of the Treasury of the United States. They shall in all Cases, except Treason, Felony and Breach of the Peace, be privileged from Arrest during their Attendance at the Session of their respective Houses, and in going to and returning from the same; and for any Speech or Debate in either House, they shall not be questioned in any other Place.

Congressional salaries are to be paid by the U.S. Treasury rather than by the members' respective states. The original salaries were $6 per day; in 1857 they were $3,000 per year. Both representatives and senators were paid a base salary of $174,000 in 2014.

Treason is defined in Article III, Section 3. A felony is any serious crime. A breach of the peace is any indictable offense less than treason or a felony. Members cannot be arrested for things they say during speeches and debates in Congress. This immunity applies to the Capitol Building itself and not to their private lives.

Clause 2: Restrictions. No Senator or Representative shall, during the Time for which he was elected, be appointed to any civil Office under the Authority of the United States, which shall have been created, or the Emoluments whereof shall have been encreased during such time; and no Person holding any Office under the United States, shall be a Member of either House during his Continuance in Office.

During the term for which a member was elected, he or she cannot concurrently accept another federal government position.

Section 7. Legislative Powers: Bills and Resolutions
Clause 1: Revenue Bills. All Bills for raising Revenue shall originate in the House of Representatives; but the Senate may propose or concur with Amendments as on other Bills.

All tax and appropriation bills for raising money have to originate in the House of Representatives. The Senate, though, often amends such bills and may even substitute an entirely different bill.

Clause 2: The Presidential Veto. Every Bill which shall have passed the House of Representatives and the Senate, shall, before it becomes a Law, be presented to the President of the United States; If he approve he shall sign it, but if not he shall return it, with his Objections to the House in which it shall have originated, who shall enter the Objections at large on their Journal, and proceed to reconsider it. If after such Reconsideration two thirds of that House shall agree to pass the Bill, it shall be sent together with the Objections, to the other House, by which it shall likewise be reconsidered, and if approved by two thirds of that House, it shall become a Law. But in all such Cases the Votes of both Houses shall be determined by Yeas and Nays, and the Names of the Persons voting for and against the Bill shall be entered on the Journal of each House respectively. If any Bill shall not be returned by the President within ten Days (Sundays excepted) after it shall have been presented to him, the Same shall be a Law, in like Manner as if he had signed it, unless the Congress by their Adjournment prevent its Return in which Case it shall not be a Law.

When Congress sends the president a bill, he or she can sign it (in which case it becomes law) or send it back to the chamber in which it originated. If it is sent back, a two-thirds majority of each chamber must pass it again for it to become law. If the president neither signs it nor sends it back within ten days, it becomes law anyway, unless Congress adjourns in the meantime.

Clause 3: Actions on Other Matters. Every Order, Resolution, or Vote to which the Concurrence of the Senate and House of Representatives may be necessary (except on a question of Adjournment) shall be presented to the President of the United States; and before the Same shall take Effect, shall be approved by him, or being disapproved by him, shall be repassed by two thirds of the Senate and House of Representatives, according to the Rules and Limitations prescribed in the Case of a Bill.

The president must have the opportunity to either sign or veto everything that Congress passes, except votes to adjourn and resolutions not having the force of law.

Section 8. The Powers of Congress
Clause 1: Taxing. The Congress shall have Power to lay and collect Taxes, Duties, Imposts and Excises, to pay the Debts and provide for the common Defence and general Welfare of the United States; but all Duties, Imposts and Excises shall be uniform throughout the United States;

Duties are taxes on imports and exports. Impost is a generic term for tax. Excises are taxes on the manufacture, sale, or use of goods.

Clause 2: Borrowing. To borrow Money on the credit of the United States;

Congress has the power to borrow money, which is normally carried out through the sale of U.S. Treasury bonds on which interest is paid.

Note that the Constitution places no limit on the amount of government borrowing.

Clause 3: Regulation of Commerce. To regulate Commerce with foreign Nations, and among the several States, and with the Indian Tribes;

This is the commerce clause, *which gives to Congress the power to regulate interstate and foreign trade. Much of the activity of Congress is based on this clause.*

Clause 4: Naturalization and Bankruptcy. To establish an uniform Rule of Naturalization, and uniform Laws on the subject of Bankruptcies throughout the United States;

Only Congress may determine how aliens can become citizens of the United States. Congress may make laws with respect to bankruptcy.

Clause 5: Money and Standards. To coin Money, regulate the Value thereof, and of foreign Coin, and fix the Standard of Weights and Measures;

Congress mints coins and prints and circulates paper money. Congress can establish uniform measures of time, distance, weight, and the like. In 1838, Congress adopted the English system of weights and measurements as our national standard.

Clause 6: Punishing Counterfeiters. To provide for the Punishment of counterfeiting the Securities and current Coin of the United States;

Congress has the power to punish those who copy American currency and pass it off as real. Currently, the penalty may be imprisonment for up to fifteen years plus fines.

Clause 7: Roads and Post Offices. To establish Post Offices and post Roads;

Post roads include all routes over which mail is carried—highways, railways, waterways, and airways.

Clause 8: Patents and Copyrights. To promote the Progress of Science and useful Arts, by securing for limited Times to Authors and Inventors the exclusive Right to their respective Writings and Discoveries;

Authors' and composers' works are protected by copyrights established by copyright law, which currently is the Copyright Act of 1976, as amended. Copyrights are valid for the life of the author or composer plus seventy years. Inventors' works are protected by patents, which vary in length of protection from fourteen to twenty years. A patent gives a person the exclusive right to control the manufacture or sale of her or his invention.

Clause 9: Lower Courts. To constitute Tribunals inferior to the supreme Court;

Congress has the authority to set up all federal courts, except the Supreme Court, and to decide what cases those courts will hear.

Clause 10: Punishment for Piracy. To define and punish Piracies and Felonies committed on the high Seas, and Offences against the Law of Nations;

Congress has the authority to prohibit the commission of certain acts outside U.S. territory and to punish certain violations of international law.

Clause 11: Declaration of War. To declare War, grant Letters of Marque and Reprisal, and make Rules concerning Captures on Land and Water;

Only Congress can declare war, although the president, as commander in chief, can make war without Congress's formal declaration. Letters of marque and reprisal authorized private parties to capture and destroy enemy ships in wartime. Since the middle of the nineteenth century, international law has prohibited letters of marque and reprisal, and the United States has honored the ban.

Clause 12: The Army. To raise and support Armies, but no Appropriation of Money to that Use shall be for a longer Term than two Years;

Congress has the power to create an army; the funds used to pay for it must be appropriated for no more than two-year intervals. This latter restriction gives ultimate control of the army to civilians.

Clause 13: Creation of a Navy. To provide and maintain a Navy;

This clause allows for the maintenance of a navy. In 1947, Congress created the U.S. Air Force.

Clause 14: Regulation of the Armed Forces. To make Rules for the Government and Regulation of the land and naval Forces;

Congress sets the rules for the military mainly by way of the Uniform Code of Military Justice, which was enacted in 1950 by Congress.

Clause 15: The Militia. To provide for calling forth the Militia to execute the Laws of the Union, suppress Insurrections and repel Invasions;

The militia is known today as the National Guard. *Both Congress and the president have the authority to call the National Guard into federal service.*

Clause 16: How the Militia Is Organized. To provide for organizing, arming, and disciplining the Militia, and for governing such Part of them as may be employed in the Service of the United States, reserving to the States respectively, the Appointment of the Officers, and the Authority of training the Militia according to the discipline prescribed by Congress;

This clause gives Congress the power to "federalize" state militia (National Guard). When called into such service, the National Guard is subject to the same rules that Congress has set forth for the regular armed services.

Clause 17: Creation of the District of Columbia. To exercise exclusive Legislation in all Cases whatsoever, over such District (not exceeding ten Miles square) as may, by Cession of particular States, and the Acceptance of Congress, become the Seat of the Government of the United States, and to exercise like Authority over all Places purchased by the Consent of the Legislature of the State in which the Same shall be, for the Erection of Forts, Magazines, Arsenals, dock-Yards, and other needful Buildings;—And

Congress established the District of Columbia as the national capital in 1791. Virginia and Maryland had granted land for the District, but Virginia's grant was returned because it was believed it would not be needed. Today, the District covers sixty-nine square miles.

Clause 18: The Elastic Clause. To make all Laws which shall be necessary and proper for carrying into Execution the foregoing Powers, and all other Powers vested by this Constitution in the Government of the United States, or in any Department or Officer thereof.

This clause—the necessary and proper clause, or the elastic clause—grants no specific powers, and thus it can be stretched to fit different circumstances. It has allowed Congress to adapt the government to changing needs and times.

Section 9. The Powers Denied to Congress
Clause 1: Question of Slavery. The Migration or Importation of such Persons as any of the States now existing shall think proper to admit, shall not be prohibited by the Congress prior to the Year one thousand eight hundred and eight, but a Tax or duty may be imposed on such Importation, not exceeding ten dollars for each Person.

"Persons" referred to slaves. Congress outlawed the slave trade in 1808.

Clause 2: Habeas Corpus. The privilege of the Writ of Habeas Corpus shall not be suspended, unless when in Cases of Rebellion or Invasion the public Safety may require it.

A writ of habeas corpus is a court order directing a sheriff or other public officer who is detaining another person to "produce the body" of the detainee so the court can assess the legality of the detention.

Clause 3: Special Bills. No Bill of Attainder or ex post facto Law shall be passed.

A bill of attainder is a law that inflicts punishment without a trial. An ex post facto law is a law that inflicts punishment for an act that was not illegal when it was committed.

Clause 4: Direct Taxes. [No Capitation, or other direct, Tax shall be laid, unless in Proportion to the Census or Enumeration herein before directed to be taken.][6]

A capitation is a tax on a person. A direct tax is a tax paid directly to the government, such as a property tax. This clause was intended to

prevent Congress from levying a tax on slaves per person and thereby taxing slavery out of existence.

Clause 5: Export Taxes. No Tax or Duty shall be laid on Articles exported from any State.

Congress may not tax any goods sold from one state to another or from one state to a foreign country. (Congress does have the power to tax goods that are bought from other countries, however.)

Clause 6: Interstate Commerce. No Preference shall be given by any Regulation of Commerce or Revenue to the Ports of one State over those of another: nor shall Vessels bound to, or from, one State, be obliged to enter, clear, or pay Duties in another.

Congress may not treat different ports within the United States differently in terms of taxing and commerce powers. Congress may not give one state's port a legal advantage over the ports of another state.

Clause 7: Treasury Withdrawals. No Money shall be drawn from the Treasury, but in Consequence of Appropriations made by Law; and a regular Statement and Account of the Receipts and Expenditures of all public Money shall be published from time to time.

Federal funds can be spent only as Congress authorizes. This is a significant check on the president's power.

Clause 8: Titles of Nobility. No Title of Nobility shall be granted by the United States: And no Person holding any Office of Profit or Trust under them, shall, without the Consent of the Congress, accept of any present, Emolument, Office, or Title, of any kind whatever, from any King, Prince, or foreign State.

No person in the United States may hold a title of nobility, such as duke or duchess. This clause also discourages bribery of American officials by foreign governments.

Section 10. Those Powers Denied to the States
Clause 1: Treaties and Coinage. No State shall enter into any Treaty, Alliance, or Confederation; grant Letters of Marque and Reprisal; coin Money; emit Bills of Credit; make any Thing but gold and silver Coin a Tender in Payment of Debts; pass any Bill of Attainder, ex post facto Law, or Law impairing the Obligation of Contracts, or grant any Title of Nobility.

Prohibiting state laws "impairing the Obligation of Contracts" was intended to protect creditors. (Shays' Rebellion—an attempt to prevent courts from giving effect to creditors' legal actions against debtors—occurred only one year before the Constitution was written.)

Clause 2: Duties and Imposts. No State shall, without the Consent of the Congress, lay any Imposts or Duties on Imports or Exports, except what may be absolutely necessary for executing its inspection Laws; and the net Produce of all Duties and Imposts, laid by any State on Imports or Exports, shall be for the Use of the Treasury of the United States; and all such Laws shall be subject to the Revision and Controul of the Congress.

---

6. Modified by the Sixteenth Amendment.

Only Congress can tax imports. Further, the states cannot tax exports.

Clause 3: War. No State shall, without the Consent of Congress, lay any Duty of Tonnage, keep Troops, or Ships of War in time of Peace, enter into any Agreement or Compact with another State, or with a foreign Power or engage in War, unless actually invaded, or in such imminent Danger as will not admit of delay.

A duty of tonnage is a tax on ships according to their cargo capacity. No states may tax ships according to their cargo unless Congress agrees. Additionally, this clause forbids any state to keep troops or warships during peacetime or to make a compact with another state or foreign nation unless Congress so agrees. A state, in contrast, can maintain a militia, but its use has to be limited to disorders that occur within the state—unless, of course, the militia is called into federal service.

ARTICLE II. (Executive Branch)

Section 1. The Nature and Scope of Presidential Power

Clause 1: Four-Year Term. The executive Power shall be vested in a President of the United States of America. He shall hold his Office during the Term of four Years, and, together with the Vice President, chosen for the same Term, be elected, as follows.

The president has the power to carry out laws made by Congress, called the executive power. He or she serves in office for a four-year term after election. The Twenty-second Amendment limits the number of times a person may be elected president.

Clause 2: Choosing Electors from Each State. Each State shall appoint, in such Manner as the Legislature thereof may direct, a Number of Electors, equal to the whole Number of Senators and Representatives to which the State may be entitled in the Congress; but no Senator or Representative, or Person holding an Office of Trust or Profit under the United States, shall be appointed an Elector.

The "Electors" are known more commonly as the "electoral college." The president is elected by electors—that is, representatives chosen by the people—rather than by the people directly.

Clause 3: The Former System of Elections. [The Electors shall meet in their respective States, and vote by Ballot for two Persons, of whom one at least shall not be an Inhabitant of the same State with themselves. And they shall make a List of all the Persons voted for, and of the Number of Votes for each; which List they shall sign and certify, and transmit sealed to the Seat of the Government of the United States, directed to the President of the Senate. The President of the Senate shall, in the Presence of the Senate and House of Representatives, open all the Certificates, and the Votes shall then be counted. The Person having the greatest Number of Votes shall be the President, if such Number be a Majority of the whole Number of Electors appointed; and if there be more than one who have such Majority, and have an equal Number of Votes, then the House of Representatives shall immediately chuse by Ballot one of them for President; and if no Person have a Majority, then from the five

highest on the List the said House shall in like Manner chuse the President. But in chusing the President, the Votes shall be taken by States, the Representation from each State having one Vote; A quorum for this Purpose shall consist of a Member or Members from two thirds of the States, and a Majority of all the States shall be necessary to a Choice. In every Case, after the Choice of the President, the Person having the greater Number of Votes of the Electors shall be the Vice President. But if there should remain two or more who have equal Votes, the Senate shall chuse from them by Ballot the Vice President.][7]

The original method of selecting the president and vice president was replaced by the Twelfth Amendment. Apparently, the framers did not anticipate the rise of political parties and the development of primaries and conventions.

Clause 4: The Time of Elections. The Congress may determine the Time of chusing the Electors, and the Day on which they shall give their Votes; which Day shall be the same throughout the United States.

Congress set the Tuesday after the first Monday in November every fourth year as the date for choosing electors. The electors cast their votes on the Monday after the second Wednesday in December of that year.

Clause 5: Qualifications for President. No person except a natural born Citizen, or a Citizen of the United States, at the time of the Adoption of this Constitution, shall be eligible to the Office of President; neither shall any Person be eligible to that Office who shall not have attained to the Age of thirty five Years, and been fourteen Years a Resident within the United States.

The president must be a natural-born citizen, be at least thirty-five years of age when taking office, and have been a resident within the United States for at least fourteen years.

Clause 6: Succession of the Vice President. [In Case of the Removal of the President from Office, or of his Death, Resignation or Inability to discharge the Powers and Duties of the said Office, the same shall devolve on the Vice President, and the Congress may by Law provide for the Case of Removal, Death, Resignation or Inability, both of the President and Vice President, declaring what Officer shall then act as President, and such Officer shall act accordingly, until the Disability be removed, or a President shall be elected.][8]

This section provided for the method by which the vice president was to succeed to the presidency, but its wording is ambiguous. It was replaced by the Twenty-fifth Amendment.

Clause 7: The President's Salary. The President shall, at stated Times, receive for his Services, a Compensation, which shall neither be encreased nor diminished during the Period for which he

---

7. Changed by the Twelfth Amendment.
8. Modified by the Twenty-fifth Amendment.

shall have been elected, and he shall not receive within that Period any other Emolument from the United States, or any of them.

The president maintains the same salary during each four-year term. Moreover, she or he may not receive additional cash payments from the government. Originally set at $25,000 per year, the salary is currently $400,000 a year plus $169,000 in various expense accounts.

Clause 8: *The Oath of Office.* Before he enter on the Execution of his Office, he shall take the following Oath or Affirmation: "I do solemnly swear (or affirm) that I will faithfully execute the Office of President of the United States, and will to the best of my Ability, preserve, protect and defend the Constitution of the United States."

The president is "sworn in" prior to beginning the duties of the office. The taking of the oath of office occurs on January 20, following the November election. The ceremony is called the inauguration. *The oath of office is administered by the chief justice of the United States Supreme Court.*

Section 2. Powers of the President
Clause 1: *Commander in Chief.* The President shall be Commander in Chief of the Army and Navy of the United States, and of the Militia of the several States, when called into the actual Service of the United States; he may require the Opinion, in writing, of the principal Officer in each of the executive Departments, upon any Subject relating to the Duties of their respective Offices, and he shall have Power to grant Reprieves and Pardons for Offences against the United States, except in Cases of Impeachment.

The armed forces are placed under civilian control because the president is a civilian but still commander in chief of the military. The president may ask for the help of the head of each of the executive departments (thereby creating the cabinet). The cabinet members are chosen by the president with the consent of the Senate, but they can be removed without Senate approval.

The president's clemency powers extend only to federal cases. In those cases, he or she may grant a full or conditional pardon, or reduce a prison term or fine.

Clause 2: *Treaties and Appointment.* He shall have Power, by and with the Advice and Consent of the Senate, to make Treaties, provided two thirds of the Senators present concur; and he shall nominate, and by and with the Advice and Consent of the Senate, shall appoint Ambassadors, other public Ministers and Consuls, Judges of the supreme Court, and all other Officers of the United States, whose Appointments are not herein otherwise provided for, and which shall be established by Law; but the Congress may by Law vest the Appointment of such inferior Officers, as they think proper, in the President alone, in the Courts of Law, or in the Heads of Departments.

Many of the major powers of the president are identified in this clause, including the power to make treaties with foreign governments (with the approval of the Senate by a two-thirds vote) and the

power to appoint ambassadors, Supreme Court justices, and other government officials. Most such appointments require Senate approval.

Clause 3: *Vacancies.* The President shall have Power to fill up all Vacancies that may happen during the Recess of the Senate, by granting Commissions which shall expire at the end of their next Session.

The president has the power to appoint temporary officials to fill vacant federal offices without Senate approval if the Congress is not in session. Such appointments expire automatically at the end of Congress's next term.

Section 3. Duties of the President
He shall from time to time give to the Congress Information of the State of the Union, and recommend to their Consideration such Measures as he shall judge necessary and expedient; he may, on extraordinary Occasions, convene both Houses, or either of them, and in Case of Disagreement between them, with Respect to the Time of Adjournment, he may adjourn them to such Time as he shall think proper; he shall receive Ambassadors and other public Ministers; he shall take Care that the Laws be faithfully executed, and shall Commission all the Officers of the United States.

Annually, the president reports on the state of the union to Congress, recommends legislative measures, and proposes a federal budget. The State of the Union speech is a statement not only to Congress but also to the American people. After it is given, the president proposes a federal budget and presents an economic report. At any time, the president may send special messages to Congress while it is in session. The president has the power to call special sessions, to adjourn Congress when its two chambers do not agree on when to adjourn, to receive diplomatic representatives of other governments, and to ensure the proper execution of all federal laws. The president further has the ability to empower federal officers to hold their positions and to perform their duties.

Section 4. Impeachment
The President, Vice President and all civil Officers of the United States, shall be removed from Office on Impeachment for, and Conviction of, Treason, Bribery, or other high Crimes and Misdemeanors.

Treason denotes giving aid to the nation's enemies. The phrase high crimes and misdemeanors *is usually considered to mean serious abuses of political power. In either case, the president or vice president may be accused by the House (called an* impeachment*) and then removed from office if convicted by the Senate. (Note that impeachment does not mean removal but rather refers to an accusation of treason or high crimes and misdemeanors.)*

ARTICLE III. (Judicial Branch)

Section 1. Judicial Powers, Courts, and Judges
The judicial Power of the United States, shall be vested in one supreme Court, and in such inferior Courts as the Congress may

from time to time ordain and establish. The Judges, both of the supreme and inferior Courts, shall hold their Offices during good Behaviour, and shall, at stated Times, receive for their Services a Compensation, which shall not be diminished during their Continuance in Office.

The Supreme Court is vested with judicial power, as are the lower federal courts that Congress creates. Federal judges serve in their offices for life unless they are impeached and convicted by Congress. The payment of federal judges may not be reduced during their time in office.

Section 2. Jurisdiction
Clause 1: Cases under Federal Jurisdiction. The judicial Power shall extend to all Cases, in Law and Equity, arising under this Constitution, the Laws of the United States, and Treaties made, or which shall be made, under their Authority;—to all Cases affecting Ambassadors, other public Ministers and Consuls;—to all Cases of admiralty and maritime Jurisdiction;—to Controversies to which the United States shall be a Party;—to Controversies between two or more States; [—between a State and Citizens of another State;—]⁹ between Citizens of different States;—between Citizens of the same State claiming Lands under Grants of different States, [and between a State, or the Citizens thereof, and foreign States, Citizens or Subjects.]¹⁰

The federal courts take on cases that concern the meaning of the U.S. Constitution, all federal laws, and treaties. They also can take on cases involving citizens of different states and citizens of foreign nations.

Clause 2: Cases for the Supreme Court. In all Cases affecting Ambassadors, other public Ministers and Consuls, and those in which a State shall be a Party, the supreme Court shall have original Jurisdiction. In all the other Cases before mentioned, the supreme Court shall have appellate Jurisdiction, both as to Law and Fact, with such Exceptions, and under such Regulations as the Congress shall make.

In a limited number of situations, the Supreme Court acts as a trial court and has original jurisdiction. These cases involve a representative from another country or involve a state. In all other situations, the cases must first be tried in the lower courts and then can be appealed to the Supreme Court. Congress may, however, make exceptions. Today, the Supreme Court acts as a trial court of first instance on rare occasions.

Clause 3: The Conduct of Trials. The Trial of all Crimes, except in Cases of Impeachment, shall be by Jury; and such Trial shall be held in the State where the said Crimes shall have been committed; but when not committed within any State, the Trial shall be at such Place or Places as the Congress may by Law have directed.

Any person accused of a federal crime is granted the right to a trial by jury in a federal court in that state in which the crime was committed. Trials of impeachment are an exception.

Section 3. Treason
Clause 1: The Definition of Treason. Treason against the United States, shall consist only in levying War against them, or, in adhering to their Enemies, giving them Aid and Comfort. No Person shall be convicted of Treason unless on the Testimony of two Witnesses to the same overt Act, or on Confession in open Court.

Treason is the making of war against the United States or giving aid to its enemies.

Clause 2: Punishment. The Congress shall have Power to declare the Punishment of Treason, but no Attainder of Treason shall work Corruption of Blood, or Forfeiture except during the Life of the Person attainted.

Congress has provided that the punishment for treason ranges from a minimum of five years in prison and/or a $10,000 fine to a maximum of death. "No Attainder of Treason shall work Corruption of Blood" prohibits punishment of the traitor's heirs.

ARTICLE IV. (Relations among the States)

Section 1. Full Faith and Credit
Full Faith and Credit shall be given in each State to the public Acts, Records, and judicial Proceedings of every other State. And the Congress may by general Laws prescribe the Manner in which such Acts, Records and Proceedings shall be proved, and the Effect thereof.

All states are required to respect one another's laws, records, and lawful decisions. There are exceptions, however. A state does not have to enforce another state's criminal code. Nor does it have to recognize another state's grant of a divorce if the person obtaining the divorce did not establish legal residence in the state in which it was given.

Section 2. Treatment of Citizens
Clause 1: Privileges and Immunities. The Citizens of each State shall be entitled to all Privileges and Immunities of Citizens in the several States.

A citizen of a state has the same rights and privileges as the citizens of another state in which he or she happens to be.

Clause 2: Extradition. A Person charged in any State with Treason, Felony, or other Crime, who shall flee from Justice, and be found in another State, shall on Demand of the executive Authority of the State from which he fled, be delivered up, to be removed to the State having Jurisdiction of the Crime.

Any person accused of a crime who flees to another state must be returned to the state in which the crime occurred.

Clause 3: Fugitive Slaves. [No Person held to Service or Labour in one State, under the Laws thereof, escaping into another, shall, in

---

9. Modified by the Eleventh Amendment.
10. Modified by the Eleventh Amendment.

Consequence of any Law or Regulation therein, be discharged from such Service or Labour, but shall be delivered up on Claim of the Party to whom such Service or Labour may be due.][11]

This clause was struck down by the Thirteenth Amendment, which abolished slavery in 1865.

Section 3. Admission of States
Clause 1: The Process. New States may be admitted by the Congress into this Union; but no new State shall be formed or erected within the Jurisdiction of any other State; nor any State be formed by the Junction of two or more States, or Parts of States, without the Consent of the Legislatures of the States concerned as well as of the Congress.

Only Congress has the power to admit new states to the Union. No state may be created by taking territory from an existing state unless the state's legislature so consents.

Clause 2: Public Land. The Congress shall have Power to dispose of and make all needful Rules and Regulations respecting the Territory or other Property belonging to the United States; and nothing in this Constitution shall be so construed as to Prejudice any Claims of the United States, or of any particular State.

The federal government has the exclusive right to administer federal government public lands.

Section 4. Republican Form of Government
The United States shall guarantee to every State in this Union a Republican Form of Government, and shall protect each of them against Invasion; and on Application of the Legislature, or of the Executive (when the Legislature cannot be convened) against domestic Violence.

Each state is promised a republican form of government—that is, one in which the people elect their representatives. The federal government is bound to protect states against any attack by foreigners or during times of trouble within a state.

ARTICLE V. (Methods of Amendment)

The Congress, whenever two thirds of both Houses shall deem it necessary, shall propose Amendments to this Constitution, or on the Application of the Legislatures of two thirds of the several States, shall call a Convention for proposing Amendments, which, in either Case, shall be valid to all Intents and Purposes, as Part of this Constitution, when ratified by the Legislatures of three fourths of the several States, or by Conventions in three fourths thereof, as the one or the other Mode of Ratification may be proposed by the Congress; Provided that no Amendment which may be made prior to the Year One thousand eight hundred and eight shall in any Manner affect the first and fourth Clauses in the Ninth Section of the First Article; and that no

State, without its Consent, shall be deprived of its equal Suffrage in the Senate.

Amendments may be proposed in either of two ways: by a two-thirds vote of each chamber (Congress) or at the request of two-thirds of the states. Ratification of amendments may be carried out in two ways: by the legislatures of three-fourths of the states or by the voters in three-fourths of the states. No state may be denied equal representation in the Senate.

ARTICLE VI. (National Supremacy)

Clause 1: Existing Obligations. All Debts contracted and Engagements entered into, before the Adoption of this Constitution shall be as valid against the United States under this Constitution, as under the Confederation.

During the Revolutionary War and the years of the Confederation, Congress borrowed large sums. This clause pledged that the new federal government would assume those financial obligations.

Clause 2: Supreme Law of the Land. This Constitution, and the Laws of the United States which shall be made in Pursuance thereof; and all Treaties made, or which shall be made, under the Authority of the United States, shall be the supreme Law of the Land; and the Judges in every State shall be bound thereby, any Thing in the Constitution or Laws of any State to the Contrary notwithstanding.

This is typically called the supremacy clause; *it declares that federal law takes precedence over all forms of state law. No government at the local or state level may make or enforce any law that conflicts with any provision of the Constitution, acts of Congress, treaties, or other rules and regulations issued by the president and his or her subordinates in the executive branch of the federal government.*

Clause 3: Oath of Office. The Senators and Representatives before mentioned, and the Members of the several State Legislatures, and all executive and judicial Officers, both of the United States and of the several States, shall be bound by Oath or Affirmation, to support this Constitution; but no religious Test shall ever be required as a Qualification to any Office or public Trust under the United States.

Every federal and state official must take an oath of office promising to support the U.S. Constitution. Religion may not be used as a qualification to serve in any federal office.

ARTICLE VII. (Ratification)

The Ratification of the Conventions of nine States shall be sufficient for the Establishment of this Constitution between the States so ratifying the Same.

Nine states were required to ratify the Constitution. Delaware was the first and New Hampshire the ninth.

---

11. Repealed by the Thirteenth Amendment.

Done in Convention by the Unanimous Consent of the States present the Seventeenth Day of September in the Year of our Lord one thousand seven hundred and Eighty seven and of the Independence of the United States of America the Twelfth. In witness whereof we have hereunto subscribed our Names,

Go. WASHINGTON
Presid't.
and deputy from Virginia

Attest William Jackson Secretary

DELAWARE
- Geo. Read
- Gunning Bedford jun
- John Dickinson
- Richard Bassett
- Jaco. Broom

MARYLAND
- James McHenry
- Dan of St. Thos. Jenifer
- Danl. Carroll

VIRGINIA
- John Blair
- James Madison Jr.

NORTH CAROLINA
- Wm. Blount
- Richd. Dobbs Spaight
- Hu. Williamson

SOUTH CAROLINA
- J. Rutledge
- Charles Cotesworth Pinckney
- Charles Pinckney
- Pierce Butler

GEORGIA
- William Few
- Abr. Baldwin

NEW HAMPSHIRE
- John Langdon
- Nicholas Gilman

MASSACHUSETTS
- Nathaniel Gorham
- Rufus King

CONNECTICUT
- Wm. Saml. Johnson
- Roger Sherman

NEW YORK
- Alexander Hamilton

NEW JERSEY
- Wh. Livingston
- David Brearley
- Wm. Paterson
- Jona. Dayton

PENNSYLVANIA
- B. Franklin
- Thomas Mifflin
- Robt. Morris
- Geo. Clymer
- Thos. FitzSimons
- Jared Ingersoll
- James Wilson
- Gouv. Morris

AMENDMENTS TO THE CONSTITUTION OF THE UNITED STATES[12]

AMENDMENT I.
(Religion, Speech, Assembly, and Petition)
Congress shall make no law respecting an establishment of religion, or prohibiting the free exercise thereof; or abridging the freedom of speech, or of the press; or the right of the people peaceably to assemble, and to petition the Government for a redress of grievances.

Congress may not create an official church or enact laws limiting the freedom of religion, speech, the press, assembly, and petition. These guarantees, like the others in the Bill of Rights (the first ten amendments), are not absolute—each may be exercised only with regard to the rights of other persons.

AMENDMENT II.
(Militia and the Right to Bear Arms)
A well regulated Militia, being necessary to the security of a free State, the right of the people to keep and bear Arms, shall not be infringed.

To protect itself, each state has the right to maintain a volunteer armed force. States and the federal government may regulate but not completely ban the possession and use of firearms by individuals.

AMENDMENT III.
(The Quartering of Soldiers)
No Soldier shall, in time of peace be quartered in any house, without the consent of the Owner, nor in time of war, but in a manner to be prescribed by law.

Before the Revolutionary War, it had been common British practice to quarter soldiers in colonists' homes. Military troops do not have the power to take over private houses during peacetime.

AMENDMENT IV.
(Searches and Seizures)
The right of the people to be secure in their persons, houses, papers, and effects, against unreasonable searches and seizures, shall not be violated, and no Warrants shall issue, but upon probable cause, supported by Oath or affirmation, and particularly describing the place to be searched, and the persons or things to be seized.

Here the word warrant *means "justification" and refers to a document issued by a magistrate or judge indicating the name, address, and possible offense committed. Anyone asking for the warrant, such as a police officer, must be able to convince the magistrate or judge that an offense probably has been committed.*

AMENDMENT V.
(Grand Juries, Self-Incrimination, Double Jeopardy, Due Process, and Eminent Domain)
No person shall be held to answer for a capital, or otherwise infamous crime, unless on a presentment or indictment of a Grand Jury, except in cases arising in the land or naval forces, or in the Militia, when in actual service in time of War or public danger; nor shall any person be subject for the same offence to be twice put in jeopardy of life or limb; nor shall be compelled in any criminal case to be a witness against himself, nor be deprived of life, liberty, or property, without due process of law; nor shall private property be taken for public use, without just compensation.

There are two types of juries. A grand jury *considers physical evidence and the testimony of witnesses and decides whether there is sufficient reason to bring a case to trial. A* petit jury *hears the case at trial and decides it. "For the same offence to be twice put in jeopardy of life or limb" means to be tried twice for the same crime. A person may not be tried for the same crime twice or forced to give evidence against herself or himself. No person's right to life, liberty, or property may be taken away except by lawful means, called the* due process of law. *Private property taken for public use must be paid for by the government.*

AMENDMENT VI.
(Criminal Court Procedures)
In all criminal prosecutions, the accused shall enjoy the right to a speedy and public trial, by an impartial jury of the State and district wherein the crime shall have been committed, which district shall have been previously ascertained by law, and to be informed of the nature and cause of the accusation; to be confronted with the witnesses against him; to have compulsory process for obtaining witnesses in his favor, and to have the Assistance of Counsel for his defence.

Any person accused of a crime has the right to a fair and public trial by a jury in the state in which the crime took place. The charges against that person must be indicated. Any accused person has the right to a lawyer to defend him or her and to question those who testify against him or her, as well as the right to call people to speak in his or her favor at trial.

AMENDMENT VII.
(Trial by Jury in Civil Cases)
In Suits at common law, where the value in controversy shall exceed twenty dollars, the right of trial by jury shall be preserved, and no fact tried by jury, shall be otherwise re-examined in any Court of the United States, than according to the rules of the common law.

A jury trial may be requested by either party in a dispute in any case involving more than $20. If both parties agree to a trial by a judge without a jury, the right to a jury trial may be put aside.

---

12. On September 25, 1789, Congress transmitted to the state legislatures twelve proposed amendments, two of which, having to do with congressional representation and congressional pay, were not adopted. The remaining ten amendments became the Bill of Rights. In 1992, the amendment concerning congressional pay was adopted as the Twenty-seventh Amendment.

AMENDMENT VIII.
(Bail, Cruel and Unusual Punishment)
Excessive bail shall not be required, nor excessive fines imposed, nor cruel and unusual punishments inflicted.

Bail is an amount of money that a person accused of a crime may be required to deposit with the court as a guaranty that she or he will appear in court when requested. The amount of bail required or the fine imposed as punishment for a crime must be reasonable compared with the seriousness of the crime involved. Any punishment judged to be too harsh or too severe for a crime is prohibited.

AMENDMENT IX.
(The Rights Retained by the People)
The enumeration in the Constitution, of certain rights, shall not be construed to deny or disparage others retained by the people.

Many civil rights that are not explicitly enumerated in the Constitution are still held by the people.

AMENDMENT X.
(Reserved Powers of the States)
The powers not delegated to the United States by the Constitution, nor prohibited by it to the States, are reserved to the States respectively, or to the people.

Those powers not delegated by the Constitution to the federal government or expressly denied to the states belong to the states and to the people. This amendment in essence allows the states to pass laws under their "police powers."

AMENDMENT XI.
(Ratified on February 7, 1795—
Suits against States)
The Judicial power of the United States shall not be construed to extend to any suit in law or equity, commenced or prosecuted against one of the United States by Citizens of another State, or by Citizens or Subjects of any Foreign State.

This amendment has been interpreted to mean that a state cannot be sued in federal court by one of its own citizens, by a citizen of another state, or by a foreign country.

AMENDMENT XII.
(Ratified on June 15, 1804—
Election of the President)
The Electors shall meet in their respective states, and vote by ballot for President and Vice-President, one of whom, at least, shall not be an inhabitant of the same State with themselves; they shall name in their ballots the person voted for as President, and in distinct ballots the person voted for as Vice-President, and they shall make distinct lists of all persons voted for as President, and of all persons voted for as Vice-President, and of the number of votes for each, which lists they shall sign and certify, and transmit sealed to the seat of the government of the United States, directed to the President of the Senate;—The President of the Senate shall, in the presence of the Senate and House of Representatives, open all the certificates and the votes shall then be counted;—The person having the greatest number of votes for President, shall be the President, if such number be a majority of the whole number of Electors appointed; and if no person have such majority, then from the persons having the highest numbers not exceeding three on the list of those voted for as President, the House of Representatives shall choose immediately, by ballot, the President. But in choosing the President, the votes shall be taken by States, the representation from each State having one vote; a quorum for this purpose shall consist of a member or members from two-thirds of the States, and a majority of all States shall be necessary to a choice. [And if the House of Representatives shall not choose a President whenever the right of choice shall devolve upon them, before the fourth day of March next following, then the Vice-President shall act as President, as in the case of the death or other constitutional disability of the President.][13]—The person having the greatest number of votes as Vice-President, shall be the Vice-President, if such number be a majority of the whole number of Electors appointed, and if no person have a majority, then from the two highest numbers on the list, the Senate shall choose the Vice-President; a quorum for the purpose shall consist of two-thirds of the whole number of Senators, and a majority of the whole number shall be necessary to a choice. But no person constitutionally ineligible to the office of President shall be eligible to that of Vice-President of the United States.

The original procedure set out for the election of president and vice president in Article II, Section 1, resulted in a tie in 1800 between Thomas Jefferson and Aaron Burr. It was not until the next year that the House of Representatives chose Jefferson to be president. This amendment changed the procedure by providing for separate ballots for president and vice president.

AMENDMENT XIII.
(Ratified on December 6, 1865—
Prohibition of Slavery)
Section 1.
Neither slavery nor involuntary servitude, except as a punishment for crime whereof the party shall have been duly convicted, shall exist within the United States, or any place subject to their jurisdiction.

Some slaves had been freed during the Civil War. This amendment freed the others and abolished slavery.

Section 2.
Congress shall have power to enforce this article by appropriate legislation.

---

13. Changed by the Twentieth Amendment.

AMENDMENT XIV.
(Ratified on July 9, 1868—
Citizenship, Due Process, and
Equal Protection of the Laws)

Section 1.

All persons born or naturalized in the United States, and subject to the jurisdiction thereof, are citizens of the United States and of the State wherein they reside. No State shall make or enforce any law which shall abridge the privileges or immunities of citizens of the United States; nor shall any State deprive any person of life, liberty, or property, without due process of law; nor deny to any person within its jurisdiction the equal protection of the laws.

Under this provision, states cannot make or enforce laws that take away rights given to all citizens by the federal government. States cannot act unfairly or arbitrarily toward, or discriminate against, any person.

Section 2.

Representatives shall be apportioned among the several States according to their respective numbers, counting the whole number of persons in each State, excluding Indians not taxed. But when the right to vote at any election for the choice of electors for President and Vice President of the United States, Representatives in Congress, the Executive and Judicial officers of a State, or the members of the Legislature thereof, is denied to any of the male inhabitants of such State, being [twenty-one][14] years of age, and citizens of the United States, or in any way abridged, except for participation in rebellion, or other crime, the basis of representation therein shall be reduced in the proportion which the number of such male citizens shall bear to the whole number of male citizens twenty-one years of age in such State.

Section 3.

No person shall be a Senator or Representative in Congress, or elector of President and Vice President, or hold any office, civil or military, under the United States, or under any State, who having previously taken an oath, as a member of Congress, or as an officer of the United States, or as a member of any State legislature, or as an executive or judicial officer of any State, to support the Constitution of the United States, shall have engaged in insurrection or rebellion against the same, or given aid or comfort to the enemies thereof. But Congress may by a vote of two-thirds of each House, remove such disability.

This provision forbade former state or federal government officials who had acted in support of the Confederacy during the Civil War to hold office again. It limited the president's power to pardon those persons. Congress removed this "disability" in 1898.

Section 4.

The validity of the public debt of the United States, authorized by law, including debts incurred for payment of pensions and bounties for services in suppressing insurrection or rebellion, shall not be questioned. But neither the United States nor any State shall assume or pay any debt or obligation incurred in aid of insurrection or rebellion against the United States, or any claim for the loss or emancipation of any slave, but all such debts, obligations and claims shall be held illegal and void.

Section 5.

The Congress shall have power to enforce, by appropriate legislation, the provisions of this article.

AMENDMENT XV.
(Ratified on February 3, 1870—
The Right to Vote)

Section 1.

The right of citizens of the United States to vote shall not be denied or abridged by the United States or by any State on account of race, color, or previous condition of servitude.

No citizen can be refused the right to vote simply because of race or color or because that person was once a slave.

Section 2.

The Congress shall have power to enforce this article by appropriate legislation.

AMENDMENT XVI.
(Ratified on February 3, 1913—Income Taxes)

The Congress shall have power to lay and collect taxes on incomes, from whatever source derived, without apportionment among the several States, and without regard to any census or enumeration.

This amendment allows Congress to tax income without sharing the revenue so obtained with the states according to their population.

AMENDMENT XVII.
(Ratified on April 8, 1913—
The Popular Election of Senators)

Section 1.

The Senate of the United States shall be composed of two Senators from each State, elected by the people thereof, for six years; and each Senator shall have one vote. The electors in each State shall have the qualifications requisite for electors of the most numerous branch of the State legislatures.

Section 2.

When vacancies happen in the representation of any State in the Senate, the executive authority of such State shall issue writs of election to fill such vacancies: *Provided,* That the legislature of any State may empower the executive thereof to make temporary appointments until the people fill the vacancies by election as the legislature may direct.

Section 3.

This amendment shall not be so construed as to affect the election or term of any Senator chosen before it becomes valid as part of the Constitution.

---

14. Changed by the Twenty-sixth Amendment.

This amendment modified portions of Article I, Section 3, that related to election of senators. Senators are now elected by the voters in each state directly. When a vacancy occurs, either the state may fill the vacancy by a special election, or the governor of the state involved may appoint someone to fill the seat until the next election.

AMENDMENT XVIII.
(Ratified on January 16, 1919—Prohibition)

Section 1.

After one year from the ratification of this article the manufacture, sale, or transportation of intoxicating liquors within, the importation thereof into, or the exportation thereof from the United States and all territory subject to the jurisdiction thereof for beverage purposes is hereby prohibited.

Section 2.

The Congress and the several States shall have concurrent power to enforce this article by appropriate legislation.

Section 3.

This article shall be inoperative unless it shall have been ratified as an amendment to the Constitution by the legislatures of the several States, as provided in the Constitution, within seven years from the date of the submission hereof to the States by the Congress.[15]

This amendment made it illegal to manufacture, sell, and transport alcoholic beverages in the United States. It was repealed by the Twenty-first Amendment.

AMENDMENT XIX.
(Ratified on August 18, 1920—Women's Right to Vote)

Section 1.

The right of citizens of the United States to vote shall not be denied or abridged by the United States or by any State on account of sex.

Section 2.

Congress shall have power to enforce this article by appropriate legislation.

Women were given the right to vote by this amendment, and Congress was given the power to enforce this right.

AMENDMENT XX.
(Ratified on January 23, 1933— The Lame Duck Amendment)

Section 1.

The terms of the President and Vice President shall end at noon on the 20th day of January, and the terms of Senators and Representatives at noon on the 3d day of January, of the years in which such terms would have ended if this article had not been ratified; and the terms of their successors shall then begin.

This amendment modified Article I, Section 4, Clause 2, and other provisions relating to the president in the Twelfth Amendment. The taking of the oath of office was moved from March 4 to January 20.

---

15. The Eighteenth Amendment was repealed by the Twenty-first Amendment.

Section 2.

The Congress shall assemble at least once in every year, and such meeting shall begin at noon on the 3d day of January, unless they shall by law appoint a different day.

Congress changed the beginning of its term to January 3. The reason the Twentieth Amendment is called the Lame Duck Amendment is that it shortens the time between when a member of Congress is defeated for reelection and when he or she leaves office.

Section 3.

If, at the time fixed for the beginning of the term of the President, the President elect shall have died, the Vice President elect shall become President. If a President shall not have been chosen before the time fixed for the beginning of his term, or if the President elect shall have failed to qualify, then the Vice President elect shall act as President until a President shall have qualified; and the Congress may by law provide for the case wherein neither a President elect nor a Vice President elect shall have qualified, declaring who shall then act as President, or the manner in which one who is to act shall be selected, and such person shall act accordingly until a President or Vice President shall have qualified.

This part of the amendment deals with problem areas left ambiguous by Article II and the Twelfth Amendment. If the president dies before January 20 or fails to qualify for office, the presidency is to be filled as described in this section.

Section 4.

The Congress may by law provide for the case of the death of any of the persons from whom the House of Representatives may choose a President whenever the right of choice shall have devolved upon them, and for the case of the death of any of the persons from whom the Senate may choose a Vice President whenever the right of choice shall have devolved upon them.

Congress has never created legislation pursuant to this section.

Section 5.

Sections 1 and 2 shall take effect on the 15th day of October following the ratification of this article.

Section 6.

This article shall be inoperative unless it shall have been ratified as an amendment to the Constitution by the legislatures of three-fourths of the several States within seven years from the date of its submission.

AMENDMENT XXI.
(Ratified on December 5, 1933— The Repeal of Prohibition)

Section 1.

The eighteenth article of amendment to the Constitution of the United States is hereby repealed.

Section 2.

The transportation or importation into any State, Territory, or possession of the United States for delivery or use therein of intoxicating liquors, in violation of the laws thereof, is hereby prohibited.

Section 3.

This article shall be inoperative unless it shall have been ratified as an amendment to the Constitution by conventions in the several States, as provided in the Constitution, within seven years from the date of the submission hereof to the States by the Congress.

The amendment repealed the Eighteenth Amendment but did not make alcoholic beverages legal everywhere. Rather, they remained illegal in any state that so designated them. Many such "dry" states existed for a number of years after 1933. Today, there are still "dry" counties within the United States, in which the sale of alcoholic beverages is illegal.

AMENDMENT XXII.
(Ratified on February 27, 1951— Limitation of Presidential Terms)

Section 1.

No person shall be elected to the office of the President more than twice, and no person who has held the office of President, or acted as President, for more than two years of a term to which some other person was elected President shall be elected to the office of President more than once. But this Article shall not apply to any person holding the office of President when this Article was proposed by the Congress, and shall not prevent any person who may be holding the office of President, or acting as President, during the term within which this Article becomes operative from holding the office of President or acting as President during the remainder of such term.

Section 2.

This article shall be inoperative unless it shall have been ratified as an amendment to the Constitution by the legislatures of three-fourths of the several States within seven years from the date of its submission to the States by the Congress.

No president may serve more than two elected terms. If, however, a president has succeeded to the office after the halfway point of a term in which another president was originally elected, then that president may serve for more than eight years, but not to exceed ten years.

AMENDMENT XXIII.
(Ratified on March 29, 1961— Presidential Electors for the District of Columbia)

Section 1.

The District constituting the seat of Government of the United States shall appoint in such manner as the Congress may direct:

A number of electors of President and Vice President equal to the whole number of Senators and Representatives in Congress to which the District would be entitled if it were a State, but in no event more than the least populous State; they shall be in addition to those appointed by the States, but they shall be considered, for the purposes of the election of President and Vice President, to be electors appointed by a State; and they shall meet in the District and perform such duties as provided by the twelfth article of amendment.

Section 2.

The Congress shall have power to enforce this article by appropriate legislation.

Citizens living in the District of Columbia have the right to vote in elections for president and vice president. The District of Columbia has three presidential electors, whereas before this amendment it had none.

AMENDMENT XXIV.
(Ratified on January 23, 1964— The Anti–Poll Tax Amendment)

Section 1.

The right of citizens of the United States to vote in any primary or other election for President or Vice President, for electors for President or Vice President, or for Senator or Representative in Congress, shall not be denied or abridged by the United States, or any State by reason of failure to pay any poll tax or other tax.

Section 2.

The Congress shall have power to enforce this article by appropriate legislation.

No government shall require a person to pay a poll tax to vote in any federal election.

AMENDMENT XXV.
(Ratified on February 10, 1967—Presidential Disability and Vice-Presidential Vacancies)

Section 1.

In case of the removal of the President from office or of his death or resignation, the Vice President shall become President.

Whenever a president dies or resigns from office, the vice president becomes president.

Section 2.

Whenever there is a vacancy in the office of the Vice President, the President shall nominate a Vice President who shall take office upon confirmation by a majority vote of both Houses of Congress.

Whenever the office of the vice presidency becomes vacant, the president may appoint someone to fill this office, provided Congress consents.

Section 3.

Whenever the President transmits to the President pro tempore of the Senate and the Speaker of the House of Representatives his written declaration that he is unable to discharge the powers and duties of his office, and until he transmits to them a written declaration to the contrary, such powers and duties shall be discharged by the Vice President as Acting President.

Whenever the president believes she or he is unable to carry out the duties of the office, she or he shall so indicate to Congress in writing. The vice president then acts as president until the president declares that she or he is again able to carry out the duties of the office.

Section 4.

Whenever the Vice President and a majority of either the principal officers of the executive departments or of such other body as Congress may by law provide, transmit to the President pro tempore of the Senate and the Speaker of the House of Representatives their written declaration that the President is unable to discharge the powers and duties of his office, the Vice President shall immediately assume the powers and duties of the office as Acting President.

Thereafter, when the President transmits to the President pro tempore of the Senate and the Speaker of the House of Representatives his written declaration that no inability exists, he shall resume the powers and duties of his office unless the Vice President and a majority of either the principal officers of the executive department or of such other body as Congress may by law provide, transmit within four days to the President pro tempore of the Senate and the Speaker of the House of Representatives their written declaration that the President is unable to discharge the powers and duties of his office. Thereupon Congress shall decide the issue, assembling within forty-eight hours for that purpose if not in session. If the Congress, within twenty-one days after receipt of the latter written declaration, or, if Congress is not in session, within twenty-one days after Congress is required to assemble, determines by two-thirds vote of both Houses that the President is unable to discharge the powers and duties of his office, the Vice President shall continue to discharge the same as Acting President; otherwise, the President shall resume the powers and duties of his office.

Whenever the vice president and a majority of the members of the cabinet believe that the president cannot carry out her or his duties, they shall so indicate in writing to Congress. The vice president shall then act as president. When the president believes that she or he is able to carry out her or his duties again, she or he shall so indicate to the Congress. However, if the vice president and a majority of the cabinet do not agree, Congress must decide by a two-thirds vote within three weeks who shall act as president.

AMENDMENT XXVI.
(Ratified on July 1, 1971— The Eighteen-Year-Old Vote)

Section 1.

The right of citizens of the United States, who are eighteen years of age or older, to vote shall not be denied or abridged by the United States or by any State on account of age.

No one over eighteen years of age can be denied the right to vote in federal or state elections by virtue of age.

Section 2.

The Congress shall have power to enforce this article by appropriate legislation.

AMENDMENT XXVII.
(Ratified on May 7, 1992—Congressional Pay)

No law, varying the compensation for the services of the Senators and Representatives, shall take effect, until an election of representatives shall have intervened.

This amendment allows the voters to have some control over increases in salaries for congressional members. Originally submitted to the states for ratification in 1789, it was not ratified until 203 years later, in 1992.

Federalism

3

A University of Nebraska professor examines a water-collecting drone that can be used to sample water from lakes, ponds, and streams that people can't easily reach. The project is funded in part by a grant from the U.S. Department of Agriculture.

AP Images/Nati Harnik

The five Learning Outcomes below are designed to help improve your understanding of this chapter. After reading this chapter, you should be able to:

■ **Learning Outcome 1:** Explain some of the benefits of the federal system for the United States.

■ **Learning Outcome 2:** Describe how the various provisions of the U.S. Constitution provide a framework for federalism.

■ **Learning Outcome 3:** Discuss how, in the early years of the republic, the United States Supreme Court confirmed the authority of the national government, and how that authority was ratified by the Civil War.

■ **Learning Outcome 4:** Define the terms *dual federalism, cooperative federalism, categorical grants, block grants*, and *fiscal federalism*.

■ **Learning Outcome 5:** Detail recent political developments and Supreme Court rulings that affect the distribution of power between the national government and the states.

(▶) **WATCH & LEARN** MindTap™ for American Government
Watch a brief "What Do You Know?" video summarizing Federalism.

Same-Sex Marriages Were Legal in Every State?

BACKGROUND

One of the most dramatic developments in recent years has been the speed with which Americans have changed their minds about same-sex marriage. In 1996, only 27 percent of those questioned in a Gallup poll supported same-sex marriage, and 68 percent were opposed. By 2013, 53 percent were in favor and 45 opposed. Gay marriage now enjoys majority support.

The Hawaii Supreme Court first put same-sex marriage on the public agenda in 1993 when it suggested that denying marriage to same-sex couples might violate the Hawaii Constitution. This ruling raised an important question. Under the U.S. Constitution, "Full Faith and Credit must be given in each State to the public Acts, Recordings, and judicial Proceedings of every other State." Does that mean if gay marriage is legal in one state, it must be recognized everywhere? The U.S. Congress tried to answer "no" to that question with the 1996 Defense of Marriage Act (DOMA). That act also stated that the national government would refuse to recognize same-sex marriages endorsed by any state.

In 2003, Massachusetts became the first state to recognize gay marriages through a ruling by the state's supreme court.[a] By Election Day 2014, same-sex marriage was legal in thirty-two states, in the District of Columbia, and on ten Indian reservations. Seven states endorsed it in 2013, a record. Also in 2013, the United States Supreme Court threw out the portion of DOMA that banned federal recognition of state-approved gay marriages. The national government must now recognize *all* state-endorsed marriages.[b]

WHAT IF SAME-SEX MARRIAGES WERE LEGAL IN EVERY STATE?

If same-sex marriage does go national, few people will be surprised. Among those who favor same-sex marriage, 85 percent now believe that legal recognition is inevitable. Even 59 percent of opponents believe that. Still, in a wide swath of conservative states, a majority of the voters continues to oppose legalization.

A number of states, especially in the South, have a history of forcibly resisting unwanted national impositions. In the 1950s and 1960s, it took federal troops to force certain southern schools and colleges to admit African Americans. We can assume that imposing same-sex marriage on a reluctant state would not require calling out the 101st Airborne (employed in the 1957 integration of Central High in Little Rock, Arkansas). Still, a few county clerks are

Should all states have to recognize same-sex marriages? Why or why not?

sure to refuse to issue licenses. Some might even refuse a court order to do so and be jailed for contempt of court. They would then be hailed as heroes by fervent opponents of gay marriage.

POPULAR ACCEPTANCE

It is not just government officials who would have to respond to same-sex marriages, however. Same-sex relationships would be more open in general. People ranging from motel desk clerks to bank loan officers, from florists to wedding-cake bakers, would not be able to avoid confronting them. Cultural conservatives who vehemently oppose gay relationships might experience enhanced alienation from American society. They might withdraw further from the broader society through such practices as homeschooling.

For Critical Analysis

1. **What impact might widespread same-sex marriage have on American culture generally?**

2. **Russia and certain African countries have recently adopted severe anti-gay laws, arguing that same-sex relationships are a form of "western corruption." What are the prospects that recognition of gay rights may spread beyond the Western Hemisphere and Europe?**

a. *Goodridge v. Department of Public Health*, 798 N.E.2nd 941 (Mass. 2003).
b. *United States v. Windsor*, 133 S.Ct. 2675 (2013).

Cavan Images/Iconica/Getty Images

In the United States, rights and powers are reserved to the states by the Tenth Amendment. In recent years, however, it may appear that the federal government, sometimes called the national or central government, predominates. That might be an exaggerated perception, for there are 89,056 separate governmental units in this nation, as you can see in Table 3–1.

Visitors from countries such as France and Spain are often awestruck by the complexity of our system of government. Consider that a criminal action can be defined by state law, by national law, or by both. Thus, a criminal suspect can be prosecuted in the state court system or in the federal court system (or both). Often, economic regulation covering exactly the same issues exists at the local level, the state level, and the national level—generating multiple forms to be completed, multiple procedures to be followed, and multiple laws to be obeyed. Many programs are funded by the national government but administered by state and local governments.

Relations between central governments and local units can be structured in various ways. *Federalism* is one of these ways. Understanding federalism and how it differs from other forms of government is important in understanding the American political system. Indeed, many political issues today would not arise if we did not have a federal form of government in which governmental authority is divided between the central government and various subunits. States, for example, might not have the right to set their own marriage laws, as we discussed in this chapter's opening *What If . . .* feature.

Federalism and Its Alternatives

There are almost two hundred independent nations in the world today. Each of these nations has its own system of government. Generally, though, we can describe how nations structure relations between central governments and local units in terms of three models: (1) the unitary system, (2) the confederal system, and (3) the federal system. The most popular, both historically and today, is the unitary system.

A Unitary System

A **unitary system** of government is the easiest to define. Unitary systems place ultimate governmental authority in the hands of the national, or central, government. Consider a typical unitary system—France. The regions, departments, municipalities, and communes in France have elected and appointed officials.

So far, the French system appears to be very similar to the U.S. system, but the similarity is only superficial. Under the unitary French system, the decisions of the lower levels of government can be overruled by the national government. The national government also can cut off the funding for local government activities. Moreover, in a unitary system such as that in France, all questions of education, police, the use of land, and welfare are handled by the national government. Britain, Egypt, Ghana, Israel, Japan, the Philippines, and Sweden—in fact, a majority of all nations—have unitary systems of government.[1]

A Confederal System

You were introduced to the elements of a **confederal system** of government in Chapter 2, when we examined the Articles of Confederation. A *confederation* is the opposite of a unitary governing system. It is a league of independent states, in which a central government or administration handles only those matters of common concern expressly delegated to it by the member states. The central government has no ability to make

LISTEN & LEARN
MindTap for American Government

Access Read Speaker to listen to Chapter 3.

Table 3–1 ▸

Governmental Units in the United States

With more than 89,000 separate governmental units in the United States today, it is no wonder that intergovernmental relations in the United States are so complicated. The number of school districts has decreased over time, but the number of special districts created for single purposes, such as flood control, has increased from about 8,000 during World War II to more than 37,000 today. *Why so many?*

Federal government	**1**
State governments and District of Columbia	**51**
Local governments	
Counties	3,031
Municipalities (mainly cities or towns)	19,522
Townships (less extensive powers)	16,364
Special districts (water, sewer, and the like)	37,203
School districts	12,884
TOTAL	**89,056**

Source: U.S. Census Bureau.

Unitary System
A centralized governmental system in which ultimate governmental authority rests in the hands of the national, or central, government.

Confederal System
A system consisting of a league of independent states, in which the central government created by the league has only limited powers over the states.

---

1. Recent legislation has altered somewhat the unitary character of the French political system. In Britain, the unitary nature of the government has been modified by the creation of the Scottish Parliament.

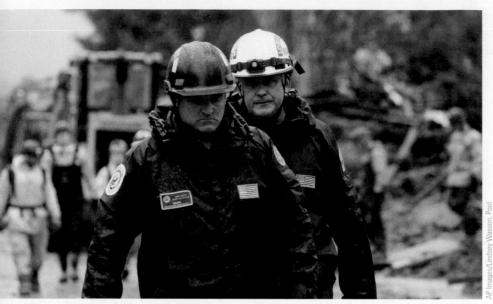

Workers from the Federal Emergency Management Agency (FEMA) join staff from Washington State in the town of Oso, site of a deadly mudslide. The mudslide buried about one square mile of land and killed at least 41 people in March 2014. *Is this an example of federalism?*

■ **Learning Outcome 1:**
Explain some of the benefits of the federal system for the United States.

laws directly applicable to member states unless the members explicitly support such laws. The United States under the Articles of Confederation was a confederal system.

Few, if any, confederations of this kind exist. One possible exception is the European Union (EU), a league of countries that has developed a large body of Europe-wide laws that all members must observe. Many members even share a common currency, the euro. Recent problems in the "Eurozone," which we describe in this chapter's *Beyond Our Borders* feature that follows, demonstrate the limits of a confederal system.

A Federal System

The federal system lies between the unitary and confederal forms of government. As mentioned in Chapter 2, in a *federal system*, authority is divided, usually by a written constitution, between a central government and regional, or subdivisional, governments (often called *constituent governments*). The central government and the constituent governments both act directly on the people through laws and through the actions of elected and appointed governmental officials. Within each government's sphere of authority, each is supreme, in theory. Thus, a federal system differs sharply from a unitary one, in which the central government is supreme and the constituent governments derive their authority from it. In addition to the United States, Australia, Brazil, Canada, Germany, India, and Mexico are examples of nations with federal systems. See Figure 3–1 that follows for a comparison of the three systems.

Figure 3–1 ▸ The Flow of Power in Three Systems of Government

In a unitary system, power flows from the central government to the local and state governments. In a confederal system, power flows in the opposite direction—from the state governments to the central government. In a federal system, the flow of power, in principle, goes both ways. *Why do you think confederal systems are rare?*

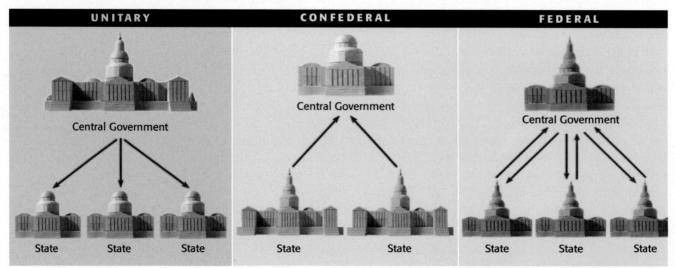

Why Federalism?

Why did the United States develop in a federal direction? Here we look at that question, as well as at some of the arguments for and against a federal form of government. As you saw in Chapter 2, the historical basis of our federal system was laid down in Philadelphia at the Constitutional Convention, where advocates of a strong national government opposed states' rights advocates. This conflict continued through to the ratifying conventions in the several states. The resulting federal system was a compromise. The supporters of the new Constitution were political pragmatists—they realized that without a federal arrangement, the new Constitution would not be ratified. The appeal of federalism was that it retained state traditions and local power while establishing a strong national government capable of handling common problems.

Beyond Our Borders

The European Union Gazes into the Abyss

The European Union (EU) is a confederation of twenty-eight countries. Seventeen of the countries share a common currency called the euro. When the euro was created in 1999, Germany—the largest Eurozone economy—demanded and received certain guarantees. The European Central Bank (ECB) was barred from aiding any national government that got into trouble. Some economists warned that the Eurozone, as designed, was inherently unstable. For many years, however, everything seemed fine.

Crisis in Greece

After 1999, investors in wealthy euro nations such as Germany and France invested larger and larger sums in the poorer euro nations. These included Greece, Ireland, Portugal, and Spain. In 2010, however, a newly elected Greek government discovered that previous administrations had "cooked the books." In fact, Greece had rolled up so much debt it would never be able to pay it all back. Much against their will, other euro nations put together a package to bail out the Greek government. But the rot did not stop with Greece. In Ireland, banks had made huge loans on home mortgages, loans that now could not be repaid. The Irish government, which had been running a substantial budget *surplus,* assumed the obligations of its banks—and discovered that it was now stuck as well. A bailout of Ireland was soon followed by a bailout of Portugal.

Crisis in the Eurozone

If nations such as Greece and Portugal had their own currencies, they could devalue them. Their debts would fall, and their exports would be more competitive. With the euro, that is impossible. Investors began to flee from the bonds issued by the poorer euro nations. Even countries with finances that ought to have been stable—such as Italy and Spain—were in danger of defaulting on their debts, simply because they could no longer borrow. The only alternative to default would be to leave the euro. Either alternative would be a disaster.

Normally, a nation in such a situation would borrow from its own central bank. But the ECB, remember, was prohibited from making such loans. By the end of 2011, however, the ECB began loaning huge sums to European banks. The banks then used the funds to buy the bonds of nations in trouble. In September 2012, the ECB announced that it would buy, from investors, as many bonds issued by troubled nations as would be necessary to save the euro.

These steps appeared to resolve the crisis. In 2014, however, the German Constitutional Court ruled that the ECB bond-buying program was unconstitutional. The German court asked the European Court of Justice to respond, delaying a final ruling. If the Germans force the ECB to stop assisting troubled nations, however, Europe will again be gazing into the abyss.

For Critical Analysis

No one worries that fiscal misbehavior by an American state could threaten the dollar. Why?

Even if the founders had agreed on the desirability of a unitary system, size and regional isolation would have made such a system difficult operationally. At the time of the Constitutional Convention, the thirteen states taken together were much larger geographically than England or France. Slow travel and communication, combined with geographic spread, contributed to the isolation of many regions within the states. It could take several weeks for all of the states to be informed about a particular political decision.

Other Arguments for Federalism

For big countries, such as Canada, India, and the United States, federalism allows many functions to be "farmed out" by the central government to the states or provinces. The lower levels of government that accept these responsibilities thereby can become the focus of political dissatisfaction rather than the national authorities. Also, even with modern transportation and communications systems, the large area or population of some nations makes it impractical to locate all political authority in one place.

Finally, federalism brings government closer to the people. It allows more direct access to, and influence on, government agencies and policies, rather than leaving the population restive and dissatisfied with a remote, faceless, all-powerful central authority.

Benefits for the United States. In the United States, federalism historically has yielded additional benefits. State governments long have been a training ground for future national leaders. Many presidents made their political mark as state governors. The states themselves have been testing grounds for new government initiatives. As United States Supreme Court justice Louis Brandeis once observed:

> It is one of the happy incidents of the federal system that a single courageous state may, if its citizens choose, serve as a laboratory and try novel social and economic experiments without risk to the rest of the country.[2]

Examples of programs pioneered at the state level include unemployment compensation, which began in Wisconsin, and air-pollution control, which was initiated in California. Today, states are experimenting with policies ranging from education reform to homeland security strategies. In recent years, states have begun experimenting with new ways of managing marijuana. Some states have decriminalized marijuana consumption. Some have legalized marijuana for medical use. Two states have now passed laws that legalize, tax, and regulate marijuana for recreational use. We take a closer look at these developments in the *Which Side Are You On?* feature that follows.

Why Should You Care about . . .

The Federal System?

Our federal system encourages debate over whether a particular issue should be a national, state, or local question. Many questions are, in fact, state or local ones, and it is easier for you to make a significant contribution to the discussion on these issues. Even in the largest states, there are many fewer people to persuade than in the nation as a whole. Attempts to influence your fellow citizens can therefore be more effective.

A fifth-grade science and math teacher in California helps a student. Some federal funds are used to help local elementary schools hire additional staff. *How much responsibility does the federal government have for elementary education?*

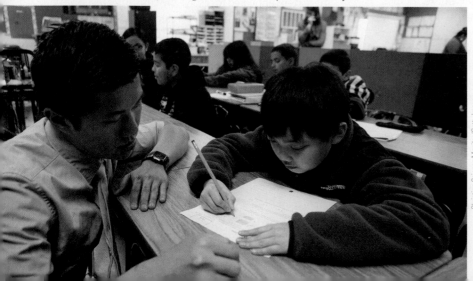

Christian Science Monitor/Getty Images

2. *New State Ice Co. v. Liebmann*, 285 U.S. 262 (1932). See the *Additional Resources* feature at the end of this chapter for information on how to look up court cases online.

Which Side Are You On?

Should Recreational Marijuana Be Legal?

Marijuana has been around for a long time. The earliest record we have of its use as a drug dates from the Third Millennium B.C.E. The drug was not criminalized in the United States until the twentieth century, however, beginning with restrictions in the District of Columbia in 1906. The Marijuana Tax Act of 1937 banned the drug nationwide. Today, the federal government classifies marijuana as a Schedule I drug, that is, a substance with a high potential for abuse and no medical uses. Seventeen states have passed decriminalization laws, however, beginning in Oregon in 1973. As of early 2014, twenty states allow the sale and use of marijuana for medical purposes. In 2012, Colorado and Washington voters approved the sale and possession of marijuana for recreational use.

So, should all states follow in their footsteps? Should the federal government change its law similarly?

Don't Go the Alcohol and Tobacco Route

Some argue that legal recreational use of marijuana will generate huge costs to society, just like the recreational use of tobacco and alcoholic beverages. Abuse of alcohol and cigarettes leads to hundreds of thousands of premature deaths a year in this country. Why add marijuana to that list? For many—an estimated 4.3 million—marijuana use is an addiction. The American Medical Association claims that heavy marijuana use in adolescents causes impairments in neurocognitive performance and

IQ. As one pundit put it, "the reason potheads appear stupid is because in fact they are becoming stupider." High school students who use marijuana tend to have lower grades and are less likely to get into college than nonsmokers.

Don't Fight Reality, Just Make It Legal

Cannabis has been illegal for decades, yet it is readily available just about everywhere. Why should we be hypocrites? A father who regularly puts away a six-pack of beer has no grounds on which to lecture a twenty-one-year-old son on smoking pot. The social cost of alcohol is a thousand times more than that of marijuana. Marijuana is also safer than alcohol—no one ever dies of an overdose of marijuana. Alcohol overdoses kill college students every year. About 40 million Americans currently break the law by smoking pot at least once a year. That is an absurd situation and fosters disrespect for the law in general. Also consider taxation—when pot is legal, state and local governments can obtain much-needed tax revenues.

For Critical Analysis

If recreational marijuana does become legal, what effect might that have on rates of alcohol consumption?

Allowance for Many Political Subcultures. The American way of life always has been characterized by a number of political subcultures, which divide along the lines of race and ethnic origin, region, wealth, education, and, more recently, degree of religious commitment and sexual preference. The existence of diverse political subcultures would appear to be incompatible with a political authority concentrated solely in a central government. Had the United States developed into a unitary system, various political subcultures certainly would have been less able to influence government behavior than they have been, and continue to be, in our federal system.

Arguments against Federalism

Not everyone thinks federalism is such a good idea. Some see it as a way for powerful state and local interests to block progress and impede national plans. Smaller political

did you know?

State governments in the United States are unitary governments. As a result, most local governments are mere creatures of the states.

units are more likely to be dominated by a single political group. (This was essentially the argument that James Madison put forth in *Federalist Paper* No. 10, which you can read in Appendix B of this text.) In fact, the dominant groups in some cities and states have resisted implementing equal rights for minority groups. Some argue, however, that the dominant factions in other states have been more progressive than the national government in many areas, such as environmental protection.

Critics of federalism also argue that too many Americans suffer as a result of the inequalities across the states. Individual states differ markedly in educational spending and achievement, crime and crime prevention, and even the safety of their buildings. Not surprisingly, these critics argue for increased federal legislation and oversight. This might involve creating national standards for education and building codes, national expenditure minimums for crime control, and similar measures.

Others see dangers in the expansion of national powers at the expense of the states. President Ronald Reagan (1981–1989) said, "The Founding Fathers saw the federalist system as constructed something like a masonry wall. The States are the bricks, the national government is the mortar. . . . Unfortunately, over the years, many people have increasingly come to believe that Washington is the whole wall."[3]

The Constitutional Basis for American Federalism

■ **Learning Outcome 2:** Describe how the various provisions of the U.S. Constitution provide a framework for federalism.

The term *federal system* cannot be found in the U.S. Constitution. Nor is it possible to find a systematic division of governmental authority between the national and state governments in that document. Rather, the Constitution sets out different types of powers. These powers can be classified as (1) the powers of the national government, (2) the powers of the states, and (3) prohibited powers. The Constitution also makes it clear that if a state or local law conflicts with a national law, the national law will prevail.

Powers of the National Government

The powers delegated to the national government include both expressed and implied powers, as well as the special category of inherent powers. Most of the powers expressly delegated to the national government are found in the first seventeen clauses of Article I, Section 8, of the Constitution. These **enumerated powers,** also called *expressed powers,* include coining money, setting standards for weights and measures, making uniform naturalization laws, admitting new states, establishing post offices and post roads, and declaring war. Another important enumerated power is the power to regulate commerce among the states—a topic we deal with later in this chapter.

The Necessary and Proper Clause. The implied powers of the national government are also based on Article I, Section 8, which states that the Congress shall have the power

> to make all Laws which shall be necessary and proper for carrying into Execution the foregoing Powers, and all other Powers vested by this Constitution in the Government of the United States, or in any Department or Officer thereof.

This clause is sometimes called the **elastic clause,** or the **necessary and proper clause,** because it provides flexibility to our constitutional system. It gives Congress the power

Enumerated Powers
Powers specifically granted to the national government by the Constitution. The first seventeen clauses of Article I, Section 8, specify most of the enumerated powers of the national government.

Elastic Clause, or Necessary and Proper Clause
The clause in Article I, Section 8, that grants Congress the power to do whatever is necessary to execute its specifically delegated powers.

3. As quoted in Edward Millican, *One United People: The Federalist Papers and the National Idea* (Lexington: The University Press of Kentucky, 1990).

to do whatever is necessary to execute its specifically delegated powers. The clause was first used in the Supreme Court decision of *McCulloch v. Maryland*[4] (discussed later in this chapter) to develop the concept of implied powers. Through this concept, the national government has succeeded in strengthening the scope of its authority to meet the many problems that the framers of the Constitution did not, and could not, anticipate.

Inherent Powers. A special category of national powers that is not implied by the necessary and proper clause consists of what have been labeled the *inherent powers* of the national government. These powers derive from the fact that the United States is a sovereign power among nations, and so its national government must be the only government that deals with other nations. Under international law, it is assumed that all nation-states, regardless of their size or power, have an inherent right to ensure their own survival. To do this, each nation must have the ability to act in its own interest among and with the community of nations—by, for instance, making treaties, waging war, seeking trade, and acquiring territory.

Note that no specific clause in the Constitution says anything about the acquisition of additional land. Nonetheless, the federal government's inherent powers allowed it to make the Louisiana Purchase in 1803 and then go on to acquire Florida, Texas, Oregon, Alaska, Hawaii, and other lands. The United States grew from a mere thirteen states to fifty states, plus several territories.

The national government has these inherent powers whether or not they have been enumerated in the Constitution. Some constitutional scholars categorize inherent powers as a third type of power, completely distinct from the delegated powers (both expressed and implied) of the national government.

> **Police Power**
> The authority to legislate for the protection of the health, morals, safety, and welfare of the people. In the United States, most police power is reserved to the states.

Powers of the State Governments

The Tenth Amendment states that the powers not delegated to the United States by the Constitution, nor prohibited by it to the states, are reserved to the states, or to the people. These are the *reserved powers* that the national government cannot deny to the states. Because these powers are not expressly listed, there is sometimes a question as to whether a certain power is delegated to the national government or reserved to the states.

State powers have been held to include each state's right to regulate commerce within its borders and to provide for a state militia. States also have the reserved power to make laws on all matters not prohibited to the states by the U.S. Constitution or state constitutions and not expressly, or by implication, delegated to the national government. Furthermore, the states have **police power**—the authority to legislate for the protection of the health, morals, safety, and welfare of the people. Their police power enables states to pass laws governing such activities as crime, marriage, contracts, education, intrastate transportation, and land use.

Mischa Richter/The New Yorker Collection/The Cartoon Bank

"They have very strict anti-pollution laws in this state."

4. 17 U.S. 316 (1819).

The ambiguity of the Tenth Amendment has allowed the reserved powers of the states to be defined differently at different times in our history. When there is widespread support for increased regulation by the national government, the Tenth Amendment tends to recede into the background. When the tide turns the other way (in favor of states' rights), the Tenth Amendment is resurrected to justify arguments supporting the states.

Prohibited Powers

The Constitution prohibits, or denies, a number of powers to the national government. For example, the national government has expressly been denied the power to impose taxes on goods sold to other countries (exports). Moreover, any power not granted expressly or implicitly to the federal government by the Constitution is prohibited to it. For example, many legal experts believe that the national government could not create a national divorce law system without a constitutional amendment. The states are also denied certain powers. For example, no state is allowed to enter into a treaty on its own with another country.

Concurrent Powers

In certain areas, the states share **concurrent powers** with the national government. Most concurrent powers are not specifically listed in the Constitution—they are only implied. An example of a concurrent power is the power to tax. The types of taxation are divided between the levels of government. For example, states may not levy a tariff (a set of taxes on imported goods). Only the national government may do this. Neither government may tax the facilities of the other. If the state governments did not have the power to tax, they would not be able to function other than on a ceremonial basis.

Additional concurrent powers include the power to borrow funds, to establish courts, and to charter banks and corporations. To a limited extent, the national government exercises police power, and to the extent that it does, police power is also a concurrent power. Concurrent powers exercised by the states are normally limited to the geographic area of each state and to those functions not granted by the Constitution exclusively to the national government.

The Supremacy Clause

The supremacy of the national constitution over subnational laws and actions is established in the **supremacy clause** of the Constitution. The supremacy clause (Article VI, Clause 2) states the following:

> *This Constitution, and the Laws of the United States which shall be made in Pursuance thereof; and all Treaties made . . . under the Authority of the United States, shall be the supreme Law of the Land; and the Judges in every State shall be bound thereby, any Thing in the Constitution or Laws of any State to the Contrary notwithstanding.*

In other words, states cannot use their reserved or concurrent powers to thwart national policies. All national and state officers, including judges, must be bound by oath to support the Constitution. Hence, any legitimate exercise of national governmental power supersedes any conflicting state action. Of course, deciding whether a conflict actually exists is a judicial matter, as you will soon learn when we discuss the case of *McCulloch v. Maryland*.

COMPARE WITH YOUR PEERS
MindTap for American Government

Access the Federalism Forum: Polling Activity—State Income Tax

did you know?

The founders of Canada in 1867 sought to create a federal system in which the central government was much more powerful than in the United States. Today, however, Canadian provinces may actually have *more* power than American states.

The National Guard can serve as an example of how federal power supersedes that of the states. Normally, the National Guard functions as a state militia under the command of the governor. It is frequently called out to assist with recovery efforts after natural disasters such as hurricanes, floods, and earthquakes. The president, however, can assume command of any National Guard unit at any time. Presidents George W. Bush and Barack Obama repeatedly "federalized" such units for deployment in Afghanistan and Iraq. In the conflicts in these countries, National Guard members and reservists made up a larger percentage of the forces on combat duty than during any previous war in U.S. history.

National government legislation in a concurrent area is said to *preempt* (take precedence over) conflicting state or local laws or regulations in that area. One of the ways in which the national government has extended its powers, particularly during the twentieth century, is through the preemption of state and local laws by national legislation. In the first decade of the twentieth century, fewer than twenty national laws preempted laws and regulations issued by state and local governments. By the beginning of the twenty-first century, the number had grown into the hundreds.

> **Interstate Compact**
> An agreement between two or more states. Agreements on minor matters are made without congressional consent, but any compact that tends to increase the power of the contracting states relative to other states or relative to the national government generally requires the consent of Congress.

Interstate Relations

So far, we have examined only the relationship between central and state governmental units. The states, however, have constant commercial, social, and other dealings among themselves. The national Constitution imposes certain "rules of the road" on interstate relations. These rules have had the effect of preventing any one state from setting itself apart from the other states. The three most important clauses governing interstate relations in the Constitution, all taken from the Articles of Confederation, require each state to do the following:

1. Give full faith and credit to every other state's public acts, records, and judicial proceedings (Article IV, Section 1).
2. Extend to every other state's citizens the privileges and immunities of its own citizens (Article IV, Section 2).
3. Agree to return persons who are fleeing from justice in another state back to their home state when requested to do so (Article IV, Section 2).

Additionally, states may enter into agreements with one another called **interstate compacts**—if consented to by Congress. In reality, congressional consent is necessary only if such a compact increases the power of the contracting states relative to other states (or to the national government). An example of an interstate compact is the Port Authority of New York and New Jersey, established by an agreement between those two states in 1921.

The entrance to the George Washington Bridge in Ft. Lee, New Jersey. The bridge is controlled by the Port Authority of New York and New Jersey, an interstate compact. In 2013, it was alleged that top advisers to New Jersey's Republican Governor Chris Christie ordered several lanes on the bridge shut to traffic. The resulting days of gridlock in Fort Lee may have been revenge against the town's mayor for not endorsing Christie for reelection. *What effect could such a scandal have on Christie's presidential prospects?*

Commerce Clause
The section of the Constitution in which Congress is given the power to regulate trade among the states and with foreign countries.

■ **Learning Outcome 3:**
Discuss how, in the early years of the republic, the United States Supreme Court confirmed the authority of the national government, and how that authority was ratified by the Civil War.

Defining Constitutional Powers—the Early Years

Although political bodies at all levels of government play important roles in the process of settling disputes over the nature of our federal system, ultimately it is the United States Supreme Court that casts the final vote. As might be expected, the character of the referee will have an impact on the ultimate outcome of any dispute. From 1801 to 1835, the Supreme Court was headed by Chief Justice John Marshall, a Federalist who advocated a strong central government. We look here at two cases decided by the Marshall Court: *McCulloch v. Maryland*[5] and *Gibbons v. Ogden*.[6] Both cases are considered milestones in the movement toward national government supremacy.

McCulloch v. Maryland (1819)

The U.S. Constitution says nothing about establishing a national bank. Nonetheless, at different times Congress chartered two banks—the First and Second Banks of the United States—and provided part of their initial capital. Thus, they were national banks. The government of Maryland imposed a tax on the Second Bank's Baltimore branch in an attempt to put that branch out of business. The branch's cashier, James William McCulloch, refused to pay the Maryland tax. When Maryland took McCulloch to its state court, the state of Maryland won. The national government appealed the case to the Supreme Court.

One of the issues before the Court was whether the national government had the implied power, under the necessary and proper clause, to charter a bank and contribute capital to it. The other important question before the Court was the following: If the bank was constitutional, could a state tax it? In other words, was a state action that conflicted with a national government action invalid under the supremacy clause?

Chief Justice Marshall held that if establishing a national bank aided the national government in the exercise of its designated powers, then the authority to set up such a bank could be implied. Having established this doctrine of implied powers, Marshall then answered the other question before the Court and established the doctrine of national supremacy. Marshall ruled that no state could use its taxing power to tax a part of the national government. If it could, "the declaration that the Constitution . . . shall be the supreme law of the land, is [an] empty and unmeaning [statement]."

Marshall's decision enabled the national government to grow and to meet problems that the Constitution's framers were unable to foresee. Today, practically every expressed power of the national government has been expanded in one way or another by use of the necessary and proper clause.

Gibbons v. Ogden (1824)

One of the most important parts of the Constitution included in Article I, Section 8, is the **commerce clause,** in which Congress is given the power "to regulate Commerce with foreign Nations, and among the several States, and with the Indian Tribes." The meaning of this clause was at issue in *Gibbons v. Ogden*.

The Background of the Case. Robert Fulton and Robert Livingston secured a monopoly on steam navigation on the waters in New York State from the New York legislature in 1803. They licensed Aaron Ogden to operate steam-powered ferryboats between New York and New Jersey. Thomas Gibbons, who had

5. 17 U.S. 316 (1819).
6. 22 U.S. 1 (1824).

obtained a license from the U.S. government to operate boats in interstate waters, decided to compete with Ogden, but he did so without New York's permission. Ogden sued Gibbons. New York's state courts prohibited Gibbons from operating in New York waters. Gibbons appealed to the Supreme Court.

There were actually several issues before the Court in this case. The first issue was how the term *commerce* should be defined. New York's highest court had defined the term narrowly to mean only the shipment of goods or the interchange of commodities, *not* navigation or the transport of people. The second issue was whether the national government's power to regulate interstate commerce extended to commerce within a state (*intrastate* commerce) or was limited strictly to commerce among the states (*interstate* commerce). The third issue was whether the power to regulate interstate commerce was a concurrent power (as the New York court had concluded) or an exclusive national power.

Marshall's Ruling. Marshall defined *commerce* as all commercial interactions—all business dealings—including navigation and the transport of people. Marshall also held that the commerce power of the national government could be exercised in state jurisdictions, even though it could not reach *solely* intrastate commerce. Finally, Marshall emphasized that the power to regulate interstate commerce was an *exclusive* national power. Marshall held that because Gibbons was duly authorized by the national government to navigate in interstate waters, he could not be prohibited from doing so by a state court.

Marshall's expansive interpretation of the commerce clause in *Gibbons v. Ogden* allowed the national government to exercise increasing authority over economic affairs throughout the land. Congress did not immediately exploit this broad grant of power. In the 1930s and subsequent decades, however, the commerce clause became the primary constitutional basis for national government regulation—as you will read later in this chapter.

States' Rights and the Resort to Civil War

The controversy over slavery that led to the Civil War took the form of a dispute over national government supremacy versus the rights of the separate states. Essentially, the Civil War brought to an ultimate and violent climax the ideological debate begun by the Federalist and Anti-Federalist parties even before the Constitution was ratified.

The Shift Back to States' Rights. As we have seen, while John Marshall was chief justice of the Supreme Court, he did much to increase the power of the national government and to reduce that of the states. During the administration of President Andrew Jackson (1829–1837), however, a shift back to states' rights began. The question of the regulation of commerce became one of the major issues in federal–state relations. When Congress passed a tariff in 1828, the state of South Carolina unsuccessfully attempted to nullify the tariff (render it void), claiming that in cases of conflict between a state and the national government, the state should have the ultimate authority over its citizens.

During the next three decades, the North and the South became even more sharply divided, especially over the slavery issue. On December 20, 1860, South Carolina formally repealed its ratification of the Constitution and withdrew from the Union. On February 4, 1861, representatives from six southern states met at Montgomery, Alabama, to form a new government called the Confederate States of America.

War and the Growth of the National Government. The ultimate defeat of the South in 1865 permanently ended the idea that a state could successfully claim the right to secede, or withdraw, from the Union. Ironically, the Civil War—brought about in large part because of the South's desire for increased states' rights—resulted in the opposite: an

When John Marshall (1755–1835) was chief justice of the United States Supreme Court, he championed the power of the federal government. *What are the most famous cases that the Marshall Court decided?*

Historical/Corbis

Dual Federalism
A model of federalism in which the states and the national government each remain supreme within their own spheres. The doctrine looks on nation and state as co-equal sovereign powers. Neither the state government nor the national government should interfere in the other's sphere.

increase in the political power of the national government. Thousands of new employees were hired to run the Union war effort and to deal with the social and economic problems that had to be handled in the aftermath of the war. A billion-dollar ($1.3 billion, which is about $19 billion in today's dollars) national government budget was passed for the first time in 1865 to cover the increased government expenditures. The first (temporary) income tax was imposed on citizens to help pay for the war.

The Civil War Amendments. The expansion of the national government's authority during the Civil War was also reflected in the passage of the Civil War amendments to the Constitution. Before the war, it was a bedrock constitutional principle that the national government should not interfere with slavery in the states. The Thirteenth Amendment, ratified in 1865, did more than interfere with slavery—it abolished the institution altogether.

The Fourteenth Amendment, ratified in 1868, defined who was a citizen of each state. It sought to guarantee equal rights under state law, stating that

> [no] State [shall] deprive any person of life, liberty, or property, without due process of law; nor deny to any person within its jurisdiction the equal protection of the laws.

In time, the courts interpreted these words to mean that the national Bill of Rights applied to state governments, a development that we will examine in Chapter 4. Finally, the Fifteenth Amendment (1870) gave African Americans the right to vote in all elections, including state elections—although a century would pass before that right was enforced in all states.

did you know?
Only after the Civil War did people commonly refer to the United States as "it" instead of "they."

The Continuing Dispute over the Division of Power

Although the outcome of the Civil War firmly established the supremacy of the national government and put to rest the idea that a state could secede from the Union, the war by no means ended the debate over the division of powers between the national government and the states.

Dual Federalism

During the decades following the Civil War, the prevailing model of federalism was what political scientists have called **dual federalism**—a doctrine that emphasizes a distinction between national and state spheres of government authority. This doctrine looks on nation and state as co-equal sovereign powers. Neither the state government nor the national government should interfere in the other's sphere.

Various images have been used to describe different configurations of federalism over time. Dual federalism is commonly depicted as a layer cake, because the state governments and the national government are viewed as separate entities, like separate layers of a cake. The two layers are physically separate; they do not mix. For the most part, advocates of dual federalism believed that the state and national governments should not exercise authority in the same areas.

John Brown (1800–1859), an advocate of abolishing slavery, led an ill-fated raid on a federal arsenal at Harper's Ferry, Virginia. Brown had hoped to set off a slave uprising. He was executed on charges of treason and murder. Today, we would doubtless call him a terrorist. *Why do some people nevertheless consider him a hero?*

Kean Collection/Staff/Getty Images

The doctrine of dual federalism represented a revival of states' rights following the expansion of national authority during the Civil War. Dual federalism, after all, was a fairly accurate model of the prewar consensus on federal–state relations. For many people, it therefore represented a return to normal.

The Civil War crisis drastically reduced the influence of the United States Supreme Court. In the prewar *Dred Scott* decision,[7] the Court had attempted to abolish the power of the national government to restrict slavery in the territories, and it also declared that African Americans could never be citizens, even if free. In so doing, the Court placed itself on the losing side of the impending conflict. After the war, Congress took the unprecedented step of exempting the entire process of southern reconstruction from judicial review. The Court had little choice but to acquiesce.

In time, the Supreme Court reestablished itself as the legitimate constitutional umpire. Its decisions tended to support dual federalism, defend states' rights, and limit the powers of the national government. The Court generally limited the exercise of police power to the states. For example, in 1918, the Court ruled that a 1916 national law banning child labor was unconstitutional because it attempted to regulate a local problem.[8] In effect, the Court placed severe limits on the ability of Congress to legislate under the commerce clause of the Constitution.

The New Deal and Cooperative Federalism

The doctrine of dual federalism receded into the background in the 1930s as the nation attempted to deal with the Great Depression. Franklin D. Roosevelt was inaugurated as president on March 4, 1933. In the previous year, nearly 1,500 banks had failed (and 4,000 more would fail in 1933). Thirty-two thousand businesses had closed down, and almost one-fourth of the labor force was unemployed. The public expected the national government to do something about the disastrous state of the economy.

The "New Deal." President Herbert Hoover (1929–1933), however, clung to the doctrine of dual federalism and insisted that unemployment and poverty were local issues. The states, not the national government, had the sole responsibility for combating the effects of unemployment and providing relief to the poor. Roosevelt did not feel bound by this doctrine, and his new Democratic administration energetically intervened in the economy. Roosevelt's "New Deal" included large-scale emergency antipoverty programs. In addition, the New Deal introduced major new laws regulating economic activity, such as the National Industrial Recovery Act of 1933, which established the National Recovery Administration (NRA).

The End of Dual Federalism. Roosevelt's expansion of national authority was challenged by the Supreme Court, which continued to adhere to the doctrine of dual federalism. In 1935, the Court ruled that the NRA program was unconstitutional.[9] The NRA had turned out to be largely unworkable and was unpopular. The Court, however, rejected the program on the ground that it regulated intrastate, not interstate, commerce. This position appeared to rule out any alternative recovery plans that might be better designed.

Learning Outcome 4:
Define the terms *dual federalism, cooperative federalism, categorical grants, block grants,* and *fiscal federalism.*

did you know?
While Southerners often defended slavery by appealing to states' rights, *Dred Scott* was an *anti-states' rights* decision—it denied Northern states the right to grant citizenship to African Americans.

Child labor was still common in the early 1900s. *Why didn't the federal government simply ban it then?*

7. *Dred Scott v. Sandford,* 60 U.S. 393 (1856).
8. *Hammer v. Dagenhart,* 247 U.S. 251 (1918). This decision was overruled in *United States v. Darby,* 312 U.S. 100 (1940).
9. *Schechter Poultry Corp. v. United States,* 295 U.S. 495 (1935).

President Franklin Delano Roosevelt (1933–1945). Roosevelt's national approach to addressing the effects of the Great Depression was overwhelmingly popular, although many of his specific initiatives were controversial. *How did the Great Depression change the political beliefs of many ordinary Americans?*

In 1937, Roosevelt proposed legislation that would allow him to add up to six new justices to the Supreme Court. Presumably, the new justices would be more friendly to the exercise of national power than the existing members were. Congressional Democrats refused to support the measure, and it failed. Still, changes to the membership of the Court from 1937 on proved as effective as the failed "court-packing scheme." After 1937 the Court ceased its attempts to limit the national government's powers under the commerce clause.

Cooperative Federalism. Some political scientists have described the era since 1937 as characterized by **cooperative federalism,** in which the states and the national government cooperate in solving complex common problems. Roosevelt's New Deal programs, for example, often involved joint action between the national government and the states. The pattern of federal–state relationships during these years gave rise to a new metaphor for federalism—that of a marble cake. Unlike a layer cake, in a marble cake the two types of cake are intermingled, and any bite contains cake of both flavors.

As an example of how national and state governments work together under the cooperative federalism model, consider Temporary Assistance for Needy Families (TANF). Created in 1997 to replace an earlier welfare program, TANF provides limited cash assistance to families with children who are living in severe poverty. Under the TANF program, the national government provides most of the funding, but state governments establish benefit levels and eligibility requirements for recipients. Local welfare offices are staffed by state, not national, employees. In return for national funding, the states must conform to a series of regulations on how the program is carried out. The states, however, have more discretion on how to distribute funds than under earlier welfare programs.

Methods of Implementing Cooperative Federalism

Even before the Constitution was adopted, the national government gave grants to the states in the form of land to finance education. The national government also provided land grants for canals, railroads, and roads. In the twentieth century, federal grants increased significantly, especially during Roosevelt's administration throughout the Great Depression and again in the 1960s, when the dollar amount of grants quadrupled. These funds were used for improvements in education, pollution control, recreation, and highways. With this increase in grants, however, came a bewildering number of restrictions and regulations.

Categorical Grants. In the 1980s, **categorical grants** were spread out across four hundred separate programs, but the five largest accounted for more than 50 percent of the revenues spent. These five programs were Medicaid (health care for the poor),

Cooperative Federalism
A model of federalism in which the states and the national government cooperate in solving problems.

Categorical Grant
A federal grant to a state or local government for a specific program or project.

highway construction, unemployment benefits, housing assistance, and welfare programs to assist mothers with dependent children and people with disabilities. For fiscal year 2014, the national government gave about $640 billion to the states. The shift toward a greater role for the central government in the United States can be seen in Figure 3–2 that follows, which shows the increase in central government spending as a percentage of total government spending.

Before the 1960s, most categorical grants by the national government were *formula grants*. These grants take their name from the method used to allocate funds. They fund state programs using a formula based on such variables as the state's needs, population, or willingness to come up with matching funds. Beginning in the 1960s, the national government began increasingly to offer *program grants*. This funding requires states to apply for grants for specific programs. The applications are evaluated by the national government, and the applications may compete with one another. Program grants give the national government a much greater degree of control over state activities than do formula grants.

Over the decades, federal grants to the states have increased significantly, as shown in Figure 3–3 that follows. One reason for this increase is that Congress has decided to offload some programs to the states and provide a major part of the funding for them. Also, Congress continues to use grants to persuade states and cities to operate programs devised by the federal government. Finally, states often are happy to apply for grants because they are relatively "free," requiring only that the state match a small portion of each grant. States can still face criticism for accepting the grants, because their matching funds may be diverted from other state projects.

Figure 3–2 ▸ **The Shift toward Central Government Spending**

In the years before the Great Depression, local governments accounted for close to three-fifths of all government spending, and the federal government accounted for only about 30 percent. After Franklin D. Roosevelt's New Deal, national spending began to rival state and local spending combined. The national share is still about 46 percent today, not counting transfers to state and local governments. The size of the pies reflects total spending. *Note that the United States entered World War II in 1941. What effect might the national security crisis leading up to the war have had on federal spending?*

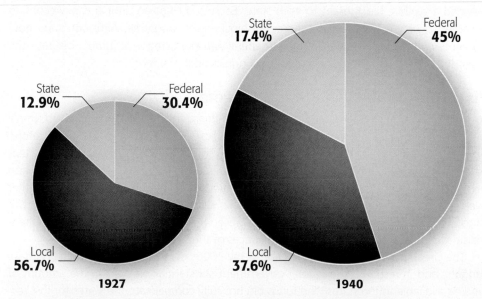

State 12.9%   Federal 30.4%
Local 56.7%
1927

State 17.4%   Federal 45%
Local 37.6%
1940

Sources: *Historical Statistics of the United States*, Bureau of the Census, and authors' calculations.

Figure 3–3 ▶ **The Rise in Federal Transfers to State and Local Governments**

The chart shows the percentage of the nation's state and local revenues supplied by the federal government. The national government has gained leverage over state and local governments by supplying an increasing share of their revenues. The drop in federal transfers from 1980 to 1990 took place during the presidency of Ronald Reagan, as we explain in "The 'New Federalism'" section later in this chapter. *What might the national government try to do with the leverage it holds over the states?*

Sources: *Historical Statistics of the United States; Statistical Abstract of the United States, 2008;* and www.usgovernmentspending.com.

Block Grants. **Block grants** lessen the restrictions on federal grants given to state and local governments by grouping a number of categorical grants under one broad heading. Governors and mayors generally prefer block grants because such grants give the states more flexibility in how the funds are spent.

One major set of block grants provides aid to state welfare programs. The Personal Responsibility and Work Opportunity Reconciliation Act of 1996 ended the Aid to Families with Dependent Children (AFDC) program. The TANF program that replaced AFDC provided a welfare block grant to each state. Each grant has an annual cap. According to some, this is one of the most successful block grant programs. Although state governments prefer block grants, Congress generally favors categorical grants because the expenditures can be targeted according to congressional priorities.

Fiscal Federalism and State Budgets

In discussions of government policy, you may have heard the word *fiscal*. This word simply means "having to do with government revenues and expenditures." **Fiscal** policy, therefore, is policy concerning taxing or borrowing—and then spending the revenues. When the federal government makes grants to state and local governments, funds raised through taxation or borrowing by one level of government (the national government) are spent by another level (state and local governments). We can speak of this process as **fiscal federalism.** With up to 20 percent of state and local revenues supplied by the federal government, fiscal federalism clearly has a major impact on the finances of the states.

The Great Recession in the first decade of the 2000s had a devastating impact on state budgets, and in response the federal government substantially increased the amount of funding available to the states. The funds did not fully compensate the states for lost revenue, however, and from 2011 on they were no longer available at all. State governments

Block Grant

A federal grant that provides funds to a state or local government for a general functional area, such as criminal justice or mental-health programs.

Fiscal

Having to do with government revenues and expenditures.

Fiscal Federalism

A process by which funds raised through taxation or borrowing by one level of government (usually the national government) are spent by another level (typically state or local governments).

cut spending and employment substantially—so much so that total government spending as a share of the economy actually fell from 2010 through 2015.

In 2011, new conservative governors in many states argued that excessively generous pension benefits for state workers were a major part of state budget problems. Many of them sponsored new laws to reduce pension benefits. Several governors also campaigned against state employee labor unions, a step that led to controversy in states such as Ohio and Wisconsin.

Feeling the Pressure—The Strings Attached to Federal Grants. No dollars sent to the states are completely free of "strings." All funds come with requirements that must be met by the states. Often, through the use of grants, the national government has been able to exercise substantial control over matters that traditionally have been under the purview of state governments. When the federal government gives federal funds for highway improvements, for example, it may condition the funds on the state's cooperation with a federal policy. This is exactly what the federal government did in the 1980s and 1990s to force the states to raise their minimum alcoholic beverage drinking age to twenty-one.

In 2012, for the first time, the United States Supreme Court placed limits on the ability of the national government to use federal grants to coerce state governments. In its ruling on the Affordable Care Act (Obamacare), the Court found that the penalties the act imposes on the states to compel them to expand the Medicaid program were excessive and unconstitutional. Under the health-care reform legislation, a state that refused to expand Medicaid would lose *all* Medicaid funding. Presumably, Congress could continue to coerce the states if it used less drastic penalties.[10]

> **Federal Mandate**
> A requirement in federal legislation that forces states and municipalities to comply with certain rules.

Why Should You Care about...

The Federal System?

In this chapter, we mention a variety of issues arising from our federal system that may concern you directly. For example, though the national government provides aid to educational programs, education is still primarily a state and local responsibility. The total amount of money spent on education is determined by state and local governments. Therefore, you can address the question of how much should be spent on education at the state or local level.

Federal Mandates. For years, the federal government has passed legislation requiring that states improve environmental conditions or the civil rights of various groups. Since the 1970s, the national government has enacted hundreds of **federal mandates** requiring the states to take some action in areas ranging from voter registration, to ocean-dumping restrictions, to the education of people with disabilities. The Unfunded Mandates Reform Act of 1995 requires the Congressional Budget Office to identify mandates that cost state and local governments more than $50 million to implement. Nonetheless, the federal government routinely continues to pass mandates for state and local governments that cost more than that to put into place. For example, the National Conference of State Legislatures has identified federal mandates to the states in transportation, health care, education, environment, homeland security, election laws, and other areas with a total cost of $29 billion per year. Water-quality mandates appear to be particularly expensive.

One way in which the national government has moderated the burden of federal mandates is by granting *waivers,* which allow individual states to try out innovative approaches to carrying out the mandates. For example, governors of several conservative states agreed to expand Medicaid as part of the Obamacare program if they received waivers. The waivers allowed them to channel the new funds through private insurance companies rather than through the state government.

10. *National Federation of Independent Business v. Sebelius,* 132 S.Ct. 2566 (2012).

Devolution
The transfer of powers from a national or central government to a state or local government.

Competitive Federalism. When state governments have authority in a particular field, there may be great variations from state to state in how they exercise that authority. Such differentials can lead to a competition among the states, which has been called *competitive federalism*. For example, it is widely believed that major corporations are more likely to establish new operations in states with a "favorable business climate." Such a climate could result from state spending on roads and other infrastructure, a well-educated workforce, and other amenities. More often, a favorable business climate means low taxes on businesses and on the executives who run those businesses.

Always and everywhere, citizens tend to favor ample government services, even as they resist the taxes necessary to fund those services. Fiscal problems can be more severe than usual in bad economic times. State governments can experience fiscal difficulties even in times of economic growth, however, and competitive federalism adds to the pressures.

■ **Learning Outcome 5:** Detail recent political developments and Supreme Court rulings that affect the distribution of power between the national government and the states.

The Politics of Federalism

As we have observed, the allocation of powers between the national and state governments continues to be a major issue. We look here at some further aspects of the ongoing conflict between national authority and states' rights in our federal system.

What Has National Authority Accomplished?

Why is it that conservatives have so often favored the states and liberals have favored the national government? One answer is that throughout American history, the expansion of national authority typically has been an engine of social change. Far more than the states, the national government has been willing to alter the status quo. The expansion of national authority during the Civil War freed the slaves—a major social revolution. During the New Deal, the expansion of national authority meant unprecedented levels of government intervention in the economy. In both the Civil War and the New Deal eras, support for states' rights was a method of opposing these changes and supporting the status quo.

Another example of the use of national power to change society occurred during the presidency of Lyndon B. Johnson (1963–1969). Johnson oversaw the greatest expansion of national authority since the New Deal. Under Johnson, a series of civil rights acts forced the states to grant African Americans equal treatment under the law. Crucially, these acts included the abolition of all measures designed to prevent African Americans from voting. Johnson's Great Society and War on Poverty programs resulted in major increases in spending by the national government. As before, states' rights were invoked to support the status quo—states' rights meant no action on civil rights and no increase in antipoverty spending.

Why Should You Care about...

The Federal System?

Do you enjoy gambling—or do you believe that the effects of gambling make it a social disaster? State law usually determines the availability of gambling. The Constitution, however, assigns American Indian affairs exclusively to the national government. As a result of this provision, federal law requires state governments to negotiate with native tribes that want to set up gambling operations.

The "New Federalism"

In the years after 1968, the **devolution** of power from the national government to the states became a major ideological theme for the Republican Party. Republican president Richard Nixon (1969–1974) advocated what he called a "New Federalism" that would devolve authority from the national government to the states. In part, the New Federalism involved the conversion of categorical grants into block grants, thereby giving state governments greater flexibility in spending. A second part of Nixon's New Federalism was *revenue sharing*. Under the revenue-sharing plan, the national government provided direct, unconditional financial support to state and local governments.

Nixon was able to obtain only a limited number of block grants from Congress. The block grants he did obtain, plus revenue sharing, substantially increased financial support to state governments. Republican president Ronald Reagan (1981–1989) was also a strong advocate of federalism, but some of his policies withdrew certain financial support from the states. Reagan was more successful than Nixon in obtaining block grants, but Reagan's block grants, unlike Nixon's, were less generous to the states than the categorical grants they replaced. Under Reagan, revenue sharing was eliminated. You can see the results of these actions in Figure 3–3 earlier.

The Politics of Federalism Today

In recent years, it has not been clear whether competing theories of federalism divide the Republicans from the

A young salesperson weighs out marijuana for a customer in a shop in Denver. Colorado legalized the commercial production and sale of marijuana beginning in 2014. Washington State passed similar legislation. *What problems may result from the fact that marijuana sales continue to be illegal under national law?*

Democrats at all, at least in practice. Consider that the passage of welfare reform legislation in 1996, which involved transferring significant control over welfare programs to the states, took place under Democratic president Bill Clinton (1993–2001). In contrast, under Republican president George W. Bush, Congress enacted the No Child Left Behind Act of 2001, which was signed into law in 2002. This act increased federal control over education and educational funding, which had traditionally been under the purview of state governments.

Beginning in 2009, however, conservative activists, especially Tea Party members, began to rediscover states' rights. One reason may be that in that year the Democrats added the presidency to their control of the U.S. House and Senate. Republicans were shut out at the national level. The ambitious program of the Obama administration also alarmed conservatives. Obama's initiatives generally involved greater federal control of the private sector, not of state and local governments. Still, many conservatives hoped that the states could be a counterweight to the newly active national government.

Federalism and the Supreme Court

The United States Supreme Court, which normally has the final say on constitutional issues, plays a major role in determining where the line is drawn between federal and state powers. Consider the decisions rendered by Chief Justice John Marshall in the cases discussed earlier in this chapter. Since the 1930s, Marshall's broad interpretation of the commerce clause has made it possible for the national government to justify its regulation of almost any activity, even when the activity appears to be completely local in character. In the 1990s and 2000s, however, the Court has evidenced a willingness to impose some limits on the national government's authority under the commerce clause and other constitutional provisions. As a result, it is difficult to predict how today's Court might rule on a particular case involving federalism.

A Trend toward States' Rights. Since the mid-1990s, the Supreme Court has tended to give greater weight to states' rights than it did during previous decades. In a widely publicized 1995 case, *United States v. Lopez,*[11] the Supreme Court held that Congress had exceeded its constitutional authority under the commerce clause when it passed the Gun-Free School Zones Act in 1990. The Court stated that the act, which banned the possession of guns within one thousand feet of any school, was unconstitutional because it attempted to regulate an area that had "nothing to do with commerce, or any sort of economic enterprise." This marked the first time in sixty years that the Supreme Court had placed a limit on the national government's authority under the commerce clause.

The Court Sends Mixed Messages. Although the Court has tended to favor states' rights in some decisions, in other decisions it has backed the federal government's position. In 2005, the Court held that the federal government's power to declare various substances to be illegal drugs superseded California's law legalizing the use of marijuana for medical treatment.[12] Yet less than a year later, the Court favored states' rights when it upheld Oregon's controversial "death with dignity" law, which allows patients with terminal illnesses to choose to end their lives early and thus alleviate suffering.[13]

Recent Supreme Court Rulings

As noted, since President Obama took office, conservatives have taken a greater interest in states' rights. A growing number of such cases have been brought before the Supreme Court. In its rulings, the Court has shown a degree of sympathy for states' rights. Yet it has rejected arguments that would transform the relationship between the states and the federal government.

Immigration. In one important opinion, the Court found that Arizona had gone too far in its attempt to subject unauthorized immigration to state authority. Under the ruling, Arizona cannot make it a crime when illegal immigrants fail to carry identification papers or attempt to find work. Arizona police cannot arrest individuals solely on suspicion of illegal status.[14]

Health-Care Reform. It was the Court's opinion on the Affordable Care Act (Obamacare) that was expected to be the most important states' rights ruling in decades. In the end, the Court's 2012 verdict was somewhat anticlimactic. It did not find that the individual mandate—a penalty imposed on those who do not buy health-care insurance—violated the police powers of the states. (The Court found that while the mandate could not be justified under

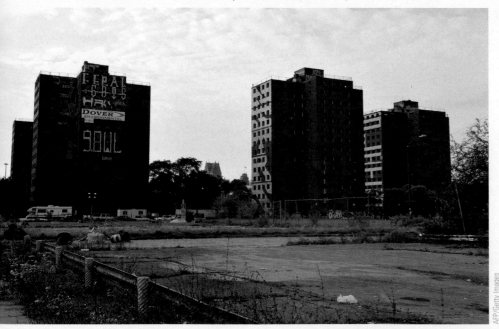

Detroit's Frederick Douglass Homes, a public housing project, is being demolished with the help of a federal grant. In 2013, the City of Detroit filed for bankruptcy—the largest municipal bankruptcy in U.S. history. *Why was Detroit's bankruptcy overseen by a federal court? (Hint—see Article I, Section 8 of the U.S. Constitution.)*

AFP/Getty Images

---

11. 514 U.S. 549 (1995).
12. *Gonzales v. Raich,* 545 U.S. 1 (2005).
13. *Gonzales v. Oregon,* 546 U.S. 243 (2006).
14. *Arizona v. United States,* 132 S.Ct. 2492 (2012).

the commerce clause, it was legitimate under the national government's power to tax.) Chief Justice John Roberts's ruling on Medicaid expansion did hearten states' rights advocates, however. By making Medicaid expansion optional for the states, the Court for the first time put limits on the ability of the federal government to coerce states by withholding grants.[15]

Same-Sex Marriage. In 2013, the Court's two rulings on same-sex marriage also tended to enhance the authority of the states. True, by refusing to rule on a California case, the Court in effect prevented the state's voters from banning same-sex marriage. Still, this step allowed all the other states to continue making their own decisions about the issue.[16] Still, because of lower-court rulings against state bans on same-sex marriages, the Court may not be able to put off much longer a ruling on whether same-sex marriage must be recognized in every state.

Also, the Court's ruling that the federal government must recognize state-approved same-sex marriages was a victory for states' rights, as well as for same-sex couples in the affected states.[17]

The Voting Rights Act. Finally, the Court's ruling on the Voting Rights Act was a striking triumph for states' rights. The 1965 act imposed certain requirements on states and localities—mostly in the South—with a history of violating the voting rights of minority group members. Such areas had to obtain preclearance from the federal government to make changes in voting procedures or districts. In June 2013, the Court effectively destroyed the preclearance system, giving all affected governments the right to set their own voting rules without restriction.[18]

15. *National Federation of Independent Business v. Sebelius,* 132 S.Ct. 2566 (2012).
16. *Hollingsworth v. Perry,* 133 S.Ct. 2652 (2013).
17. *United States v. Windsor,* 133 S.Ct. 2675 (2013).
18. *Shelby County v. Holder,* 570 U.S. ___ (2013).

CONNECT
WITH YOUR CLASSMATES
MindTap for American Government

Access the Federalism Forum:
Discussion Board—Patient
Protection and Affordable Care Act

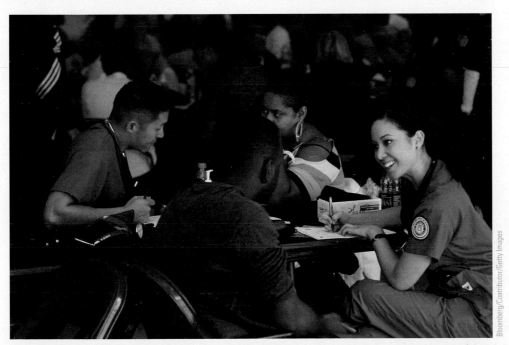

Patients consult with nurses at a CareHarbor Clinic in the Los Angeles Sports Arena. Care Harbor is supported by charitable contributions and provides medical services to very low income persons. *What effect might the Affordable Care Act have on these services?*

How You Can Make a Difference

In our modern era, the number of ways in which you can communicate your opinion is vast. You can post a response on any of thousands of blogs. You could develop your own mini-video and post it on YouTube. Politicians use Facebook and Twitter to organize their supporters and often have thousands of online "friends." This can provide you with the opportunity to present your views to someone who might be able to act on them.

If you want to effect policy change at the state or local level, however, the local newspaper, in both its paper and its online formats, continues to be essential. Blogs, YouTube, and other online venues tend to be nationally and even internationally oriented. Most newspapers, however, are resolutely local and are the natural hub for discussions of local issues. Most papers allow responses and comments on their Web sites, and you can make a point by contributing in that fashion. Nothing, however, will win you a wider audience than an old-fashioned letter to the editor. Use the following rules to compose an effective communication:

- Use a computer, and double-space the lines. Use a spelling checker and grammar checker.

- Include a lead topic sentence that is short, to the point, and powerful.

- Keep your thoughts on target—choose only one topic to discuss. Make sure it is newsworthy and timely.

- Make sure your communication is concise; never let it exceed a page and a half in length (double-spaced).

- If you know that facts were misstated or left out in current news stories about your topic, supply the facts. The public wants to know.

- Don't be afraid to express moral judgments. You can go a long way by appealing to the reader's sense of justice.

- Personalize the communication by bringing in your own experiences, if possible.

- If you are writing a letter, sign it and give your address (including your e-mail address) and your telephone number. Comments posted to blogs and other communications may have their own rules for identifying yourself. Follow them.

- If writing a letter, send or e-mail it to the editorial office of the newspaper of your choice. Almost all publications now have e-mail addresses. Their Web sites usually give information on where you can send mail.

Key Terms

block grant 92

categorical grant 90

commerce clause 86

concurrent powers 84

confederal system 77

cooperative federalism 90

devolution 94

dual federalism 88

elastic clause, or necessary and proper clause 82

enumerated powers 82

federal mandate 93

fiscal 92

fiscal federalism 92

interstate compact 85

police power 83

supremacy clause 84

unitary system 77

Chapter Summary

Learning Outcome 1 There are three basic models for ordering relations between central governments and local units: (a) a unitary system (in which ultimate power is held by the national government), (b) a confederal system (in which ultimate power is retained by the states), and (c) a federal system (in which governmental powers are divided between the national government and the states).

Learning Outcome 2 The Constitution expressly grants certain powers to the national government in Article I, Section 8. In addition to these enumerated powers, the national government has implied and inherent powers. Implied powers are those that are reasonably necessary to carry out the powers expressly given to the national government. Inherent powers are those held by the national government by virtue of its being a sovereign state with the right to preserve itself.

The Tenth Amendment to the Constitution states that powers not delegated to the United States by the Constitution, nor prohibited by it to the states, are reserved to the states, or to the people. In certain areas, the Constitution provides for concurrent powers (such as the power to tax), which are powers that are held jointly by the national and state governments. The Constitution also denies certain powers to both the national government and the states.

The supremacy clause of the Constitution states that the Constitution, congressional laws, and national treaties are the supreme law of the land. States cannot use their reserved or concurrent powers to override national policies.

Learning Outcome 3 Chief Justice John Marshall's expansive interpretation of the necessary and proper clause of the Constitution in *McCulloch v. Maryland* (1819), along with his affirmation of the supremacy clause, enhanced the power of the national government. Marshall's broad interpretation of the commerce clause in *Gibbons v. Ogden* (1824) further extended the powers of the national government.

The controversy over slavery that led to the Civil War took the form of a fight over national government supremacy versus the rights of the separate states.

Learning Outcome 4 Since the Civil War, federalism has evolved through at least two general phases: dual federalism and cooperative federalism. In dual federalism, each of the states and the federal government remain supreme within their own spheres. The era since the Great Depression has sometimes been labeled one of cooperative federalism, in which states and the national government cooperate in solving complex common problems.

Categorical grants from the federal government to state governments help finance many projects. By attaching special conditions to federal grants, the national government can effect policy changes in areas typically governed by the states. Block grants usually have fewer strings attached, thus giving state and local governments more flexibility in using the funds. Federal mandates—laws requiring states to implement certain policies—have generated controversy.

Learning Outcome 5 Traditionally, conservatives have favored states' rights, and liberals have favored national authority. In part, this is because the national government has historically been an engine of change. In recent years, rulings by the United States Supreme Court have tended to emphasize the rights of the states as compared to the powers of the federal government.

Master the concept of Federalism with MindTap™ for American Government

 REVIEW MindTap™ for American Government
Access Key Term Flashcards for Chapter 3.

TEST YOURSELF MindTap™ for American Government
Take the Wrap It Up Quiz for Chapter 3.

 STAY CURRENT MindTap™ for American Government
Access the KnowNow blog and customized RSS for updates on current events.

STAY FOCUSED MindTap™ for American Government
Complete the Focus Activities for Federalism.

Additional Resources

The federal courts have a major impact on how federalism has been interpreted and implemented in the United States. In this chapter and continuing through the rest of the text, you will find many references to court cases, typically ones decided by the United States Supreme Court. A good way to find out more about the American political system is to learn about key cases.

You'll notice in the footnotes that there is a standard format for citing cases. Consider *New State Ice Co. v. Liebmann*, cited on page 80. In addition to the name of the case, the citation includes the mysterious term "285 U.S. 262 (1932)." This case was decided in 1932, and "U.S." is an abbreviation for *United States Reports*, the official edition of the decisions of the Supreme Court. The volume number is "285," and "262" is the page number on which the decision begins.

You may not need the full citation when you want to investigate cases, however. Simply type the name of the case into a search engine such as Google. You'll see articles describing the case and its importance. Wikipedia, for example, has articles on most important cases. Other sites provide the text of the ruling.

Sometimes, the name of the case is not enough to locate it. What if the name is *United States v. Johnson*? Twelve cases by that name are important enough to merit articles in Wikipedia. If you are searching for such a case, you'll want to enter the full citation into the search engine— for example, "*United States v. Johnson* 457 U.S. 537 (1982)."

Online Resources

- The *New York Times* sponsors a series on the United States Civil War that uses contemporary accounts, diaries, and images. To follow it on Twitter, go to twitter.com/NYTcivilwar.
- The Reality Based Community is a good Web site for thoughtful discussions of drug policies, including the pros and cons of marijuana legalization. See it at www.samefacts.com.

Books

Doonan, Michael. *American Federalism in Practice: The Formulation and Implementation of Contemporary Health Policy.* Washington: Brookings Institution Press, 2013. Doonan, a professor at Brandeis U., explains how federal-state relations have shaped American health-care policies.

Martin, Alyson, and Nushin Rashidian. *A New Leaf: The End of Cannabis Prohibition.* New York: The New Press, 2014. The authors, award-winning journalists, report from nearly every state, interviewing patients, growers, doctors, entrepreneurs, politicians, activists, and regulators.

Pierceson, Jason. *Same-Sex Marriage in the United States: The Road to the Supreme Court.* Lanham, Maryland: Rowman & Littlefield Publishers, 2013. Pierceson, a political science professor at U. Illinois, describes the dramatic cultural and legal shifts in U.S. opinion on same-sex marriage.

Video

The Civil War—The PBS documentary series that made director Ken Burns famous. *The Civil War*, first shown in 1990, marked a revolution in documentary technique. Photographs, letters, eyewitness memoirs, and music are used to bring the war to life. The DVD version was released in 2002.

Waiting to Inhale: Marijuana, Medicine and the Law—A 2010 documentary on the controversy over legalizing marijuana in the United States for medical purposes. The film portrays patients and activists on both sides of this battle.

Quiz

Multiple Choice and Fill-Ins

Learning Outcome 1 Explain some of the benefits of the federal system for the United States.

1. One reason the founders chose a federal system is that:
  a. there were no supporters of states' rights.
  b. the United States was already large geographically, and it would have been difficult to govern just from the national capital.
  c. the thirteen states were smaller geographically than France, so a federal system was appropriate.

2. The system of government in the United States that existed before the adoption of the Constitution was called a
_____ _____.

Learning Outcome 2 Describe how the various provisions of the U.S. Constitution provide a framework for federalism.

3. When both the national government and the state governments share certain powers, we call them:
  a. prevailing powers.
  b. concurrent powers.
  c. constitutional powers.

4. Each state must give full _____ ___ _____ to other states' public acts, records, and judicial proceedings.

Learning Outcome 3 Discuss how, in the early years of the republic, the United States Supreme Court confirmed the authority of the national government, and how that authority was ratified by the Civil War.

5. In the Supreme Court case of *McCulloch v. Maryland* (1819), the Court clearly established:
  a. that the Constitution is the supreme law of the land.
  b. that state governments can tax the national government.
  c. that the national government can tax the state governments.

6. The Supreme Court case of *Gibbons v. Ogden* (1824) involved regulation of _____ commerce.

Learning Outcome 4 Define the terms *dual federalism, cooperative federalism, categorical grants, block grants*, and *fiscal federalism*.

7. When the federal (national) government sends dollars to state governments, those funds:
  a. are given without any restrictions.
  b. are to be returned to the federal government at a later date.
  c. come with many "strings" attached.

8. When monies are raised through taxation or borrowing by the national government but then are spent by the state governments, this is an example of _____ _____.

Learning Outcome 5 Detail recent political developments and Supreme Court rulings that affect the distribution of power between the national government and the states.

9. When ruling on the Affordable Care Act (Obamacare) in 2012, the Supreme Court:
  a. found the act to be entirely constitutional.
  b. found the act to be entirely unconstitutional.
  c. found the act to be mostly constitutional.

10. The transfer of powers from a central or national government to a state or local one is called _____.

Essay Questions

1. Traditionally, conservatives have favored states' rights and liberals have favored national authority. Can you think of modern-day issues in which these long-standing preferences might be reversed, with conservatives favoring national authority and liberals favoring states' rights? Explain.

2. Some members of the Tea Party movement want to repeal the Seventeenth Amendment, which provides for electing U.S. senators by popular vote. If the amendment were repealed, state legislatures would choose each state's senators. Advocates of repeal argue that it would strengthen the power of the states within the federal system. Are they right—and would such a change have good or bad consequences? Explain.

Civil Liberties

4

A coalition opposed to surveillance by the National Security Agency marches to the U.S. Capitol.

Bill Clark/CQ-Roll Call Group/Getty Images

The six Learning Outcomes below are designed to help improve your understanding of this chapter. After reading this chapter, you should be able to:

- **Learning Outcome 1:** Describe the Bill of Rights and how it came to be applied to state governments as well as the national government.

- **Learning Outcome 2:** Explain how the First Amendment's establishment clause and free exercise clause guarantee our freedom of religion.

- **Learning Outcome 3:** Specify the limited circumstances in which the national and state governments may override the principles of free speech and freedom of the press.

- **Learning Outcome 4:** Provide the constitutional basis of the right to privacy, and explain how the principle has been applied to the abortion and right-to-die controversies.

- **Learning Outcome 5:** Cite examples of how recent security concerns have affected our civil liberties.

- **Learning Outcome 6:** Identify the constitutional rights of those who are accused of a crime, explain the *Miranda* and exclusionary rules, and describe the current status of the death penalty.

(▶) **WATCH & LEARN** MindTap® for American Government

Watch a brief "What Do You Know?" video summarizing Civil Liberties.

What If...

Roe v. Wade Were Overturned?

BACKGROUND

The Bill of Rights and other provisions of the U.S. Constitution are the ultimate protections of our civil rights and liberties. But how do these rights work in practice? How do we determine what our rights are in any given situation? One way is through *judicial review,* the power of the United States Supreme Court or other courts to declare laws and other acts of government unconstitutional.

Supreme Court cases are often hotly contested, and the decision in the 1973 case *Roe v. Wade* is one of the most contentious ever handed down. In the *Roe v. Wade* case, the Court declared that a woman's constitutionally protected right to privacy includes the right to have an abortion. The Court concluded that the states cannot restrict a woman's right to an abortion during the first three months of pregnancy. Forty years later, however, the debate over the legality of abortion still rages in the United States.

WHAT IF *ROE V. WADE* WERE OVERTURNED?

If the Supreme Court overturned *Roe v. Wade,* the authority to regulate abortion would fall again to the states. Before the *Roe v. Wade* case, each state decided whether abortion would be legal within its borders. State legislatures made the laws that covered abortion.

Simply overturning *Roe v. Wade* would not make abortion in the United States illegal overnight. In many states, abortion rights are very popular, and the legislatures in those states would not consider measures to ban abortion or to further restrict access to abortion. Some states have laws that would protect abortion rights even if *Roe v. Wade* were overturned. Access to abortions would likely continue in the West Coast states and in much of the Northeast. In most of the South and parts of the Midwest, however, abortion could be seriously restricted or even banned.

Already, twenty-seven states require a waiting period between when a woman receives counseling and when the procedure is performed. Eleven states require counseling that includes information generally considered to be incorrect by the medical profession, such as the proposition that abortions can cause breast cancer. Some states have "trigger laws" that would immediately outlaw abortion if *Roe v. Wade* were overturned.

After the 2010 elections, in which conservative, right-to-life candidates won victories in many state legislative elections, the volume of anti-abortion legislation exploded. In the following three years, thirty states passed more than 200 laws. A dozen states have banned abortions after twenty weeks of pregnancy. In

Texas, restrictive laws in 2013 closed about one-third of the state's abortion clinics. Some United States Supreme Court justices have said that they expect eventually to hear the Texas case.

Women living in conservative states such as the Dakotas, Kentucky, and Mississippi face serious difficulties in obtaining an abortion. Still, if abortion were banned, these women could cross state lines to obtain an abortion. It is also probable that if states could outlaw abortion, most existing state laws restricting the procedure would become irrelevant. The states that have passed such laws are generally the same states that would make abortion illegal.

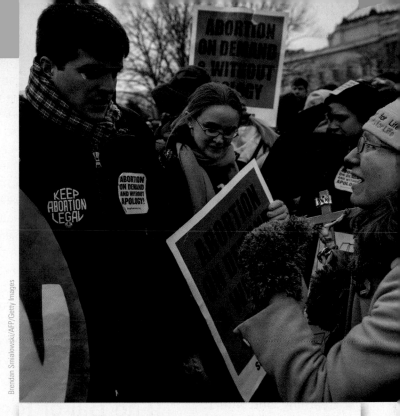

Brendan Smialowski/AFP/Getty Images

Pro-life and pro-choice activists argue in front of the Supreme Court building. *Is one of these sides winning? If so, why?*

For Critical Analysis

1. Why do you think that abortion has remained a contentious topic for the forty-plus years since the *Roe v. Wade* decision? Should that decision be revisited? Why or why not?

2. What political consequences could result from overturning *Roe v. Wade*? How might people's opinions change about abortion? About the Supreme Court?

"The land of the free." When asked what makes the United States distinctive, Americans will commonly say that it is a free country. Americans have long believed that limits on the power of government are an essential part of what makes this country free. Recall from Chapter 1 that restraints on the actions of government against individuals are generally referred to as *civil liberties.* The first ten amendments to the U.S. Constitution—the Bill of Rights—place such restraints on the national government. Of these amendments, none is more famous than the First Amendment, which guarantees freedom of religion, speech, and the press, as well as other rights.

Most other democratic nations have laws to protect these and other civil liberties, but none of the laws is quite like the First Amendment. Take the issue of "hate speech." What if someone makes statements that stir up hatred toward a particular race or other group of people? In Germany, where memories of Nazi anti-Semitism remain alive, such speech is unquestionably illegal. In the United States, the issue is not so clear. The courts have often extended constitutional protection to this kind of speech.

In this chapter, we describe the civil liberties provided by the Bill of Rights and some of the controversies that surround them. We initially look at the First Amendment. We also discuss the right to privacy, which is at the heart of the abortion issue introduced in the *What If . . .* feature that opened this chapter. We also examine the rights of defendants in criminal cases.

■ **Learning Outcome 1:** Describe the Bill of Rights and how it came to be applied to state governments as well as the national government.

The Bill of Rights

As you read through this chapter, bear in mind that the Bill of Rights, like the rest of the Constitution, is relatively brief. The framers set forth broad guidelines, leaving it up to the courts to interpret these constitutional mandates and apply them to specific situations. Thus, judicial interpretations shape the true nature of the civil liberties and rights that we possess. Because judicial interpretations change over time, so do our liberties and rights. As you will read in the following pages, there have been many conflicts over the meaning of such simple phrases as *freedom of religion* and *freedom of the press.*

To understand what freedoms we actually have, we need to examine how the courts—and particularly the United States Supreme Court—have resolved some of those conflicts. One important conflict was over the issue of whether the Bill of Rights in the federal Constitution limited the powers of state governments as well as those of the national government.

Extending the Bill of Rights to State Governments

Many citizens do not realize that, as originally intended, the Bill of Rights limited only the powers of the national government. At the time the Bill of Rights was ratified, there was little concern over the potential of state governments to curb civil liberties. For one thing, state governments were closer to home and easier to control. For another, most state constitutions already had bills of rights. Rather, the fear was of the potential tyranny of the national government. The Bill of Rights begins with the words, "Congress shall make no law . . . ." It says nothing about states making laws that might abridge citizens' civil liberties. In 1833, the United States Supreme Court held that the Bill of Rights did not apply to state laws.[1]

We mentioned that most states had bills of rights. These bills of rights were similar to the national one, but there were some differences. Furthermore, each state's judicial system interpreted the rights differently. Citizens in different states, therefore, effectively had different sets of civil liberties. It was not until after the Fourteenth Amendment was

---

1. *Barron v. Baltimore,* 32 U.S. 243 (1833).

ratified in 1868 that civil liberties guaranteed by the national Constitution began to be applied to the states. Section 1 of that amendment provides, in part, as follows:

> No State shall . . . deprive any person of life, liberty, or property, without due process of law . . .

Incorporation of the Fourteenth Amendment

There was no question that the Fourteenth Amendment applied to state governments. For decades, however, the courts were reluctant to define the liberties spelled out in the national Bill of Rights as constituting "due process of law," which was protected under the Fourteenth Amendment. Not until 1925, in *Gitlow v. New York*,[2] did the United States Supreme Court hold that the Fourteenth Amendment protected the freedom of speech guaranteed by the First Amendment to the Constitution from state infringement.

Only gradually did the Supreme Court accept the **incorporation theory**—the view that most of the protections of the Bill of Rights are incorporated into the Fourteenth Amendment's protection against state government actions. Table 4–1 that follows shows the rights that the Court has incorporated into the Fourteenth Amendment and the case in which it first applied each protection. As you can see in the table, in the fifteen

Incorporation Theory
The view that most of the protections of the Bill of Rights apply to state governments through the Fourteenth Amendment's due process clause.

2. 268 U.S. 652 (1925).

Table 4–1 ▶ **Incorporating the Bill of Rights into the Fourteenth Amendment**

The Bill of Rights provides that "No Soldier shall, in time of peace be quartered in any house, without the consent of the Owner. . ." *Why has the Supreme Court never incorporated that right into the Fourteenth Amendment?*

Year	Issue	Amendment Involved	Court Case
1925	Freedom of speech	I	*Gitlow v. New York*, 268 U.S. 652.
1931	Freedom of the press	I	*Near v. Minnesota*, 283 U.S. 697.
1932	Right to a lawyer in capital punishment cases	VI	*Powell v. Alabama*, 287 U.S. 45.
1937	Freedom of assembly and right to petition	I	*De Jonge v. Oregon*, 299 U.S. 353.
1940	Freedom of religion	I	*Cantwell v. Connecticut*, 310 U.S. 296.
1947	Separation of church and state	I	*Everson v. Board of Education*, 330 U.S. 1.
1948	Right to a public trial	VI	*In re Oliver*, 333 U.S. 257.
1949	No unreasonable searches and seizures	IV	*Wolf v. Colorado*, 338 U.S. 25.
1961	Exclusionary rule	IV	*Mapp v. Ohio*, 367 U.S. 643.
1962	No cruel and unusual punishment	VIII	*Robinson v. California*, 370 U.S. 660.
1963	Right to a lawyer in all criminal felony cases	VI	*Gideon v. Wainwright*, 372 U.S. 335.
1964	No compulsory self-incrimination	V	*Malloy v. Hogan*, 378 U.S. 1.
1965	Right to privacy	I, III, IV, V, IX	*Griswold v. Connecticut*, 381 U.S. 479.
1966	Right to an impartial jury	VI	*Parker v. Gladden*, 385 U.S. 363.
1967	Right to a speedy trial	VI	*Klopfer v. North Carolina*, 386 U.S. 213.
1969	No double jeopardy	V	*Benton v. Maryland*, 395 U.S. 784.
2010	Right to bear arms	II	*McDonald v. Chicago*, 561 U.S. 3025.

years following the *Gitlow* decision, the Supreme Court incorporated into the Fourteenth Amendment the other basic freedoms (of the press, assembly, the right to petition, and religion) guaranteed by the First Amendment. It took time for the Supreme Court to require the states to accept other liberties. Only in 2010 did the Court rule that the states were obligated to recognize an individual's right to bear arms. Even with that ruling, the national and state governments retain the power to regulate the ownership of firearms. We examine a major gun-regulation topic in the *Which Side Are You On?* feature that follows.

Which Side Are You On?

Should We Ban Assault-Type Weapons?

The Second Amendment to the United States Constitution provides a right to keep and bear arms. In 2008, the United States Supreme Court found this to be a right enjoyed by individuals. The national government therefore lacks the power to ban handguns completely. In 2010, the rule was imposed on the states.[a]

In December 2012, a young man in Connecticut stole his mother's semiautomatic Bushmaster XM15 rifle, which had a magazine holding thirty rounds of bullets. He murdered her and then attacked Sandy Hook Elementary School, killing twenty-six students and staff. In July 2012, in Aurora, Colorado, a shooter used a hundred-round drum in a semiautomatic rifle to kill or wound most of his seventy victims before the weapon jammed. They were attending a midnight showing of the Batman film *The Dark Knight Rises*. Such violence has prompted calls to ban the assault-type weapons used in these crimes. Is such a ban desirable? Is it even constitutional?

Nobody Needs These Weapons for Hunting or Protection

Those in favor of banning the sale of assault-type weapons argue that such a step does not violate the Second Amendment. After all, who really needs these military-type weapons? Semiautomatic weapons based on military assault rifles are not optimized for hunting. They are second-rate deer rifles and completely useless for waterfowl. These firearms are not ideal for target shooting either—they are not used in international and Olympic competition.

The use of such weapons for self-defense is problematic. A handgun is more portable, and a shotgun is easier to aim. So, why do so many people want such weapons? Some argue that

buyers are fulfilling fantasies. The dream is that the guns will be used to protect homes and families after a collapse of civilization, or even to rebel against the government. Let's base gun laws on reality instead. These weapons have no place in America's homes and businesses.

Banning Assault-Type Weapons Will Have No Effect

Those who oppose a ban observe that the vast majority of firearm deaths result from weapons that would not be subject to the proposed ban on assault-style weapons. In 1994, Congress passed the Federal Assault Weapons Ban. Two leading researchers concluded that the ban had no detectable impact on murder rates, which have fallen since the ban expired in 2004.

An alternative to a ban on assault-style weapons would be to limit the size of the magazines that hold ammunition. Proponents of such legislation argue that no one needs a thirty- or hundred-round magazine for hunting, target shooting, or self-protection. Still, such a law would not have prevented the disaster at Virginia Tech in 2007. In that instance, the shooter fired 176 rounds from multiple ten- and fifteen-round magazines. If magazines were limited to ten rounds, shooters could just arm themselves with multiple magazines.

For Critical Analysis

Does the Second Amendment give all Americans the right to bear arms of any type at all times in any location? Why or why not?

a. *District of Columbia v. Heller*, 554 U.S. 570 (2008); and *McDonald v. Chicago*, 561 U.S. 3025 (2010).

Freedom of Religion

In the United States, freedom of religion consists of two main principles that are presented in the First Amendment. The **establishment clause** prohibits the establishment of a church that is officially supported by the national government, thus guaranteeing a division between church and state. The **free exercise clause** constrains the national government from prohibiting individuals from practicing the religion of their choice.

The Separation of Church and State—The Establishment Clause

The First Amendment to the Constitution states, in part, that "Congress shall make no law respecting an establishment of religion." In the words of Thomas Jefferson, the *establishment clause* was designed to create a "wall of separation between Church and State." As interpreted by the United States Supreme Court, the establishment clause in the First Amendment means at least the following:

> *Neither a state nor the federal government can set up a church. Neither can pass laws which aid one religion, aid all religions, or prefer one religion over another. Neither can force nor influence a person to go to or to remain away from church against his will or force him to profess a belief or disbelief in any religion. No person can be punished for entertaining or professing religious beliefs or disbeliefs, for church attendance or nonattendance. No tax in any amount, large or small, can be levied to support any religious activities or institutions, whatever they may be called, or whatever form they may adopt to teach or practice religion. Neither a state nor the federal government can, openly or secretly, participate in the affairs of any religious organizations or groups and vice versa.*[3]

The establishment clause covers all conflicts about such matters as the legality of giving state and local government aid to religious organizations and schools, allowing or requiring school prayers, teaching evolution versus creationist theories that reject evolution, placing religious displays in schools or public places, and discriminating against religious groups in publicly operated institutions.

Aid to Church-Related Schools. In the United States, almost 11 percent of school-age children attend private schools, of which about 80 percent have religious affiliations. The United States Supreme Court has tried to draw a fine line between permissible public aid to students in church-related schools and impermissible public aid to religion. These issues have arisen most often at the elementary and secondary levels.

In 1971, in *Lemon v. Kurtzman,*[4] the Court ruled that direct state aid could not be used to subsidize religious instruction. The Court in

Establishment Clause

The part of the First Amendment prohibiting the establishment of a church officially supported by the national government. It determines the legality of giving state and local government aid to religious organizations and schools, allowing or requiring school prayers, and teaching evolution versus creationism.

Free Exercise Clause

The provision of the First Amendment guaranteeing the free exercise of religion. The provision constrains the national government from prohibiting individuals from practicing the religion of their choice.

■ **Learning Outcome 2:**
Explain how the First Amendment's establishment clause and free exercise clause guarantee our freedom of religion.

Demonstrators at the Capitol Building in Frankfort, Kentucky, in 2013, urge the governor to veto a controversial religious freedom bill. Opponents believe that the legislation will make it easier to discriminate against lesbian and gay individuals under the guise of religious freedom. *Are there ever circumstances in which people have a legitimate right to discriminate?*

---

3. *Everson v. Board of Education,* 330 U.S. 1 (1947).
4. 403 U.S. 602 (1971).

Charles Barsotti/The New Yorker Collection

"I'm taking my voucher and going to circus school."

the *Lemon* case gave its most general pronouncement on the constitutionality of government aid to religious schools, stating that (1) the aid had to be secular (nonreligious) in aim, (2) it could not have the primary effect of advancing or inhibiting religion, and (3) the government must avoid "an excessive government entanglement with religion." All laws that raise issues under the establishment clause are now subject to the three-part *Lemon* test. How the test is applied, however, has varied over the years.

In a number of cases, the Supreme Court has held that state programs helping church-related schools are unconstitutional. In other cases, however, the Supreme Court has allowed states to use tax funds for lunches, textbooks, diagnostic services for speech and hearing problems, standardized tests, computers, and special educational services for disadvantaged students attending religious schools.

School Vouchers. An ongoing controversy concerning the establishment clause has to do with school vouchers. Some people believe that the public schools are failing to educate our children adequately. One proposed solution to the problem has been for state and local governments to issue school vouchers. These vouchers represent state-issued funds that can be used to purchase education at any school, public or private. At issue is whether voucher programs violate the establishment clause.

In 2002, the United States Supreme Court held that a voucher program in Cleveland, Ohio, did not violate the establishment clause. The Court concluded that because the vouchers could be used for public as well as private schools, the program did not unconstitutionally entangle church and state.[5] The Court's 2002 decision was encouraging to those who support school choice, whether it takes the form of school vouchers or tuition tax credits to offset educational expenses in private schools.

Today, a variety of states allow public funds to be used for private school expenses. Some have small-scale voucher or scholarship programs for a limited number of students, frequently special-needs students. A growing number of states provide tax deductions for private school expenses. Interest in such programs became more widespread in 2011, after the 2010 elections gave conservatives control of many state governments.

Still, voucher programs have also been eliminated in several jurisdictions. In 2007, Utah voters rejected a voucher plan that was created earlier that year by the state legislature. In March 2009, the U.S. Congress voted to halt a voucher program in the District of Columbia.

The Issue of School Prayer—*Engel v. Vitale*. Do the states have the right to promote religion in general, without making any attempt to establish a particular religion? That is the question raised by school prayer and was the precise issue presented in 1962 in *Engel v. Vitale*,[6] the so-called Regents' Prayer case in New York. The State Board of Regents of New York had suggested that a prayer be spoken aloud in the public schools at the beginning of each day. The recommended prayer was as follows:

---

5. *Zelman v. Simmons-Harris*, 536 U.S. 639 (2002).
6. 370 U.S. 421 (1962).

*Almighty God, we acknowledge our dependence upon Thee,
And we beg Thy blessings upon us, our parents, our teachers,
and our Country.*

Such a prayer was implemented in many New York public schools.

The parents of a number of students challenged the action of the regents, maintaining that it violated the establishment clause of the First Amendment. At trial, the parents lost. On appeal, however, the Supreme Court ruled that the regents' action was unconstitutional because "the constitutional prohibition against laws respecting an establishment of a religion must mean at least that in this country it is no part of the business of government to compose official prayers for any group of the American people to recite as part of a religious program carried on by any government."

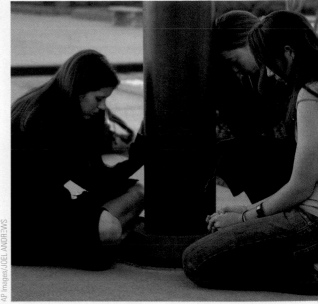

These high school students pray around the school flagpole before class in Lufkin, Texas. *Do their actions violate the separation of church and state?*

The Debate over School Prayer Continues. Although the Supreme Court has ruled repeatedly against officially sponsored prayer and Bible-reading sessions in public schools, other means for bringing some form of religious expression into public education have been attempted. In 1985, the Supreme Court struck down as unconstitutional an Alabama law authorizing one minute of silence for prayer or meditation in all public schools.[7] The Court concluded that the law violated the establishment clause because it was "an endorsement of religion lacking any clearly secular [non-religious] purpose."

Since then, the lower courts have interpreted the Supreme Court's decision to mean that states can require a moment of silence in the schools as long as they make it clear that the purpose of the law is secular, not religious.

Forbidding the Teaching of Evolution. For many decades, certain religious groups have opposed the teaching of evolution in the schools. To these groups, evolutionary theory directly counters their religious belief that human beings did not evolve but were created fully formed, as described in the biblical story of the creation. State and local attempts to forbid the teaching of evolution, however, have not passed constitutional muster in the eyes of the United States Supreme Court. For example, in 1968 the Supreme Court held that an Arkansas law prohibiting the teaching of evolution violated the establishment clause because it imposed religious beliefs on students.[8]

Nonetheless, state and local groups around the country continue their efforts against the teaching of evolution. Some school districts have considered teaching the creationist theory of "intelligent design" as an alternative explanation of the origin of life. Proponents of intelligent design contend that evolutionary theory has "gaps" that can be explained only by the existence of an intelligent creative force (God).

The federal courts took up the issue of intelligent design in 2005. The previous year, the Dover Area Board of Education in Pennsylvania had voted to require the presentation of intelligent design as an explanation of the origin of life. In December 2005, a U.S. district court ruled that the Dover mandate was unconstitutional.[9] All of the school board members who endorsed intelligent design were voted out of office.

Since 2005, advocates of intelligent design have made continued attempts to introduce their doctrine into the public schools. They have had some success, notably in laws passed in Louisiana in 2008 and in Tennessee in 2012. Intelligent design advocates have

---

7. *Wallace v. Jaffree*, 472 U.S. 38 (1985).
8. *Epperson v. Arkansas*, 393 U.S. 97 (1968).
9. *Kitzmiller v. Dover Area School District*, 400 F.Supp.2d 707 (M.D.Pa. 2005).

The National Christmas Tree and the National Hanukkah Menorah share space on the Ellipse in Washington, D.C. *Would a judge approve this display?*

adopted the slogan "teach the controversy" as a way of introducing creationism alongside evolution. Opponents argue, however, that there *is* no controversy among biologists. Rather, the controversy is political and religious, and if it is taught at all it should be covered in social science or politics classes.

Religious Displays on Public Property. On a regular basis, the courts are asked to determine whether religious symbols placed on public property violate the establishment clause. A frequent source of controversy is the placement of a crèche, or nativity scene, on public property during the Christmas season. The Supreme Court has allowed some displays but prohibited others. In general, a nativity scene is acceptable if it is part of a broader display that contains secular objects such as lights, Christmas trees, Santa Claus figures, and reindeer. A stand-alone crèche is not acceptable.[10] A related issue is whether the Ten Commandments exhibit may be displayed on public property. As with nativity displays, acceptability turns on whether the Ten Commandments is part of a larger secular display or whether the context is overtly religious.

The Free Exercise Clause

The First Amendment constrains Congress from prohibiting the free exercise of religion. Does this *free exercise clause* mean that no type of religious practice can be prohibited or restricted by government? Certainly, a person can hold any religious belief that he or she wants, or a person can have no religious belief. When, however, religious *practices* work against public policy and the public welfare, the government can act. For example, regardless of a child's or parent's religious beliefs, the government can require vaccinations.

Churches and other religious organizations are tax-exempt bodies, and as a result they are not allowed to endorse candidates for office or make contributions to candidates' campaigns. Churches are allowed to take positions on ballot proposals, however, and may contribute to referendum campaigns. For example, both the Latter-Day Saints (the Mormons) and the Roman Catholic Church were able to fund the campaign for California's 2008 Proposition 8, a measure to ban same-sex marriage.

The Internal Revenue Service (IRS) rarely bothers to threaten the tax-exempt status of a church based on simple candidate endorsements, however. For example, in October 2012, about 1,400 ministers collectively endorsed Republican presidential candidate Mitt Romney in a deliberate challenge to the 1954 law that prohibits such endorsements. The IRS did not respond. In 1995, however, the IRS did revoke the tax-exempt status of Branch Ministries, Inc., and in 2000 a federal district court supported the revocation.[11] Branch

10. *Lynch v. Donnelly*, 465 U.S. 668 (1984).
11. *Branch Ministries v. Rossetti*, 211 F.3d 137 (D.C.Cir. 2000).

Ministries went far beyond simply endorsing a candidate from the pulpit. The church had used tax-exempt income to buy newspaper advertisements denouncing Democratic presidential candidate Bill Clinton.

Freedom of Expression

Perhaps the most frequently invoked freedom that Americans have is the right to free speech and a free press. Each of us has the right to have our say, and all of us have the right to hear what others say. For the most part, Americans can criticize public officials and their actions without fear of reprisal by any branch of our government.

No Prior Restraint

Restraining an activity before that activity has actually occurred is called **prior restraint.** When expression is involved, prior restraint means censorship, as opposed to subsequent punishment. Prior restraint of expression would require, for example, that a permit be obtained before a speech could be made, a newspaper published, or a movie or TV show exhibited. Most, if not all, Supreme Court justices have been very critical of any governmental action that imposes prior restraint on expression.

One of the most famous cases concerning prior restraint was *New York Times v. United States,*[12] the so-called Pentagon Papers case. In 1971, the *Times* and the *Washington Post* were about to publish the Pentagon Papers, an elaborate secret history of the U.S. government's involvement in the Vietnam War (1965–1975). The secret documents had been obtained illegally by a disillusioned former Pentagon official. The government wanted a court order to bar publication of the documents, arguing that national security was threatened and that the documents had been stolen. The newspapers argued that the public had a right to know the information contained in the papers and that the press had the right to inform the public. The Supreme Court ruled six to three in favor of the newspapers' right to publish the information. This case affirmed the no-prior-restraint doctrine.

The Protection of Symbolic Speech

Not all expression is in words or in writing. Articles of clothing, gestures, movements, and other forms of nonverbal expressive conduct are considered **symbolic speech.** Such speech is given substantial protection today by our courts. For example, in a landmark decision issued in 1969, *Tinker v. Des Moines School District,*[13] the United States Supreme Court held that the wearing of black armbands by students in protest against the Vietnam War was a form of speech protected by the First Amendment.

Flag Burning. In 1989, the Supreme Court ruled that state laws that prohibited the burning of the American flag as part of a peaceful protest also violated the freedom of expression protected by the First Amendment.[14] Congress responded by passing the Flag Protection Act of 1989, which was ruled unconstitutional by the Supreme Court in 1990.[15] Congress and President George H. W. Bush immediately pledged to work for a constitutional amendment to "protect our flag"—an effort that has yet to be successful.

■ **Learning Outcome 3:** Specify the limited circumstances in which the national and state governments may override the principles of free speech and freedom of the press.

Prior Restraint
Restraining an activity before it has actually occurred. When expression is involved, this means censorship.

Symbolic Speech
Expression made through articles of clothing, gestures, movements, and other forms of nonverbal conduct. Symbolic speech is given substantial protection by the courts.

12. 403 U.S. 713 (1971).
13. 393 U.S. 503 (1969).
14. *Texas v. Johnson,* 488 U.S. 884 (1989).
15. *United States v. Eichman,* 496 U.S. 310 (1990).

This ad for cigarettes appeared in 1946. Despite protection of commercial speech, it would be impossible for such an ad to appear today. *Why?*

Cross Burning. In 2003, the Supreme Court concluded in a Virginia case that a state, consistent with the First Amendment, may ban cross burnings carried out with the intent to intimidate. The Court reasoned that historically, cross burning was a sign of impending violence, and a state has the right to ban threats of violence. The Court also ruled, however, that the state must prove intimidation and cannot infer it from the cross burnings themselves. In an impassioned dissent, Justice Clarence Thomas, who is African American and usually one of the Court's most conservative members, argued that cross burnings should be automatic evidence of intent to intimidate.[16]

The Protection of Commercial Speech

Commercial speech usually is defined as advertising statements. Can advertisers use their First Amendment rights to prevent restrictions on the content of commercial advertising? Until the 1970s, the Supreme Court held that such speech was not protected at all by the First Amendment. By the mid-1970s, however, more and more commercial speech had been brought under First Amendment protection. According to Justice Harry A. Blackmun, "Advertising, however tasteless and excessive it sometimes may seem, is nonetheless dissemination of information as to who is producing and selling what product for what reason and at what price."[17] Nevertheless, the Supreme Court will consider a restriction on commercial speech valid as long as it (1) seeks to implement a substantial government interest, (2) directly advances that interest, and (3) goes no further than necessary to accomplish its objective. In particular, a business engaging in commercial speech can be subject to liability for factual inaccuracies in ways that do not apply to noncommercial speech.

Attempts to Ban Subversive or Advocacy Speech

Over the past hundred years, the United States Supreme Court has established, in succession, a number of doctrines regarding language allegedly subversive to the public order. Descriptions of these doctrines follow.

Commercial Speech
Advertising statements, which increasingly have been given First Amendment protection.

16. *Virginia v. Black,* 538 U.S. 343 (2003).
17. *Virginia State Board of Pharmacy v. Virginia Citizens Consumer Council, Inc.,* 425 U.S. 748 (1976).

The Clear and Present Danger Test. In 1919, the Supreme Court ruled that when a person's remarks create a clear and present danger to the peace or public order, they can be curtailed constitutionally. Justice Oliver Wendell Holmes used this reasoning when examining the case of a socialist who had been convicted of violating the Espionage Act by distributing a leaflet that opposed the military draft.[18] (The conviction was upheld.) According to the *clear and present danger test*, expression may be restricted if evidence exists that such expression would cause a dangerous condition, actual or imminent, that Congress has the power to prevent.

> **Imminent Lawless Action Test**
> The current standard established by the Supreme Court for evaluating the legality of advocacy speech. Such speech can be forbidden only when it is "directed to inciting . . . imminent lawless action."

The Bad Tendency Rule. Over the course of the twentieth century, the Supreme Court modified the clear and present danger rule, limiting the constitutional protection of free speech in 1925 and 1951, and then broadening it substantially in 1969. In *Gitlow v. New York*,[19] the Court reintroduced the earlier *bad tendency rule,* which placed greater restrictions on speech than Justice Holmes's formulation. According to this rule, speech may be curtailed if there is a possibility that such expression might lead to some "evil."

In the *Gitlow* case, a member of a left-wing group was convicted of violating New York State's criminal anarchy statute when he published and distributed a pamphlet urging the violent overthrow of the U.S. government. In its majority opinion, the Supreme Court held that the First Amendment afforded protection against state incursions on freedom of expression—the first time that the First Amendment was ever invoked against a state government (see the discussion of incorporation theory earlier). Nevertheless, Gitlow could be punished legally because his expression would tend to bring about evils that the state had a right to prevent.

The Imminent Lawless Action Test. Some claim that the United States did not achieve true freedom of political speech until 1969. In that year, in *Brandenburg v. Ohio*,[20] the Supreme Court overturned the conviction of a Ku Klux Klan leader for violating a state statute. The statute prohibited anyone from advocating "the duty, necessity, or propriety of sabotage, violence, or unlawful methods of terrorism as a means of accomplishing industrial or political reform." The Court held that the guarantee of free speech does not permit a state "to forbid or proscribe [disallow] advocacy of the use of force or of law violation except where such advocacy is directed to inciting or producing imminent [immediate] lawless actions and is likely to incite or produce such action." The **imminent lawless action test** enunciated by the Court is a difficult one for prosecutors to meet. As a result, the Court's decision significantly broadened the protection given to advocacy speech.

The Eclipse of Obscenity as a Legal Category

Traditionally, state and federal statutes made it a crime to disseminate obscene materials. But what is *obscenity*? Justice Potter Stewart once stated that even though he could not define obscenity, "I know it when I see it." The legal system needs a more precise definition than that, however.

The Rise and Fall of *Miller v. California*. In 1973, in *Miller v. California*,[21] Chief Justice Warren Burger created a list of requirements that must be met for material to be legally obscene. Material is obscene if (1) the average person finds that it violates contemporary community standards, (2) the work taken as a whole appeals to a prurient interest in sex, (3) the work shows patently offensive sexual conduct, and (4) the work lacks serious

---

18. *Schenck v. United States,* 249 U.S. 47 (1919).
19. 268 U.S. 652 (1925).
20. 395 U.S. 444 (1969).
21. 413 U.S. 5 (1973).

redeeming literary, artistic, political, or scientific merit. The definition of *prurient interest* would be determined by "community standards," thus leaving the definition to local and state authorities.

The Court's ruling came down at a time when popular attitudes toward obscenity were undergoing a revolution. A few years earlier, literary works regarded as masterpieces by critics could be banned from the U.S. mail, from import, and from sale. Such works included *Lady Chatterley's Lover* by D. H. Lawrence and *Ulysses* by James Joyce. By the 1980s, however, it was possible in almost every corner of the country to buy or rent pornographic videotapes that left nothing to the imagination.

Internet Pornography. The rise of the Internet in the 1990s sealed the fate of obscenity as a useful legal category. Conventional pornography on the Internet was essentially impossible to police. Congress attempted to spare children from exposure to Internet pornography by laws passed in 1996 and 1998, but the Court found this legislation to be unconstitutional.[22] In 2000, Congress was more successful with the Children's Internet Protection Act, which requires public schools and libraries to install filtering software to prevent children from viewing Web sites with "adult" content. This law was upheld.[23] Young people today, however, are not dependent on libraries for Internet access. Free Wi-Fi, for use by laptops, tablets, and smartphones, is available almost everywhere.

Remaining Restrictions. Pornography can still be limited by the private sector—for example, most mainstream movie theaters will not show a film that has received a "No Children 17 or Under Admitted" (NC-17) rating from the Motion Picture Association of America. The government also retains the right to place restrictions on media it controls, such as the broadcast spectrum. Therefore, restrictions on radio and broadcast television remain.

Pornography That Exploits Minors. The government has also successfully outlawed materials that show sexual performance by minors. In 1990, the Court ruled that states can criminalize the possession of child pornography. The Court reasoned that the ban on private possession is justified because owning the material constitutes a form of child abuse.[24] This legal reasoning, however, reveals just how barren the concept of obscenity had become. Child abuse was the crime—not obscenity. As a result, the law makes no attempt to ban depictions of sexual performance by children in literary works such as Vladimir Nabokov's *Lolita* or in obvious cartoons such as Japanese *hentai*. Novels and cartoons do not involve the exploitation of actual, identifiable children.

Unprotected Speech: Slander

Can you say anything you want about someone else? Not really. Individuals are protected from **defamation of character,** which is defined as wrongfully hurting a person's good reputation. The law imposes a general duty on all persons to refrain from making false, defamatory statements about others. Breaching this duty orally is the wrongdoing called *slander.* Breaching it in writing is the wrongdoing called *libel,* which we discuss later. The government itself does not bring charges of slander or libel. Rather, the defamed person may bring a civil (as opposed to a criminal) suit for damages.

Defamation of Character
Wrongfully hurting a person's good reputation. The law imposes a general duty on all persons to refrain from making false, defamatory statements about others.

---

22. *Reno v. American Civil Liberties Union,* 521 U.S. 844 (1997); *American Civil Liberties Union v. Ashcroft,* 542 U.S. 646 (2004).
23. *United States v. American Library Association,* 539 U.S. 194 (2003).
24. *Osborne v. Ohio,* 495 U.S. 103 (1990).

Legally, **slander** is the public uttering of a false statement that harms the good reputation of another. Public uttering means that the defamatory statement is made to, or within the hearing of, a person other than the defamed party. If one person calls another dishonest, manipulative, and incompetent to his or her face when no one else is around, that does not constitute slander. If, however, a third party accidentally overhears defamatory statements, the courts have generally held that this constitutes a public uttering and therefore slander.

Student Speech

In recent years, high school and university students at public institutions have faced a variety of free speech challenges. Court rulings on these issues have varied by the level of school involved. Elementary schools, in particular, have great latitude in determining what kinds of speech are appropriate for their students. High school students have more free speech rights than do elementary students, and college students have the most speech rights of all.

Rights of Public School Students. High schools can impose restrictions on speech that would not be allowed in a college setting or in the general society. For example, high school officials may censor publications such as newspapers and yearbooks produced by the school's students. Courts have argued that a school newspaper is an extension of the school's educational mission, and thus subject to control by the school administration.

One of the most striking rulings to illustrate the power of school officials was handed down by the Supreme Court in 2007. An Alaska high school student had displayed a banner reading "Bong Hits 4 Jesus" on private property across from the school as students on the school grounds watched the Winter Olympics torch relay. The school principal crossed the street, seized the banner, and suspended the student from school. The Supreme Court later held that the school had an "important—indeed, perhaps compelling—interest" in combating drug use that allowed it to suppress the banner.[25] The Court's decision was widely criticized.

College Student Activity Fees. Should a college student have to subsidize, through student activity fees, organizations that promote causes that the student finds objectionable? In 2000, this question came before the Supreme Court in a case brought by several University of Wisconsin students. The students argued that their mandatory student activity fees—which helped to fund liberal causes with which they disagreed, including gay rights—violated their First Amendment rights of free speech, free association, and free exercise of religion.

To the surprise of many, the Supreme Court rejected the students' claim and ruled in favor of the university. The Court stated that "the university may determine that its mission is well served if students have the means to engage in dynamic discussions of philosophical, religious, scientific, social and political subjects in their extracurricular life. If the university reaches this conclusion, it is entitled to impose a mandatory fee to sustain an open dialogue to these ends."[26]

One possible response to high school censorship of student newspapers is to start an alternative paper off-campus. At a school in Washington State, students have done exactly that. Here, an editor works on the next edition of the alternative student paper. This case has led to lawsuits and proposed state legislation. *What are the downsides of creating an independent publication?*

---

25. *Morse v. Frederick*, 551 U.S. 393 (2007).
26. *Board of Regents of the University of Wisconsin System v. Southworth*, 529 U.S. 217 (2000).

Libel
A written defamation of a person's character, reputation, business, or property rights.

Actual Malice
Either knowledge of a defamatory statement's falsity or a reckless disregard for the truth.

Campus Speech and Behavior Codes. Another free speech issue is the legitimacy of campus speech and behavior codes at some state universities. These codes prohibit so-called hate speech—abusive speech attacking persons on the basis of their ethnicity, race, or other criteria. For example, a University of Michigan code banned "any behavior, verbal or physical, that stigmatizes or victimizes an individual on the basis of race, ethnicity, religion, sex, sexual orientation, creed, national origin, ancestry, age, marital status, handicap," or Vietnam-veteran status. A federal court found that the code violated students' First Amendment rights.[27] Although the courts generally have held, as in the University of Michigan case, that campus speech codes at state institutions are unconstitutional restrictions on the right to free speech, such codes continue to exist.

The Right to Assemble and to Petition the Government

The First Amendment prohibits Congress from making any law that abridges "the right of the people peaceably to assemble, and to petition the Government for a redress of grievances." Inherent in such a right is the ability of private citizens to communicate their ideas on public issues to government officials, as well as to other individuals. The Supreme Court has often put this freedom on a par with freedom of speech and freedom of the press. Nonetheless, it has allowed municipalities to require permits for parades, sound trucks, and demonstrations so that public officials can control traffic or prevent demonstrations from turning into riots.

The freedom to demonstrate became a major issue in 1978 when the American Nazi Party sought to march through Skokie, Illinois, a largely Jewish suburb with many Holocaust survivors. The Supreme Court let stand a lower court's ruling that the city of Skokie had violated the Nazis' First Amendment guarantees by denying them a permit to march.[28]

An issue that has surfaced in recent decades is whether communities can prevent gang members from gathering together on the streets without violating their right of assembly or associated rights. For example, in a 1997 case, the California Supreme Court upheld a lower court's order preventing gang members from appearing in public together.[29] In 1999, however, the United States Supreme Court held that a Chicago "anti-loitering" ordinance violated the constitutional right to due process of law because, among other things, it left too much power to the police to determine what constituted "loitering."[30]

Freedom of the Press

Freedom of the press can be regarded as a special instance of freedom of speech. Of course, at the time of the framing of the Constitution, the press meant only newspapers, pamphlets, magazines, and books. As technology has modified the ways in which we disseminate information, the laws touching on freedom of the press have been modified. What can and cannot be printed still occupies an important place in constitutional law, however.

Defamation in Writing. **Libel** is defamation in writing or in pictures, signs, films, or any other communication. As with slander, libel occurs only if the defamatory statements are observed by a third party. If one person writes a private letter to another wrongfully accusing him or her of embezzling funds, that does not constitute libel.

A 1964 case, *New York Times Co. v. Sullivan*,[31] explored an important question regarding libelous statements made about public officials. The Supreme Court held that only when a statement against a public official is made with **actual malice**—that is, with either knowledge of its falsity or a reckless disregard for the truth—can damages be obtained.

---

27. *Doe v. University of Michigan,* 721 F.Supp. 852 (1989).
28. *Smith v. Collin,* 439 U.S. 916 (1978).
29. *Gallo v. Acuna,* 14 Cal.4th 1090 (1997).
30. *City of Chicago v. Morales,* 527 U.S. 41 (1999).
31. 376 U.S. 254 (1964).

The standard set by the Court in the *New York Times* case has since been applied to **public figures** generally. Public figures include not only public officials but also any persons, such as movie stars, who are generally in the public limelight. Statements made about public figures usually are related to matters of general public interest. They are made about people who substantially affect all of us. Furthermore, public figures generally have some access to a public medium for answering disparaging falsehoods about themselves, whereas private individuals do not. For these reasons, public figures have a greater burden of proof in defamation cases than do private individuals.

The Internet has vastly expanded the number of published statements by the general citizenry, including anonymous comments. As a result, today libelous statements can be hard even to track down, much less prosecute. In addition, libel is more difficult to prove in the United States than in many other countries. We take a brief look at British libel law in this chapter's *Beyond Our Borders* feature that follows.

> **Public Figure**
> A public official or any other person, such as a movie star, known to the public because of his or her position or activities.

Beyond Our Borders

The Trouble with British Libel Law

Because Americans value free speech highly, it is not easy to sue someone for libel successfully. Britain, in contrast, has a much lower standard for proving libel.

The Difference between U.S. and British Laws

To succeed in a libel suit in the United States, the *plaintiff,* the person who is suing, has to prove that the offending speech was false and published with reckless disregard for the truth. In contrast, British law assumes that any offending speech is false. It is the writer or author who must prove that it is in fact true in order to prevail against a libel charge.

In the past, Britain was willing to hear cases in which the alleged libel took place in another country. As a result, Britain became the international destination of choice for those who wished to file libel suits. For example, a Tunisian businessperson sued Al Arabiya, a satellite television network based in Dubai and broadcasting in Arabic, in London. The Tunisian disputed allegations that he had ties to terrorist groups. A court awarded the plaintiff $325,000.

A further problem is that defending oneself against a libel suit in Britain is very expensive. A wealthy plaintiff can wind up bankrupting a defendant even if the plaintiff's case is weak.

The United States Fights Back

In reaction to easy libel lawsuits in Britain, some states and cities in the United States adopted laws to protect their citizens. One example is New York State's Libel Terrorism Protection Act. It protects New York–based publishers and writers from the enforcement of most foreign libel judgments. In 2010, Congress passed a law that makes foreign libel judgments unenforceable in U.S. courts unless the judgments are in accord with the First Amendment.

Reforming British Libel Law

In time, British libel practices became enough of a scandal that Parliament adopted a new law, the Defamation Act of 2013. Businesses can now prove defamation only if they have suffered serious financial loss. New rules reduce the legal costs of small plaintiffs and defendants. An "honest opinion" defense has been created. Finally, courts have sought to curb "libel tourism" by limiting foreigners to defending the reputation that they have *in Britain*. Unfortunately, the British province of Northern Ireland refused to adopt the new law, potentially giving libel tourism a new home.

For Critical Analysis

British newspapers argue that reducing the costs of small plaintiffs will expose the press to more libel suits. Is this a problem? Why or why not?

A Free Press versus a Fair Trial: Gag Orders. Another major issue relating to freedom of the press concerns media coverage of criminal trials. The Sixth Amendment to the Constitution guarantees the right of criminal suspects to a fair trial. In other words, the accused have rights. The First Amendment guarantees freedom of the press. What if the two rights appear to be in conflict?

Jurors may be influenced by reading news stories about the trial in which they are participating. In the 1970s, judges increasingly issued **gag orders,** orders that restricted the publication of news about a trial in progress or even a pretrial hearing to protect the accused's right to a fair trial. In a landmark 1976 case, *Nebraska Press Association v. Stuart,*[32] the Supreme Court unanimously ruled that a Nebraska judge's gag order had violated the First Amendment's guarantee of freedom of the press. Despite the *Nebraska Press Association* ruling, the Court has upheld gag orders when it believed that publicity was likely to harm a defendant's right to a fair trial. Given how easy it is for a modern juror to access social media through a smartphone, however, gag orders may have become pointless.

Films, Radio, and TV. As we have noted, in only a few cases has the Supreme Court upheld prior restraint of published materials. The Court's reluctance to accept prior restraint is less evident with respect to motion pictures. In the first half of the twentieth century, films were routinely submitted to local censorship boards. Only in 1952 did the Court find that motion pictures were covered by the First Amendment.[33] In contrast, the Court extended full protection to the Internet almost immediately by striking down provisions of the 1996 Telecommunications Act.[34] Cable TV received broad protection in 2000.[35]

While the Court has held that the First Amendment is relevant to radio and television, it has never extended full protection to these media. The Court has used a number of arguments to justify this stand—initially, the scarcity of broadcast frequencies. The Court later held that the government could restrict "indecent" programming based on the "pervasive" presence of broadcasting in the home.[36] On this basis, the Federal Communications Commission (FCC) has the authority to fine broadcasters for indecency or profanity. The extent of the FCC's authority to penalize broadcasters for such infractions is unclear, however. A Supreme Court ruling in 2012 overturned a specific penalty imposed by the FCC without addressing the fundamental constitutional question.

Los Angeles soccer star David Beckham did not succeed in his libel suit against In Touch *magazine. What legal standard makes it more difficult for a celebrity to win a libel suit?*

■ **Learning Outcome 4:**
Provide the constitutional basis of the right to privacy, and explain how the principle has been applied to the abortion and right-to-die controversies.

The Right to Privacy

No explicit reference is made anywhere in the Constitution to a person's right to privacy. Until the second half of the 1900s, the courts did not take a very positive approach toward the right to privacy. In the 1960s, the highest court began to modify the majority view. In 1965, in *Griswold v. Connecticut,*[37] the Supreme Court overturned a Connecticut law that effectively prohibited the use of contraceptives, holding that the law violated the right to privacy. Justice William O. Douglas formulated a unique way of reading this right into the Bill of Rights. He claimed that the First, Third, Fourth, Fifth, and Ninth Amendments created "penumbras, formed by emanations [shadows, formed by the light] from those

Gag Order
An order issued by a judge restricting the publication of news about a trial or a pretrial hearing to protect the accused's right to a fair trial.

32. 427 U.S. 539 (1976).
33. *Joseph Burstyn, Inc. v. Wilson*, 343 U.S. 495 (1952).
34. *Reno v. American Civil Liberties Union*, 521 U.S. 844 (1997).
35. *United States v. Playboy Entertainment Group*, 529 U.S. 803 (2000).
36. *FCC v. Pacifica Foundation*, 438 U.S. 726 (1978). In this case, the Court banned seven swear words (famously used by the late comedian George Carlin) during hours when children could hear them.
37. 381 U.S. 479 (1965).

guarantees that help give them life and substance," and he went on to describe zones of privacy that are guaranteed by these rights. When we read the Ninth Amendment, we can see the foundation for his reasoning: "The enumeration in the Constitution, of certain rights, shall not be construed to deny or disparage [belittle] others retained by the people." In other words, just because the Constitution, including its amendments, does not specifically talk about the right to privacy does not mean that this right is denied to the people.

Privacy Rights and Abortion

Historically, abortion was not a criminal offense before the "quickening" of the fetus (the first movement of the fetus in the uterus, usually between the sixteenth and eighteenth weeks of pregnancy). During the latter half of the nineteenth century, however, state laws became more severe. By 1973, performing an abortion at any time during pregnancy was a criminal offense in a majority of the states.

Roe v. Wade. In 1973, in *Roe v. Wade*,[38] the United States Supreme Court accepted the argument that the laws against abortion violated "Jane Roe's" right to privacy under the Constitution. The Court held that during the first trimester (three months) of pregnancy, abortion was an issue solely between a woman and her physician. The state could not limit abortions except to require that they be performed by licensed physicians. During the second trimester, to protect the health of the mother, the state was allowed to specify the conditions under which an abortion could be performed. During the final trimester, the state could regulate or even outlaw abortions except when they were necessary to preserve the life or health of the mother.

After the *Roe* case, the Supreme Court issued decisions in a number of cases defining and redefining the boundaries of state regulation of abortion. During the 1980s, the Court twice struck down laws that required a woman who wished to have an abortion to undergo counseling designed to discourage abortions. In the late 1980s and early 1990s, however, the Court took a more conservative approach. For example, in 1989 the Court upheld a Missouri statute that, among other things, banned the use of public hospitals or other taxpayer-supported facilities for performing abortions.[39] In 1992, the Court upheld a Pennsylvania law that required preabortion counseling, a waiting period of twenty-four hours, and, for girls under the age of eighteen, parental or judicial permission.[40] As a result, abortions are now more difficult to obtain in some states than others, as noted in the chapter-opening *What If . . .* feature.

Protests at Abortion Clinics. Because of several episodes of violence attending protests at abortion clinics, in 1994 Congress passed the Freedom of Access to Clinic Entrances Act. The act prohibits protesters from blocking entrances to such clinics. In 1997, the Supreme Court upheld the constitutionality of prohibiting protesters from entering a fifteen-foot "buffer zone" around abortion clinics and from giving unwanted counseling to those entering the clinics.[41] In a 2000 decision, the Court upheld a Colorado law requiring demonstrators to stay at

This protester stands in front of the Planned Parenthood center in Aurora, Illinois. *What limits are placed on anti-abortion protesters?*

KEEP ABORTION OUT OF AURORA

FAMILIESAGAINSTPLANNEDPARENTHOOD.ORG

AP Images/Stacie Freudenberg

---

38. 410 U.S. 113 (1973). Jane Roe was not the real name of the woman in this case. It is a common legal pseudonym used to protect a person's privacy.
39. *Webster v. Reproductive Health Services*, 492 U.S. 490 (1989).
40. *Planned Parenthood v. Casey*, 505 U.S. 833 (1992).
41. *Schenck v. ProChoice Network*, 519 U.S. 357 (1997).

least eight feet away from people entering and leaving clinics unless people consented to be approached. In 2014, however, the Court found that a thirty-five-foot buffer zone established by Massachusetts was too extensive.[42]

Partial-Birth Abortion. Another issue in the abortion controversy concerns "partial-birth" abortion. A partial-birth abortion, which physicians call intact dilation and extraction, is a procedure that can be used during the second trimester of pregnancy. Abortion rights advocates claim that in limited circumstances the procedure is the safest way to perform an abortion and that the government should never outlaw specific medical procedures. Opponents argue that the procedure has no medical merit and that it ends the life of a fetus that might be able to live outside the womb.

In 2000, the Supreme Court addressed this issue when it reviewed a Nebraska law banning partial-birth abortions. The Court invalidated the Nebraska law on the ground that, as written, the law could be used to ban other abortion procedures and contained no provisions for protecting the health of the pregnant woman.[43]

In 2003, legislation similar to the Nebraska statute was passed by the U.S. Congress and signed into law by President George W. Bush. In 2007, the Supreme Court, with several changes in membership since the 2000 ruling, upheld the federal law in a five-to-four vote, effectively reversing its position on partial-birth abortion.[44]

The Controversy Continues. Abortion continues to be a divisive issue. During the early years of the twenty-first century, abortion opponents concentrated on state ballot proposals that could lay the groundwork for an eventual challenge to *Roe*. They were not very successful, however. In one 2011 example, in Mississippi, a conservative state, voters rejected a measure that would have outlawed all abortions and some forms of birth control. Abortion opponents have been more successful in winning new restrictions passed by state legislatures. New state laws became especially common after the 2010 elections, when Republicans took over many state legislative chambers.

Privacy Rights and the "Right to Die"

A 1976 case involving Karen Ann Quinlan was one of the first publicized "right-to-die" cases.[45] The parents of Quinlan, a young woman who had been in a coma for nearly a year and who had been kept alive during that time by a respirator, wanted her respirator removed. The ruling of the New Jersey Supreme Court, *In re Quinlan,* was that the right to privacy includes the right of a patient to refuse treatment and that patients unable to speak can exercise that right through a family member or guardian. In 1990, the Supreme Court took up the issue. In *Cruzan v. Director, Missouri Department of Health,*[46] the Court stated that a patient's life-sustaining treatment can be withdrawn at the request of a family member only if there is "clear and convincing evidence" that the patient did not want such treatment.

What If There Is No Living Will? Since the 1976 *Quinlan* decision, most states have enacted laws permitting people to designate their wishes concerning life-sustaining procedures in "living wills" or durable health-care powers of attorney. These laws and the Supreme Court's *Cruzan* decision have resolved the right-to-die controversy for situations in which the patient has drafted a living will. Disputes are still possible if there is no living will.

42. *Hill v. Colorado,* 530 U.S. 703 (2000) and *McCullen v. Coakley,* ___ U.S. ___ (2014).
43. *Stenberg v. Carhart,* 530 U.S. 914 (2000).
44. *Gonzales v. Carhart,* 550 U.S. 124 (2007).
45. 70 N.J. 10 (1976).
46. 497 U.S. 261 (1990).

An example is the case of Terri Schiavo. The husband of the Florida woman who had been in a persistent vegetative state for more than a decade sought to have her feeding tube removed on the basis of oral statements that she would not want her life prolonged in such circumstances. Schiavo's parents fought this move in court but lost on the ground that a spouse, not a parent, is the appropriate legal guardian for a married person. Although the Florida legislature passed a law allowing Governor Jeb Bush to overrule the courts, the state supreme court held that the law violated the state constitution.[47] The federal courts agreed with the Florida state courts, and Schiavo died shortly thereafter.

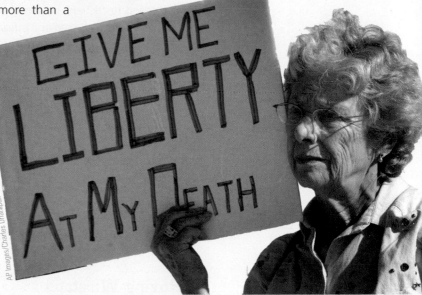

AP Images/Charles Dharapak

Physician-assisted suicide continues to be an emotional issue for many Americans. Only three states allow such action by physicians. *Does the Constitution give any guidelines about the "right-to-die" controversy?*

Physician-Assisted Suicide. In the 1990s, another issue surfaced: Do privacy rights include the right of terminally ill people to end their lives through physician-assisted suicide? Until 1996, the courts consistently upheld state laws that prohibited this practice. In 1996, after two federal appellate courts ruled that state laws banning assisted suicide were unconstitutional, the issue reached the United States Supreme Court.

In 1997 the Court stated that the liberty interest protected by the Constitution does not include a right to commit suicide, with or without assistance. In effect, the Supreme Court left the decision as to whether to permit the practice to the states.[48] Since then, assisted suicide has been allowed in only five states—Montana, New Mexico, Oregon, Vermont, and Washington. In 2006, the Supreme Court upheld Oregon's physician-assisted suicide law against a challenge from the George W. Bush administration.[49]

Civil Liberties versus Security Issues

■ **Learning Outcome 5:**
Cite examples of how recent security concerns have affected our civil liberties.

As former Supreme Court justice Thurgood Marshall once said, "Grave threats to liberty often come in times of urgency, when constitutional rights seem too extravagant to endure." Not surprisingly, antiterrorist legislation since the attacks on September 11, 2001, has eroded certain basic rights, in particular the Fourth Amendment protections against unreasonable searches and seizures.

The USA Patriot Act

The most significant piece of antiterrorism legislation, the USA Patriot Act, was originally passed in October 2001. In 2006, when the act was renewed, a heated debate emerged. While many Americans believe that the Patriot Act is a necessary safety measure to prevent future terrorist attacks, others argue that the act endangers long-established civil liberties guaranteed by the Constitution.

Much of the blame for the government's failure to anticipate the 9/11 attacks was assigned to a lack of cooperation among government agencies. A major goal of the Patriot Act was to lift interagency barriers to cooperation, especially between

did you know?

In 2013, public opinion polls showed that Americans were more concerned about restrictions on civil liberties than they were about protection from terrorism. This was the first time since the attacks of 9/11 that surveys reported this result.

---

47. *Bush v. Schiavo,* 885 So.2d 321 (Fla. 2004).
48. *Washington v. Glucksberg,* 521 U.S. 702 (1997).
49. *Gonzales v. Oregon,* 546 U.S. 243 (2006).

the Federal Bureau of Investigation and the Central Intelligence Agency. The Patriot Act also eased restrictions on the government's authority to investigate and arrest suspected terrorists. Law enforcement officials can secretly search a suspect's home and monitor a suspect's Internet activities, phone conversations, financial records, and book purchases. For the first time in American history, the government can open a suspect's mail.

The Patriot Act also authorized National Security Letters (NSLs), which are subpoenas issued by the FBI itself and which do not require probable cause or judicial oversight. In addition, an individual or financial institution that is served with such a warrant cannot speak about the government's investigation to anyone. Thus, many argue that this provision of the Patriot Act contradicts the First Amendment by making free speech a crime. In addition to First Amendment issues, this provision raises the concern that no one would be allowed to blow the whistle on abuses of the government's powers. As a result of these concerns, a U.S. district court found the NSL provisions of the Patriot Act to be unconstitutional in 2004 and again in 2007.[50] Finally, if the government decides to take a suspected terrorist into custody, the suspect can be summarily denied bail—a potential breach of the Eighth Amendment.

Roving Wiretaps

One civil liberties issue involves legislation that allows the government to conduct "roving" wiretaps. Previously, only specific telephone numbers, cell phone numbers, or computers could be tapped. Now a person under suspicion can be monitored electronically no matter what form of electronic communication he or she uses. Such roving wiretaps appear to be inconsistent with the Fourth Amendment, which requires a judicial warrant to describe the *place* to be searched, not just the person.

One of the goals of the framers was to avoid *general* searches. Further, once a judge approves an application for a roving wiretap, when, how, and where the monitoring occurs is left to the discretion of law enforcement agents. As an unavoidable result, a third party may have access to the conversations and e-mails of hundreds of people who falsely believe them to be private.

National Security Agency Surveillance

Shortly after September 11, 2001, President George W. Bush issued an executive order authorizing the National Security Agency (NSA) to conduct secret surveillance without court warrants, even warrants from special security courts. The NSA was to monitor phone calls and other communications between foreign parties and persons within the United States when one of the parties had suspected links to terrorist organizations. News of the secret program came out in December 2005. The program was intensely criticized by civil liberties groups.

In 2007, Congress passed a law to authorize the warrantless NSA wiretaps. The law expired in 2008, however, and its reauthorization was held up by a dispute as to whether telephone companies should receive blanket immunity from lawsuits stemming from their past cooperation with the wiretaps. When it finally passed, the reauthorization protected the telephone companies.

Recent Revelations of NSA Activity

In June 2013, leaks provided by Edward Snowden, an employee of a federal contractor, revealed that NSA surveillance was far more extensive than previously assumed. Among the most striking discoveries was that the NSA gathers information on *every* domestic phone call made in the United States and certain other countries. The NSA does not record

---

50. *Doe v. Ashcroft*, 334 F.Supp.2d 471 (S.D.N.Y. 2004); and *Doe v. Gonzales*, 500 F.Supp.2d 379 (S.D.N.Y. 2007).

the contents of U.S. domestic calls, but rather the *metadata,* which includes the time of the call, the number of the caller, and the number of the phone that was called.

Collecting Actual Data. Under a second program, PRISM, the NSA collected information from the Web sites of corporations, including Apple, Google, Facebook, Microsoft, Skype, and others. This data collection was undertaken without the knowledge of the companies involved. A third revelation was of major espionage actions against European countries. These included bugging the offices of the European Union in advance of trade talks between the United States and that organization.

The NSA also bugged the cell phones of a wide variety of world leaders, including Brazil's president Dilma Rousseff and Germany's chancellor Angela Merkel. Dozens of additional reports, covering matters great and small, were released in subsequent months. For example, it was revealed that the NSA had recorded every phone call made in one year in an unidentified foreign country—not just the metadata but the actual conversations. The recordings included millions of calls made by or to U.S. citizens.

Consequences of the Revelations. Snowden fled to Russia. Meanwhile, reports based on the materials he released resulted in an outcry by U.S. civil libertarians. The Obama administration defended the NSA programs, noting—correctly—that they had been authorized by secret courts. In addition, former NSA director Michael Hayden bluntly stated that the Fourth Amendment, which prohibits unreasonable searches, "is not an international treaty." Foreigners, in other words, had no privacy rights that the U.S. government was bound to respect.

As you might imagine, citizens of foreign countries, especially in Europe, found such statements to be alarming. Several nations announced initiatives aimed at protecting the privacy of data belonging to their own citizens. Such steps could cut into the sales of American high-tech firms. Currently, through "cloud computing" services, U.S. companies such as Google and Microsoft store vast amounts of data belonging to people and corporations not just in America, but around the world. In the future, individuals and firms in Germany, for example, might limit their use of cloud computing to servers located in Germany. Some have even asked whether U.S.-made hardware and software might be subject to NSA tampering. (Similar suspicions have been raised about Chinese-made equipment.)

National Security and the Civil Liberties of Immigrants

For many U.S. citizens, immigration—especially unauthorized or illegal immigration—is a national security issue. The terrorist attacks on September 11, 2001, reinforced the belief that the civil liberties of noncitizens should be limited. Among the most obvious characteristics of the terrorists who perpetrated the 9/11 attacks is that they were all foreign citizens. Still, legal immigrants who are not citizens have rights. The Bill of Rights contains no

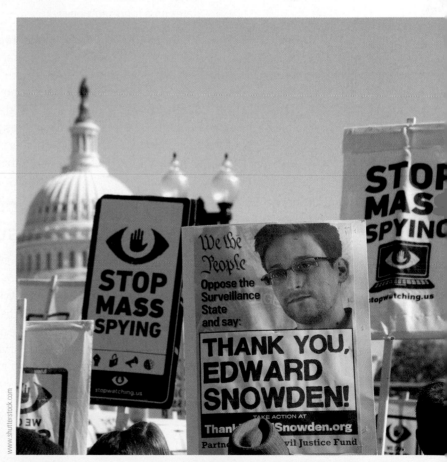

Opponents of national security surveillance support Edward Snowden, the leaker who exposed NSA activities. *Is Snowden a hero or a traitor? In either case, why?*

language that limits its protections to citizens. The Fourteenth Amendment specifies that all *persons* (as opposed to all *citizens*) shall enjoy "due process of law."

Illegal immigrants are subject to deportation. In 1903, however, the Supreme Court ruled that the government could not deport someone without a hearing that meets constitutional due process standards.[51] Today, most people facing deportation are entitled to a hearing before an immigration judge, to representation by a lawyer, and to the right to see the evidence presented against them. The government must prove that its grounds for deportation are valid.

Limits to the Rights of Deportees: Due Process. Despite the language of the Fourteenth Amendment, the courts have often deferred to government assertions that noncitizens cannot make constitutional claims. The Antiterrorism and Effective Death Penalty Act passed by Congress in 1996 was especially restrictive. The government was given the right to deport noncitizens for alleged terrorism without any court review of the deportation order. Further, the government is now allowed to deport noncitizens based on secret evidence that the deportee is not permitted to see.

Limits to the Rights of Deportees: Freedom of Speech. A case in 1999 involved a group of noncitizens associated with the Popular Front for the Liberation of Palestine (PFLP). The PFLP had carried out terrorist acts in Israel, but there was no evidence of criminal conduct by the group arrested in the United States. In this case, the Supreme Court ruled that aliens have no First Amendment rights to object to deportation, even if the deportation is based on their political associations.[52] This ruling also covers permanent residents—noncitizens with "green cards" that allow them to live and work in the United States on a long-term basis.

Limits to the Rights of Deportees: *Ex Post Facto* Laws. Article I, Section 9, of the Constitution prohibits *ex post facto* laws—laws that inflict punishments for acts that were not illegal when they were committed. This provision may not apply in deportation cases, however. The 1996 law mentioned earlier provided mandatory deportation for noncitizens convicted of an aggravated felony, even if the crime took place before 1996. Under the 1996 law, permanent residents have been deported to nations that they left when they were small children. In some cases, deported persons did not even speak the language of the country to which they were deported.

■ **Learning Outcome 6:**
Identify the constitutional rights of those who are accused of a crime, explain the *Miranda* and exclusionary rules, and describe the current status of the death penalty.

The Great Balancing Act: The Rights of the Accused versus the Rights of Society

The United States has one of the highest murder rates in the industrialized world. It is not surprising, therefore, that many citizens have extremely strong opinions about the rights of those accused of violent crimes. When an accused person, especially one who has confessed to some criminal act, is set free because of an apparent legal "technicality," many people believe that the rights of the accused are being given more weight than the rights of society and of potential or actual victims. Why, then, give criminal suspects rights? The answer is partly to avoid convicting innocent people, but mostly because due process of law and fair treatment benefit everyone who comes in contact with law enforcement or the courts.

The courts and the police must constantly engage in a balancing act of competing rights. The basis of all discussions about the appropriate balance is, of course, the U.S. Bill

---

51. *Yamataya v. Fisher,* 189 U.S. 86 (1903).
52. *Reno v. Arab-American Anti-Discrimination Committee,* 525 U.S. 471 (1999).

of Rights. The Fourth, Fifth, Sixth, and Eighth Amendments deal specifically with the rights of criminal defendants.

Rights of the Accused

The basic rights of criminal defendants are outlined below. When appropriate, the specific constitutional provision or amendment on which a right is based is also given.

Limits on the Conduct of Police Officers and Prosecutors.
- No unreasonable or unwarranted searches and seizures (Amendment IV).
- No arrest except on probable cause (Amendment IV).
- No coerced confessions or illegal interrogation (Amendment V).
- No entrapment.
- On questioning following an arrest, a suspect must be informed of her or his rights.

Defendant's Pretrial Rights.
- **Writ of *habeas corpus*** (Article I, Section 9).
- Prompt **arraignment** (Amendment VI).
- Legal counsel (Amendment VI).
- Reasonable bail (Amendment VIII).
- To be informed of charges (Amendment VI).
- To remain silent (Amendment V).

Trial Rights.
- Speedy and public trial before a jury (Amendment VI).
- Impartial jury selected from a cross section of the community (Amendment VI).
- Trial atmosphere free of prejudice, fear, and outside interference.
- No compulsory self-incrimination (Amendment V).
- Adequate counsel (Amendment VI).
- No cruel and unusual punishment (Amendment VIII).
- Appeal of convictions.
- No double jeopardy (Amendment V).

Extending the Rights of the Accused

During the 1960s, the Supreme Court, under Chief Justice Earl Warren, significantly expanded the rights of accused persons. In *Gideon v. Wainwright,*[53] a case decided in 1963, the Court held that if a person is accused of a felony and cannot afford an attorney, an attorney must be made available to the accused person at the government's expense. Although the Sixth Amendment to the Constitution provides for the right to counsel, the Court had previously held that only criminal defendants in capital (death penalty) cases automatically had a right to free legal counsel.

Miranda v. Arizona. In 1966, the Court issued its decision in *Miranda v. Arizona.*[54] The case involved Ernesto Miranda, who was charged with the kidnapping and rape of a young woman. After questioning, Miranda confessed and was later convicted. Miranda's

53. 372 U.S. 335 (1963).
54. 384 U.S. 436 (1966).

Why Should You Care about...

Civil Liberties?

The Bill of Rights includes numerous provisions that protect persons who are suspected of criminal activity. You may be the most law-abiding person in the world, but that will not guarantee that you will never be stopped, searched, or arrested by the police. Sooner or later, the great majority of all citizens will have some kind of interaction with the police. People who do not understand their rights or how to behave toward law enforcement officers can find themselves in serious trouble. The advice in the *How You Can Make a Difference* feature at the end of this chapter therefore provides key survival skills for life in the modern world.

Writ of *Habeas Corpus*
Habeas corpus means, literally, "you have the body." A writ of *habeas corpus* is an order that requires jailers to bring a prisoner before a court or a judge and explain why the person is being held.

Arraignment
The first act in a criminal proceeding, in which the defendant is brought before a court to hear the charges against him or her and enter a plea of guilty or not guilty.

A murder suspect at his trial in Vermont. After conviction, his lawyers appealed, claiming that police questioned him without first reading him Miranda warnings, and that the trial court admitted into testimony statements he made in the hospital to police. *Does this individual have a chance of winning a new trial? Why or why not?*

lawyer appealed his conviction, arguing that the police had never informed Miranda that he had a right to remain silent and a right to be represented by counsel. The Court, in ruling in Miranda's favor, enunciated the now-familiar *Miranda* rights. Today, *Miranda* rights statements typically take the following form:

> *You have the right to remain silent. Anything you say can and will be used against you in a court of law. You have the right to speak to an attorney. If you cannot afford an attorney, one will be appointed for you. Do you understand these rights as they have been read to you?*

Exceptions to the *Miranda* Rule. As part of a continuing attempt to balance the rights of accused persons against the rights of society, the Supreme Court has made a number of exceptions to the *Miranda* rule. As one example, in an important 1991 decision, the Court stated that a suspect's conviction will not be automatically overturned if the suspect was coerced into making a confession. If the other evidence admitted at trial is strong enough to justify the conviction without the confession, then the fact that the confession was obtained illegally can effectively be ignored.[55]

The Exclusionary Rule

At least since 1914, judicial policy has prohibited the admission of illegally seized evidence at trials in federal courts. This is the so-called **exclusionary rule.** Improperly obtained evidence, no matter how telling, cannot be used by prosecutors. This includes evidence obtained by police in violation of a suspect's *Miranda* rights or of the Fourth Amendment.

The Fourth Amendment protects against unreasonable searches and seizures and provides that a judge may issue a search warrant to a police officer only on *probable cause* (a demonstration of facts that permit a reasonable belief that a crime has been committed). The courts must determine what constitutes an "unreasonable" search and seizure.

The reasoning behind the exclusionary rule is that it forces police officers to gather evidence properly, in which case their due diligence will be rewarded by a conviction. Nevertheless, the exclusionary rule has always had critics who argue that it permits guilty persons to be freed because of innocent procedural errors by the police.

This rule was first extended to state court proceedings in a 1961 United States Supreme Court decision, *Mapp v. Ohio.*[56] In this case, the Court overturned the conviction of Dollree Mapp for the possession of obscene materials. Police found pornographic books in her apartment after searching it without a search warrant and despite her refusal to let them in. Under the Fourth Amendment, search warrants must describe the persons

did you know?

In 2013, for the first time in four decades, a majority of Americans in a public opinion poll endorsed legalizing the use of marijuana.

Exclusionary Rule
A judicial policy prohibiting the admission at trial of illegally obtained evidence.

---

55. *Arizona v. Fulminante,* 499 U.S. 279 (1991).
56. 367 U.S. 643 (1961).

or things to be seized. Nonetheless, officers are entitled to seize items not mentioned in the search warrant if the materials are in "plain view" and reasonably appear to be contraband or evidence of a crime.[57]

During the past several decades, the Supreme Court has diminished the scope of the exclusionary rule by creating exceptions to its applicability. For example, in 1984 the Court held that illegally obtained evidence could be admitted at trial if law enforcement personnel could prove that they would have obtained the evidence legally anyway. In another case decided in the same year, the Court held that a police officer who used a technically incorrect search warrant form to obtain evidence had acted in good faith and therefore the evidence was admissible at trial. The Court thus created the "good faith" exception to the exclusionary rule. In 2009, for example, the Court found that the good faith exception applies when an officer makes an arrest based on an outstanding warrant in another jurisdiction, even if the warrant in question was based on a clerical error.[58]

The Death Penalty

Capital punishment remains one of the most debated aspects of our criminal justice system. Those in favor of the death penalty maintain that it serves as a deterrent to serious crime and satisfies society's need for justice and fair play. Those opposed to the death penalty do not believe it has any deterrent value and hold that it constitutes a barbaric act in an otherwise civilized society.

Cruel and Unusual Punishment? The Eighth Amendment prohibits "cruel and unusual punishment." Throughout history, the phrase referred to torture and to executions that prolonged the agony of dying. The Supreme Court has never interpreted "cruel and unusual" as prohibiting all forms of capital punishment in all circumstances. Many people came to believe, however, that the imposition of the death penalty was random and arbitrary, and in 1972 the Supreme Court agreed, in *Furman v. Georgia.*[59]

The Supreme Court's 1972 decision stated that the death penalty, as then applied, violated the Eighth and Fourteenth Amendments. The Court also ruled that capital punishment is not necessarily cruel and unusual if the criminal has killed or attempted to kill someone. In its opinion, the Court invited the states to enact more precise laws so that the death penalty would be applied more consistently. By 1976, twenty-five states had adopted a two-stage, or *bifurcated,* procedure for capital cases. In the first stage, a jury determines the guilt or innocence of the defendant for a crime that has been determined by statute to be punishable by death. If the defendant is found guilty, the jury reconvenes in the second stage and considers all relevant evidence to decide whether the death sentence is, in fact, warranted.

In 1976, in *Gregg v. Georgia,*[60] the Supreme Court ruled in favor of Georgia's bifurcated process, holding that the state's legislative guidelines had removed the ability of a jury to "wantonly and freakishly impose the death penalty." The Court upheld similar procedures in Texas and Florida, establishing a "road map"

New York Daily News/Getty Images

Front page of the New York *Daily News*, April 23, 2013. Dzhokhar Tsarnaev was accused of bombing the Boston Marathon on April 15. Three died and 264 were injured, many badly. *Is revenge a legitimate reason for imposing the death penalty?*

57. *Texas v. Brown,* 460 U.S. 730 (1983); and *Horton v. California,* 496 U.S. 128 (1990).
58. *Herring v. United States,* 555 U.S. 135 (2009).
59. 408 U.S. 238 (1972).
60. 428 U.S. 153 (1976).

for all states to follow that would assure them protection from lawsuits based on Eighth Amendment grounds.

The Death Penalty Today.   Today, thirty-two states and the federal government have capital punishment laws based on the guidelines established by the *Gregg* case (see Figure 4–1 that follows). State governments are responsible for almost all executions in this country. At this time, there are about 3,100 prisoners on death row across the nation.

The number of executions per year reached a high in 1998 at ninety-eight and then began to fall. Some believe that the declining number of executions reflects the waning support among Americans for the imposition of the death penalty. In 1994, polls indicated that 80 percent of Americans supported the death penalty in cases involving murder. Recent polls, however, suggest that this number has dropped to about 60 percent.

The decline in the number of executions may be due in part to the Supreme Court's 2002 ruling in *Ring v. Arizona*.[61] The Court held that only juries, not judges, could impose the death penalty, thus invalidating the laws of five states that allowed judges to make this decision. The ruling meant that the death sentences of 168 death row inmates would have to be reconsidered by the relevant courts. The sentences of many of these inmates have been commuted to life in prison.

---

61. 536 U.S. 548 (2002).

Figure 4–1 ▸ **The States and the Death Penalty: Executions since 1976 and the Death Row Population**

Today, as shown in this figure, eighteen states have abolished the death penalty. The District of Columbia, Puerto Rico, Guam, and the U.S. Virgin Islands also have no death penalty. In Connecticut, Maryland, and New Mexico, abolition of the death penalty was not retroactive. Therefore, these states still have inmates on death row. *Why might some Americans have become more skeptical about the death penalty?*

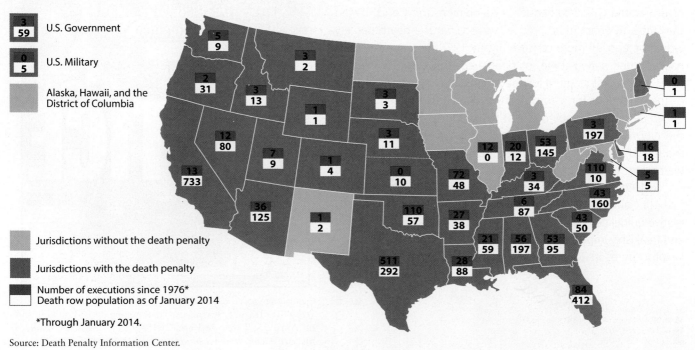

U.S. Government

U.S. Military

Alaska, Hawaii, and the District of Columbia

Jurisdictions without the death penalty

Jurisdictions with the death penalty

Number of executions since 1976*
Death row population as of January 2014

*Through January 2014.

Source: Death Penalty Information Center.

Time Limits for Death Row Appeals. In 1996, Congress passed the Anti-Terrorism and Effective Death Penalty Act. The law limits access to the federal courts for defendants convicted in state courts. It also imposes a severe time limit on death row appeals. Many are concerned that the shortened appeals process increases the possibility that innocent persons may be put to death. Recently, DNA testing has shown that some innocent people may have been convicted unjustly of murder. Since 1973, more than one hundred prisoners have been freed from death row after new evidence suggested that they were convicted wrongfully. On average, it takes about seven years to exonerate someone on death row. Currently, however, the time between conviction and execution has been shortened from an average of ten to twelve years to an average of six to eight years.

Methods of Execution. The most recent controversy concerning the death penalty is whether execution by injecting the condemned prisoner with lethal drugs is a cruel and unusual punishment. Lethal injection is currently used in almost all executions. Evidence exists that when performed incompetently, death by lethal injection can be extremely painful. Some death penalty opponents have claimed that the procedure is painful in so many instances that it constitutes cruel and unusual punishment. The United States Supreme Court took up this matter in a Kentucky case in 2007. In 2008, it ruled by a seven-to-two margin that Kentucky's method of execution by lethal injection was constitutional.[62]

---

62. *Baze v. Rees,* 553 U.S. 35 (2008).

did you know?

In eighteenth-century England, pocket picking and similar crimes were punishable by the death penalty.

CONNECT WITH YOUR CLASSMATES
MindTap™ for American Government

Access the Civil Liberties Forum: Discussion Board—Eighth Amendment Rights

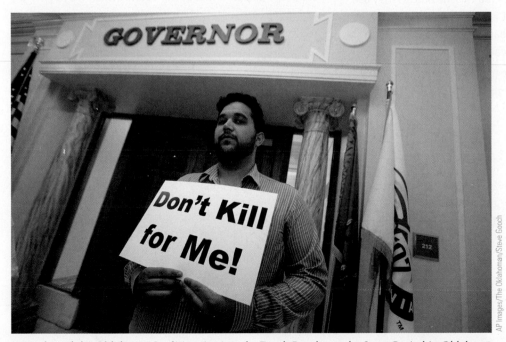

A member of the Oklahoma Coalition Against the Death Penalty at the State Capitol in Oklahoma City in 2014. Oklahoma has had serious difficulty obtaining the drugs used for execution by lethal injection. *Why might pharmaceutical companies be reluctant to supply such drugs?*

How You Can Make a Difference

How should you behave if you are stopped by police officers?

- Your civil liberties protect you from having to provide information other than your name and address.

- Normally, even if you have not been placed under arrest, the officers have the right to frisk you for weapons, and you must let them proceed. The officers cannot, however, check your person or your clothing further if, in their judgment, no weaponlike object is produced.

- The officers may search you only if they have a search warrant or probable cause to believe that a search will likely produce incriminating evidence. What if the officers do not have probable cause or a warrant? Physically resisting their attempt to search you can lead to disastrous results. It is best simply to refuse orally to give permission for the search, if possible in the presence of a witness.

- Being polite is better than acting out of anger and making the officers irritable. It is usually advisable to limit what you say to the officers. If you are arrested, it is best to keep quiet until you can speak with a lawyer.

- If you are in your car and are stopped by the police, the same fundamental rules apply. Always be ready to show your driver's license and car registration.

- You may be asked to get out of the car. The officers may use a flashlight to peer inside if it is too dark to see otherwise. None of this constitutes a search. A true search requires either a warrant or probable cause.

- No officer has the legal right to search your car simply to find out if you may have committed a crime. Police officers can conduct searches that are incident to lawful arrests, however.

- If you are in your home and a police officer with a search warrant appears, you can ask to examine the warrant before granting entry. A warrant that is correctly made out will state the place or persons to be searched, the object sought, and the date of the warrant (which should be no more than ten days old). It will also bear the signature of a judge or magistrate. If the warrant is in order, you need not make any statement.

- If you believe the warrant to be invalid, or if no warrant is produced, you should make it clear orally that you have not consented to the search, if possible in the presence of a witness. If the search later is proved to be unlawful, normally any evidence obtained cannot be used in court.

- Officers who attempt to enter your home without a search warrant can do so only if they are pursuing a suspected felon into the house. Rarely is it advisable to give permission for a warrantless search.

- You, as the resident, must be the one to give permission if any evidence obtained is to be considered legal. A landlord, manager, or head of a college dormitory cannot give legal permission. A roommate, however, can give permission for a search of his or her room, which may allow the police to search areas where you have belongings.

- If you are a guest in a place that is being legally searched, you may be legally searched as well. But unless you have been placed under arrest, you cannot be compelled to go to the police station or get into a squad car.

Key Terms

Chapter Summary

Learning Outcome 1 Originally, the Bill of Rights limited only the power of the national government, not that of the states. Gradually and selectively, however, the Supreme Court accepted the incorporation theory, under which no state can violate most provisions of the Bill of Rights.

Learning Outcome 2 The First Amendment protects against government interference with freedom of religion by requiring a separation of church and state (under the establishment clause) and by guaranteeing the free exercise of religion. Controversial issues that arise under the establishment clause include aid to church-related schools, school prayer, the teaching of evolution versus creationism, school vouchers, the placement of religious displays on public property, and discrimination against religious speech. The government can interfere with the free exercise of religion only when religious practices work against public policy or the public welfare.

Learning Outcome 3 The First Amendment protects against government interference with freedom of speech, which includes symbolic speech (expressive conduct). The Supreme Court has been especially critical of government actions that impose prior restraint on expression. Commercial speech (advertising) by businesses has received limited First Amendment protection. Restrictions on expression are permitted when the expression may incite imminent lawless action. Other speech that has not received First Amendment protection includes expression judged to be obscene or slanderous.

The First Amendment protects against government interference with the freedom of the press, which can be regarded as a special instance of freedom of speech. Speech by the press that does not receive protection includes libelous statements. Publication of news about a criminal trial may be restricted by a gag order in some circumstances.

Learning Outcome 4 Under the Ninth Amendment, rights not specifically mentioned in the Constitution are not necessarily denied to the people. Among these unspecified rights protected by the courts is a right to privacy, which has been inferred from the First, Third, Fourth, Fifth, and Ninth Amendments. Whether an individual's privacy rights include a right to an abortion or a "right to die" continues to provoke controversy.

Learning Outcome 5 Another major challenge concerns the extent to which Americans must forfeit civil liberties to control terrorism. Partially in response to alleged national security concerns, the civil rights of noncitizens in deportation cases are quite limited.

Learning Outcome 6 The Constitution includes protections for the rights of persons accused of crimes. Under the Fourth Amendment, no one may be subject to an unreasonable search or seizure or be arrested except on probable cause. Under the Fifth Amendment, an accused person has the right to remain silent. Under the Sixth Amendment, an accused person must be informed of the reason for his or her arrest. The accused also has the right to adequate counsel, even if he or she cannot afford an attorney, and the right to a prompt arraignment and a speedy and public trial before an impartial jury selected from a cross section of the community.

In *Miranda v. Arizona* (1966), the Supreme Court held that criminal suspects, before interrogation by law enforcement personnel, must be informed of the right to remain silent and the right to be represented by counsel.

The exclusionary rule forbids the admission in court of illegally obtained evidence. There is a "good faith exception" to the exclusionary rule: evidence need not be thrown out owing to, for example, a clerical error in a database. Under the Eighth Amendment, cruel and unusual punishment is prohibited. Whether the death penalty is cruel and unusual punishment continues to be debated.

Master the concept of Civil Liberties with MindTap™ *for American Government*

 REVIEW MindTap™ **for American Government**
Access Key Term Flashcards for Chapter 4.

 TEST YOURSELF MindTap™ **for American Government**
Take the Wrap It Up Quiz for Chapter 4.

STAY CURRENT MindTap™ **for American Government**
Access the KnowNow blog and customized RSS for updates on current events.

 STAY FOCUSED MindTap™ **for American Government**
Complete the Focus Activities for Civil Liberties.

Additional Resources

Today, the online world offers opportunities for Americans to easily access information about the nature of their civil liberties, how they originated, and how they may be threatened by various government actions.

Online Resources

- A key asset in learning about our civil liberties is the Web site of the American Civil Liberties Union (ACLU). Find it at aclu.org.
- Another organization of interest when studying civil liberties issues is the Civil Liberties Defense Center (CLDC), which you can follow at cldc .org.
- For a different take on civil liberties, check out the Web site of the Liberty Counsel at www.lc.org. This conservative group describes itself as "a nonprofit religious civil liberties education and legal defense organization established to preserve religious freedom."
- The largest group advocating robust Second Amendment rights is the National Rifle Organization (NRA). Its Web site is at nra.org.
- You can find current information on Internet privacy issues at the Electronic Privacy Information Center's Web site. Find it at epic.org.

Books

Bernstein, Nell. *Burning Down the House: The End of Juvenile Prison.* New York: The New Press, 2014. Bernstein, an award-winning journalist, argues in favor of shutting down the nation's juvenile prisons on the grounds that imprisoning children is brutal and counterproductive.

Harding, Luke. *The Snowden Files: The Inside Story of the World's Most Wanted Man.* New York: Vintage Paperback, 2014. Harding is a journalist at the *Guardian,* the British newspaper that printed Edward Snowden's revelations about the NSA. Harding's entertaining account reads like a spy novel.

Temple, Ralph J. *Life, Liberty and the Pursuit of Happiness.* Brooklyn, N.Y.: Akashic Books, 2014. Written in essay form, this work is the autobiography of one of the ACLU's top civil rights and civil liberties lawyers. Temple recounts his efforts representing the Rev. Dr. Martin Luther King, Jr., pediatrician Dr. Benjamin Spock, singer Joan Baez, and others.

Video

Assaulted: Civil Rights under Fire—Released in 2013, this film, narrated by the rapper Ice-T, presents arguments against gun control legislation. In an unusual twist, Ice-T describes how African Americans have been denied access to weapons throughout U.S. history.

War on Whistleblowers: Free Press and the National Security State—This 2013 documentary by Robert Greenwald exposes the threatening realities now faced by whistleblowers and the press when national security is involved. The film firmly defends the four whistleblowers it covers. Note, however, that many Americans who strongly support national security may view these individuals as criminals.

Quiz

Multiple Choice and Fill-Ins

Learning Outcome 1 Describe the Bill of Rights and how it came to be applied to state governments as well as the national government.

1. As originally intended, the Bill of Rights limited the powers of:
   a. only the state governments.
   b. both the national government and the state governments.
   c. only the national government.

2. Since 1925, the Supreme Court has gradually accepted the _____ _____ and has therefore extended the Bill of Rights to cover state governments under the Fourteenth Amendment's due process clause.

Learning Outcome 2 Explain how the First Amendment's establishment clause and free exercise clause guarantee our freedom of religion.

3. Religious displays on public property are:
   a. always acceptable.
   b. never acceptable.
   c. acceptable as part of a broader display that contains non-religious elements.

4. Our freedom of religion is based on two clauses in the First Amendment. These are the _____ ___ _____ _____ clauses.

Learning Outcome 3 Specify the limited circumstances in which the national and state governments may override the principles of free speech and freedom of the press.

5. If you utter a false statement that harms the good reputation of another, it is called slander and such expression is:
   a. always protected under the First Amendment.
   b. unprotected speech and a potential basis for a lawsuit.
   c. prosecuted as a felony in most states.

6. When governments attempt to ban certain types of clothing, gestures, and other forms of expressive conduct, they are attempting to ban _____ _____.

Learning Outcome 4 Provide the constitutional basis of the right to privacy, and explain how the principle has been applied to the abortion and right-to-die controversies.

7. The right to privacy:
   a. is explicitly guaranteed by the original text of the Constitution.
   b. is explicitly guaranteed by the Fifth Amendment to the Constitution.
   c. has been inferred from other rights by the Supreme Court.

8. The Supreme Court has ruled that the decision as to whether to permit the practice of assisted suicide must be left to the _____.

Learning Outcome 5 Cite examples of how recent security concerns have affected our civil liberties.

9. The Supreme Court has significantly limited the rights of non-citizens in cases that involve:
   a. deportation.
   b. employment.
   c. freedom of religion.

10. The most significant antiterrorism legislation is the _____ _____ _____.

Learning Outcome 6 Identify the constitutional rights of those who are accused of a crime, explain the *Miranda* and exclusionary rules, and describe the current status of the death penalty.

11. Illegally seized evidence is not admissible at trial because of the:
    a. exclusionary rule.
    b. *Miranda* rule.
    c. writ of *habeas corpus*.

12. Cruel and unusual punishment is prohibited by the _____ _____.

Essay Questions

1. The courts have never held that the provision of military chaplains by the armed forces is unconstitutional, despite the fact that chaplains are religious leaders who are employed by and under the authority of the U.S. government. What arguments might the courts use to defend the military chaplain system?

2. In a surprisingly large number of cases, arrested individuals do not choose to exercise their right to remain silent. Why might a person not exercise his or her *Miranda* rights?

Civil Rights

5

A six-year-old takes a picture of the Rev. Dr. Martin Luther King, Jr. Memorial while her three-year-old brother watches.
Photo by Mark Wilson/Getty Images

The six Learning Outcomes below are designed to help improve your understanding of this chapter. After reading this chapter, you should be able to:

- **Learning Outcome 1:** Summarize the historical experience of African Americans, state how the separate-but-equal doctrine was abolished, and describe the consequences of the civil rights movement.

- **Learning Outcome 2:** Define the different levels of scrutiny used by the Supreme Court in civil rights cases, and describe recent rulings on affirmative action.

- **Learning Outcome 3:** Discuss the history and current status of Latinos, American Indians, and Asian Americans.

- **Learning Outcome 4:** Contrast the goals of the women's suffrage movement with the goals of modern feminism.

- **Learning Outcome 5:** Summarize the recent revolution in the rights enjoyed by gay men and lesbians.

- **Learning Outcome 6:** Evaluate the rights and status of juvenile citizens.

WATCH & LEARN MindTap™ for American Government
Watch a brief "What Do You Know?" video summarizing Civil Rights.

134

What If...

We Deported Most Unauthorized Immigrants?

BACKGROUND

Today, about 11 million unauthorized immigrants live in the United States. Whether they are called illegal immigrants, illegal aliens, or undocumented workers, for many Americans they represent a problem. Most unauthorized immigrants come from Latin America, with more than 50 percent of them from Mexico alone. For years, Congress has made various attempts at resolving the illegal immigrant issue. Yet nothing has happened. Many proposals have involved programs to move illegal immigrants onto a path that ends in legal status or even citizenship. In contrast, states such as Alabama and Arizona have passed their own very strict immigration laws.

The hostility of many Republicans to illegal immigration has pushed Latino voters toward the Democrats. President Obama, however, has in practice taken a hard line on undocumented workers. He has deported 2 million persons, more than any other president. As a result of these deportations and the lack of jobs due to the recent Great Recession, the number of illegal immigrants has been stable for several years.

WHAT IF WE DEPORTED MOST UNAUTHORIZED IMMIGRANTS?

Suppose that the federal government expanded its current deportation effort into a program aimed at identifying and deporting every last unauthorized immigrant. Some say that this would be simply following current immigration laws to the letter. Others contend, however, that the United States would suffer from the repercussions of such a policy for years.

To implement such a policy, the government would have to hire hundreds of thousands of additional immigration officers. New prisons would be needed to hold those arrested while they awaited deportation. Expenditures would increase by many billions of dollars per year. Other government programs might have to be cut to fund the expanded deportation program.

SURPRISE—SUCH A PROGRAM MIGHT KILL JOBS

Deportation proponents argue that with fewer illegal immigrants, American citizens would have access to more jobs. Most economists disagree. The number of jobs in the economy is not fixed. There is no static "lump of labor" to be shared out. When the economy grows, the number of jobs rises. Legal and illegal immigrants alike add to net employment because they not only work, they also spend. They buy lodging, food, and entertainment. This spending adds to the demand for goods and services, which leads to more employment, not less. These workers also pay taxes. If they were deported they would no longer pay these taxes.

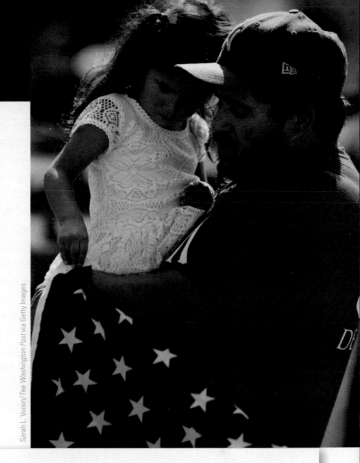

This three-year-old was born in the United States, but her parents are undocumented. *Do the parents still risk deportation?*

Major industries such as agriculture are dependent on undocumented workers. A team at the University of Alabama recently estimated that Alabama's stiff immigration law may cost the state almost $2.5 billion per year. A study at UCLA predicted that mass deportation would reduce California tax revenues by 8.5 percent and would shrink the state economy by tens of billions of dollars per year. If the projections for states such as Alabama and California were extended to the entire nation, the reduced economic activity resulting from mass deportation could trigger an economic recession.

THE EFFECT ON CIVIL RIGHTS

A successful mass deportation effort would require that police have the ability to "stop and ask." Everyone would have to produce proof of legal status. Questioning could not be limited to unauthorized immigrants. Latinos who are U.S. citizens would be singled out. Many non-Hispanic citizens might be caught in the net as well.

For Critical Analysis

1. If mass deportations were initiated, what might happen to the cost of farm produce?

2. Why has the immigration issue remained a political "hot potato" for decades?

135

did you know?

At the time of the American Revolution, African Americans made up 21 percent of the American population, compared to about 13 percent today.

■ **Learning Outcome 1:** Summarize the historical experience of African Americans, state how the separate-but-equal doctrine was abolished, and describe the consequences of the civil rights movement.

Civil Rights

Generally, all rights rooted in the Fourteenth Amendment's guarantee of equal protection under the law.

In spite of the words set forth in the Declaration of Independence that "all Men are created equal," the concept of equal treatment under the law was a distant dream in our nation's early years. In fact, the majority of the population had few rights at that time. As you learned in Chapter 2, the framers of the Constitution permitted slavery to continue. Slaves thus were excluded from the political process. Women also were excluded for the most part, as were Native Americans, African Americans who were not slaves, and even white men who did not own property.

Today, in contrast, we have numerous civil rights. Equality is at the heart of the concept of civil rights. Generally, the term **civil rights** refers to the rights of all Americans to equal protection under the law, as provided for by the Fourteenth Amendment to the Constitution. Although the terms *civil rights* and *civil liberties* are sometimes used interchangeably, scholars make a distinction between the two. As discussed in Chapter 4, civil liberties are basically limitations on government. They specify what the government *cannot* do. Civil rights, in contrast, specify what the government *must* do to ensure equal protection and freedom from discrimination.

The history of civil rights in America is the story of the struggle of various groups to be free from discriminatory treatment. In this chapter, we look at two movements that had significant consequences for civil rights in America: the civil rights movement of the 1950s and 1960s and the women's movement, which began in the mid-1800s and continues today. Each of these movements resulted in legislation that secured important basic rights for all Americans—the right to vote and the right to equal protection under the laws.

As you read in the chapter-opening *What If . . .* feature, most of the 11 million unauthorized immigrants in the United States come from Latin America. In this chapter, we look at some of the issues facing Latino Americans, and also American Indians and Asian Americans. In addition, other groups have suffered—and continue to suffer—from discrimination of one kind or another. These include Muslim Americans, persons with disabilities, and older Americans. The fact that any group is not singled out for special attention in the following pages should not be construed to mean that its struggle for equality is any less significant than the struggles of those groups that we do discuss.

The African American Experience and the Civil Rights Movement

Before 1863, the Constitution protected slavery and made equality impossible in the sense in which we use the word today. The system of slavery, however, did not survive the American Civil War (1861–1865).

Ending Servitude

With the emancipation of the slaves by President Abraham Lincoln's Emancipation Proclamation in 1863 and the passage of the Thirteenth, Fourteenth, and Fifteenth Amendments during the Reconstruction period (1865–1877) following the Civil War, constitutional inequality was ended.

Constitutional Amendments. The Thirteenth Amendment (1865) states that neither slavery nor involuntary servitude shall exist within the United States. The Fourteenth Amendment (1868) tells us that *all* persons born or naturalized in the United States are citizens of the United States. It states, furthermore, that "[n]o State shall make or enforce any law which shall abridge the privileges or immunities of citizens of the United States;

nor shall any State deprive any person of life, liberty, or property, without due process of law; nor deny to any person within its jurisdiction the equal protection of the laws." Note the use of the terms *citizen* and *person* in this amendment. *Citizens* have political rights, such as the right to vote and run for political office. Citizens also have certain privileges or immunities (see Chapter 3). All *persons,* however, including noncitizen immigrants, have a right to due process of law and equal protection under the law. We discuss the Fourteenth Amendment in greater detail later in this chapter.

Finally, the Fifteenth Amendment (1870) reads as follows: "The right of citizens of the United States to vote shall not be denied or abridged by the United States or by any State on account of race, color, or previous condition of servitude."

The Civil Rights Acts of 1865 to 1875. From 1865 to 1875, Congress passed a series of civil rights acts to enforce the Thirteenth, Fourteenth, and Fifteenth Amendments. The Civil Rights Act of 1866 implemented the extension of citizenship to anyone born in the United States and gave African Americans full equality before the law. The Enforcement Act of 1870 set out specific criminal penalties for interfering with the right to vote as protected by the Fifteenth Amendment and by the Civil Rights Act of 1866.

First Lady Michelle Obama attends the unveiling of a bust of African American leader Sojourner Truth in the U.S. Capitol Building.

Equally important was the Civil Rights Act of 1872, known as the Anti–Ku Klux Klan Act. This act made it a federal crime for anyone to use law or custom to deprive an individual of rights, privileges, and immunities secured by the Constitution or by any federal law. The Second Civil Rights Act, passed in 1875, declared that everyone is entitled to full and equal enjoyment of public accommodations, theaters, and other places of public amusement, and it imposed penalties on violators.

did you know?

The original Constitution failed to describe the status of *citizen* or how this status could be acquired.

The Ineffectiveness of the Early Civil Rights Laws

The Reconstruction statutes, or civil rights acts, ultimately did little to secure equality for African Americans. Both the *Civil Rights Cases* and the case of *Plessy v. Ferguson* (discussed next) effectively nullified these acts. Additionally, various barriers were erected that prevented African Americans from exercising their right to vote.

**CONNECT
WITH YOUR CLASSMATES**
MindTap™ for American Government

Access the Civil Rights Forum: Discussion Board—Minority Rights Protection

The *Civil Rights Cases.* The United States Supreme Court invalidated the 1875 Second Civil Rights Act when it held, in the *Civil Rights Cases*[1] of 1883, that the enforcement clause of the Fourteenth Amendment (which states that "[n]o State shall make or enforce any law which shall abridge the privileges or immunities of citizens") was limited to correcting official actions by states. Thus, the discriminatory acts of *private* citizens were not illegal. ("Individual invasion of individual rights is not the subject matter of the Amendment.") The 1883 Supreme Court decision met with widespread approval by whites throughout most of the United States.

Twenty years after the Civil War, the white majority was all too willing to forget about the Civil War amendments to the U.S. Constitution and the civil rights legislation of the 1860s and 1870s. The other civil rights laws that the Court did not specifically invalidate became dead letters in the statute books, although they were never officially repealed by Congress.

---

1.   109 U.S. 3 (1883).

Separate-but-Equal Doctrine

The doctrine holding that separate-but-equal facilities do not violate the equal protection clause of the Fourteenth Amendment to the U.S. Constitution.

White Primary

A state primary election that restricted voting to whites only. It was outlawed by the Supreme Court in 1944.

Grandfather Clause

A device used by southern states to disenfranchise African Americans. It restricted voting to those whose grandfathers had voted before 1867.

Poll Tax

A special tax that had to be paid as a qualification for voting. In 1964, the Twenty-fourth Amendment to the Constitution outlawed the poll tax in national elections, and in 1966 the Supreme Court declared it unconstitutional in state elections as well.

Literacy Test

A test administered as a precondition for voting, often used to prevent African Americans from exercising their right to vote.

Plessy v. Ferguson: **Separate but Equal.** A key decision during this period concerned Homer Plessy, a Louisiana resident who was one-eighth African American. In 1892, he boarded a train in New Orleans. The conductor made him leave the car, which was restricted to whites, and directed him to a car for nonwhites. At that time, Louisiana had a statute providing for separate railway cars for whites and African Americans.

Plessy went to court, claiming that such a statute was contrary to the Fourteenth Amendment's equal protection clause. In 1896, the United States Supreme Court rejected Plessy's contention in *Plessy v. Ferguson*.[2] The Court concluded that the Fourteenth Amendment "could not have been intended to abolish distinctions based upon color, or to enforce social . . . equality." The Court stated that segregation alone did not violate the Constitution: "Laws permitting, and even requiring, their separation in places where they are liable to be brought into contact do not necessarily imply the inferiority of either race to the other." So was born the **separate-but-equal doctrine.**

Plessy v. Ferguson became the judicial cornerstone of racial discrimination throughout the United States. Even though *Plessy* upheld segregated facilities in railway cars only, it was assumed that the Supreme Court was upholding segregation everywhere. The result was a system of racial segregation, particularly in the South—supported by state and local "Jim Crow" laws. (Jim Crow was an insulting term for African Americans derived from a song-and-dance show.) These laws required separate drinking fountains; separate seats in theaters, restaurants, and hotels; separate public toilets; and separate waiting rooms for the two races. "Separate" was indeed the rule, but "equal" was never enforced, nor was it a reality.

Voting Barriers. The brief voting enfranchisement of African Americans ended after 1877, when the federal troops that occupied the South during the Reconstruction era were withdrawn. White supremacist politicians regained control of state governments and, using everything except race as a formal criterion, passed laws that effectively deprived African Americans of the right to vote. By using the ruse that political parties were private entities, the Democratic Party managed to keep black voters from its primaries. The **white primary** was upheld by the Supreme Court until 1944 when the Court ruled it a violation of the Fifteenth Amendment.[3]

Another barrier to African American voting was the **grandfather clause,** which restricted voting to those who could prove that their grandfathers had voted before 1867. **Poll taxes** required the payment of a fee to vote. Thus, poor African Americans—as well as poor whites—who could not afford to pay the tax were excluded from voting. Not until the Twenty-fourth Amendment to the Constitution was ratified in 1964 was the poll tax eliminated as a precondition to voting. **Literacy tests** were also used to deny the vote to African Americans. Such tests asked potential voters to read, recite, or interpret complicated texts, such as a section of the state constitution, to the satisfaction of local registrars—who were, of course, rarely satisfied with the responses of African Americans.

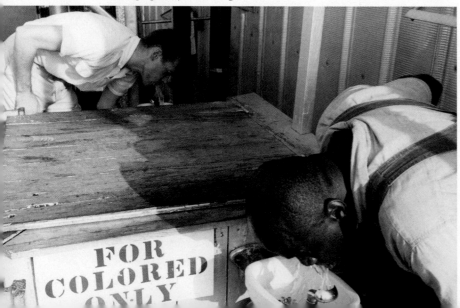

Segregated drinking fountains were common in southern states in the late 1800s and during the first half of the twentieth century. *What landmark Supreme Court case made such segregated facilities legal?*

© Bettmann/Corbis

2. 163 U.S. 537 (1896).
3. *Smith v. Allwright*, 321 U.S. 649 (1944).

Extralegal Methods of Enforcing White Supremacy.

The second-class status of African Americans was also a matter of social custom, especially in the South. In their interactions with southern whites, African Americans were expected to observe an informal but detailed code of behavior that confirmed their inferiority. The code was backed up by the common practice of *lynching*—mob action to murder an accused individual, usually by hanging and sometimes accompanied by torture. Of course, lynching was illegal, but southern authorities rarely prosecuted these cases, and white juries would not convict.

The End of the Separate-but-Equal Doctrine

As early as the 1930s, several court rulings began to chip away at the separate-but-equal doctrine. The United States Supreme Court did not explicitly overturn *Plessy v. Ferguson* until 1954, however, when it issued one of the most famous judicial decisions in U.S. history.

Alabama governor George Wallace speaks in the doorway of a campus building at the University of Alabama in Tuscaloosa in 1963. He is refusing to allow African American students entry into the school despite a federal court order. *Why were Southern leaders so opposed to integration?*

In 1951, Oliver Brown decided that his eight-year-old daughter, Linda Carol Brown, should not have to go to an all-nonwhite elementary school twenty-one blocks from her home, when there was a white school only seven blocks away. The National Association for the Advancement of Colored People (NAACP), formed in 1909, decided to support Oliver Brown.[4] The outcome would have a monumental impact on American society.

Brown v. Board of Education of Topeka.

The 1954 unanimous decision of the United States Supreme Court in *Brown v. Board of Education of Topeka*[5] established that the segregation of races in the public schools violates the equal protection clause of the Fourteenth Amendment. Chief Justice Earl Warren said that separation implied inferiority, whereas the majority opinion in *Plessy v. Ferguson* had said the opposite.

The following year, in *Brown v. Board of Education*[6] (sometimes called the second *Brown* decision), the Court declared that the lower courts needed to ensure that African Americans would be admitted to schools on a nondiscriminatory basis "with all deliberate speed."

did you know?

The NAACP's lawyer in *Brown v. Board of Education* was Thurgood Marshall. In 1967, President Lyndon B. Johnson named Marshall to be the first black member of the United States Supreme Court.

Reactions to School Integration.

The white South did not let the Supreme Court ruling go unchallenged. Governor Orval Faubus of Arkansas used the state's National Guard to block the integration of Central High School in Little Rock in September 1957. Finally, President Dwight Eisenhower had to federalize the Arkansas National Guard and send in the Army's 101st Airborne Division to quell the violence. Central High became integrated.

Universities in the South remained segregated. When James Meredith, an African American student, attempted to enroll at the University of Mississippi in Oxford in 1962, violence flared there, as it had in Little Rock. The white riot at Oxford was so intense that President John F. Kennedy was forced to send in 30,000 U.S. combat troops, a larger force than the one then stationed in Korea. Ultimately, peace was restored, and Meredith began attending classes.

---

4. *NAACP* is pronounced "N-double A-C-P."
5. 347 U.S. 483 (1954).
6. 349 U.S. 294 (1955).

De Jure Segregation
Racial segregation that occurs because of laws or administrative decisions by public agencies.

De Facto Segregation
Racial segregation that occurs because of past social and economic conditions and residential racial patterns.

Civil Disobedience
A nonviolent, public refusal to obey allegedly unjust laws.

De Jure and De Facto Segregation

The kind of segregation faced by Linda Carol Brown and James Meredith is called **de jure segregation,** because it is the result of discriminatory laws or government actions. (*De jure* is Latin for "by law.") A second kind of public school segregation was common in many northern communities—**de facto segregation.** This term refers to segregation that is not due to an explicit law but results from other causes, such as residential patterns. Neighborhoods inhabited almost entirely by African Americans naturally led to *de facto* segregation of the public schools.

Discrimination was still involved, however. In many communities, landlords would only rent to African Americans in specific districts, and realtors would not allow them to view houses for sale outside of these zones. In other words, nongovernmental discrimination confined African Americans to all-black districts, which became known as *ghettos*.[7]

One method used by federal courts in the 1970s and 1980s to address both *de jure* and *de facto* segregation in the public schools was to bus students from black neighborhoods into white ones, and vice versa. Busing proved to be enormously unpopular. In the mid-1970s, about three-fourth of all whites opposed the policy, as did almost half of all African Americans. By the 1990s, federal courts were backing away from the practice. The desegregation of U.S. public schools peaked in 1988, and since then the schools have grown more segregated. Indeed, today, school admissions policies that favor minority applicants in an attempt to reduce *de facto* segregation may end up being challenged on equal protection grounds. (For a further discussion of this issue, see the section on affirmative action later in this chapter.)

The Civil Rights Movement

The *Brown* decisions applied only to public schools. Not much else in the structure of existing segregation was affected. In December 1955, an African American woman, Rosa Parks, boarded a public bus in Montgomery, Alabama. When the bus became crowded, Parks was asked to move to the rear of the bus, the "colored" section. She refused and was arrested. But that was not the end of the matter. For an entire year, African Americans boycotted the Montgomery bus line. The protest was headed by a twenty-seven-year-old Baptist minister, Dr. Martin Luther King, Jr. In 1956, a federal district court issued an injunction prohibiting the segregation of buses in Montgomery. The era of civil rights protests had begun.

In 1955, Rosa Parks was arrested for refusing to give up her seat on a Montgomery, Alabama, bus and move to the colored section. *What happened after her arrest?*

AP Photo/Montgomery County Sheriff's Office

King's Philosophy of Nonviolence. In the following year, 1957, King formed the Southern Christian Leadership Conference (SCLC). King advocated nonviolent **civil disobedience** as a means to achieve racial justice. The SCLC used tactics such as demonstrations and marches, as well as nonviolent, public disobedience of unjust laws. King's followers successfully used these methods to gain wider public acceptance of their cause.

Nonviolent Demonstrations. For the next decade, African Americans and sympathetic whites engaged in sit-ins, freedom rides, and freedom marches. In the beginning, such demonstrations were often met with violence, and the contrasting image

7. *Ghetto* was originally the name of a district in Venice, Italy, in which Venetian Jews were required to live.

of nonviolent African Americans and violent, hostile whites created strong public support for the civil rights movement. When African Americans in Greensboro, North Carolina, were refused service at a Woolworth's lunch counter, they organized a sit-in that was aided day after day by other African Americans and by sympathetic whites. Within six months of the first sit-in at the Greensboro Woolworth's, hundreds of lunch counters throughout the South were serving African Americans. The sit-in technique also was successfully used to integrate interstate buses and their terminals, as well as railroads engaged in interstate transportation.

The March on Washington. In August 1963, African American leaders A. Philip Randolph and Bayard Rustin organized the massive March on Washington for Jobs and Freedom. Before nearly a quarter-million white and African American spectators and millions watching on television, Dr. Martin Luther King, Jr., told the world: "I have a dream that my four little children will one day live in a nation where they will not be judged by the color of their skin but by the content of their character."

Another Approach—Black Power. Not all African Americans agreed with King's philosophy of nonviolence. Black Muslims and other African American separatists advocated a more militant stance and argued that desegregation should not result in cultural assimilation. During the 1950s and 1960s, when King was spearheading nonviolent protests and demonstrations to achieve civil rights for African Americans, black power leaders such as Malcolm X insisted that African Americans should "fight back" instead of turning the other cheek. Indeed, some would argue that without the fear generated by black militants, a "moderate" such as King would not have garnered such widespread support from white America.

Modern Civil Rights Legislation

Attacks on demonstrators using police dogs, cattle prods, high-pressure water hoses, beatings, and bombings—plus the March on Washington—all led to an environment in which Congress felt compelled to act on behalf of African Americans. The second era of civil rights acts, sometimes referred to as the second Reconstruction period, was under way.

The Civil Rights Act of 1964. The Civil Rights Act of 1964, the most far-reaching bill on civil rights in modern times, banned discrimination on the basis of race, color, religion, gender, or national origin. The major provisions of the act were as follows:

1. It outlawed arbitrary discrimination in voter registration.
2. It barred discrimination in public accommodations, such as hotels and restaurants, which have operations that affect interstate commerce.
3. It authorized the federal government to sue to desegregate public schools and facilities.
4. It expanded the power of the Civil Rights Commission, which had been created in 1957, and extended its life.
5. It provided for the withholding of federal funds from programs administered in a discriminatory manner.
6. It established the right to equality of opportunity in employment.

Title VII of the Civil Rights Act of 1964 is the cornerstone of employment-discrimination law. It prohibits discrimination in employment based on race, color, religion, gender, or national origin. Under Title VII, executive orders were issued that banned employment discrimination by

In August 1963, a quarter-million whites and blacks descended on Washington, D.C., for a massive March for Jobs and Freedom. *Who was the most important speaker at that event?*

AP Photo

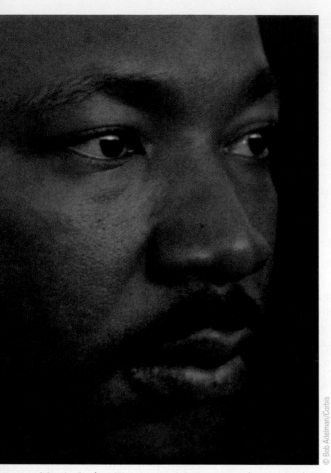

Martin Luther King in a quiet moment as he prepared to speak in Montgomery, Alabama. *What type of resistance against segregation did King advocate?*

firms that received any federal funding. The 1964 Civil Rights Act created the Equal Employment Opportunity Commission (EEOC) to administer Title VII. It was not until 1972, however, that Congress gave the EEOC the right to sue employers, unions, and employment agencies. Litigation then became an important agency activity.

The Voting Rights Act of 1965. As late as 1960, only 29 percent of African Americans of voting age were registered in the southern states, in stark contrast to 61 percent of whites. The Voting Rights Act of 1965 addressed this issue. The act had two major provisions. The first outlawed discriminatory voter-registration tests. The second authorized federal registration of voters and federally administered voting procedures in any political subdivision or state that discriminated electorally against a particular group. The act also provided that certain political subdivisions could not change their voting procedures and election laws without federal approval—a provision revoked by the Supreme Court in 2013.

The act targeted counties, mostly in the South, in which fewer than 50 percent of the eligible population were registered to vote. Federal voter registrars were sent to those areas to register African Americans who had been kept from voting by local registrars. Within one week after the act was passed, forty-five federal examiners were sent to the South. A massive voter-registration drive covered the country.

Urban Riots. Even as the civil rights movement was experiencing its greatest victories, a series of riots swept through African American inner-city neighborhoods. The riots were primarily civil insurrections, although these disorders were accompanied by large-scale looting of stores. Inhabitants of the affected neighborhoods attributed the riots to racial discrimination. The riots dissipated much of the goodwill toward the civil rights movement that had been built up earlier in the decade among northern whites. Together with widespread student demonstrations against the Vietnam War (1965–1975), the riots pushed many Americans toward conservatism.

The Civil Rights Act of 1968 and Other Housing Reform Legislation. Martin Luther King, Jr., was assassinated on April 4, 1968. Despite King's message of peace, his death was followed by the most widespread rioting to date. Nine days after King's death, President Lyndon Johnson signed the Civil Rights Act of 1968, which banned discrimination in most housing and provided penalties for those attempting to interfere with individual civil rights (giving protection to civil rights workers, among others). Subsequent legislation added enforcement provisions to the federal government's rules against discriminatory mortgage-lending practices.

Consequences of Civil Rights Legislation

As a result of the Voting Rights Act of 1965 and its amendments, and the large-scale voter-registration drives in the South, the number of African Americans registered to vote climbed dramatically. By 1980, 56 percent of African Americans of voting age in the South were registered. In recent national elections, turnout by African American voters has come very close to the white turnout. In 2008, with an African American on the presidential ballot, African American turnout exceeded that of whites for the first time in history.[8]

---

8. One widely reported study claimed that African American turnout did not quite match that of whites, but this conclusion was based on an overestimate of the number of African Americans eligible to vote.

Political Participation by African Americans. Today, there are more than ten thousand African American elected officials in the United States. The movement of African American citizens into high elected office has been sure, if exceedingly slow. Notably, recent polling data show that most Americans do not consider race a significant factor in choosing a president. In 1958, when a Gallup poll first asked whether respondents would be willing to vote for an African American as president, only 38 percent of the public said yes. By 2008, this number had reached 94 percent. This high figure may have been attained, at least in part, because of the emergence of African Americans of presidential caliber. Of course, Barack Obama, first elected president in 2008 on the Democratic ticket, is African American. Earlier, two Republican African Americans were also mentioned as presidential possibilities: Colin Powell, formerly chair of the Joint Chiefs of Staff and later secretary of state under President George W. Bush; and Condoleezza Rice, who succeeded Powell at the State Department.

Differing Perspectives. Even today, however, race consciousness continues to divide African Americans and white Americans. Whether we are talking about media stereotyping, racial profiling, or academic achievement, the black experience is different from the white one. As a result, African Americans often view the nation and many specific issues differently than their white counterparts do. In survey after survey, when blacks are asked whether they have achieved racial equality, few believe that they have. In contrast, whites are much more likely than blacks to believe that racial equality has been achieved.

One of the most troubling contrasts between the races is their differing experiences with the criminal justice system. African Americans, especially men, are far more likely to be arrested and imprisoned than whites. There is widespread disagreement about the reasons for this phenomenon, as you will see in this chapter's *Which Side Are You On?* feature that follows.

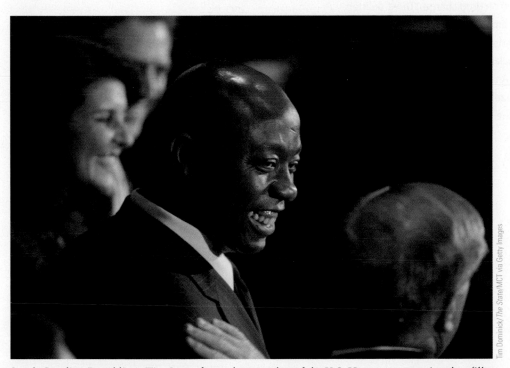

South Carolina Republican Tim Scott, formerly a member of the U.S. House, was appointed to fill a vacant U.S. Senate seat in December 2012. *Why are most African American members of Congress Democrats?*

Which Side Are You On?

Is the Criminal Justice System Discriminatory?

Since 1980, the rate of drug arrests of African Americans in forty large American cities has increased 250 percent, compared to 75 percent among whites. African Americans make up about 13 percent of the U.S. population. Nonetheless, they represent more than 50 percent of sentenced drug offenders. Nationwide, 43 percent of all inmates in state and federal prisons are black. In New York City, the most recent data show that police have made about 575,000 pedestrian stops in a year, of which 55 percent have targeted African Americans. Yet black citizens are only 23 percent of that city's population. Not surprisingly, many believe that the criminal justice system is unfair to African Americans, and in fact, New York's current mayor Bill de Blasio has taken steps to curb "stop-and-frisk" practices that target African Americans.

The System Is Unfair

Those who believe that the system is discriminatory point to a number of statistics. About the same percentage of black and white poll respondents admit to using illegal drugs—between 8.5 and 9 percent. Yet African Americans are three times more likely than whites to be arrested on drug charges. Three-quarters of those sentenced for drug crimes are African American. More than four out of five drug arrests are for simple possession of a banned substance—so the racial disparity in arrests cannot be due to a large class of African American drug dealers. Under former New York City mayor Michael Bloomberg, the police department dramatically increased the number of minor drug arrests.

Such targeting tactics result in blacks being arrested for drug possession at seven times the rate of whites. How can that be fair?

But Racism Is Not the Explanation

Some observers, however, argue that the disparities just described are legitimate. Certainly, the black-versus-white statistics are clear. But to blame racism is misguided. Police personnel go where the easy "collars" are. As a Chicago police chief admitted, "There is as much cocaine in the stock exchange as there is in the black community. But those guys are harder to catch. Those deals are done in office buildings [and] in someone's home. But the guy standing on the corner, he has almost got a sign on his back. These guys are just arrestable." District attorneys also know they can get higher conviction rates because residents of low-income communities usually cannot hire expensive legal help. Further, some experts contend that trading drugs openly on the streets leads to other crimes, including crimes of violence. This is not true of drug sales that take place in homes and offices. Low-income neighborhoods benefit when open drug markets are shut down. Indeed, homicide rates are now falling in such areas.

For Critical Analysis

What effect would legalizing or decriminalizing drugs have on the relationship between minority group members and the criminal justice system?

■ **Learning Outcome 2:**
Define the different levels of scrutiny used by the Supreme Court in civil rights cases, and describe recent rulings on affirmative action.

Civil Rights and the Courts

As you have just learned, our modern understanding of civil rights developed over a period of many years, and decisions by the United States Supreme Court were crucial in establishing that understanding. Over time, the Supreme Court developed a series of standards to use when deciding cases of alleged discrimination: strict scrutiny, intermediate scrutiny, and rational basis review.

The Fourteenth Amendment

The Fourteenth Amendment to the U.S. Constitution, adopted in 1869 following the Civil War, is the main constitutional basis for civil rights legislation and court decisions. In Chapter 4, we discussed the due process clause of the Fourteenth Amendment:

> *No State shall . . . deprive any person of life, liberty, or property, without due process of law . . . .*

This language mirrors that of the Fifth Amendment, which binds the federal government:

> *No person shall . . . be deprived of life, liberty, or property, without due process of law . . . .*

The due process clause was crucial to extending the civil liberties contained in the Bill of Rights to cover the actions of the individual states. The courts have made use of this clause in civil rights cases as well. As a guarantee of civil rights, however, the next clause in the Fourteenth Amendment is at least as important:

> *. . . nor deny to any person within its jurisdiction the equal protection of the laws.*

The principal effect of *Plessy v. Ferguson,* described earlier, was to make the equal protection clause almost a dead letter in cases involving discrimination against individuals. Today, in contrast, the equal protection clause serves as the foundation of a sizable body of law.

Strict Scrutiny and Suspect Classifications. Federal courts use three standards when engaging in judicial review of laws or executive actions. The most exacting of these, **strict scrutiny,** is employed when fundamental rights are at stake, such as those guaranteed by the Bill of Rights. Strict scrutiny also comes into play when laws are based on a **suspect classification.** The original suspect class was race. As these terms suggest, the courts are suspicious of, and will strictly scrutinize, any attempt by a government body to treat persons of different races in different ways. A recent study suggested that 70 percent of all legal challenges based on strict scrutiny have succeeded in striking down the law or action in question. Religion and national origin are also suspect classifications. To be acceptable under the strict scrutiny standard, a law must pass three tests:

- It must be justified by a *compelling government interest.* National security is an example of such an interest.
- It must be *narrowly tailored* to meet that interest.
- It must be the *least restrictive means* of accomplishing the goal in question. In other words, restrictions on rights such as freedom of speech must not exceed what is absolutely necessary.

The Supreme Court introduced the standard of strict scrutiny in 1944 in *Korematsu v. United States.*[9] This was the case in which the Court ruled that the federal government had the right to force West Coast Japanese Americans into detention camps purely on the basis of race. National security was cited as the compelling government interest. The irony could hardly be greater—the Court established the standard of strict scrutiny in the course of approving one of the greatest acts of racial discrimination in American history. In later years, however, the Court

---

Strict Scrutiny

A judicial standard for assessing the constitutionality of a law or government action when the law or action threatens to interfere with a fundamental right or potentially discriminates against members of a suspect classification.

Suspect Classification

A classification, such as race, religion, or national origin, that triggers strict scrutiny by the courts when a law or government action potentially discriminates against members of the class.

COMPARE WITH YOUR PEERS
MindTap˙ for American Government

Access the Civil Rights Forum: Polling Activity—Civil Rights Protection

---

Why Should You Care about...

Civil Rights?

Why should you, as an individual, care about civil rights? Some people may think that discrimination is a problem only for members of racial or ethnic minorities. Actually, almost everyone can be affected. Consider that in some instances, white men have actually experienced "reverse discrimination"—and have obtained redress for it. Also, discrimination against women is common, and women constitute half the population. Even if you are male, you probably have female friends or relatives whose well-being is of interest to you.

---

9. 323 U.S. 214 (1944). Fred Korematsu's conviction was overturned in 1983. In 1988, the U.S. Congress apologized for the internments and granted $20,000 in compensation to each surviving prisoner.

Intermediate Scrutiny
The standard used by the
courts to determine whether
a law or government action
improperly discriminates
against women. Also known
as *exacting scrutiny*.

Rational Basis Review
The standard used by the
courts to determine the
constitutionality of a law
or government action if
neither strict scrutiny nor
intermediate scrutiny applies.

Affirmative Action
A policy in educational
admissions and job hiring
that gives special attention
or compensatory treatment to
traditionally disadvantaged
groups in an effort to
overcome present effects of
past discrimination.

would use the standard as a major tool in outlawing racial discrimination. *Brown v. Board of Education* was only one of many rulings that employed strict scrutiny on behalf of civil rights.

Intermediate, or Exacting, Scrutiny. As you will learn in a subsequent section, the women's movement that arose in the 1960s led to a large number of suits claiming that various laws, policies, and government actions improperly discriminated against women. The courts were often sympathetic to such arguments. Still, the Supreme Court was reluctant to define sex or gender as a suspect classification equivalent to race. Instead of extending the standard of strict scrutiny to discrimination against women, the Court established a new standard—**intermediate scrutiny**—in a 1976 ruling. In that case, the Court ruled that Oklahoma could not ban men from drinking low-alcohol beer until they turned twenty-one, while women were allowed to drink this type of beer at the age of nineteen.[10] In addition to gender, illegitimacy is also a classification subject to intermediate scrutiny.

To pass the intermediate scrutiny test, a law or government action "must further an important government interest by means that are substantially related to that interest." This standard is easier to meet than the three-part standard established for strict scrutiny. In later years, the Court tightened the test by requiring an "exceedingly persuasive justification" for gender-based discrimination.[11] The Court has come to also use the term *exacting scrutiny* when referring to the standard.

Rational Basis Review. In cases where neither strict scrutiny nor intermediate scrutiny are appropriate, the courts use **rational basis review** as a standard. This test requires that an action or law be "rationally related" to a "legitimate government interest." The legitimate interest does not have to be the interest cited by the government. If the courts can imagine a possible legitimate interest, the law stands. Rational basis review does not involve assessing the usefulness of laws. As Justice Thurgood Marshall observed on several occasions, "The Constitution does not prohibit legislatures from enacting stupid laws."[12]

If a court can find no legitimate interest at all, however, a law or action can fail even this test. For example, as you will learn later in this chapter, courts have found that certain laws penalizing gay men and lesbians—and even bans on same-sex marriage—fail the rational basis test. Rational basis review was introduced in a 1938 decision in which the Court affirmed the right of the federal government to ban a dairy product known as *filled milk* from interstate commerce.[13]

The Courts Address Affirmative Action

As noted earlier in this chapter, the Civil Rights Act of 1964 prohibited discrimination against any person on the basis of race, color, national origin, religion, or gender. The act also established the right to equal opportunity in employment. A basic problem remained, however: minority groups and women, because of past discrimination, often lacked the education and skills to compete effectively in the marketplace. In 1965, the federal government attempted to remedy this problem by implementing the concept of affirmative action. **Affirmative action** policies attempt to "level the playing field" by giving special

---

10. *Craig v. Boren*, 429 U.S. 190 (1976).
11. *Mississippi University for Women v. Hogan*, 458 U.S. 718 (1982).
12. As quoted in Justice Stevens' concurrence to *New York State Board of Elections v. Lopez Torres*, 552 U.S. 196 (2008).
13. *United States v. Carolene Products Company*, 304 U.S. 144 (1938). *Filled milk* is milk in which the dairy fat has been replaced by other fats, typically vegetable oils. This product was frequently banned in the 1920s and 1930s. It is legal today, however, and it is widely used in ice cream and baked goods.

preferences in educational admissions and employment decisions to groups that have been discriminated against in the past.

Implementing Affirmative Action. In 1965, President Lyndon Johnson issued Executive Order 11246, which mandated affirmative action policies to remedy the effects of past discrimination. All government agencies, including those of state and local governments, were required to implement such policies. Additionally, affirmative action requirements were imposed on companies that sell goods or services to the federal government and on institutions that receive federal funds, such as universities. Affirmative action policies were also required whenever an employer had been ordered to develop such a plan by a court or by the Equal Employment Opportunity Commission because of evidence of past discrimination. Finally, labor unions that had been found to discriminate against women or minorities in the past were required to establish and follow affirmative action plans.

Affirmative action programs have been controversial because they allegedly result in discrimination against "majority" groups, such as white males (or discrimination against other minority groups that may not be given preferential treatment under a particular affirmative action program). At issue in the current debate over affirmative action programs is whether such programs, because of their discriminatory nature, violate the equal protection clause of the Fourteenth Amendment to the Constitution.

The *Bakke* Case. The first United States Supreme Court case addressing the constitutionality of affirmative action examined a program implemented by the University of California at Davis. Allan Bakke, a white student who had been turned down for medical school at the Davis campus, discovered that his academic record was better than those of some of the minority applicants who had been admitted to the program. He sued the University of California regents, alleging **reverse discrimination.** The UC Davis Medical School had held sixteen places out of one hundred for educationally "disadvantaged students" each year, and the administrators at that campus admitted to using race as a criterion for admission for those particular slots.

In 1978, the Supreme Court handed down its decision in *Regents of the University of California v. Bakke.*[14] The Court did not rule against affirmative action programs. Rather, it held that Bakke must be admitted to the medical school because its admissions policy had used race as the sole criterion for the sixteen "minority" positions. Justice Lewis Powell, speaking for the Court, indicated that while race can be considered "as a factor" among others in admissions (and presumably hiring) decisions, race cannot be the sole factor. So affirmative action programs, but not quota systems, were upheld as constitutional.

Additional Limits on Affirmative Action. A number of cases decided during the 1980s and 1990s placed further limits on affirmative action programs. In a landmark decision in 1995, *Adarand Constructors, Inc. v. Peña,*[15] the Supreme Court held that any federal, state, or local affirmative action program that uses racial or ethnic classifications as

Reverse Discrimination
The situation in which an affirmative action program discriminates against those who do not have minority status.

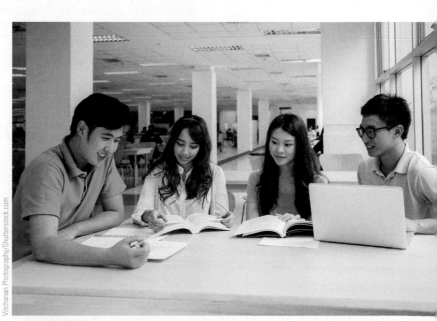
Asian college students studying at the library. *Are Asian American students helped or hurt by affirmative action programs?*

14. 438 U.S. 265 (1978).
15. 515 U.S. 200 (1995).

the basis for making decisions is subject to strict scrutiny by the courts. (We described the strict scrutiny standard earlier in this section.) The Court's opinion in the *Adarand* case means that an affirmative action program cannot make use of quotas or preferences for unqualified persons. In addition, once the program has succeeded in achieving the purpose it was tailored to meet, the program must be changed or dropped.

In 2003, in two cases involving the University of Michigan, the Supreme Court indicated that limited affirmative action programs continued to be acceptable and that diversity was a legitimate goal. The Court struck down the affirmative action plan used for undergraduate admissions at the university, which automatically awarded a substantial number of points to applicants based on minority status.[16] At the same time, it approved the admissions plan used by the law school, which took race into consideration as part of a complete examination of each applicant's background.[17]

The End of Affirmative Action? Despite the position taken by the Supreme Court in the University of Michigan Law School case, affirmative action is subject to serious threats. A variety of states have banned all state-sponsored affirmative action programs. These include Michigan, which banned such programs through a ballot initiative in 2006. Others include Arizona, California, Florida, Nebraska, Oklahoma, and Washington. Voters in Colorado rejected such a measure in 2008, however. While a federal appeals court overturned the Michigan ban, in 2014 the Supreme Court endorsed the right of state voters to ban such programs.[18]

In 2007, the Supreme Court tightened the guidelines for permissible affirmative action programs. In rejecting school integration plans in Seattle, Washington, and Louisville, Kentucky, the Court found that race could not be used as a "tiebreaker" when granting admission to a school.[19]

Today, the future of affirmative action programs is in doubt. State attempts to ban such programs are not the greatest threat. Rather, affirmative action faces a possible change of heart by the Supreme Court. It is conceivable that in coming years the Court may find that affirmative action programs can no longer survive the strict scrutiny standard when they are applied to a suspect classification such as race. Still, in a recent affirmative action case, the Court stopped short of such a step. In June 2013, in *Fisher v. University of Texas,* the Court sent the case back to the federal appeals court with instructions to decide it under existing law. Affirmative action, the Court said, could be used for purposes of diversity, but only when no alternative way of reaching that goal is available.[20] The ruling did not affect affirmative action programs at private schools and colleges.

■ **Learning Outcome 3:** Discuss the history and current status of Latinos, American Indians, and Asian Americans.

Experiences of Other Minority Groups

In a single chapter, it is not possible to describe the experiences of all groups of Americans who have had to struggle for civil rights. Still, three of the largest groups deserve mention: Hispanic Americans, or Latinos, are now the nation's largest minority group by population. Asian Americans are the third largest group, after African Americans. American Indians are notable for their unusual and troubled history, and of course because they were here first.

---

16. *Gratz v. Bollinger,* 539 U.S. 244 (2003).
17. *Grutter v. Bollinger,* 539 U.S. 306 (2003).
18. *Schuette v. Coalition to Defend Affirmative Action,* _____ U.S. _____ (2014).
19. *Parents Involved in Community Schools v. Seattle School District No. 1,* 551 U.S. 701 (2007).
20. 133 S.Ct. 2411 (2013)

Latinos and the Immigration Issue

The most striking characteristic of Latinos is that many of them are relatively recent immigrants. A century ago, most immigrants to the United States came from Europe. Today, most come from Latin America and Asia. New immigrants from Spanish-speaking countries have significantly increased the Latino proportion of the U.S. population. Table 5–1 that follows shows the leading countries of origin for the foreign-born population in the United States.

The law recognizes that Latinos have been subjected to many of the same forms of ill treatment as African Americans, so Latinos are usually grouped with African Americans and American Indians in laws and programs that seek to protect minorities from discrimination or to address the results of past discrimination.

Political Participation by Latinos. The civil rights movement focused primarily on the rights of African Americans, but the legislation resulting from the movement ultimately benefited nearly all minority groups. The Civil Rights Act of 1964, for example, prohibits discrimination against any person because of race, color, or national origin. Subsequent amendments to the Voting Rights Act of 1965 extended its protections to Latino Americans, Asian Americans, Native Americans, and Native Alaskans. Latino political participation has increased in recent years, and they have gained political power in several states. Latinos do not vote at the same rate as African Americans, in large part because many Latinos are immigrants who are not yet citizens. Still, there are now about five thousand Latino elected officials in the United States.

Unauthorized Immigration. Illegal immigration—or unauthorized immigration, to use the language of the Department of Homeland Security—has been a major national issue for many years. Latinos, especially those migrating from Mexico, constitute the majority of individuals entering the United States without permission. In addition, many unauthorized immigrants enter the country legally, as tourists or students, and then fail to return home when their visas expire.

Naturally, the unauthorized population is hard to count. The Pew Research Hispanic Trends Project believes that the population has stabilized at about 11 million in recent years. Figures from the Department of Homeland Security are somewhat higher. Unauthorized immigrants typically come to the United States to work, and until the economic crisis of 2008 their labor had been in high demand. Before the Immigration Reform and Control Act of 1986, there was no law against hiring foreign citizens who lacked proper papers. We list the top ten countries supplying unauthorized immigrants to the United States in Table 5–2, and the top ten countries for legal immigrants in Table 5–3.

Until recently, laws penalizing employers were infrequently enforced. As we explained in the chapter-opening *What If . . .* feature, however, the Obama administration has stepped up enforcement of these laws substantially. In addition, several states have adopted laws that impose severe penalties on businesses that employ unauthorized workers. As a result, agricultural businesses in some states have begun to report labor shortages.

Characteristics of the Undocumented Population. Studies of unauthorized immigrants have revealed that a large share of them eventually return to their home countries, where they frequently set up small businesses or retire. Many send remittances back to relatives in their homeland. In 2011, Mexico received $23 billion in such remittances. In these ways, unauthorized immigrants are acting as immigrants

Table 5–1 ▶ **Top Eleven Countries of Origin for the Foreign-Born Population**

Hispanic countries are shown in red.
Why are there no European countries on this list?

Mexico	11,700,000
China	2,200,000
India	1,800,000
Philippines	1,800,000
El Salvador	1,200,000
Vietnam	1,200,000
Cuba	1,100,000
Korea	1,100,000
Dominican Republic	900,000
Canada	800,000
Guatemala	800,000
ALL COUNTRIES	40,000,000

Source: U.S. Bureau of the Census. Figures are for 2010.

Table 5–2 ▶ **Top Ten Countries of Birth for Unauthorized Immigrants**

Of necessity, these figures are rough estimates. Hispanic countries are shown in red. *Given high rates of poverty in Africa, why don't more Africans come to America?*

Mexico	6,800,000
Guatemala	660,000
El Salvador	620,000
Honduras	380,000
China	280,000
Philippines	270,000
India	240,000
Korea	230,000
Ecuador	210,000
Vietnam	170,000
ALL COUNTRIES	11,510,000

Source: U.S. Department of Homeland Security. Figures are for 2011.

Table 5–3 ▶ **Top Ten Countries of Origin for Legal Immigrants**

The following figures are for a single year only. Legal immigrants are persons obtaining official permanent resident status in that year. Hispanic countries are shown in red. *In time, could immigrants from Asia each year outnumber Latinos?*

Mexico	146,406
China	81,784
India	66,434
Philippines	57,327
Dominican Republic	41,566
Cuba	32,820
Vietnam	28,304
Haiti	22,818
Colombia	20,931
South Korea	20,846
ALL COUNTRIES	1,031,631

Source: U.S. Department of Homeland Security. Figures are for 2012.

to the United States always have. Throughout American history, immigrants frequently returned home or sent funds to relatives in the "old country."

Unauthorized immigrants often live in mixed households, in which one or more members of a family have lawful resident status, but others do not. A woman from Guatemala with permanent resident status, for example, might be married to a Guatemalan man who is in the country illegally. Often, the parents in a family are unauthorized, while the children, who were born in the United States, possess American citizenship. Mixed families mean that deporting the illegal immigrant will either break up a family or force one or more American citizens into exile.

The Agony of the American Indian

Whether living on rural reservations or in urban neighborhoods, American Indians have long experienced high rates of poverty. There is much history behind this problem. (In recent years, a majority of American Indians have come to prefer the term *American Indian*—or even, simply, *Indian*—to *Native American*. Still, both terms are in use.)

The Demographic Collapse. During the years after Columbus arrived in America, native population numbers—both in the future United States and in the Americas generally—experienced one of the most catastrophic collapses in human history. The Europeans brought with them Old World diseases to which Native Americans had no immunity. A person who was able to resist one disease might die from another. By one estimate, 90 percent of the inhabitants of the New World died. For their part, the Europeans had no idea what caused diseases and did not understand what was happening. When the Pilgrims landed at Plymouth in 1620, the coast of New England was lined with empty Indian village sites. The villages had been abandoned because of an epidemic touched off by shipwrecked French sailors in 1616.

American Indians in the Nineteenth and Twentieth Centuries. In the United States, the American Indian population continued to decrease through the nineteenth century—a time when the European American and African American populations were experiencing explosive growth. The decrease was largely due to the concentration of Native Americans into ever-smaller territories. The U.S. Indian population bottomed out at 250,000 at the end of the nineteenth century. Since that time, however, it has recovered substantially. The figure is about 3.2 million today, possibly close to the number living here before Columbus.

American Indians faced additional challenges. A federal policy of "assimilation" adopted in the late 1880s resulted in further loss of territory and the suppression of traditional cultures. Indians did not become U.S. citizens until 1924.

In the late twentieth century, some native tribes hit upon a new strategy for economic development—gambling casinos on reservation lands. This strategy was possible because the U.S. Constitution grants the responsibility for Indian relations to the national government. As a result, reservations are not subject to the full authority of the states in which they are located.

Asian Americans

Asian Americans are probably better integrated into the broader society than any other racial minority. Collectively, Americans with ancestors from China, India, Japan, Korea, the Philippines and Vietnam have above-average incomes. Some smaller national groups, however, continue to struggle economically.

This member of the Ute tribe attends a ceremony for Ute and Comanche leaders. *About how many Native Americans are there today?*

As a result of these successes, it may be hard for today's students to realize just how powerful anti-Asian prejudice was a century ago. For example, Justice John Marshall Harlan, in his dissent to *Plessy v. Ferguson,* stated just a few paragraphs after his famous words that our Constitution is "color-blind," that Chinese people are members of "a race so different from our own" that it is permissible to deny them citizenship. In fact, Chinese American immigrants and their children were denied citizenship throughout the nineteenth century. Only in 1898 did the Supreme Court rule that Chinese Americans born in the United States must be recognized as citizens, in accordance with the Fourteenth Amendment.[21]

The Chinese Exclusion Act. Immigrants from China began arriving in California at the time of the 1849 Gold Rush. Almost all were young men who worked in mines and in railroad construction. The absence of women meant that the Chinese American population grew very slowly. Hostility among white Californians was severe, and anti-Chinese

---

21. *United States v. Wong Kim Ark,* 169 U.S. 649 (1898).

riots were common. In time, Chinese Americans became confined largely to urban Chinatowns and to menial labor. In 1882, the Chinese Exclusion Act banned all further immigration from China. The act was not repealed until 1943.

The Japanese in America. Immigration from Japan was also banned in 1924. By that time, Japanese Americans had become a major ethnic group in Hawaii. In California, some Japanese Americans were able to advance economically by setting up businesses or becoming truck farmers. Almost all of these businesses were lost after 1942, however, when West Coast Japanese were forced into internment camps. Of those interned, 62 percent were U.S. citizens. Japanese Americans were not allowed to leave until 1945, near the end of World War II. The Supreme Court justified the internment in *Korematsu v. United States*, described earlier.

Asian Americans and College Admissions. A current issue faced by Asian Americans is the question of admissions to highly selective colleges and universities. Princeton sociologist Thomas Espenshade has calculated that for Asian Americans to obtain equal consideration at elite colleges, they must outperform whites on SAT tests by 140 points (out of 1600). Top schools deny that they employ quotas. Still, in one way or another, these schools appear to be limiting the number of Asian Americans in their student bodies.

Lingering Social and Economic Disparities

According to census data, social and economic disparities between U.S. racial and ethnic groups persist. Mean incomes in black households are only 59 percent of the incomes in non-Hispanic white households, and incomes of Hispanic households are just 69 percent of those of non-Hispanic whites. White adults were also more likely than black and Hispanic adults to have college degrees and to own their own homes. Whites are also less likely to live in poverty—Figure 5–1 that follows shows the poverty rates for various groups. The recent collapse of the housing market also hit minority households much

Figure 5–1 ▶ **Persons in Poverty in the United States by Race and Hispanic Origin**

Blacks, Hispanics, and American Indians are more likely than whites or Asians to have incomes below the poverty line. Children are substantially more likely than adults to live in families with incomes below the poverty line. *Why are children more likely to live in poverty?*

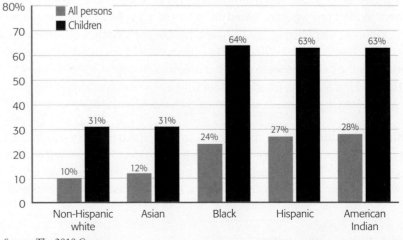

Source: The 2010 Census

harder than white ones. While median non-Hispanic white households lost 16 percent of their net assets in the crash, the figure for African Americans was 53 percent and for Hispanics, 66 percent.

It follows from these figures that America has some distance to go before the effects of past discrimination are erased. Still, the nation has come a long way already. It is also worth remembering that discrimination against minority groups is a worldwide problem. We describe a group in Europe that has experienced discrimination in the *Beyond Our Borders* feature that follows.

Women's Struggle for Equal Rights

Like African Americans and other minorities, women have had to struggle for equality. During the first phase of this struggle, the primary goal of women was to obtain the right to vote.

■ **Learning Outcome 4:**
Contrast the goals of the women's suffrage movement with the goals of modern feminism.

Beyond Our Borders

Europe's Roma People

The Roma people live throughout Europe, and to a lesser extent in the Americas. These are the people formerly known as Gypsies. (That term is now considered to be offensive.) The native language of the Roma is Romani. The ancestors of the Roma came from north India, and they arrived in Europe more than one thousand years ago. Roma are most numerous in eastern European nations such as Bulgaria, Romania, Hungary, and Serbia, but hundreds of thousands also live in Britain, France, Spain, and elsewhere in western Europe. The Roma are a nationality, but they do not have a homeland in which they are the majority. They have faced systematic discrimination almost everywhere they live.

Expulsions Are Common

A major problem for the Roma in western Europe is expulsion. In principle, the European Union guarantees freedom of movement between countries. An exception can be made for persons who may become dependent on welfare, however, and nations such as France place almost all Roma in that category. Throughout France, Roma have seen their campsites, where dozens of families live, routinely demolished by local police. France expels on average 20,000 Roma each year, sending them back to eastern Europe.

No Way Out of Poverty

Often, Roma leave eastern Europe not necessarily in search of employment, but to avoid persecution. Hate crimes against Roma are common in eastern Europe. Roma are typically accused of being thieves. Local communities in Slovakia and other countries have built walls to separate Roma settlements from the rest of the citizenry. In Hungary, a far-right political party recently called for mass internment of all Roma.

Even when Roma migrate to western Europe, they remain poor, and the future is not bright. Roma are often suspicious of the outside world, and do not take advantage of what opportunities may be available. Many Roma children never attend school, and when they do, they are frequently placed in classes for the mentally handicapped. In spite of Europe's "Decade of Roma Inclusion" launched in 2005, the Roma remain excluded just about everywhere on the continent.

For Critical Analysis

Even though there are an estimated 1 million ethnic Roma living in the United States, no one here ever speaks of a "Gypsy problem." Why not?

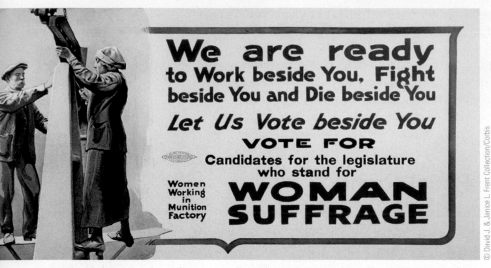

© David J. & Janice L. Frent Collection/Corbis

Women did not get the right to vote throughout the United States until 1920. Prior to that, though, there was a strong women's suffrage movement. This cardboard poster is asking voters to support candidates who favor women's right to vote.

Early Women's Political Movements

In 1848, Lucretia Mott and Elizabeth Cady Stanton organized the first women's rights convention in Seneca Falls, New York. The three hundred people who attended approved a Declaration of Sentiments: "We hold these truths to be self-evident: that all men and women are created equal." In the following twelve years, groups that supported women's rights held seven conventions in different cities in the Midwest and East.

Women's Suffrage Associations. In 1869, after the Civil War, Susan B. Anthony and Stanton formed the National Woman Suffrage Association. In their view, women's **suffrage**—the right to vote—was a means to achieve major improvements in the economic and social situation of women in the United States. In other words, the vote was to be used to seek broader goals.

Lucy Stone, however, a key founder of the rival American Woman Suffrage Association, believed that the vote was the only major issue. In 1880, the two organizations joined forces. The resulting National American Woman Suffrage Association had only one goal—the enfranchisement of women—but it made little progress.

The Nineteenth Amendment. The Congressional Union, founded in the early 1900s by Alice Paul, adopted a national strategy of obtaining an amendment to the U.S. Constitution. The Union employed militant tactics. It sponsored large-scale marches and civil disobedience—which resulted in hunger strikes, arrests, and jailings. Finally, in 1920, the Nineteenth Amendment was passed: "The right of citizens of the United States to vote shall not be denied or abridged by the United States or by any State on account of sex." (Today, the word *gender* is typically used instead of *sex*.)

The Modern Women's Movement

Historian Nancy Cott contends that the word *feminism* first began to be used around 1910. At that time, **feminism** meant, as it does today, political, social, and economic equality for women—a radical notion that gained little support then.

After gaining the right to vote in 1920, women engaged in little independent political activity until the 1960s. The civil rights movement of that decade resulted in a growing awareness of rights for all groups, including women. Increased participation in the workforce gave many women greater self-confidence. Additionally, the publication of Betty Friedan's *The Feminine Mystique* in 1963 focused national attention on the unequal status of women in American life.

In 1966, Friedan and others formed the National Organization for Women (NOW). Many observers consider the founding of NOW to be the beginning of the modern women's movement—the feminist movement.

Feminism gained additional impetus from young women who entered politics to support the civil rights movement or to oppose the Vietnam War (1965–1975). Many of them found that despite the egalitarian principles of these movements, women remained in

did you know?

NOW is the National Organization *for* Women—not "*of* Women"—so that men can be members.

Suffrage
The right to vote; the franchise.

Feminism
The movement that supports political, economic, and social equality for women.

second-class positions. These young women sought their own movement. In the late 1960s, "women's liberation" organizations began to spring up on college campuses. Women also began organizing independent "consciousness-raising groups" in which they discussed how gender issues affected their lives. The new women's movement experienced explosive growth, and by 1970 it had emerged as a major social force.

The Equal Rights Amendment. The initial focus of the modern women's movement was to eradicate gender inequality through a constitutional amendment. The proposed Equal Rights Amendment (ERA), which was first introduced in Congress in 1923 by leaders of the National Women's Party (a successor to the Congressional Union), states as follows: "Equality of rights under the law shall not be denied or abridged by the United States or by any state on account of sex." For years, the amendment was not even given a hearing in Congress, but finally it was approved by both chambers and sent to the state legislatures for ratification in 1972. The necessary thirty-eight states failed to ratify the ERA within the time specified by Congress, however. To date, efforts to reintroduce the amendment have not succeeded.

Women's rights advocates on the march in 1977. Among the most prominent leaders are Representative Bella Abzug (D., N.Y.) wearing a lei and her trademark hat, and Betty Friedan on the far right. *What successes did the feminist movement enjoy?*

During the national debate over the ratification of the ERA, a women's countermovement emerged. Some women perceived the goals pursued by NOW and other liberal women's organizations as a threat to their way of life. One leader of the countermovement was Republican Phyllis Schlafly. The "Stop ERA" campaign of her conservative organization, Eagle Forum, found significant support among fundamentalist religious groups and various other conservative organizations.

Additional Women's Issues. While NOW concentrated on the ERA, a large number of other women's groups, many of them entirely local, addressed a spectrum of added issues. One of these was the issue of *domestic violence*—that is, assaults within the family. Typically, this meant husbands or boyfriends assaulting their wives or girlfriends. During the 1970s, feminists across the country began opening *battered women's shelters* to house victims of abuse.

Abortion soon emerged as a key concern. Almost the entire organized women's movement united behind the "freedom-of-choice" position, at the cost of alienating potential women's rights supporters who favored the "right-to-life" position instead. Because abortion was a national issue, the campaign was led by national organizations such as NARAL Pro-Choice America, formerly the National Abortion and Reproductive Rights Action League.

Another issue—pornography—tended to divide the women's movement rather than unite it. While a majority of feminists found pornography demeaning to women, many were also strong supporters of free speech. Others, notably activists Andrea Dworkin and Catharine Mackinnon, believed that pornography was so central to the subjugation of women that First Amendment protections should not apply.

Challenging Gender Discrimination in the Courts. When ratification of the ERA failed, women's rights organizations began a campaign to win national and state laws that would guarantee the equality of women. This more limited campaign met with much success. Women's rights organizations also challenged discriminatory statutes and policies in the federal courts, contending that **gender discrimination** violated the Fourteenth Amendment's equal protection clause. Employing the intermediate scrutiny standard, the United States Supreme Court has invalidated many such statutes and policies. For

Gender Discrimination
Any practice, policy, or procedure that denies equality of treatment to an individual or to a group because of gender.

Female Marine recruits during boot camp at Parris Island, S.C., in 2013. Days before, a new Defense Department order allowed women to join ground combat units. About 6 percent of enlisted Marines are female. *Might that number grow? Why or why not?*

example, in 1977 the Court held that police and firefighting units cannot establish arbitrary rules, such as height and weight requirements, that tend to keep women from participating in those occupations.[22] In 1983, the Court ruled that life insurance companies cannot charge different rates for women and men.[23]

Congress sought to guarantee equality of treatment in education by passing Title IX of the Education Amendments of 1972, which states: "No person in the United States shall, on the basis of sex, be excluded from participation in, be denied the benefits of, or be subjected to discrimination under any education program or activity receiving Federal financial assistance." Title IX's best-known and most controversial impact has been on high school and collegiate athletics, although the original statute made no reference to athletics.

Women in the Military. One of the most controversial issues involving women's rights has been the role of women in the armed forces. Many believe that the ERA failed because of the fear that women might be drafted (forced) into military service. Currently, no draft exists, but to this day young American men must register for it. Women do not face such a requirement.

A recent issue has been whether women should be allowed to serve in military combat units. In the past, women were not allowed to join such units. Due to the fluid nature of modern combat, however, women in support positions have often found themselves in firefights anyway. In January 2013, the Department of Defense lifted the Combat Exclusion Policy, and in the future women will be able to compete for assignment to combat units. Participation in such units is usually a requirement for promotion to top military positions.

Women in Politics Today

The efforts of women's rights advocates have helped to increase the number of women holding political offices at all levels of government.

Women in Congress. Although a men's club atmosphere still prevails in Congress, the number of women holding congressional seats has increased significantly in recent years. Elections during the 1990s brought more women to Congress than either the Senate or the House had seen before.

In 2001, for the first time, a woman was elected to a leadership post in Congress—Nancy Pelosi of California became the Democrats' minority whip in the U.S. House of Representatives. In 2002, she was elected minority leader. In 2006, she was chosen to be the first woman Speaker of the House in the history of the United States—although she was forced to drop back to minority leader again in 2010 when the Republicans regained control of the House.

Women in the Executive and Judicial Branches. In 1984, for the first time, a woman, Geraldine Ferraro, became the Democratic nominee for vice president. In 2008, Hillary Clinton mounted a major campaign for the Democratic presidential nomination, and Sarah Palin became the Republican nominee for vice president. Recent Gallup polls show that close to 90 percent of Americans said they would vote for a qualified woman for president if she was nominated by their party.

22. *Dothard v. Rawlinson*, 433 U.S. 321 (1977).
23. *Arizona v. Norris*, 463 U.S. 1073 (1983).

Increasing numbers of women are also being appointed to cabinet posts. President George W. Bush appointed several women to cabinet positions, including Condoleezza Rice as his secretary of state in 2005. President Barack Obama named his former rival Hillary Clinton to be secretary of state and added six other women to his cabinet.

Increasing numbers of women are sitting on federal judicial benches as well. President Ronald Reagan (1981–1989) was credited with a historic first when he appointed Sandra Day O'Connor to the United States Supreme Court in 1981. (O'Connor retired in 2006.) President Bill Clinton also appointed a woman, Ruth Bader Ginsburg, to the Court. In 2009, President Obama named Sonia Sotomayor to the Court. She became the third woman and first Hispanic to serve. In 2010, Obama appointed Elena Kagan to the Court, bringing the number of women currently serving on the Court to three.

Gender-Based Discrimination in the Workplace

Traditional cultural beliefs concerning the proper role of women in society continue to be evident not only in the political arena but also in the workplace. Since the 1960s, however, women have gained substantial protection against discrimination through laws that require equal employment opportunities and equal pay.

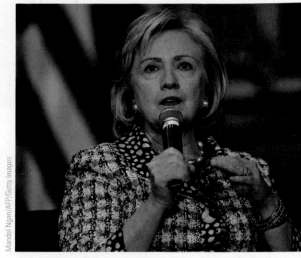

Former Secretary of State Hillary Clinton speaks at Georgetown University in Washington, D.C., in 2013. She is the overwhelming favorite to win the 2016 Democratic presidential nomination. *Why does she have so much support?*

Title VII of the Civil Rights Act of 1964. Title VII of the Civil Rights Act of 1964 prohibits gender discrimination in employment and has been used to strike down employment policies that discriminate against employees on the basis of gender. In 1978, Congress amended Title VII to expand the definition of gender discrimination to include discrimination based on pregnancy.

Sexual Harassment. The United States Supreme Court has also held that Title VII's prohibition of gender-based discrimination extends to **sexual harassment** in the workplace. One form of sexual harassment occurs when job opportunities, promotions, salary increases, and the like are given in return for sexual favors. Another form of sexual harassment, called hostile-environment harassment, occurs when an employee is subjected to sexual conduct or comments that interfere with the employee's job performance or are so pervasive or severe as to create an intimidating, hostile, or offensive environment.

Wage Discrimination. Although Title VII and other legislation since the 1960s has mandated equal employment opportunities for men and women, women continue to earn less, on average, than men do.

The Equal Pay Act, which was enacted in 1963, basically requires employers to provide equal pay for substantially equal work. In other words, males cannot legally be paid more than females who perform essentially the same job.

The Equal Pay Act did not address the fact that certain types of jobs traditionally held by women pay lower wages than the jobs usually held by men. For example, more women than men are salesclerks and nurses, whereas more men than women are construction workers and truck drivers. Even if all clerks performing substantially similar jobs for a company earned the same salaries, they typically would still be earning less than the company's truck drivers.

When Congress passed the Equal Pay Act in 1963, a woman, on average, made 59 cents for every dollar earned by a man. By the mid-1990s, this amount had risen to 75 cents. Figures recently released by the U.S. Department of Labor indicate, though, that since then there has been little change. By 2012, women were still earning, on average, 77 cents for every dollar earned by men.

Sexual Harassment
Unwanted physical or verbal conduct or abuse of a sexual nature that interferes with a recipient's job performance, creates a hostile work environment, or carries with it an implicit or explicit threat of adverse employment consequences.

2014 Elections

Women and Minority Group Members

Voters in 2014 continued to elect a more diverse group of candidates to Congress. For the first time, the number of women in Congress passed the 100 mark. The 89 elected that year joined 16 returning senators for a total of 105 women. Representatives newly elected in 2014 included Utah's Mia Love, the first black Republican woman in the House. Love is also a Mormon and the daughter of Haitian immigrants. In New York, 30-year-old Republican Elise Stefanik became the youngest woman ever elected to Congress. The number of women increased even though 2014 was a Republican year, and the Republicans in Congress are considerably whiter and more male than the Democrats. Only 22 women elected to the House were Republican.

The number of African Americans and Latinos in Congress also continued to advance. African Americans were up three to a total of 46, including three Republicans. In the Senate, Tim Scott became the first elected African American Republican since shortly after the Civil War. (He had earlier been appointed to the seat by Republican governor Nikki Haley—herself the daughter of immigrants from India.) A record 32 Latinos were elected to Congress. Asian American representation held steady at eleven. As in previous elections, African American and Latino voters were strong supporters of the Democrats. Asian Americans, however, seem to have given the Democrats only modest majorities, a change from 2012 when they were strongly Democratic.

Seven members of Congress are now openly gay, lesbian, or bisexual, the same as in the last Congress. For the first time ever, there are no white Democrats representing the deep South. And in New Hampshire, Republican Scott Brown became the first man to lose to two different women in consecutive senate campaigns.

■ **Learning Outcome 5:** Summarize the recent revolution in the rights enjoyed by gay men and lesbians.

did you know?

The word *lesbian* is derived from the Greek island Lesbos, home of Sappho, a female poet. Her poetry proclaimed her love for women.

The Rights and Status of Gay Males and Lesbians

On June 27, 1969, patrons of the Stonewall Inn, a New York City bar popular with gay men and lesbians, responded to a police raid by throwing beer cans and bottles because they were angry at what they felt was unrelenting police harassment. In the ensuing riot, which lasted two nights, hundreds of gay men and lesbians fought with police. Before Stonewall, the stigma attached to homosexuality and the resulting fear of exposure had tended to prevent most gay men and lesbians from engaging in activism. In the months immediately after Stonewall, however, the Gay Liberation Front and the Gay Activist Alliance were formed, and similar groups sprang up in other parts of the country.

Growth in the Gay Male and Lesbian Rights Movement

The Stonewall incident marked the beginning of the movement for gay and lesbian rights. Since then, gay men and lesbians have formed thousands of organizations to exert pressure on legislatures, the media, schools, churches, and other organizations to recognize their right to equal treatment.

To a great extent, lesbian and gay groups have succeeded in changing public opinion—and state and local laws—that pertain to their status and rights. Nevertheless, they continue to struggle against age-old biases against homosexuality, often rooted in deeply held religious beliefs, and the rights of gay men and lesbians remain an extremely divisive issue in American society.

State and Local Laws Targeting Gay Men and Lesbians

Before the Stonewall incident, forty-nine states had sodomy laws that made various kinds of sexual acts, including homosexual acts, illegal (Illinois, which had repealed its sodomy law in 1962, was the only exception). During the 1970s and 1980s, more than half of these laws were either repealed or struck down by the courts.

Lawrence v. Texas. The states—mostly in the South—that resisted the movement to abolish sodomy laws received a boost in 1986 with the Supreme Court's decision in *Bowers v. Hardwick*.[24] In that case, the Court upheld, by a five-to-four vote, a Georgia law that made homosexual conduct between two adults a crime. In 2003, however, the Court reversed its earlier position with its decision in *Lawrence v. Texas*.[25] In this case, the Court held that laws against sodomy violate the due process clause of the Fourteenth Amendment. The Court stated: "The liberty protected by the Constitution allows homosexual persons the right to choose to enter upon relationships in the confines of their homes and their own private lives and still retain their dignity as free persons." *Lawrence v. Texas* invalidated the sodomy laws that remained on the books in fourteen states.

In the summer of 1969, gay men and lesbians who frequented a New York City bar called the Stonewall Inn had had enough. They were tired of unrelenting police harassment. For two nights, they fought with police. *What movement resulted from the riots?*

State Actions. Today, thirty-two states, the District of Columbia, and more than 180 cities and counties have enacted laws protecting lesbians and gay men from discrimination in employment in at least some workplaces. Many of these laws also ban discrimination in housing, in public accommodation, and in other contexts.

In contrast, Colorado adopted a constitutional amendment in 1992 to invalidate all state and local laws protecting homosexuals from discrimination. Ultimately, however, the Supreme Court ruled against the amendment, because it violated the equal protection clause of the U.S. Constitution by denying to homosexuals in Colorado—but to no other Colorado residents—"the right to seek specific protection of the law."[26]

The Gay Community and Politics. Politicians at the national level have not overlooked the potential significance of homosexual issues in American politics. While

did you know?

Hungarian writer Karl-Maria Kertbeny, living in Berlin, coined the word *homosexual* in 1869. He argued that German sodomy laws violated the "rights of man," and that homosexuality was inborn and unchangeable.

---

24. 478 U.S. 186 (1986).
25. 539 U.S. 558 (2003).
26. *Romer v. Evans,* 517 U.S. 620 (1996).

Lesbian and gay male midshipmen at the Naval Academy in Annapolis, Maryland. The midshipmen say they are more comfortable since the repeal of the "Don't Ask, Don't Tell" policy. *Do such officers still need to worry about how their sexual orientation might affect their careers?*

conservative politicians generally have been critical of efforts to secure gay and lesbian rights, liberals, by and large, have been speaking out for gay rights in the past thirty years. In 1980, the Democratic platform included a gay plank for the first time.

Gay Men and Lesbians in the Military

Until recently, the armed forces viewed homosexuality as incompatible with military service. In 1993, however, President Bill Clinton announced a new policy, described as "don't ask, don't tell." Enlistees would not be asked about their sexual orientation, and gay men and lesbians would be allowed to serve in the military so long as they did not declare that they were gay men or lesbians or commit homosexual acts. The new policy was a compromise—Clinton had promised during his presidential campaign to repeal outright the long-standing ban on lesbian and gay military service. Despite the new policy, large numbers of gay men and lesbians were expelled from the military in subsequent years.

During his 2008 presidential campaign, Barack Obama promised to repeal "don't ask, don't tell" and allow lesbians and gay men to serve openly, but throughout 2010, Congress failed to act on legislation that would repeal the policy gradually. Public opinion was running ahead of the government, however—by December 2010, respondents in a typical public opinion poll supported the right of gay men and lesbians to serve openly by a margin of 77 to 21 percent.

In September 2010, a U.S. district court judge ruled that "don't ask, don't tell" was unconstitutional and issued an injunction that would prohibit its enforcement.[27] A federal court of appeals then stayed (suspended) the injunction. Faced with the possibility that the courts might force the immediate abolition of "don't ask, don't tell," in December Congress finally passed the gradual repeal legislation that had been tied up for most of 2010. "Don't ask, don't tell" was phased out in 2011.

Same-Sex Marriage

One of the hottest political issues today is whether gay and lesbian couples should be allowed to marry. New developments in this area are constant, and several may have taken place by the time you read this text.

Defense of Marriage Act.   Controversy over this issue flared up in 1993 when the Hawaii Supreme Court ruled that denying marriage licenses to gay couples might violate the equal protection clause of the Hawaii Constitution.[28] In response, the U.S. Congress passed the Defense of Marriage Act of 1996, which bans federal recognition of lesbian and gay couples and allows state governments to ignore same-sex marriages performed in other states. (Chapter 3's *What If . . .* feature discussed the Defense of Marriage Act in greater depth.)

27. *Log Cabin Republicans v. United States,* 716 F.Supp.2d 884 (C.D. Cal. 2010).
28. *Baehr v. Lewin,* 852 P.2d 44 (Hawaii 1993).

In 1999, the Vermont Supreme Court ruled that gay couples are entitled to the same benefits of marriage as opposite-sex couples.[29] Subsequently, in April 2000, the Vermont legislature passed a law permitting gay and lesbian couples to form "civil unions." The law entitled partners forming civil unions to receive some three hundred state benefits available to married couples, including the rights to inherit a partner's property and to decide on medical treatment for an incapacitated partner. It did not, however, entitle those partners to receive any benefits allowed to married couples under federal law, such as spousal Social Security benefits. In subsequent years, a number of states permitted civil unions. In time, however, most of these states also legalized same-sex marriages. As a result, by early 2014, of the states making any provision for same-sex couples, Colorado and Nevada were the only ones to stop short of marriage and to offer civil unions instead. (Wisconsin provided more limited benefits.)

State Recognition of Same-Sex Marriages. Massachusetts was the first state to recognize gay marriage. In 2003, the Massachusetts Supreme Judicial Court ruled that same-sex couples have a right to civil marriage under the Massachusetts state constitution.[30] In June 2008, through a ruling by the state supreme court, California became the second state to legalize same-sex marriages. In November of that year, however, California voters approved Proposition 8, a state constitutional amendment that banned the marriages. Interestingly, marriages performed between June and November 2008 continued to be valid, but no additional marriages were allowed.

In October 2008, the Connecticut Supreme Court required the state to recognize same-sex marriages. The Iowa Supreme Court followed in 2009. That same year, New Hampshire became the first state to legalize such marriages through legislation. By 2012, when Maine, Maryland, and Washington became the first states to adopt gay marriage through popular vote, nine states and the District of Columbia had joined the movement. By mid-2014, nineteen states were on board. In Oregon and Pennsylvania, same-sex marriages became legal because state governments declined to appeal court rulings overturning state bans.

Same-Sex Marriage and the Federal Courts. By 2013, dozens of cases involving same-sex marriage were working their way through the federal courts. In 2010, Vaughn Walker, a federal district judge in California, ruled that Proposition 8 violated the U.S. Constitution because it singled out a particular group to deprive it of a right. In 2013, the United States Supreme Court refused to rule on the case.[31] The Court thus preserved Judge Walker's decision that Proposition 8 was unconstitutional. By not ruling, the Supreme Court also refused to extend same-sex marriage rights to any other state. While the Court in effect reversed a vote of the California citizenry, every sign was that California was ready to change its mind on gay marriage anyway.

An interesting detail of the California case is that Judge Walker explicitly based his ruling on the rational basis test. He found, in other words, that the government had no legitimate interest in banning same-sex marriage. In other cases, federal courts have applied the intermediate

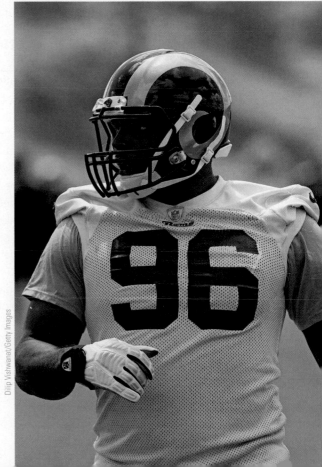

Michael Sam of the St. Louis Rams participates in a rookie minicamp in 2014. He was the first openly gay player to be drafted by a National Football League team. *Why might football have been slower than some other institutions to accept gay individuals?*

Dilip Vishwanat/Getty Images

29. *Baker v. Vermont,* 744 A.2d 864 (Vt. 1999).
30. *Goodridge v. Department of Public Health,* 798 N.E.2d 941 (Mass. 2003).
31. *Hollingsworth v. Perry,* 133 S.Ct. 2652 (2013).

Mario Tama/Getty Images

Two women laugh while waiting to get married in New York City, on the day after the Supreme Court struck down parts of the Defense of Marriage Act (DOMA). *Why has public opinion on same-sex marriage reversed itself so dramatically and quickly?*

scrutiny test. The appropriate level of scrutiny for ruling on gay and lesbian discrimination cases, therefore, is yet to be determined.

Also in 2013, in *United States v. Windsor*, the Supreme Court found that the provision of the Defense of Marriage Act that banned federal recognition of same-sex marriages performed by the states was unconstitutional.[32] This ruling was of enormous value to same-sex couples in states that permitted them to marry.

Toward a National Ruling. In December 2013, a federal district court judge in Utah ruled that the state's constitutional amendment banning same-sex marriage violated the U.S. Constitution.[33] The United States Supreme Court stayed (suspended) this ruling pending decisions by higher federal courts. The Utah ruling opened the floodgates. By mid-2014, federal courts had authorized same-sex marriage in fourteen states where the practice had previously been banned. In all states except Oregon and Pennsylvania (which refused to appeal the rulings) the orders in favor of same-sex marriage were stayed (postponed) pending a decision by the United States Supreme Court. Still, in five states, hundreds of same-sex couples managed to obtain marriage licenses before the stays went into effect. The federal government announced that it would recognize these marriages. Lawsuits challenging bans on same-sex marriage had been filed in every state of the union in which the practice was still illegal.

In October 2014, the Supreme Court refused to take up any of the cases provisionally decided by U.S. appeals courts. All stays were lifted, and within weeks same-sex marriage was legal in thirty-two states. Legalization was expected in other states as well. The Court's ability to keep dodging this issue depended on unanimity among the various district appeals courts. Experts were confident that eventually an appeals court would rule against same-sex marriage, forcing the Supreme Court to act.

---

32. 570 U.S. ____ (2013).
33. *Kitchen v. Herbert*, ____ F.Supp.2d ____ (D.Utah 2013).

The Rights and Status of Juveniles

Approximately 75 million Americans—about 24 percent of the total population—are under eighteen years of age. Depending on the topic, the definition of *child* can range from a person under age sixteen to a person under age twenty-one. However defined, children in the United States have fewer rights and protections than adults.

The reason for this lack of rights is the presumption of society that children basically are protected by their parents. This is not to say that children are the property of the parents. Rather, an overwhelming case in favor of *not* allowing parents to control the actions of their children must be presented before children can be given authorization to act without parental consent (or before the state can be authorized to act on children's behalf without regard to their parents' wishes).

Supreme Court decisions affecting children's rights began a process of slow evolution with *Brown v. Board of Education of Topeka,* the landmark civil rights case of 1954 discussed earlier in this chapter. In the *Brown* case, the Court granted children the status of rights-bearing persons. In the 1967 case *In re Gault,*[34] the Court expressly held that children have a constitutional right to be represented by counsel at the government's expense in a criminal action. Five years later, the Court acknowledged that "children are 'persons' within the meaning of the Bill of Rights. We have held so over and over again."[35]

Voting Rights and the Young

The Twenty-sixth Amendment to the Constitution, ratified on July 1, 1971, reads as follows:

> *The right of citizens of the United States, who are eighteen years of age or older, to vote shall not be denied or abridged by the United States or by any State on account of age.*

---

34. 387 U.S. 1 (1967).
35. *Wisconsin v. Yoder,* 406 U.S. 205 (1972).

When children are at risk, local or state agencies sometimes take over their care. *Under what circumstances might the government take such an action?*

Civil Law

The law regulating conduct between private persons over noncriminal matters, including contracts, domestic relations, and business interactions.

Criminal Law

The law that defines crimes and provides punishment for violations. In criminal cases, the government is the prosecutor.

Majority

The age at which a person is entitled by law to the right to manage her or his own affairs.

Common Law

Judge-made law that originated in England from decisions shaped according to prevailing customs. Decisions were applied to similar situations and thus gradually became common to the nation.

Before this amendment was ratified, the age at which citizens could vote was twenty-one in most states. One of the arguments used for granting suffrage to eighteen-year-olds was that, because they could be drafted to fight in the country's wars, they had a stake in public policy. At the time, the example of the Vietnam War was paramount. Even though persons between ages eighteen and twenty-one now have the right to vote, their rates of turnout in elections are much lower than the rates posted by older voters.

The Rights of Children in Civil and Criminal Proceedings

Civil law relates to such matters as contracts among private individuals, domestic relations, and business transactions. **Criminal law** relates to crimes against society that are defined by legislatures and prosecuted by a public official, such as a district attorney. Different procedural rules and judicial safeguards apply under civil and criminal laws.

Civil Rights of Juveniles. The civil rights of children are defined by state laws. The legal definition of **majority**—the age at which a person is entitled by law to the right to manage his or her own affairs—varies from eighteen to twenty-one years of age, depending on the state. As a rule, an individual who is legally a minor cannot be held responsible for contracts that he or she forms with others. In most states, only contracts entered into for so-called *necessaries* (things necessary for subsistence, such as food and clothing), can be enforced against minors. Also, when minors engage in negligent behavior, typically their parents are liable. If, for example, a minor destroys a neighbor's fence, the neighbor may bring a suit against the child's parent but not against the child.

Civil law also encompasses the area of child custody. Child-custody rulings traditionally have given little weight to the wishes of the child. Courts have maintained the right to act on behalf of the child's "best interests" but have sometimes been constrained from doing so by the "greater" rights possessed by adults. For instance, a widely publicized Supreme Court ruling awarded legal custody of a two-and-a-half-year-old Michigan resident to an Iowa couple, the child's biological parents. A Michigan couple, who had cared for the child since shortly after her birth and who had petitioned to adopt the child, lost out in the custody battle. The Court agreed that the law allowed it to consider only the parents' rights and not the child's best interests.[36]

Children's rights and their ability to articulate their rights for themselves in custody matters were strengthened, however, by several well-publicized rulings involving older children. In one case, for example, an eleven-year-old Florida boy filed suit in his own name, assisted by his own privately retained legal counsel, to terminate his relationship with his biological parents and to have the court affirm his right to be adopted by foster parents. The court granted his request, although it did not agree procedurally with the method by which the boy initiated the suit.[37]

Criminal Rights of Juveniles. One of the main requirements for an act to be criminal is intent. The law has given children certain defenses against criminal prosecution because of their presumed inability to have criminal intent. Under the **common law,** children up to seven years of age were considered incapable of committing a crime because they did not have the moral sense to understand that they were doing wrong. Children between the ages of seven and fourteen were also presumed to be incapable of committing a crime, but this presumption could be challenged by showing that the child understood the wrongful nature of the act. Today, states vary in their approaches. Most states retain the

did you know?

The first juvenile court in the United States opened in Chicago on July 3, 1899.

---

36. *DeBoer by Darrow v. DeBoer*, 509 U.S. 1301 (1993).
37. *Kingsley v. Kingsley*, 623 So.2d 780 (Fla.App. 1993).

common law approach, although age limits vary from state to state. Other states have simply set a minimum age for criminal responsibility.

Juvenile Court Systems. All states have juvenile court systems that handle children below the age of criminal responsibility who commit delinquent acts. The aim of juvenile courts is allegedly to reform rather than to punish. In states that retain the common law approach, children who are above the minimum age but are still juveniles can be turned over to the criminal courts if the juvenile court determines that they should be treated as adults. Children sent to juvenile court do not have the right to trial by jury or to post bail.

Felony Cases. Although minors usually do not have the full rights of adults in criminal proceedings, they have certain advantages. In felony cases, which include, among others, cases involving manslaughter, murder, armed robbery, and assault, juveniles traditionally were not tried as adults. (A **felony** is a serious crime punishable in most jurisdictions by a prison sentence longer than one year.) They were often sentenced to probation or "reform" school for a relatively short term regardless of the seriousness of their crimes.

Today, however, most states allow juveniles to be tried as adults (often at the discretion of the judge) for certain crimes, such as murder. When they are tried as adults, they are given due process of law and tried for the crime, rather than being given the paternalistic treatment reserved for a juvenile delinquent.

A youth under arrest. *What rights does this person have?*

Juveniles and the Death Penalty. Juveniles who are tried as adults may also face adult penalties. These used to include the death penalty. In 2005, however, the United States Supreme Court ruled that executing persons who were under the age of eighteen when they committed their crimes would constitute cruel and unusual punishment. The Court contended that sixteen- and seventeen-year-olds do not have a fully developed sense of right and wrong, nor do they necessarily understand the full gravity of their misdeeds.[38] In May 2010, the Court also ruled that juveniles who commit crimes in which no one is killed may not be sentenced to life in prison without the possibility of parole.[39]

> **Felony**
> A serious crime punishable in most jurisdictions by a prison sentence longer than one year.

---

38. *Roper v. Simmons,* 543 U.S. 551 (2005).
39. *Graham v. Florida,* 130 S.Ct. 2011 (2010).

How You Can Make a Difference

Anyone applying for a job may be subjected to a variety of possibly discriminatory practices based on race, color, gender, religion, age, sexual preference, or disability. There may be tests, some of which could have a discriminatory effect. At both the state and the federal levels, the government continues to examine the fairness and validity of criteria used in screening job applicants. As a result, there are ways of addressing the problem of discrimination.

If you believe that you have been discriminated against by a potential employer, consider the following steps:

1. Evaluate your own capabilities, and determine if you are truly qualified for the position.

2. Analyze the reasons why you were turned down. Would others agree with you that you have been the object of discrimination, or would they uphold the employer's claim?

3. If you still believe that you have been treated unfairly, you have recourse to several agencies and services.

You should first speak to the human resources director of the company and explain politely that you believe you have not been evaluated adequately. If asked, explain your concerns clearly. If necessary, go into explicit detail, and indicate that you may have been discriminated against.

If a second evaluation is not forthcoming, contact your local state employment agency. If you still do not obtain adequate help, contact one or more of the following state agencies, usually listed in your telephone directory under "State Government":

1. If a government entity is involved, a state ombudsperson or citizen aide may be available to mediate.

2. You can contact the state civil rights commission, which at least should give you advice, even if it does not wish to take up your case.

3. The state attorney general's office normally has a division dealing with discrimination and civil rights.

4. There may be a special commission or department specifically set up to help you, such as a women's status commission or a commission on Hispanics or Asian Americans. If you are a woman or a member of such a minority group, contact these commissions.

Finally, at the national level, you can contact:

Equal Employment Opportunity Commission
131 M St. NE
Washington, DC 20507
202-663-4900
eeoc.gov

Key Terms

affirmative action 146
civil disobedience 140
civil law 164
civil rights 136
common law 164
criminal law 164
de facto segregation 140

de jure segregation 140
felony 165
feminism 154
gender discrimination 155
grandfather clause 138
intermediate scrutiny 146
literacy test 138

majority 164
poll tax 138
rational basis review 146
reverse discrimination 147
separate-but-equal
doctrine 138
sexual harassment 157

strict scrutiny 145
suffrage 154
suspect classification 145
white primary 138

Chapter Summary

Learning Outcome 1 Before the Civil War, most African Americans were slaves, and slavery was protected by the Constitution. Constitutional amendments after the Civil War ended slavery, and African Americans gained citizenship, the right to vote, and other rights. This protection was largely a dead letter by the 1880s, however, and African American inequality continued.

Segregation was declared unconstitutional by the Supreme Court in *Brown v. Board of Education of Topeka* (1954), in which the Court stated that separation implied inferiority. In 1955, the modern civil rights movement began with a boycott of segregated public transportation in Montgomery, Alabama. The Civil Rights Act of 1964 banned discrimination on the basis of race, color, religion, gender, or national origin in employment and public accommodations. The Voting Rights Act of 1965 outlawed discriminatory voter-registration tests and authorized federal voter registration.

Learning Outcome 2 Civil rights are protected by the Fourteenth Amendment to the U.S. Constitution and, in particular, by the due process and equal protection clauses. The courts have developed a series of tests to use when considering cases of possible discrimination. Strict scrutiny, the most rigorous of these, applies to such suspect classifications as race, religion, and national origin. Intermediate, or exacting, scrutiny is employed in cases involving women's rights. Rational basis review, used when strict or exacting scrutiny does not apply, is the easiest test to meet.

Affirmative action programs have been controversial because they may lead to reverse discrimination against majority groups or even other minority groups. United States Supreme Court decisions have limited affirmative action programs, and several states now ban state-sponsored affirmative action.

Learning Outcome 3 Today, most immigrants come from Asia and Latin America, especially Mexico. Many are unauthorized immigrants (also called illegal aliens or undocumented workers). Latinos and American Indians benefit from the same antidiscrimination measures as African Americans. American Indians suffered a demographic collapse upon the arrival of the Europeans in the New World. They continue to face high levels of poverty. Asian Americans have frequently enjoyed economic success, despite prejudice that in past years was severe.

Learning Outcome 4 In the early history of the United States, women had no political rights. After the first women's rights convention in 1848, the women's movement gained momentum. Not until 1920, however, when the Nineteenth Amendment was ratified, did women obtain the right to vote nationwide. The modern women's movement began in the 1960s in the wake of the civil rights and anti–Vietnam War movements. Efforts to secure the ratification of the Equal Rights Amendment failed, but the women's movement has been successful in obtaining new laws, changes in social customs, and increased political representation for women.

The number of women in Congress and in other government bodies increased significantly in the 1990s and 2000s. Federal government efforts to eliminate gender discrimination in the workplace include Title VII of the Civil Rights Act of 1964, which prohibits gender-based discrimination, including sexual harassment on the job. Wage discrimination continues to be a problem for women.

Learning Outcome 5 During the 1970s and 1980s, sodomy laws that criminalized specific sexual practices were repealed or struck down by the courts in nearly half of the states. In 2003, a United States Supreme Court decision invalidated all remaining sodomy laws nationwide. Many states and cities have laws prohibiting at least some types of discrimination based on sexual orientation. The military's "don't ask, don't tell" policy, now repealed, fueled extensive controversy, as have same-sex marriages, which have been legalized in a growing number of states.

Learning Outcome 6 Children have few rights and protections, in part because it is presumed that their parents protect them. The Twenty-sixth Amendment grants the right to vote to those ages eighteen or older. Minors have some defense against criminal prosecution because of their presumed inability to have criminal intent below certain ages. For those under the age of criminal responsibility, there are state juvenile courts. When minors are tried as adults, they are entitled to the procedural protections afforded to adults and are usually subject to adult penalties.

Master the concept of Civil Rights with MindTap™ *for American Government*

 REVIEW MindTap™ **for American Government**
Access Key Term Flashcards for Chapter 5.

 TEST YOURSELF MindTap™ **for American Government**
Take the Wrap It Up Quiz for Chapter 5.

 STAY CURRENT MindTap™ **for American Government**
Access the KnowNow blog and customized RSS for updates on current events.

 STAY FOCUSED MindTap™ **for American Government**
Complete the Focus Activities for Civil Rights.

Additional Resources

Today, thanks to the Internet, information on civil rights issues is literally at your fingertips. A host of Web sites offer data on the extent to which groups discussed in this chapter are protected under state and federal laws. You can also find many advocacy sites that describe what you can do to help promote the rights of a certain group.

Online Resources

- Twitter contains a large number of hashtags devoted to civil rights. You could check out #civilrights, #womensrights, or #gayrights.
- An excellent source of information on issues facing African Americans is the Web site of the National Association for the Advancement of Colored People (NAACP). Find it at naacp.org.
- The National Organization for Women (NOW) offers online information and updates on the status of women's rights. You can locate its Web site at now.org.
- You can access the Web site of the Human Rights Campaign, the nation's largest gay and lesbian political organization, by going to hrc .org.
- If you are interested in children's rights and welfare, you can visit the Web site of the Children's Defense Fund at www.childrensdefense.org.

Books

Kundnani, Arun. *The Muslims Are Coming! Islamophobia, Extremism, and the Domestic War on Terror.* Brooklyn, N.Y.: Verso, 2014. Kundnani argues that Islamophobia on the part of law enforcement personnel has been counterproductive in combating terrorism and has resulted in a variety of abuses. Kundnani is on the faculty of New York University and John Jay College.

Mayeri, Serena. *Reasoning from Race: Feminism, Law, and the Civil Rights Revolution.* Cambridge, Mass.: Harvard University Press, 2014. Mayeri, a professor at the University of Pennsylvania Law School, charts how feminists borrowed strategies and legal concepts from the civil rights movement.

Risen, Clay. *The Bill of the Century: The Epic Battle for the Civil Rights Act.* New York: Bloomsbury Press, 2014. The passage of the Civil Rights Act of 1964 has often been credited to the political leadership of President Lyndon Johnson and the moral force of Dr. Martin Luther King, Jr. According to Risen, a *New York Times* editor, passage depended on a much broader cast of characters, both inside and outside of Congress.

Video

Eyes on the Prize: America's Civil Rights Years 1954–1965—Narrated by civil rights veteran Julian Bond, this six-hour television series is one of the most highly regarded video histories of the civil rights movement ever. It was released in 2010.

Miss Representation—This highly acclaimed 2011 documentary shows how the media's emphasis on youth and beauty makes it harder for women to gain equality and to win leadership positions. The all-star cast includes Margaret Cho, Katie Couric, Geena Davis, Rachel Maddow, Nancy Pelosi, Condoleezza Rice, and Gloria Steinem.

Quiz

Multiple Choice and Fill-Ins

Learning Outcome 1 Summarize the historical experience of African Americans, state how the separate-but-equal doctrine was abolished, and describe the consequences of the civil rights movement.

1. The separate-but-equal doctrine was announced by the Supreme Court:
   a. in *Plessy v. Ferguson*.
   b. in *Roe v. Wade*.
   c. nowhere, because the Supreme Court never addressed the issue.

2. Past barriers to African American voting included grandfather clauses, poll taxes, and _____ _____.

Learning Outcome 2 Define the different levels of scrutiny used by the Supreme Court in civil rights cases, and describe recent rulings on affirmative action.

3. Affirmative action programs have assisted groups that had been discriminated against in the past. In educational admissions and employment, these programs:
   a. awarded preferences to minority group members.
   b. relied on numerical quotas to improve outcomes.
   c. involved federal grants to complying institutions.

4. The Fourteenth Amendment requires that no state shall deprive any person of life, liberty, or property, without _____ _____ __ _____.

Learning Outcome 3 Discuss the history and current status of Latinos, American Indians, and Asian Americans.

5. In the years following the European discovery of America, the number of Native Americans:
   a. rose because of the introduction of new foodstuffs.
   b. fell because of the introduction of new diseases.
   c. remained about the same for many years.

6. Currently, the country providing the largest number of immigrants to the United States is _____.

Learning Outcome 4 Contrast the goals of the women's suffrage movement with the goals of modern feminism.

7. The Equal Rights Amendment today requires:
   a. that women be treated equally to men.
   b. that women be treated equally in the labor market.
   c. nothing at all, because the Equal Rights Amendment never passed.

8. Among the most controversial issues raised by the modern feminist movement are whether pornography should be banned and whether women should have the right to _____ __ _____.

Learning Outcome 5 Summarize the recent revolution in the rights enjoyed by gay men and lesbians.

9. The Defense of Marriage Act (DOMA) provided for all of the following except:
   a. states were not required to recognize same-sex marriages conducted in other states.
   b. states were not required to recognize divorces obtained in other states.
   c. the federal government was barred from recognizing same-sex marriages when awarding benefits or collecting taxes.

10. Since 2011, _____ _____ __ _____ can openly serve in the U.S. military.

Learning Outcome 6 Evaluate the rights and status of juvenile citizens.

11. Very young children may not be charged with crimes because:
    a. they lack the ability to form criminal intent.
    b. their parents must be charged instead.
    c. such charges would not be in the best interest of the child.

12. In 1971, because of the _____ _____, citizens eighteen and older were given the right to vote.

Essay Questions

1. Not all African Americans agreed with the philosophy of nonviolence espoused by Dr. Martin Luther King, Jr. Advocates of black power called for a more militant approach. Can militancy make a movement more effective (possibly by making a more moderate approach seem like a reasonable compromise), or is it typically counterproductive? Either way, why?

2. The prevention of terrorist acts committed by adherents of radical Islamism is a major policy objective today. Can we defend ourselves against such acts without abridging the civil rights and liberties of American Muslims and immigrants from predominantly Muslim countries? What measures that might be undertaken by the authorities are legitimate? Which are not?

Public Opinion and Political Socialization

6

High school students in Philadelphia participate in a game that promotes political awareness. *How can schools encourage responsible citizenship?*
AP Photo/H. Rumph Jr.

The four Learning Outcomes below are designed to help improve your understanding of this chapter. After reading this chapter, you should be able to:

- **Learning Outcome 1:** Define *public opinion, consensus opinion,* and *divided opinion,* and discuss major sources of political socialization, including the family, schools, the media, and political events.

- **Learning Outcome 2:** Identify the effects of various influences on voting behavior, including education, income, religion, race/ethnicity, gender, and geography.

- **Learning Outcome 3:** Describe the characteristics of a scientific opinion poll, and list some of the problems pollsters face in obtaining accurate results.

- **Learning Outcome 4:** Consider the effect that public opinion may have on the political process.

(▶) **WATCH & LEARN** MindTap™ for American Government

Watch a brief "What Do You Know?" video summarizing Public Opinion and Political Socialization.

What If...

Politicians Really Listened to the Polls?

BACKGROUND

How do we know about popular opinion? For the most part, we must rely on public opinion polling. Of course, politicians are aware of public opinion. Indeed, many of them use polling to determine what positions they should take during an election campaign. Once elected, though, it is not clear how much senators and members of the House really do listen to public opinion.

On a few issues, politicians clearly do respond to popular opinion. On others, however, the Washington, D.C., political elites—politicians, columnists, think tank pundits, major fundraisers, and others—take a different approach. On these issues, rather than paying attention to polls, elites are apparently drawing their own conclusions about what is good for the country. Policymaking might be more conservative on some issues—and more liberal on others—if politicians really tried to respond to popular opinion.

Linda D. Epstein/MCT/Getty Images

When voters tried to contact members of Congress during a threatened debt default, many Web sites were not available. *When might a member of Congress seek to dodge the voters?*

WHAT IF POLITICIANS REALLY LISTENED TO THE POLLS?

According to the Pew Research Center, 75 percent of those polled believe that it would be positive for our society if more Americans were religious. About the same percentage believe that religion is losing its influence on American life. Almost three quarters believe that the state of U.S. moral values is getting worse.

About 60 percent of Americans believe that progressives have gone too far in trying to keep religion out of the schools and government. If politicians really listened to these polls, they would find ways to allow more religion in our public school systems. Three quarters of Americans favor a constitutional amendment to allow "voluntary prayer" in the public schools—that is, prayer led by teachers from which students could theoretically opt out. Yet somehow, this amendment never seems to make it to the floor of the House or Senate.

WHAT SHOULD WE DO TO CUT THE DEFICIT?

If Americans are more conservative than political elites on religion in the schools, they are more liberal on a few economic issues. Opinion polls regularly report that voters want to reduce the deficit—the excess of the federal government's spending over and above its income. It's widely believed among elites that we therefore need to cut rates of "entitlement spending," programs such as Social Security and Medicaid. Reporters from newspapers such as the *Washington Post* regularly report this need as if it were a fact, not an opinion. Pew Research, however, in a poll on the deficit, reported that 41 percent of respondents wanted to *increase* Social Security spending. Only 10 percent wanted to see it cut. While Social Security was among the most popular federal programs, a majority of those polled opposed cutting *anything* except foreign aid.

A unique poll by the Program for Public Consultation at the University of Maryland let respondents work through an interactive budget exercise in which they were forced to confront the realities of taxing and spending. Respondents did cut the deficit. Still, a majority also increased Social Security benefits slightly. It was the only program so treated. Respondents supported large cuts to defense spending—and tax increases on the wealthy that go well beyond anything that Democrats have recently advocated. These are not policies with much elite support.

For Critical Analysis

1. Even if politicians wanted to listen to the public on religion in the schools, how could they get around Supreme Court decisions that stand in their way?

2. Why do you think a majority of voters opposes cuts to most federal government programs?

LISTEN & LEARN

MindTap™ for American Government

Access Read Speaker to listen to Chapter 6.

In a democracy, the ability of the people to freely express their opinions is fundamental. Americans can express their opinions in many ways. They can write letters to newspapers. They can share their ideas in online forums on Facebook, blogs, and tweets. They can organize politically. They can vote. They can respond to opinion polls.

Both the Republicans and the Democrats found out how important public opinion can be in 2013. In an attempt to halt the implementation of Obamacare, House Republicans in September refused to fund the government. On October 1, therefore, 800,000 federal employees were sent home, and another 1.3 million "essential employees" were required to work without pay. Democrats refused to negotiate. Under growing public pressure, the Republicans passed a funding bill on October 16. Opinion polls predicted that the Republicans would take a heavy beating in the next elections.

The Obamacare Web site—HealthCare.gov—also opened for business on October 1. The plan was that Americans who did not have health-care insurance through their employer or through a program such as Medicare could use the new site to buy insurance. The site, however, was almost completely dysfunctional. It took a new team of computer programmers two months to repair the site to the point where customers could use it. A few problems took even more time to resolve. Some consumers also found that they could not keep their previous insurance plan because it did not meet newly established standards. An earlier statement by President Obama that everyone could keep their existing plan came back to haunt him. By the end of October, the Democrats had completely lost the edge in popularity they had gained from the government shutdown crisis.

There is no doubt that public opinion can be powerful. The extent to which public opinion affects policymaking is not always so clear, however, as we see in the chapter-opening *What If . . .* feature. For example, suppose that public opinion strongly supports a certain policy. If political leaders adopt that position, is it because they are responding to public opinion or because they share the public's beliefs?

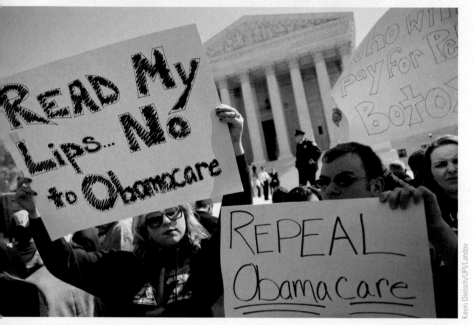

Public opinion can be strongly divided. *Why is that so with health care reform legislation?*

Kevin Dietsch/UPI/Landov

■ **Learning Outcome 1:**
Define *public opinion, consensus opinion,* and *divided opinion,* and discuss major sources of political socialization, including the family, schools, the media, and political events.

Public Opinion
The aggregate of individual attitudes or beliefs shared by some portion of the adult population.

Consensus
General agreement among the citizenry on an issue.

Public Opinion and Political Socialization

There is no single public opinion, because there are many different "publics." In a nation of 320 million people, there may be innumerable gradations of opinion on an issue. What we do is describe the distribution of opinions about a particular question. Thus, we define **public opinion** as the aggregate of individual attitudes or beliefs shared by some portion of the adult population.

Consensus and Divided Opinion

Typically, public opinion is distributed among several different positions, and the distribution of opinion can tell us how divided the public is on an issue and whether compromise is possible. When polls show that a large proportion of the American public appears to express the same view on an issue, we say that a **consensus** exists, at least at the moment the poll was taken. Figure 6–1 that follows shows a pattern of opinion that might be called consensual. Issues on which the public holds widely differing attitudes result in **divided opinion** (see Figure 6–2 that follows). Sometimes, a poll shows a distribution of opinion indicating that most Americans either have no information about the issue or do not care enough about the issue to formulate a position.

An interesting question arises as to when private opinion becomes public opinion. Everyone probably has a private opinion about the competence of the president, as well as private opinions about more personal concerns, such as the state of a neighbor's lawn. We say that private opinion becomes public opinion when the opinion is publicly expressed and concerns public issues. When someone's private opinion becomes so strong that the individual is willing to take action, then the opinion becomes public opinion.

Forming Public Opinion: Political Socialization

Most Americans are willing to express opinions on political issues when asked. How do people acquire these opinions and attitudes? Typically, views that are expressed as political opinions are acquired through the process of **political socialization.** By this, we mean that people acquire their political beliefs and values, often including their party identification, through relationships with their families, friends, and co-workers.

The most important early sources of political socialization are the family and the schools. Individuals' basic political orientations are formed in the family if other family members hold strong views. When the adults in a family view politics as relatively unimportant and describe themselves as independent voters or disaffected from the political system, however, children may receive very little political socialization.

Divided Opinion
Public opinion that is polarized between two quite different positions.

Political Socialization
The process by which people acquire political beliefs and values.

Figure 6–1 ▶ **Consensus Opinion**

Question: Do you think that Russia's actions in Ukraine are or are not a violation of international law?

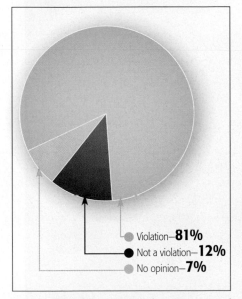

Violation—**81%**
Not a violation—**12%**
No opinion—**7%**

Do you think Russia's President Putin cared whether the annexation of Crimea was a violation of international law? Why or why not?

Source: CNN/ORC Poll, Mar. 7-9, 2014

Figure 6–2 ▶ **Divided Opinion**

Question: Do you think it is likely or not likely that there will be a new cold war between the United States and Russia in the next few years?

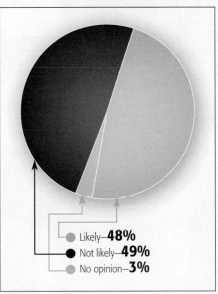

Likely—**48%**
Not likely—**49%**
No opinion—**3%**

Why would the United States be reluctant to become militarily involved in Ukraine?

In the past few decades, more and more sources of information about politics have become available to all Americans, especially to young people through the Web. Thus, although their basic outlook on the political system still may be formed by early family influences, young people are now exposed to many other sources of information about issues and values. This greater access to information may explain why young Americans are often more liberal than their parents on certain social issues, such as gay rights.

The Family. Not only do our parents' political beliefs, values, and actions affect our opinions, but the family also links us to other factors that affect opinion, such as race, social class, educational environment, and religious beliefs. How do parents transmit their political values to their offspring?

Studies suggest that the influence of parents is due to two factors: communication and receptivity. Parents communicate their feelings and preferences to their children constantly. Because children have such a strong need for parental approval, they are very receptive to their parents' views.

Children are less likely to influence their parents, because parents expect deference from their children.[1] Nevertheless, other studies show that if children are exposed to political ideas at school and in the media, they will share these ideas with their parents, giving the parents what some scholars call a "second chance" at political socialization.

Education as a Source of Political Socialization. From the early days of the republic, schools were perceived to be important transmitters of political information and

---

1. Barbara A. Bardes and Robert W. Oldendick, *Public Opinion: Measuring the American Mind,* 4th ed. (Belmont, Calif.: Wadsworth Publishing Co., 2012), p. 73.

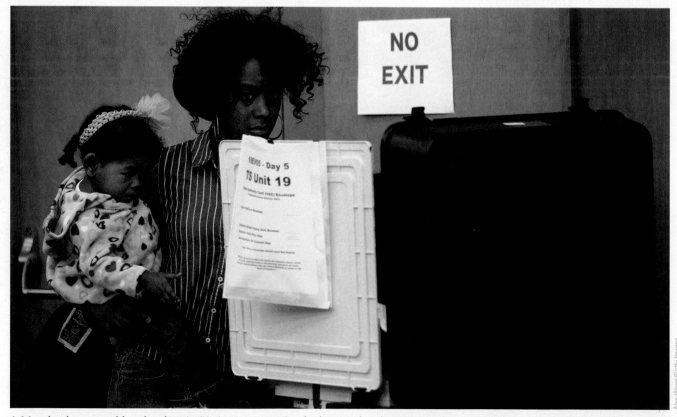

A Maryland voter and her daughter in 2012. Hurricane Sandy disrupted early voting in that state. *What kinds of voters tend to turn out even in very bad weather?*

attitudes. Children in the primary grades learn about their country mostly in patriotic ways. They learn about the Pilgrims, the flag, and some of the nation's presidents. In the middle grades, children learn additional historical facts and come to understand the structure of government and the functions of the president, judges, and Congress. By high school, students have a more complex understanding of the political system, may identify with a political party, and may take positions on issues.

Generally, the more education a person receives, the more likely it is that the person will be interested in politics, be confident in his or her ability to understand political issues, and be an active participant in the political process.

Peers and Peer Group Influence. Once a child enters school, the child's friends become an important influence on behavior and attitudes. For children and for adults, friendships and associations in **peer groups** affect political attitudes. We must, however, separate the effects of peer group pressure on opinions and attitudes in general from the effects of peer group pressure on political opinions. For the most part, associations among peers are nonpolitical. Political attitudes are more likely to be shaped by peer groups when those groups are involved directly in political activities. Individuals who join an interest group based on ethnic identity, for example, may find a common political bond through working for the group's civil liberties and rights.

Opinion Leaders' Influence. We are all influenced by those with whom we are closely associated or whom we hold in high regard—friends at school, family members and other relatives, and teachers. In a sense, these people are **opinion leaders,** but on an *informal* level. That is, their influence on our political views is not necessarily intentional or deliberate. We are also influenced by *formal* opinion leaders, such as presidents, lobbyists, congresspersons, news commentators, and religious leaders, who have as part of their jobs the task of swaying people's views.

The Media and Public Opinion

Clearly, the **media**—newspapers, television, radio, and Internet sources—strongly influence public opinion. This is because the media inform the public about the issues and events of our times and thus have an **agenda-setting** effect. To borrow from Bernard Cohen's classic statement about the media and public opinion, the media may not be successful in telling people what to think, but they are "stunningly successful in telling their audience what to think about."[2] The media's influence will be discussed in more detail in Chapter 9.

The Popularity of the Media. Today, many contend that the media's influence on public opinion has grown to equal that of the family. For example, in her analysis of the role played by the media in American politics,[3] media scholar

> **Peer Group**
> A group whose members share common social characteristics. These groups play an important part in the socialization process, helping to shape attitudes and beliefs.
>
> **Opinion Leader**
> One who is able to influence the opinions of others because of position, expertise, or personality.
>
> **Media**
> The channels of mass communication.
>
> **Agenda Setting**
> Determining which public-policy questions will be debated or considered.

Pastor Rick Warren, author of *The Purpose Driven Life*, speaks to a conference on AIDS in Washington, D.C. *Is Warren an opinion leader?*

2. Bernard C. Cohen, *The Press and Foreign Policy* (Princeton, N.J.: Princeton University Press, 1963), p. 81.
3. Doris A. Graber, *On Media: Making Sense of Politics* (Boulder, Colo.: Paradigm Publishers, 2011).

Fairness Doctrine
A Federal Communications Commission rule enforced between 1949 and 1987 that required radio and television to present controversial issues in a manner that was (in the commission's view) honest, equitable, and balanced.

Generational Effect
The long-lasting effect of the events of a particular time on the political opinions of those who came of political age at that time.

Doris A. Graber points out that high school students, when asked where they obtain the information on which they base their views, mention the mass media far more than they mention their families, friends, and teachers. This trend may significantly alter the nature of the media's influence on public debate in the future.

The Impact of the New Media. The extent to which new forms of media have supplanted older ones—such as newspapers and the major broadcast networks—has been a major topic of discussion for several years. New forms include not only the World Wide Web, but also talk radio and cable television. Talk radio would seem to be a very dated medium, given that radio first became important early in the twentieth century. Between 1949 and 1987, however, the Federal Communications Commission (FCC) enforced the **Fairness Doctrine,** which required radio and television to present controversial issues in a manner that was (in the FCC's view) honest, equitable, and balanced. Modern conservative talk radio took off only after the Fairness Doctrine was abolished.

The impact of the various forms of new media appears to vary considerably. Talk radio and cable networks such as Fox News have given conservatives new methods for promoting their views and socializing their audiences. It is probable, however, that such media mostly strengthen the beliefs of those who are already conservative, rather than recruiting new members to the political right. A similar observation is often made about political blogs on the Internet, although in this medium liberals may be even better represented than conservatives. Blogs appear to radicalize their readers, rather than turn conservatives into liberals or vice versa. Indeed, cable news, talk radio, and political blogs are widely blamed for the increased polarization that has characterized American politics in recent years.

The impact of social networking sites such as Facebook is more ambiguous. Facebook does have strongly political "pages" that, in effect, are political blogs. Many interactions on Facebook, however, are between members of peer groups, such as students who attend a particular school or individuals who work in the same profession. Such groups are more likely to contain a variety of views than are groups explicitly organized around a political viewpoint. Facebook, in other words, may enhance peer group influence and even serve as a force for political moderation.

did you know?

In a poll, 21 percent of respondents agreed that a UFO crashed in Roswell, New Mexico, in 1947, and that the U.S. government covered it up.

Facebook founder Mark Zuckerberg marches with his employees in San Francisco's Gay Pride Parade. *How are leaders of the new media different from leaders of the old?*

Political Events and Public Opinion

Generally, older Americans tend to be somewhat more conservative than younger Americans—particularly on social issues but also, to some extent, on economic issues. This effect probably occurs because older adults are likely to retain the social values that they learned at a younger age. The experience of marriage and raising a family also has a measurable conservatizing effect. Young people, especially today, are more liberal than their grandparents on social issues, such as on the rights of gay men and lesbians and on racial and gender equality. Nevertheless, a more important factor than a person's age is the impact of momentous political events that shape the political attitudes of an entire generation. When events produce such a long-lasting result, we refer to it as a **generational effect** (also called a *cohort effect*).

Shutterstock/Kobby Dagan

Historical Events. Working class voters who grew up in the 1930s during the Great Depression were likely to form lifelong attachments to the Democratic Party, the party of Franklin D. Roosevelt. In the 1960s and 1970s, the war in Vietnam, the *Watergate break-in,* and the subsequent presidential cover-up fostered widespread cynicism toward government. (The Watergate break-in was the 1972 illegal entry into Democratic National Committee offices by members of President Richard Nixon's reelection organization.) There is evidence that the years of economic prosperity under President Ronald Reagan during the 1980s led many young people to identify with the Republican Party. The high levels of support that younger voters have given to Barack Obama during his presidential campaigns may be good news for the Democratic Party in future years, even if it has not helped the Democrats during midterm elections when the president is not on the ballot.

> **Socioeconomic Status**
> The value assigned to a person due to occupation or income. An upper-class person, for example, has high socioeconomic status.

The Political Mood. A number of political scientists believe that they can make some broad generalizations about events that tug voters to the political right or the political left. One such proposition is that the public mood swings in a more liberal direction when the federal government is successful, especially in handling economic issues. Presumably, the identification of liberalism with active government means that the image of liberalism improves when the government is successful. Likewise, the trend is toward conservatism during periods of perceived governmental failure.[4] The presidencies of Republican Gerald Ford (1974–1977) and Democrat Jimmy Carter (1977–1981) provide examples of failure. In those years, the government appeared to be incapable of addressing huge rises in prices, gasoline shortages, and other problems. The resulting trend toward conservatism culminated in the election of Republican Ronald Reagan (1981–1989) as president.

A second apparent tendency is that when the government seems to be introducing conservative policies—which usually means that a Republican is president—public sentiment drifts to the left. When governance is perceived to be liberal—which typically means there is a Democratic president—opinion moves to the right. This tendency and the success/failure dynamic just mentioned can reinforce each other or balance each other out. As an example, Reagan's presidency was both conservative and successful. As a result, the public mood, which was quite conservative at the time that Reagan was first elected, shifted back toward the center during his two terms in office. Eventually, voters picked Democrat Bill Clinton (1993–2001) as president.

Political Preferences and Voting Behavior

A major indicator of voting behavior is, of course, party identification. In addition, a variety of socioeconomic and demographic factors also appear to influence political preferences. These factors include education, income and **socioeconomic status,** religion, race/ethnicity, gender, geographic region, and similar traits. People who share the same religion, occupation, or any other demographic trait are likely to influence one another and may also have common political concerns that follow from the common characteristic.

Other factors, such as perception of the candidates and issue preferences, are closely connected to the electoral process itself. Table 6–1 that follows illustrates the impact of some of these variables on voting behavior.

■ **Learning Outcome 2:**
Identify the effects of various influences on voting behavior, including education, income, religion, race/ethnicity, gender, and geography.

---

4. For data on the public mood, see James A. Stimpson, *Public Opinion in America: Moods, Cycles, and Swings,* 2d ed. (Boulder, Colo.: Westview Press, 1999), plus annual updates through 2012 at www.unc.edu/~jstimson/Welcome.html.

Table 6–1 ▸ **Voters by Groups in Presidential Elections, 1996–2012 (in Percentages)**
Why do African Americans and Hispanics tend to support Democrats?

	1996		2000		2004		2008		2012	
	Clinton (Dem.)	Dole (Rep.)	Gore (Dem.)	Bush (Rep.)	Kerry (Dem.)	Bush (Rep.)	Obama (Dem.)	McCain (Rep.)	Obama (Dem.)	Romney (Rep.)
Total Vote	49	41	48	48	48	51	53	46	50	48
Gender										
Men	43	44	42	53	44	55	49	48	45	52
Women	54	38	54	43	51	48	56	43	55	44
Race										
White	43	46	42	54	41	58	43	55	39	59
Black	84	12	90	8	88	11	95	4	93	6
Hispanic	72	21	67	31	58	40	67	31	71	27
Educational Attainment										
Not a high school graduate	59	28	59	39	50	50	63	35	64	35
High school graduate	51	35	48	49	47	52	52	46	51	48
College graduate	44	46	45	51	46	52	50	48	47	51
Postgraduate education	52	40	52	44	54	45	58	40	55	42
Religion										
White Protestant	36	53	34	63	32	68	34	65	30	69*
Catholic	53	37	49	47	47	52	54	45	50	48
Jewish	78	16	79	19	75	24	78	21	69	30
White evangelical	NA	NA	NA	NA	21	79	24	74	21	78
Union Status										
Union household	59	30	59	37	59	40	59	39	58	40
Family Income										
Under $15,000	59	28	57	37	63	37	73	25	NA	NA
$15,000–29,000	53	36	54	41	57	41	60	37	63	35**
$30,000–49,000	48	40	49	48	50	49	55	43	57	42
Over $50,000	44	48	45	52	43	56	49	49	45	53
Size of Place of Residence										
Population over 500,000	68	25	71	26	60	40	70	28	69	29
Population 50,000 to 500,000	50	39	57	40	50	50	59	39	58	40
Population 10,000 to 50,000	48	41	38	59	48	51	45	53	42	56
Rural	44	46	37	59	39	60	45	53	37	61

Figures do not sum to 100 because of "other" or "no response" answers.
*In 2012, Protestant or "other Christian."
**In 2012, below $30,000.
NA = Not asked.
Sources: The National Election Pool, as reported by CBS, the *New York Times*, CNN, Fox News, and Politico.

Party Identification and Demographic Influences

With the possible exception of race, party identification has been the most important determinant of voting behavior in national elections. Party affiliation is influenced by family and peer groups, by generational effects, by the media, and by the voter's assessment of candidates and issues.

In the middle to late 1960s, party attachment began to weaken. Whereas independent voters were only a little more than 20 percent of the eligible electorate during the 1950s, they constituted more than 30 percent of all voters by the mid-1990s, and their numbers have grown since that time. New voters are likely to identify themselves as independent voters, although they may be more ready to identify with one of the major parties by their mid-thirties. There is considerable debate among political scientists over whether those who call themselves independents are truly so: when asked, a majority say that they are "leaning" toward one party or the other. (For further discussion of party affiliation, see Chapter 8.)

Demographic influences reflect the individual's personal background and place in society. Some factors, such as race and (for most people) religion, have to do with the family into which a person was born. Others may be the result of choices made throughout an individual's life: place of residence, educational achievement, and profession. It is also clear that many of these factors are interrelated. People who have more education typically have higher incomes and may hold professional jobs. Similarly, children born into wealthier families are far more likely to complete college than are children from poor families.

Educational Achievement. In the past, having a college education tended to be associated with voting for Republicans. In recent years, however, this correlation has become weaker. In particular, individuals with a postgraduate education—more than a bachelor's degree—have become predominantly Democratic. Many people with postgraduate degrees are professionals, such as physicians, attorneys, and college instructors. Usually, a postgraduate degree is an occupational requirement for professionals.

Despite the recent popularity of the master of business administration (MBA) degree, businesspersons are more likely to have only a bachelor's degree or no degree at all. They are also much more likely to vote Republican.

Also, a higher percentage of voters with only a high school education voted Republican in the last four presidential elections, compared with the pattern in previous elections, in which that group of voters tended to favor Democrats more strongly.

Economic Status. Family income is a strong predictor of economic liberalism or conservatism. Those with low incomes tend to favor government action to benefit the poor or to promote economic equality. Those with high incomes tend to oppose government intervention in the economy or to support it only when it benefits business. On political issues, therefore, the traditional political spectrum shown in Chapter 1, Table 1 is a useful tool. The rich often tend toward the right, and the poor often lean toward the left.

If we examine cultural as well as economic issues, however, the four-cornered ideological grid provided in Chapter 1, Figure 1 becomes important. It happens that upper-class voters are more likely to endorse cultural liberalism and lower-class individuals are more likely to favor cultural conservatism. Support for the right to have an abortion, for example, rises with income. It follows that

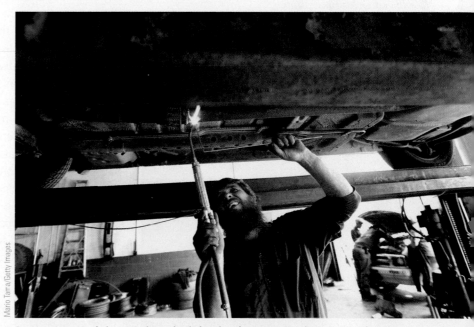

Some sections of the U.S. have high levels of poverty, such as in Owsley County, Kentucky, where this auto mechanic lives. *How does family income influence feelings about government?*

Mario Tama/Getty Images

libertarians—those who oppose government action on both economic and social issues—are concentrated among the wealthier members of the population. (Libertarians constitute the upper-right-hand corner of the grid in Figure 1–1 in Chapter 1.) Those who favor government action both to promote traditional moral values and to promote economic equality—economic liberals, cultural conservatives—are concentrated among groups that are less well off. (This group fills up the lower-left-hand corner of the grid.) As you might conclude from the chapter-opening *What If . . .* feature, those who are economic liberals and cultural conservatives tend to lack political clout.

That said, it remains generally true that the higher a person's income, the more likely that person will be to vote Republican. Manual laborers, factory workers, and especially union members are more likely to vote Democratic. There are no hard-and-fast rules, however. Many very poor individuals are devoted Republicans, just as some extremely wealthy people support the Democratic Party.

Religious Denomination. Traditionally, scholars have examined the impact of religion on political attitudes by dividing the population into such categories as Protestant, Catholic, and Jewish. In recent decades, however, such a breakdown has become less valuable as a means of predicting someone's political preferences. It is true that Jewish voters, as they were in the past, are notably more liberal than members of other groups, on both economic and cultural issues. Persons reporting no religion are very liberal on social issues but have mixed economic views.

Protestants and Non-Hispanic Catholics, however, have grown closer to each other politically in recent years. This represents something of a change—in the late 1800s and early 1900s, northern Protestants were distinctly more likely to vote Republican, and northern Catholics were more likely to vote Democratic. Even now, in a few parts of the country, Protestants and Catholics tend to line up against each other when choosing a political party.

Religious Commitment and Beliefs. Today, two factors turn out to be major predictors of political attitudes among members of the various Christian denominations. One factor is the degree of religious commitment, as measured by such actions as regular churchgoing. The other is the degree to which the voter adheres to religious beliefs that (depending on the denomination) can be called conservative, evangelical, or fundamentalist. High scores on either factor are associated with cultural conservatism on political issues—that is, with beliefs that place a high value on social order. (See Chapter 1 for a discussion of the contrasting values of order and liberty.)

Voters who are more devout, regardless of their church affiliation, tend to vote Republican, while voters who are less devout are more often Democrats. In the 2012 presidential elections, for example, Protestants who attended church weekly gave 70 percent of their votes to Republican candidate Mitt Romney, compared with 55 percent of those who attended church less often. Among Catholics, there was a similar pattern: 57 percent of Catholics who attended church weekly voted for Romney, while 42 percent of Catholics who were not regular churchgoers voted for him. Exit polls following the 2010 congressional elections showed the same pattern. There is an exception to this trend: African Americans of all religious tendencies have been strongly supportive of Democrats.

The politics of Protestant Americans who can be identified as holding evangelical or fundamentalist beliefs deserve special

did you know?

Americans who profess a religion other than Christianity are now 6 percent of the population, up from 4 percent in 2007.

Do most Jewish voters vote for liberal or for conservative candidates?

Leland Bobbé/Corbis

attention. Actually, a majority of American Protestants can be characterized as evangelical. Not all are politically conservative. Some are politically liberal, such as former Democratic presidents Jimmy Carter and Bill Clinton. Fundamentalists are a subset of evangelicals who believe in a number of doctrines not held by all evangelicals. In particular, fundamentalists believe in biblical inerrancy—that is, that every word of the Bible is literally true. In politics, fundamentalists are notably more conservative than other evangelicals. Liberal fundamentalists are rare indeed.[5]

Race and Ethnicity. Although African Americans, on average, are somewhat conservative on certain cultural issues, such as same-sex marriage and abortion, they tend to be more liberal than whites on social-welfare matters, civil liberties, and even foreign policy. African Americans voted principally for Republicans until Democrat Franklin Roosevelt's New Deal in the 1930s. Since then, they have largely identified with the Democratic Party. Indeed, Democratic presidential candidates have received, on average, more than 80 percent of the African American vote since 1956. Barack Obama's support among African Americans has been overwhelming.

Most Asian American groups lean toward the Democrats, although Vietnamese Americans are strongly Republican. Most Vietnamese Americans left Vietnam because of the Communist victory in the Vietnam War, and their strong anticommunism translates into conservative politics.

Muslim American immigrants and their descendants make up an interesting category.[6] In 2000, a majority of Muslim Americans of Middle Eastern ancestry voted for Republican George W. Bush because they shared his cultural conservatism. By 2012, the issues of Muslim civil liberties and discrimination against Muslims had turned Islamic voters into one of the nation's most Democratic blocs.

The Hispanic Vote. The diversity among Hispanic Americans has resulted in differing political behavior. The majority of Hispanic Americans vote Democratic. Cuban Americans, however, are often Republican. Most Cuban Americans left Cuba because of Fidel Castro's Communist regime. As in the example of the Vietnamese, anticommunism leads to political conservatism. By 2012, however, increasing numbers of young Cuban Americans were supporting the Democrats.

In 2004, as you saw in Table 6–1, Republican presidential candidate George W. Bush may have received almost 40 percent of the Latino vote. In 2008, however, Barack Obama won more than two-thirds of the Latino vote, a substantially larger number than his showing among non-Hispanic whites. Why did Latino support for the Republicans fall so greatly? In a word: immigration. Bush favored a comprehensive immigration reform that would have granted unauthorized immigrants a path to citizenship. Most Republicans in Congress refused to support Bush on this issue. The harsh rhetoric of some Republicans on this issue convinced many Latinos that the Republicans were hostile to Hispanic interests.

In 2012, according to one poll, Obama's support among Hispanics reached 75 percent, an all-time high. At the same time, Hispanics were

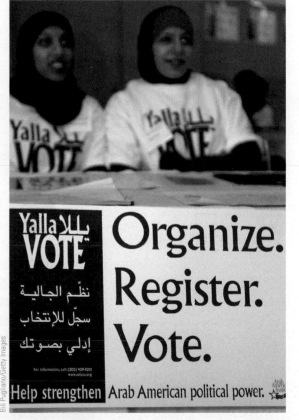

Bill Pugliano/Getty Images

Arab American activists promote voter registration in Dearborn, Michigan, a city with a substantial Arab American population. *What kinds of issues might sway the "Arab vote"?*

5. Douglas A. Sweeney, *The American Evangelical Story: A History of the Movement.* (Grand Rapids, Mich.: Baker Academic, 2005).
6. At least one-third of U.S. Muslims actually are African Americans whose ancestors have been in this country for a long time. In terms of political preferences, African American Muslims are more likely to resemble other African Americans than to resemble Muslim immigrants from the Middle East.

Gender Gap
The difference between the percentage of women who vote for a particular candidate and the percentage of men who vote for the candidate.

a growing share of the voting population—10 percent, up from 9 percent in 2008 and 8 percent in 2004. These trends were widely seen as a serious problem for the Republican Party. Following the elections, several leading Republicans began to take a much more positive line toward unauthorized immigrants.

The Gender Gap. Women won the right to vote in all states in 1920, and all the way through the 1960 elections they gave somewhat more support to Republicans than men did. From 1964 through 1976, women did not demonstrate a clear partisan preference. Beginning in 1980, however, with the election of Ronald Reagan, scholars began to detect a **gender gap**. Women were now favoring the Democrats, as you can see in Figure 6–3 that follows. In 2012, 55 percent of women voted for Democrat Barack Obama, compared with 45 percent of men, a margin of 10 percentage points.

Women's attitudes also appear to differ from those of their male counterparts on a range of issues other than presidential preferences. They are much more likely than men to oppose capital punishment and the use of force abroad. Studies also have shown that women are more concerned about risks to the environment, more supportive of social welfare, and more in agreement with extending civil rights to gay men and lesbians than are men.

Geographic Region. Finally, where you live can influence your political attitudes. In 2012, many commentators suggested that the white working class was hostile to Obama. This conclusion was not entirely accurate. In a pre-election poll by the Public Religion Research Institute, neither Obama nor Romney held a statistically significant lead among white working class voters in the East, Midwest, or West. In the South, however, Romney's margin was 62 percent to 22 percent (16 percent were undecided). Regardless of region, opposition to Obama was strongest among those who saw themselves culturally as Southerners—that is, as persons who identified with the losing side in the American Civil War.

The split between the city and the country is almost as important as the one between the North and the South. In 2012, Obama did far better than Romney in large cities. The northern states that Romney carried were often heavily rural.

did you know?

Britain had a major gender gap for much of the twentieth century—because women were much more likely than men to support the Conservative Party rather than the more left-wing Labour Party.

Figure 6–3 ▶ The Gender Gap in Presidential Elections

The gender gap is the difference between the percentage of women and the percentage of men voting for a given candidate, conventionally the Democrat. From 1980 on, the gender gap has always favored the Democrats. *Why might men be more attracted to Republicans?*

2012: Barack Obama (D) versus Mitt Romney (R)
2008: Barack Obama (D) versus John McCain (R)
2004: John Kerry (D) versus George W. Bush (R)
2000: Al Gore (D) versus George W. Bush (R)
1996: Bill Clinton (D) versus Bob Dole (R)
1992: Bill Clinton (D) versus George H. W. Bush (R)
1988: Michael Dukakis (D) versus George H. W. Bush (R)
1984: Walter Mondale (D) versus Ronald Reagan (R)
1980: Jimmy Carter (D) versus Ronald Reagan (R)

Percentage points

Source: Center for American Women and Politics

Election-Specific Factors

Factors such as perception of the candidates and issue preferences may have an effect on how people vote in particular elections. Candidates and issues can change greatly, and voting behavior can therefore change as well.

Perception of the Candidates. A candidate's image seems to be important in a voter's choice, especially for a presidential candidate. To some extent, voter attitudes toward candidates are based on emotions (such as trust) rather than on any judgment about experience or policy. In some years, voters have been attracted to a candidate who appeared to share their concerns and worries. In other years, voters have sought a candidate who appeared to have high integrity and honesty. Voters have been especially attracted to these candidates in

Thursday 43 percent. Was the president really more popular on Tuesday and Wednesday? Almost certainly not. These variations are simply artifacts of the polling process—so much "statistical noise."

The Difficulty of Obtaining Accurate Results

Reputable polling organizations devote a substantial amount of effort to ensuring that their samples are truly random. If they succeed, then the accuracy of their results should be limited only by sampling error. Unfortunately, obtaining a completely random sample of the population is difficult. Poll takers must consider that women are more likely to answer the telephone than men. Some kinds of people, such as students and low-income individuals, are relatively hard to contact.

Weighting the Sample. Polling firms address this problem of obtaining a true random sample by weighting their samples. That is, they correct for differences between the sample and the public by adding extra "weight" to the responses of underrepresented groups. For example, 20 percent of the respondents in a survey might state that they are evangelical Christians. Based on other sources of information, however, the poll taker believes that the true share of evangelicals in the target population is 25 percent. Therefore, the responses of the evangelical respondents receive extra weight so that they make up 25 percent of the reported result.

It is relatively easy to correct a sample for well-known demographic characteristics, such as education, gender, race, ethnicity, religion, and geography. It is much harder—and more dangerous—to adjust for political ideology, partisan preference, or likelihood of voting. The formulas that firms use to weight their responses are typically trade secrets and are never disclosed to the public or the press.

House Effects. One consequence of the use of secret in-house weighting schemes is that the results reported by one polling firm may differ from those reported by another in a systematic way. Pollster A might consistently rate the chances of Republican candidates as 2 percentage points higher than does pollster B. This could happen because pollster A thinks that turnout among Republican voters will be high, whereas pollster B predicts a lower turnout. Alternatively, pollster A may simply believe that there are more Republicans in the electorate. A consistent difference in polling results between firms is known as a **house effect**. (*House* here means the organization or firm, as when referring to casinos.) House effects are measured by comparing a firm's results with the average results of all other poll takers.

Some polling organizations have ties to one of the major political parties. Not surprisingly, many such firms have house effects that favor their parties. Such relationships do not always exist, however. Some party-linked pollsters exhibit no discernible house effect, and some firms that are known for their independence do demonstrate such an effect. Further, a house effect does not mean that a firm's results are in error. It could be noticing something important that its rivals have missed.

> **House Effect**
> In public opinion polling, an effect in which one polling organization's results consistently differ from those reported by other poll takers.

"Never mind what the voters are saying. What are the pollsters saying?"

did you know?

Research has demonstrated that poll respondents are more likely to give correct answers to factual questions if they are paid for being right, and they are even more accurate if they are encouraged to say "I don't know."

COMPARE WITH YOUR PEERS
MindTap· for American Government

Access the Public Opinion and Political Socialization Forum: Polling Activity—New York Times Instant Polls

How Accurate Are the Results?   We show the historical accuracy record of Gallup, perhaps the most famous pollster, in Figure 6–4 that follows. Despite all of the practical difficulties involved in poll taking, the major polling organizations have usually enjoyed a good record in predicting the outcome of presidential contests. Many major firms predicted the outcome of the 2012 presidential elections—and most of the U.S. Senate races—with considerable accuracy. Some poll takers, however, including two major firms, reported results that were embarrassingly inaccurate.

Gallup seriously overestimated voter turnout among Republicans and underestimated Democratic turnout. Gallup made major corrections at the last minute when it became clear that its models were inaccurate, but its predictions were still off. Rasmussen overweighted Republican respondents, in effect double-counting a bloc of Republican voters who identified as independents. Both pollsters predicted that Romney would win. He did not. Figure 6–5 that follows shows the 2012 predictions of several prominent pollsters.

Additional Problems with Polls

Public opinion polls are snapshots of opinions and preferences at a specific moment in time and as expressed in response to a specific question. Given that definition, it is fairly easy to understand situations in which the polls are wrong. For example, opinion polls leading up to the 1980 presidential elections showed President Jimmy Carter defeating challenger Ronald Reagan. Only a few analysts noted the large number of "undecided" respondents a week before the elections. Those voters shifted massively to Reagan at the last minute, and Reagan won the election.

The famous photo, nearby, of Harry Truman showing the front page of the newspaper that declared his defeat in the 1948 presidential election is another tribute to the weakness of polling. Again, the poll that predicted his defeat was taken more than a week before Election Day. Truman won the election with 49.9 percent of the vote.

Poll Questions.   It makes sense to expect that the results of a poll will reflect the questions that are asked. Depending on what question is asked, voters could be said either to support a particular proposal or to oppose it. One of the problems with many polls is the yes/no answer format. For example, suppose that a poll question asks, "Do you support President Obama's policies toward Syria?" Respondents who have a complicated view of

Figure 6–4 ▶ Gallup Poll Accuracy Record

This chart compares the percentage of the vote received by the winning presidential candidate with Gallup's final prediction. *Is Gallup still the "gold standard" among poll takers? Why or why not?*

Sources: *The Gallup Poll Monthly*, November 1992; *Time*, November 21, 1994; *The Wall Street Journal*, November 6, 1996; and authors' updates.

these events, as many people do, have no way of indicating their true position because "yes" and "no" are the only possible answers.

How a question is phrased can change the polling outcome dramatically. The Roper polling organization once asked a double-negative question that was very hard to understand: "Does it seem possible or does it seem impossible to you that the Nazi extermination of the Jews never happened?" The survey results showed that 20 percent of Americans seemed to doubt that the Holocaust ever occurred. When the Roper organization rephrased the question more clearly, the percentage of doubters dropped to less than 1 percent.

Respondents' answers are also influenced by the order in which questions are asked, by the possible answers from which the respondents are allowed to choose, and, in some cases, by their interaction with the interviewer. To a certain extent, people try to please the interviewer. They answer questions about which they have no information and avoid some answers to try to measure up to the interviewer's expectations.

Unscientific and Fraudulent Polls. A perennial issue is the promotion of surveys that are unscientific or even fraudulent. All too often, a magazine or Web site asks its readers to respond to a question—and then publishes the answers as if they were based on a scientifically chosen random sample. Other news media may then publicize the survey as if it were a poll taken by such reliable teams as Gallup, CBS and the *New York Times,* or the *Wall Street Journal* and NBC. Critical consumers should watch out for surveys with self-selected respondents and other types of skewed samples. These so-called polls may be used to deliberately mislead the public.

In recent years, polling experts have made a number of allegations of outright polling fraud. In these cases, so-called polling firms have been accused of reporting results without ever conducting any actual surveys. The numbers have been simply made up, out of thin air. After a challenge by polling experts, one such company ceased issuing polls and quietly disappeared. Another poll taker was sued by its largest customer, a major political blog. The blogger claimed that the pollster was making up its results. (The case was settled out of court.)

Figure 6–5 ▸ **Barack Obama's Predicted Margin of Victory over Mitt Romney in the 2012 Presidential Elections**

The eleven polls on this chart were conducted immediately before the elections. Two polling firms had ties to a political party. *Why might Obama have done better than many pollsters predicted?*

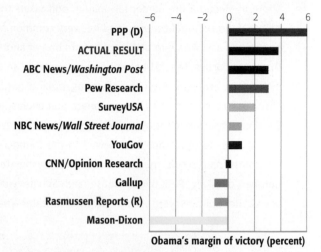

Obama's margin of victory (percent)

Sources: FiveThirtyEight and RealClearPolitics blogs.

President Harry Truman holds up the front page of the *Chicago Daily Tribune* issue that predicted his defeat on the basis of a Gallup poll. Truman, of course, defeated Dewey. The Gallup poll was completed more than a week before the election, so it missed a shift by undecided voters to Truman. *Why would a newspaper today be unlikely to make such an inaccurate prediction and put it on newsstands?*

AP Photo/Byron Rollins

2014 Elections

Polling Accuracy in the 2014 Elections

Midterm elections are harder for opinion poll takers to forecast than presidential contests, and it is very common for the polls taken as a whole to be biased toward one or another of the major parties. The 2014 elections were certainly an example of that problem. After the elections, polling guru Nate Silver calculated that the average Senate poll overestimated Democratic performance by 4 percentage points. The average poll of races for governor was skewed to the Democrats by 3.4 points. As a result, most poll takers underestimated the number of likely Republican House and Senate victories. Several Republicans were elected governor in states where no one thought they had a chance, such as Maryland. Senate polls were especially off in Arkansas, Kansas, Kentucky, and Virginia. Indeed, the Virginia race was a shocker. Democratic incumbent Mark Warner was supposed to be a shoo-in, leading by 10 percentage points. In the end, Republican Ed Gillespie was only about 17,000 votes away from winning. One factor in this result appears to have been very low turnout—Virginia had one of the lowest turnout rates of any major Senate contest. Some Warner supporters may have thought he didn't need their vote. In any event, this result should help keep pollsters humble.

did you know?

A straw poll conducted by patrons of Harry's New York Bar in Paris has an almost unbroken record of predicting the outcomes of U.S. presidential contests.

Push Polls. Some campaigns have used "push polls," in which the respondents are given misleading information in the questions asked to persuade them to vote against a candidate. The practice has spread throughout all levels of U.S. politics—local, state, and federal. In 1996, in a random survey of forty-five candidates, researchers found that thirty-five of them claimed to have been victimized by negative push-polling techniques used by their opponents.[7] Now even advocacy groups, as well as candidates for political offices, are using push polls. Push polling was prevalent during the congressional campaigns in 2010 and 2014, and the 2012 presidential and congressional campaigns.

Technology and Opinion Polls

Public opinion polling is based on scientific principles, particularly the principle of randomness. Today, technological advances allow polls to be taken over the Internet, but serious questions have been raised about the ability of pollsters to obtain truly random samples using this medium. The same was said not long ago when another technological breakthrough changed public opinion polling—the telephone.

The Advent of Telephone Polling. During the 1970s, telephone polling began to predominate over in-person polling. Obviously, telephone polling is less expensive than sending interviewers to poll respondents in their homes. Additionally, telephone

---

7.   Karl T. Feld, "When Push Comes to Shove: A Polling Industry Call to Arms," *Public Perspective,* September/October 2001, p. 38.

interviewers do not have to worry about safety problems, which is particularly important for interviewers working in high-crime areas. Finally, telephone interviews can be conducted relatively quickly. They allow politicians or the media to poll one evening and report the results the next day.

In recent years, many polling firms that rely on the telephone have begun employing automatic scripts read by a machine, the so-called *robopolls*. Polls of this type are much cheaper and easier to set up than traditional polls using live interviewers. Many observers also believe, however, that robopolls are substantially less accurate than traditional surveys.

Telephone Polling Problems. Somewhat ironically, the success of telephone polling has created major problems for the technique. The telemarketing industry in general has become so pervasive that people increasingly refuse to respond to telephone polls. More than 40 percent of households now use either caller ID or some other form of call screening. This has greatly reduced the number of households that polling organizations can reach.

For most telephone polls, the nonresponse rate has increased to as high as 80 percent. Such a high nonresponse rate undercuts confidence in the survey results. In most cases, polling only 20 percent of those on the list cannot lead to a random sample. Even more important for politicians is the fact that polling organizations are not required to report their response rates.

The Cell Phone Problem. An additional problem for telephone polling is the popularity of cell phones. Cellular telephone numbers are not always included in random-digit dialing programs and are not listed in telephone directories. Furthermore, pollsters cannot legally use robopolling to contact cell phone users. Also, individuals with cell phones may be located anywhere in the United States or the world, thus confounding attempts to reach people in a particular area. As more people, and especially younger Americans, choose to use only a cell phone and do not have a landline at all, polling accuracy is further reduced because these individuals are ignored by many polls.

A final problem for telephone pollsters that results from new technologies: many savvy Web users now rely on Skype and other voice-over-Internet services for their telephone calls. Skype allows users to see each other through the camera built into modern laptop computers, tablets, and cell phones. Groups of users can participate in videoconferences, viewing each other in separate windows on the screen. Skype's competitors include Ekiga, Empathy, Google Talk, and Linphone. Currently, *no* polling firm has discovered a way to survey voice-over-Internet users.

College Republicans work the polls in Virginia. *How might young Republicans view issues differently from older ones?*

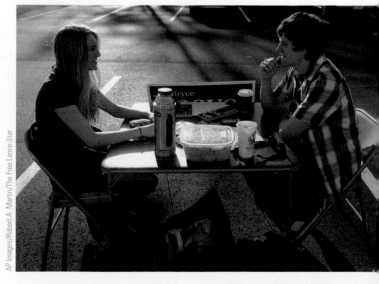

AP Images/Robert A. Martin/The Free Lance-Star

Enter Internet Polling. Obviously, Internet polling is not done on a one-on-one basis, because there is no voice communication. In spite of the potential problems, the Harris poll, a widely respected national polling organization, conducted online polls during the 1998 elections. Its election predictions were accurate in many states. Nonetheless, it made a serious error in one southern gubernatorial election. The Harris group subsequently refined its techniques and continues to conduct online polls. This organization believes that proper weighting of the results will achieve the equivalent of a random-sample poll.

How Representative Is the Internet? Public opinion experts, however, argue that the Harris poll procedure violates the mathematical basis of random sampling. Even so, the

Why Should You Care about...

Public Opinion?

Knowing what makes a poll accurate is important if you ever plan to participate in politics, even at the local level. Successful participation depends on knowing what your fellow citizens are thinking. If large numbers of other people agree with you that a particular policy needs to be changed, there may be a good chance that the policy can actually be altered. If almost no one agrees with you on a particular issue, there may be no point in trying to change policy immediately. The best you can do is to try to sway the opinions of others, in the hope that someday enough people will agree with you to make policy changes possible.

Internet population is looking more like the rest of America: almost as many women go online as men (76 percent of women and 80 percent of men), 71 percent of African American adults are online, and so are 68 percent of Hispanics (compared with 80 percent of non-Hispanic whites).[8]

"Nonpolls" on the Internet. Even if organizations such as the Harris poll succeed in obtaining the equivalent of a random sample when polling on the Internet, another problem will remain: the proliferation of "nonpolls" on the Internet. Every media outlet that maintains a Web site allows users to submit their opinions. A variety of organizations and for-profit companies send so-called polls to individuals through e-mail. Mister Poll bills itself as the Internet's largest online polling database. Mister Poll allows you to create your own polls just for fun and to include them on your home page. Like many other polling sites, Mister Poll asks questions on various issues and solicits answers from those who log on to its Web site. Although the Mister Poll site states, "None of these polls is scientific," sites such as this one undercut the efforts of legitimate pollsters to use the Internet scientifically.

■ **Learning Outcome 4:**
Consider the effect that public opinion may have on the political process.

Public Opinion and the Political Process

Public opinion affects the political process in many ways. Politicians, whether in office or in the midst of a campaign, see public opinion as important to their careers. The president, members of Congress, governors, and other elected officials realize that strong support by the public as expressed in opinion polls is a source of power in dealing with other politicians. It is more difficult for a senator to say no to the president if the president is immensely popular and if polls show approval of the president's policies. Public opinion also helps political candidates identify voters' most important concerns and may help them shape their campaigns successfully.

Political Culture and Public Opinion

Americans are divided into a multitude of ethnic, religious, regional, and political subgroups. Given the diversity of American society and the wide range of opinions contained within it, how is it that the political process continues to function without being stalemated by conflict and dissension?

One explanation is rooted in the concept of the American political culture, which can be described as a set of attitudes and ideas about the nation and the government. As discussed in Chapter 1, our political culture is widely shared by Americans of many different backgrounds. To some extent, it consists of symbols, such as the American flag, the Liberty Bell, and the Statue of Liberty. The elements of our political culture also include certain shared beliefs about the most important values in the American political system, including liberty, equality, and property.

Political Culture and Support for Our Political System. The political culture provides a general environment of support for the political system. If the people share certain beliefs about the system and a reservoir of good feeling exists toward the institutions of government, the nation will be better able to weather periods of crisis.

---

8. Pew Internet and American Life Project, August 2011 survey.

Political Trust. The political culture also helps Americans evaluate their government's performance. **Political trust,** the degree to which individuals express trust in political institutions, has been measured by a variety of polling questions. One of these is whether the respondent is satisfied with "the way things are going in the United States." Figure 6–6 that follows shows the responses to this question over time, which correspond to political developments. During the successful presidency of Republican Ronald Reagan, satisfaction levels rose from a fairly dismal 20 percent range to around 50 percent. Republican George H. W. Bush (1989–1993) enjoyed high levels of satisfaction until 1992, when rates fell back to the 20 percent range. This fall reflected the economic problems and other difficulties that handed the presidency to Democrat Bill Clinton.

Clinton's two terms appear to have been mostly a success, as satisfaction levels rose to as high as 70 percent. Under Republican George W. Bush (2001–2009), however, satisfaction levels slowly fell. In October 2008, at the peak of the crisis in the financial industry, satisfaction bottomed out at an unprecedented 7 percent.

Public Opinion about Government

A vital component of public opinion in the United States is the considerable ambivalence with which the public regards many major national institutions. Figure 6–7 that follows shows trends from 1993 to 2014 in opinion polls asking respondents how much confidence they had in the institutions listed. Over the years, military and religious organizations have ranked highest. Note, however, the decline in confidence in churches in 2002 following sex-abuse allegations against a number of Catholic priests. The public has consistently had more confidence in the military than in any of the other institutions shown in Figure 6–7. In 2002 and 2003, confidence in the military soared even higher, most likely because of the military's role in the war on terrorism.

Confidence in Other Institutions. The United States Supreme Court and the public schools have scored well over time. Less confidence is expressed in television, organized labor, and big business. From 2007 on, confidence in Congress almost disappeared. By 2013, the figure was down to 10 percent, an all-time low.

At times, popular confidence in all institutions may rise or fall, reflecting optimism or pessimism about the general state of the nation. For example, a Gallup poll in 2008

Political Trust
The degree to which individuals express trust in the government and political institutions, usually measured through a specific series of survey questions.

Figure 6–6 ▸ **Political Satisfaction Trend**

Question: In general, are you satisfied or dissatisfied with the way things are going in the United States at this time?

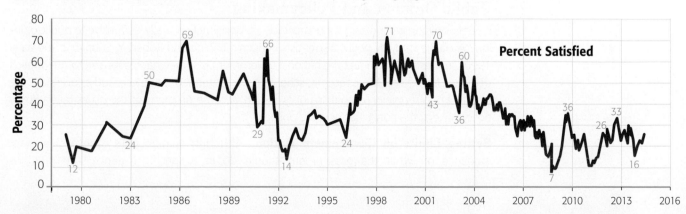

Satisfaction hit a minor peak of 33 percent on Election Day 2012, the highest number in several years before or since. *Why might satisfaction have been greater on that day?*

Source: Gallup polls, 1979 through 2014.

Figure 6-7 ▶ **Confidence in Institutions Trend**

Question: I am going to read a list of institutions in American society. Please tell me how much confidence you, yourself, have in each one: a great deal, quite a lot, some, or very little?

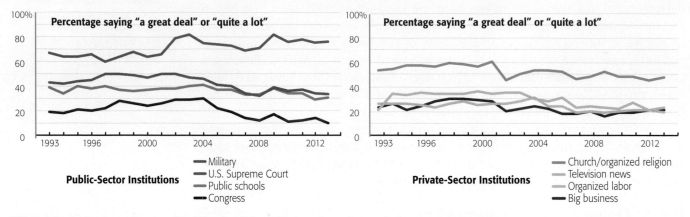

Why might the Supreme Court and public schools be at least moderately popular?
Source: Gallup polls over time.

---

following the onset of the Great Recession showed that the level of national satisfaction with the state of the nation had dropped to 14 percent—the lowest rating since 1992.

The Most Important Problem. Although people may not have much confidence in government institutions, they nonetheless turn to government to solve what they perceive to be the major problems facing the country. Table 6–2 that follows, which is based on Gallup polls conducted from the years 1985 to 2014, shows that the leading problems have changed over time. The public tends to emphasize problems that are immediate and that have been the subject of many stories in the media. When coverage of a particular problem increases suddenly, the public is more likely to see that as the most important problem. Thus, the fluctuations in the "most important problem" cited in Table 6–2 may, at times, be attributed to media agenda setting. In other years, however, the nation's leading problem has been so obvious that media attention is a minor factor. The Great Recession, which began in December 2007, is one example.

Public Opinion and Policymaking

If public opinion is important for democracy, are policymakers really responsive to public opinion? A classic study by political scientists Benjamin I. Page and Robert Y. Shapiro in the early 1990s suggested that in fact the national government is somewhat responsive to the public's demands for action.[9] More recently, scholars have contended that these studies overstate the effect of public opinion on public policy, in part because on many of the issues taken up by policymakers, the public has no clear opinions.[10]

Setting Limits on Government Action. Although opinion polls cannot give exact guidance on what the government should do in a specific instance, the opinions

---

9. Benjamin I. Page and Robert Y. Shapiro, *The Rational Public: Fifty Years of Trends in Americans' Policy Preferences* (Chicago: University of Chicago Press, 1992).
10. Paul Burstein, "Why Estimates of the Impact of Public Opinion on Public Policy Are Too High: Empirical and Theoretical Implications," *Social Forces*, Vol. 84, No. 4, June 2006, pp. 2273–2289.

Table 6–2 ▸ **Most Important Problem Trend, Present to 1985**

Why might politicians (and dissatisfaction with government in general) have moved to the top of the list in 2014?

2014	Politicians, economy	1999	Crime, violence
2013	Economy, unemployment	1998	Crime, violence
2012	Economy, unemployment	1997	Crime, violence
2011	Economy, unemployment	1996	Budget deficit
2010	Economy, unemployment	1995	Crime, violence
2009	Economy	1994	Crime, violence, health care
2008	Economy, war in Iraq	1993	Health care, budget deficit
2007	War in Iraq, health care	1992	Unemployment, budget deficit
2006	War in Iraq, terrorism	1991	Economy
2005	War in Iraq	1990	War in Middle East
2004	War in Iraq, economy	1989	War on drugs
2003	Terrorism, economy	1988	Economy, budget deficit
2002	Terrorism, economy	1987	Unemployment, economy
2001	Economy, education	1986	Unemployment, budget deficit
2000	Morals, family decline	1985	Fear of war, unemployment

Sources: *New York Times*/CBS News poll, January 1996; and Gallup polls, 1985 through 2014. This poll is usually conducted in January.

measured in polls may set an informal limit on government action. For example, consider the highly controversial issue of abortion. Most Americans are moderates on this issue. They do not approve of abortion as a means of birth control, but they do feel that it should be available under certain circumstances. Yet sizable groups of people express very intense feelings both for and against legalized abortion. Many politicians also hold polarized beliefs on the topic of abortion. Political party platforms take firm positions on abortion.

The strong words, however, are not matched with strong actions. At the national level, abortion policies have been roughly stable for years. Politicians know that radical changes to abortion policies would offend the opinions of the moderate majority. In this example, as in many others, public opinion does not make public policy. Rather, it restrains officials from taking truly unpopular actions. If officials do act in the face of public opposition, the consequences will be determined at the ballot box.

Citizens of foreign nations cannot vote in U.S. elections, but popular opinion in other countries can sometimes be an important consideration when our government establishes its foreign policies. We look at current world reactions to the U.S. government in the *Beyond Our Borders* feature that follows.

The Public versus the Policymakers. To what degree should public opinion influence policymaking? It would appear that members of the public view this issue differently than policy leaders do. Polls indicate that whereas a majority of the public feel that public opinion should have a great deal of influence on policy, a majority of policy leaders hold

Beyond Our Borders

What Do Foreign Nations Think about Us?

For a long time, residents of foreign nations have often had negative attitudes about the United States. Such attitudes are almost inevitable given that the United States is the most powerful nation on earth. Confidence in the United States reached new lows during the George W. Bush administration, however. Our war in Iraq was widely unpopular. In 2008, many people also blamed the United States for the financial crisis. British confidence in Bush, for example, was just 16 percent in 2008. The Pew Research Center reported that only nine of twenty-three nations polled reported that half or more of their residents had a favorable opinion of the United States.

The "Obama Bounce" Wears Off

The election of President Barack Obama improved foreign perceptions of this country substantially. To look again at Britain, in 2009 confidence in the U.S. president was at 86 percent, a dramatic turnaround in one year. Even in some Muslim nations, opinions of the U.S. government showed initial improvement.

By 2013, however, the honeymoon was over. British confidence in Obama was down to 72 percent. A British poll reported that only 46 percent thought that the United States had a positive impact on the world. Residents of other European countries had similar reactions. In most Muslim nations, views of the United States were abysmal. For example, only 11 percent of

Pakistanis and 16 percent of Egyptians had a favorable opinion of the American government. Still, America remained quite popular in Africa.

Drones and Spooks

It was probably inevitable that foreign citizens would fall out of love with Obama, but several specific problems seemed to have strengthened the disenchantment. One issue was U.S. drone missile strikes targeted at extremists in Pakistan, Somalia, and Yemen. In thirty-one of thirty-nine nations, at least half of those surveyed disapproved of the strikes.

A second issue was the revelation that our National Security Agency (NSA) was collecting cell phone data all over the world. After Germans discovered that the NSA had hacked Chancellor Angela Merkel's cell phone, support for Obama fell from 75 percent to 43 percent. Other European countries and nations such as Brazil also were highly critical of U.S. spying.

For Critical Analysis

Why does it matter what foreign nations think about us?

did you know?

Only 16 percent of Egyptians believe that Osama bin Laden's al Qaeda group was behind the 9/11 terrorist attacks. Of those polled, 43 percent believed Israel was responsible, and 12 percent blamed the U.S. government.

the opposite position. Why would a majority of policy leaders not want to be strongly influenced by public opinion? One answer to this question is that public opinion polls can provide only a limited amount of guidance to policymakers.

The Limits of Polling. Policymakers cannot always be guided by opinion polls. In the end, politicians must make their own choices. When they do so, their choices necessarily involve trade-offs. If politicians vote for increased spending to improve education, for example, by necessity fewer resources are available for other worthy projects. Moreover, to make an informed policy choice requires an understanding not only of the policy area but also of the consequences of any given choice. Public opinion polls very rarely ensure that those polled have such information.

Finally, government decisions cannot be made simply by adding up individual desires. Politicians engage in "horse trading" with each other. Politicians also know that they cannot satisfy every desire of every constituent. Therefore, each politician attempts to maximize the net benefits to his or her constituents, while keeping within the limits of whatever the politician believes the government can afford.

A Policy Example: Contraception Insurance

Many policy issues could be used to demonstrate the limits of public opinion's effect on policymakers. One example is a controversy that first surfaced in 2012: whether employers should be required to include coverage for birth control methods—contraception—in the insurance plans offered to their employees.

Under the health-care reform legislation adopted in 2010, it was left to the executive branch to define which medical services had to be covered by qualifying plans. In February 2012, the Obama administration ruled that religious bodies such as churches that opposed birth control in principle did not need to pay for health insurance plans that covered contraception. Institutions such as hospitals and schools that were owned or controlled by churches, however, would be required to provide coverage like all other employers.

The Controversy.   The Obama ruling was denounced by religious bodies, including the Catholic Church, that oppose contraception and also control hospitals and colleges. The issue was quickly picked up by Republicans in Congress, who accused the administration of trampling on religious freedom. Defenders of the ruling argued in response that exempting religiously owned hospitals and schools from the mandate would mean that employers could force their own religious principles on their employees. In the end, the Obama administration came up with a compromise under which contraception would still be covered by insurance, but religiously controlled institutions would not have to pay for the coverage. Many Catholic hospitals and colleges accepted this plan, but the Catholic bishops and a number of Catholic institutions sued to overturn it.

The Supreme Court Takes Up the Issue.   In 2013, the Supreme Court accepted a case dealing with contraception insurance. This case raised a broader issue—not whether religiously controlled institutions could be exempt from coverage, but whether *any* business could obtain such exemption. The owners of Hobby Lobby Stores objected to the coverage requirement based on their religious beliefs. Hobby Lobby, however, is a for-profit corporation with no affiliation to a religious organization. In June 2014, the Court ruled that family-owned corporations such as Hobby Lobby could indeed demand a religious exemption.[11] This decision did not resolve the question of whether the administration's compromise offer to church-controlled schools and hospitals was acceptable.

Public Opinion and the Controversy.   What effect did public opinion have on this dispute? That is hard to say, because it is not clear what the opinion of the public actually was. Popular attitudes were determined overwhelmingly by whether the topic of the controversy was religious freedom or the right of women to reproductive health care. Consider two polls taken by CBS News/*The New York Times*. An initial poll asked whether the insurance plans of religiously affiliated institutions should be required to cover contraception. Respondents supported coverage by 61 percent to 31 percent. One month later, the polling question included the language "opt out based on religious and moral objections." This time, respondents agreed by 57 percent to 36 percent that the institutions ought to be able to opt out.

These differing survey results emphasize the important concept of **framing.** The public response to a particular issue may depend largely on how the question is framed—in

Framing
Establishing the context of a polling question or a media report. Framing can mean fitting events into a familiar story or activating preconceived beliefs.

---

11. *Burwell v. Hobby Lobby,* 573 U.S. _____ (2014).

this example, whether the issue is framed as a question of women's health rights or a question of religious freedom. Indeed, the contraception insurance issue soon became a political battle to determine which frame would predominate. We look at another example of the importance of framing in this chapter's *Which Side Are You On?* feature that follows.

Which Side Are You On?

Do We Really Need to Spend More on Schools?

A common theme among Democratic candidates is that the nation needs to spend more on public schools. Funds spent on education are a form of investment—a better-educated workforce is more productive, and that leads to a higher standard of living for everyone. Around the world, nations have a larger per capita income when their students complete more years of education. Many Americans believe that our current public schools are not doing enough to educate our children to a high standard. The question remains, however: Are more dollars the solution to problems in public schools? Many conservatives believe that extra spending on the schools will not change educational outcomes. How the public responds to these arguments depends, to a great degree, on how the question is framed.

Spending on Schools Is Already High Enough

Those who oppose additional spending on public schools argue that educational outcomes around the country are poorly related to spending. Some opponents contend that many voters support more spending for public schools because the question is framed too simplistically. After all, education is a good thing, and who doesn't want more of a good thing? A recent survey by the journal *Education Next* reported that 65 percent of respondents favored spending more on public schools.

When these same respondents were informed that current levels of spending amount to an average of $12,922 per student every year, however, support for additional spending fell to 49 percent. When they were asked whether taxes to fund public schools should increase, only 35 percent supported the increase. If people aren't reminded that there is no such thing as a free lunch, they can be tempted to think that the way to fix the problems in public schools is to spend more. When voters are given a more accurate way to frame the problem, they will think again.

The Schools Have Suffered Too Many Cuts

Supporters of school spending have a ready criticism for the conclusions advanced in the *Education Next* study. They contend that the pollsters did not impose a more accurate frame on the question, but a misleading one. A cost of almost $13,000 per pupil may sound like a lot to some respondents—but these people have not been given information on what things actually cost. To make sense of a figure such as $13,000, respondents would need to receive detailed information on school budgets.

Putting the question in terms of higher taxes can also be misleading. At the federal level, at least, additional educational dollars can be freed by restraining the growth of other programs. Finally, "spending more on the schools" is not an accurate description of what has happened in recent years. As a result of our troubled economy, states and school systems across the country have been forced to reduce their budgets. More than 100,000 teachers have been laid off. Per capita spending on students is now below $12,500. The real issue isn't increased spending. Rather, the issue is restoring what has been cut. That is the frame we should use.

For Critical Thinking

Conservatives have pointed out that public school spending is poorly related to educational outcomes. Some liberals claim, however, that to equalize outcomes, we would have to spend *more* on schools that contain larger numbers of poor and troubled students than on other schools, and that this rarely happens. Does this argument make any sense? Why or why not?

How You Can Make a Difference

As a critical consumer, you need to be aware of what makes one set of public opinion poll results valid and other results useless or even dangerously misleading.

- Pay attention only to opinion polls that are based on scientific, or random, samples. In these samples, a known probability is used to select each person interviewed.

- Do not give credence to the results of opinion polls that consist of shopping-mall interviews or the like. The main problem with this kind of opinion taking is that not everyone has an equal chance of being in the mall when the interview is conducted. Also, it is almost certain that the people in the mall are not a reasonable cross section of a community's entire population.

- Probability samples are useful because you can calculate the range within which the results would have fallen if everybody had been interviewed. Well-designed samples will allow the pollster to say, for example, that he or she is 95 percent sure that in February 2009, 58 percent of the public, plus or minus 3 percentage points, opposed giving aid to U.S. automakers that were in danger of going bankrupt.

- Pay attention as well to how people were contacted for the poll—by mail, by telephone, in person in their homes, or in some other way. Because of its lower cost, polling firms have turned more and more to telephone interviewing. This method can produce accurate results, but it has its disadvantages—as discussed earlier in this chapter.

- One problem is that telephone interviews typically need to be short and to deal with questions that are fairly easy to answer. Interviews in person are better for getting useful information about why a particular response was given. They take much longer to complete, however.

- Results from mailed questionnaires should be taken with a grain of salt. Usually, only a small percentage of people send them back. When viewers or listeners of television or radio shows are encouraged to call in their opinions to an 800 telephone number, the polling results are meaningless.

- Users of the Internet also have an easy way to make their views known. Only people with access to computers and who are interested in the topic will take the trouble to respond, however, and that group may not be representative of the general public.

Key Terms

agenda setting 175
consensus 172
divided opinion 173
Fairness Doctrine 176
framing 195

gender gap 182
generational effect 176
house effect 185
media 175
opinion leader 175

opinion poll 183
peer group 175
political socialization 173
political trust 191
public opinion 172

sampling error 184
socioeconomic status 177

Chapter Summary

Learning Outcome 1 Public opinion is the aggregate of individual attitudes or beliefs shared by some portion of the adult population. A consensus exists when a large proportion of the public appears to express the same view on an issue. Divided opinion exists when the public holds widely different attitudes on an issue. Sometimes, a poll shows a distribution of opinion indicating that most people either have no information about an issue or are not interested enough in the issue to form a position on it.

People's opinions are formed through the political socialization process. Important factors in this process are the family, educational experiences, peer groups, opinion leaders, the media, and political events. The influence of the media as a socialization factor may be growing relative to the influence of the family.

Learning Outcome 2 Party identification is one of the most important indicators of voting behavior. Voting behavior is also influenced by demographic factors, such as education, economic status, religion, race and ethnicity, gender, and geographic region. Finally, voting behavior is influenced by election-specific factors, such as perception of the candidates and issue preferences.

Learning Outcome 3 Most descriptions of public opinion are based on the results of opinion polls. The accuracy of polls depends on sampling techniques. An accurate poll includes a representative sample of the population being polled and ensures randomness in the selection of respondents.

Problems with polls include sampling error, the difficulty in obtaining a truly representative sample, the issue of whether responses are influenced by the phrasing and order of questions asked, the use of a yes/no format for answers to the questions, and the interviewer's techniques. Many people are concerned about the use of push polls (in which the questions "push" the respondent toward a particular candidate). "Polls" that rely on self-selected respondents are inherently inaccurate and should be discounted.

Advances in technology have changed polling techniques over the years. During the 1970s, telephone polling became widely used. Today, largely because of extensive telemarketing, people often refuse to answer calls, and nonresponse rates in telephone polling have skyrocketed. Many poll takers also fail to include cell phone users. Due to the difficulty of obtaining a random sample in the online environment, Internet polls are often "nonpolls." Whether Internet polling can overcome this problem remains to be seen.

Learning Outcome 4 Public opinion affects the political process in many ways. The political culture provides a general environment of support for the political system, allowing the nation to weather periods of crisis. The political culture also helps Americans to evaluate their government's performance. At times, the level of trust in government has been relatively high. At other times, the level of trust has declined steeply. Similarly, Americans' confidence in government institutions varies over time, depending on a number of circumstances. Generally, though, Americans turn to government to solve what they perceive to be the major problems facing the country. In 2012, Americans ranked the economy and unemployment as the two most significant problems facing the nation.

Public opinion also plays an important role in policymaking. Although polling data show that a majority of Americans would like policy leaders to be influenced to a great extent by public opinion, politicians cannot always be guided by opinion polls. This is because the respondents often do not understand the costs and consequences of policy decisions or the trade-offs involved in making such decisions. How issues are framed has an important influence on popular attitudes.

Master the concept of Public Opinion and Political Socialization with MindTap™ for American Government

REVIEW MindTap™ for American Government
Access Key Term Flashcards for Chapter 6.

TEST YOURSELF MindTap™ for American Government
Take the Wrap It Up Quiz for Chapter 6.

STAY CURRENT MindTap™ for American Government
Access the KnowNow blog and customized RSS for updates on current events.

STAY FOCUSED MindTap™ for American Government
Complete the Focus Activities for Public Opinion and Political Socialization.

Additional Resources

The Internet is an excellent source for finding polling reports and data. All of the major polling organizations have Web sites that include news releases about polls they have conducted. Many sites make the polling data available for free to users. A few require that a user pay a subscription fee before accessing the polling archives on the site.

Online Resources

- Government and Politics on Facebook has almost 200,000 "likes" and is a major gateway to dozens of other sites. You can find it at www.facebook.com/govtpolitics.
- The Polling Report Web site offers polls and their results organized by topic. It is up to date and easy to use. To find it, go to www.pollingreport.com.
- The Gallup organization's Web site offers not only polling data but also information on how polls are constructed, conducted, and interpreted. See it at www.gallup.com.
- The Pew Research Center, a major public opinion research group, sponsors projects on journalism, the Internet, religion, Hispanics, global attitudes, and other topics. For a home page with links to all projects, visit www.pewresearch.org.
- Real Clear Politics is known for its "poll of polls," which aggregates results from leading pollsters in the run-up to elections. The site also aggregates polls on the president's job approval rating and other indicators. Although the site is run by conservatives, it offers opinion pieces from multiple media sources on its home page. Go to www.realclearpolitics.com.

Books

Burstein, Paul. *American Public Opinion, Advocacy, and Policy in Congress: What the Public Wants and What It Gets.* New York: Cambridge University Press, 2014. Burstein, a sociology professor at the University of Washington, attempts to determine the effect of popular opinion on legislation by "working backward." He first chooses a representative sample of bills, and then estimates how much influence the public had on the outcome.

Citrin, Jack, and David O. Sears. *American Identity and the Politics of Multiculturalism (Cambridge Studies in Public Opinion and Political Psychology).* New York: Cambridge University Press, 2014. The authors study how ethnic and racial minorities respond to the concept of multiculturalism. They find strong patriotism and support for assimilation among all groups. Citrin is a political science professor at UC Berkeley, and Sears is a professor at UCLA.

Perrin, Andrew J. *American Democracy: From Tocqueville to Town Halls to Twitter.* London: Polity Press, 2014. Perrin, a University of North Carolina sociologist, discusses how American democracy is based on a shared political culture.

Video

Purple State of Mind—A 2009 film, in which two old friends, college roommates, take different political roads—one left, the other right. They meet again and explore their differences.

Wag the Dog—A 1997 film that provides a very cynical look at the importance of public opinion. The film, which features Dustin Hoffman and Robert De Niro, follows the efforts of a presidential political consultant who stages a foreign policy crisis to divert public opinion from a sex scandal in the White House.

Quiz

Multiple Choice and Fill-Ins

Learning Outcome 1 Define *public opinion, consensus opinion,* and *divided opinion,* and discuss major sources of political socialization, including the family, schools, the media, and political events.

1. We can best define *public opinion* as:
   a. beliefs held by moderate voters.
   b. beliefs shared by both Republicans and Democrats.
   c. the aggregate of individual beliefs shared by some portion of adults.

2. If you are influenced in your political attitudes by your friends and co-workers, that means that a _____ _____ affects your attitudes.

Learning Outcome 2 Identify the effects of various influences on voting behavior, including education, income, religion, race/ethnicity, gender and geography.

3. The gender gap refers to:
   a. the difference in college attendance rates for males and females.
   b. the tendency for women to be more likely to vote for a particular candidate than men.
   c. the tendency for men to dominate the political process.

4. With the possible exception of race, _____ _____ is the most important determinant of voting behavior in national elections.

Learning Outcome 3 Describe the characteristics of a scientific opinion poll, and list some of the problems pollsters face in obtaining accurate results.

5. One way to compensate for underrepresented groups in a polling sample is to:
   a. eliminate all answers from those who are part of the underrepresented group.
   b. reduce the weight given to the underrepresented group so that it does not count excessively.
   c. compensate by adding extra weight to the responses of the underrepresented group.

6. When one polling organization's results consistently differ from those of other poll takers, we call this the _____ effect.

Learning Outcome 4 Consider the effect that public opinion may have on the political process.

7. The trend in political satisfaction in this country has:
   a. always been very high.
   b. fallen since around 2001.
   c. risen since around 2001.

8. The same polling question can result in different responses depending on how that question is _____.

Essay Questions

1. Years ago, people with postgraduate degrees were more likely to vote for Republican than Democratic candidates, but in recent years, highly educated voters have been trending Democratic. Why might physicians and lawyers be more likely to vote Democratic than in the past? For what reasons might college professors lean Democratic?

2. Why do you think the American people express a relatively high degree of confidence in the military as an institution? Why do people express less confidence in Congress than in other major institutions? Could people be holding various institutions to different standards, and if so, what might these standards be?

Interest Groups

7

In New York City, interest groups rally in favor of unionizing fast-food workers and raising the minimum wage. *Which groups would probably oppose such demands?*
Andrew Burton/Getty Images

The five Learning Outcomes below are designed to help improve your understanding of this chapter. After reading this chapter, you should be able to:

- **Learning Outcome 1:** Describe the basic characteristics of interest groups, and provide three major reasons why Americans join them.
- **Learning Outcome 2:** List the major types of interest groups, especially those with economic motivations.
- **Learning Outcome 3:** Evaluate the factors that make some interest groups especially effective.
- **Learning Outcome 4:** Discuss direct and indirect interest group techniques.
- **Learning Outcome 5:** Describe the main ways in which lobbyists are regulated.

▶ WATCH & LEARN MindTap· for American Government
Watch a brief "What Do You Know?" video summarizing Interest Groups.

What If...

The Minimum Wage Were Really High?

BACKGROUND

A minimum wage is the lowest wage rate that an employer can legally pay. The national minimum wage is set by Congress. Currently, it is $7.25 per hour. Twenty states have minimum wages that are higher than that. At $9.32 per hour, Washington State has the highest minimum wage. Seattle has just established a $15.00 minimum wage. Australia has the world's highest such wage—$22.74 in U.S. dollars.

Increases in the minimum wage are always controversial. In 2014, President Obama ordered a $10.10 minimum wage for federal contractors. He also proposed such a wage for all workers. With that, the debate was on.

Obviously, hiking the minimum wage raises the pay of the lowest-paid workers. These workers become more expensive to hire. It is basic economics that ordinarily, if something costs more people will buy less of it. In principle, a higher minimum wage should therefore reduce the number of low-wage jobs. It is not clear, though, whether modest increases in the minimum wage do in fact have a measurable effect on employment.

Indeed, the impact of a minimum wage hike on employment is very controversial. Interest groups of all kinds have a stake in this issue. Lobbyists for the restaurant and retail industries argue that even the lowest increase will cost many jobs. Labor and liberal interest groups contend that the impact of a modest raise is too small to measure. Still, every economist agrees that if you raise the minimum wage high enough, there will be consequences. The political question is, "how high is too high?" Without trying to answer that question, we can ask what the effects of a very high minimum wage might be.

WHAT IF THE MINIMUM WAGE WERE REALLY HIGH?

Certainly, a really high minimum wage would lift many of the working poor out of poverty. Another likely outcome of such a minimum wage is less income inequality. We can also predict that among people earning the minimum wage who remain employed, there would be less turnover—workers would stay longer in such jobs. A very high minimum wage could also lead some employers to increase the performance that they expect from workers, however.

BUSINESSES THAT EMPLOY LOW-WAGE WORKERS

Many minimum-wage workers are in food service, especially fast-food restaurants, as well as various retail stores. If the minimum wage were really high, the profits in such industries would most

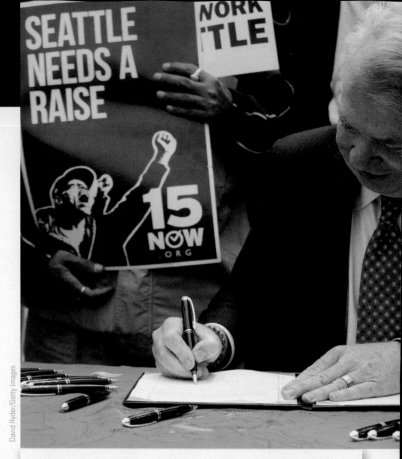

Seattle mayor Ed Murray signs an ordinance raising the minimum wage in that city to $15.00. *Why are wages high in Washington State?*

likely fall. It is quite possible that these businesses would raise their prices to recoup the lost profits. Consequently, consumers might see higher prices for hamburgers and pizza, as well as budget clothing from Walmart. Of course, the people who rely the most on such products are other low-income workers.

THE YOUNG AND THE UNSKILLED

A really high minimum wage almost certainly would affect low-skilled workers, including many teenagers. No businessperson will consistently pay a worker a wage rate that exceeds the value of that worker's output. Teenage unemployment, particularly among minorities, might rise. Teenagers who cannot find a minimum-wage job would lose out on the opportunity to learn basic work skills that could help them find better jobs later.

For Critical Analysis

1. Is it possible that a very high minimum wage would ultimately result in more automation in the fast food industry? Why or why not?

2. In polls, 90 percent of Democrats and 53 percent of Republicans support a higher minimum wage. Why might such legislation be popular?

The structure of American government invites the participation of **interest groups** at various stages of the policymaking process. Americans can form groups in their neighborhoods or cities and lobby the city council or their state government. They can join statewide groups or national groups and try to influence government policy through Congress or through one of the executive agencies or cabinet departments. Representatives of large corporations may seek to influence members of Congress or the president personally at social events or fund-raisers. All of these practices were in use during the debate over raising the minimum wage, discussed in the chapter-opening *What If. . .* feature. When attempts to influence government through the executive and legislative branches fail, interest groups can turn to the courts, filing suits in state or federal courts to achieve their political objectives.

The large number of "pressure points" in American government helps to explain why there are so many—more than one hundred thousand—interest groups at work in our society. Another reason for the multitude of interest groups is that the right to join a group is protected by the First Amendment to the U.S. Constitution (see Chapter 4). Not only are all people guaranteed the right "peaceably to assemble," but they are also guaranteed the right "to petition the Government for a redress of grievances." This constitutional provision encourages Americans to form groups and to express their opinions to the government or to their elected representatives as members of these groups. The constitutional protection of groups is one reason that it would be very difficult to satisfy the occasional demand that **lobbyists**—persons hired to represent interest groups to the government—be banned.

Interest Group Fundamentals

Interest groups play a significant role in American government at all levels. As you will read later in this chapter and in Chapter 9, one of the ways in which interest groups attempt to influence government policies is through campaign contributions to members of Congress who intend to run for reelection. It is the interplay between campaign financial assistance and legislation favorable to specific interests that has caused some observers to claim that Congress has been sold to the highest bidder. Certainly, devising a system in which campaigns can be financed *without* jeopardizing objectivity on the part of members of Congress is a major challenge for our nation today.

Interest Groups: A Natural Phenomenon

Alexis de Tocqueville observed in the early 1830s that "in no country of the world has the principle of association been more successfully used or applied to a greater multitude of objectives than in America."[1] The French traveler was amazed at the degree to which Americans formed groups to solve civic problems, establish social relationships, and speak for their economic or political interests. Perhaps James Madison, when he wrote *Federalist Paper* No. 10 (see Appendix B), had already judged the character of his country's citizens similarly. He supported the

***

1. Alexis de Tocqueville, *Democracy in America*, Vol. 1 [1835], ed. Phillips Bradley (New York: Knopf, 1980), p. 191.

LISTEN & LEARN
MindTap® for American Government

Access Read Speaker to listen to Chapter 7.

■ **Learning Outcome 1:** Describe the basic characteristics of interest groups, and provide three major reasons why Americans join them.

Interest Group
An organized group of individuals sharing common objectives who actively attempt to influence policymakers.

Lobbyist
An organization or individual who attempts to influence legislation and the administrative decisions of government.

Lobbyists hold a lunch meeting in Washington, D.C. *Why does lobbying have constitutional protection?*

Linda Davidson/The Washington Post via Getty Images

These women wanted the right to vote in 1900. *Did they have many supporters then?*

creation of a large republic with many states to encourage the formation of multiple interests. The multitude of interests, in Madison's view, would work to discourage the formation of an oppressive majority interest.

Poll data show that more than two-thirds of all Americans belong to at least one group or association. Although the majority of these affiliations could not be classified as "interest groups" in the political sense, Americans certainly understand the principles of working in groups.

Today, interest groups range from the elementary school parent-teacher association and the local "Stop the Sewer Plant Association" to the statewide association of insurance agents. They include small groups such as local environmental organizations and national groups such as the American Civil Liberties Union, the National Education Association, and the American League of Lobbyists.

Interest Groups and Social Movements

Interest groups are often spawned by mass **social movements.** Such movements represent demands by a large segment of the population for change in the political, economic, or social system. A social movement is often the first expression of latent discontent with the existing system. It may be the authentic voice of weaker or oppressed groups in society that do not have the means or standing to organize as interest groups. For example, the women's movement of the early 1800s suffered disapproval from most mainstream political and social leaders. Because women were unable to vote or take an active part in the political system, it was difficult for women who desired greater freedoms to organize formal groups. After the Civil War, when more women became active in professional life, organizations seeking to win women the right to vote came into being.

African Americans found themselves in an even more disadvantaged situation after the end of the Reconstruction period (1865–1877). They were unable to exercise political rights in many southern states, and their participation in any form of organization could lead to economic ruin, physical harassment, or even death. The civil rights movement of the 1950s and 1960s was clearly a social movement. To be sure, several formal organizations worked to support the movement—including the Southern Christian Leadership Conference, the National Association for the Advancement of Colored People, and the Urban League—but only a social movement could generate the kinds of civil disobedience that took place in hundreds of towns and cities across the country.

Social movements may generate interest groups with specific goals. In the example of the women's movement of the 1960s, the National Organization for Women was formed in part out of a demand to end gender-segregated job advertising in newspapers.

Why Do Americans Join Interest Groups?

One puzzle that has fascinated political scientists is why some people join interest groups, while many others do not. Everyone has some interest that could benefit from government action. For many individuals, however, those concerns remain unorganized interests, or **latent interests.**

According to political theorist Mancur Olson,[2] it simply may not be rational for individuals to join most groups. In his classic work on this topic, Olson introduced the idea of

Social Movement
A movement that represents the demands of a large segment of the public for political, economic, or social change.

Latent Interests
Public-policy interests that are not recognized or addressed by a group at a particular time.

---

2. Mancur Olson, *The Logic of Collective Action* (Cambridge, Mass.: Harvard University Press, 1965).

the "collective good." This concept refers to any public benefit that, if available to any member of the community, cannot be denied to any other member, whether or not he or she participated in the effort to gain the good.

Although collective benefits are usually thought of as coming from such public goods as clean air and national defense, benefits are also bestowed by the government on subsets of the public. Price subsidies to dairy farmers and loans to college students are examples. Olson used economic theory to propose that it is not rational for interested individuals to join groups that work for *group* benefits. In fact, it is often more rational for the individual to wait for others to procure the benefits and then share them. How many community college students, for example, join the American Association of Community Colleges, an organization that lobbies the government for increased financial aid to students? The difficulty interest groups face in recruiting members when the benefits can be obtained without joining the groups is referred to as the **free rider problem.**

If so little incentive exists for individuals to join together, why are there thousands of interest groups lobbying in Washington? According to the logic of collective action, if the contribution of an individual *will* make a difference to the effort, then it is worth it to the individual to join. Thus, smaller groups, which seek benefits for only a small proportion of the population, are more likely to enroll members who will give time and funds to the cause. Larger groups, which represent general public interests (the women's movement or the American Civil Liberties Union, for example), will find it relatively more difficult to get individuals to join. People need an incentive—material or otherwise—to participate.

Solidary Incentives. Interest groups offer **solidary incentives** for their members. Solidary benefits include companionship, a sense of belonging, and the pleasure of associating with others. Although the National Audubon Society was originally founded to save the snowy egret from extinction, today most members join to learn more about birds and to meet and share their pleasure with other individuals who enjoy bird-watching as a hobby. Even though the incentive might be solidary for many members, this organization nonetheless also pursues an active political agenda, working to preserve the environment and to protect endangered species. Still, most members may not play any part in working toward larger, more national goals unless the organization can convince them to take political action or unless some local environmental issue arises.

Material Incentives. For other individuals, interest groups offer direct **material incentives.** A case in point is AARP (formerly the American Association of Retired Persons), which provides discounts, insurance plans, and organized travel opportunities for its members. Because of its exceptionally low dues ($16 annually) and the benefits gained through membership, AARP has become the largest—and a very powerful—interest group in the United States. AARP can claim to represent the interests of millions of senior citizens and can show that they actually have joined the group. For most seniors, the material incentives outweigh the membership costs.

Another example of such an interest group is the American Automobile Association (AAA). Most people who join this organization do so for its emergency roadside assistance and trip planning.

Free Rider Problem
The difficulty interest groups face in recruiting members when the benefits they achieve can be gained without joining the group.

Solidary Incentive
A reason or motive that follows from the desire to associate with others and to share with others a particular interest or hobby.

Material Incentive
A reason or motive based on the desire to enjoy certain economic benefits or opportunities.

did you know?
At least half of all lobbyists in Washington, D.C., are women.

CONNECT WITH YOUR CLASSMATES
MindTap for American Government

Access the Interest Groups Forum: Discussion Board—Participation in Interest Groups

Purposive Incentive
A reason for supporting or participating in the activities of a group that is based on agreement with the goals of the group. For example, someone with a strong interest in human rights might have a purposive incentive to join Amnesty International.

Many members may not realize that the AAA is also a significant interest group seeking to shape laws that affect drivers.

Many other interest groups offer indirect material incentives for their members. Such groups as the American Dairy Association and the National Association of Automobile Dealers do not give discounts or "freebies" to their members, but they do offer indirect benefits and rewards by, for example, protecting the material interests of their members from government policymaking that is injurious to their industry or business.

Purposive Incentives. Interest groups also offer the opportunity for individuals to pursue political, economic, or social goals through joint action. **Purposive incentives** offer individuals the satisfaction of taking action when the goals of a group correspond to their beliefs or principles. The individuals who belong to a group focusing on the abortion issue or gun control, for example, do so because they feel strongly enough about the issues to support the group's work with money and time.

Some scholars have argued that many people join interest groups simply for the discounts, magazine subscriptions, and other tangible benefits and are not really interested in the political positions taken by the groups. According to William P. Browne, however, research shows that people really do care about the policy stance of an interest group. Representatives of a group seek people who share the group's views and then ask them to join. As one group leader put it, "Getting members is about scaring the hell out of people."[3] People join the group and then feel that they are doing something about a cause that is important to them.

did you know?

Firms lobbying for the American Jobs Creation Act, which created a tax holiday for earnings repatriated from abroad, gained a return of $220 for every $1 they spent lobbying.

■ **Learning Outcome 2:**
List the major types of interest groups, especially those with economic motivations.

Types of Interest Groups

Thousands of groups exist to influence government. Among the major types of interest groups are those that represent the main sectors of the economy. In addition, a number of environmental groups and "public-interest" organizations have been formed to protect the environment and represent the needs of the general citizenry. Other types of groups include many "single-issue" groups, ideological groups, and groups based on race, sex, or sexual orientation. The interests of foreign governments and foreign businesses are represented in the American political arena as well. The names of some major interest groups are shown in Table 7–1 that follows.

Economic Interest Groups

More interest groups are formed to represent economic interests than any other set of interests. The variety of economic interest groups mirrors the complexity of the American economy. Major sectors that seek influence in Washington, D.C., include business, agriculture, labor unions, government workers, and professionals.

Business Interest Groups. Thousands of business groups and trade associations work to influence government policies that affect their respective industries. "Umbrella groups" represent

This twenty-four-year-old Pennsylvania dairy farmer has a Penn State degree in agriculture. He has taken over the farm from his father, who died two years ago. Why is it hard to become a farmer if you were not raised in a farm family?

AP Photo, Erie Times-News, Greg Wohlford

3. William P. Browne, *Groups, Interests, and U.S. Public Policy* (Washington, D.C.: Georgetown University Press, 1998), p. 23.

Table 7–1 ▶ A List of Effective Interest Groups

Do you know people who are members of any of these groups?

Business
- American Bankers Association
- American Farm Bureau Federation
- American Hospital Association
- America's Health Insurance Plans
- Business Roundtable
- Chamber of Commerce of the United States
- National Association of Home Builders
- National Association of Manufacturers (NAM)
- Pharmaceutical Research and Manufacturers of America

Labor
- American Federation of Labor–Congress of Industrial Organizations (AFL-CIO)
- American Federation of State, County, and Municipal Employees (AFSCME)
- Change to Win (a federation of labor unions)
- International Brotherhood of Teamsters
- National Education Association (NEA)
- Service Employees International Union

Professional
- American Association for Justice (trial lawyers)
- American Medical Association (AMA, representing physicians)
- National Association of Realtors

Identity
- AARP (formerly the American Association of Retired Persons)
- League of United Latin American Citizens (LULAC)
- National Association for the Advancement of Colored People (the NAACP, representing African Americans)
- National Organization for Women (NOW)

Environmental
- National Audubon Society
- National Wildlife Federation
- Nature Conservancy
- Sierra Club

Other
- American Civil Liberties Union (ACLU)
- American Israel Public Affairs Committee (AIPAC)
- American Legion (veterans)
- American Society for the Prevention of Cruelty to Animals (ASPCA)
- Amnesty International USA (human rights)
- Consumers Union
- Handgun Control, Inc. (favors gun control)
- Mothers Against Drunk Driving (MADD)
- NARAL Pro-Choice America
- National Rifle Association (NRA)
- National Right to Life Committee

collections of businesses or other entities. For example, the National Association of Manufacturers is an umbrella group that represents manufacturing concerns. Some business groups are decidedly more powerful than others. Consider the U.S. Chamber of Commerce, which represents about 3 million member companies. It can bring constituent influence to bear on every member of Congress.

Agricultural Interest Groups. American farmers and their employees represent less than 1 percent of the U.S. population. In spite of this, farmers' influence on legislation beneficial to their interests has been significant. Farmers have succeeded in their aims because they have very strong interest groups. For example, the American Farm Bureau Federation, or Farm Bureau, established in 1919, represents more than 5.5 million families (a majority of whom are not actually farm families) and is usually seen as conservative. Another important agricultural interest organization is the National Farmers' Union (NFU), which is considered more liberal.

Agricultural interest groups have probably been more successful than any other groups in obtaining subsidies from American taxpayers. U.S. farm subsidies are expected to cost taxpayers almost $20 billion a year over the next decade.

did you know?
The American food processing industry slaughters up to 9 billion chickens each year.

Labor Movement
The economic and political expression of working-class interests.

In the past, the "farm bill" that authorizes these payments was a bipartisan exercise, with farm-state Republicans and Democrats cooperating closely. A new farm bill was due in 2012, but the severe political polarization of today's Congress delayed legislation until 2014. The new law abolished *direct payments*, which paid farmers of certain crops whether or not they actually grew the crops. In exchange, subsidies for crop insurance were raised considerably.

As expensive as U.S. agricultural supports may be, many other nations provide their farmers with even greater subsidies. We provide some figures in the *Beyond Our Borders* feature that follows.

Labor Interest Groups. Interest groups representing the **labor movement** date back to at least 1886, when the American Federation of Labor (AFL) was formed. In 1955, the AFL joined forces with the Congress of Industrial Organizations (CIO). Today, the combined AFL-CIO is a large federation with a membership of about 10 million workers and an active political arm called the Committee on Political Education. In a sense, the AFL-CIO is a union of unions.

The AFL-CIO remained the predominant labor union organization for fifty years. The AFL-CIO experienced discord within its ranks during 2005, however, as four key unions left

Beyond Our Borders

How Foreign Countries Subsidize Agriculture

U.S. agricultural subsidies have often been controversial. In the 1930s, when subsidies began, many farmers were seriously impoverished. With today's large farms and high commodity prices, this is no longer true. It is worth noting, however, that the United States is far from the greatest sinner in the farm subsidy game. Most wealthy nations and some middle-income nations provide larger subsidies. Figure 7–1 shows the size of farm subsidies as a percentage of total agricultural production. We give a single figure for the European Union, a confederation of twenty-eight countries with a Common Agricultural Policy (CAP). While the CAP is generous, it was more so in the past. In the 1980s, it paid out subsidies worth 40 percent of production.

Figure 7–1 ▶ **Agricultural Subsidies as a Percent of Production Value**

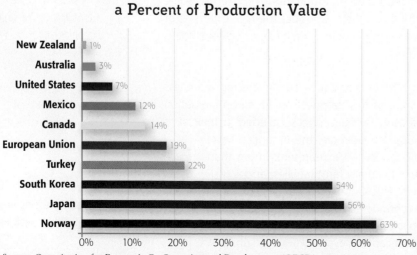

Source: Organisation for Economic Co-Operation and Development (OECD).

Country	Percent
New Zealand	1%
Australia	3%
United States	7%
Mexico	12%
Canada	14%
European Union	19%
Turkey	22%
South Korea	54%
Japan	56%
Norway	63%

For Critical Analysis

Some African countries tax farmers to support people who live in cities. If those countries were on this chart, their figures would actually be negative. Why might such nations have policies so different from those of wealthier countries?

the federation and formed the Change to Win Coalition. Today, Change to Win has a membership of about 4 million workers. Many labor advocates fear that the split will reduce organized labor's influence.

Labor's Decline. Even before the split, the role of unions in American society had been waning, as witnessed by the decline in union membership (see Figure 7–2 that follows). In the age of automation and with the rise of the **service sector,** blue-collar workers in basic industries (auto, steel, and the like) represent a smaller and smaller percentage of the total working population.

Because of this decline in the industrial sector of the economy, national unions are looking to nontraditional areas for their membership, including migrant farmworkers, service workers, and especially public employees—such as police officers, firefighting personnel, teachers, college professors, and even graduate assistants. Indeed, public-sector unions make up an ever-greater share of the labor movement.

Public Employee Unions. The degree of unionization in the private sector has declined over the past fifty years, but this decline has been partially offset by growth in the unionization of public employees. Figure 7–2 displays the growth in public-sector unionization. With a total membership of more than 7 million, public-sector unions are a powerful force.

Charley Galley/Getty Images

These writers are members of the Writers Guild of America in Hollywood, California. *If you were to classify this interest group, what kind would it be?*

Figure 7–2 ▶ **Decline in Union Membership, 1948 to Present**

The percentage of the total workforce that consists of labor union members has declined greatly over the past forty years. The percentage of government workers who are union members, however, increased significantly in the 1960s and 1970s and has remained stable since. (Note that the percentage of the workforce that consists of union members, as shown on this chart, is several points lower than the percentage of workers represented by a union, because most unions represent some nonmembers.) *Why could it be easier to organize a union in the public sector than the private sector?*

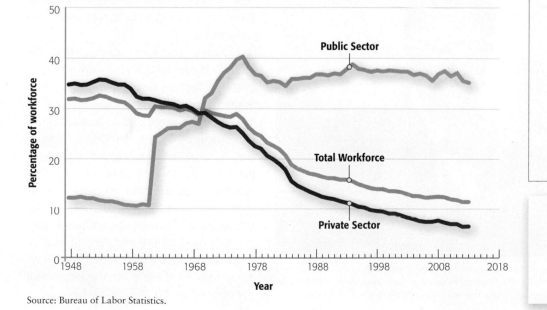

Source: Bureau of Labor Statistics.

did you know?

With about 3 million workers, the National Education Association (NEA) is the largest labor union in the country. Some NEA locals do not function as unions, but all are part of a major interest group lobbying for education funding and teacher's rights.

Service Sector
The sector of the economy that provides services—such as health care, banking, and education—in contrast to the sector that produces goods.

Over the years, public employee unions have sometimes been involved in strikes. Most of these strikes are illegal, because almost no public employees have the right to strike. In recent years, conservatives have taken a strong stand against public employee unions, in particular teachers' unions such as the National Education Association and the American Federation of Teachers. In some states, mostly in the South, bargaining with public sector unions is prohibited. In 2011 and 2012, Republican governors in several Midwestern states—notably Ohio and Wisconsin—attempted to restrict or abolish the bargaining rights of public employees. The cost of public employee pension funds has also been an issue, as we report in the *Which Side Are You On?* feature that follows.

The Political Environment Faced by Labor. The success or failure of attempts to form unions depends greatly on popular attitudes. Many business-oriented conservatives have never accepted unions as legitimate institutions. In states where this position is widely held, local laws and practices can make it hard for labor to organize. For example, Georgia and North Carolina are major manufacturing states, but the percentages of union members in these two conservative states are 5.3 percent and 3 percent, respectively. States where the voting public is more sympathetic to labor, such as California and New York, have unionization rates of 16.4 percent and 24.4 percent, respectively. These rates are more typical of the world's wealthy nations than are the rates in conservative southern states.

Interest Groups of Professionals. Many professional organizations exist, including the American Bar Association, the Association of General Contractors of America, the Institute of Electrical and Electronics Engineers, and others. Some professional groups, such as those representing lawyers and physicians, are more influential than others because of their ability to restrict entry into their professions. Lawyers have a unique advantage—a large number of members of Congress share their profession.

The Unorganized Poor. Some have argued that the system of interest group politics leaves out poor Americans. If they are members of the working poor, they may hold two or more jobs just to survive, leaving them no time to participate in interest groups. Consequently, some scholars suggest that interest groups and lobbyists are the privilege of upper-middle-class Americans and those who belong to unions or other special groups.

Others, however, observe that the poor do obtain benefits from government. Without federal tax and spending programs aimed at low-income persons, as many as 25 percent of U.S. families would have incomes below the official poverty line. If you take into account all benefits that low-income families obtain, that number drops to about 10 percent. True, the poor cannot represent themselves. But for decades, liberal groups and, especially, religious groups have lobbied on behalf of those suffering from poverty. These interest groups have done for the poor what the poor cannot do for themselves.

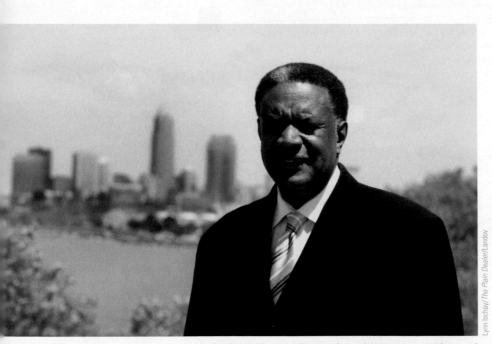

Lynn Ischay/*The Plain Dealer*/Landov

Reverend Tony Minor is a lobbyist for Lutheran Metropolitan Ministries in Ohio and pastor of a Cleveland church. Many religious lobbyists are more interested in advocating for the poor than in issues such as same-sex marriage. *Why might this be so?*

Which Side Are You On?

Are State and Local Government Pensions Too Generous?

It's well known that government employees—whether they work for federal, state, or local governments—receive better benefits than most people employed by private businesses. That includes pension benefits. Recently, articles in *USA Today* and other publications claimed that state governments had incurred at least a trillion dollars in unfunded pension liabilities. After the 2010 elections, a number of Republican governors and state legislatures went on the warpath against state employees and state employee pensions in particular. This raises the question: Do state and local government workers, in fact, receive pensions that are too generous?

Public Sector Workers Are the New Elite

Those who believe that state and local government employees are getting too good of a deal say that these workers have better pay, benefits, vacations, and job security than workers employed in the private sector. Many state and local government employees retire earlier than their counterparts in the private sector. Above all, their pension benefits are considerably more generous than in the private sector. Government employees typically have "defined benefit" plans under which their pension income is guaranteed. Private-sector workers more often have "defined contribution" plans, under which their benefits can rise and fall with the stock market.

Often, state employees receive a promotion during their last year of work to ensure that their annual pension payments are greater. Unless you are a chief executive officer, that won't happen in the private sector. Take California as one example. In recent years, spending on retirement benefits has grown at three times the rate of state revenues. The cost now exceeds $5.7 billion annually for schoolteachers alone. The result: fewer taxpayer dollars for public schools, higher education, and highways. It is unfair that government workers get a better deal than the rest of us.

Pensions Aren't Bankrupting the States

Those who support government workers agree that many state and local governments provide generous compensation to their employees. But those employees on average perform tasks that require more education than the average employee in the private sector. Professors, teachers, health-care workers, and even police officers need to be well educated or trained. Nationwide, current state and local pension payments are about 3 percent of total spending. Unless a government is very badly managed (admittedly, some are), pensions shouldn't "break the bank."

Many pension plans were underfunded recently for a good reason. When the stock market tanked in 2008, so did the value of the funds set aside for pensions. Since then, however, the stock market has enjoyed a complete recovery. On average, state and local governments could pay out benefits for the next fifteen years without even making additional contributions to pension funds. Of course, state and local governments add to the pension funds every year. Most states also require that employees make substantial contributions to their own plans.

We shouldn't be worrying that government employee pensions are too generous. Rather, we should be trying to improve pensions of ordinary workers in the private sector.

For Critical Analysis

Do you believe that state government employees are indeed an overpaid labor aristocracy—or do attacks on state employees' compensation divert us from focusing on the true aristocracy, the wealthiest 1 percent? In either case, why?

Environmental Groups

Environmental interest groups are not new. We have already mentioned the National Audubon Society, which was founded in 1905 to protect the snowy egret from the commercial demand for hat decorations. The patron of the Sierra Club, John Muir, worked for the creation of national parks more than a century ago. But the blossoming of national environmental groups with mass memberships did not occur until the 1970s.

Today's Environmental Groups. Since the first Earth Day, organized in 1972, many interest groups have sprung up to protect the environment in general or unique ecological niches. The groups range from the National Wildlife Federation, with a membership of more than 4 million and an emphasis on education, to the more elite Environmental Defense Fund, with a membership of five hundred thousand and a focus on influencing federal policy. The Nature Conservancy uses members' contributions to buy up threatened natural areas and then either gives them to state or local governments or manages them itself. Other groups include the more radical Greenpeace Society and Earth First.

Global Warming. The topic of global warming has become a major focus for environmental groups in recent years. This issue has pitted environmentalists against other interest groups to a much greater degree than in the past. Environmentalists often find themselves in opposition to economic interests representing industries that release "greenhouse" gases into the atmosphere. Indeed, the reaction against environmentalism has been strong enough in such coal-oriented states as West Virginia to transform them politically. Once a Democratic bastion, West Virginia now usually supports Republicans in presidential contests.

Public-Interest Groups

Public interest is a difficult term to define because, as we noted in Chapter 6, there are many publics in our nation of about 320 million. It is almost impossible for one particular public policy to benefit everybody, which in turn makes it practically impossible to define the public interest. Nonetheless, over the past few decades, a variety of lobbying organizations have been formed "in the public interest."

The Consumer Movement. As an organized movement, consumerism began in 1936 with the founding of the Consumers Union, which continues to publish the popular magazine *Consumer Reports.* The movement had antecedents dating back to the earliest years of the twentieth century, when investigative journalists known as "muckrakers" exposed exploitative working conditions and unsafe products in a variety of industries. Upton Sinclair's 1906 novel *The Jungle,* which revealed abuses of the workforce and unsanitary conditions in the meatpacking industry, was a classic of this genre.

Consumerism took off during the 1960s, a time of social ferment marked by the civil rights, antiwar, and feminist movements. Ralph Nader, who gained notice by exposing unsafe automobiles, was a key figure in the consumer

---

Public Interest
The best interests of the overall community; the national good, rather than the narrow interests of a particular group.

did you know?

The names of many interest groups suggest goals opposite from the organization's true objectives—for example, the Palm Oil Truth Foundation does not seek to expose the dangers of palm oil use, but to expand the use of palm oil in food and oppose action against global warming.

A Consumers Union (CU) technician tests the effects of shampoo samples on hair. *How important are CU's recommendations?*

Yvonne Hemsey/Getty Images

movement. Nader was a major sponsor of a series of new organizations. These included the Public Interest Research Groups (PIRGs)—campus organizations that emerged in the early 1970s and continue to provide students with platforms for civic engagement. Other new groups included the Consumer Federation of America (1968) and Public Citizen (1971).

Partly in response to the PIRG organizations and other groups, several conservative public-interest legal foundations have sprung up that are often pitted against liberal groups in court. Some of these are the Pacific Legal Foundation, the National Right to Work Legal Defense Foundation, the Institute for Justice, and the Mid-Atlantic Legal Foundation.

Other Public-Interest Groups.   One of the largest public-interest groups is Common Cause, founded in 1968. Its goal is to reorder national priorities toward "the public" and to make governmental institutions more responsive to the needs of the public. Another public-interest group is the League of Women Voters, founded in 1920. Although officially nonpartisan, it has lobbied for the Equal Rights Amendment and for government reform.

Other Interest Groups

A number of interest groups focus on just one issue. Single-interest groups, being narrowly focused, may be able to call attention to their causes because they have simple, straightforward goals and because their members tend to care intensely about the issues. Thus, such groups can easily motivate their members to contact legislators or to organize demonstrations in support of their policy goals.

The abortion debate has created groups opposed to abortion (such as the National Right to Life Committee) and groups in favor of abortion rights (such as NARAL Pro-Choice America). Further examples of single-issue groups are the National Rifle Association of America, the National Right to Work Committee (an antiunion group), and the American Israel Public Affairs Committee (a pro-Israel group).

Ideological Groups.   Among the most important interest groups are those that unite citizens around a common ideological viewpoint. Americans for Democratic Action, for example, was founded in 1947 as a home for liberals who were explicitly anti-Communist. On the political right, Americans for Tax Reform, organized by Grover Norquist, has been successful in persuading almost all leading Republicans to sign a pledge promising never to vote to raise taxes. The various organizations making up the Tea Party movement are widely seen as ideological interest groups. (Some observers, however, believe that the movement is better considered as a faction of the Republican Party rather than a series of interest groups.)

Identity Groups.   Still other groups represent Americans who share a common identity, such as membership in a particular race or ethnic group. The NAACP, founded in 1909 as the National Association for the Advancement of Colored People, represents African Americans. The National Organization for Women (NOW) has championed women's rights since 1966.

Grover Norquist of Americans for Tax Reform displays a pledge against tax increases that most Republicans in Congress have signed. The mask is of Guy Fawkes, who tried to blow up the English Parliament in 1605. *Was Fawkes a terrorist?*

Why Should You Care about...

Interest Groups?

Some interest groups focus on issues that concern only a limited number of people. Others, however, are involved in causes in which almost everyone has a stake. Gun control is an issue that concerns a large number of people. The question of whether the possession of handguns should be regulated is at the heart of a long-running heated battle among organized interest groups. The fight is fueled by the 1 million gun incidents occurring in the United States each year—murders, suicides, assaults, accidents, and robberies in which guns are involved.

Elderly Americans can be considered to have a common identity. AARP is one of the most powerful interest groups in Washington, D.C., and, according to some, the strongest lobbying group in the United States. It is certainly the nation's largest interest group, with a membership of about 40 million. AARP has accomplished much for its members over the years. It played a significant role in the creation of Medicare and Medicaid, as well as in obtaining annual cost-of-living increases in Social Security payments. (Medicare pays for medical expenses incurred by those who are at least sixty-five years of age; Medicaid provides health-care support for the poor.) In 2009 and 2010, AARP strongly supported the Democratic health-care reform bills and argued against those who feared that the new legislation might harm the Medicare program.

Foreign Interest Groups

Homegrown interest groups are not the only players in the game. Washington, D.C., is also the center for lobbying by foreign governments as well as private foreign interests. The governments of the largest U.S. trading partners, such as Canada, the European Union (EU) countries, Japan, and South Korea, maintain substantial research and lobbying staffs. Even smaller nations, such as those in the Caribbean, engage lobbyists when vital legislation affecting their trade interests is considered.

The Influence of Interest Groups

At any time, thousands of interest groups are attempting to influence state legislatures, governors, Congress, and members of the executive branch of the U.S. government. How powerful are these groups—and what influence do they have on policy and our democratic institutions?

■ **Learning Outcome 3:**
Evaluate the factors that make some interest groups especially effective.

What Makes an Interest Group Powerful?

What characteristics make some interest groups more powerful than others and more likely to have influence over government policy? Generally, interest groups attain a reputation for being powerful through their membership size, financial resources, leadership, and cohesiveness.

Size and Resources. No legislator can deny the power of an interest group that includes thousands of his or her own constituents among its members. Labor unions and organizations such as AARP and the American Automobile Association are able to claim voters in every congressional district. Having a large membership—about 10 million in the case of the AFL-CIO—carries a great deal of weight with government officials. AARP now has about 40 million members and a budget of more than a billion dollars for its operations. In addition, AARP claims to represent all older Americans, who constitute close to 20 percent of the population, whether they join the organization or not.

Having a large number of members, even if the individual membership dues are relatively small, provides an organization with a strong financial base. Those funds pay for lobbyists, television advertisements, e-mailings to members, a Web site, pages on Facebook, Twitter feeds, and many other resources that help an interest group make its point to politicians. The business organization with the largest membership is probably the U.S. Chamber of Commerce, which represents about 3 million businesses. The Chamber uses

President Obama shakes hands with leaders of the American Israel Public Affairs Committee after a speech. *Why does Israel have so much support among Americans?*

its members' dues to pay for staff and lobbyists, as well as a sophisticated communications network so that it can contact members in a timely way. All of the members can check the Chamber's Web site to get updates on the latest legislative proposals.

Other organizations may have fewer members but nonetheless can muster significant financial resources. The pharmaceutical lobby, which represents many of the major drug manufacturers, is one of the most powerful interest groups in Washington due to its financial resources. This interest group has more than 1,250 registered lobbyists and spent large sums in the 2014 cycle for lobbying and campaign expenditures.

Leadership. Money is not the only resource that interest groups need. Strong leaders who can develop effective strategies are also important. For example, the American Israel Public Affairs Committee (AIPAC) has long benefited from strong leadership. AIPAC lobbies Congress and the executive branch on issues related to U.S.-Israeli relations, as well as general foreign policy in the Middle East. AIPAC has been successful in promoting the close relationship that the two nations have enjoyed, which includes foreign aid that the United States annually bestows on Israel, now about $3.6 billion per year. Despite its modest membership size, AIPAC has won bipartisan support for its agenda and is consistently ranked among the most influential interest groups in America.

Other interest groups, including some with few financial resources, succeed in part because they are led by individuals with charisma and access to power. Sometimes, choosing a leader with a particular image can be an effective strategy for an organization. The National Rifle Association (NRA) had more than organizational

Why Should You Care about...

Interest Groups?

The problem of crime is central to the gun control issue. Public opinion poll respondents cited crime as one of the nation's most important problems throughout the 1990s, and it continues to be a major concern today. Does the easy availability of handguns promote crime? Or are guns part of the problem of crime—or part of the solution? Either way, the question is important to you personally. Even if you are fortunate enough not to be victimized by crime, you will probably find yourself limiting your activities from time to time out of a fear of crime.

skills in mind when it elected the late actor Charlton Heston as its president. The strategy of using an actor identified with powerful roles as the spokesperson for the organization worked to improve its image.

Cohesiveness. Regardless of an interest group's size or the amount of funds in its coffers, the motivation of an interest group's members is a key factor in determining how powerful it is. If the members of a group hold their beliefs strongly enough to send letters to their representatives, join a march on Washington, or work together to defeat a candidate, that group is considered powerful.

Although groups that oppose abortion rights have had modest success in influencing policy, they are considered powerful because their members are vocal and highly motivated. Of course, the existence of countervailing pro-choice groups limits their influence. Other measures of cohesion include the ability of a group to get its members to contact Washington quickly or to give extra funds when needed. The U.S. Chamber of Commerce excels at both of these strategies. In comparison, AARP cannot claim that it can get many of its 40 million members to contact their congressional representatives, but it does seem to have some influence on the opinions of older Americans and their views of political candidates.

Interest Groups and Representative Democracy

The role played by interest groups in shaping national policy has caused many to question whether we really have a democracy at all. Most interest groups have a middle-class or upper-class bias. Members of interest groups can afford to pay the membership fees, are generally fairly well educated, and normally participate in the political process to a greater extent than the "average" American.

Furthermore, leaders of interest groups tend to constitute an "elite within an elite" in the sense that they usually are from a higher social class than other group members. The most powerful interest groups—those with the most resources and political influence—are primarily business, trade, and professional groups. In contrast, public-interest groups and civil rights groups make up only a small percentage of the interest groups lobbying Congress.

Interest Groups: Elitist or Pluralist? Remember from Chapter 1 that the elite theory of politics presumes that most Americans are uninterested in politics and are willing to let a small, elite group of citizens make decisions for them. Pluralist theory, in contrast, views politics as a struggle among various interest groups to gain benefits for their members. The pluralist approach views compromise among various competing interests as the essence of political decision making. In reality, neither theory fully describes American politics. If interest groups led by elite, upper-class individuals are the dominant voices in Congress, then what we see is a conflict among elite groups—which would lend as much support to the elitist theory as to the pluralist approach.

Interest Group Influence. The results of lobbying efforts—congressional bills—do not always favor the interests of the most powerful groups, however. In part, this is because not all interest groups have an equal influence on government. Each group has a different combination of resources to use in the policymaking process. While some groups are composed of members who have high social status and significant economic resources, such as the National Association of Manufacturers, other groups derive influence from their large memberships. AARP, for example, has more members than any other interest group. Still other groups, such as environmentalists, have causes that can claim strong public support even from people who have no direct stake in

did you know?

On average, there are now sixty lobbyists for each member of Congress.

the issue. Groups such as the National Rifle Association are well organized and have highly motivated members. This enables them to channel a stream of letters, e-mails, and tweets toward Congress with a few days' effort.

Even the most powerful interest groups do not always succeed in their demands. Whereas the U.S. Chamber of Commerce may be accepted as having a justified interest in the question of business taxes, many legislators might feel that the group should not engage in the debate over the future of Social Security. In other words, groups are seen as having a legitimate concern in the issues closest to their interests but not necessarily in broader issues. This may explain why some of the most successful groups are those that focus on very specific issues—such as tobacco farming, funding of abortions, and handgun control—and do not get involved in larger conflicts.

Complicating the question of interest group influence is the fact that many groups' lobbyists are former colleagues, friends, or family members of current members of Congress.

Supporters of the "open carry" of firearms order drinks at a coffee shop in Texas. *Could the actions of this group be counterproductive? Why or why not?*

Concentrated Benefits, Dispersed Costs. We noted earlier that when an interest is shared by a small number of individuals, it may be easier to organize them into a group. One reason for this effect is known as *concentrated benefits and dispersed costs.* If a special law, such as a tax break, helps a relatively small number of people, those who receive the benefit will fight hard to keep or enlarge it. Other citizens, who pay for the benefit, may have little motivation to oppose it. For members of the majority, after all, the cost can be a matter of pennies. In other words, there is an *enthusiasm gap* between supporters and opponents of any given subsidy or tax break.

Sugar producers, for example, benefit greatly from restrictions on sugar imports. They work hard to ensure that these restrictions continue. Yet for sugar consumers—all the rest of us—the price of sugar is a trivial matter. End users of sugar have little incentive to organize. Still, when many interest groups are able to obtain benefits, the total impact on our representative democracy can be large.

Interest Groups and the Political Parties

Political scientists draw a distinction between interest groups and political parties. Parties nominate candidates for office, contest elections, and seek to operate the government. Interest groups do not seek to operate the government, even though they often support candidates who will promote their interests if elected.

Interest Groups and Party Coalitions. The separation between interest groups and political parties is not as sharp as some political models suggest, however. A party, after all, consists not only of candidates for office, elected officials, party officials, and party activists. A party also includes all of the people who identify with and support that party. Party supporters include millions of ordinary, unaffiliated citizens—and these supporters include interest groups as well.

Direct Technique
An interest group activity that involves personal interaction with government officials to further the group's goals.

Indirect Technique
A strategy employed by interest groups that uses third parties to influence government officials.

A large number of interest groups are closely linked to one or another of the major political parties. To examine the broad coalition that normally supports the Democrats, for example, you need to consider labor unions, organized minority groups, ideological organizations, and many other interests. Take labor. Although the percentage of workers who belong to a labor union has declined, unions continue to support sympathetic candidates for Congress and for state office. The AFL-CIO and many individual unions have large political budgets, which they use to help Democratic candidates nationwide. Labor can offer a candidate (such as President Obama) a corps of volunteers in addition to campaign contributions.

On the Republican side, major business groups such as the U.S. Chamber of Commerce are normally considered to be part of the Republican coalition. Other members include ideological groups such as Americans for Tax Reform and various Tea Party organizations.

Nonpartisan Interest Groups. Years ago, business interests would endorse friendly Democrats, and unions could and did endorse many sympathetic Republicans. With today's polarized politics, however, the number of labor-friendly Republican candidates approaches zero, and the number of Democrats who can win business endorsements is down as well.

Nevertheless, even today, many interest groups maintain their independence. These groups stay nonpartisan for several reasons. A group such as AIPAC hopes to win support for Israel from members of both parties. Other interest groups may find that they are not in full agreement with either major party. A Catholic organization, for example, might favor the Republicans to oppose abortion, but ally with the Democrats to support those in poverty. In short, like individual Americans, interest groups can be Republican, Democratic, or independent.

■ **Learning Outcome 4:** Discuss direct and indirect interest group techniques.

Interest Group Strategies

Interest groups employ a wide range of techniques and strategies to promote their policy goals. Although few groups are successful at persuading Congress and the president to endorse their programs completely, many are able to block—or at least weaken—legislation injurious to their members. The key to success for interest groups is access to government officials. To gain such access, interest groups and their representatives try to cultivate long-term relationships with legislators and government officials. The best of these relationships are based on mutual respect and cooperation. The interest group provides the official with sources of information and assistance, and the official in turn gives the group opportunities to express its views.

The techniques used by interest groups can be divided into direct and indirect techniques. With **direct techniques,** the interest group and its lobbyists approach officials personally to present their case. With **indirect techniques,** in contrast, the interest group uses the general public or individual constituents to influence the government on behalf of the interest group.

Direct Techniques

Lobbying, publicizing ratings of legislative behavior, building alliances, and providing campaign assistance are four direct techniques used by interest groups.

Lobbying Techniques. As you might have guessed, the term *lobbying* comes from the activities of private citizens regularly congregating in the lobbies of legislative chambers to petition legislators. In the latter part of the 1800s, railroad and industrial groups openly bribed state legislators to pass legislation beneficial to their interests, giving lobbying a well-deserved bad name. Most lobbyists today are professionals. They are either consultants to a company or interest group or members of one of the Washington, D.C., law firms that specialize in providing lobbying services. Such firms employ hundreds of former members of Congress and former government officials who are valued for their network of contacts in Washington. As Ed Rollins, a former White House aide, put it, "I've got many friends who are all through the agencies and equally important, I don't have many enemies. . . . I tell my clients I can get your case moved to the top of the pile."[4] Lobbyists of all types are becoming more numerous. The number of lobbyists in Washington, D.C., has more than doubled since 2000.

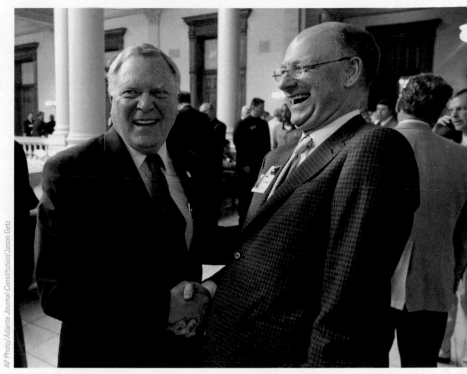

AP Photo/Atlanta Journal-Constitution/Jason Getz

Georgia governor Nathan Deal (on the left) meets with a lobbyist during a session of that state's legislature. *Why would he willingly be photographed with lobbyists?*

Common Activities. Lobbyists engage in an array of activities to influence legislation and government policy. These activities include the following:

- Meeting privately with public officials. Although they are acting on behalf of their clients, lobbyists often furnish needed information to senators and representatives (and government agency appointees). It is to the lobbyists' advantage to provide useful information so that the policymakers will rely on them in the future.
- Testifying before congressional committees for or against proposed legislation.
- Testifying before executive rulemaking agencies—such as the Federal Trade Commission or the Consumer Product Safety Commission—for or against proposed rules.
- Assisting legislators or bureaucrats in drafting legislation or prospective regulations. Especially at the state level, lobbying firms have been known to write up the complete text of a bill, which is then passed by the legislature.
- Inviting legislators to social occasions, such as cocktail parties, boating expeditions, and other events, including conferences at exotic locations.
- Providing political information to legislators and other government officials. Sometimes, the lobbyists have better information than the party leadership about how other legislators are going to vote.
- Suggesting nominations for federal appointments to the executive branch.

COMPARE WITH YOUR PEERS
MindTap™ for American Government

Access the Interest Groups Forum: Polling Activity—Regulating Interest Groups

The Ratings Game. Many interest groups attempt to influence the overall behavior of legislators through their rating systems. Each year, these interest groups identify the legislation that they consider most important to their goals and then monitor how legislators vote on it. Legislators receive scores based on their votes. The usual ratings scheme ranges from 0 to 100 percent. In the scheme of the liberal Americans for Democratic Action, for example, a rating of 100 means that a member of Congress voted with the group on every issue and is, by that measure, very liberal.

---

4. As quoted in H. R. Mahood, *Interest Groups in American National Politics: An Overview* (New York: Prentice Hall, 2000), p. 51.

"Please understand, I don't sell access to the government, I merely sell access to the guys who **do** sell access to the government."

Building Alliances.   Another direct technique used by interest groups is to form a coalition with other groups concerned about the same legislation. Often, these groups will set up a paper organization with an innocuous name to represent their joint concerns. In the early 1990s, for example, environmental, labor, and consumer groups formed an alliance called the Citizens Trade Campaign to oppose the passage of the North American Free Trade Agreement.

Members of such a coalition share expenses and multiply the influence of their individual groups by combining their efforts. Other advantages of forming a coalition are that it blurs the specific interests of the individual groups involved and makes it appear that larger public interests are at stake. These alliances also are efficient devices for keeping like-minded groups from duplicating one another's lobbying efforts.

Campaign Assistance.   Interest groups have additional strategies to use in their attempts to influence government policies. Groups recognize that the greatest concern of legislators is to be reelected, so they focus on the legislators' campaign needs. Associations with large memberships, such as labor unions, are able to provide workers for political campaigns, including precinct workers to get out the vote, volunteers to put up posters and pass out literature, and people to staff telephone banks at campaign headquarters.

Candidates vie for the groups' endorsements in a campaign. Gaining those endorsements may be automatic, or it may require that the candidates participate in debates or interviews with the interest groups. An interest group usually publicizes its choices in its membership publication, and the candidate can use the endorsement in her or his campaign literature.

did you know?

In 2013–2014, finance was the number-one business sector making political contributions. Health-care businesses came in second.

Citizens United v. FEC.   In 2010, the United States Supreme Court shook up the campaign-finance system when it issued its opinion in *Citizens United v. FEC*.[5] The Court ruled that corporations (and implicitly, unions) may spend freely to support or oppose

---

5.   130 S.Ct. 876 (2010).

2014 Elections

The Impact of Interest Groups

Conservative special interest super PACs appeared to have a much better year in 2014 than they did in 2012. In the previous elections, most of the candidates funded by organizations such as Karl Rove's American Crossroads lost. The super PACs were more successful in 2014. This may have been because they spent some dollars on get-out-the-vote drives rather than television ads. More likely, 2014 was just a Republican year, and that party would have done better regardless of outside spending. Several issues illustrate the limits of special interest contributions. Consider immigration reform. It is strongly supported by the

Republican-leaning U.S. Chamber of Commerce and other business interests. Labor also backs it. Although many congressional Republicans are pro-business, anti-immigration cultural conservatives continue to have the power to block any legislation. Special interests were more successful in blocking threatening ballot proposals. For example, proposals in Colorado and Oregon would have required the labeling of foods containing *genetically modified organism* (GMO) ingredients. Companies such as Monsanto that produce GMO seeds spent prodigiously—and successfully—to kill these proposals.

political candidates, so long as they do not contribute directly to candidate campaigns. The new freedom to make "independent expenditures" eases decades-old limits on corporate participation in federal elections. The Court held that the independent expenditures were a form of constitutionally protected free speech. The Court's decision was criticized by President Obama and many others. Some critics argued that the Court was granting to corporations rights that should only be given to flesh-and-blood humans. As it turned out, the main beneficiaries of the new rules were not corporations, but ideological interest groups that were often funded by extremely wealthy individuals. You will learn much more about campaign finance in Chapter 9.

Indirect Techniques

Interest groups can also try to influence government policy by working through others, who may be constituents or the general public. Indirect techniques mask an interest group's own activities and make the effort appear to be spontaneous. Furthermore, legislators and government officials are often more impressed by contacts from constituents than from an interest group's lobbyist.

Generating Public Pressure. In some instances, interest groups try to produce a "groundswell" of public pressure to influence the government. Such efforts may include advertisements in national magazines and newspapers, mass mailings, television publicity, and demonstrations. The Internet, social media, and satellite links make communication efforts even more effective. Interest groups may commission polls to find out what the public's sentiments are and then publicize the results. The intent of this activity is to convince policymakers that public opinion supports the group's position.

Some corporations and interest groups also engage in a practice that might be called **climate control.** With this strategy, public relations efforts are aimed at improving the public image of the industry or group and are not necessarily related to any specific political issue. Contributions by corporations and groups in support of public television programs, sponsorship of special events, and commercials extolling the virtues of corporate research are some ways of achieving climate control. For example, to improve its image in the wake of litigation against tobacco companies, Philip Morris began advertising its assistance to community agencies, including halfway houses for teen offenders and shelters for battered women. By building a reservoir of favorable public opinion, groups believe that their legislative goals will be less likely to encounter opposition from the public.

Using Constituents as Lobbyists. An interest group may also use constituents of elected officials to lobby for the group's goals. In the "shotgun" approach, the interest group tries to mobilize large numbers of constituents to write, phone, or send e-mails and tweets to their legislators or to the president. Often, the group provides language that constituents can use in the communication, thus sparing people from the need to compose a message of their own. These efforts are effective on Capitol Hill only when the number of responses is very large, however, because legislators know that the voters did not initiate the communications on their own when many communications use exactly the same wording. Artificially manufactured grassroots activity has been aptly labeled *astroturf lobbying.*

A more powerful variation of this technique uses only important constituents. With this approach, known as the "rifle" technique or the "Utah plant manager theory," the interest group might, for example, ask the manager of a local plant in Utah to contact the senator from Utah. Because the constituent is seen as influential and responsible for many jobs, the legislator is more likely to listen carefully to the constituent's concerns about legislation than to a paid lobbyist.

Climate Control
The use of public relations techniques to create favorable public opinion toward an interest group, industry, or corporation.

did you know?
Lobbyists have their own lobbying organization, the American League of Lobbyists.

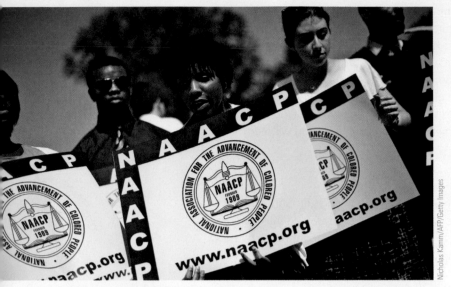

Members of the NAACP oppose a Supreme Court ruling that struck down part of the Voting Rights Act of 1965. *How effective are demonstrations?*

Unconventional Forms of Pressure. Sometimes, interest groups may employ forms of pressure that are outside the ordinary political process. These can include marches, rallies, or demonstrations. Such assemblies, as long as they are peaceful, are protected by the First Amendment. In Chapter 5, we described the civil disobedience techniques of the African American civil rights movement in the 1950s and 1960s. The 1963 March on Washington in support of civil rights was one of the most effective demonstrations ever organized. The women's suffrage movement of the early 1900s also employed marches and demonstrations to great effect.

Demonstrations, however, are not always peaceable. Violent demonstrations have a long history in America, dating back to the antitax Boston Tea Party described in Chapter 2. The Vietnam War (1965–1975) provoked a large number of demonstrations, some of which were violent. Violent demonstrations can be counterproductive—instead of putting pressure on the authorities, they may simply alienate the public. For example, historians continue to debate whether the demonstrations against the Vietnam War were effective or counterproductive.

Another unconventional form of pressure is the **boycott**—a refusal to buy a particular product or deal with a particular business. To be effective, boycotts must command widespread support. One example was the African American boycott of buses in Montgomery, Alabama, in 1955, described in Chapter 5. Another was the boycott of California grapes that were picked by nonunion workers, as part of a campaign to organize Mexican American farmworkers. The first grape boycott lasted from 1965 to 1970. A series of later boycotts was less effective.

■ **Learning Outcome 5:** Describe the main ways in which lobbyists are regulated.

Regulating Lobbyists

Congress made its first attempt to control lobbyists and lobbying activities through Title III of the Legislative Reorganization Act of 1946, otherwise known as the Federal Regulation of Lobbying Act. The law actually provided for public disclosure more than for regulation, and it neglected to specify which agency would enforce its provisions. The 1946 legislation defined a *lobbyist* as any person or organization that received funds to be used principally to influence legislation before Congress. Such persons and organizations were supposed to "register" their clients and the purposes of their efforts, and to report quarterly on their activities.

The legislation was tested in a 1954 Supreme Court case, *United States v. Harriss,*[6] and was found to be constitutional. The Court agreed that the lobbying law did not violate due process, freedom of speech or of the press, or the freedom to petition. The Court narrowly construed the act, however, holding that it applied only to lobbyists who were influencing federal legislation *directly*.

The Results of the 1946 Act

The immediate result of the act was that a minimal number of individuals registered as lobbyists. National interest groups, such as the National Rifle Association and the American

Boycott
A form of pressure or protest—an organized refusal to purchase a particular product or deal with a particular business.

6. 347 U.S. 612 (1954).

Petroleum Institute, could employ hundreds of staff members who were, of course, working on legislation but register only one or two lobbyists who were engaged *principally* in influencing Congress. There were no reporting requirements for lobbying the executive branch, federal agencies, the courts, or congressional staff. Approximately seven thousand individuals and organizations registered annually as lobbyists, although most experts estimated that ten times that number were actually employed in Washington to exert influence on the government.

The Reforms of 1995

The reform-minded Congress of 1995–1996 overhauled the lobbying legislation, fundamentally changing the ground rules for those who seek to influence the federal government. The Lobbying Disclosure Act, passed in 1995, included the following provisions:

- A *lobbyist* is defined as anyone who spends at least 20 percent of his or her time lobbying members of Congress, their staffs, or executive-branch officials.
- Lobbyists must register with the clerk of the House and the secretary of the Senate.
- Semiannual reports must disclose the general nature of the lobbying effort.
- The requirements exempt "grassroots" lobbying efforts and those of tax-exempt organizations, such as religious groups.

Also in 1995, both the House and the Senate adopted new rules on gifts and travel expenses provided by lobbyists. The House adopted a flat ban on gifts, while the Senate established limits—senators were prohibited from accepting any gift with a value of more than $50 and from accepting gifts worth more than $100 from a single source in a given year. These gift rules stopped the broad practice of taking members of Congress to lunch or dinner at high-priced restaurants, but the various exemptions and exceptions have allowed much gift giving to continue.

Lobbying Scandals and the Reforms of 2007

The regulation of lobbying resurfaced as an issue in 2005 after a number of scandals. When the Democrats took control of Congress in January 2007, one of their initial undertakings was ethics and lobbying reform. In the first one hundred hours of the session, the House tightened its rules on gifts and on travel funded by lobbyists. The Senate followed shortly thereafter.

In September 2007, President George W. Bush signed the Honest Leadership and Open Government Act. Under the new law, lobbyists must report quarterly, and the registration threshold is $10,000 in spending per quarter. Organizations must report coalition activities if they contribute more than $5,000 to a coalition. The House and the Senate must now post lobbying information in a searchable file on the Internet. In a significant alteration to legislative practices, "earmarked" expenditures, commonly called "pork," must now be identified and made public. This last change may not have immediately had its intended effect of reducing earmarks, however. Many legislators are actually proud of their pork and happy to tell the folks back home all about it. In 2011, the Republican majority in the House banned earmarks that benefit a particular business, but this rule tended to drive pork underground rather than eliminating it completely.

Recent Developments

During his first presidential campaign, Barack Obama claimed that there would be no former lobbyists in his administration. He later amended that statement to say that former lobbyists could not work in areas where they had recently lobbied. Upon election, Obama made a considerable show of denying lobbyists access to administration officials. Many Washington insiders considered Obama's positions absurd and predicted that he would not be able to adhere to them. The insiders were correct: Obama was soon issuing countless waivers that allowed former lobbyists to serve in official posts.

How You Can Make a Difference

Consider gun laws. Almost every year, Congress and the various state legislatures debate measures that would alter gun laws for the nation or for the individual states. As a result, there are plenty of opportunities to get involved.

- Issues in the debate include child-safety features on guns and the regulation of gun dealers who sell firearms at gun shows. Proponents of gun control seek safety locks and more restrictions on gun purchases.

- Proponents of firearms claim that possessing firearms is a constitutional right and meets a vital defense need for individuals. They contend that the problem lies not in the sale and ownership of weapons but in their use by criminals.

- The Coalition to Stop Gun Violence takes the position that handguns "serve no valid purpose, except to kill people." In contrast, the National Rifle Association (NRA) of America supports the rights of gun owners. The NRA, founded in 1871, is currently one of the most powerful single-issue groups in the United States. The NRA believes that gun laws will not reduce the number of crimes. It is illogical to assume, according to the NRA, that persons who refuse to obey laws prohibiting rape, murder, and other crimes will obey a gun law.

- In recent years, gun rights advocates have been strikingly successful in accomplishing their objectives. One sign of this is the affirmation by the United States Supreme Court that individuals have a constitutional right to bear arms.

- The NRA and other organizations have also been effective in winning state laws that allow citizens to carry concealed weapons in an ever-greater number of environments, including college campuses.

- To find out more about the NRA's positions, go to www.nra .org.

- Organizations that advocate gun controls include the Coalition to Stop Gun Violence and the Brady Campaign to Prevent Gun Violence. You can locate the first of these organizations at csgv.org and the second at www.brady campaign.org

Key Terms

boycott 222	indirect technique 218	lobbyist 203	service sector 209
climate control 221	interest group 203	material incentive 205	social movement 204
direct technique 218	labor movement 208	public interest 212	solidary incentive 205
free rider problem 205	latent interests 204	purposive incentive 206	

Chapter Summary

Learning Outcome 1 An interest group is an organization whose members share common objectives and actively attempt to influence government policy. Interest groups proliferate in the United States because they can influence government at many points in the political structure and because they offer solidary, material, and purposive incentives to their members. Interest groups are often created out of social movements.

Learning Outcome 2 Major types of interest groups include business, agricultural, labor, public employee, professional, and environmental groups. Other important groups may be considered public-interest, single-interest, ideological, and identity groups. In addition, foreign governments and corporations lobby our government.

Learning Outcome 3 Factors that can help make an interest group effective include membership size, financial resources, strong leadership, and cohesion around specific issues. The existence of interest groups has been seen as confirming both the elite theory and the pluralist theory of American politics. Many groups are considered to be part of the coalitions that support the two major parties.

Learning Outcome 4 Interest groups use direct and indirect techniques to influence government. Direct techniques include testifying before committees and rulemaking agencies, providing information to legislators, rating legislators' voting records, building alliances, and aiding political campaigns. Indirect techniques to influence government include campaigns to rally public sentiment, letter-writing campaigns, efforts to influence the climate of opinion, and the use of constituents to lobby for the group's interest. Unconventional methods of applying pressure include demonstrations and boycotts.

Learning Outcome 5 The 1946 Legislative Reorganization Act was the first attempt to control lobbyists and their activities through registration requirements. The United States Supreme Court narrowly construed the act as applying only to lobbyists who directly seek to influence federal legislation.

In 1995, Congress approved new legislation requiring anyone who spends 20 percent of his or her time influencing legislation to register as a lobbyist. Also, any organization spending more than $24,500 semiannually and any individual who is paid more than $6,000 semiannually for his or her work must register. Semiannual reports must include the names of clients, the bills in which they are interested, and the branches of government contacted. The lobbying efforts of grassroots and tax-exempt organizations are exempt from the rules.

In 2007, in response to lobbying scandals, Congress tightened rules on giving gifts to legislators and increased reporting requirements for lobbyists to four times a year. Under the 2007 reform legislation, lobbyists now have to report contributions to coalition efforts. Congress has created a searchable online database of lobbying information.

Master the concept of Interest Groups with MindTap™ for American Government

 REVIEW MindTap™ for American Government
Access Key Term Flashcards for Chapter 7.

TEST YOURSELF MindTap™ for American Government
Take the Wrap It Up Quiz for Chapter 7.

 STAY CURRENT MindTap™ for American Government
Access the KnowNow blog and customized RSS for updates on current events.

STAY FOCUSED MindTap™ for American Government
Complete the Focus Activities for Interest Groups.

Additional Resources

Today, almost every interest group or association has its own Web site. To find one, use your favorite search engine (such as Google), and search for the association by name. For a sense of the variety of interest groups that have Web sites, take a look at one or two of those listed here. Most groups are also active on Facebook and Twitter.

Online Resources

- You can learn more about the labor movement by visiting the AFL-CIO's site at www.aflcio.org. For a business perspective, try the U.S. Chamber of Commerce at www.uschamber.com.
- AARP (formerly the American Association of Retired Persons), a powerful group, can be found at www.aarp.org.
- It's worth taking a look at the site of the American Israel Public Affairs Committee—go to www.aipac.org.
- Information on environmental issues is available at a number of sites. The Environmental Defense Fund's site can be found at www.edf.org. You can also go to the Natural Resources Defense Council's site at www.nrdc.org.

Books

Dubofsky, Melvyn, and Foster Rhea Dulles. *Labor in America: A History.* Wheeling, Ill.: Harlan Davidson, 2010. This work is probably the best general history of American labor. Dubofsky, a history professor at Binghamton University, has given the text a complete update.

Holyoake, Thomas T. *Interest Groups and Lobbying: Pursuing Political Interests in America.* Boulder, Colo.: Westview Press, 2014. In this in-depth study of interest groups, Holyoake cites the benefits as well as the disadvantages that these groups provide. Holyoake is a professor of political science at California State University, Fresno.

Moss, Michael. *Salt Sugar Fat: How the Food Giants Hooked Us.* New York: Random House Trade Paperbacks, 2014. An investigative reporter for the *New York Times,* Moss contends that cheap, calorie-rich, processed food has led us to become the world's most obese nation. Moss argues that while food safety is heavily regulated, the government has been industry's best partner in encouraging Americans to become more dependent on processed foods.

Video

Sixty Minutes: The Lobbyist's Playbook—Jack Abramoff, the notorious former lobbyist, spent more than three years in prison for his crimes. In this 2011 excerpt from the well-known CBS News show, Leslie Stahl interviews Abramoff. He believes that the reforms passed after his conviction have had little effect on lobbying.

Moyers & Company: United States of ALEC—The American Legislative Exchange Council (ALEC) is an alliance of corporations and conservative state politicians that designs model laws for states to adopt. In this 2012 episode, journalist Bill Moyers contends that much of ALEC's legislation seeks to increase corporate profits at the public's expense.

Quiz

Multiple Choice and Fill-Ins

Learning Outcome 1 Describe the basic characteristics of interest groups, and provide three major reasons why Americans join them.

1. When individuals benefit by the actions of an interest group but do not support that group, they are:
    a. free riders.
    b. freeloaders.
    c. usually just waiting to join the group.

2. When individuals have definite interests, but choose not to become a member of an interest group that represents these interests, their concerns are called _____ interests.

Learning Outcome 2 List the major types of interest groups, especially those with economic motivations.

3. Union membership in the United States has:
    a. been growing, especially since 2000.
    b. stayed about the same since the Great Depression.
    c. been declining in recent years, except in the public sector.

4. The U.S. Chamber of Commerce is an example of a _____ interest group.

Learning Outcome 3 Evaluate the factors that make some interest groups especially effective.

5. Some factors that make an interest group powerful include:
    a. urban location and financial resources.
    b. membership size, financial resources, and cohesion of its members on key issues.
    c. membership size and attention to a broad range of interests.

6. Interest groups have been described as examples of both the _____ and _____ theories of politics.

Learning Outcome 4 Discuss direct and indirect interest group techniques.

7. Direct interest group techniques include:
    a. using constituents as lobbyists and organizing demonstrations.
    b. meeting with officials and making campaign contributions.
    c. organizing boycotts and filing lawsuits.

8. Some interest groups hire public relations firms to improve the public image of an industry or a group. This is called _____ _____.

Learning Outcome 5 Describe the main ways in which lobbyists are regulated.

9. A difficulty in limiting the effect of lobbying is:
    a. opposition to new legislation by Democratic members of Congress.
    b. opposition to new legislation by Republican presidents.
    c. many legislators are proud of "pork" spending and are happy to tell their constituents all about it.

10. Most lobbying today is undertaken by _____, who often work in Washington, D.C., law firms.

Essay Questions

1. "If guns are outlawed, only outlaws will have guns." This is a key slogan used by opponents of gun control. How much truth do you think there is to this slogan? Explain your reasoning.

2. About half of the paid lobbyists in Washington are former government staff members or former members of Congress. Why would interest groups employ such people? Why might some reformers want to limit the ability of interest groups to employ them? On what basis might an interest group argue that such limits are unconstitutional?

Answers to questions: 1. a, 2. latent, 3. c, 4. business, 5. b, 6. elite/pluralist, 7. b, 8. climate control. 9. c, 10. professionals.

Political Parties

8

A political science major adorns her cap with a Republican elephant and a Democratic donkey while waiting for commencement at the University of Georgia.

Athens *Banner-Herald*, David Manning/AP Images

The five Learning Outcomes below are designed to help improve your understanding of this chapter. After reading this chapter, you should be able to:

■ **Learning Outcome 1:** Cite some of the major activities of U.S. political parties, and discuss how they are organized.

■ **Learning Outcome 2:** Explain how the history of U.S. political parties has led to the two major parties that exist today.

■ **Learning Outcome 3:** Summarize key differences between the policies and supporters of the major parties.

■ **Learning Outcome 4:** Give reasons why the two-party system has endured in America, and evaluate the impact of third parties on U.S. politics.

■ **Learning Outcome 5:** Discuss some of the ways in which support for the parties can change, and explain the increasing importance of independents.

▶ **WATCH & LEARN** MindTap™ **for American Government**
Watch a brief "What Do You Know?" video summarizing Political Parties.

What If...

We Chose Candidates through Bipartisan Primary Elections?

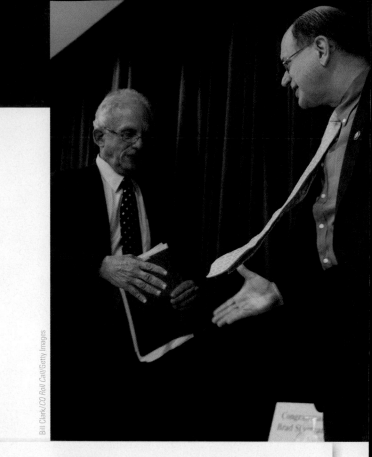

BACKGROUND

In recent years, American politics have been characterized by severe political polarization. Supporters of the two major political parties have often seen the other party as not merely mistaken, but evil. One common result of polarization is competition among candidates to be the most unwavering advocate of their party's philosophy. We see such contests during *primary elections,* in which voters choose the candidates who will represent each party in the November general election.

Is there a way to eliminate such "purity" contests? California and Washington recently adopted systems designed to do just that. Under a "Top Two Candidates" primary system, all candidates appear on a single ballot. Candidates can list their party but are not required to do so. More than one candidate from each party can appear on the ballot. The two candidates receiving the most votes—regardless of party—then appear on the general election ballot. In the general election, two Republicans might face each other in a conservative district. In a highly Democratic district, the top two finishers could both be Democrats.

WHAT IF WE CHOSE CANDIDATES THROUGH BIPARTISAN PRIMARY ELECTIONS?

A Top Two Candidates primary could increase voter participation. Parties would no longer have the option of controlling who votes for their candidates in the primary election. Candidates therefore would need to appeal to a broader range of opinion. The assumption is that candidates would take more moderate stands to appeal to independents or members of the other party. For example, in a conservative district, two Republican candidates might be forced to compete on the basis of who could add the most independent and even Democratic voters to their Republican support.

THE MAJOR POLITICAL PARTIES MIGHT SUFFER

A Top Two Candidates election could reduce the influence of the two major parties. According to Ron Nehring, a former chair of the California Republican Party, "It's a misnomer to call this an open primary. It's the abolition of primaries." Indeed, a Top Two election is not really a partisan primary—it is not a way in which parties can decide whom to support. Rather, it can be viewed as the first half of a two-part general election process.

Still, under the Top Two system, political parties would continue to have the right to endorse candidates for the various offices. The parties could publicize these candidates and could

These two Democrats were forced to run against each other for a California U.S. House seat in 2012. At a later event, they almost got into a fight. *Why might California's Top Two Candidates system lead to more moderate candidates?*

spend, within legal limits, as much as they wanted in campaigning for them. The parties could not, however, automatically place their preferred candidates on the November ballot.

WHAT WOULD HAPPEN TO CAMPAIGN SPENDING?

Some predict that if every state used a Top Two system, fewer campaign dollars would be spent. These people believe that partisan politics leads to more campaign spending. Candidates and their supporters spend whatever they can for negative, mudslinging ads on television and the Internet. Others contend that more, rather than less, spending would be necessary, because candidates would have to reach the entire electorate, not just a part of it.

For Critical Analysis

1. If you were a relatively unknown candidate, would you prefer a Top Two Candidates system or an ordinary partisan primary? Why?

2. Assume you are a California Republican in a heavily Democratic congressional district. How could you best influence the outcome of your Top Two election?

The state of the political parties is a matter of constant concern for the media. Even when an election is relatively far off, commentators obsessively assess the relative fortunes of the Republican and Democratic parties. As elections draw closer, polls concentrate on determining which political party individual voters "belong" to or support. Prior to an election, a typical poll usually asks the following question: "Do you consider yourself to be a Republican, a Democrat, or an independent?" For many years, Americans were divided fairly evenly among these three choices. Today, about 40 percent of all voters call themselves **independents.** Of course, independents are not represented as such in Congress, and three-quarters or more of all independents lean toward either the Republicans or the Democrats. Still, the power of independents might be enhanced if changes were made in the way that we choose candidates, as discussed in the chapter-opening *What If . . .* feature.

After the elections are over, the media publish the election results. Among other things, Americans learn which party will control the presidency and how many Democrats and Republicans will be sitting in the House of Representatives and the Senate when the new Congress convenes.

Notice that earlier, when discussing party membership, we put the word *belong* in quotation marks. We did this because hardly anyone actually "belongs" to a political party in the sense of being a card-carrying member. To become a member of a political party, you do not have to pay dues, pass an examination, or swear an oath of allegiance. Therefore, we can ask an obvious question: If it takes almost nothing to be a member of a political party, what, then, is a political party?

LISTEN & LEARN
MindTap™ for American Government

Access Read Speaker to listen to Chapter 8.

Independent
A voter or candidate who does not identify with a political party.

Political Party
A group of political activists who organize to win elections, operate the government, and determine public policy.

Policy Demanders
Individuals or interest group members who participate in political parties with the intent to see that certain policies are adopted or specific groups favored.

Political Parties in the United States

A **political party** might be formally defined as a group of political activists who organize to win elections, operate the government, and determine public policy. Political parties are thus quite different from interest groups, which seek to influence, not run, the government.

As we explain later in greater detail, a party includes elected officials who ran under the party's banner, officers of the party organization itself, and party supporters. These supporters may be ordinary citizens who do nothing more than regularly vote for the party's candidates. Supporters also include individuals and interest groups who are much more active than that. In *The Party Decides*, a modern classic book, a team of political scientists has argued that **policy demanders** are a key part of any major party. Policy demanders are interest group members or other ideologically motivated individuals who participate in parties with the intent to see that certain policies are adopted, or at least specific groups favored.[1]

■ **Learning Outcome 1:**
Cite some of the major activities of U.S. political parties, and discuss how they are organized.

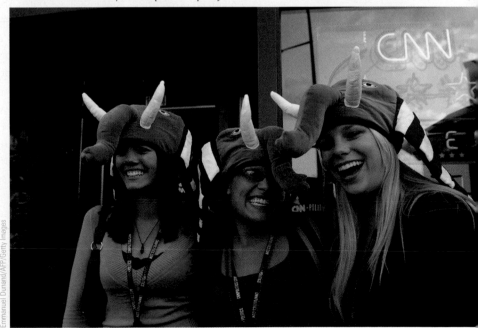

Republican Party supporters at the Republican National Convention. *What does it take to become a member of a U.S. political party?*

---

1. Marty Cohen et al., *The Party Decides: Presidential Nominations before and after Reform* (Chicago: University of Chicago Press, 2008).

Emmanuel Dunand/AFP/Getty Images

Party-in-the-Electorate
Those members of the general public who identify with a political party or who express a preference for one party over another.

Party Organization
The formal structure and leadership of a political party, including election committees; local, state, and national executives; and paid professional staff.

Functions of Political Parties in the United States

Political parties in the United States engage in a wide variety of activities, many of which are discussed in this chapter. Through these activities, parties perform a number of functions for the political system. These functions include the following:

1. *Recruiting candidates for public office.* Because it is the goal of parties to gain control of government, they must work to recruit candidates for all elective offices.
2. *Organizing and running elections.* Although elections are a government activity, political parties actually organize voter-registration drives, recruit volunteers to work at the polls, provide much of the campaign activity to stimulate interest in the election, and work to increase voter participation.
3. *Presenting alternative policies to the electorate.*
4. *Accepting responsibility for operating the government.* When a party elects the president or governor—or the majority of the members of a legislative body—it accepts the responsibility for running the government. This includes developing linkages among elected officials in the various branches of government to gain support for policies and their implementation.
5. *Acting as the organized opposition to the party in power.* The "out" party, or the one that does not control the government, is expected to articulate its own policies and oppose the winning party when appropriate.

The major functions of American political parties are carried out by a small, relatively loose-knit nucleus of party activists. This arrangement is quite different from the more highly structured, mass-membership organization typical of many European parties. American parties concentrate on winning elections rather than on signing up large numbers of deeply committed, dues-paying members who believe passionately in the party's program.

The Three Faces of a Party

Although American parties are known by a single name and, in the public mind, have a common historical identity, each party really has three major components. The first component is the **party-in-the-electorate.** This phrase refers to all those individuals who claim an attachment to the political party. They need not participate in election campaigns. Rather, the party-in-the-electorate is the large number of Americans who feel some loyalty to the party or who use partisanship as a cue to decide who will earn their vote. Party membership is not really a rational choice. Rather, it is an emotional tie somewhat analogous to identifying with a region or a baseball team. Although individuals may hold a deep loyalty to or identification with a political party, there is no need for members of the party-in-the-electorate to speak out publicly, to contribute to campaigns, or to vote all Republican or all Democratic. Nevertheless, the party leaders pay close attention to their members in the electorate.

The second component, the **party organization,** provides the structural framework for the political party by recruiting volunteers to become party leaders, identifying potential candidates, and organizing caucuses, conventions, and election campaigns for its candidates, as will be discussed in more detail shortly. It is the party organization and its active workers that keep the party functioning

Representative Joaquin Castro (D., Texas) speaks at the Democratic State Convention in 2014. *Why is the Latino vote important to the future of the Democrats?*

TEXAS ✦ DEMOCRATS

between elections, as well as ensure that the party puts forth electable candidates and clear positions in the elections. If the party-in-the-electorate declines in numbers and loyalty, the party organization must try to find a strategy to rebuild the grassroots following.

The **party-in-government** is the third component of American political parties. The party-in-government consists of those elected and appointed officials who identify with a political party. Generally, elected officials do not also hold official party positions within the formal organization, although they often have the informal power to appoint party executives.

The Party-in-the-Electorate

The party-in-the-electorate consists of everyone who identifies with the party in question who is not an elected official or part of the formal party organization. The party-in-the-electorate does not just consist of ordinary Americans, however, but of elites—motivated interests, media personalities, fundraisers, and prominent figures of all types who identify with a party but who are not part of its formal organization and are not elected officials.

As we have noted, the party-in-the-electorate includes policy demanders. In the Democratic Party, for example, teachers' unions function as policy demanders who favor increased spending on education and policies that benefit teachers. Among the Republicans, a variety of policy demanders oppose legislation that would grant legal status to unauthorized immigrants.

Another elite group is opinion leaders. Radio talk show host Rush Limbaugh, for example, holds no office in the government or the Republican Party, but his ideological influence is substantial. Other Republican opinion leaders include Fox News commentator Bill O'Reilly, *Washington Post* columnist George Will, and Erick Erickson of the RedState blog. Democratic opinion leaders include MSNBC commentator Rachel Maddow, *New York Times* economics columnist Paul Krugman, and Markos Moulitsas of the Daily Kos blog.

Other elite individuals include fundraisers and large-scale contributors. In recent years, the Democrats and the Republicans have enjoyed roughly equal success in fundraising, but most of the truly famous individual fundraisers have been Republicans. They include organizers such as Karl Rove of American Crossroads, and persons who are major contributors all by themselves, such as the brothers Charles and David Koch. Finally, one elite group is heavily Democratic—entertainment celebrities ranging from Leonardo DiCaprio and Natalie Portman through the Dixie Chicks and Bruce Springsteen.

The Party Organization

Each of the American political parties is often seen as having a pyramid-shaped organization, with the national chairperson and committee at the top and the local precinct chairperson on the bottom. This structure, however, does not accurately reflect the relative power of the individual components of the party organization. If it did, the national chairperson of the Democratic Party or the Republican Party, along with the national committee, could simply dictate how the organization was to be run, just as if it were ExxonMobil or Apple. In reality, the political parties have a confederal structure, in which each unit has significant autonomy and is linked only loosely to the other units.

The National Party Organization. Each party has a national organization, the most conspicuous part of which is the **national convention,** held every four years. The convention is used to officially nominate the presidential and vice-presidential candidates. In addition, the **party platform** is developed at the national convention. The platform sets forth the party's position on the issues and makes promises to initiate certain policies if the party wins the presidency.

Party-in-Government
All of the elected and appointed officials who identify with a political party.

National Convention
The meeting held every four years by each major party to select presidential and vice-presidential candidates, write a platform, choose a national committee, and conduct party business.

Party Platform
A document drawn up at each national convention, outlining the policies, positions, and principles of the party.

National Committee

A standing committee of a national political party established to direct and coordinate party activities between national party conventions.

State Central Committee

The principal organized structure of each political party within each state. This committee is responsible for carrying out policy decisions of the party's state convention.

After the convention, the platform sometimes is neglected or ignored when party candidates disagree with it. Because candidates are trying to win votes from a wide spectrum of voters, it can be counterproductive to emphasize the fairly narrow and sometimes controversial goals set forth in the platform. Still, once elected, the parties do try to carry out platform promises, and many of the promises eventually become law. Of course, some general goals, such as economic prosperity, are included in the platforms of both parties.

Convention Delegates. The party convention provides the most striking illustration of the difference between the ordinary members of a party, or party identifiers, and party activists. As a series of studies by the *New York Times* shows, delegates to the national party conventions are different from ordinary party identifiers. Delegates to the Democratic National Convention often take stands on issues that are far more liberal than the positions of ordinary Democratic voters. Delegates to the Republican National Convention are often more conservative than ordinary Republicans. Why does this happen? In part, it is because a person, to become a delegate, must be appointed by party leaders or gather votes in a primary election from party members who care enough to vote in a primary.

In addition, the primaries generally pit presidential candidates against one another on intraparty issues. Competition within each party tends to pull candidates away from the center, and delegates even more so.

The National Committee. At the national convention, each of the parties formally chooses a national standing committee, elected by the individual state parties. This **national committee** directs and coordinates party activities during the following four years.

One of the jobs of the national committee is to ratify the presidential nominee's choice of a national chairperson, who in principle acts as the spokesperson for the party. The national chairperson and the national committee plan the next campaign and the next convention, obtain financial contributions, and publicize the national party.

Picking a National Chairperson. In general, the party's presidential candidate chooses the national chairperson. (If that candidate loses, however, the chairperson is often changed.) The national chairperson performs such jobs as establishing a national party headquarters, raising campaign funds and distributing them to state parties and to candidates, and appearing in the media as a party spokesperson. The national chairperson, along with the national committee, attempts to maintain some sort of communication among the different levels of the party organization.

The State Party Organization. Because every state party is unique, it is impossible to describe what an "average" state political party is like. Nonetheless, state parties have several organizational features in common. Each state party has a chairperson, a committee, and a number of local organizations. In theory, the role of the **state central committee**—the principal organized structure of each political party within each state—is similar in the various states. The committee has responsibility for carrying out the policy decisions of the party's state convention.

Also, like the national committee, the state central committee has control over the use of party campaign funds during political campaigns. Usually, the state central committee has little, if any, influence on party candidates once they are elected.

Local Party Machinery: The Grassroots. The lowest layer of party machinery is the local organization, supported by district leaders, precinct or ward captains, and party workers.

Patronage and City Machines. In the 1800s, the institution of **patronage**—the rewarding of the party faithful with government jobs or contracts—held the local organization together. For immigrants and the poor, the political machine often furnished important services and protections. The big-city machine was the archetypal example. The last big-city political machine to exercise substantial power was run by Chicago mayor Richard J. Daley (1955–1978), who was also an important figure in national Democratic politics. City machines are now dead, mostly because their function of providing social services (and reaping the reward of votes) has been taken over by state and national agencies.

Local Party Organizations Today. Local political organizations are still able to provide the foot soldiers of politics—individuals who pass out literature and get out the vote on Election Day, which can be crucial in local elections. In many regions, local Democratic and Republican organizations still exercise some patronage, such as awarding courthouse jobs, contracts for street repair, and other lucrative construction contracts. The constitutionality of awarding—or not awarding—contracts on the basis of political affiliation has been subject to challenge, however. The Supreme Court has ruled that firing or failing to hire individuals because of their political affiliation is an infringement of the employees' First Amendment rights to free expression.[2] Local party organizations are also the most important vehicles for recruiting young adults into political work, because political involvement at the local level offers activists many opportunities to gain experience.

> **Patronage**
> The rewarding of faithful party workers and followers with government employment or contracts.

---

2. *Rutan v. Republican Party of Illinois*, 497 U.S. 62 (1990).

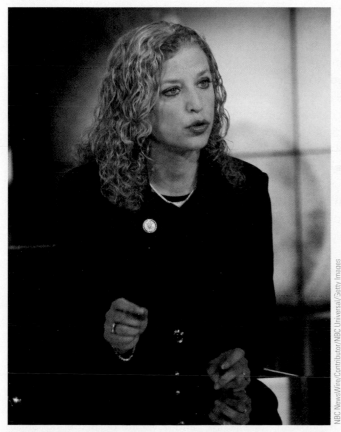

Representative Debbie Wasserman Schultz (D., Florida) is the chairperson of the Democratic National Committee.

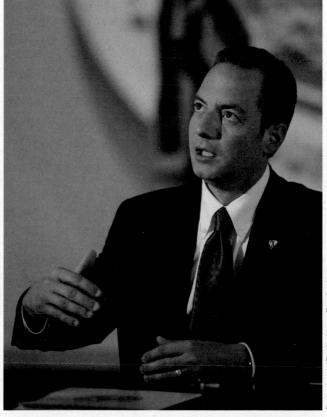

Reince Priebus is the chairperson of the Republican National Committee.

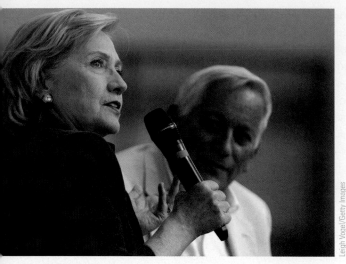

Hillary Rodham Clinton speaks in Aspen, Colorado, in 2014. *Why is Clinton a strong candidate for president in 2016?*

The Party-in-Government

After the election is over and the winners are announced, the focus of party activity shifts from getting out the vote to organizing and controlling the government. As you will see in Chapter 10, party membership plays an important role in the day-to-day operations of Congress, with partisanship determining everything from office space to committee assignments and power on Capitol Hill. For the president, the political party furnishes a pool of qualified applicants for political appointments to run the government. (Although it is uncommon to do so, presidents can and occasionally do appoint executive personnel, such as cabinet members, from the opposition party.) Judicial appointments also offer a great opportunity to the winning party. For the most part, presidents are likely to appoint federal judges from their own party.

Divided Government. All of these party appointments suggest that the winning political party, whether at the national, state, or local level, has a great deal of control in the American system. The degree of control that a winning party can actually exercise, however, depends on several factors. At the national level, an important factor is whether the party controls both the executive and the legislative branches of government. If it does, the party leadership in Congress may be reluctant to exercise congressional checks on presidential powers. If Congress cooperates in implementing legislation approved by the president, the president, in turn, will not feel it necessary to exercise the veto power. Certainly, this situation existed while the Republicans controlled both the legislative and the executive branches of government from January 2003 to January 2007, and when the Democrats controlled the government in the two years following Obama's inauguration in January 2009.

The winning party has less control over the government when the government is divided. A **divided government** is one in which the executive and legislative branches are controlled by different parties. After the 2010 elections, this was the situation facing the nation. Even though the Democrats still controlled the presidency and the U.S. Senate, they could not pass legislation unless it was also supported by the Republicans in the House. Although House Republicans could not pass legislation either, they energetically sought to use what bargaining power they had.

The Limits of Party Unity. There are other ways in which the power of the parties is limited. Consider how major laws are passed in Congress. Traditionally, legislation was rarely passed by a vote strictly along party lines. Although most Democrats might oppose a bill, for example, some Democrats would vote for it. Their votes, combined with the votes of Republicans, were often enough to pass the bill. Similarly, support from some Republicans enabled bills sponsored by the Democrats to pass.

One reason that the political parties traditionally found it so hard to rally all of their members in Congress to vote along party lines was that candidates who won most elections largely did so on their own, without significant help from a political party. A candidate generally gained a nomination through her or his own hard work and personal political organization. In many other countries, most candidates are selected by the party organization, not by primary elections. This means, though, that in the United States the parties have very little control over the candidates who run under the party labels. In fact, a candidate could run as a Republican, for example, and advocate beliefs repugnant to the national party, such as racism. No one in the Republican Party organization could stop this person from being nominated or even elected.

did you know?

The political party with the most seats in the House of Representatives chooses the Speaker of the House, makes any new rules it wants, obtains a majority of the seats on each important committee, chooses committee chairs, and hires most of the congressional staff.

Divided Government
A situation in which one major political party controls the presidency and the other controls one or more chambers of Congress, or in which one party controls a state governorship and the other controls part or all of the state legislature.

Party Polarization. In recent years, it has become increasingly difficult for legislators in either party to obtain support for important legislation from members of the other party. More and more, voting takes place strictly along party lines. Discipline within the party caucuses has never been greater. The Republicans, who took the lead in the development of party unity, presented a united front throughout much of the 1990s. By 2009, the Democrats had largely caught up, although even then the party's congressional delegation contained a number of dissidents, notably the conservative Blue Dog caucus in the U.S. House. One reason for party-line voting is that political overlap between the two parties has essentially vanished. Political scientists calculated that by 2009, the most conservative Blue Dog Democrat in the House was still more liberal than the most liberal Republican—if a term such as *liberal Republican* still makes any sense.

For much of the twentieth century, however, liberal Republicans were a real presence in the nation's politics, and so were extremely conservative Democrats. Millions of Americans formed their party attachments not through ideology, but on the basis of tradition and sentiment. Old-stock New England Yankees were Republicans because New England Yankees had always been Republicans. White southerners were, by and large, Democrats because that party affiliation was part of what it meant to be a southerner. Ideologically, however, most of the southerners were well to the right of the average Yankee. Likewise, Yankee Republicans were, on average, more liberal than most southern Democrats. Today, liberal Yankees are usually Democrats, and conservative southerners are Republicans.

Blocking Tactics. One effect of the new polarization is that interpersonal relationships between members of the parties have deteriorated. True, some senators and representatives are able to maintain friendships across party lines, but such friendships have become less common. A second effect is the growing tactic of blocking bills to make the other party appear ineffective, without any attempt to reach a compromise. Republicans pioneered this tactic in the 1990s under House Speaker Newt Gingrich in an attempt to embarrass Democratic president Bill Clinton, and they tried it again under President Obama with varying degrees of success.

Democrats contended that the tactic demonstrated Republican irresponsibility. It is also possible to propose—rather than oppose—legislation for political ends, however. For example, in 2010 the Democrats introduced an immigration reform package, in the apparent hopes that it would mobilize their support among Latino voters, even though it had little chance of passing or even coming to a vote.

A History of Political Parties in the United States

The United States has a **two-party system,** and that system has been around since before 1800. The function and character of the political parties, as well as the emergence of the two-party system itself, have much to do with the unique historical forces operating from this country's beginning as an independent nation.

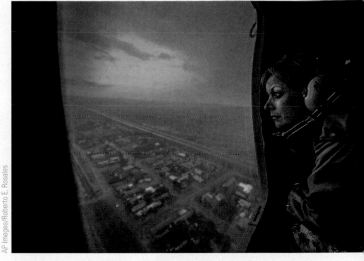

Republican governor Susana Martinez of New Mexico gets a bird's eye view of flooding in the city of Las Vegas, New Mexico. The massive flooding prompted her to declare a state of emergency. *How can Republicans maximize their support among Latinos?*

Two-Party System
A political system in which only two parties have a reasonable chance of winning.

■ **Learning Outcome 2:**
Explain how the history of U.S. political parties has led to the two major parties that exist today.

"I think it was an election year."

Thomas Jefferson was particularly adamant about his dislike of political parties. Nonetheless, he helped create a new party that we call the Jeffersonian Republicans. *Why did he find it necessary to engage in party politics?*

Generally, we can divide the evolution of our nation's political parties into seven periods:

1. The formation of parties, from 1789 to 1816.
2. The era of one-party rule, from 1816 to 1828.
3. The period from Andrew Jackson's presidency to the eve of the Civil War, from 1828 to 1856.
4. The Civil War and post–Civil War period, from 1856 to 1896.
5. The Republican ascendancy and the progressive period, from 1896 to 1932.
6. The New Deal period, from 1932 to about 1968.
7. The modern period, from approximately 1968 to the present.

The Formative Years: Federalists and Anti-Federalists

The first partisan political division in the United States occurred before the adoption of the Constitution. As you will recall from Chapter 2, the Federalists were those who pushed for the adoption of the Constitution, whereas the Anti-Federalists were against ratification.

In September 1796, George Washington, who had served as president for two terms, decided not to run again. In his farewell address, he made a somber assessment of the nation's future. Washington felt that the country might be destroyed by the "baneful [harmful] effects of the spirit of party." He viewed parties as a threat to both national unity and the concept of popular government.

Nevertheless, in the years after the ratification of the Constitution, Americans came to realize that some permanent mechanism would be necessary to identify candidates for office and represent political differences among the people. The result was two political parties.

Federalists and Republicans. One party was the Federalists, which included John Adams, the second president (1797–1801). The Federalists represented commercial interests such as merchants and large planters. They supported a strong national government.

Thomas Jefferson led the other party, which came to be called the Republicans, or Jeffersonian Republicans. (These Republicans should not be confused with the later Republican Party of Abraham Lincoln.[3]) Jefferson's Republicans represented artisans and farmers. They strongly supported states' rights. In 1800, when Jefferson defeated Adams in the presidential contest, one of the world's first peaceful transfers of power from one party to another was achieved.

The One-Party Interlude. From 1800 to 1820, a majority of U.S. voters regularly elected Jeffersonian Republicans to the presidency and to Congress. By 1816, the Federalist Party had nearly collapsed, and two-party competition did not really exist at the national level. Because there was no real political opposition to the Jeffersonian Republicans and thus little political debate, the administration of James Monroe (1817–1825) came to be known as the *era of good feelings.*

Democrats and Whigs

Organized two-party politics returned after 1824. Following the election of John Quincy Adams as president, the Jeffersonian Republican Party split in two. The supporters of Adams called themselves National Republicans. The supporters of Andrew Jackson, who defeated Adams in 1828, formed the **Democratic Party.** Later, the National Republicans took the name **Whig Party,** which had been a traditional name for British liberals. The

did you know?

An anti-immigrant, anti-Catholic secret society dubbed the "know-nothings" entered politics as the American Party in the 1840s. In the 1856 presidential elections, know-nothing candidate Millard Fillmore carried Maryland.

Democratic Party
One of the two major American political parties evolving out of the Republican Party of Thomas Jefferson.

Whig Party
A major party in the United States during the first half of the nineteenth century, formally established in 1836. The Whig Party was anti-Jackson and represented a variety of regional interests.

---

3. To avoid confusion, some scholars refer to Jefferson's party as the Democratic-Republicans, but this name was never used during the time that the party existed.

Whigs stood for, among other things, federal spending on "internal improvements," such as roads.

The Democrats opposed this policy. The Democrats, who were the stronger of the two parties, favored personal liberty and opportunity for the "common man." It was understood implicitly that the "common man" was a white man—hostility toward African Americans was an important force holding the disparate Democratic groups together.[4]

The Civil War Crisis

In the 1850s, hostility between the North and the South over the issue of slavery divided both parties. The Whigs were the first to split in two. The Whigs had been the party of an active federal government, but Southerners had come to believe that "a government strong enough to build roads is a government strong enough to free your slaves." The southern Whigs therefore ceased to exist as an organized party. In 1854, the northern Whigs united with antislavery Democrats and members of the radical antislavery Free Soil Party to found the modern **Republican Party.**

The Post–Civil War Period

After the Civil War, the Democratic Party was able to heal its divisions. Southern resentment of the Republicans' role in defeating the South and fears that the federal government would intervene on behalf of African Americans ensured that the Democrats would dominate the white South for the next century. It was in this period that the Republicans adopted the nickname **GOP,** which stands for "grand old party."

Cultural Politics. Northern Democrats feared a strong government for other reasons. The Republicans thought that the government should promote business and economic growth, but many Republicans also wanted to use the power of government to impose evangelical Protestant moral values on society. Democrats opposed what they saw as culturally coercive measures. Many Republicans wanted to limit or even prohibit the sale of alcoholic beverages. They favored the establishment of public schools—with a Protestant curriculum. As a result, Catholics were strongly Democratic.

The Triumph of the Republicans. In this period, the parties were very evenly matched in strength. In the 1890s, however, the Republicans gained a decisive edge. In that decade, the Populist movement emerged in the West and South to champion the interests of small farmers, who were often greatly in debt. Populists supported inflation, which benefited debtors by reducing the real value of outstanding debts. In 1896, when William Jennings Bryan became the Democratic candidate for president, the Democrats embraced populism.

As it turned out, the few western farmers who were drawn to the Democrats by this step were greatly outnumbered by urban working class voters who believed that inflation would reduce the purchasing power of their paychecks and who therefore became Republicans. William McKinley, the Republican candidate, was elected with a solid majority of the votes. Figure 8–1 that follows shows the states taken by Bryan and McKinley. Political scientists use the term *realignment* to refer to this kind of large-scale change in support for the two major parties. (Realignment is discussed in more detail later in this chapter.) From 1896 until 1932, the GOP was successful in presenting itself as the party that knew how to manage the economy.

Andrew Jackson earned the name "Old Hickory" for his exploits during the War of 1812. In 1828, Jackson was elected president as the candidate of the new Democratic Party. *What policies held the new party together?*

> **Republican Party**
> One of the two major American political parties. It emerged in the 1850s as an antislavery party and consisted of former northern Whigs and antislavery Democrats.
>
> **GOP**
> A nickname for the Republican Party; stands for "grand old party."

Abraham Lincoln ran on the Republican ticket for president in 1860. *What political groups banded together to form the modern Republican Party?*

---

4. Edward Pessen, *Jacksonian America: Society, Personality, and Politics* (Homewood, Ill.: Dorsey Press, 1969). See especially pages 246–247. The small number of free blacks who could vote were overwhelmingly Whig.

Figure 8–1   ▶   **The 1896 Presidential Elections**

In 1896, the agrarian, populist appeal of Democrat William Jennings Bryan (blue states) won western states for the Democrats at the cost of losing more populous eastern states to Republican William McKinley (red states). This pattern held in subsequent presidential elections. *Why was populism a losing ideology?*

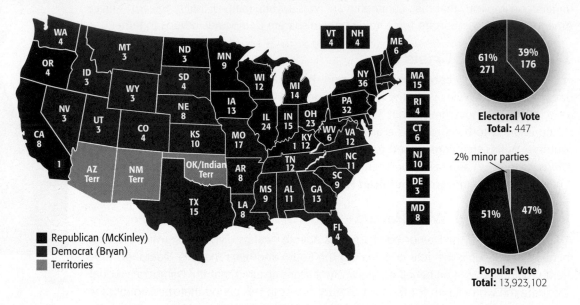

Republican (McKinley)
Democrat (Bryan)
Territories

Electoral Vote
Total: 447

61%
271

39%
176

2% minor parties

51%

47%

Popular Vote
Total: 13,923,102

The Progressive Interlude

In the early 1900s, a spirit of political reform arose in both major parties. Called *progressivism,* this spirit was compounded of a fear of the growing power of large corporations and a belief that honest, impartial government could regulate the economy effectively. In 1912, the Republican Party temporarily split as former Republican president Theodore Roosevelt campaigned for the presidency on a third-party Progressive ticket. The Republican split permitted the election of Woodrow Wilson, the Democratic candidate, along with a Democratic Congress.

Like Roosevelt, Wilson considered himself a progressive, although he and Roosevelt did not agree on how progressivism ought to be implemented. Wilson's progressivism marked the beginning of a radical change in Democratic policies. Dating back to its very foundation, the Democratic Party had been the party of limited government. Under Wilson, the Democrats became for the first time at least as receptive as the Republicans to government action in the economy. (Wilson's progressivism did not extend to race relations—for African Americans, the Wilson administration was something of a disaster.)

The New Deal Era

The Republican ascendancy resumed after Wilson left office. It ended with the election of 1932, in the depths of the Great Depression. Republican Herbert Hoover was president when the Depression began in 1929. Although Hoover took some measures to fight the Depression, they fell far short of what the public demanded. Significantly, Hoover opposed federal relief for the unemployed and the destitute. In 1932, Democrat Franklin D. Roosevelt was elected president by an overwhelming margin. As with the election of 1896, the vote in 1932 constituted a major political realignment.

President Woodrow Wilson (1913–1921) considered himself a progressive. *Did he change Democratic policies very much?*

The Great Depression shattered the working class belief in Republican economic competence. Under Roosevelt, the Democrats began to make major interventions in the economy in an attempt to combat the Depression and to relieve the suffering of the unemployed. Roosevelt's New Deal relief programs were open to all citizens, both black and white. As a result, African Americans began to support the Democratic Party in large numbers—a development that would have stunned any American politician of the 1800s.

Roosevelt's political coalition was broad enough to establish the Democrats as the new majority party, in place of the GOP. In the 1950s, Republican Dwight D. Eisenhower, the leading U.S. general during World War II, won two terms as president. Otherwise, with minor interruptions, the Democratic ascendancy lasted until about 1968.

An Era of Divided Government

The New Deal coalition managed the unlikely feat of including both African Americans and whites who were hostile to African American advancement. This balancing act came to an end in the 1960s, a decade that was marked by the civil rights movement, by several years of "race riots" in major cities, and by increasingly heated protests against the Vietnam War (1965–1975). For many economically moderate, socially conservative voters, especially in the South, social issues had become more important than economic ones, and these individuals left the Democratic Party. These voters outnumbered the new voters who joined the Democrats—newly enfranchised African Americans and former liberal Republicans in New England and the upper Midwest.

The Parties in Balance. The result, after 1968, was a slow-motion realignment that left the nation almost evenly divided in politics. In presidential elections, the Republicans had more success than the Democrats. Until the 1990s, Congress remained Democratic, but official party labels can be misleading. Some of the Democrats were southern conservatives who normally voted with the Republicans on issues. As these conservative Democrats retired, they were largely replaced by Republicans. In 1994, Republicans were able to take control of both the House and the Senate for the first time in many years.

Red State, Blue State. Nothing demonstrated the nation's close political divisions more clearly than the 2000 presidential elections. Democratic presidential candidate Al Gore won the popular vote, but lost the electoral college by a narrow margin to Republican George W. Bush. The closeness of the vote in the electoral college led the press to repeatedly publish the map of the results state by state. Commentators discussed at length the supposed differences between the Republican "red states" and the Democratic "blue states."

An interesting characteristic of the red state–blue state division is that it is an almost exact reversal of the presidential elections of 1896 (see Figure 8–1 earlier in this section). Except for the state of Washington, every state that supported Democrat William Jennings Bryan in 1896 supported Republican George W. Bush in 2000 and 2004. This reversal parallels the transformation of the Democrats from an anti–civil rights to a pro–civil rights party and from a party that supported limited government to a party that favors expanded positive government action.

> **did you know?**
> The Democrats and the Republicans each had exactly one woman delegate at their conventions in 1900.

The Two Major U.S. Parties Today

Not only was the presidential election of 2000 very close, but the partisan balance in the U.S. Congress was also very close in the opening years of the twenty-first century. It is true

■ **Learning Outcome 3:** Summarize key differences between the policies and supporters of the major parties.

that from 1995 until the elections of 2006, the Republicans generally controlled Congress. Their margins of control, however, were very narrow.

A Series of Wave Elections

From time to time, voters demonstrate that they are relatively dissatisfied with the performance of one or another of the major parties. This dissatisfaction can produce a "wave" of support for the other party. Unlike realignments, the effects of wave elections are temporary. The first decade of the twenty-first century was marked by a series of wave elections in which the voters punished first one party and then the other.

Wave Elections Sweep Out the Republicans. By 2006, ever-larger numbers of voters came to believe that U.S. intervention in Iraq had been a mistake. In the 2006 midterm elections, the Democrats took control of the U.S. House and Senate in a wave election. In September 2008, a worldwide financial panic turned what had been a modest recession into the greatest economic downturn since the Great Depression of the 1930s. The political consequences were inevitable. In November, Democratic presidential candidate Barack Obama was elected with one of the largest margins in recent years.

Democrats in Trouble. By 2010, the Democrats had lost popularity. In the midterm elections of 2010, the Republicans benefited from one of the strongest wave elections in decades and took control of the House. The Democrats retained control of the Senate.

It is likely that some voters now blamed the Democrats for the state of the economy. Many observers, however, argued that independents turned away from the Democrats in the belief that the party was expanding the scope of the federal government to an unacceptable degree. In particular, the Democratic health-care reform package was crucial in fostering the perception of the party as being committed to "big government."

Republican Overreach. The incoming class of Republican House members in 2011 included a large contingent loyal to the Tea Party movement, and many incumbent members aligned themselves with the movement as well. These legislators were pledged to oppose any compromise with the Democrats—even though the Democratic Party still controlled the Senate and the presidency.

The uncompromising spirit of the Republicans received a major test in 2011, when House Republicans refused to lift the nation's debt ceiling unless the Democrats accepted large cuts in spending. President Obama and House Speaker John Boehner reached a compromise, but the threat to the nation's ability to meet its obligations severely damaged the popularity of everyone concerned.

The 2012 Elections. In 2012, Obama was reelected by a clear margin—four percentage points in the popular vote. We show the state-by-state results in Figure 8–2 that follows. While the voters favored the Democrats, the results were hardly a crushing blow to the Republicans. Mitt Romney, the Republican candidate, had done well. The Republicans lost seats in Congress but remained in control of the House.

Still, exit polls showed that Hispanics now cast 10 percent of the vote, a new high, and Obama won 71 percent of that vote. Some political observers argued that the Republicans should modify their immigration policies in an attempt to court Latinos. Others pointed to a deeper problem. Government programs are widely popular among most Hispanics, and also among the growing population of Asian Americans. Republicans were simply not doing well with groups that were growing in numbers—an ominous sign for the future.

COMPARE WITH YOUR PEERS
MindTap™ for American Government

Access the Political Parties Forum: Polling Activity—Hurricane Sandy and Politics

CONNECT WITH YOUR CLASSMATES
MindTap™ for American Government

Access the Political Parties Forum: Discussion—Working Together after Elections

Figure 8–2   ▶   **The 2012 Presidential Elections**

In the 2012 presidential elections, Barack Obama received a majority of the electoral college votes, outdoing Mitt Romney by a convincing margin. Although Obama lost two states that he had won in the 2008 presidential elections, the regional political preferences remained similar to those of previous elections. *Why might state partisan preferences be relatively stable?*

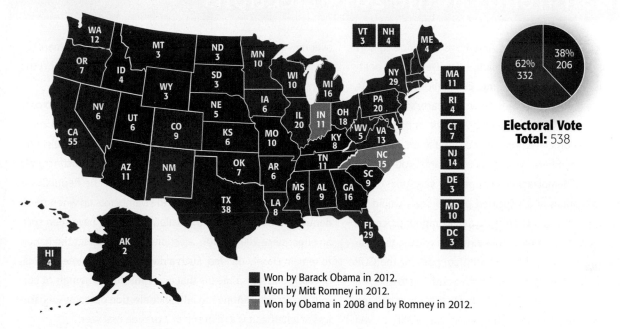

- Won by Barack Obama in 2012.
- Won by Mitt Romney in 2012.
- Won by Obama in 2008 and by Romney in 2012.

The Parties' Core Constituents

Who are the people that support the two major parties? You learned in Chapter 6 how demographic factors affect support for the two parties. Democrats receive disproportionate support not only from the least well-educated voters but also from individuals with advanced degrees. Businesspersons are much more likely to vote Republican than are labor union members. The Jewish electorate is heavily Democratic; white evangelical Christians who are regular churchgoers tend to be Republicans. Hispanics are strongly Democratic, and African Americans are overwhelmingly so. City dwellers tend to be Democrats, and rural people tend to be Republicans. Such tendencies represent the influences of economic interests and cultural values, which are often in conflict with each other.

Core Economic Interests

A coalition of the labor movement and various racial and ethnic minorities has been a major part of Democratic Party support since the presidency of Franklin D. Roosevelt. The social programs and increased government intervention in the economy that made up Roosevelt's New Deal were intended to ease the pressure of economic hard times on these groups. This goal remains important for many Democrats today. In general, Democratic identifiers are more likely to approve of social-welfare spending, to support government regulation of business, and to endorse measures to

Why Should You Care about...

Political Parties?

Political parties do affect your everyday life, if often indirectly. Consider that whichever political party has the most members in each chamber of Congress dominates that body. Thus, a political party's success can lead to new laws and regulations that affect your life. You might have to pay higher or lower taxes, receive a better or worse deal on a student loan, or face greater or lesser employment opportunities upon graduation.

2014 Elections

Partisan Trends in the 2014 Elections

The 2014 elections suggest that Americans continue to sort themselves into opposing political camps. The Democratic political "brand" is now so toxic among Evangelicals and white Southerners that it is hard to see how the party's reputation could fall any further. The Republican brand, for its part, is ever more toxic among other sections of the population, including minority group members, young people, and voters with advanced degrees. Democrats have hoped for years that growing numbers of Latinos and educated professionals would tip the electorate in their direction. This demographic process is indeed underway. To a considerable extent, however, the process has been counteracted by growing support for the GOP among older white voters, especially in the South but to a degree in northern regions as well. These facts raise some questions: Which effect will be stronger—the Republican ability to win over new white voters, or the growth of Democratic elements in the population? Will the recent tendency of youth to support the Democrats save that party in the end?

The sorting of the voters by age has helped create two contrasting electorates. Midterm voters are now older and more conservative than the ones who turn out in presidential election years. (In the past, the two electorates were not as distinct.) We may continue to have a see-saw effect, with the Republicans favored in the midterms and with the Democrats up when presidential candidates are on the ballot. In fact, we have seen such an effect since 2008. Across elections, we can expect the nation to remain closely divided. Such a division will promote political gridlock, and it also means that economic fundamentals or current events will continue to influence election outcomes regardless of whether it is a midterm or a presidential year.

improve the situation of minorities. Republicans are more supportive of the private marketplace and believe more strongly in an ethic of self-reliance and limited government.

During the administrations of Democrat Bill Clinton (1993–2001) and Republican George W. Bush (2001–2009), it seemed for several years that the major parties had come to a consensus on the size of government. To be sure, the GOP continued to accuse Democrats of being the party of "big government." It was Clinton, however, who led the effort to reform the welfare system, cutting benefits. Bush, in contrast, added drug coverage to the Medicare program and increased federal support for public schools through the No Child Left Behind law. With the arrival of the Obama administration, however, the parties appeared to revert to their traditional positions on the size of government.

Cultural Politics

In recent years, cultural values have played a significant role in defining the beliefs of the two major parties. For example, in 1987 Democrats were almost as likely to favor stricter abortion laws (40 percent) as Republicans were (48 percent). Today, Republicans are twice as likely to favor stricter abortion laws (50 percent to 25 percent).

Cultural Politics and Socioeconomic Status. Some years ago, Thomas Frank reported seeing the following bumper sticker at a gun show in Kansas City: "A working person voting for the Democrats is like a chicken voting for Colonel Sanders." (Colonel Sanders is the iconic founder of KFC, a chain of fried-chicken restaurants.) In light of the economic traditions of the two parties, this seems to be an odd statement. In fact, the sticker is an exact reversal of an earlier one directed against the Republicans.

You can make sense of such a sentiment by remembering what you learned in Chapter 6—although economic conservatism is associated with higher incomes, social conservatism is relatively more common among lower-income groups. The individual who displayed the bumper sticker, therefore, was in effect claiming that cultural concerns—in this example, presumably the right to own handguns—were far more important than economic ones. Frank argues that cultural conservatives view themselves as embattled "ordinary Americans" under threat from a liberal, cosmopolitan elite.[5] Of course, the election of Barack Obama and a strongly Democratic Congress in 2008 certainly magnified such fears.

The Regional Factor in Cultural Politics. Conventionally, some parts of the country are viewed as culturally liberal, and others as culturally conservative. On a regional basis, cultural liberalism (as opposed to economic liberalism) may be associated with economic dynamism. The San Francisco Bay Area can serve as an example. The greater Bay Area contains Silicon Valley, the heart of the high-tech industry. It has the highest per capita personal income of any metropolitan area in America. It also is one of the most liberal regions of the country. San Francisco liberalism is largely cultural—one sign of this liberalism is that the city has been called the "capital" of gay America.

To further illustrate this point, we can compare the political preferences of relatively wealthy states with those of relatively poor ones. Of the fifteen states with the highest per capita personal incomes in 2012, twelve voted for Democrat Barack Obama in the presidential elections of that year. Of the fifteen with the lowest per capita incomes in 2012, thirteen voted for Republican Mitt Romney.

Given these data, it seems hard to believe that upper-income voters really are more Republican than lower-income ones. Still, within any given state or region, upscale voters are more likely to be Republican regardless of whether the area as a whole leans Democratic or Republican. States that vote Democratic are often northern states that contain large cities. At least part of this **reverse-income effect** may simply be that urban areas are more prosperous, culturally liberal, and Democratic than the countryside, and that the North is more prosperous, culturally liberal, and Democratic than the South.

Party Divisions and Party Unity

As we have observed, for much of American history the two major political parties were broad coalitions that included individuals with widely varying political beliefs. Today, however, members of the major parties demonstrate a striking degree of political convergence.

A college student describes the importance of Pell Grant scholarships at the 2012 Democratic National Convention. *Why is the youth vote significant?*

did you know?

In his first inaugural address, Thomas Jefferson proclaimed that "We are all Republicans, we are all Federalists."

Reverse-Income Effect
A tendency for wealthier states or regions to favor the Democrats and for less wealthy states or regions to favor the Republicans. The effect appears paradoxical because it reverses traditional patterns of support.

5. Thomas Frank, *What's the Matter with Kansas? How Conservatives Won the Heart of America* (New York: Holt, 2005).

Yet despite their ideological unity, the parties are made up of a variety of different kinds of people.

Different Kinds of Democrats. In addition to members of the working class and various racial and ethnic minority groups, the Democrats have long included middle to upper-middle-class "reform" elements that are drawn to specific issues. By the late twentieth century, these Democrats were likely to be anti-war or interested in the environment, women's rights, or other causes. During the Vietnam War (1965–1975), differences between "regulars" and anti-war insurgents almost tore the Democrats apart.

Typically, Democratic regulars with working class appeal have beaten issue-oriented liberals in presidential nomination contests. In the last decades of the twentieth century, however, many white working class Democrats became Republicans, even as the number of well-educated liberals in the party grew. As a result, Barack Obama could narrowly win the 2008 Democratic nomination even though Hillary Clinton had more working class support. Still, political differences between Obama and Clinton—and their supporters— were almost nonexistent. In contrast to the Vietnam War era, today different kinds of Democrats tend to have similar politics.

Different Kinds of Republicans. Observers have long distinguished three kinds of Republicans. One bloc of GOP voters, often called the Religious Right, is energized by conservative religious beliefs. These conservatives are often evangelical Protestants but may also be Catholics, Mormons, or adherents of other faiths. For these voters, moral issues such as abortion and gay marriage are key. Another group of Republicans is more oriented toward economic issues and business concerns. These voters often are small-business owners or have some other connection to commercial enterprise. Such voters oppose high tax rates and are concerned about government regulations that interfere with the conduct of business.

While these two groups of Republicans have different concerns, it is relatively easy for a Republican politician to appeal to both with a platform that is both culturally conservative and pro-business. A third type of Republican, however, is strongly libertarian. These voters dislike government regulation of social issues as well as economic ones. They may also oppose U.S. intervention in foreign conflicts. This group is much smaller than the Religious Right or the pro-business bloc and has little influence on party policy. Therefore, Republican politicians with national ambitions may find that they must play down any libertarian tendencies they actually embrace.

Phil Robertson, a star of the *Duck Dynasty* television series, addresses the 2014 Republican Leadership Conference in New Orleans. *How might Republicans react to Robertson's statements about the sinfulness of homosexual behavior?*

Bill Haber/AP Images

Radicals and Moderates. In the twenty-first century, differences within the parties were less likely to take the form of disputes over the issues, and more likely to pit moderates against radicals. This division was particularly conspicuous among the Republicans. In 2010 and 2012, Tea Party activists and other ideological groups sought to purge the Republicans of so-called RINOs (Republicans in name only). In 2013, Republican House Speaker John Boehner experienced serious difficulties in controlling the more radical members of his party in the House. One result was that in 2014, groups such as the U.S. Chamber of Commerce organized to support more moderate—and potentially more successful—conservatives in congressional primary elections.

Forces Promoting Party Unity. We remarked earlier that cultural conservatism has propelled some white working class voters out of the Democratic Party and into the Republican ranks. Psychologists who study politics have noted a consequence of such transitions: voters who change parties due to cultural issues soon change their economic views to match their new party. After all, it is not comfortable to hold progressive economic views while participating in a conservative party. This variety of discomfort has been described as a kind of *cognitive dissonance*, the mental stress that results from holding contradictory views. The impulse toward political unity becomes conspicuous when an issue that previously was nonpartisan becomes partisan. Global warming, or climate change, can serve as an example. As recently as fifteen years ago, opinions on this topic crossed ideological lines. Today, almost all progressives believe that climate change is a problem, and almost all conservatives believe that it is not. Ezra Klein, writing in the Vox blog, explains why this is so:

> *Imagine what would happen to [conservative personality] Sean Hannity if he decided tomorrow that climate change was the central threat facing the planet. Initially, his viewers would think he was joking. But soon, they'd begin calling in furiously. . . He would lose friendships, viewers, and money. He could ultimately lose his job. And along the way he would cause himself immense personal pain as he systematically alienated his closest political and professional allies.[6]*

For most people, maintaining social relationships is far more important than taking a particular position on an issue. As another example, it could be equally difficult for a San Francisco progressive to defend crops altered by genetic engineering (GMO crops). Have these forces resulted in parties that are too radical? We address that issue in the *Which Side Are You On?* feature that follows.

Why Has the Two-Party System Endured?

There are several reasons why two major parties have dominated the political landscape in the United States for almost two centuries. These reasons have to do with (1) the historical foundations of the system, (2) political socialization and practical considerations, (3) the winner-take-all electoral system, and (4) state and federal laws favoring the two-party system.

The Historical Foundations of the Two-Party System

As we have seen, at many times in American history one preeminent issue or dispute has divided the nation politically. In the beginning, Americans were at odds over ratifying the Constitution. After the Constitution went into effect, the power of the federal government became the major national issue. Thereafter, the dispute over slavery divided the nation, North versus South. At times—for example, in the North after the Civil War—cultural differences have been important, with advocates of government-sponsored morality (such as banning alcoholic beverages) pitted against advocates of personal liberty.

During much of the twentieth century, economic differences were preeminent. In the New Deal period, the Democrats became known as the party of the working class, while the Republicans became known as the party of the middle and upper classes and commercial interests. In situations like these, when politics is based on an argument between two opposing points of view, advocates of each viewpoint can mobilize most effectively by forming a single, unified party. The result is a two-party system. When such a system has been in existence for almost two centuries, it becomes difficult to imagine an alternative.

Political Socialization and Practical Considerations

Given that the majority of Americans identify with one of the two major political parties, it is not surprising that most children learn at a fairly young age to think of themselves

■ **Learning Outcome 4:**
Give some of the reasons why the two-party system has endured in America, and evaluate the impact of third parties on U.S. politics.

6. www.vox.com/2014/4/6/5556462/brain-dead-how-politics-makes-us-stupid

Which Side Are You On?

Are the Parties Becoming Too Radical?

In recent years, political rhetoric seemed to reach new heights of hysteria. Many Americans on the political right believed that President Obama was foreign-born and ineligible to be president—even though Obama produced his Hawaii birth certificate and the birth was announced in Honolulu newspapers. In one poll, a majority of Republicans affirmed that Obama was a Muslim.

Meanwhile, the Democrats in Congress pushed through their health-care reform program, a massive change in how we fund one-sixth of the nation's economy. No national consensus existed in support of the program, but the Democrats proceeded regardless.

Irresponsible rhetoric, adventurous legislation—were these manifestations of a new radical spirit? Some observers contend that they were.

The Parties Have Never Been So Radical

Those who believe that our politics exhibits unprecedented levels of radicalism point to the extreme language used on the Web, on the airwaves, and in Congress. In addition, both parties seem willing to undertake ideologically motivated steps that can only hurt them. If passing health-care legislation that will damage you politically is not radical, what is?

On their side, Republicans sought to purge their party of candidates showing the least sign of moderation, even when purity meant losing elections. In a 2012 primary election, for example, Tea Party Republicans defeated U.S. senator Richard Lugar, a popular moderate who was running for a seventh term in office. The

Republican winner, Richard Mourdock, then went down to defeat after making unfortunate remarks on the topic of rape.

Radicalism Exists, All Right, but It Is Not New

Anyone who thinks that the beliefs of the far right are unprecedentedly "out there" needs to learn more history. In 1958, Robert Welch, leader of the right-wing John Birch Society, claimed in all seriousness that Republican president Dwight D. Eisenhower was a "dedicated, conscious agent of the Communist conspiracy." That beats anything we've heard recently from a prominent figure.

As for the Democrats, passage of health-care legislation doesn't mean that the party has become more radical. It only means that with large majorities in the House and Senate, the party found itself in a position to pass measures it had supported for decades. If the Republicans had the power to win certain long-sought objectives supported by all wings of the party, they would surely do the same.

For Critical Analysis

Suppose that the United States Supreme Court were to reverse itself on *Roe v. Wade*, thus giving the national and state governments the power to outlaw abortions. How might the Republican Party, with its strong right-to-life platform, respond to such a ruling? How might Republicans who support freedom of choice react to their party's actions?

Plurality
A number of votes cast for a candidate that is greater than the number of votes for any other candidate but not necessarily a majority.

as either Democrats or Republicans. This generates a built-in mechanism to perpetuate a two-party system. Also, most politically oriented people who aspire to work for change consider that the only realistic way to capture political power in this country is to be either a Republican or a Democrat.

The Winner-Take-All Electoral System

At almost every level of government in the United States, the outcome of elections is based on the **plurality,** winner-take-all principle. In a plurality system, the winner is the person who obtains the most votes, even if that person does not receive a majority (more than 50 percent) of the votes. Whoever gets the most votes gets everything. Most legislators in the United States are elected from single-member districts in which only one person represents the constituency, and the candidate who finishes second in such an election receives nothing for the effort.

Presidential Voting. The winner-take-all system also operates in the election of the U.S. president. Recall that the voters in each state do not vote for a president directly but vote for **electoral college** delegates who are committed to the various presidential candidates. These delegates are called *electors*.

In all but two states (Maine and Nebraska), if a presidential candidate wins a plurality in the state, then *all* of the state's electoral votes go to that candidate. This is known as the *unit rule*. For example, suppose that the electors pledged to a particular presidential candidate receive a plurality of 40 percent of the votes in a state. That presidential candidate will receive all of the state's votes in the electoral college. Minor parties have a difficult time competing under such a system. Because voters know that minor parties cannot win any electoral votes, they often will not vote for minor-party candidates, even if the candidates are in tune with them ideologically.

> **Electoral College**
> A group of persons, called electors, who are selected by the voters in each state. This group officially elects the president and the vice president of the United States.

Why Should You Care about...

Political Parties?

Political parties play an important role at the state and local level, in addition to their importance in national politics. A state legislature controlled by the Democrats will create and implement different policies than one controlled by the Republicans, and vice versa. These policies can affect the amount of tuition you pay, the speed limits on your state's highways, and much else.

Popular Election of the Governors and the President. In most of Europe, the chief executive (usually called the prime minister) is elected by the legislature, or parliament. If the parliament contains three or more parties, as is usually the situation, two or more of the parties can join together in a coalition to choose the prime minister and the other leaders of the government. In the United States, however, the people elect the president and the governors of all fifty states. There is no opportunity for two or more parties to negotiate a coalition. Here, too, the winner-take-all principle discriminates powerfully against any third party.

Proportional Representation. Many other nations use a system of proportional representation. If, during the national election, party X obtains 12 percent of the vote, party Y gets 43 percent of the vote, and party Z gets the remaining 45 percent of the vote, then party X gets 12 percent of the seats in the legislature, party Y gets 43 percent of the seats, and party Z gets 45 percent of the seats.

Some nations implement proportional representation by creating districts that elect multiple representatives. Such a system, however, can require the creation of districts that are uncomfortably large. The nation of Israel, for example, is a single, large electoral district. Every party runs nationwide.

Congressional pages carry the electoral college votes to the House chamber where the election of Barack Obama as the forty-fourth president of the United States was certified on January 8, 2009. *What effect does the electoral college have on the political system?*

Bill Clark/*Roll Call*/Getty Images

An alternate system is to let voters choose both a local representative and a preferred party. Germany uses such a system to elect members of the Bundestag, its parliament. Suppose that the Green Party wins the support of 10 percent of the voters in a particular German state, but only a few Greens win in their local districts. If this happens, enough Greens will be added from the party's statewide list of candidates to boost its Bundestag delegation to 10 percent of the total from that state. Regardless of how proportional representation is implemented, the system gives smaller parties a greater incentive to organize than in the United States.

State and Federal Laws Favoring the Two Parties

Many state and federal election laws offer a clear advantage to the two major parties. In some states, the established major parties need to gather fewer signatures to place their candidates on the ballot than minor parties or independent candidates do. The criterion for determining how many signatures will be required is often based on the total party vote in the last general election, thus penalizing a new political party that did not compete in that election.

At the national level, minor parties face different obstacles. All of the rules and procedures of both chambers of Congress divide committee seats, staff members, and other privileges on the basis of party membership. A legislator who is elected on a minor-party ticket, such as the Conservative Party of New York, must choose to be counted with one of the major parties to obtain a committee assignment.

The Federal Election Commission (FEC) rules for campaign financing also place restrictions on minor-party candidates. Such candidates are not eligible for federal matching funds in either the primary or the general election. In the 1980 elections, John Anderson, running for president as an independent, sued the FEC for campaign funds. The commission finally agreed to repay part of his campaign costs after the election in proportion to the votes he received. Giving funds to a candidate when the campaign is over is, of course, much less helpful than providing funds while the campaign is still under way.

The Role of Minor Parties in U.S. Politics

For the reasons just discussed, minor parties have a difficult, if not impossible, time competing within the American two-party political system. Still, minor parties have played an important role in our political life. Parties other than the Republicans or Democrats are usually called **third parties.** (Technically, of course, there could be fourth, fifth, or sixth parties as well, but we use the term *third party* because it has endured.) Third parties can come into existence in a number of ways. They may be founded from scratch by individuals or groups who are committed to a particular interest, issue, or ideology. They can split off from one of the major parties when a group becomes dissatisfied with the major party's policies. Finally, they can be organized around a particular charismatic leader and serve as that person's vehicle for contesting elections.

Frequently, third parties have acted as barometers of change in the political mood, forcing the major parties to recognize new issues or trends in the thinking of Americans. Political scientists believe that third parties have acted as safety valves for dissident groups, preventing major confrontations and political unrest. In some instances, third parties have functioned as way stations for voters en route from one of the major parties to the other. Table 8–1 lists significant third-party presidential campaigns in American history, and Table 8–2 provides a brief description of third-party beliefs.

did you know?

In a bipartisan vote, the lower house of the Indiana legislature passed a bill in 1897 that, among other things, set the value of the mathematical constant π (pi) as 3.2. (The true approximate value, to four decimal places, is 3.1416.) The bill was then buried in the Indiana Senate.

Third Party
A political party other than the two major political parties (Republican and Democratic).

Table 8–1 ▶ **The Most Successful Third-Party Presidential Campaigns since 1864**

The following list includes all third-party candidates winning more than 5 percent of the popular vote or any electoral votes since 1864. (We ignore isolated "unfaithful electors" in the electoral college who failed to vote for the candidate to which they were pledged.)

Year	Major Third Party	Third-Party Presidential Candidate	Percent of the Popular Vote	Electoral Votes	Winning Presidential Candidate and Party
1892	Populist	James Weaver	8.5	22	Grover Cleveland (D)
1912	Progressive	Theodore Roosevelt	27.4	88	Woodrow Wilson (D)
	Socialist	Eugene Debs	6.0	—	
1924	Progressive	Robert LaFollette	16.6	13	Calvin Coolidge (R)
1948	States' Rights	Strom Thurmond	2.4	39	Harry Truman (D)
1960	Independent Democrat	Harry Byrd	0.4	15*	John F. Kennedy (D)
1968	American Independent	George Wallace	13.5	46	Richard Nixon (R)
1980	National Union	John Anderson	6.6	—	Ronald Reagan (R)
1992	Independent	Ross Perot	18.9	—	Bill Clinton (D)
1996	Reform	Ross Perot	8.4	—	Bill Clinton (D)

*Byrd received fifteen electoral votes from unpledged electors in Alabama and Mississippi.

Source: *Dave Leip's Atlas of U.S. Presidential Elections* at **www.uselectionatlas.org.**

Table 8–2 ▶ **Policies of Selected American Third Parties since 1864**

Populist: This pro-farmer party of the 1890s advocated progressive reforms. It also advocated replacing gold with silver as the basis of the currency in hopes of creating a mild inflation in prices. (It was believed by many that inflation would help debtors and stimulate the economy.)

Socialist: This party advocated a "cooperative commonwealth" based on government ownership of industry. It was pro-labor, often antiwar, and in later years, anti-Communist. It was dissolved in 1972 and replaced by nonparty advocacy groups (Democratic Socialists of America and Social Democrats USA).

Communist: This left-wing breakaway from the Socialists was the U.S. branch of the worldwide Communist movement. The party was pro-labor and advocated full equality for African Americans. It was also closely aligned with the Communist-led Soviet Union, which provoked great hostility among most Americans.

Progressive: This name was given to several successive splinter parties built around individual political leaders. Theodore Roosevelt, who ran in 1912, advocated federal regulation of industry to protect consumers, workers, and small businesses. Robert LaFollette, who ran in 1924, held similar views.

American Independent: Built around George Wallace, this party opposed any further promotion of civil rights and advocated a militant foreign policy. Wallace's supporters were mostly former Democrats who were soon to be Republicans.

Libertarian: This party opposes most government activity.

Reform: The Reform Party was initially built around businessman H. Ross Perot but later was taken over by others. Under Perot, the party was a middle-of-the-road group opposed to federal budget deficits. Under Patrick Buchanan, it came to represent right-wing nationalism and opposition to free trade.

Green: The Greens are a left-of-center pro-environmental party. They are also generally hostile to globalization.

Ideological Third Parties. The longest-lived third parties have been those with strong ideological foundations that are typically at odds with the majority mind-set. The Socialist Party is an example. The party was founded in 1901 and lasted until 1972, when it was finally dissolved. (A smaller party later took up the name.) The Socialists were never very popular in the United States. Indeed, the term *socialist* has recently gained currency as a conservative insult directed at President Obama. In Europe, however, socialist parties became very important, and *socialist* is merely a description. We take a look at the "real" socialists in the *Beyond Our Borders* feature that follows.

Ideology has at least two functions in such parties. First, the members of the party regard themselves as outsiders and look to one another for support—ideology provides great psychological cohesiveness. Second, because the rewards of ideological commitment are partly psychological, these parties do not think in terms of immediate electoral success. A poor showing at the polls therefore does not dissuade either the leadership or the grassroots participants from continuing their quest for change in American government (and, ultimately, American society).

Today's active ideological parties include the Libertarian Party and the Green Party. As you learned in Chapter 1, the Libertarian Party supports a *laissez-faire* ("let it be") capitalist economic program, together with a hands-off policy on regulating matters of moral conduct. The Green Party began as a grassroots environmentalist organization with affiliated political parties across North America and Western Europe. It was established in the United States as a national party in 1996 and nominated Ralph Nader to run for president in 2000. Nader campaigned against what he called "corporate greed," advocated universal health

did you know?

By the mid-1990s in England, the Monster Raging Loony Party had become strong enough to regularly win fourth place in special parliamentary elections.

Beyond Our Borders

The Real Socialists

Not many American politicians accept the socialist label, although Vermont senator Bernie Sanders answers to it. In most Western European nations, however, the main left-of-center party comes out of the socialist tradition. Examples include the British Labour Party, the Socialist Party of France, and the Social Democratic Party of Germany. A hundred years ago, these parties were much more radical than they are today. Most called for the abolition of capitalism. Instead, the state, democratically elected by the people, would own the factories and shops, the banks and railroads. (Some socialists advocated ownership by employee cooperatives instead.) Karl Marx was a patron saint of the movement. Many of these parties—most notably the British Labour Party—were tightly linked to labor unions.

From 1918 to 1920, some of the radical fervor left the socialist parties as revolutionaries withdrew to form the new communist movement. In Russia, the communists actually succeeded in replacing capitalism with government ownership, but their methods were so brutal as to taint everything they did. In time, experiments revealed that government ownership of businesses

was not helpful in democratic countries either. In the years following World War II, one by one the socialist parties formally gave up the goal of replacing capitalism. What was left was a commitment to a strong welfare state and to the labor movement.

Despite their growing moderation, substantial differences remain between Western European socialists and American liberals. Socialists continue to champion a much larger and more active government than liberals ever would. European tax burdens prove the point.

For Critical Analysis

Socialist parties were far more effective at winning elections after World War II than before the war. What might have been the reason?

insurance, and promoted environmental concerns. He ran again for president as an independent in 2004 and 2008.

Splinter Parties. Some of the most successful minor parties have been those that split from major parties. The impetus for these **splinter parties,** or factions, has usually been a situation in which a particular personality was at odds with the major party. The most successful of these splinter parties was the "Bull Moose" Progressive Party, formed in 1912 to support Theodore Roosevelt for president. The Republican national convention of that year denied Roosevelt the nomination, despite the fact that he had won most of the primaries. He therefore left the GOP and ran against Republican "regular" William Howard Taft in the general election. Although Roosevelt did not win the election, he did split the Republican vote so that Democrat Woodrow Wilson became president.

Former presidential candidate Ross Perot addresses the first California statewide convention of the Reform Party in 1996. Perot said, "We're creating a new party because a majority of the American people want a new party." *Was that true? Why or why not?*

Third parties have also been formed to back individual candidates who were not rebelling against a particular party. H. Ross Perot, for example, who challenged Republican George H. W. Bush and Democrat Bill Clinton for the presidency in 1992, had not previously been active in a major party. Perot's supporters probably would have split their votes between Bush and Clinton had Perot not been in the race. In theory, Perot ran in 1992 as a nonparty independent. In practice, he had to create a campaign organization. By 1996, Perot's organization was formalized as the Reform Party.

The Impact of Minor Parties. Third parties have rarely been able to affect American politics by actually winning elections. (One exception is that third-party and independent candidates have occasionally won races for state governorships—for example, Jesse Ventura was elected governor of Minnesota on the Reform Party ticket in 1998.) Instead, the impact of third parties has taken two forms. First, third parties can influence one of the major parties to take up one or more issues. Second, third parties can determine the outcome of a particular election by pulling votes from one of the major-party candidates in what is called the "spoiler effect."

Influencing the Major Parties. One of the most clear-cut examples of a major party adopting the issues of a minor party took place in 1896, when the Democratic Party took over the Populist demand for "free silver"—that is, a policy of coining enough new money to create an inflation. As you learned earlier in this chapter, however, absorbing the Populists cost the Democrats votes overall.

Affecting the Outcome of an Election. The presidential elections of 2000 were one instance in which a minor party may have altered the outcome. Green Party candidate Ralph Nader received almost one hundred thousand votes in Florida, a majority of which would probably have gone to Democrat Al Gore if Nader had not been in the race.

The real question, however, is not whether the Nader vote had an effect—clearly, it did—but whether the effect was important. The problem is that in elections as close as the presidential elections of 2000, any factor with an impact on the outcome can be said to have determined the results.

Mechanisms of Political Change

In the future, could one of the two parties decisively overtake the other and become the "natural party of government"? The Republicans held this status from 1896 until 1932, and the Democrats enjoyed it for many years after the election of Franklin D. Roosevelt in 1932.

> **Splinter Party**
> A new party formed by a dissident faction within a major political party. Often, splinter parties have emerged when a particular personality was at odds with the major party.

■ **Learning Outcome 5:**
Discuss some of the ways in which support for the parties can change, and explain the increasing importance of independents.

Realignment

One mechanism by which a party might gain dominance is **realignment.** In this process, major constituencies shift their allegiance from one party to another, creating a long-term alteration in the political environment. Realignment has often been associated with particular elections, called *realigning elections*. The election of 1896, which established a Republican ascendancy, was clearly a realigning election. So was the election of 1932, which made the Democrats the leading party.

Realignments in American Politics.   A number of myths exist about the concept of realignment. One is that in realignment a newly dominant party must replace the previously dominant party. Actually, realignment could easily strengthen an already dominant party. Alternatively, realignment could result in a tie. This has happened—twice. One example was the realignment of the 1850s, which resulted in Abraham Lincoln's election as president in 1860. After the Civil War, the Republicans and the Democrats were almost evenly matched nationally.

The most recent realignment—which also resulted in two closely matched parties—was a gradual process that took place over many years. In 1968, Republican presidential candidate Richard Nixon adopted a "southern strategy," aimed at drawing dissatisfied southern Democrats into the Republican Party.[7] At the presidential level, the strategy was an immediate success, although years would pass before the Republicans could gain dominance in the South's delegation to Congress or in state legislatures. Another milestone in the progress of the Republican realignment was Ronald Reagan's sweeping victory in the presidential elections of 1980.

Is Realignment Still Possible?   The sheer size of our nation, combined with the inexorable pressure toward a two-party system, has resulted in parties made up of voters with conflicting interests or values. The pre–Civil War party system involved two parties—Whigs and Democrats—with support in both the North and the South. This system could survive only by burying, as deeply as possible, the issue of slavery. We should not be surprised that the structure eventually collapsed. The Republican ascendancy of 1896–1932 united capitalists and industrial workers under the Republican banner, despite serious economic conflicts between the two. The New Deal Democratic coalition after 1932 brought African Americans and ardent segregationists into the same party.

For realignment to occur, a substantial body of citizens must come to believe that their party can no longer represent their interests or values. The problem must be fundamental and not attributable to the behavior of an individual politician. It is not easy to identify large groups of Republicans or Democrats today who might reach such a conclusion.

In recent years, however, a number of small-scale realignments have taken place. Chapter 7 described a state-level realignment in West Virginia. Many West Virginia voters switched from the Democrats to the Republicans in the belief that Democratic environmentalists were "anti-coal." Muslims of Middle Eastern ancestry provide another small-scale example. This group formerly had a Republican majority, but during the last decade, many Muslim Republicans decided that the Democrats were more likely to protect Muslim rights and interests.

Realignment
A process in which a substantial group of voters switches party allegiance, producing a long-term change in the political landscape.

---

7. The classic work on Nixon's southern strategy is Kirkpatrick Sales, *The Emerging Republican Majority* (New Rochelle, N.Y.: Arlington House, 1969).

Dealignment

Among political scientists, one common argument has been that realignment is no longer likely because voters are not as committed to the two major parties as they were in the 1800s and early 1900s. In this view, called **dealignment** theory, large numbers of independent voters may result in political volatility, but the absence of strong partisan attachments means that it is no longer easy to "lock in" political preferences for decades.

Independent Voters. Figure 8–3 that follows shows trends in **party identification,** as measured by standard polling techniques from 1944 to the present. The chart displays a rise in the number of independent voters throughout the period combined with a fall in support for the Democrats from the mid-1960s on. The decline in Democratic identification may be due to the consolidation of Republican support in the South since 1968, a process that by now is substantially complete. In any event, the traditional Democratic advantage in party identification has largely vanished.

Not only has the number of independents grown over the last half century, but voters are also less willing to vote a straight ticket—that is, to vote for all the candidates of one party. In the early twentieth century, **straight-ticket voting** was nearly universal. By midcentury, 12 percent of voters engaged in **split-ticket voting**—voting for candidates of two or more parties for different offices, such as voting for a Republican presidential candidate and a Democratic congressional candidate. By the 1970s and 1980s, 25 to 30 percent of all ballots cast in presidential election years were split-ticket. A major reason was that many voters, especially in the South, were pairing a Republican for president with a conservative Democrat for Congress. In recent years, conservative Democrats have become scarce, and the incidence of split-ticket voting has ranged only from 17 to 19 percent.

Not-So-Independent Voters. A problem with dealignment theory is that many of the "independent" voters are not all that independent. For some time, about one-third of the voters who classified themselves as independents typically voted Democratic, and

Dealignment
A decline in party loyalties that reduces long-term party commitment.

Party Identification
Linking oneself to a particular political party.

Straight-Ticket Voting
Voting exclusively for the candidates of one party.

Split-Ticket Voting
Voting for candidates of two or more parties for different offices, such as voting for a Republican presidential candidate and a Democratic congressional candidate.

Figure 8–3 ▶ **Party Identification from 1944 to the Present**

Why would people who usually support one of the two major parties still call themselves independents?

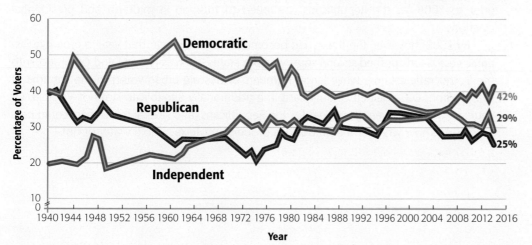

Sources: *Gallup Report*, August 1995; *New York Times*/CBS poll, June 1996; *Gallup Report*, February 1998; The Pew Research Center for the People and the Press, November 2003; Gallup polls, 2004 through 2014.

another one-third typically voted Republican. The remaining third consisted of true independents and became known as **swing voters**—they could swing back and forth
between the parties.

By 2014, the Democrats were a few points ahead when independent "leaners" were
added to their core supporters. The relatively modest number of true independents—
currently a tenth of the total electorate—raises a strategic question for the parties. Is it
more important to sway the independents, or can a party obtain better results by improving voter turnout among its natural supporters? The answer to that question has varied
by election.

Tipping

Political transformation can also result from changes in the composition of the electorate.
Even when groups of voters never change their party preferences, if one group becomes
more numerous over time, it can become dominant for that reason alone. We call this kind
of demographically based change **tipping.**

Tipping in Massachusetts and California. Consider Massachusetts, where for generations Irish Catholics confronted Protestant Yankees in the political arena. Most of the
Yankees were Republicans, and most of the Irish were Democrats. The Yankees were
numerically dominant from the founding of the state until 1928. In that year, for the first
time, Democratic Irish voters came to outnumber the Republican Yankees. Massachusetts,
which previously had been one of the most solidly Republican states, became one of the
most reliably Democratic states in the nation.

California may have experienced a tipping effect during the 1990s. From 1952
through 1988, California normally supported Republican presidential candidates. Since
1992, however, no GOP presidential candidate has managed to carry California. The
improved performance of the Democrats in California is almost certainly a function of
demography. In 1999, California became the third state, after Hawaii and New Mexico, in
which non-Hispanic whites do not make up a majority of the population.

Tipping in the Twenty-First Century? It is possible that states other than California
may tip to a different party in future years. John B. Judis and Ruy Teixeira have argued that
the Democrats are poised to become the new majority party due to a growth in the number of liberal professionals and Hispanic immigrants.[8] This thesis attracted much ridicule
prior to 2006, as the Republicans continued to triumph in midterm and presidential
elections.

By 2008, however, the thesis had become more credible. In that year, a growing Hispanic vote clearly pushed several southwestern states, such as Nevada and Colorado, into
the Democratic column, while larger numbers of upscale urban voters in the suburbs of
Washington, D.C., helped Obama carry the traditionally Republican state of Virginia. Of
course, 2010 was a very good year for the Republicans, and several more years could pass
before we know whether the predictions of Judis and Teixeira hold water or not.

8. John B. Judis and Ruy Teixeira, *The Emerging Democratic Majority* (New York: Scribner, 2004).

How You Can Make a Difference

How would you like to exercise a small amount of real political power yourself—power that goes beyond simply voting in an election? You might be able to become a delegate to a county, district, or even state party convention.

- Many of these conventions nominate candidates for various offices. For example, in Michigan, the state party conventions nominate the candidates for the Board of Regents of the state's three top public universities. The regents set university policies, so these are nominations in which students have an obvious interest.

- In Michigan, if you are elected as a party precinct delegate, you can attend your party's state convention. In much of the country, there are more openings for precinct-level delegates than there are people willing to serve.

- In such circumstances, almost anyone can become a delegate by collecting a handful of signatures on a nominating petition or by mounting a small-scale write-in campaign.

- You are then eligible to take part in one of the most educational political experiences available to an ordinary citizen. You will get a firsthand look at how political persuasion takes place, how resolutions are written and passed, and how candidates seek out support among their fellow party members.

- If you are interested in committing yourself, check with your local county committee about the rules you must follow.

Key Terms

dealignment 253
Democratic Party 236
divided government 234
electoral college 247
GOP 237
independent 229
national committee 232
national convention 231

party identification 253
party-in-government 231
party-in-the-electorate 230
party organization 230
party platform 231
patronage 233
plurality 246
policy demanders 229

political party 229
realignment 252
Republican Party 237
reverse-income effect 243
splinter party 251
split-ticket voting 253
state central
  committee 232

straight-ticket voting 253
swing voters 254
third party 248
tipping 254
two-party system 235
Whig Party 236

Chapter Summary

Learning Outcome 1 A political party is a group of political activists who organize to win elections, operate the government, and determine public policy. Political parties recruit candidates for public office, organize and run elections, present alternative policies to the voters, assume responsibility for operating the government, and act as the opposition to the party in power.

A political party consists of three components: the party-in-the-electorate, the party organization, and the party-in-government. Each party component maintains linkages to the others to keep the party strong. Each level of the party—local, state, and national—has considerable autonomy. The national party organization is responsible for holding the national convention in presidential election years, writing the party platform, choosing the national committee, and conducting party business.

The party-in-government comprises all of the elected and appointed officeholders of a party. Increased ideological coherence in both major parties has resulted in growing political polarization.

Learning Outcome 2 The evolution of our nation's political parties can be divided into seven periods: (a) the formation of political parties from 1789 to 1816; (b) the era of one-party rule from 1816 to 1828; (c) the period from Andrew Jackson's presidency to the eve of the Civil War, from 1828 to 1856; (d) the Civil War and post–Civil War period, from 1856 to 1896; (e) the Republican ascendancy and progressive period, from 1896 to 1932; (f) the New Deal period, from 1932 to about 1968; and (g) the modern period, from approximately 1968 to the present. Throughout most of the modern period, the parties have been closely matched in strength.

Learning Outcome 3 Many of the differences between the two parties date from the time of Franklin D. Roosevelt's New Deal. The Democrats have advocated government action to help labor and minorities, and the Republicans have championed self-reliance and limited government. Today, cultural differences are at least as important as economic issues in determining party allegiance. While the two major parties are made up of various types of voters, both have become more politically unified in recent years.

Learning Outcome 4 Two major parties have dominated the political landscape in the United States for almost two centuries. The reasons for this include (a) the historical foundations of the system, (b) political socialization and practical considerations, (c) the winner-take-all electoral system, and (d) state and federal laws favoring the two-party system. For these reasons, minor parties have found it extremely difficult to win elections.

Minor, or third, parties have emerged from time to time, sometimes as dissatisfied splinter groups from within major parties, and have acted as barometers of change in the political mood. Third parties can affect the political process (even if they do not win) if major parties adopt their issues or if they determine which major party wins an election.

Learning Outcome 5 One mechanism of political change is realignment, in which major blocs of voters switch allegiance from one party to another. Realignments were manifested in the elections of 1896 and 1932. Some scholars speak of dealignment—that is, the loss of strong party attachments. In fact, the share of the voters who describe themselves as independents has grown, and the share of self-identified Democrats has shrunk. Many independents actually vote as if they were Democrats or Republicans, however. Demographic change can also "tip" a district or state from one party to another.

Master the concept of Political Parties with MindTap™ *for American Government*

REVIEW MindTap™ **for American Government**
Access Key Term Flashcards for Chapter 8.

TEST YOURSELF MindTap™ **for American Government**
Take the Wrap It Up Quiz for Chapter 8.

STAY CURRENT MindTap™ **for American Government**
Access the KnowNow blog and customized RSS for updates on current events.

STAY FOCUSED MindTap™ **for American Government**
Complete the Focus Activities for Political Parties.

Additional Resources

Today's political parties use the Internet to attract voters, organize campaigns, obtain campaign contributions, and the like. Voters, in turn, can go online to learn more about specific parties and their programs. Those who use the Internet for information on the parties, though, need to exercise some caution. Even the official party sites are filled with misinformation or outright lies about the policies and leaders of the other party. Besides the parties' official sites, there are satirical sites mimicking the parties, sites distributing misleading information about the parties, and sites that are raising money for their own causes rather than for political parties.

Online Resources

- The political parties all have Web sites. You can locate the Republican National Committee at www.gop.com or the Democratic National Committee by entering www.democrats.org.
- The two leading third parties are the Libertarian Party and the Green Party. Find their Web sites at www.lp.org and www.greenparty.org respectively.
- Ron Gunzburger's Politics1 site provides a list of more than forty U.S. parties, almost all of them tiny. Go to www.politics1.com.
- The Pew Research Center for the People and the Press offers survey data online on how the parties fared during the most recent elections, voter typology, and numerous other issues. Visit its site at www.people-press.org.

Books

Gairdner, William D. *The Great Divide: Why Liberals and Conservatives Will Never, Ever Agree.* New York: Encounter Books, 2015. Gairdner argues that the divide between liberalism and conservatism has grown so great that those holding either ideology can barely speak to one another. A Canadian businessman, Gairdner draws his examples from Europe as well as North America.

Geismer, Lily. *Don't Blame Us: Suburban Liberals and the Transformation of the Democratic Party.* Princeton, N.J., Princeton University Press, 2014. Geismer traces the reorientation of modern liberalism and the Democratic Party away from their roots in labor union halls of northern cities to white-collar professionals in postindustrial high-tech suburbs. Geismer is a history professor at Claremont McKenna College.

Gould, Lewis L. *The Republicans: A History of the Grand Old Party.* New York: Oxford University Press, 2014. In this thoroughly updated edition of a classic, Gould, a professor at the University of Texas, portrays the almost 180-degree shifts in GOP policy over the decades.

Video

House of Cards—This celebrated series premiered in 2013 on the streaming service Netflix. Kevin Spacey stars as Frank Underwood, a ruthless and conniving Democratic member of the U.S. House. By 2014, *House of Cards* received more than thirty recognitions, including nominations for the Emmy, Writer's Guild, and Golden Globe awards.

A Third Choice—An award-winning 2011 PBS documentary, *A Third Choice* provides a colorful look at the history of third parties and how they changed America.

Quiz

Multiple Choice and Fill-Ins

Learning Outcome 1 Cite some of the major activities of U.S. political parties, and discuss how they are organized.

1. The three faces of a political party include:
   a. the party-in-the-electorate, the party organization, and the members of the party.
   b the party organization, the party-in-government, and the party-in-the-electorate.
   c. the party-in-government, the party-in-the-electorate, and the lobbyists for that party.

2. Both political parties have _____ _____ that direct and coordinate party activities during the four years after each presidential election.

Learning Outcome 2 Explain how the history of U.S. political parties has led to the two major parties that exist today.

3. The New Deal era under Democratic President Franklin D. Roosevelt occurred:
   a. at the beginning of the twentieth century.
   b. during the 1960s.
   c. during the Great Depression of the 1930s.

4. The first organized political parties in the United States were _____ and the _____ _____.

Learning Outcome 3 Summarize key differences between the policies and supporters of the major parties.

5. Two major types of Republicans are:
   a. members of the Religious Right and business-oriented economic conservatives.
   b. members of the Religious Right and organized labor.
   c. supporters of the Tea Party movement and Hispanics.

6. When voters are temporarily dissatisfied with the performance of one or another of the major parties, the result may be a _____ election.

Learning Outcome 4 Give reasons why the two-party system has endured in America, and evaluate the impact of third parties on U.S. politics.

7. At almost every level of government in this country, the outcome of elections is based on the plurality voting system, which means that:
   a. the candidate with the largest number of votes wins, even if the winner does not receive 50 percent or more of the votes.
   b. when no one receives 50 percent of the vote, a runoff election is held.
   c. there is no need for everyone to vote in each election.

8. The two most important third parties that remain active today are the _____ and _____ parties.

Learning Outcome 5 Discuss some of the ways in which support for the parties can change, and explain the increasing importance of independents.

9. The presidential elections of 1932, in which Democrat Franklin D. Roosevelt carried all but six states, were an example of:
   a. political dealignment.
   b. the establishment of divided government.
   c. a realigning election.

10. In an election, when a voter casts ballots for candidates of two or more parties, we call this _____-_____ voting.

Essay Questions

1. Do you support (or lean toward) one of the major political parties today? If so, would you have supported the same party in the late 1800s—or would you have supported a different party? Explain your reasoning.

2. In America, party candidates for national office are typically chosen through primary elections. In some other countries, a party's central committee picks the party's candidates. How might primary elections limit the ability of parties to present a united front on the issues?

Campaigns and Elections

9

New Yorkers in Times Square celebrate the reelection of President Barack Obama in 2012.

Scott Eells/Bloomberg via Getty Images

The five learning outcomes below are designed to help improve your understanding of this chapter. After reading this chapter, you should be able to:

- **Learning Outcome 1:** Discuss who runs for office and how campaigns are managed.
- **Learning Outcome 2:** Describe the current system of campaign finance.
- **Learning Outcome 3:** Summarize the process of choosing a president of the United States.
- **Learning Outcome 4:** Explain the mechanisms through which voting takes place on Election Day.
- **Learning Outcome 5:** Discuss voter turnout in the United States and the types of people most likely to vote.

▶ **WATCH & LEARN** MindTap® for American Government

Watch a brief "What Do You Know?" video summarizing Campaigning for Office and Elections.

What If...

Campaign Lies Were Illegal?

BACKGROUND

Campaign falsehoods have been with us for as long as there have been elections. You could call some of them lies. You might call others exaggerations. Whatever they are, many Americans believe that they are examples of free speech and thus protected by the First Amendment. Yet today, fifteen states have laws on their books that criminalize willful false political speech that attacks an opponent during a campaign. For example, Ohio's law against political lies makes them punishable by a fine of up to $5,000 and a jail term of up to six months. In other words, this law has "teeth." The courts have usually taken a dim view of such laws, however. In 2014, the United States Supreme Court ruled unanimously that a group that felt threatened by the Ohio law had the right to challenge the law in court.[a]

WHAT IF CAMPAIGN LIES WERE ILLEGAL?

What if the courts had accepted such laws? Supporters of criminalizing political lies argue that such legislation would lead to more honest campaigning. We would expect that the threat of serious penalties would discourage gross falsehoods during a campaign. Political advertisements might avoid groundless accusations that, say, a candidate supported abortion. (That, in fact, was the issue in the Ohio case.) It might be dangerous to claim that a candidate didn't deserve the medals he won while serving in the military—an accusation made against presidential candidate John Kerry in 2004. Someone could get into serious trouble by forging documents that question a candidate's service in the National Guard—accusations against President George W. Bush in 2004 may have been based on such a forgery.

WHAT IF CANDIDATES LIE ABOUT THEMSELVES?

Presumably, if political lies were against the law, it would also be illegal for candidates to lie about their own backgrounds. What if a politician claimed, falsely, to have won the Medal of Honor? In fact, in 2005 Congress passed the Stolen Valor Act, which criminalized false claims to have received military honors.[b] In 2012, the Supreme Court ruled that such a law violated the First Amendment. The Court's vote was six to three, however, raising the possibility that a Court with a different membership might have come to a different conclusion.

THE IMPACT ON THE COURT SYSTEM

We could expect that if some states, or even the federal government, criminalized political lies, we would see hundreds, if not thousands, of lawsuits during every campaign season. Many candidates would use such suits to attack their opponents. Every two years, then, the courts would have to deal with a flurry of suits, many of them frivolous, which would use up their limited resources.

LESS POLITICAL HUMOR?

In a brief sent to the Supreme Court on the Ohio case, political satirist P.J. O'Rourke wrote: "The law at issue undermines the First Amendment's protection of the serious business of making politics funny. Laws, like Ohio's here . . . do not replace truthiness, satire, and snark with high-minded ideas and 'just the facts.' Instead, they chill speech such that spin becomes silent." One person's political lie, in other words, can be another person's political humor.

A demonstration in Washington, D.C. *Are there any circumstances in which political speech should be limited? Why or why not?*

For Critical Analysis

1. If laws outlawing campaign lies were universal in America, how could the courts decide what is a political lie as opposed to a simple exaggeration?

2. If you were in a hard-fought campaign, how might you use such laws to improve your chances of winning?

---

a. *Susan B. Anthony List v. Driehaus*, ___ U.S. ___ (2014).
b. *United States v. Alvarez*, 132 S.Ct. 2537 (2012).

Free elections are the cornerstone of the American political system. Voters choose one candidate over another to hold political office by casting ballots in local, state, and federal elections. In 2012, the voters chose Democrats Barack Obama and Joe Biden to be president and vice president of the United States for the following four years. In 2014, voters elected all of the members of the House of Representatives and one-third of the members of the Senate. The campaigns were bitter, long, and expensive.

Voters and candidates frequently criticize the American electoral process. It is said to favor wealthier candidates, to further the aims of special interest groups, and to be dominated by older voters and those with better education and higher incomes. Campaign fund-raising has grown by leaps and bounds as the United States Supreme Court has progressively reduced limits on the fund-raising process.

Campaigns are also seen as excessively bitter, with negative campaign ads playing a major role. Several states have responded to such negativity with new legislation that outlaws lies during political campaigns. We discussed this legislation in the chapter's opening *What If . . .* feature.

■ **Learning Outcome 1:**
Discuss who runs
for office and how
campaigns are managed.

The Twenty-First-Century Campaign

There are thousands of elective offices in the United States. Although the major political parties strive to provide a slate of candidates for every election, recruiting candidates is easier for some offices than for others. Political parties may have difficulty finding candidates for the board of the local water control district, for example, but they generally find a sufficient number of candidates for county commissioner or sheriff. The "higher" the office and the more prestige attached to it, the more candidates are likely to want to run. In many areas of the country, however, one major party may be considerably stronger than the other is. In those situations, the minority party may have difficulty finding nominees for elections in which victory is unlikely.

The presidential campaign provides the most colorful and exciting look at candidates and how they prepare to compete for office—in this instance, the highest office in the land. The men and women who wanted to be the Republican candidate in the 2012 presidential campaign faced a long and obstacle-filled path. First, they needed to raise sufficient funds to tour the nation, particularly the states with early **presidential primaries,** to see if they had enough local supporters. They needed funds to create an organization and win primary votes. Finally, when nominated as the party's candidate, the winner required funds to finance a successful campaign for president. Always, at every turn, there was the question of whether there were enough funds to effectively compete against their opponents, and eventually against President Barack Obama.

Who Is Eligible?

There are few constitutional restrictions on who can be elected to national office in the United States. As detailed in the Constitution, the formal requirements are as follows:

1. *President.* Must be a natural-born citizen, have attained the age of thirty-five years, and be a resident of the country for fourteen years by the time of inauguration.
2. *Vice president.* Must meet the same requirements as the president and also not be a resident of the same state as the president.[1]
3. *Senator.* Must be a citizen for at least nine years, have attained the age of thirty by the time of taking office, and be a resident of the state from which elected.

Presidential Primary

A statewide primary election of delegates to a political party's national convention, held to determine a party's presidential nominee.

---

1. Technically, a presidential and vice-presidential candidate on the same ticket can be from the same state, but if they are, one of the two must forfeit the electoral votes of his or her home state.

4. *Representative.* Must be a citizen for at least seven years, have attained the age of twenty-five by the time of taking office, and be a resident of the state from which elected.

The qualifications for state legislators are set by the state constitutions and likewise include age, place of residence, and citizenship. (Usually, the requirements for the upper chamber of a legislature are somewhat higher than those for the lower chamber.) The legal qualifications for serving as governor or in other state offices are similar.

Who Runs?

In spite of these minimal legal qualifications for office at both the national and the state levels, a quick look at the slate of candidates in any election—or at the current members of Congress—will reveal that not all segments of the population enjoy these opportunities equally. Holders of political office in the United States are predominantly white and

Democratic president Barack Obama and Republican presidential candidate Mitt Romney campaigning in 2012. *How might undecided voters make up their minds about these candidates?*

male. Until the twentieth century, presidential candidates were exclusively of northern European origin and of Protestant heritage.[2] Laws that effectively denied voting rights made it impossible to elect African American public officials in many areas in which African Americans constituted a significant portion of the population. As a result of the passage of major civil rights legislation in the 1960s, however, the number of African American public officials has increased throughout the United States, and in a groundbreaking vote, the nation elected an African American president in 2008.

Women as Candidates. Until recently, women generally were considered to be appropriate candidates only for lower-level offices, such as state legislator or school board member. The past twenty years have seen a tremendous increase in the number of women who run for office, not only at the state level but for the U.S. Congress as well. Figure 9–1 that follows shows the increase in female candidates. In 2014, 175 women ran for the House or Senate on major-party tickets, and 89 were elected. Today, a majority of Americans say they would vote for a qualified woman for president of the United States. Indeed, Hillary Clinton came close to winning the Democratic presidential nomination in 2008, a year in which the eventual Democratic nominee was favored to win the general election, and she may run again in 2016.

Professional Status. Political campaigning and officeholding are easier for some occupational groups than for others, and political involvement can make a valuable contribution to certain careers. Lawyers, for example, have more flexible schedules than do many other professionals, can take time off for campaigning, and can leave their jobs to hold public office full time. Furthermore, holding political office is good publicity for their professional

did you know?
We have had a Native American vice president. Herbert Hoover's vice president, Charles Curtis, claimed Kaw, Osage, and Pottawatomie ancestry.

2. A number of early presidents were Unitarian. The Unitarian Church is not Protestant, but it is historically rooted in the Protestant tradition.

practice. Perhaps most important, many jobs that lawyers aspire to—federal or state judge-ships, state's attorney offices, or work in a federal agency—can be attained by political appointment.

Managing the Campaign

After the candidates have been nominated, typically through a **primary election,** the most exhausting and expensive part of the election process begins—the **general election** campaign, which actually fills the offices at stake. Political campaigns are becoming more complex and more sophisticated with every election. Even with the most appealing of candidates, today's campaigns require a strong organization with (1) expertise in political polling and marketing, (2) professional assistance in fund-raising, accounting, and financial management, and (3) technological capabilities in every aspect of the campaign.

The Changing Campaign. The goal is the same for all campaigns—to convince voters to choose a candidate or a slate of candidates for office. In recent decades, the typical campaign for high office has no longer been centered on the party but on the candidate. The candidate-centered campaign emerged in response to changes in the electoral system, the increased importance of television in campaigns, technological innovations such as the Internet, and the increased cost of campaigning.

To run a successful and persuasive campaign, the candidate's organization must be able to raise funds for the effort, obtain coverage from the media, and produce and pay for political commercials and advertising. In addition, the organization needs to schedule the candidate's time effectively, convey the candidate's position on the issues to the voters, and conduct research on the opposing candidate. Finally, the campaign must get the voters to go to the polls.

Figure 9–1 ▶ **Women Running for Congress (and Winning)**

Why are women still well in the minority in both chambers of Congress?

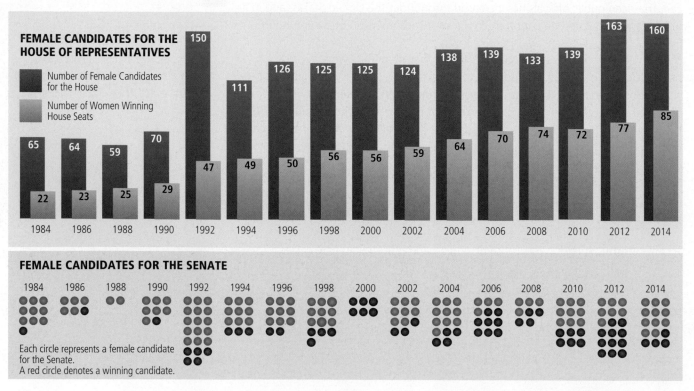

When party identification was stronger among voters and before the advent of television campaigning, a strong party organization at the local, state, or national level could furnish most of the services and expertise that the candidate needed. Parties used their precinct organizations to distribute literature, register voters, and get out the vote on election day. Less effort was spent on advertising each candidate's positions and character, because the party label presumably communicated that information to many voters.

Still, even though modern parties cannot provide the level of services that they did many years ago, parties remain central to the elections system. The high levels of political polarization seen in recent years mean that each major party is a strong ideological rallying point. The party organization as such may be less important, but for politicians, party identification is more important than ever. Also, the candidate-centered campaign does not change the fact that candidates for top national and state positions must normally win the support of their party in a primary election.

The Professional Campaign. Whether the candidate is running for the state legislature, for the governor's office, for the U.S. Congress, or for the presidency, every campaign has some fundamental tasks to accomplish. Today, in national elections most of these tasks are handled by paid professionals rather than volunteers or amateur politicians.

The most sought-after and possibly the most criticized campaign expert is the **political consultant,** who, for a large fee, takes charge of the candidate's campaign. Political consultants began to displace volunteer campaign managers in the 1960s, about the same time that television became a force in campaigns. The paid consultant devises a campaign strategy and theme, oversees advertising, and plans media appearances. The consultants and the firms they represent are not politically neutral. Most will work only for candidates from one party.

The Strategy of Winning. In the United States, unlike some European countries, there are no rewards for a candidate who comes in second. The winner takes all. Candidates seek to capture all the votes of their party's supporters, to convince a majority of independent voters to vote for them, and to gain some votes from supporters of the other party. To accomplish these goals, candidates must consider their visibility, their message, and their campaign strategy.

Candidate Visibility and Appeal. One of the most important concerns is how well known the candidate is. If she or he is a highly visible incumbent, there may be little need for campaigning except to remind voters of the officeholder's good deeds. If, however, the candidate is an unknown challenger or a largely unfamiliar character who is opposing a well-known public figure, the campaign requires a strategy to get the candidate before the public.

The Use of Opinion Polls. One of the major sources of information for both the media and the candidates is opinion polls. Poll taking is

> **Political Consultant**
> A paid professional hired to devise a campaign strategy and manage a campaign.

did you know?
Since 1945, the stock market (the Dow Jones Industrial Average) has gone up an average of 5.5 percent in years when a Republican was president—and 15.3 percent when the president was a Democrat.

CONNECT WITH YOUR CLASSMATES
MindTap™ for American Government

Access the Campaigning for Office and Elections Forum: Discussion— Electing Incumbents

Two of the best-known political consultants are Mary Matalin for the Republicans and James Carville for the Democrats. They happen to be married to each other. *What functions do they perform?*

Heather Wines/CBS via Getty Images

Focus Group

A small group of individuals who are led in discussion by a professional consultant in order to gather opinions on and responses to candidates and issues.

Political Action Committee (PAC)

A committee set up by and representing a corporation, labor union, or special interest group. PACs raise and give campaign donations.

Hatch Act

An act passed in 1939 that restricted the political activities of government employees. It also prohibited a political group from spending more than $3 million in any campaign and limited individual contributions to a campaign committee to $5,000.

■ **Learning Outcome 2:** Describe the current system of campaign finance.

widespread during the primaries. Presidential hopefuls have private polls taken to make sure that there is at least some chance they could be nominated and, if nominated, elected. During the presidential campaign itself, polling is even more frequent. Polls are taken not only by the regular pollsters—Gallup, Pew Research, and others—but also privately by each candidate's campaign organization. These private polls are for the exclusive and confidential use of the candidate and his or her campaign organization. As the election approaches, many candidates use *tracking polls,* which are polls taken almost every day, to find out how well they are competing for votes. Tracking polls enable consultants to fine-tune advertising and the candidate's speeches in the last days of the campaign.

Focus Groups. Another tactic used by campaign organizations to gain insights into public perceptions of the candidate is the **focus group.** The ten to fifteen ordinary citizens who make up the group discuss the candidate or certain political issues. Professional consultants who conduct the discussion select focus group members from specific target groups in the population—for example, working women, blue-collar men, senior citizens, or young voters.

Recent campaigns have tried to reach groups such as "soccer moms," "Walmart shoppers," or "NASCAR dads."[3] The group discusses personality traits of the candidate, political advertising, and other candidate-related issues. Focus groups can reveal more emotional responses to candidates or the deeper anxieties of voters—feelings that consultants believe often are not tapped by more impersonal telephone surveys. The campaign then can shape its messages to respond to those feelings and perceptions.

Financing the Campaign

The connection between money and elections is a sensitive issue in American politics. The belief is widespread that large campaign contributions by special interests corrupt the political system. Indeed, spending reached unprecedented heights during the 2011–2012 election cycle. In 2012, total spending for the presidential races alone reached $2.6 billion. Even though no presidential candidates were on the ballot in the 2014 midterm elections, spending was almost as high as it was in 2012. These funds had to be provided by the candidates and their families, borrowed, or raised by contributions from individuals, organizations, or **political action committees (PACs).** PACs are committees set up under federal or state law for the express purpose of making political donations.

The way campaigns are financed has changed dramatically in the past several years. For decades, candidates and political parties had to operate within the constraints imposed by complicated laws regulating campaign financing. Some of these constraints still exist, but recent developments have opened up the process to a striking degree. Today, there are no limits on how much any person or institution can invest in the political process, and only modest limits on how this spending can take place.

The Evolution of the Campaign Finance System

Throughout much of early American history, campaign financing was unregulated. No limits existed on contributions, and no data were collected on campaign funding. During the twentieth century, however, a variety of federal corrupt practices acts were adopted to regulate campaign financing. The first, passed in 1925, contained many loopholes and proved to be ineffective. The **Hatch Act** (Political Activities Act) of 1939 is best known

---

3. NASCAR stands for the National Association for Stock Car Auto Racing.

for restricting the political activities of civil servants. The act also made it unlawful for a political group to spend more than $3 million in any campaign and limited individual contributions to a campaign committee to $5,000. Of course, such restrictions were easily circumvented by creating additional political organizations.

The Federal Election Campaign Act. The Federal Election Campaign Act (FECA) of 1971, which became effective in 1972, replaced all past laws. The act restricted the amount that could be spent on campaign advertising. It also limited the amount that candidates could contribute to their own campaigns and required disclosure of all contributions and expenditures over $100. In principle, the FECA limited the role of labor unions and corporations in political campaigns.

Amendments to the FECA passed in 1974 created the **Federal Election Commission (FEC).** This commission consists of six bipartisan administrators whose duty is to enforce compliance with the requirements of the act. The 1974 amendments also placed limits on the sums that individuals and committees could contribute to candidates.

The principal role of the FEC today is to collect data on campaign contributions. Candidate committees must file periodic reports with the FEC listing who contributed, how much was spent, and for what it was spent. As an enforcement body, however, the FEC is conspicuously ineffective and typically does not determine that a campaign has violated the rules until the elections are over, if then.

The original FECA of 1971 limited the amount that each individual could spend on his or her own behalf. The Supreme Court overturned the provision in 1976, in *Buckley v. Valeo*,[4] stating that it was unconstitutional to restrict in any way the amount congressional candidates could spend on their own behalf. The Court later extended this principle to state elections as well.

Political Action Committees. Changes to the FECA in 1974 and 1976 allowed corporations, labor unions, and other interest groups to set up political action committees (PACs) to raise funds for candidates. PACs can contribute up to $5,000 to each candidate in each election. Each corporation or each union is limited to one PAC. The number of PACs grew significantly after 1976, as did the amounts that they spent on elections. Since the 1990s, however, the number of traditional PACs has leveled off because interest groups and activists have found alternative mechanisms for funneling resources into campaigns.

Issue Advocacy Advertising. Business corporations, labor unions, and other interest groups have also developed ways of making independent expenditures that are not coordinated with those of a candidate or political party. A common tactic is **issue advocacy** advertising, which promotes positions on issues rather than candidates. Although promoting issue positions aligns very closely with promoting candidates who

> **Federal Election Commission (FEC)**
> The federal regulatory agency with the task of enforcing federal campaign laws. As a practical matter, the FEC's role is largely limited to collecting data on campaign contributions.
>
> **Issue Advocacy**
> Advertising paid for by interest groups that support or oppose a candidate or a candidate's position on an issue without mentioning voting or elections.

did you know?
Abraham Lincoln sold pieces of fence rail that he had split as political souvenirs to finance his campaign.

Media mogul Rupert Murdoch (left) and major conservative contributor David Koch (right) attend *Time* magazine's gala celebrating the one hundred most influential people in the world. The party was held at New York City's Lincoln Center in 2014. *Why might some people make large political contributions?*

4. 424 U.S. 1 (1976).

"Most of all, I want to thank the people of my district for their unflagging support and disturbingly short term memories."

support those positions, the courts repeatedly have held that interest groups have a First Amendment right to advocate their positions. Political parties may also make independent expenditures on behalf of candidates.

Soft Money. Interest groups and PACs hit upon the additional strategy of generating **soft money**—that is, campaign contributions to political parties that escaped the limits of federal or state election law. No limits existed on contributions to political parties for activities such as voter education and voter-registration drives. This loophole enabled the parties to raise millions of dollars from corporations and individuals.

The Rise and Fall of the McCain-Feingold Act. The Bipartisan Campaign Reform Act of 2002, also known as the McCain-Feingold Act after its chief sponsors in the Senate, took effect on the day after the midterm elections of 2002. The law sought to regulate the new campaign finance practices developed since the passage of the FECA. It banned soft money at the federal level, but it did not ban such contributions to state and local parties. It attempted to curb issue advocacy advertising, but also increased the sums that individuals could contribute directly to candidates.

The constitutionality of the 2002 act was immediately challenged. In December 2003, the Supreme Court upheld almost all of the clauses of the act.[5] In 2007, however, the Court eased the act's restrictions on issue advocacy ads when it ruled that only those ads "susceptible of no reasonable interpretation other than as an appeal to vote for or against a specific candidate" could be restricted prior to an election.[6] Finally, in 2010, *Citizens United v. FEC*[7] swept away almost all remaining restrictions on independent expenditures, leading to the system we have today.

The Current Campaign Finance Environment

As of 2014, political campaigns are financed in two distinct ways. One of these is spending by the candidate's own committee. Contributions made directly to a candidate's committee are subject to limitations: An individual can donate no more than $2,500 to a candidate in a single election, and contributions by committees are limited as well. In exchange for these limits, candidates have almost complete control over how their own campaign money is spent.

Another way in which campaigns are financed is through **independent expenditures.** These funds may be spent on advertising and other political activities, but in theory the expenditures cannot be coordinated with those of a candidate. No limits exist on how much can be spent in this fashion. This two-part system is the direct result of the 2010 *Citizens United v. FEC* ruling by the Supreme Court.

Citizens United v. FEC. In January 2010, the Supreme Court ruled that corporations, unions, and nonprofits may spend freely to support or oppose candidates, so long as the expenditures are made independently and are not coordinated with candidate campaigns.

Soft Money
Campaign contributions unregulated by federal or state law, usually given to parties and party committees to help fund general party activities.

Independent Expenditures
Nonregulated contributions from PACs, organizations, and individuals. The funds may be spent on advertising or other campaign activities, so long as those expenditures are not coordinated with those of a candidate.

---

5. *McConnell v. FEC*, 540 U.S. 93 (2003).
6. *FEC v. Wisconsin Right to Life*, 551 U.S. 449 (2007).
7. 558 U.S. 310 (2010).

The ruling overturned campaign-finance laws dating back decades. Democrats, plus many journalists and bloggers, accused the Court of granting corporations rights that ought to be exercised only by flesh-and-blood humans. Republicans and others defended the ruling as protecting freedom of speech. Two months later, a federal court of appeals held that it was not possible to limit contributions to independent-expenditure groups based on the size of the contribution.[8]

Super PACs. These rulings led directly to a new type of political organization: the **super PAC.** Traditional PACs, which continue to exist, are set up to represent a corporation, labor union, or special interest group. The super PAC, in contrast, is established to aggregate unlimited contributions by individuals and organizations and then funnel these sums into independent expenditures. By 2011, every major presidential candidate had a super PAC. It soon became clear that the supposed independence of these organizations is a fiction. Presidential super PACs are usually chaired by individuals who are closely associated with the candidate. Frequently, the chair is a former top member of the candidate's campaign.

A variety of other super PACs were established as well. These groups were often oriented toward a party, rather than a candidate. Such super PACs might seek, for example, to support Republican or Democratic candidates for the U.S. Senate, or to intervene within a particular party. The super PAC founded by the Club for Growth, for example, devotes its considerable resources to supporting strong conservatives in Republican primaries and to running negative advertisements against more moderate Republicans.

One interesting development in 2011–2012 was the tendency for super PACs to be supported primarily by very wealthy individuals, rather than by corporations or other organizations. The funding was still provided by business interests but came from individuals who owned corporations, not from the corporations themselves. A striking example of this phenomenon was $20 million in contributions to the super PAC of Republican presidential candidate Newt Gingrich, former Speaker of the U.S. House.

The contribution, supplied by casino magnate Sheldon Adelson and his wife, amounted to almost half of all the funds that Gingrich raised throughout the entire primary season. Without this contribution, Gingrich would have been forced to end his campaign much earlier than he actually did. Are super PACs such as these bad for democracy? We address that question in this chapter's *Which Side Are You On?* feature that follows.

The 527 Organization. Well before *Citizens United,* interest groups realized that they could set up new organizations outside the parties to encourage voter registration and to run issue ads aimed at energizing supporters. So long as these committees did not endorse candidates, they faced no limits on fundraising. These tax-exempt groups, called 527 organizations after the section of the tax code that provides for them, first made a major impact during the 2003–2004 election cycle.

> **Super PAC**
> A political organization that aggregates unlimited contributions by individuals and organizations to be spent independently of candidate committees.

COMPARE WITH YOUR PEERS
MindTap™ for American Government

Access the Campaigning for Office and Elections Forum: Polling Activity—Super PACs and Elections

Toru Yamanaka/AFP/Getty Images

Larry Ellison, CEO of Oracle Corporation, is most famous for his business success and his impressive degree of self-regard. He is also a major campaign contributor. *What do high-tech firms want from the government?*

---

8. *Speechnow v. FEC,* 599 F.3d 686 (D.C.Cir. 2010).

Which Side Are You On?

Do Super PACs Hurt Our Democracy?

The 2010 Supreme Court decision *Citizens United v. FEC* allowed corporations, unions, and individuals to donate unlimited sums to entities that are "independent" of the candidates. So was born the super PAC. A super PAC can raise sums without limit. Those monies can be spent on both positive and negative campaign ads. Not surprisingly, some very rich people donated millions of dollars to various super PACs during 2011 and 2012. During the 2011–2012 presidential election cycle, outside groups spent an estimated $1.3 billion. Most of these funds were used for negative advertising in the "battleground states." About 65 percent of the funds were spent on Republican candidates. Is this spending harmful to our democracy?

Just Another Way for Big Money to Rule America

Those who oppose super PACs argue that money should not determine the outcome of elections. Super PACs allow America's millionaires and billionaires to donate unlimited funds to influence the outcome of congressional and presidential elections. How can the "little people" keep up? Super PACs are supposed to be independent, but in reality, the majority are run by candidates' former staff members. Obama's super PAC, Priorities USA Action, was organized by two ex–White House staffers, Bill Burton and Sean Sweeney. The pro-Romney super PAC, Restore Our Future, was managed by Romney's former lawyer.

Almost all the advertising purchased by super PACs is negative—the candidates can remain upbeat while their super PACs do the dirty work. These attack ads are themselves a corruption of the political process. Finally, due to the rise of 501(c)4 organizations (described in the text), some super PACs manage to hide the identity of many of their donors. A number of public-interest groups have called for a constitutional amendment to overturn *Citizens United*. We need some such step to keep the United States from becoming a republic of the rich, by the rich, and for the rich.

Money Alone Can't Buy Elections

Those who support super PACs argue that people should have the right to say whatever they want. Corporations and unions are made up of individuals, and so organizations as well as individuals should be able to express their views by donating to campaign organizations.

Does money buy elections? When it comes to super PACs, at least, the dollars do not seem to have made that much difference in 2012. Consider some spectacular super PAC failures. Casino owner Sheldon Adelson and his wife spent at least $98 million, most of it in donations to super PACs. They spent $20 million to win the Republican presidential nomination for Newt Gingrich (he lost), and $20 million in the general election to support Mitt Romney (he lost, too).

Consider also American Crossroads, managed by conservative strategist Karl Rove. Only 1.3 percent of the $104 million that American Crossroads spent in the general election helped produce a winner. Almost all of the Senate candidates supported by American Crossroads lost. Past a certain point, spending on television ads is just wasted.

For Critical Analysis

Some have argued that limits on campaign spending violate First Amendment guarantees of freedom of speech. How strong is this argument?

Since then, they have largely been replaced by super PACs, but a number continue to be active to the present day.

The 501(c)4 Organization. In the 2007–2008 election cycle, campaign-finance lawyers began recommending a new type of independent group—the 501(c)4 organization, which, like the 527 organization, is named after the relevant provision of the tax code. A 501(c)4 is ostensibly a "social welfare" group and, unlike a 527, is not required to disclose the identity of its donors or to report spending to the Federal Election Commission (FEC).

Lawyers then began suggesting that 501(c)4 organizations claim a special exemption that would allow the organization to ask people to vote for or against specific candidates as long as a majority of the group's effort was devoted to issues. Only those funds spent directly to support candidates had to be reported to the FEC, and the 501(c)4 could continue to conceal its donors.

One result was to make it all but impossible to determine exactly how much was spent by independent groups in elections since 2008. Critics claimed that 501(c)4s were being used illegally. The FEC has never ruled on their validity, however. Like the 527 organizations, 501(c)4 groups were eclipsed by super PACs in 2011–2012, but they continue to be a valuable tool for those donors who prefer to conceal their political contributions. For the top independent committees contributing to federal candidates in 2014, see Table 9–1 that follows.

Table 9–1 ▶ **The Fifteen Top Groups Making Independent Expenditures during the 2014 Cycle**

Independent expenditures only. Some groups, such as the party committees, have designated only a small part of their total fundraising as independent expenditures. *Does this list suggest that either of the two major parties has an advantage?*

Committee	Affiliation	Raised by October 2014	Type	Disclosure of Contributors
National Republican Congressional Committee	Republican	$64,591,859	Party committee	full
Democratic Congressional Campaign Committee	Democratic	$55,037,623	Party committee	full
Democratic Senatorial Campaign Committee	Democratic	$47,150,656	Party committee	full
Crossroads GPS and American Crossroads	Republican (Karl Rove)	$46,876,858	501c, Super PAC	partial
Senate Majority PAC	Democratic	$42,611,228	Super PAC	full
U.S. Chamber of Commerce	business	$33,554,401	501c	none
National Republican Senatorial Committee	Republican	$31,678,951	Party committee	full
House Majority PAC	Democratic	$21,598,144	Super PAC	full
National Rifle Association	gun rights	$19,927,656	PAC	full
Ending Spending Action Fund	conservative	$19,572,162	Super PAC	partial
NextGen Climate Action	environment (Tom Steyer)	$19,313,475	Super PAC	full
Freedom Partners Action Fund	conservative (Koch brothers)	$18,997,147	Super PAC	partial
League of Conservation Voters	environment	$17,389,444	501c, Super PAC	partial
National Association of Realtors	business	$10,306,180	Super PAC	none
Put Alaska First PAC	Senator Mark Begich (D)	$9,881,324	Super PAC	full

Source: Center for Responsive Politics.

Candidate Committees. Despite the limits on contributions to candidate committees, these organizations continued to collect large sums. The committees of major-party presidential nominees, such as Mitt Romney and Barack Obama, were able to amass well beyond $1 billion each, often from relatively small contributions.

Candidate committees at all levels received a boost in April 2014 as a result of the Supreme Court's latest ruling on campaign finance. The Court continued to hold that limits on the amount that any one individual could contribute to any one candidate were permissible. An overall cap on the total amount that an individual could contribute, however, was unconstitutional. In other words, there can be no limit on the number of different candidates a wealthy individual can support. A billionaire could, for example, give the $2,600 maximum contribution to every single candidate of a particular party running for the U.S. Congress. The ruling also freed up the amounts that individuals could give to the political parties.[9] The likely consequence will be to divert some funds away from super PACs and to candidate and party committees.

The Decline and Fall of Public Financing. From 1976 through 2004, most presidential candidates relied on a system of public funding financed by a checkoff on federal income tax forms. This system provided funds to match what a candidate could raise during the primary season. During the general election campaign, the system would pay for a candidate's entire campaign. Publicly funded candidates, however, could not raise funds independently for the general election or exceed the program's overall spending limits.

The system began to break down after 2000, when many candidates rejected public support during the primaries in the belief that they could raise larger sums privately. In 2008, Barack Obama became the first candidate since the program was founded to opt out of federal funding for the general elections as well. By 2012, the public financing system was essentially out of business. None of the major candidates in either party was willing to use it. Public funds continued to be available to support the parties' national conventions, but in 2012 Congress revoked funding for conventions in future election years.

From 2012 on, a division of effort developed between candidate committees and outside organizations such as super PACs. Candidate committees would run positive advertisements that portrayed the candidate to best advantage. Independent organizations would run negative ads aimed at tearing down the candidate's opponents. The belief was that because super PACs and other groups were technically independent, a candidate could deny responsibility for the negative campaign. Over time, however, such denials grew less and less credible.

■ **Learning Outcome 3:**
Summarize the process of choosing a president of the United States.

Running for President: The Longest Campaign

The American presidential election is the culmination of two different campaigns: the presidential primary campaign and the general election campaign following the party's national convention. Traditionally, both the primary campaigns and the final campaigns take place during the first ten months of an election year. Increasingly, though, the states are holding their primaries earlier in the year, which has motivated the candidates to begin their campaigns earlier as well. Indeed, candidates in the 2012 presidential races began campaigning in early 2011, thus launching one of the longest presidential campaigns to date in U.S. history.

---

9. *McCutcheon v. FEC,* 572 U.S. ___ (2014).

Primary elections were first organized in 1904 in Wisconsin for state officials. The purpose of the primary was to open the nomination process to ordinary party members and to weaken the influence of party bosses. Until 1968, however, there were fewer than twenty primary elections for the presidency. They were often *"beauty contests,"* in which the candidates competed for popular votes but the results did not control the selection of delegates to the national convention. National conventions were meetings of the party elite—legislators, mayors, county chairpersons, and loyal party workers—who were mostly appointed to their delegations. The leaders of large blocs of delegates could direct their delegates to support a favorite candidate.

Reforming the Presidential Primaries

In recent decades, the character of the presidential primary process and the makeup of the national convention have changed dramatically. The public, rather than party elites, now generally controls the nomination process. After the disruptive riots outside the doors of the 1968 Democratic convention in Chicago, many party leaders pushed for serious reforms of the convention system.

The Democratic National Committee appointed a special commission to study the problems of the presidential primary system. During the next several years, the group—called the McGovern-Fraser Commission—formulated new rules for delegate selection that had to be followed by state Democratic parties beginning in 1972.

The reforms instituted by the Democratic Party, which were mostly imitated by the Republicans, revolutionized the nomination process for the presidency. The most important changes require that a majority of the convention delegates be elected by the voters in primary elections, in caucuses held by local parties, or at state conventions. Delegates are normally pledged to a particular candidate, although the pledge is not always formally binding at the convention. The delegation from each state must also include a proportion of women, younger party members, and representatives of the minority groups within the party. At first, almost no special privileges were given to party leaders and elected party

did you know?

Obama's reelection in 2012 meant that we have now had three presidents in a row elected for two terms. That hasn't happened in 200 years (the last example was Jefferson, Madison, and Monroe).

2014 Elections

Financing the Congressional Races

Spending on races for the U.S. House and Senate came to about $4 billion in 2013 and 2014. This sum set a new record. State contests were also expensive, especially races for governor. In the very close race for governor of Florida, spending easily passed the $100 million mark. In California, one ballot proposal would require drug testing for doctors. Another would require insurers to receive approval for rate hikes from the state insurance commissioner. Physicians and insurance companies opposed to these two measures raised more than $100 million. The proposals lost.

A major development was the growth in so-called dark money—independent expenditures by groups, often conservative, that do not identify their contributors. *The New York Times* estimated that more than half of political television commercials were bought by groups that conceal their donors. Journalists got a glimpse behind the curtain when files of a secretive Republican governors committee accidentally became public. It turned out that corporations such as Coca-Cola, Exxon Mobil, Microsoft, and Walmart were giving millions to the campaigns of Republican governors. This development was new—before the advent of dark money, such corporations were often reluctant to make political donations, presumably to avoid offending their customers. Of course, as Table 9–1 shows, in 2014 Democrats were not exactly short of funds either.

Superdelegate

A party leader or elected official who is given the right to vote at the party's national convention. Superdelegates are not selected at the state level.

Invisible Primary

The pre-primary campaign to win supporters among elected officials, fund raisers, interest groups, and opinion leaders.

officials, such as senators and governors. In 1984, however, many of these individuals returned to the Democratic convention as **superdelegates.**

In an interesting recent development, a number of foreign political parties have decided to adopt versions of the American primary system. What benefits do these parties hope to gain by such a step? We examine that question in the *Beyond Our Borders* feature that follows.

The Invisible Primary

Before the primary season even begins, presidential candidates must begin lining up as much support within their party as is possible. In the example of the 2012 Republican primaries, leading Republicans such as Mitt Romney were effectively in campaign mode as early as 2010. Romney was running in what has been called the **invisible primary,** the pre-primary campaign to win supporters among elected officials, fund raisers, interest groups, and opinion leaders. If a candidate can win the invisible primary, his or her chances in the actual primaries go way up.

During 2011, polls showed dramatic shifts in popular opinion about the Republican candidates. Most of these shifts were due to candidate performances in the long series of

Beyond Our Borders

Foreign Parties Are Adopting the U.S. Primary System

In the past, the American primary election system was unique among the world's democracies. Today, though, a number of political parties throughout the world are adopting some type of primary election to choose their candidate for chief executive officer.

French Socialists Lead the Way

Official members of the French Socialist Party have to pay annual dues equal to one-tenth of their monthly income. Given that, it is surprising that there are even 120,000 official party members. Traditionally, those party members picked the Socialist candidate for president of France. That's better than making such a decision in "a smoke-filled room," but not by much. In 2011, though, the Socialists "went to the people" by conducting *les primières* (the primaries). Almost three million French citizens who were willing to endorse leftist values participated in choosing François Hollande as their candidate. He is now president of France.

Canada's Liberal Party Joins In

In 2013, Canada's Liberal Party (a party with centrist views) staged a primary vote open to anyone who stated that she or he was a supporter of the party's values. The primary was held online and by telephone. Hundreds of thousands participated in

choosing the party's leader, Justin Trudeau. He will become prime minister of Canada if the Liberals win the next national election. The list of those who participated in the primary will be a valuable campaign tool in that election.

More Primaries to Come

We can expect to see more primaries taking place in other countries for a simple reason: Primaries provide political parties with information about supporters. These supporters can then be solicited not only for campaign funds, but for activities such as "getting out the vote." Parties can mine data gleaned from primaries to develop better relationships with their supporters—both actual and potential. Major parties in Argentina and Italy have employed primary-style mechanisms for choosing their leader, and the British Labour Party will adopt a similar system for its next leadership election.

For Critical Analysis

How might a political party's opponents sabotage the primaries in France or Canada?

Republican debates held in 2011. In the end, though, Romney prevailed. From the beginning, he had much more support among Republican leaders than anyone else. Republicans have typically rallied around the presumptive candidate, and they did so again in 2012. Indeed, to find candidates who won the presidential nomination while actually *losing* the invisible primary, you have to go back to Democratic candidates George McGovern in 1972 and Jimmy Carter in 1976.

Primaries and Caucuses

Various types of primaries are used by the states. One notable difference is between proportional and winner-take-all primaries. Another important consideration is whether independent voters can take part in a primary. Some states also use caucuses and conventions to choose candidates for various offices.

Direct and Indirect Primaries. A **direct primary** is one in which voters decide party nominations by voting directly for candidates. In an **indirect primary,** voters instead choose convention delegates, and the delegates determine the party's candidate in the general election. Delegates may be pledged to a particular candidate. Indirect primaries are used almost exclusively in presidential elections. Most candidates in state and local elections are chosen by direct primaries.

Proportional and Winner-Take-All Primaries. Most primaries are *winner-take-all.* *Proportional* primaries are used mostly to elect delegates to the national conventions of the two major parties—delegates who are pledged to one or another candidate for president. Under the proportional system, if one candidate for president wins 40 percent of the vote in a primary, that candidate receives about 40 percent of the pledged delegates.

In recent years, the Democrats have used the proportional system for all of their presidential primaries and caucuses. For the most part, the Republicans have relied on the winner-take-all principle. In 2012, however, the Republican National Committee ruled that any state choosing national convention delegates before April 1 would be required to use the proportional system. States voting later could adopt whatever method they preferred. A number of early-voting states, such as Arizona and Florida, refused to follow the rules and used winner-take-all systems. They were penalized. Still, a majority of the states now allocate Republican National Convention delegates on a proportional basis.

Closed Primary. A closed primary is one of several types of primaries distinguished by how independent voters are handled. In a **closed primary,** only declared members of a party can vote in that party's primary. In other words, voters must declare their party affiliation, either when they register to vote or at the primary election. In a closed-primary system, voters cannot cross over into the other party's primary in order to nominate the weakest candidate of the opposing party or to affect the ideological direction of that party.

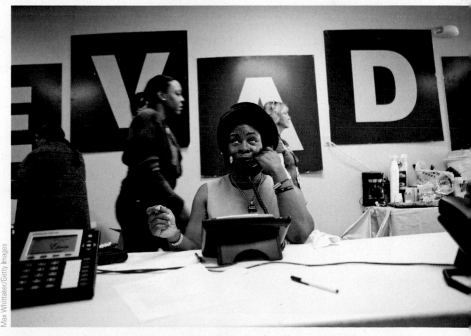

A campaign volunteer at a Romney-Ryan phone bank calls voters on Election Day in Reno, Nevada. *How can a get-out-the-drive help a candidate?*

Direct Primary

A primary election in which voters decide party nominations by voting directly for candidates.

Indirect Primary

A primary election in which voters choose convention delegates, and the delegates determine the party's candidate in the general election.

Closed Primary

A type of primary in which the voter is limited to choosing candidates of the party of which he or she is a member.

Open Primary. In an **open primary,** any voter can vote in either party's primary without declaring a party affiliation. Basically, the voter makes the choice in the privacy of the voting booth. The voter must, however, choose one party's list from which to select candidates.

Blanket Primary. A *blanket primary* is one in which the voter can vote for candidates of more than one party. Until 2000, a few states, including Alaska, California, and Washington, had blanket primaries. In 2000, however, the United States Supreme Court abolished the system. The Court ruled that the blanket primary violated political parties' First Amendment right of association. Because the nominees represent the party, party members—not the general electorate—should have the right to choose the party's nominee.[10]

Run-Off Primary. Some states have a two-primary system. If no candidate receives a majority of the votes in the first primary, the top two candidates must compete in another primary, called a *run-off primary.*

The "Top-Two" Primary. Louisiana has long used a special type of primary for filling some offices. Under the system, all candidates appear on a single ballot. A party cannot prevent a candidate from appearing on the primary ballot—an insurgent Republican, for example, could appear on the ballot alongside the party-supported Republican. The two candidates receiving the most votes, regardless of party, then move on to the general election. Following the abolition of the blanket primary, the state of Washington adopted this system. In 2008, the United States Supreme Court upheld the new plan.[11] In 2010, Californians voted to use the type of primary, beginning in 2012. (For more detail on this type of primary, see the *What If . . .* feature in Chapter 8.)

Conventions. While primary elections are the most common way in which a party's candidates are selected, there are other procedures in use. State party conventions may nominate candidates for various offices. Those who attend meetings below the statewide level may participate in nominating candidates as well. The most famous of such meetings are the caucuses that help nominate a party's candidate for president of the United States.

Open Primary

A primary in which any registered voter can vote (but must vote for candidates of only one party).

Caucus

A meeting of party members to select candidates and propose policies.

Caucuses. In 2012, sixteen states relied at least in part on **caucuses** for choosing delegates to the Republican and Democratic national conventions. Some of these states used a combined system. Strictly speaking, the caucus system is actually a convention system. In North Dakota, for example, local citizens, who need not be registered as party members, gather in party meetings, called caucuses, at the precinct level. They choose delegates to district conventions. The district conventions elect delegates to the state convention, and the state convention actually chooses the delegates to the national convention. The national delegates, however, are pledged to reflect the presidential preferences that voters expressed at the caucus level.

UC Davis students line up at a campus polling place in Davis, California, on Election Day 2012. *Should students vote where they attend school or where their parents live? In either case, why?*

10. *California Democratic Party v. Jones,* 530 U.S. 567 (2000).
11. *Washington State Grange v. Washington State Republican Party,* 552 U.S. 442 (2008).

Front-Loading the Primaries

When potential presidential candidates realized that winning as many primary elections as possible guaranteed them the party's nomination for president, their tactics changed dramatically. Candidates began to concentrate on building organizations in states that held early, important primary elections. By the 1970s, candidates recognized that winning early contests, such as the Iowa caucuses and the New Hampshire primary election (both now held in January), meant that the media instantly would label the winner as the **front-runner,** thus increasing the candidate's media exposure and escalating the pace of contributions to his or her campaign.

The Rush to Be First. The state political parties began to see that early primaries had a much greater effect on the outcome of the presidential contest than did later ones. Accordingly, in successive presidential elections, more and more states moved their primaries into the first months of the year, a process known as **front-loading** the primaries. One result was a series of "Super Tuesdays," when multiple states held simultaneous primaries. In 2008, twenty-four states held their primaries or caucuses on February 5, making it the largest Super Tuesday ever. So many states were in play on February 5 that it was impossible for the candidates to campaign strongly in all of them. Rather than winning more attention, many Super Tuesday states found that they were ignored. Because the Democratic race was not decided until the very end of the process in June, the later Democratic primaries, such as those in Indiana, North Carolina, Ohio, Pennsylvania, and Texas, were hotly contested.

Front-loading, in short, had become counterproductive. As a result, in 2012 Super Tuesday was held on March 6, a month later than in 2008. Ten states participated instead of twenty-four.

The National Parties Seek to Regain Control. The process of front-loading the primaries alarmed many observers, who feared that a front-runner might wrap up the nomination before voters were able to make a thorough assessment of the candidates. In the many months between the early primaries and the general election, the voters might come to regret their decision.

In response, the national Democratic and Republican parties took steps to regain control of the primary schedule. Such steps included a ban on primaries or caucuses held before a specified date. States would need special permission to choose delegates before that date. Traditional lead-off states such as Iowa and New Hampshire were allowed to go first, and a limited number of other states also received such permission.

Not all states were willing to follow the official schedule, however. In principle, the national parties had all the power they needed to enforce the rules—they could cut the number of delegates a state was authorized to send to the national convention, or even refuse to seat a state delegation altogether. The two national committees found it politically difficult to impose tough punishments, however.

On to the National Convention

Presidential candidates have been nominated by the convention method in every election since 1832. Extra delegates are allowed from states that had voting majorities for the party in the preceding elections. Parties also accept delegates from the District of Columbia, the territories, and U.S. citizens living abroad.

Front-Runner
The presidential candidate who appears to be ahead at a given time in the primary season.

Front-Loading
The practice of moving presidential primary elections to the early part of the campaign to maximize the impact of these primaries on the nomination.

did you know?

2012 was the first election since 1976 with no Bushes or Clintons running for president or vice president—and it is possible we could have both a Clinton and a Bush running for president in 2016.

**CONNECT
WITH YOUR CLASSMATES**
MindTap for American Government

Access the Campaigning for Office and Elections Forum: Discussion—Bringing the Party Together after Primaries

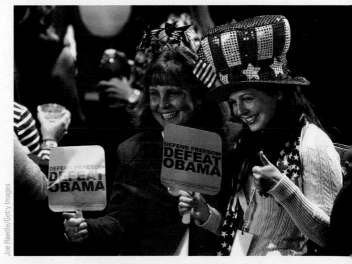

Mitt Romney supporters at his election night event in Boston in 2012. *What kinds of Americans tended to support the Republican candidate?*

Joe Raedle/Getty Images

Credentials Committee
A committee used by political parties at their national conventions to determine which delegates may participate. The committee inspects the claim of each prospective delegate to be seated as a legitimate representative of his or her state.

Elector
A member of the electoral college, which selects the president and vice president. Each state's electors are chosen in each presidential election year according to state laws.

did you know?

The 1976 Republican National Convention, where incumbent president Gerald Ford narrowly defeated former California governor Ronald Reagan, was the last major-party convention at which the party's nominee was not decided before the convention began.

A Texas delegate at the 2012 Democratic National Convention in Charlotte, North Carolina. *What kinds of Americans tended to support the Democratic candidate?*

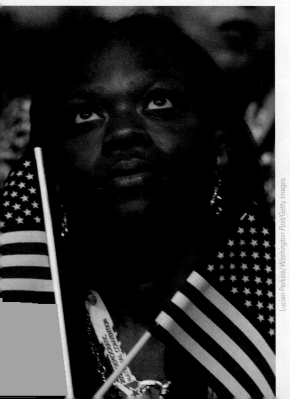

Seating the Delegates. At the convention, each political party uses a **credentials committee** to determine which delegates may participate. Controversy may arise when rival groups claim to be the official party organization. For example, the Mississippi Democratic Party split in 1964 at the height of the civil rights movement, and two sets of delegates were selected. After much debate, the credentials committee seated the mixed-race, pro–civil rights delegation and excluded those who represented the traditional "white" party.

Convention Activities. Most delegates arrive at the convention committed to a presidential candidate. No convention since 1952 has required more than one ballot to choose a nominee. Conventions normally last four days, but in both 2008 and 2012 the Republican convention was shortened to three days due to hurricanes. On each night, featured speakers seek to rally the party faithful and draw in uncommitted voters who are watching on television. In 2012, about 25 million viewers saw presidential candidate Mitt Romney speak to the Republican convention. At the Democratic convention, almost 36 million Americans tuned in to see President Obama, and 25 million watched the nomination address by former president Bill Clinton.

Public opinion polls following each convention showed a definite "bounce" for the Democrats but not for the Republicans. Some attributed this result to Clinton—his speech was widely considered to be unusually effective.

The Electoral College

Some people who vote for the president and vice president think that they are voting directly for a candidate. In actuality, they are voting for **electors** who will cast their ballots in the electoral college. Article II, Section 1, of the Constitution outlines in detail the method of choosing electors for president and vice president. The framers of the Constitution did not want the president and vice president to be selected by the "excitable masses." Rather, they wished the choice to be made by a few supposedly dispassionate, reasonable men (but not women).

The Choice of Electors. Electors are selected during each presidential election year. The selection is governed by state laws. After the national party convention, the electors are pledged to the candidates chosen. Each state's number of electors equals that state's number of senators (two) plus its number of representatives. The total number of electors today is 538, equal to 100 senators, 435 members of the House, and 3 electors for the District of Columbia. (The Twenty-third Amendment, ratified in 1961, added electors for the District of Columbia.)

The Electors' Commitment. A plurality of voters in a state chooses a slate of electors (except in Maine and Nebraska, where electoral votes are partly based on congressional districts). Those electors are pledged to cast their ballots on the first Monday after the second Wednesday in December in the state capital for the presidential and vice-presidential candidates of their party. The Constitution does not, however, *require* the electors to cast their ballots for the candidates of their party, and on rare occasions so-called *faithless electors* have voted for a candidate to whom they were not pledged.

The ballots are counted and certified before a joint session of Congress early in January. The candidates who receive a majority (270) of the electoral votes are certified as president-elect and vice president-elect. According to the Constitution, if no candidate receives a majority of the electoral votes, the election of the president is decided in the House of Representatives from among the candidates with the three highest numbers of votes, with each state having one vote (decided by a plurality of each state delegation). The selection of the vice president is determined by the Senate in a choice between the two candidates with the most votes, each senator having one vote. The House was required to choose the president in 1801 (Thomas Jefferson) and again in 1825 (John Quincy Adams).

Problems with the Electoral College System. It is possible for a candidate to become president without obtaining a majority of the popular vote. There have been many presidents in our history who did not win a majority of the popular vote, including Abraham Lincoln, Woodrow Wilson, Harry Truman, John F. Kennedy, Richard Nixon (in 1968), Bill Clinton, and George W. Bush (in 2000). Such an event becomes more likely when there are important third-party candidates.

Perhaps more distressing is the possibility of a candidate's being elected when an opposing candidate receives a plurality of the popular vote. This has occurred on four occasions—in the elections of John Quincy Adams in 1824, Rutherford B. Hayes in 1876, Benjamin Harrison in 1888, and George W. Bush in 2000. All of these candidates won elections in which an opponent received more popular votes than they did. Such results have led to calls for replacing the electoral college with a popular-vote system.

Abolishing the college would require a constitutional amendment, however, and the likelihood of such an amendment is remote. As an alternative, the National Popular Vote movement advocates an interstate compact to bypass the existing system. This proposal would require each participating state to cast all of its electoral votes for the candidate who receives the most popular votes nationwide. The plan will go into effect if the number of participating states grows to the point at which these states can elect a majority of the electoral college. As of mid-2014, ten states and the District of Columbia had joined the compact.

> **Australian Ballot**
> A secret ballot prepared, distributed, and tabulated by government officials at public expense. Since 1888, all states have used the Australian ballot rather than an open, public ballot.
>
> **Office-Block, or Massachusetts, Ballot**
> A form of general election ballot in which candidates for elective office are grouped together under the title of each office. It emphasizes voting for the office and the individual candidate, rather than for the party.

COMPARE WITH YOUR PEERS
MindTap for American Government

Access the Campaigning for Office and Elections Forum: Polling Activity—Presidential Election Process

How Are Elections Conducted?

The United States uses the **Australian ballot**—a secret ballot that is prepared, distributed, and counted by government officials at public expense. Since 1888, all states have used the Australian ballot. Before that, many states used the alternatives of oral voting or differently colored ballots prepared by the parties. Obviously, knowing which way a person was voting made it easy to apply pressure on the person to change his or her vote, and vote buying was common.

■ **Learning Outcome 4:**
Explain the mechanisms through which voting takes place on Election Day.

Office-Block and Party-Column Ballots

Two types of Australian ballots are used in the United States in general elections. The first, called an **office-block ballot,** or sometimes a **Massachusetts ballot,** groups all the candidates for a particular elective office under the title of that office. Parties dislike the office-block ballot because it places more emphasis on the office than on the party. It discourages straight-ticket voting and encourages split-ticket voting. Most states now use this type of ballot.

Sometimes, ballots are disputed and must be recounted. This occurred after the votes were tallied for the U.S. senatorial candidates in Minnesota in 2008. *Is there any way to reform the voting process to avoid such disputes?*

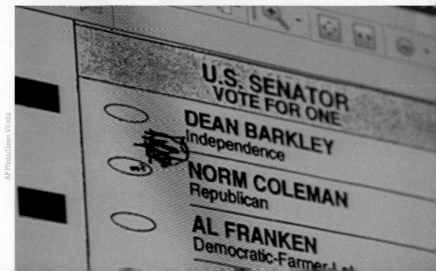

AP Photo/Dawn Villella

A **party-column ballot** is a form of general election ballot in which all of a party's candidates are arranged in one column under the party's label and symbol. It is also called an **Indiana ballot.** In some states, it allows voters to vote for all of a party's candidates for local, state, and national offices by simply marking a single "X" or by pulling a single lever. Because it encourages straight-ticket voting, the two major parties favor this form. When a party has an exceptionally strong presidential or gubernatorial candidate to head the ticket, the use of the party-column ballot increases the **coattail effect** (the influence of a popular candidate on the success of other candidates on the same party ticket).

> **Party-Column, or Indiana, Ballot**
>
> A form of general election ballot in which all of a party's candidates for elective office are arranged in one column under the party's label and symbol. It emphasizes voting for the party, rather than for the office or individual.
>
> **Coattail Effect**
>
> The influence of a popular candidate on the success of other candidates on the same party ticket.

Voting by Mail

Voting by mail has been accepted for absentee ballots for many decades (for example, for individuals who are doing business away from home or for members of the armed forces). Recently, several states have offered mail ballots to all of their voters. The rationale for using the mail ballot is to make voting easier for the voters and increase turnout. Oregon has gone one step further: since 1998, that state has employed postal ballots exclusively, and there are no polling places. (Voters who do not prepare their ballot in time for the U.S. Postal Service to deliver it can drop off their ballots at drop boxes on Election Day.) In addition, most counties in Washington State now use mail ballots exclusively. By national standards, voter turnout in these two states has been high, but not exceptionally so.

Voting Fraud and Voter ID Laws

Voting fraud is something regularly suspected but seldom proved. Voting in the 1800s, when secret ballots were rare and people had a cavalier attitude toward the open buying of votes, was probably much more conducive to fraud than modern elections are. Still, some observers claim that the potential for voting fraud is high in many states, particularly through the use of phony voter registrations and absentee ballots. Other observers claim, however, that errors due to fraud are trivial in number and that a few mistakes are inevitable in a system involving millions of voters. These people argue that an excessive concern with voting fraud makes it harder for minorities and poor people to vote.

> **did you know?**
>
> When President Grover Cleveland lost the election of 1888, his wife told the White House staff to change nothing because the couple would be back in four years—and she was right.

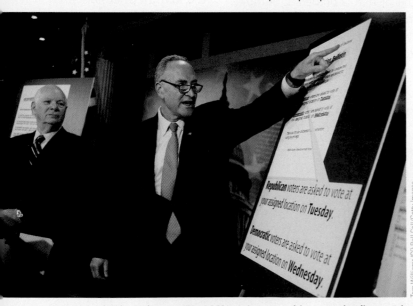

Senator Charles Schumer (D., N.Y.) points to a blowup of a flyer with misleading voting information. Schumer cosponsored a bill to make the distribution of fraudulent election material a federal offense. *How likely is it that a voter would be misled by such a flyer?*

Voter ID Requirements. In recent years, many states have adopted laws requiring enhanced proof of identity before voters can cast their ballots. Indiana imposed what was then the nation's toughest voter identification (ID) law in 2005. Indiana legislators claimed that they were motivated by a desire to prevent voting fraud, but critics argued that they were really trying to suppress voter turnout among minority group members and the poor—the individuals least likely to possess adequate identification. In 2008, the United States Supreme Court upheld the Indiana voter ID law.[12]

Voting Restrictions during the 2012 Election Cycle. In the wake of the Court's ruling, dozens of states moved to tighten voter ID requirements. Republicans provided almost all of the support for the new ID laws. In 2011 and 2012, nineteen states enacted voter ID requirements, and eleven of these states

---

12. *Crawford v. Marion County Election Board*, 553 U.S. 181 (2008).

mandated photo IDs. Not all of these laws were actually in effect on Election Day, however. In Wisconsin, a state court held that the new law violated the state constitution. In Maine and Ohio, voters repealed new voting laws before the November elections.

Also, until 2013, most southern states with a history of racial discrimination had to obtain preclearance from the federal government for any significant change to their voting laws and procedures under the 1965 Voting Rights Act. The Department of Justice refused to preclear voter ID laws in South Carolina and Texas on the ground that the laws impose a greater burden on minority voters than on whites. More than 239,000 registered voters in South Carolina lacked the identification needed to vote under that state's proposed law. As we explain in a later section of this chapter, however, in June 2013 the United States Supreme Court effectively suspended the preclearance procedure. As a result, many southern states were able to implement strict voter ID laws in time for the 2014 elections.

The Impact of Restrictive Voting Laws on Voter Turnout. In any election, the number of Americans who fail to vote is very large. Any factor that affects voter turnout, therefore, can have a major impact on election results. Heavy voter turnout among conservatives, for example, made 2010 a banner year for the Republicans. In 2012, a belief by minority group members that their voting rights were at risk seems to have increased minority turnout measurably. If the new voting laws really were meant to reduce the Democratic vote in 2012, they apparently backfired.

Turning Out to Vote

In 2012, the number of Americans eligible to vote was about 221.9 million people. Of that number, about 130.3 million, or 58.7 percent of the eligible population, actually cast a ballot. When voter turnout is this low, it means, among other things, that the winner of a close presidential election may be voted in by less than a third of those eligible to vote.

Figure 9–2 that follows shows **voter turnout** for presidential and congressional elections from 1910 to 2014. Each of the peaks in the figure represents voter turnout in a

> **Voter Turnout**
> The percentage of citizens taking part in the election process; the number of eligible voters that actually "turn out" on election day to cast their ballots.

> **did you know?**
> In the 2012 elections, Obama won 77 percent of all counties with a Whole Foods Market, and just 29 percent of all counties with a Cracker Barrel Old Country Store.

> ■ **Learning Outcome 5:**
> Discuss voter turnout in the United States and the types of people most likely to vote.

Figure 9–2 ▶ **Voter Turnout for Presidential and Midterm Elections, 1910–2014**

The peaks represent voter turnout in presidential election years; the troughs represent voter turnout in off-presidential election years. *Why might voter turnout have picked up in recent years?*

Note: Prior to 1948, the voting-age population is used as a proxy for the population eligible to vote.

Sources: Historical Data Archive, Inter-university Consortium for Political and Social Research; Michael P. McDonald and Samuel L. Popkin, "The Myth of the Vanishing Voter," *American Political Science Review,* Vol. 95, No. 4 (December 2001), p. 966, and the United States Elections Project.

Midterm Elections

National elections in which candidates for president are not on the ballot. In midterm elections, voters choose all members of the U.S. House of Representatives and one-third of the members of the U.S. Senate.

Voting-Age Population

The number of people of voting age living in the country at a given time, regardless of whether they have the right to vote.

Vote-Eligible Population

The number of people who, at a given time, enjoy the right to vote in national elections.

presidential election. Thus, we can also see that turnout for congressional elections is influenced greatly by whether there is a presidential election in the same year. Whereas voter turnout during the presidential elections of 2012 was 58.7 percent, as noted, it was only 41.6 percent in the **midterm elections** of 2010.

The same is true at the state level. When there is a race for governor, more voters participate in the elections than when only state legislators are on the ballot. Voter participation rates in gubernatorial elections are also greater in presidential election years. The average turnout in state elections is about 14 percentage points higher when a presidential election is held.

Now consider local elections. In races for mayor, city council, county auditor, and the like, it is fairly common for only 25 percent or less of the electorate to vote. Is something amiss here? It would seem that people should be more likely to vote in elections that directly affect them. At the local level, each person's vote counts more (because there are fewer voters). Furthermore, the issues—crime control, school bonds, sewer bonds, and the like—touch the immediate interests of the voters. In reality, however, potential voters are most interested in national elections when a presidential choice is involved. Otherwise, voter participation in our representative government is very low (and, as we have seen, it is not overwhelmingly high even in presidential elections).

The Effect of Low Voter Turnout

There are two schools of thought concerning low voter turnout. Some view low voter participation as a threat to our democratic republic. Too few individuals are deciding who wields political power in society. In addition, low voter participation presumably signals apathy about the political system in general. It also may signal that potential voters simply do not want to take the time to learn about the issues.

Others are less concerned about low voter participation. They contend that low voter participation simply indicates more satisfaction with the status quo. Also, they believe that representative democracy is a reality even if a very small percentage of eligible voters vote. If everyone who does not vote thinks that the outcome of the election will accord with his or her own desires, then representative democracy is working. The nonvoters are obtaining the type of government—with the type of people running it—that they want to have anyway.

did you know?

Noncitizens were allowed to vote in some states until the early 1920s.

Why Should You Care about...

Elections?

Why bother to vote? After all, the electorate is large and many elections are not close. If you do vote, however, you increase the amount of attention that politicians pay to people like you. When Congress, state legislatures, or city councils consider new laws and regulations, these bodies typically give more weight to the interests of groups that are more likely to vote. Your vote adds, to a small degree, to the voter turnout for your constituency. It therefore increases the chances of legislation that benefits you or that meets with your approval.

The Voting-Age Population and the Vote-Eligible Population

In the past, the press and even many political scientists calculated voter turnout by taking the number of people who vote as a percentage of the nation's **voting-age population.** Until about 1972, this was a reasonable way to obtain an approximate figure for turnout. In recent decades, however, turnout figures based on the voting-age population have become less and less reliable. The problem is that the voting-age population is not the same as the population of eligible voters, the **vote-eligible population.** The figure for the voting-age population includes felons and ex-felons who have lost the right to vote. Above all, it includes a large number of new immigrants who are not yet citizens. Finally, it does not include Americans living abroad, who can cast absentee ballots.

In 2012, the voting-age population included 3.2 million ineligible felons and ex-felons and an estimated 20.5 million noncitizens. It did not include 4.7 million Americans abroad. The

In general, a person must register well in advance of an election, although voters in Idaho, Iowa, Maine, Minnesota, New Hampshire, Wisconsin, and Wyoming are allowed to register up to, or even on, Election Day. North Dakota has no voter registration at all.

Some argue that registration requirements are responsible for much of the nonparticipation in our political process. There also is a partisan dimension to the debate over registration and nonvoting. Republicans generally fear that an expanded electorate would help to elect more Democrats—because more Democrats than Republicans are the kinds of persons who have trouble registering.

Voter-Registration Drives. Given the registration system, voter-registration drives are a familiar part of the political landscape. In the year leading up to any presidential or midterm election, public-interest groups and political organizations fan out across the land to register new voters. Registration drives are particularly common on college campuses and in low-income neighborhoods, where large numbers of unregistered voters may be found.

Long seen as noncontroversial, voter-registration drives suddenly became a political issue in 2010, when Acorn, a community-organizing group, was accused of violating election laws in its campaigns. Conservatives claimed that Acorn posed a major threat to the integrity of the voting process. Liberals contended that the controversy was overblown. Still, Acorn was forced to dissolve in 2010. Many former members later organized new groups.

In 2011 and 2012, Republican-controlled legislatures in a number of states tightened the laws governing voter-registration drives. Florida adopted the most stringent of these laws. In that state, organizations conducting registration drives were required to hand in all new registrations within forty-eight hours on penalty of a $50 fine for each late form. No allowance was made for days when state offices are closed—thus effectively banning voter registration on Fridays and any Saturday falling in a three-day weekend. Early voting days were also drastically curtailed. As a result, the League of Women Voters and Rock the Vote, major sponsors of voter-registration drives, suspended activities in Florida and sued to block the new law. The political parties, however, vowed to press on. In May 2012, a federal district judge suspended most of the voter registration requirements.

The Voting Rights Act. As we discussed in Chapter 5, the Voting Rights Act was enacted in 1965 to ensure that African Americans had equal access to the polls. Section 5 of the act requires that new voting practices or procedures in jurisdictions with a history of discrimination in voting have to be approved by the national government before being implemented.

Section 5 permits jurisdictions to "bail out" of coverage if they can demonstrate a clean record on discrimination during the previous ten years. By 2009, however, seventeen Virginia counties were the only jurisdictions in the country to successfully bail out. In June 2009, the Supreme Court permitted a Texas utility district to file for a bailout and strongly indicated that relief from the requirements of the act should be granted more freely.[14]

In June 2013, in *Shelby County v. Holder*, the Supreme Court effectively invalidated the requirement that changes to voting procedures in covered states and districts receive preclearance.[15] The Court did not throw out Section 5. Rather, it overturned Section 4, which determined which states and localities should be covered by Section 5. The Court contended that Section 4, which dated back to the 1960s, was obsolete. In principle, Congress could adopt a new set of Section 4 formulas based on more current conditions. The chances of such legislation making its way through a polarized Congress, however, seemed slight.

African American and liberal leaders accused the Court of engaging in one of the most sweeping examples of conservative judicial activism ever. The Voting Rights Act had been reaffirmed by Congress in 2006, with the House supporting it by 390 to 33 and the Senate by 98 to 0.

---

14. *Northwest Austin Municipal Utility District No. One v. Holder*, 557 U.S. 193 (2009).
15. 570 U.S. ___ (2013).

How You Can Make a Difference

What do you have to do to register and cast a vote?

- In general, you must be a citizen of the United States, at least eighteen years old on or before Election Day, and a resident of the state in which you intend to register.

- A number of states require that you meet a minimum-residency requirement. The minimum-residency requirement is very short in some states. No state requires more than thirty days. Thirty states do not have any minimum-residency requirement.

- Nearly every state also specifies a closing date by which you must be registered before an election. You may not be able to vote if you register too close to the day of the election. The closing date for registration varies from Election Day itself to thirty days before the election. In North Dakota, no registration is necessary.

- In most states, your registration can be revoked if you do not vote within a certain number of years or do not report a change of address. Federal regulations place limits on how purges are conducted.

- Look at voter registration in Texas as an example. If you live in Texas, you may have registered to vote when you obtained your Texas driver's license. If not, you can find a voter registration form online by searching on "texas vrapp."

- You must mail the application to the voter registrar in your county. (The registrar's address appears on the form after you finish filling it out.) Applications are also available at post offices, libraries, and other government offices. Your application must be postmarked thirty days before Election Day.

Key Terms

Australian ballot 277
caucus 274
closed primary 273
coattail effect 278
credentials committee 276
direct primary 273
elector 276
Federal Election Commission (FEC) 265
focus group 264

front-loading 275
front-runner 275
general election 262
Hatch Act 264
independent expenditures 266
indirect primary 273
invisible primary 272
issue advocacy 265
midterm elections 280

office-block, or Massachusetts, ballot 277
open primary 274
party-column, or Indiana, ballot 278
political action committee (PAC) 264
political consultant 263
presidential primary 260

primary election 262
registration 282
soft money 266
superdelegate 272
super PAC 267
vote-eligible population 280
voter turnout 279
voting-age population 280

Chapter Summary

Learning Outcome 1 The legal qualifications for holding political office are minimal at both the state and the local levels, but holders of political office still are predominantly white and male and are likely to be from the professional class.

American political campaigns are lengthy and extremely expensive. In the past decade, they have become more candidate centered than party centered in response to technological innovations and decreasing party identification.

Candidates have begun to rely on paid professional consultants to perform the various tasks necessary to wage a political campaign. The crucial task of professional political consultants is image building. The campaign organization devises a campaign strategy to maximize the candidate's chances of winning. Candidates use public opinion polls and focus groups to gauge their popularity and to test the mood of the country.

Learning Outcome 2 Under current conditions, finance for federal campaigns is supplied in two ways: candidate committees and independent expenditures. Candidate committees are under the complete control of the candidate. They have few limits on how they can spend their resources, but individual and organizational contributions to the committees face strict limits. Presidential candidate committees formerly accepted public financing, but candidates no longer participate in that system because they can raise more funds on their own. Independent organizations are not allowed to coordinate their expenditures with candidate campaigns, although this restriction is something of a fiction. These groups, which include super PACs and 501(c)4 organizations, can raise unlimited sums. Modern independent groups are the result of a 2010 Supreme Court ruling, *Citizens United v. FEC.*

Learning Outcome 3 After the Democratic convention of 1968, the McGovern-Fraser Commission formulated new rules for primaries, which were adopted by Democrats and, in most cases, by Republicans. These reforms opened up the nomination process for the presidency to all voters.

A presidential primary is a statewide election to help a political party determine its presidential nominee at the national convention. Some states use the caucus method of choosing convention delegates. The primary campaign recently has been shortened to the first few months of the election year.

A voter technically does not vote directly for president but instead chooses between slates of presidential electors. In most states, the slate that wins the most popular votes throughout the state gets to cast all the electoral votes for the state. The candidate receiving a majority (270) of the electoral votes wins.

Learning Outcome 4 The United States uses the Australian ballot, a secret ballot that is prepared, distributed, and counted by government officials. In recent years, several states have passed laws requiring photo IDs in order to vote and imposing other restrictions on voting. These laws have been very controversial.

Learning Outcome 5 Voter participation in the United States is often considered to be low, especially in elections that do not feature a presidential contest. Turnout is lower when measured as a percentage of the voting-age population than it is when measured as a percentage of the population actually eligible to vote. There is an association between voter turnout and a person's age, education, and income level.

In colonial times, only white males with a certain minimum amount of property were eligible to vote. The suffrage issue has concerned, at one time or another, most groups in the United States. Today, to register to vote, a person must satisfy citizenship, age, and residency requirements. Each state has different qualifications.

Master the concepts of Campaigning for Office and Elections with MindTap™ *for American Government*

REVIEW MindTap™ **for American Government**
Access Key Term Flashcards for Chapter 9.

TEST YOURSELF MindTap™ **for American Government**
Take the Wrap It Up Quiz for Chapter 9.

STAY CURRENT MindTap™ **for American Government**
Access the KnowNow blog and customized RSS for updates on current events.

STAY FOCUSED MindTap™ **for American Government**
Complete the Focus Activities for Campaigning for Office and Elections.

Additional Resources

Today's voters have a significant advantage over those in past decades. It is now possible to obtain extensive information about candidates and issues simply by going online. Some sites present point-counterpoint articles about the candidates or issues in an upcoming election. Other sites support some candidates and positions and oppose others. The candidates themselves all have Web sites that you can visit if you want to learn more about them and their positions.

Online Resources

- For detailed information about current campaign-financing laws and for the latest filings of finance reports, find the site maintained by the Federal Election Commission at www.fec.gov.
- To locate excellent reports on where campaign money comes from and how it is spent, be sure to view the site of the Center for Responsive Politics at www.opensecrets.org.
- Another Web site for investigating voting records and campaign financing information is run by Project Vote Smart. Find it at www.votesmart.org.
- One of the best people to follow for information on elections is statistics guru Nate Silver. He is the founder of the FiveThirtyEight blog at fivethirtyeight.com.

Books

Halperin, Mark, and John Heilemann. *Double Down: Game Change 2012.* New York: Penguin Books, 2014 (paperback). This work, by journalists Halperin and Heilemann, is the most celebrated report on the presidential elections of 2012. It offers inside information on every candidate.

Lee, Caroline W., Michael McQuarrie, Edward T. Walker, and Craig Calhoun. *Democratizing Inequalities: Dilemmas of the New Public Participation.* New York: NYU Press, 2015. Four sociologists contend that the benefits of political participation are limited by the structure of American politics. Popular participation may even reinforce elite power in unexpected ways.

Mattes, Kyle, and David P. Redlawsk. *The Positive Case for Negative Campaigning.* Chicago, University of Chicago Press, 2015. In this comprehensive treatment, the authors make the case that negative campaigning provides voters with valuable information. The authors are professors of political science, Mattes at the University of Iowa and Redlawsk at Rutgers.

Video

Scandal—A celebrated ABC drama series, *Scandal* stars Kerry Washington as political consultant Olivia Pope. A former presidential staff member, Pope's crisis management firm tries to protect the public images of the nation's political elite. Pope is usually successful, but we the viewers learn all the real dirt.

Veep—This award-winning series premiered in 2012 on HBO. *Veep* is a comedy starring Julia Louis-Dreyfus as U.S. vice president Selina Meyer. The hapless vice president, a former and possibly future presidential candidate, is forever one step away from catastrophe.

Quiz

Multiple Choice and Fill-Ins

Learning Outcome 1 Discuss who runs for office and how campaigns are managed.

1. To be eligible to serve as president of the United States, you must be:
   a. a natural-born citizen, a resident of the country for twenty-five years, and at least forty-two years old.
   b. a naturalized citizen, a resident of the country for twenty-five years, and at least thirty-five years old.
   c. at least thirty-five years old, a natural-born citizen, and a resident of the country for fourteen years.

2. The most sought-after (and most criticized) campaign expert is the _____ _____, who for a large fee takes over the candidate's campaign.

Learning Outcome 2 Describe the current system of campaign finance.

3. Today, presidential candidates do not accept matching public funds because:
   a. candidates can raise far more outside of the public system than they would receive if they participated in it.
   b. once candidates accept public funds for the primaries, they must match public funds in a ratio of two to one for the general elections.
   c. public funds are no longer available.

4. The Supreme Court ruling that was most important in creating our current campaign finance system was _____ *v. FEC*.

Learning Outcome 3 Summarize the process of choosing a president of the United States.

5. In an indirect primary:
   a. voters decide party nominations by voting directly for candidates.
   b. voters make no decisions directly about convention delegates.
   c. voters choose convention delegates, and those delegates determine the party's candidate in the general election.

6. In a/an _____ _____, any voter can vote in either party primary without declaring a party affiliation.

Learning Outcome 4 Explain the mechanisms through which voting takes place on Election Day.

7. In the United States today, all states use secret ballots that are prepared, distributed, and counted by government officials at public expense. This system is called:
   a. the Australian ballot.
   b. the Massachusetts ballot.
   c. the office-block ballot.

8. A/an _____ - _____ ballot groups all the candidates for a particular elective office under the title of that office.

Learning Outcome 5 Discuss voter turnout in the United States and the types of people most likely to vote.

9. In colonial times, the right to vote was typically limited to persons who were:
   a. of English ancestry.
   b. adult white males.
   c. adult white males who owned at least some property.

10. In statistics on voter participation, the voting-age population is typically larger than the _____ - _____ population.

Essay Questions

1. Many observers believe that holding so many presidential primary elections at such an early point in an election year is a serious problem. How might the problem be resolved? Also, is it fair and appropriate that New Hampshire always holds the first presidential primary and Iowa always conducts the first caucuses? Why or why not?

2. Some people are more likely to vote than others. Older persons vote more frequently than younger people. Wealthy voters make it to the polls more often than poor voters. What might cause older and wealthier individuals to exhibit greater turnout?

Answers to questions: 1. c, 2. political consultant, 3. a, 4. *Citizens United*, 5. c, 6. open primary, 7. a, 8. office-block, 9. c, 10. vote-eligible.

The Media

10

Members of the press take photos and video of the Obama administration's proposed 2015 budget.
Brendan Smialowski/AFP/Getty Images

The four Learning Outcomes below are designed to help improve your understanding of this chapter. After reading this chapter, you should be able to:

- **Learning Outcome 1:** Describe the different types of media and the changing roles that they play in American society.

- **Learning Outcome 2:** Summarize the impact of the media on the political process.

- **Learning Outcome 3:** Explain the relationship between the government and the media, and in particular the Internet.

- **Learning Outcome 4:** Discuss the question of opinion and bias in the mainstream media and alternative media such as talk radio.

▶ **WATCH & LEARN** MindTap™ for American Government
Watch a brief "What Do You Know?" video summarizing Media and Politics.

What If...

There Were No Newspapers?

BACKGROUND

At the end of the Revolutionary War, Americans could buy any of a total of forty-three newspapers. By 1910, newspapers throughout the country looked much as they do today. Currently, however, many newspapers face extinction. Great newspapers in Chicago, Minneapolis, Philadelphia, and other cities have filed for bankruptcy protection. Some, such as the *Baltimore Examiner* and the *Cincinnati Post,* have folded completely. Some people have speculated that, ultimately, newspapers will disappear altogether. What would such a world look like?

WHAT IF THERE WERE NO NEWSPAPERS?

The trend is already here. Since 1994, the share of Americans saying they read a daily newspaper has dropped from almost 60 percent to around 30 percent. If this trend continues, newspapers could for the most part vanish. Gone, too, would be their reporters and management.

By 2010, for the first time, more people obtained their national and international news from the Internet than from newspapers. Obviously, without newspapers, everyone would obtain their news from the Internet, broadcast and cable television, and to a lesser extent, news magazines. Without newspapers, these other sources of news would increase in size, scope, and availability.

THE DEATH OF THE STANDARD NEWS PACKAGE

When you open a metropolitan newspaper today, it has a "newspaper look." When you visit that newspaper's Web site, it often has the same look, one that dates back a hundred years. You'll find a mixture of local, national, business, sports, and international news, plus weather forecasts. What you see online is not much different from what is in print, although it may be easier to access.

If newspapers disappeared, the conventional news package also would disappear. People would find their news using online portals such as Yahoo and Google News. Their news format consists of headlines, a sentence, and a link. Such operations are cheap to run. Google News has no editors as such—everything is automated. Of course, if newspapers disappeared, Google News would not be able to access newspaper stories. Such stories would have to be found elsewhere online.

NEWS BLOGS AND CABLE NEWS CHANNELS WOULD GAIN VIEWERS

Without newspapers, news blogs would grow. Already, the Huffington Post (nicknamed HuffPost) has a total staff of 850. It has an unpaid army of about three thousand bloggers.

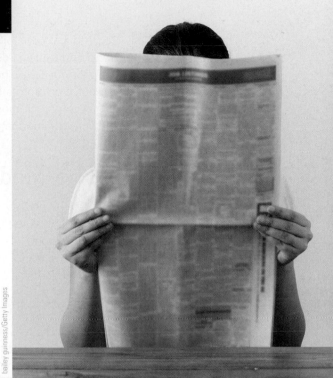

Why are young people giving up on newspapers?

As of 2014, Fox News was the most popular cable news channel, but we also have MSNBC, CNN, and others. Without newspapers, more people would obtain some of their news from these cable sources. New cable news channels might pop up to serve niche audiences.

LOCAL NEWS WITHOUT NEWSPAPERS

Newspaper owners claim that it is not possible to obtain local news without the services of a local newspaper. Yet start-up companies are now creating "hyperlocal" news sites. These sites let people zoom in on what is happening in their neighborhoods. Check out berkeleyside.com for coverage of Berkeley, California; arlnow.com for Arlington, Virginia; or www.everyblock.com for Chicago. These sites collect links to articles and blogs and often obtain data from municipal governments and other local sources.

For Critical Analysis

1. Would the quality of news gathering diminish if newspapers no longer existed?

2. Many news blogs are definitely biased and often proud of it. Should this attitude worry us? Why or why not?

LISTEN & LEARN

MindTap™ **for American Government**

Access Read Speaker to listen to Chapter 10.

■ **Learning Outcome 1:** Describe the different types of media and the changing roles that they play in American society.

did you know?

The first "wire" story transmitted by telegraph was sent in 1846.

The study of people and politics must take into account the role played by the media. Historically, the print media played the most important role in informing public debate. The print media developed, for the most part, our understanding of how news is to be reported. Today, however, 69 percent of Americans use television news as their primary source of information. In addition, the Internet has become a major source for news, political communication, and fund-raising. The Internet is now the second most widely used source of information—34 percent of all persons consider it their primary source of news.

The Media and Politics

Only 22 percent of the public now relies on newspapers as a primary news source, and newspapers are facing serious problems, as you can see from the chapter-opening *What If . . .* feature. As Internet use grows, the system of gathering and sharing news and information is changing from one in which the media have a primary role to one in which the individual citizen may play a greater part.

The Roles of the Media

The mass media perform a number of different functions in any country. In the United States, we can list at least six media functions. Almost all of them can have political implications, and some are essential to the democratic process. These functions are: (1) entertainment, (2) reporting the news, (3) identifying public problems, (4) socializing new generations, (5) providing a political forum, and (6) making profits.

Entertainment. By far the greatest number of radio and television hours are dedicated to entertaining the public. The battle for prime-time ratings indicates how important successful entertainment is to the survival of networks and individual stations. A number of network shows have a highly political content. Many younger people have reported that they get much of their political information from two programs on the Comedy Central network, hosted by Jon Stewart and Stephen Colbert. Both are liberal, although as part of his routine, Colbert pretends to be a conservative. (Colbert has recently moved to CBS to be the host of the *Late Show*.)

For many Americans, especially younger ones, the Internet has replaced television as a source of entertainment. While much time on the Internet may be spent chatting with friends on Skype or watching television programs online, politics is often a topic. YouTube, in particular, offers a large number of politically oriented videos, many of which are satirical. Talk radio and television shows that feature talk-radio personalities are another form of politically oriented

Many young people get their television news from Stephen Colbert and Jon Stewart on the Comedy Central network. In 2015, Colbert became host of the *Late Show* on CBS. *What are the politics of these two individuals?*

Win McNamee/Getty Images

entertainment—one that is dominated by the political right.

Reporting the News. A primary function of the mass media in all their forms is the reporting of news. The media provide words and pictures about events, facts, personalities, and ideas. The protections of the First Amendment are intended to keep the flow of news as free as possible, because it is an essential part of the democratic process. If citizens cannot obtain unbiased information about the state of their communities and their leaders' actions, how can they make voting decisions? One of the most incisive comments about the importance of the media was made by James Madison, who said, "A people who mean to be their own governors must arm themselves with the power knowledge gives. A popular government without popular information or the means of acquiring it, is but a prologue to a farce or a tragedy or perhaps both."[1]

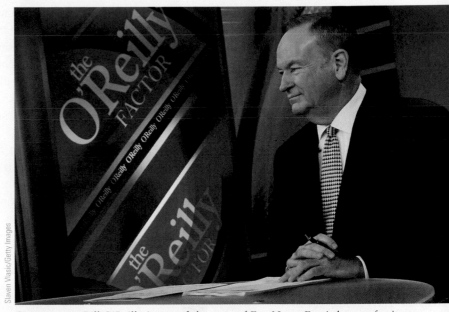

Commentator Bill O'Reilly is one of the stars of Fox News. Fox is known for its conservative slant on the news, and it is also more popular than its competitors. *Why might this be?*

Identifying Public Problems. The power of the media is important not only in revealing what the government is doing but also in determining what the government ought to do—in other words, in setting the **public agenda.** The mass media identify public issues. An example is the release of convicted sex offenders into residential neighborhoods after the end of their prison terms. The media have influenced the passage of legislation, such as "Megan's Law," which requires police to notify neighbors about the release and/or resettlement of certain sex offenders. American journalists also work in a long tradition of uncovering public wrongdoing, corruption, and bribery, and of bringing such wrongdoing to the public's attention.

Closely related to this investigative function is that of presenting policy alternatives. Public policy is often complex and difficult to make entertaining, but programs devoted to public policy are often scheduled for prime-time television, especially on cable networks. For its part, the Web offers an enormous collection of political sites, with policy proposals representing every point of view.

Agenda-setting by the media is enhanced by the various ways in which it can present the news. At the very end of Chapter 6, we introduced the concept of *framing*. The media can affect the public response to a particular issue by how it frames the issue—that is, by what kinds of facts it includes in the reporting. A similar concept is **priming**, that is, embedding the issue in a particular story line. Attitudes toward spending on the poor, for example, can be altered by stories that present poor people who are victims of bad luck—or who are suffering mostly due to their own behavioral problems.

Socializing New Generations. As mentioned in Chapter 6, the media strongly influence the beliefs and opinions of Americans. Because of this influence, the media play a significant role in the political socialization of the younger generation and of immigrants to this country. Through the transmission of historical information (sometimes fictionalized), the presentation of American culture, and the portrayal of the diverse regions and groups in

Public Agenda
Issues that are perceived by the political community as meriting public attention and governmental action.

Priming
A way in which the media can alter public perceptions of an issue—by embedding that issue in particular examples or stories.

---

1. James Madison, "Letter to W. T. Barry" (August 4, 1822), in Gaillard P. Hunt, ed., *The Writings of James Madison*, Vol. 103 (1910).

Why Should You Care about...

The Media?

Even if you do not plan to engage in political activism, you have a stake in ensuring that your beliefs are truly your own and that they represent your values and interests. To guarantee this result, you need to obtain accurate information from the media and avoid being swayed by subliminal appeals, loaded terms, or outright bias. If you do not take care, you could find yourself voting for a candidate who is opposed to what you believe in or voting against ballot propositions that are in your interest.

did you know?

Female representation in newsrooms has changed very little since 1999—in fact, it has fallen from 37 percent to 36 percent.

Marie Colvin, an American, was a foreign correspondent for Britain's *Sunday Times* for two decades. She lost the sight in one eye in Sri Lanka in 2001 and was killed in Syria in 2012. *Why would fighters target journalists?*

AP Images/*Sunday Times*

the United States, the media teach young people and immigrants about what it means to be an American. Many children's television shows are designed not only to entertain young viewers but also to instruct them in the moral values of American society.

On the Internet, young Americans participate in political forums, obtain information for writing assignments, and, in general, acquire much of their political socialization.

Providing a Political Forum. As part of their news function, the media also provide a political forum for leaders and the public. Candidates for office use news reporting to sustain interest in their campaigns, while officeholders use the media to gain support for their policies or to present an image of leadership. Presidential trips abroad are one way for the chief executive to get colorful, positive, and exciting news coverage that makes the president look "presidential." The media also offer ways for citizens to participate in public debate, through letters to the editor, blog posts, Twitter, and other channels.

Making Profits. Most of the news media in the United States are private, for-profit corporate enterprises. In general, profits are made as a result of charging for advertising. Advertising revenues usually are related directly to circulation or to listener/viewer ratings.

Several well-known media outlets, in contrast, are publicly owned—public television stations in many communities and National Public Radio. These operate without extensive commercials, are locally supported, and are often subsidized by the government and corporations.

Pressure by Advertisers. For the most part, however, the media depend on advertisers to obtain revenues to make profits. Consequently, reporters may feel pressure from media owners and from advertisers. If an important advertiser does not like the political bent of a particular newspaper reporter, for example, the reporter could be asked to alter his or her "style" of writing.

In one example, a harsh review of a country singer was removed from the Web site of an alternative weekly when concert promoters threatened never to advertise in the weekly again. In another instance, advertiser pressure on a firearms industry trade magazine led to the firing of a columnist and the resignation of the magazine's editor. The columnist had argued that Second Amendment rights are subject to regulation. In some foreign nations, threats to journalists are much more severe, as we describe in the *Beyond Our Borders* feature that follows.

Newspapers in Crisis. Lately, newspapers have found it increasingly difficult to make a profit. Newspaper revenues have fallen because online services such as Craigslist have taken over a greater share of classified advertising. The recent economic crisis, which depressed advertising spending, pushed many large daily newspapers over the edge. Newspapers in Chicago, Denver, and Seattle went out of business. Even some famous papers, such as the *New York Times,* the *Chicago Tribune,* and the *Boston Globe,* were in serious financial trouble.

Although all major newspapers are now online, they have found it difficult to turn a profit on their Web editions. News sites typically cannot sell enough advertising to meet their costs. In response to this problem, many newspapers have begun charging for online access, a process dubbed *retreating behind a paywall.* Access charges, however, reduce the number of users who are willing to view a site. Major publications such as the *New York Times* (shown later in this chapter) and the *Wall Street Journal* have been able to set up paywalls without losing an excessive number of customers, but less famous newspapers have not been so successful.

Content Providers versus Aggregators. On the Internet, news organizations that employ reporters and create articles are known as **content providers**, because they provide original content. Unfortunately for the content providers, they collect only a small share of the total revenue from online advertising. Most ad revenue goes to **aggregators**, such as

> **Content Provider**
> On the Internet, an individual or organization that generates original content.
>
> **Aggregator**
> A Web site that provides search and aggregation services, but creates little or no original content.

Beyond Our Borders

Threats to Journalists around the World

In the United States, we take it for granted that our reporters can investigate any subject and present the results without fearing for their lives or their freedom. Not so in many other countries. In the last few years, hundreds of journalists have been kidnapped or killed, and several thousand have been physically threatened or injured because of the stories they were reporting. In addition, many governments have imprisoned journalists in response to their reporting. Half of them were jailed in just three countries: Turkey, Iran, and China.

Russia—Always in the News

Over the past ten years, the independent press has almost completely disappeared in Russia. In several high-profile cases, investigative reporters who were critical of the current regime have been murdered. These crimes are conspicuously unsolved. Until recently, one of the few remaining independent sources of opinion was VKontakte, a type of Russian Facebook founded by Pavel Durov. In 2014, however, Durov was forced out and fled the country. VKontakte is now controlled by two of Russian president Putin's personal friends. Under a new law, if you have a blog with more than 3,000 readers, you must register as a formal news organization and obey Russia's restrictive press laws.

The Muslim World

A ghastly civil war continues in Syria. In recent years, up to seventy journalists per year have been killed openly. In addition, almost three dozen others have "gone missing" and are widely presumed to be dead. Still others have been jailed, not only by the Assad government but by rebel organizations as well. The Committee to Protect Journalists declared in 2014 that Syria was the world's most dangerous country for journalists.

In Egypt, authorities continue to jail reporters and to charge them with terrorist activities. Those detained have included journalists from Australia, Canada, and of course, Egypt. The growing unrest in Iraq has also led to an increase in unsolved murders of reporters. In one recent year, ten journalists were killed.

In Pakistan, members of the press live under the constant threat of murder, injury, or harassment. Since 2008, at least three dozen journalists have been killed in Pakistan either because of their reporting on the military or on the Islamic rebels in that country. Pakistan's government has rarely, if ever, solved any of these murder cases.

For Critical Analysis

Can you think of other countries where journalists may be under constant threat?

Google, that provide search and aggregation services, but generate little or no original content. In particular, Google itself collects a full 41 percent of all online ad revenue. Google's ad revenue is substantially greater than the total ad revenue, print and online, of all the newspapers in the nation put together. In other words, there is no absolute shortage of ad revenue—the problem is that it does not go to the content providers. Of course, without content providers, there is nothing to aggregate. We provided additional details on the troubles of the newspaper industry in the *What If . . .* feature that introduced this chapter.

Television versus the New Media

As we explained earlier, new forms of media are displacing older ones as sources of information on politics and society in general. Although it is only recently that newspapers have experienced severe economic difficulties, they were losing ground to television as early as the 1950s. Today, the Internet has begun to displace television.

New Patterns of Media Consumption. Not everyone, however, migrates to new media at the same rate. Among Americans older than sixty-five years of age, only 11 percent obtain information about political campaigns by going online, up from 5 percent in 2000. In this older generation, 31 percent still rely on a daily newspaper, although that is down from 58 percent in 2000.[2]

The media consumption patterns of *early adopters* of new technology are different. Some older high-income persons are among the early adopters, but the new media are most popular among youth. Indeed, many younger people have abandoned e-mail, relying on Facebook, texting, and other systems for messages. Many have moved on from Facebook to newer, more innovative social-networking platforms. Television becomes something to watch only if you cannot find online the program you want to see.

Young early adopters may find much of the older media irrelevant to their lives. It does not matter whether national television news shows are willing to pay personalities such as Diane Sawyer or Matt Lauer millions of dollars if you never watch these shows. Yet television news, cable networks, talk radio, and other older forms of media are not irrelevant to American politics. Older voters outnumber younger ones by a wide margin.

As of 2015, about 103 million Americans were age fifty or older. U.S. residents age eighteen through twenty-nine numbered about 54 million. Older voters are more likely to make it to the polls—and many early adopters of new media technology are too young to vote. It follows that television remains essential to American politics.

The Continuing Influence of Television. Television's continuing influence on the political process today is recognized by all who engage in that process. Television news is often criticized for being superficial, particularly compared with the detailed coverage available in newspapers and magazines. In fact, television news is constrained by its technical characteristics, the most important being the limitations of time—stories must be reported in only a few minutes.

Ezra Klein became famous as editor of Wonkblog, a *Washington Post* Web site. In 2014, he co-founded Vox, an independent blog for in-depth news (www.vox.com). *How can such a site support itself financially?*

2. Pew Research Center for the People & the Press, "Cable Leads the Pack as Campaign News Source," February 7, 2012.

The most interesting aspect of television—and of online videos—is that it relies on pictures rather than words to attract the viewer's attention. Therefore, video that is chosen for a particular political story has exaggerated importance. Viewers do not know what other photos may have been taken or what other events may have been recorded—they see only those appearing on their screens. Video clips, whether they appear on network news or YouTube, can also use well-constructed stories to exploit the potential for drama. Some critics suggest that there is pressure to produce television news that has a story line, like a novel or movie. The story should be short, with exciting pictures and a clear plot. In extreme cases, the news media are satisfied with a **sound bite,** a several-second comment selected or crafted for its immediate impact on the viewer.

It has been suggested that these formatting characteristics of video increase its influence on political events. As you are aware, real life is usually not dramatic, nor do all events have a plot that is neat or easily understood. Political campaigns are continuing events, lasting perhaps as long as two years. The significance of their daily turns and twists is only apparent later. The "drama" of Congress, with its 535 players and dozens of important committees and meetings, is also difficult for the media to present. Television requires, instead, dozens of daily three-minute stories.

> **Sound Bite**
> A brief, memorable comment that easily fits into news broadcasts.

> **did you know?**
> A full 69 percent of those who watch Bill O'Reilly on Fox News call themselves conservative, while 57 percent of those viewing Rachel Maddow on MSNBC consider themselves liberal.

The Media and Political Campaigns

■ **Learning Outcome 2:** Summarize the impact of the media on the political process.

All forms of the media—television, newspapers, radio, magazines, online services—have a significant political impact on American society. It is not too much of an exaggeration to say that almost all national political figures, starting with the president, plan every public appearance and statement to attract media coverage.

Television Coverage

Although younger voters get a relatively small share of their news from television, it remains the primary news source for older voters. Therefore, candidates and their consultants spend much of their time devising strategies that use television to their benefit. Three types of TV coverage are generally employed in campaigns for the presidency and other offices: political advertising (including negative ads), management of news coverage, and campaign debates.

Political Advertising. Political advertising has become increasingly important for the profitability of television station owners. Hearst Television, for example, obtains more than 10 percent of its revenues from political ads during an election year. During the 2012 presidential elections, total spending exceeded $7 billion. Among other expenses, candidates purchased more than 3 million campaign advertisements.

Negative Advertising. Perhaps one of the most effective political ads of all time was a thirty-second spot created by President Lyndon Johnson's media adviser in 1964. Johnson's opponent in the campaign was Barry Goldwater, a conservative Republican candidate known for his expansive views on the role of the U.S. military. In this ad, a little girl stood in a field of daisies. As she held a daisy, she pulled the petals off and quietly counted to herself. Suddenly, when she reached number ten, a deep bass voice cut in and began a countdown: "10, 9, 8, 7, 6 . . . ." When the voice intoned "zero," the mushroom cloud of an atomic bomb began to fill the screen. Then President Johnson's voice was heard: "These are the stakes. To make a world in which all of God's children can live, or to go into the dark. We must either love each other or we must die."

These are stills of a short television advertisement used by presidential candidate Lyndon Johnson in 1964. The daisy girl ad contrasted the innocence of childhood with the horror of an atomic bomb. *How effective was this negative TV ad?*

At the end of the commercial, the message read, "Vote for President Johnson on November 3."

Since the daisy girl advertisement, negative advertising has come into its own. In recent elections, an ever-increasing percentage of political ads have been negative in nature.

The public claims not to like negative advertising, but as one consultant put it, "Negative advertising works." Negative ads can backfire, however, when there are three or more candidates in the race, a typical state of affairs in the early presidential primaries. If one candidate attacks another, the attacker as well as the candidate who is attacked may come to be viewed negatively by the public. A candidate who "goes negative" may thus unintentionally boost the chances of a third candidate who is not part of the exchange.

The Kentucky Opportunity Coalition runs an ad showing Senator Mitch McConnell (R., Ky.) shaking hands with a Vietnam veteran. The underlying footage, from McConnell's campaign Web site, is freely available to anyone. The law prohibits candidates from coordinating with outside support groups, but this activity does not appear to qualify. *Should it?*

Management of News Coverage. Using political advertising to get a message across to the public is a very expensive tactic. Coverage by the news media, however, is free. The campaign simply needs to ensure that coverage takes place. In recent years, campaign managers have shown increasing sophistication in creating newsworthy events for journalists to cover.

The campaign staff uses several methods to try to influence the quantity and type of coverage the campaign receives. First, the staff understands the technical aspects of media coverage—camera angles, necessary equipment, timing, and deadlines—and plans political events to accommodate the press. Second, the campaign organization is aware that political reporters and their sponsors—networks, newspapers, or blogs—are in competition for the best stories and can be manipulated through the granting of favors, such as a personal interview with the candidate. Third, the scheduler in the campaign has the important task of planning events that will be photogenic and interesting enough for the evening news.

A related goal, although one that is more difficult to attain, is to convince reporters that a particular interpretation of an event is true. Today, the art of putting the appropriate **spin** on a story or event is highly developed. Press advisers, often referred to as **spin doctors,** try to convince journalists that the advisers' interpretations of the political events are correct. For example, the Obama administration and the Republicans engaged in a major spinning duel over the Affordable Care Act (Obamacare) in 2013 and 2014. The health insurance Web site organized by the federal government was dysfunctional for months, which meant that initial signups for insurance were quite low. By April 2014, however, applications substantially exceeded predictions due to a last-minute rush to sign up. The Republican spin pointed to the initial problems. The Democratic spin emphasized the number of persons who were eventually able to obtain insurance. Journalists have begun to report on the different spins placed on events and on how candidates and office-holders try to manipulate news coverage.

Going for the Knockout Punch—Televised Presidential Debates. In presidential elections, perhaps just as important as political advertisements and general news coverage is the performance of the candidate in televised presidential debates. After the first such debate in 1960, in which John Kennedy, the young senator from Massachusetts, took on the vice president of the United States, Richard Nixon, candidates became aware of the great potential of television for changing the momentum of a campaign. In general, challengers have much more to gain from debating than do incumbents. Challengers hope that the incumbent will make a mistake in the debate and undermine the "presidential" image. Incumbent presidents are loath to debate their challengers because it puts their opponents on an equal footing with them, but the debates have become so widely anticipated that it is difficult for an incumbent to refuse to participate.

The 2011–2012 Republican Primary Debates. Presidential candidates have often debated during primary election campaigns. Traditionally, such debates have not attracted much interest, but the Republican presidential primary race in 2011 and 2012 was a dramatic exception. Between May 2011 and March 2012, the Republicans held twenty-seven debates, shown on such networks as ABC, CNN, Fox News, and NBC. The number of viewers frequently exceeded 5 million, and many more watched the debates in reruns and online.

The debates shaped the course of the Republican campaigns in 2011. The political context was the belief of many strong conservatives that Mitt Romney, the eventual winner, was not really one of them. Romney, therefore, was challenged by a series of anti-Romney candidates. Texas governor Rick Perry, African American businessman Herman Cain, former U.S. House Speaker Newt Gingrich, and former Pennsylvania senator Rick Santorum each had his day in the sun. All of these candidacies proved to be flawed in one way or another, however, and in the end Romney prevailed without great difficulty.

A family watches the 1960 Kennedy-Nixon debates on television. After the debate, TV viewers thought Kennedy had won, whereas radio listeners thought Nixon had the edge. *Why have televised presidential debates become major media events?*

> **Spin**
> An interpretation of campaign events or election results that is favorable to the candidate's campaign strategy.
>
> **Spin Doctor**
> A political campaign adviser who tries to convince journalists of the truth of a particular interpretation of events.

Obama-Romney Debates. The 2012 presidential debates in October turned out to be among the more consequential debates in years. Obama's team had tried to present Romney as a rich financier who cared only for the interests of other wealthy Americans. Through September, this characterization appeared to be damaging Romney's campaign. In the first of three debates, however, Romney was successful in presenting himself as compassionate, reasonable, and above all, moderate. Obama, meanwhile, gave the appearance of being half asleep. Obama did much better in the next two debates. Romney's performance in the first debate tightened up the elections for a time, but by Election Day the effects had largely worn off.

The Internet, Blogging, and Podcasting

Today, the campaign staff of every candidate running for a significant political office includes an Internet campaign strategist—a professional hired to create and maintain the campaign Web site, social media accounts, blogs, and podcasts (blogs and podcasts will be discussed shortly). The work of this strategist includes designing a user-friendly and attractive Web site for the candidate, managing the candidate's e-mail, Twitter, and Facebook communications; tracking campaign contributions made through the site, hiring bloggers to push the candidate's agenda on the Web, and monitoring Web sites for favorable or unfavorable comments or video clips about the candidate.

Additionally, all major interest groups in the United States now use the Internet to promote their causes. Prior to elections, various groups engage in issue advocacy from their Web sites. At little or no cost, they can promote positions taken by favored candidates and solicit contributions.

Online Fund-raising. Two politicians stand out as pioneers of online fund-raising. The first of these was Ron Paul, a Republican member of Congress from Texas, who ran for president several times on a strongly libertarian platform. Paul's support was especially strong among heavy Internet users, and these supporters introduced the idea of the *moneybomb.* The San José *Mercury News* described a moneybomb as "a one-day fund-raising frenzy." Two moneybomb events in late 2007 raised more than $10 million for the Paul campaign.

Paul's fund-raising success was overshadowed in 2008, however, by Barack Obama's online fund-raising machine. In that year, Obama obliterated every political fund-raising and spending record in history. In total, his campaign raised more than $650 million, much of it in small donations solicited through the Internet. A key characteristic of successful Internet campaigns has been decentralization. The nature of the Internet has allowed candidates to assemble thousands of individual activists who serve as fund-raisers.

Obama was even more dependent on small Internet donations in 2012 than he had been in 2008, in part because his campaign rhetoric aimed at the wealthy led to a precipitous drop in donations from high-income individuals. Romney's campaign, in contrast, found it easy to collect large donations but initially had difficulties with smaller donors.

Blogging. Within the past few years, politicians have also felt obligated to post regular blogs on their Web

An image from the *New York Times* Web site. *Does it make sense for the* Times *to charge for access to its site?*

sites. The word **blog** comes from *Web log,* a regular updating of one's ideas at a specific Web site. Of course, many people besides politicians are also posting blogs. Not all of the millions of blogs posted daily are political in nature. Many are, though, and they can have a dramatic influence on events, giving rise to the term *blogosphere politics.*

Blogs are clearly threatening the mainstream media. They can be highly specialized, highly political, and highly entertaining. And they are cheap. The *Washington Post* requires thousands of employees, paper, and ink to generate its offline product and incurs delivery costs to get it to readers. A larger blogging organization such as Vox can generate its content with only about twenty reporters.

Blogs versus Magazines. Originally, blogs were the work of a single individual, describing that person's opinions and experiences. The Conscience of a Liberal, Paul Krugman's blog on economics and politics, is a modern example. Today, however, most of the highly popular political blogs are team efforts. In many cases, they were founded by an individual blogger who later hired additional contributors. It can be hard to distinguish such blogs from online magazines, given that a magazine and a team blog both contain original content from multiple writers. Indeed, some sites are divided into two parts: one designated as a magazine and the other as a collection of blog posts.

A further complication is the difficulty in distinguishing between a blog with multiple authors and an aggregation site. The largest political site on the Web, the Huffington Post, is visited by more than 100 million individuals each month. The Huffington Post (www. huffingtonpost.com) gained fame as an aggregator of material from mainstream news organizations, but today its 850 employees generate large amounts of original material. The site is also famous for its veritable army of unpaid bloggers. Is the "HuffPost" an aggregator, an online newsmagazine, or a blogging site? It appears to be all three. We list a variety of interesting blogs in Table 10–1 that follows.

Table 10–1 ▶ **Selected Political Blog Sites**
Which of these sites could also be called an online magazine?

Progressive	
The American Prospect	prospect.org
The Conscience of a Liberal	https://twitter.com/nytimeskrugman
The Daily Kos	www.dailykos.com
Mother Jones	motherjones.com
TalkingPointsMemo	talkingpointsmemo.com
ThinkProgress	thinkprogress.org
Conservative	
American Thinker	www.americanthinker.com
Breitbart News Network	www.breitbart.com
The Daily Caller	dailycaller.com
National Review Online	www.nationalreview.com
PJ Media	pjmedia.com
Townhall	townhall.com

Blog
From Web log. A Web site where an individual or group posts regular updates on their ideas or experiences.

Podcasting
A method of distributing multimedia files, such as audio or video files, for downloading onto mobile devices or personal computers.

Comments. Many, but not all, blog posts—and also articles in online newspapers and magazines—allow readers to comment on the post or article. Comments can be a way to build a community around a small blog, enhancing its influence. Sites with a huge readership drawn from the general public, however, experience problems with comments. They can quickly deteriorate into "flame wars" in which partisans of the left and right insult each other instead of entering useful observations. Even a blog with a relatively small readership, such as The Reality-Based Community (www.samefacts.com), can face this problem if it deals with a controversial topic such as policies toward illegal drugs. Short of shutting down the comments sections, one solution is to *moderate* the comments—to publish only those comments approved by a moderator. For most blogs, however, this procedure involves an unacceptable amount of effort.

Podcasting. Once blogs—written words—became well established, it was only a matter of time before they ended up as spoken words. Enter **podcasting,** so called because the first Internet-communicated spoken blogs were downloaded onto Apple's iPods. Podcasts, though, can be heard on a computer or downloaded onto any portable listening device. Podcasting can also include videos. Hundreds of thousands of podcasts are now generated every day. Basically, anyone who has an idea can easily create a podcast and make it available for downloading. Like blogs, podcasting threatens traditional media sources. Publications that sponsor podcasts find it hard to make them profitable.

Although politicians have been slower to adopt this form of communication, many now are using podcasts to keep in touch with their constituents, and there are currently tens of thousands of political podcasts.

■ **Learning Outcome 3:** Explain the relationship between the government and the media, and in particular the Internet.

Government Regulation of the Media

The United States has one of the freest presses in the world. Nonetheless, regulation of the media, particularly of the electronic media, does exist. We discussed some aspects of

2014 Elections

The Media and the Elections

Social media continue to play a growing role in the political process. According to Pew Research, voters are almost three times as likely to track candidates on social media as during the 2010 midterms. Smart phones are now used by 28 percent of voters to keep up with election news. Voters who are active online are also more likely to engage in activities such as donating money or volunteering. Further, according to the *Washington Post*, almost half of all "persuadable" voters said what they read online affected their vote. Republicans tend to prefer Facebook, while Democrats dominate Twitter.

Increased political polarization has a major effect on where liberals and conservatives get their news. According to another Pew study, 47 percent of consistent conservatives name Fox News as their top source of information about government and politics. Among liberals, favorite sources were more diverse, with CNN, National Public Radio, MSNBC, and the *New York Times* all frequently mentioned. Some sources, such as the London *Economist* and the *Wall Street Journal*, were rated as trustworthy by liberals and conservatives. In contrast, the Buzzfeed Web site was rated untrustworthy by everyone.

this regulation in Chapter 4, when we examined First Amendment rights and the press. Another issue follows from concentrated ownership of the media.

Concentrated Ownership of the Media

Many rules by the Federal Communications Commission (FCC) have dealt with ownership of news media, such as how many TV stations a network can own. In 1996, Congress passed legislation that had far-reaching implications for the communications industry—the Telecommunications Act. The act ended the rule that kept telephone companies from entering the cable business and other communications markets. What this means is that a single corporation—whether Time Warner or Disney—can offer long-distance and local telephone services, cable television, satellite television, Internet services, and, of course, libraries of films and entertainment. The act opened the door to competition and led to more options for consumers, who now can choose among multiple competitors for all of these services delivered to the home. At the same time, it launched a race among competing companies to control media ownership.

Media Conglomerates. Many media outlets are now owned by corporate conglomerates. A single entity may own a television network; the studios that produce shows, news, and movies; and the means to deliver that content to the home via cable, satellite, or the Internet. The question to be faced in the future is how to ensure competition in the delivery of news so that citizens have access to multiple points of view from the media.

Today, all of the prime-time television networks are owned by major American corporations and are part of corporate conglomerates. The Turner Broadcasting/CNN network was purchased by a major corporation, Time Warner. Fox Broadcasting Company has always been a part of Rupert Murdoch's publishing and media empire. Many of these companies have also formed partnerships with computer software makers, such as Microsoft, for joint electronic-publishing ventures.

Rebekah Brooks was the editor of Britain's *News of the World* newspaper during a phone-hacking scandal. *Why would a newspaper want to engage in such hacking?*

The greatest concern advanced by observers of concentrated media ownership is that it could lead to a decline in democratic debate. Also, media owners might use their power to steer the national agenda in a direction that they prefer. Indeed, several news organizations have clear conservative or liberal viewpoints. Among the most famous and successful of these is Fox News, part of Rupert Murdoch's operation. Murdoch's U.S. newspapers and networks have not been shy about promoting conservative politics. Some observers, however, believe that the emergence of independent news Web sites, blogs, and podcasts provides an ample counterweight to the advocacy of media moguls.

Murdoch's dominance has been more of an issue in Britain, where newspapers, radio networks, and television networks owned by his News International enjoy a very large share of the total market. For years, politicians in all major British parties believed that it was potentially fatal to get on the wrong side of the Murdoch empire. In 2011, however, Murdoch's position was seriously undercut by a major scandal. Apparently, staff at Murdoch's *News of the World,* Britain's best-selling Sunday paper, illegally hacked into the cell phones of hundreds of people, including crime victims, celebrities, and members of the royal family. Bribery of police officers was also alleged. The *News of the World* was forced to close as a result of these revelations, and several News International executives faced criminal charges.

Government Control of Content

The First Amendment does not mention electronic media, which did not exist when the Bill of Rights was written. For many reasons, the

AP Photo

Internet Service Provider (ISP)
A company or organization that provides Internet connectivity to end users or to servers.

Network Neutrality
The principle that an ISP should treat all Internet traffic equally.

government has much greater control over electronic media than it does over print media. The Federal Communications Commission (FCC) regulates communications by radio, television, wire, and cable. For many years, the FCC has controlled the number of radio stations, even though technologically we could have many more radio stations than now exist. Also, the FCC created the environment in which for many decades the three major TV networks (NBC, CBS, and ABC) dominated broadcasting.

On the face of it, the First Amendment would seem to apply to all media. In fact, the United States Supreme Court has often been slow to extend free speech and free press guarantees to new media. For example, in 1915 the Court held that "as a matter of common sense," free speech protections did not apply to movies. Only in 1952 did the Court find that motion pictures were covered by the First Amendment.[3] In contrast, the Court extended full protection to the Internet almost immediately by striking down provisions of the 1996 Telecommunications Act.[4] For more details on government control of content in radio and television, see the section "Freedom of Expression" in Chapter 4.

The Issue of Network Neutrality

The Internet is widely regarded as a triumph of unregulated enterprise, but it has been tied to the federal government from the start. The Internet is directly descended from ARPAnet, a project of the Advanced Research Projects Agency within the Department of Defense. Initially, ARPAnet linked computers at four universities—the first message to cross the net was sent in October 1969 from UCLA to Stanford. Only in 1988 was the Internet opened up to commercial users.

Even though the federal government was responsible for the Internet's creation, Internet pioneers were remarkably successful in preventing the government from imposing regulations that might limit the freedom of users. For example, Web sites and communication services are largely exempt from responsibility for the actions of their users, just as a telephone company is not liable when users commit crimes using telephones.

Who Pays for the Internet? Almost all funding for the Internet comes from the individuals and organizations that connect to it. An individual or organization may purchase connectivity from an **Internet Service Provider (ISP)**. Your ISP then purchases connectivity from an intermediate ISP, which in turn purchases connectivity from an Internet *backbone*, often provided by a telephone company. The more you pay, the better your connection. A corporation such as Google or Netflix that provides huge volumes of net services through computers called *servers* will clearly have to buy massive amounts of connectivity. Funds flow in one direction: from the periphery—end users or servers—through ISPs to the backbones.

Network Neutrality. The principle of **network neutrality,** or net neutrality, is that an ISP should treat all traffic equally. It should not block or degrade access to Web sites, for example ones that compete with the ISP's own telephone or TV services. Nor should it create special "fast lanes" that allow favored content to load more quickly than the rest. The fundamental structure of the Internet has tended to enforce the network neutrality principle. If an ISP attempted to block access to a site, for example, angry users would switch to a different ISP. Congress has never written the network neutrality principle into law, however. Attempts by the executive branch to write net neutrality rules have been struck down by the courts, most recently in 2014.[5]

---

3. *Joseph Burstyn, Inc. v. Wilson*, 343 U.S. 495 (1952).
4. *Reno v. American Civil Liberties Union*, 521 U.S. 844 (1997).
5. *Verizon v. FCC*, 740 F.3d 623 (D.C. Cir. 2014).

Monopoly ISPs. Back in the days when people connected to the Internet using dial-up modems, users often had dozens of ISPs vying for their business. Today, however, for many customers high-speed broadband service is available only from a cable TV company such as Comcast that has a local monopoly, and cell phone providers such as Verizon Wireless. Secure in the knowledge that it would be difficult for its customers to switch to a different company, large ISPs have explored the possibility of charging services such as Netflix for expedited transit. Recently, in fact, Netflix agreed to pay for a special dedicated high-volume line connecting it with Comcast. Under these arrangements, Internet funding no longer flows only from the periphery toward the center, but also from one Internet customer to another.

"Welcome to 'All About the Media,' where members of the media discuss the role of the media in media coverage of the media."

Should Network Neutrality Be Enforced by Law? As a result, network neutrality has recently become a public issue. Given the attitude of the courts, enforcement of network neutrality in the future may require either new laws passed by Congress or a completely new regulatory approach by the FCC. Advocates of the principle contend that net neutrality has eased the creation of new services such as Facebook, YouTube, and Dropbox. Opponents argue that enforcing net neutrality will discourage investment in Internet infrastructure.

Some observers, however, worry less about monopoly ISPs or U.S. government regulation than about the impact of foreign governments on the Internet. We describe this issue in the *Which Side Are You On?* feature that follows.

Opinion and Bias in the Media

Almost every news operation has an opinion section. Traditionally, newspapers and other media have tried carefully to separate opinion pieces from "straight news." Newer media may blur the distinction. In recent years, many media observers have worried that opinion is "taking over" and displacing news sources that try to be objective. Many blogs, for example, are almost pure opinion, even if in the course of delivering that opinion they also provide some facts. Another media format in which opinion is dominant is talk radio, which we describe in the following section. A final concern is whether media that purport to report the facts, including network news, cable news, and newspaper Web sites, are free of bias.

■ **Learning Outcome 4:**
Discuss the question of opinion and bias in the mainstream media and alternative media such as talk radio.

Talk Radio

The most conspicuous characteristic of talk radio is that it is almost completely dominated by conservatives, many of whom are quite radical. Most of the top twenty radio talk shows feature conservative politics. None of the top talk-show hosts are liberal. Talk-show hosts do not pretend to be reporters or journalists. Rather, they are entertainment personalities who entertain their audiences with red-meat politics. Exaggeration for effect is typical, and language that would be unacceptable in other contexts is commonplace.

Repeal of the Fairness Doctrine. Talk radio as it exists today would be impossible if the FCC had not repealed the *fairness doctrine* in 1987. As we explained in Chapter 6, under the doctrine anyone holding a broadcast license had to present controversial issues of public importance in a way that was (in the view of the FCC) honest, equitable, and balanced. With such a rule, it would be almost impossible for a radio network to broadcast anything like the *Rush Limbaugh Show*, even if it were matched with a liberal counterpart.

COMPARE WITH YOUR PEERS
MindTap‾ **for American Government**

Access the Media and Politics Forum: Polling Activity—Fair and Balanced Media

Which Side Are You On?

Do Foreign Governments Threaten the Internet?

One of the major reasons that the Internet has experienced explosive worldwide growth is that in general, governments do not control it. To be sure, every country with an authoritarian regime tries, with more or less success, to control its citizens' Internet access. Witness China, home of the so-called Great Firewall of China. A huge number of foreign Web sites are blocked. Bloggers and tweeters can be certain that government censors are analyzing their political statements.

The one government that maintains some control of the Internet is the U.S. government, which makes sense given that it was the Internet's initial sponsor. The Internet Corporation for Assigned Names and Numbers (ICANN) is currently responsible to the U.S. Commerce Department. ICANN oversees the system of assigning Internet domain names and addresses worldwide. When the Obama administration announced in early 2014 that it would give up control of ICANN, a controversy erupted. Some argued that if the U.S. government did not control ICANN, foreign governments would take over. Is this a realistic danger?

The Edge of the Wedge

According to opponents of relinquishing any control of ICANN, the future of an open Internet would then be bleak. The fear is that if the United States were to give up control of the Internet naming system, a United Nations (UN) body such as the International Telecommunication Union (ITU) might assume control instead. The ITU, however, is controlled by governments. This includes authoritarian regimes such as China, Iran, and Russia. Such governments might try to ban Web site addresses of dissident groups. These governments have been able to keep their citizens from accessing unapproved Web sites, but currently they cannot undermine access to the Internet in other countries.

That might change if the ITU were involved—authoritarian governments could form a coalition to restrict access to the Internet. Already, the ITU has voted to let governments close off their own citizens' access to the global Internet. China and Russia want the ITU to ban anonymity on the Web and to tax international access to sites such as Google and Facebook. UN involvement in running the Internet threatens its very essence.

Much Ado about Nothing

Not everyone believes the end of the open Internet is just around the corner. ICANN gets much attention because non-technical people can understand its job of distributing names. Yet other Internet bodies may be more important. For example, the Internet Engineering Taskforce (IETF) a group mainly of engineers, develops standards for Internet protocols and is not affiliated with any government. The World Wide Web Consortium (3WC) is another non-governmental group that helps to maintain international standards for the Web. Still other groups help the Internet run fluidly and efficiently without government interference.

The Obama administration has responded to criticism of its plan to give up control of ICANN—criticism leveled by Democrats such as Bill Clinton as well as Republicans. The Commerce Department will now retain control for up to four years. If it does yield authority, it will be to a nongovernmental "geek squad" such as the IETF or the 3WC. The United States, the European Union, and even nations such as Brazil are united in opposing any role for the UN.

For Critical Analysis

How could UN control of the Internet threaten net neutrality?

The Talk-Radio Style Migrates to Television. Until recently, television networks, including cable networks, saw the rhetoric typical of talk-radio hosts as unacceptable. That sense of propriety has retreated in the last several years. Some credit the *Glenn Beck* show on Fox News for breaking down the barriers to uninhibited speech. Beck's emotional style and apocalyptic views helped make him one of the nation's most politically polarizing figures. Beck is no longer with Fox, but remains a significant radio and television personality. Another major radio host who has extended his reach to television is Sean Hannity.

The Impact of Talk Radio. It has been said that conservative talk radio was the Tea Party before there was a Tea Party movement. Certainly, talk radio has played a role in pushing the Republican Party to the right. Hosts such as Limbaugh and Michael Savage have devoted much energy to hunting *RINOs*, that is, "Republicans in Name Only."

As you will learn shortly, many conservatives believe that progressives dominate the "mainstream media." The overwhelming conservative dominance of talk radio, however, makes it harder to argue that the media as a whole has a liberal bias. No other media format can match the partisan vehemence of talk radio.

In 2009, after the Democratic sweep in the 2008 elections, a number of liberals raised the question of whether the fairness doctrine ought to be reinstated. President Obama and the Democratic leadership in Congress, however, quickly put an end to this notion. True, the Supreme Court has held that the fairness doctrine is constitutional.[6] Yet most Americans today would consider its reestablishment to be a serious violation of the right to free speech. Conservative talk radio, in short, is here to stay.

Bias in the Media

For decades, the contention that the mainstream media have a liberal **bias** has been repeated time and again. Bernard Goldberg, formerly a CBS broadcaster and now a commentator for Fox News, is among the most prominent of these critics. Goldberg argues that liberal bias, which "comes naturally to most reporters," has given viewers reason to distrust the big news networks.

A number of studies appear to back up this claim. For example, research at the University of Connecticut has shown that journalists consider themselves Democrats three times as often as they identify with the Republicans. A recent Gallup poll reports that 47 percent of the public thinks that the news media are too liberal, while 13 percent see the media as too conservative. These views are strongly associated with the politics of the respondent: 75 percent of Republicans believe the media are too liberal, while only 20 percent of Democrats think that is true.

Other observers claim that, on the whole, the media actually have a conservative bias, especially in their coverage of economic issues. In an analysis of visual images on television news, political scientist Maria Elizabeth Grabe concluded that "image bites" (as opposed to sound bites) more often favor the Republicans.[7]

Other Theories of Media Bias. Some writers have concluded that the mainstream media are really biased toward stories that involve conflict and drama—the better to attract viewers. Still others contend the media are biased against "losers," and when a candidate falls behind in a race, his or her press quickly becomes negative. The Republican primary campaigns in 2011 and 2012 provided many opportunities for candidates to complain about such bias, as one candidate after another shot up in the polls, only to be rejected by opinion poll respondents a month or two later.

AP Photo/Dr. Scott M. Lieberman

Conservative radio talk-show host and Fox TV personality Sean Hannity has increased his audience regularly. *What could be the reason conservatives dominate the talk radio format?*

Bias
An inclination or preference that interferes with impartial judgment.

---

6. *Red Lion Broadcasting v. FCC*, 395 U.S. 367 (1969).
7. Maria Elizabeth Grabe and Erik Page Bucy, *Image Bite Politics: News and the Visual Framing of Elections* (New York: Oxford University Press, 2009).

Why Should You Care about...

The Media?

Television, print media, and the Internet provide a wide range of choices for Americans who want to stay informed. Still, a substantial amount of what you read and see is colored either by the subjectivity of editors and bloggers or by the demands of profit making. Even when journalists themselves are relatively successful in an attempt to remain objective, they will of necessity give airtime to politicians and interest group representatives who are far from impartial. You need the ability to determine what motivates the players in the political game and to what extent they are "shading" the news or even propagating outright lies. You also need to determine which news sources are reliable.

did you know?

The career guidance Web site Career Cast.com has rated "newspaper reporter" as the fifth-worst job available. It was the lowest-ranking job that did not require hard physical labor. "Software engineer" won for best job.

A Scientific Test for Bias? Communications professor Tim Groeling has devised a test for media bias that may provide accurate results regardless of whether political events favor the Democrats or the Republicans. He has examined how ABC, CBS, NBC, and Fox News reported public opinion polls that assessed the job performances of Democratic president Bill Clinton and Republican president George W. Bush. Confirming what many suspect, Groeling found that ABC, CBS, and NBC gave Clinton more favorable coverage than Bush—and that Fox gave Bush more favorable coverage than Clinton.[8]

Bias and Professionalism. While many journalists may be Democrats at heart, most operate under a code of professional ethics that dictates "objectivity" and a commitment to the truth. Journalists may not always succeed in living up to such a code, but it helps that it exists.

As we have observed, many media outlets have an explicit political point of view. This is especially common in the blogosphere, but it is true of some cable news channels as well. Fox News, for example, takes pride in avoiding what it sees as the liberal bias of the mainstream media.

Some progressives, however, have accused Fox and other conservative outlets of allowing politics to interfere with their objectivity. They argue that conservatives find liberal bias even in reporting that is scrupulously accurate. In the words of humorist Stephen Colbert, "Reality has a well-known liberal bias." An example was the widespread refusal of conservative media to believe opinion polls that showed Barack Obama leading in the 2012 presidential race.

Other observers contend that the issue of media bias is declining in importance due to the rise of the Internet. Today's technologically savvy media consumers can easily find information from a wide variety of sources, mainstream and alternative, liberal and conservative. The best answer to bias may be a willingness to consult a wide range of sources.

---

8. Tim Groeling, "Who's the Fairest of Them All? An Empirical Test for Partisan Bias on ABC, CBS, NBC, and Fox News," *Presidential Studies Quarterly*, December 2008, p. 631.

Bloomberg via Getty Images

The four major networks, including NBC, report the news throughout every 24-hour cycle. *Why is the importance of network news going to diminish in the future?*

How You Can Make a Difference

To become a critical news consumer, you must develop a critical eye and ear.

- For example, ask yourself what stories are given prominence at the top of a newspaper Web site.

- For a contrast to most daily papers, visit the sites of publications with explicit points of view, such as the *National Review* (search on "national review") or the *New Republic* (search on "tnr"). Take note of how they handle stories.

- Sources such as blogs often have strong political preferences, and you should try to determine what these are. Does a blog merely give opinions, or does it back up its arguments with data? It is possible to select anecdotes to support almost any argument—does a particular anecdote represent typical circumstances, or is it a rare occurrence highlighted to make a point?

- Watching the evening news can be far more rewarding if you look at how much the news depends on video effects. You will note that stories on the evening news tend to be no more than three minutes long, that stories with excellent videos get more attention, and that considerable time is taken up with "happy talk" or human interest stories.

- Another way to critically evaluate news coverage is to compare how the news is covered by different outlets. For example, you might compare the coverage of events on Fox News with the presentation on MSNBC, or compare the radio commentary of Rush Limbaugh with that of National Public Radio's *All Things Considered.*

- Fairness and Accuracy in Reporting is a media watchdog with a strong liberal viewpoint. Visit it at fair.org.

- Accuracy in Media takes a combative conservative position on media issues. Find its site at www.aim.org.

Key Terms

aggregator 293
bias 305
blog 299
content provider 293

Internet Service Provider (ISP) 302
network neutrality 302
podcasting 300

priming 291
public agenda 291
sound bite 295

spin 297
spin doctor 297

Chapter Summary

Learning Outcome 1 The media are enormously important in American politics today. They perform a number of functions, including (a) entertainment, (b) news reporting, (c) identifying public problems, (d) socializing new generations, (e) providing a political forum, and (f) making profits.

Learning Outcome 2 The political influence of the media is most obvious during political campaigns. Today's campaigns use political advertising and expert management of news coverage. For presidential candidates, how they appear in presidential debates is of major importance. Internet blogs, podcasts, and Web sites such as YouTube are transforming today's political campaigns.

Learning Outcome 3 Despite the First Amendment and our free speech traditions, the U.S. government has always engaged in at least some regulation of the media. Past regulation has sought to address concentrated ownership and the content of broadcast media. A current issue is whether the government should enforce net neutrality on the Internet.

Learning Outcome 4 Frequently, the mainstream media have been accused of liberal bias, although some observers contend that these accusations result from true stories that offend conservatives. Other possible media biases include a bias against political "losers." For many, the dominance of opinion over reporting in blogs and on talk radio is also a matter of concern.

Master the concept of Media and Politics with MindTap™ for American Government

REVIEW MindTap™ **for American Government**
Access Key Term Flashcards for Chapter 10.

STAY CURRENT MindTap™ **for American Government**
Access the KnowNow blog and customized RSS for updates on current events.

TEST YOURSELF MindTap™ **for American Government**
Take the Wrap It Up Quiz for Chapter 10.

STAY FOCUSED MindTap™ **for American Government**
Complete the Focus Activities for Media and Politics.

Additional Resources

The Internet offers great opportunities to those who want to access the news. All of the major news organizations, including radio and television stations and newspapers, are online. Even foreign sources can now be accessed online within a few seconds. To gain an international perspective on the news, you can check foreign news Web sites in English. The following sites all have broad worldwide coverage:

Online Resources

- For the British Broadcasting Corporation, go to www.bbc.com.
- China Network Television is surprisingly informative, given that it is owned by a Communist-controlled government. You can check out its biases at english.cntv.cn.
- For the Japan Broadcasting Corporation, visit www3.nhk.or.jp/nkhworld.
- Al Jazeera is the Arab world's number-one television news network. See it at www.aljazeera.com.
- The German magazine *Der Spiegel* is online at www.spiegel.de/international.

Books

Brock, George. *Out of Print: Newspapers, Journalism and the Business of News in the Digital Age.* Philadelphia: Kogan Page, 2013. Brock examines the past, present, and future of a fragile industry battling a perfect storm of falling circulation, reduced advertising revenue, and free news aggregators. He argues that despite all the problems, journalism can flourish in the new communications age. Brock heads the Graduate School of Journalism at London's City University.

McCombs, Maxwell. *Setting the Agenda: Mass Media and Public Opinion.* Malden, Mass.: Polity, 2014. McCombs, a professor at the University of Texas, describes the mass media's important and often controversial role in determining which topics receive public attention.

Schiffrin, Anya, ed. *Global Muckraking: 100 Years of Investigative Journalism from Around the World.* New York: The New Press, 2014. This groundbreaking book by a noted journalist presents key examples of world-changing reporting, spanning one hundred years and every continent. Vivid writing portrays a century of struggle for basic human rights in Argentina, China, India, Nigeria, Ukraine, and many other nations.

Video

All the President's Men—A film, produced by Warner Bros. in 1976, starring Dustin Hoffman and Robert Redford as the two *Washington Post* reporters, Carl Bernstein and Bob Woodward, who broke the story on the Watergate scandal. The film is an excellent portrayal of the *Washington Post* newsroom and the decisions that editors make in such situations.

The Social Network—In this 2010 Hollywood blockbuster, director David Fincher tells the story of Facebook founder Mark Zuckerberg. The film received eight Academy Award nominations and won three Oscars, including one for best adapted screenplay. It swept the Golden Globe awards, winning for best drama, best director, and best screenplay.

Quiz

Multiple Choice and Fill-Ins

Learning Outcome 1 Describe the different types of media and the changing roles that they play in American society.

1. Television remains a key medium in American politics because:
   a. it is the number-one source of information for older voters, who dominate the electorate.
   b. young people are avoiding the Internet as a source of information.
   c. television advertisements are not that expensive to buy.

2. A major problem facing newspapers today is that they cannot collect enough online _____ _____.

Learning Outcome 2 Summarize the impact of the media on the political process.

3. The first televised major-party presidential debates were held between:
   a. Democrat Lyndon Johnson and Republican Barry Goldwater in 1964.
   b. Democrat Jimmy Carter and Republican Ronald Reagan in 1980.
   c. Democrat John F. Kennedy and Republican Richard Nixon in 1960.

4. A campaign press advisor who tries to convince reporters of a particular interpretation of an event is called a _____ _____.

Learning Outcome 3 Explain the relationship between the government and the media, and in particular the Internet.

5. The United States Supreme Court found that the First Amendment applied to motion pictures:
   a. In 1915, shortly after the movies were invented.
   b. In 1952.
   c. In 1996, when it struck down provisions of the Telecommunications Act.

6. The principle that all traffic on the Internet should be treated equally is called _____ _____.

Learning Outcome 4 Discuss the question of opinion and bias in the mainstream media and alternative media such as talk radio.

7. Critics of the mainstream media have often accused it of exhibiting which of the following forms of bias:
   a. bias against conservatives, bias against losers, and bias in favor of conflict and drama.
   b. bias against Democrats, bias in favor of religion, and bias in favor of whoever is president.
   c. bias against science, bias against entertainment figures, and bias in favor of minority group members.

8. For more than two decades, the most popular conservative radio talk-show host has been _____ _____.

Essay Questions

1. Individuals who respond to blog posts sometimes enter comments that are deliberately designed to foster disruption. Why might people engage in such behavior? (Consider also the prevalence of hostile and even threatening responses to posts by women on controversial topics.)

2. Conservatives have long accused traditional media outlets of having a liberal bias. Are they correct? If so, to what degree? Regardless of whether this particular accusation is correct, what other kinds of bias might affect the reporting of prominent journalists? To the extent that the press exhibits political bias, what factors might cause this bias?

The Congress

11

Schoolchildren watch as the space shuttle *Discovery* makes its last flight—a fly-by over the Capitol building atop a 747. The shuttle was then retired to the Smithsonian's Udvar Hazy Center in Virginia.

Linda Davidson/The *Washington Post* via Getty Images

The five learning outcomes below are designed to help improve your understanding of this chapter. After reading this chapter, you should be able to:

- **Learning Outcome 1:** Describe the various roles played by Congress and the constitutional basis of its powers.
- **Learning Outcome 2:** Explain some of the differences between the House and the Senate and some of the privileges enjoyed by members of Congress.
- **Learning Outcome 3:** Examine the implications of apportioning House seats.
- **Learning Outcome 4:** Describe the committee structure of the House and the Senate and the key leadership positions in each chamber.
- **Learning Outcome 5:** Discuss the process by which a bill becomes law and how the federal government establishes its budget.

▶ **WATCH & LEARN** MindTap® for American Government

Watch a brief "What Do You Know?" video summarizing The Congress.

What If...

We Used Proportional Representation to Elect the House?

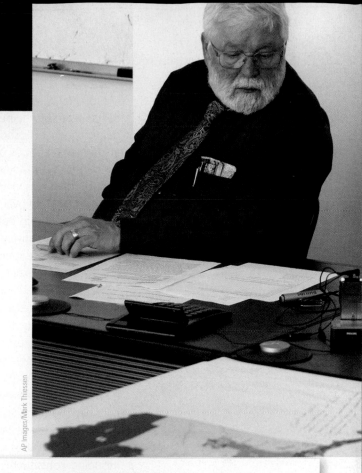

AP Images/Mark Thiessen

BACKGROUND

It used to be that Americans chose their representatives. Today, though, representatives seem to be choosing their voters, through *gerrymandering*. In most states, district lines are drawn after each census by party leaders in the state legislature. If one party dominates, it will maximize the number of safe seats for its members. As we have noted, 2010 was a good year for the Republicans—and 2010 was a census year. Republicans, therefore, controlled a majority of the state legislatures. As you might expect, the resulting gerrymanders favored the Republicans.

In 2012, Democratic candidates for the U.S. House in Pennsylvania received about 70,000 more votes than the Republicans. Still, Pennsylvania elected thirteen Republicans and only five Democrats. Nationally, the Republicans kept control of the U.S. House even though they received fewer votes overall than the Democrats. In other years, the Democrats have been responsible for their own egregious gerrymanders. Such outcomes have caused some to call for nonpartisan state boards to draw congressional districts. There is another solution, however, used around the world.

WHAT IF WE USED PROPORTIONAL REPRESENTATION TO ELECT THE HOUSE?

Proportional representation (PR) is designed to ensure that the number of candidates elected from each major party matches the popular vote for that party. PR is an alternative to the pure "first-past-the-post" system used in Britain, Canada, and the United States. In our system, the candidate with the largest number of votes—a *plurality*—always wins. If a party with substantial support is in the minority everywhere, it will elect no representatives.

Many forms of PR exist, but let's look at one of the simplest. Congress could pass a law creating, say, two hundred new seats in the House. These seats would be distributed among the states as the Constitution requires, but no new districts would be created. Each of the new seats would be filled on a statewide basis. Voters would not fill these seats directly. Instead, the extra seats would be filled based on how many votes each party won in the *district* seats. (This plan would not yield perfect proportional representation, but it would be close.)

IMMEDIATE CONSEQUENCES

One result of such a system would be to make gerrymandering pointless. That, of course, is what PR is designed to do. A second result would be more Republicans elected from Democratic states,

A court forced Alaska to redo its state legislative districts in 2013.

and more Democrats from Republican ones. Some might hope that would have a moderating effect. If at-large candidates were selected in partisan primaries, though, they would probably resemble the district candidates. Another result is that a large state such as California would almost surely elect some Green and Libertarian candidates based on the statewide vote for these parties.

A BIGGER HOUSE

If we implemented PR by adding two hundred seats to the House, it would have 635 members, not 435. You might consider that a large chamber, but by international standards it is not. The British House of Commons has 650 members, the German Bundestag has 620, and the French National Assembly has 577. A U.S. House with 635 members would fit right in. One result: we might see more of our representatives, because there would be more of them.

For Critical Analysis

1. How would members of the existing House react to a proposal to substantially increase the size of their chamber?

2. Would a PR system such as the one described be constitutional? (Hint: See Clause 1, Section 4, Article I, of the Constitution.)

311

Constituent

A person represented by a legislator or other elected or appointed official.

Bicameralism

The division of a legislature into two separate assemblies.

Most Americans view Congress in a less-than-flattering light. In recent years, Congress has appeared to be deeply split, highly partisan in its conduct, and not very responsive to public needs. Polls show that recently, as few as 9 percent of the public have had a favorable opinion about Congress as a whole. In one poll, respondents rated traffic jams, root canal operations, and cockroaches more favorably than Congress. (Congress did beat Fidel Castro, meth labs, and the Ebola virus.) Yet individual members of Congress often receive much higher approval ratings from the voters in their districts. This is one of the paradoxes of the relationship between the people and Congress. Members of the public hold the institution in relatively low regard compared with the satisfaction they express with their individual representatives.

Part of the explanation for these seemingly contradictory appraisals is that members of Congress spend considerable time and effort serving their **constituents.** If the federal bureaucracy makes a mistake, the office of the constituent's senator or representative tries to resolve the issue. On a personal level, what most Americans see, therefore, is the work of these local representatives in their home states.

Congress, however, was created to work not just for local constituents but also for the nation as a whole. As shown in the chapter-opening *What If . . .* feature, changes might be possible in the way we elect members of Congress that could encourage members to consider the national interest more closely. Understanding the nature of the institution and the process of lawmaking is an important part of understanding how the policies that shape our lives are made. In this chapter, we describe the functions of Congress, including constituent service, representation, lawmaking, and oversight of the government. We review how the members of Congress are elected and how Congress organizes itself when it meets. We also examine how bills pass through the legislative process and become laws, and how the federal budget is established.

■ **Learning Outcome 1:**
Describe the various roles played by Congress and the constitutional basis of its powers.

The Nature and Functions of Congress

The founders of the American republic believed that the bulk of the power that would be exercised by a national government should be in the hands of the legislature. The leading role envisioned for Congress in the new government is apparent from its primacy in the Constitution. Article I deals with the structure, the powers, and the operation of Congress.

Bicameralism

The **bicameralism** of Congress—its division into two legislative houses—was in part the result of the Connecticut Compromise, which tried to balance the large-state population advantage, reflected in the House, and the small-state demand for equality in policy-making, which was satisfied in the Senate. Beyond that, the two chambers of Congress also reflected the social class biases of the founders. They wished to balance the interests and the numerical superiority of the common citizens with the property interests of the less numerous landowners, bankers, and merchants.

They achieved this goal by providing that members of the House of Representatives should be elected directly by "the People," whereas members of the Senate were to be chosen by the elected representatives sitting in state legislatures, who were more likely to be members of the elite. (The latter provision was changed in 1913 by the passage of the Seventeenth Amendment, which provides that senators are also to be elected directly by the people.)

did you know?

In 1856, South Carolina representative Preston Brooks attacked Senator Charles Sumner (R., Mass.) on the Senate floor. Sumner almost bled to death. Two days earlier, Sumner had delivered an intense anti-slavery speech in which he characterized the attacker's cousin, Senator Andrew Butler (D., S.C.), as a "pimp for slavery."

The logic of the bicameral Congress was reinforced by differences in length of tenure. Members of the House are required to face the electorate every two years, whereas senators can serve for a much more secure term of six years—even longer than the four-year term provided for the president. Furthermore, the senators' terms are staggered so that only one-third of the senators face the electorate every two years, along with all of the House members.

The bicameral Congress was designed to perform certain functions for the political system. These functions include lawmaking, representation, service to constituents, oversight (regulatory supervision), public education, and conflict resolution. Of these, the two most important and the ones that most often interfere with each other are lawmaking and representation.

The Lawmaking Function

The principal and most obvious function of any legislature is **lawmaking.** Congress is the highest elected body in the country charged with making binding rules for all Americans. This does not mean, however, that Congress initiates most of the ideas for legislation that it eventually considers. A majority of the bills that Congress acts on originate in the executive branch, and many other bills are traceable to interest groups and political party organizations. In dealing with legislation, members engage in compromise and *logrolling* (offering to support a fellow member's bill in exchange for that member's promise to support your bill in the future). Through such tactics, as well as debate and discussion, backers of legislation attempt to fashion a winning majority coalition.

Traditionally, logrolling often involved agreements to support another member's legislative **earmarks,** also known as *pork*. Earmarks are special provisions in legislation to set aside funds for projects that have not passed an impartial evaluation by agencies of the executive branch. (Normal spending projects pass through such evaluations.) Recent attempts to ban pork have not succeeded in eliminating the process altogether but have significantly reduced its frequency.

Lawmaking
The process of establishing the legal rules that govern society.

Earmarks
Special provisions in legislation to set aside funds for projects that have not passed an impartial evaluation by agencies of the executive branch. Also known as *pork*.

Representation
The function of members of Congress as elected officials representing the views of their constituents as well as larger national interests.

The Representation Function

Representation includes both representing the desires and demands of the constituents in the member's home district or state and representing larger national interests, such as the nation's security or the environment. Because the interests of constituents in a specific district may be at odds with the demands of national policy, the representation function is often a source of conflict for individual lawmakers—and sometimes for Congress as a whole. For example, although it may be in the interest of the nation to reduce defense spending by closing military bases, such closures are not in the interest of the states and districts that will lose jobs and local spending. Every legislator faces votes that set local representational issues against lawmaking realities.

How should the legislators fulfill the representation function? There are several views on how this task should be accomplished.

Senator Elizabeth Warren (D., Mass.) listens as then-Federal Reserve chair Ben Bernanke answers a question at a hearing of the Senate Banking, Housing, and Urban Affairs Committee. *Why might Warren's strong criticisms of banks be popular?*

Pete Marovich/Bloomberg via Getty Images

Trustee

A legislator who acts according to her or his conscience and the broad interests of the entire society.

Instructed Delegate

A legislator who is an agent of the voters who elected him or her and who votes according to the views of constituents regardless of personal beliefs.

Casework

Personal work for constituents by members of Congress.

Ombudsperson

A person who hears and investigates complaints by private individuals against public officials or agencies. (From the Swedish word *ombudsman*, meaning "representative.")

Oversight

The process by which Congress follows up on laws it has enacted to ensure that they are being enforced and administered in the way Congress intended.

The Trustee View of Representation. One approach to the question of how representation should be achieved is that legislators should act as **trustees** of the broad interests of the entire society. They should vote against the narrow interests of their constituents if their conscience and their perception of national needs so dictate. For example, in 2011 Congress approved trade agreements with Colombia, Panama, and South Korea, despite the widely held belief that such agreements cost Americans jobs.

The Instructed-Delegate View of Representation. Directly opposed to the trustee view of representation is the notion that members of Congress should behave as **instructed delegates.** That is, they should mirror the views of the majority of the constituents who elected them. For this approach to work, however, we must assume that constituents actually have well-formed views on the issues that are decided in Congress and, further, that they have clear-cut preferences about these issues. Neither condition is likely to be satisfied very often.

Generally, most legislators hold neither a pure trustee view nor a pure instructed-delegate view. Typically, they combine both perspectives in a pragmatic mix.

Service to Constituents Individual members of Congress are expected by their constituents to act as brokers between private citizens and the imposing, often faceless federal government. This function of providing service to constituents usually takes the form of **casework.** The legislator and her or his staff spend a considerable portion of their time in casework activities, such as tracking down a missing Social Security payment, explaining the meaning of particular bills to people who may be affected by them, promoting a local business interest, or interceding with a regulatory agency on behalf of constituents who disagree with proposed agency regulations.

Legislators and many analysts of congressional behavior regard this **ombudsperson** role as an activity that strongly benefits the members of Congress. A government characterized by a large, confusing bureaucracy and complex public programs offers innumerable opportunities for legislators to come to the assistance of (usually) grateful constituents.

did you know?

Fewer than three in ten people can name the House member from their district, and fewer than half can name even one of the two senators from their state.

The Oversight Function

Oversight of the bureaucracy is essential if the decisions made by Congress are to have any force. **Oversight** is the process by which Congress follows up on the laws it has enacted to ensure that they are being enforced and administered in the way Congress intended. This is done by holding committee hearings and investigations, changing the size of an agency's budget, and cross-examining high-level presidential nominees to head major agencies.

Senators and representatives traditionally have seen their oversight function as a critically important part of their legislative activities. In part, oversight is related to the concept of constituency service, particularly when Congress investigates alleged arbitrariness or wrongdoing by bureaucratic agencies.

A problem with oversight is that it has become entangled in partisan politics. During the past two decades, members of Congress have tended to ease up on oversight whenever the president is of their political party. In contrast, oversight can become intense, and even excessive, when the president faces a chamber of Congress that is controlled by the other party. For example, in 2014 the Republicans launched a series of investigations of the Obama administration. One was based on the belief that the administration had deliberately targeted conservative groups for inspection by the Internal Revenue Service. Another sought to identify improper conduct during and after an attack on the U.S. consulate in Benghazi, Libya, in which four Americans were killed.

The Public-Education Function

Educating the public is a function that Congress performs whenever it holds public hearings, exercises oversight of the bureaucracy, or engages in committee and floor debate on such major issues and topics as immigration, oil pipelines, and the concerns of small businesses. In so doing, Congress presents a range of viewpoints on pressing national questions. Congress also decides what issues will come up for discussion and decision. This **agenda setting** is a major facet of its public-education function.

The Conflict-Resolution Function

Congress is commonly seen as an institution for resolving conflicts within American society. Organized interest groups and spokespersons for different racial, religious, economic, and ideological interests look on Congress as an access point for airing their grievances and seeking help. This puts Congress in the position of trying to resolve the differences among competing points of view by passing laws to accommodate as many interested parties as possible. To the extent that Congress meets pluralist expectations in accommodating competing interests, it tends to build support for the entire political process. Failure, however, tends to bring the political process into disrepute.

The Powers of Congress

The Constitution is both highly specific and extremely vague about the powers that Congress may exercise. The first seventeen clauses of Article I, Section 8, specify most of the **enumerated powers** of Congress—that is, powers expressly given to that body.

Enumerated Powers. The enumerated, or expressed, powers of Congress include the right to:

- Impose a variety of taxes, including tariffs on imports.
- Borrow funds.
- Regulate interstate commerce and international trade.
- Establish procedures for naturalizing citizens.
- Make laws regulating bankruptcies.
- Coin (and print) currency, and regulate its value.
- Establish standards of weights and measures.
- Punish counterfeiters.
- Establish post offices and post roads.
- Regulate copyrights and patents.
- Establish the federal court system.
- Punish illegal acts on the high seas.
- Declare war.
- Raise and regulate an army and a navy.
- Call up and regulate the state militias to enforce laws, to suppress insurrections, and to repel invasions.
- Govern the District of Columbia.

The most important of the domestic powers of Congress, listed in Article I, Section 8, are the rights to impose taxes, to spend, and to regulate commerce. The most important foreign policy power is the power to declare war. Other sections of the

Agenda Setting
Determining which public-policy questions will be debated or considered.

Enumerated Power
A power specifically granted to the national government by the Constitution. The first seventeen clauses of Article I, Section 8, specify most of the enumerated powers of Congress.

COMPARE WITH YOUR PEERS
MindTap‾ for American Government

Access the Congress Forum: Polling Activity—The Power to Declare War

Daniel Mihailescu/AFP/Getty Images

U.S. soldiers attend the opening ceremony of a U.S. military transit center in Romania in 2014. The center supports the movement of U.S. Army personnel into and out of Afghanistan and other European and Central Asian operating areas. *What powers does Congress have over the use of the U.S. military?*

Constitution allow Congress to establish rules for its own members, to regulate the electoral college, and to override a presidential veto. Congress may also regulate the extent of the Supreme Court's authority to review cases decided by the lower courts, regulate relations among states, and propose amendments to the Constitution.

Powers of the Senate. Some functions are restricted to one chamber. The Senate must advise on, and consent to, the ratification of treaties and must accept or reject presidential nominations of ambassadors, Supreme Court justices, other federal judges, and "all other Officers of the United States." But the Senate may delegate to the president or lesser officials the power to make lower-level appointments.

These specific powers granted to the Senate mean that the Senate is a more powerful chamber than the House. The United States is unique among the world's economically advanced nations in that its "upper house"—the Senate—is more powerful than the "lower house." In every nation with a parliamentary system, the lower house in effect chooses the nation's chief executive officer, the prime minister. We describe a few of the world's upper houses in the *Beyond Our Borders* feature that follows.

Constitutional Amendments. Amendments to the Constitution provide for other congressional powers. Congress must certify the election of a president and a vice president or itself choose those officers if no candidate has a majority of the electoral vote (Twelfth Amendment). It may levy an income tax (Sixteenth Amendment) and determine who will be acting president in case of the death or incapacity of the president or vice president (Twentieth Amendment and Twenty-fifth Amendment).

Beyond Our Borders

The Exceptional Power of the U.S. Senate

Political scientists refer to the U.S. Senate as the "upper house" of Congress. Each senator represents an entire state and is one out of only a hundred, so he or she commands more prestige and press than a representative. The Senate is also more powerful than the "lower house"—the House of Representatives. The Senate must approve treaties. It advises and consents to presidential appointments. The House does not have such powers. In most of the world, however, the "lower house" is far more powerful than the upper one. (Latin America is the one region of the world where the U.S. model dominates.) Consider some examples:

• Canada has a Senate, but it mainly revises legislation passed by the lower house, the House of Commons. Only on rare occasions does it reject such bills altogether. Its seats are entirely filled by appointment—members are often former cabinet members and provincial leaders.
• In Britain, the House of Lords is almost powerless. Until 1958, all seats were inherited, thereby giving that body no democratic legitimacy. Finally, in 1999, all but ninety-two of the hereditary peers were expelled, and today, most members are appointed "life peers." The Lords are limited to making minor improvements to bills passed by the House of Commons.
• The senate in France, which is elected by local government officials, has an excellent wine cellar, but that is about it. When Charles de Gaulle became French president in 1959, he wondered aloud about the senate: "What is that little thing?"

For Critical Analysis

Why is the Senate so powerful in the United States?

The Necessary and Proper Clause. Beyond these numerous specific powers, Congress enjoys the right under Clause 18 of Article I, Section 8 (the "elastic," or "necessary and proper," clause), "to make all Laws which shall be necessary and proper for carrying into Execution the foregoing Powers [of Article I], and all other Powers vested by this Constitution in the Government of the United States, or in any Department or Officer thereof." As discussed in Chapter 3, this vague statement of congressional responsibilities has provided, over time, the basis for a greatly expanded national government. It has also constituted, at least in theory, a check on the expansion of presidential powers.

House–Senate Differences and Congressional Perks

Congress is composed of two markedly different—but co-equal—chambers. Although the Senate and the House of Representatives exist within the same legislative institution, each has developed certain distinctive features that clearly distinguish one from the other. A summary of these differences is given in Table 11–1 that follows.

Size and Rules

The central difference between the House and the Senate is simply that the House is much larger than the Senate. The House has 435 voting representatives, plus delegates from the District of Columbia, Puerto Rico, Guam, American Samoa, and the Virgin Islands, compared with just 100 senators. This size difference means that a greater number of formal rules are needed to govern activity in the House, whereas correspondingly looser procedures can be followed in the less-crowded Senate.

■ **Learning Outcome 2:** Explain some of the differences between the House and the Senate and some of the privileges enjoyed by members of Congress.

Table 11–1 ▶ **Differences between the House and the Senate**

Some of these differences are provided for in the Constitution, while others are not. *Can you tell which ones are from the Constitution?*

House	Senate
Members chosen from local districts	Members chosen from an entire state
Two-year term	Six-year term
Originally elected by voters	Originally (until 1913) elected by state legislatures
May impeach (indict) federal officials	May convict federal officials of impeachable offenses
Larger (435 voting members)	Smaller (100 members)
More formal rules	Fewer rules and restrictions
Debate limited	Debate extended
Less prestige and less individual notice	More prestige and more media attention
Originates bills for raising revenues	Has power to advise the president on, and to consent to, presidential appointments and treaties
Local or narrow leadership	National leadership
More partisan	Somewhat less party loyalty

Rules Committee

A standing committee of the House of Representatives that provides special rules under which specific bills can be debated, amended, and considered by the House.

Hastert Rule

A rule adopted by Republicans in the U.S. House, under which a Republican Speaker will not bring a measure to the floor for a vote unless it has the support of a majority of the Republican members.

Filibuster

The use of the Senate's tradition of unlimited debate as a delaying tactic to block a bill.

Reconciliation

A special rule that can be applied to budget bills sent from the House of Representatives to the Senate. Reconciliation measures cannot be filibustered.

This difference is most obvious in the rules governing debate on the floors of the two chambers. The Senate usually permits extended debate on all issues that arise before it. In contrast, the House generally operates with an elaborate system in which its **Rules Committee** proposes time limitations on debate for any bill, and a majority of the entire body accepts or modifies those suggested time limits. As a consequence of its stricter time limits on debate, the House, despite its greater size, often is able to act on legislation more quickly than the Senate.

An additional practice in the House that affects its ability to legislate is the **Hastert Rule,** which is named after a former Speaker. Under this rule, a Republican Speaker will not allow a bill to reach the floor for a vote unless it has the support of a "majority of the majority." That means that the Speaker will block a bill that could pass with votes from both parties if that bill is not supported by at least half of the Republican members. Although the Hastert Rule is a Republican concept, Democratic Speakers have also blocked legislation that did not have the support of a majority of the Democrats. Further, even Republican Speakers will violate the rule when it is absolutely necessary. Speaker John Boehner, for example, abandoned the Hastert Rule to end the government shutdown in October 2013.

As a consequence of the larger size of the House, representatives generally cannot achieve as much individual recognition and public prestige as can members of the Senate. Senators are better able to gain media exposure and to establish careers as spokespersons for large national constituencies.

Debate and Filibustering

The Senate tradition of the **filibuster,** or the use of unlimited debate as a blocking tactic, dates back to 1790.[1] In that year, a proposal to move the U.S. capital from New York to Philadelphia was stalled by such time-wasting maneuvers. This unlimited-debate tradition—which also existed in the House until 1811—is not absolute, however.

Cloture. Under Senate Rule 22, debate may be ended by invoking *cloture*. Cloture shuts off discussion on a bill. Amended in 1975 and 1979, Rule 22 states that debate may be closed off on a bill if sixteen senators sign a petition requesting it and if, after two days have elapsed, three-fifths of the entire membership (sixty votes, assuming no vacancies) vote for cloture. After cloture is invoked, each senator may speak on a bill for a maximum of one hour before a vote is taken.

Increased Use of the Filibuster. Traditionally, filibusters were rare, and the tactic was employed only on issues of principle. Filibustering senators spoke for many hours, sometimes reading names from a telephone book. By the twenty-first century, however, filibusters could be invoked without such speeches, and senators were threatening to filibuster almost every significant piece of legislation to come before the body. The threats were sufficient to create a new, ad hoc rule that important legislation needed the support of sixty senators, not fifty. As a result of the increased use of the filibuster, some senators have called for its abolition. We discuss that topic in this chapter's *Which Side Are You On?* feature that follows.

Reconciliation. An additional way of bypassing the filibuster is known as **reconciliation.** Budget bills sent from the House of Representatives to the Senate can be handled under special reconciliation rules that do not permit filibusters. Under the rules, reconciliation can be used *only* to handle budgetary matters. Also, in principle, the procedure is to be

did you know?

Felons are not barred from serving in Congress, though a chamber can expel a convicted member by a two-thirds vote.

---

1. *Filibuster* comes from a Spanish word for pirate, which in turn came from the Dutch term *vrijbuiter,* or freebooter. The word was first used in 1851 to accuse senators of pirating or hijacking debate.

Which Side Are You On?

Is It Time to Get Rid of the Filibuster?

It is not in the Constitution, but it is an important institution. It is the filibuster, and it follows from Senate Rule 22, which allows for unlimited debate. Throughout American history, senators could tie up the Senate's business by talking indefinitely. In 1975, Rule 22 was revised. Since that year, a vote by sixty senators is required to stop floor debate instead of the previous sixty-seven. A second significant change in Senate practice developed, however—today, senators don't actually have to *talk* to hold a filibuster. All they have to do to maintain a filibuster is to announce that a filibuster exists. The practical effect has been to create a new rule that all important legislation requires sixty votes in the Senate. Some want the filibuster abolished. Others do not agree.

The Filibuster Is Not Even Constitutional

Critics of the filibuster argue that it has no constitutional basis and implicitly violates many actual provisions of the Constitution. After all, the Constitution requires a *supermajority*—more than a simple majority—only for special situations such as ratifying treaties, proposing constitutional amendments, overriding presidential vetoes, and convicting impeached officials.

Consider this statement by Alexander Hamilton in *Federalist Paper* No. 75: "All provisions which require more than a majority of any [legislative] body to its resolutions have a direct tendency to embarrass the operations of the government and an indirect one to subject the sense of the majority to that of the minority." Hamilton was writing about a proposal to require that more than half of a chamber's members be present to convene a session, but his argument certainly applies to whether a body should need more than a majority of its members to take a vote.

The Filibuster as Damage Control

True, filibusters today are not as colorful as they were before 1975, when senators were forced to read out of a telephone book or even wear diapers to keep a filibuster going. Yet the current filibuster system continues to provide an important protection for minority rights. Why shouldn't Congress be forced to obtain broad support for important legislation? It would be dangerous to allow major taxation and spending measures to be decided by a bare majority vote. Public opinion polling has shown that the filibuster is quite popular among the public at large. Clearly, Americans see the importance of slowing down legislation created by only a single party in Congress. The filibuster still serves a useful purpose, so let's keep it.

For Critical Analysis

What would be likely to happen if the filibuster were abolished?

invoked only for measures that would have the net effect of reducing the federal deficit. This last restriction, however, has frequently been avoided by misleading bookkeeping.

One of the most striking examples of reconciliation took place in March 2010, when the Democrats used the procedure to make a series of amendments to the just-passed Affordable Care Act, also known as Obamacare. Reconciliation was necessary because at the end of January, the Republicans won a special U.S. Senate election, thus reducing the number of Democratic senators to fifty-nine.

The Nuclear Option. It takes sixty senators to invoke cloture. Senate rules, however, can be changed by a simple majority vote. It is possible, therefore, to limit or abolish the filibuster by a majority vote. In the past, such an act would have been considered an unthinkable violation of Senate tradition. In the polarized Congress of the twenty-first century, however, very few procedural tricks are still unthinkable.

Philip Scott Andrews/*The New York Times*

Senator Marco Rubio (R., Fla.) has been mentioned as a possible presidential candidate in 2016. If he wins nomination, he will be the first Latino candidate on a major party ticket. *Is Rubio's ethnicity likely to have any impact on his political positions?*

In 2005, after Democratic senators blocked a vote on a series of Republican judicial candidates, the Republican leadership threatened to suspend the rules through a majority vote. Such a procedure was dubbed the *nuclear option,* in comparison to the most extreme option in warfare. A bipartisan group of senators known as the "gang of fourteen" arranged a compromise settlement. Filibusters of nominees were to be reserved for "extraordinary circumstances."

In November 2013, Democrats contended that Republicans had violated this understanding. At that time, fifty-nine executive branch nominees and seventeen judicial nominees were awaiting confirmation. No compromise was reached, and so Democrats voted to abolish filibusters against all executive branch nominees and judicial nominees other than to the Supreme Court. The rules change did not affect use of the filibuster against proposed legislation. Despite the change, Republican senators were still able to delay Democratic nominees in 2013 and 2014 through various procedural maneuvers.

Congresspersons and the Citizenry: A Comparison

Members of the Senate and the House of Representatives are not typical American citizens. Members of Congress are older than most Americans, partly because of constitutional age requirements and partly because a good deal of political experience normally is an advantage in running for national office. Members of Congress are also disproportionately white, male, and trained in high-status occupations. Lawyers are by far the largest occupational group among congresspersons, although the proportion of lawyers in the House is lower now than it was in the past.

Compared with the average American citizen, members of Congress are well paid. Annual congressional salaries are now $174,000. Increasingly, members of Congress are also much wealthier than the average citizen. Whereas about 3 percent of Americans have assets exceeding $1 million (not including their homes), almost half of the members of Congress are millionaires. Table 11–2 that follows summarizes selected characteristics of the members of Congress.

CONNECT WITH YOUR CLASSMATES
MindTap™ for American Government

Access the Congress Forum: Discussion—Representation in Congress

Table 11-2 ▶ **Characteristics of the 113th Congress, 2013–2015**

Why might it be difficult to determine the wealth of a member of Congress?

Characteristic	U.S. Population	House	Senate
Age (median)	36.8	61.3	59.9
Percentage minority	34.9	19.3	7
Religion			
Percentage church or synagogue members	66.4	90.3	92
Percentage Roman Catholic	23.9	30.3	27
Percentage Protestant	51.3	51.0	54
Percentage Jewish	1.7	4.6	10
Percentage female	50.7	19.5	20
Percentage with advanced degrees			
Persons age 25 or above only	10.1	61.1	73
Occupation			
Percentage lawyers of those employed	0.8	34.3	53
Family income			
Percentage of families earning over $50,000 annually	44.9	100.0	100
Personal wealth*			
Percentage with assets over $1 million	4.7	32.0	50

*113th Congress.
Sources: CIA Factbook, 2010; Census Bureau; Association of Religion Data Archives; *Congressional Quarterly*; and authors' updates.

did you know?

As of January 2013, for the first time in history, white men were a minority among Democrats in Congress.

Perks and Privileges

Legislators have many benefits that are not available to most people. These range from subsidized meals in the congressional dining rooms to free postage to free parking at Washington, D.C., airports.

Permanent Professional Staffs. More than thirty thousand people are employed in the Capitol Hill bureaucracy. About half of them are personal and committee staff members. The personal staff includes office clerks and assistants; professionals who deal with media relations, draft legislation, and satisfy constituency requests for service; and staffers who maintain local offices in the member's home district or state.

The average Senate office on Capitol Hill employs about thirty staff members, and twice that number work on the personal staffs of senators from the most populous states. House office staffs typically are about half as large as those of the Senate. The number of staff members has increased dramatically since 1960.

Congress also benefits from the expertise of the professional staffs of agencies that were created to produce information for members of the House and Senate. For example, the Congressional Research Service, the Government Accountability Office, and the Congressional Budget Office all provide reports, audits, and policy recommendations for review by members of Congress.

did you know?

Before the Republicans reorganized House services in 1995, all members had buckets of ice delivered to their offices each day, at an annual cost of $500,000.

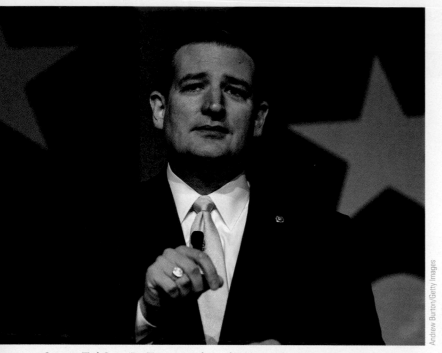

Senator Ted Cruz (R., Texas) speaks at the 2013 Values Voter Summit, held by the conservative Family Research Council. Cruz has frequently staked out positions that are more conservative than those of the Senate's Republican leadership. *How might he benefit from taking such positions?*

Congressional Caucuses: Another Source of Support. The typical member of Congress is part of a variety of caucuses. The most important caucuses are those established by the parties in each chamber. These Democratic and Republican meetings provide information to the members and devise legislative strategy for the party. Other caucuses have been founded, such as the Democratic Study Group and the Congressional Black Caucus, to support subgroups of members. Many caucuses are established to promote special interests, such as the Potato Caucus and the Sportsmen's Caucus. These caucuses deal with a limited range of legislation. Ideological caucuses, in contrast, may take up any issue. Two of the most important ideological caucuses are the conservative Tea Party Caucus and the liberal Progressive Caucus, both in the House.

Privileges and Immunities under the Law. Members of Congress also benefit from a number of special constitutional protections. Under Article I, Section 6, of the Constitution, for example, "for any Speech or Debate in either House, they shall not be questioned in any other Place." The "speech or debate" clause means that a member may make any allegations or other statements he or she wishes in connection with official duties and normally not be sued for libel or slander or otherwise be subject to legal action.

■ **Learning Outcome 3:** Examine the implications of apportioning House seats.

Congressional Elections and Apportionment

The process of electing members of Congress is decentralized. Congressional elections are conducted by the individual state governments. The states, however, must conform to the rules established by the U.S. Constitution and by federal statutes. The Constitution states that representatives are to be elected every second year by popular ballot, and the number of seats awarded to each state is to be determined every ten years by the results of the census. Each state has at least one representative, with most congressional districts having about seven hundred thousand residents. Senators are elected by popular vote (since the passage of the Seventeenth Amendment) every six years. Approximately one-third of the seats are chosen every two years. Each state has two senators.

Under Article I, Section 4, of the Constitution, state legislatures are given control over "the Times, Places and Manner of holding Elections for Senators and Representatives"; however, "the Congress may at any time by Law make or alter such Regulations."

Only states can elect members of Congress. Therefore, territories such as Puerto Rico and Guam are limited to electing nonvoting delegates to the House. The District of Columbia is also represented only by a nonvoting delegate.

Candidates for Congressional Elections

Congressional campaigns have changed considerably in the past two decades. Like all other campaigns, they are much more expensive, with the average cost of a winning

Representative Marcy Kaptur is the most senior member of Ohio's congressional delegation as well as the longest-serving woman in the House. *How strongly are representatives motivated by the desire to win reelection?*

Senate campaign now $9 million and a winning House campaign averaging more than $1.5 million. In addition, large sums are spent on congressional campaigns by independent committees, as explained in Chapter 9. Once in office, legislators spend time almost every day raising funds for their next campaign.

Most candidates for Congress must win the nomination through a direct primary, in which those who identify with a particular party vote for the candidate who will be on the party ticket in the general election. To win the primary, candidates may take more liberal or more conservative positions to get the votes of "party identifiers." In the general election, they may moderate their views to attract the votes of independents and voters from the other party.

Presidential Effects. Congressional candidates are always hopeful that a strong presidential candidate on their ticket will have "coattails" that will sweep in senators and representatives of the same party. (In fact, in some recent presidential elections coattail effects have not materialized at all.) One way to measure the coattail effect is to look at the subsequent midterm elections, held in the even-numbered years following the presidential contests. In these years, voter turnout falls sharply. The party controlling the White House frequently loses seats in Congress in the midterm elections, in part because the coattail effect ceases to apply. Table 11–3 that follows shows the pattern for midterm elections since 1946.

The Power of Incumbency. The power of incumbency in the outcome of congressional elections cannot be overemphasized. Figure 11–1 that follows shows that a sizable majority of representatives and senators who decide to run for reelection are successful. This conclusion holds for both presidential-year and midterm elections. Even in 2010, when the Republicans made very large gains, most incumbents were safe.

Table 11–3 ▶ **Midterm Gains and Losses by the Party of the President, 1946–2014**

What effect might voter turnout have had on these numbers?

	Seats Gained or Lost by the Party of the President in the House of Representatives	
Year	**President's Party**	**Outcome**
1946	D.	-55
1950	D.	-29
1954	R.	-18
1958	R.	-47
1962	D.	-4
1966	D.	-47
1970	R.	-12
1974	R.	-48
1978	D.	-15
1982	R.	-26
1986	R.	-5
1990	R.	-8
1994	D.	-52
1998	D.	+5
2002	R.	+5
2006	R.	-30
2010	D.	-64
2014	D.	-15

Reapportionment
The allocation of seats in the House of Representatives to each state after a census.

Redistricting
The redrawing of the boundaries of the congressional districts within each state.

Figure 11–1 ▶ **The Power of Incumbency**

You can see a small increase in the number of legislators who failed to be reelected in 2010. *What happened in that year?*

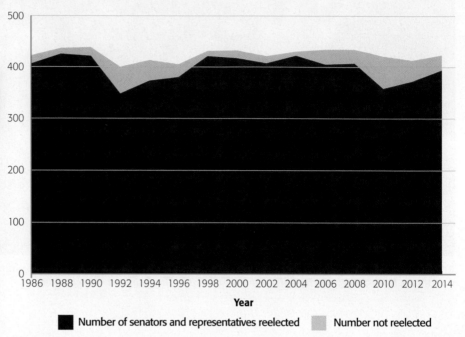

■ Number of senators and representatives reelected   ■ Number not reelected

Sources: Norman Ornstein, Thomas E. Mann, and Michael J. Malbin, *Vital Statistics on Congress, 2001–2002* (Washington, D.C.: The AEI Press, 2002); and authors' updates.

Apportionment of the House

Two of the most complicated aspects of congressional elections are apportionment issues—**reapportionment** (the allocation of seats in the House to each state after a census) and **redistricting** (the redrawing of the boundaries of the districts within each state). In a landmark six-to-two vote in 1962, the United States Supreme Court made the creation of state legislative districts a *justiciable* (that is, a review-able) *question.*[2] The Court did so by invoking the Fourteenth Amendment principle that no state can deny to any person "the equal protection of the laws." In 1964, the Court held that both chambers of a state legislature must be designed so that all districts are equal in population.[3] Later that year, the Court applied this "one person, one vote" principle to U.S. congressional districts on the basis of Article I, Section 2, of the Constitution, which requires that members of the House be chosen "by the People of the several States."[4]

Severe malapportionment of congressional districts before 1964 resulted in some districts containing two or three times the population of other districts in the same state, thereby diluting the effect of a vote cast in the more populous districts. This system generally benefited the conservative residents of rural areas and small towns and harmed the interests of the more heavily populated and liberal cities.

2. *Baker v. Carr,* 369 U.S. 186 (1962). The word *justiciable* is pronounced juhs-*tish*-a-buhl.
3. *Reynolds v. Sims,* 377 U.S. 533 (1964).
4. *Wesberry v. Sanders,* 376 U.S. 1 (1964).

2014 Elections

Party Control of Congress after the 2014 Elections

As noted in Chapter 1, the Republican Party did very well in the 2014 midterm elections. In the Senate, it now held 54 seats to 46 for the Democrats. In the House, the Republicans won 249 seats to the Democrats' 186. What effects would the new composition of Congress have in 2015 and 2016? Some hoped that in the House, more Republicans would allow Speaker John Boehner to exercise greater control over his often unruly flock. The number of Republican rebels needed to take away Boehner's majority would be larger, thus limiting the power of the Tea Party. Others doubted that this effect would materialize. In the Senate, the new Republican majority would be able to block any Obama appointees by a simple majority vote, thus reversing the effect of the *nuclear option* described earlier in this chapter. This Republican capability might provoke a major political crisis if a member of the Supreme Court were to die or retire. Conceivably, the vacant seat could prove impossible to fill. Observers doubted that the Senate would extend the nuclear option and abolish the filibuster for ordinary legislation. Any bills passed this way would be subject to the president's veto, and Republican leader Mitch McConnell was known to be a strong supporter of the filibuster.

Gerrymandering. Although the general issue of apportionment has been dealt with fairly successfully by the one person, one vote principle, the **gerrymandering** issue has not yet been resolved. This term refers to the legislative-boundary-drawing tactics that were used under Elbridge Gerry, the governor of Massachusetts, in the 1812 elections. (See Figure 11–2 that follows.) A district is said to have been gerrymandered when its shape is altered substantially to determine which party will win it.

In 1986, the Supreme Court heard a case that challenged gerrymandered congressional districts in Indiana. The Court ruled for the first time that redistricting for the political benefit of one group could be challenged on constitutional grounds. In this specific case, *Davis v. Bandemer*,[5] however, the Court did not agree that the districts had been drawn unfairly, because it could not be proved that a group of voters would consistently be deprived of influence at the polls as a result of the new districts.

In 2004, the United States Supreme Court reviewed an obviously political redistricting scheme in Pennsylvania. The Court concluded, however, that the federal judiciary would not address purely political gerrymandering claims.[6] Two years later, the Supreme Court reached a similar conclusion with respect to most of the new congressional districts created by the Republicans in the Texas legislature in 2003. Again, except for one district in Texas, the Court refused to intervene in what was clearly a political gerrymandering plan.[7] Still, gerrymandering is widely seen as unfair. For that reason several states have passed laws aimed at abolishing the process by establishing nonpartisan redistricting boards.

> **Gerrymandering**
> The drawing of legislative district boundary lines for the purpose of obtaining partisan advantage. A district is said to be gerrymandered when its shape is manipulated to determine which party will win it.

---

5. 478 U.S. 109 (1986).
6. *Vieth v. Jubelirer*, 541 U.S. 267 (2004).
7. *League of United Latin American Citizens v. Perry*, 548 U.S. 399 (2006).

Figure 11-2 ▶ **The Original Gerrymander**

The practice of "gerrymandering"—the excessive manipulation of the shape of a legislative district to benefit a certain incumbent or party—is probably as old as the republic, but the name originated in 1812. In that year, the Massachusetts legislature carved out of Essex County a district that historian John Fiske said had a "dragonlike contour." When the painter Gilbert Stuart saw the misshapen district, he penciled in a head, wings, and claws and exclaimed, "That will do for a salamander!" Editor Benjamin Russell replied, "Better say a Gerrymander" (after Elbridge Gerry, then governor of Massachusetts). *Why might the authors of this gerrymander have been reluctant to divide local governments between districts, as is regularly done today?*

Source: *Congressional Quarterly's Guide to Congress*, 3d ed. (Washington, D.C.: Congressional Quarterly Press, 1982), p. 695.

How Gerrymandering Works. Congressional and state legislative redistricting decisions are often made by a small group of political leaders within a state legislature. Typically, their goal is to shape voting districts in such a way as to maximize their party's chances of winning state legislative seats, as well as seats in Congress. Two of the techniques in use are called *packing* and *cracking*. By employing powerful computers and software, voters supporting the opposing party are "packed" into as few districts as possible or the opposing party's supporters are "cracked" into different districts.

Figure 11–3 that follows illustrates the redistricting process. In these three examples, sixty-four individuals must be distributed among four districts, each of which has a population of sixteen. Two political parties are involved: the O Party and the X Party.

In Example 1, supporters of the two parties are sorted so that each differently colored district contains only one kind of voter. Such a pattern sometimes appears when the members of a state legislature are most interested in preserving the seats of incumbents, regardless of party. In this example, it would be almost impossible to dislodge a sitting member in a general election. Example 2 is the reverse case. Every district is divided evenly between the parties, and even a very slight swing toward one of the parties could give that party all four seats.

Figure 11-3 ▶ **Examples of Districting**

Why might a nonpartisan redistricting board tend to favor solutions such as example 2?

o	o	o	o	x	x	x	x
o	o	o	o	x	x	x	x
o	o	o	o	x	x	x	x
o	o	o	o	x	x	x	x
x	x	x	x	o	o	o	o
x	x	x	x	o	o	o	o
x	x	x	x	o	o	o	o
x	x	x	x	o	o	o	o

Example 1. A "bipartisan gerrymander" aimed at protecting incumbents in both the O Party and the X Party.

o	o	o	o	x	x	x	x
o	o	o	o	x	x	x	x
o	o	o	o	x	x	x	x
o	o	o	o	x	x	x	x
x	x	x	x	o	o	o	o
x	x	x	x	o	o	o	o
x	x	x	x	o	o	o	o
x	x	x	x	o	o	o	o

Example 2. An unstable system. All districts have the same number of supporters in each party.

o	o	o	o	x	x	x	x
o	o	o	o	x	x	x	x
o	o	o	o	x	x	x	x
o	o	o	o	x	x	x	x
x	x	x	x	o	o	o	o
x	x	x	x	o	o	o	o
x	x	x	x	o	o	o	o
x	x	x	x	o	o	o	o

Example 3. A classic partisan gerrymander. The X Party is almost guaranteed to carry three districts.

Example 3 is a classic partisan gerrymander benefiting the X Party. The orange district in the lower right is an example of packing—the maximum possible number of supporters of the O Party are packed into that district. The other three districts are examples of cracking. The O Party supporters are cracked so that they do not have a majority in any of the three districts. In these districts, the X Party has majorities of eleven to five, ten to six, and eleven to five.

"Minority–Majority" Districts.   Under the mandate of the Voting Rights Act of 1965, the Justice Department issued directives to states after the 1990 census instructing them to create congressional districts that would maximize the voting power of minority groups—that is, create districts in which minority group voters were the majority. The result was a number of creatively drawn congressional districts.

Many of these "minority–majority" districts were challenged in court by citizens who claimed that creating districts based on race or ethnicity alone violates the equal protection clause of the Constitution. In 2001, for example, the Supreme Court reviewed, for a second time, a case involving North Carolina's Twelfth District.

The district was 165 miles long, following Interstate 85 for the most part. According to a local joke, the district was so narrow that a car traveling down the interstate highway with both doors open would kill most of the voters in the district. In 1996, the Supreme Court had held that the district was unconstitutional because race had been the dominant factor in drawing the district's boundaries. Shortly thereafter, the boundaries were redrawn, but the district was again challenged as a racial gerrymander. In 2001, however, the Supreme Court held that there was insufficient evidence that race had been the dominant factor when the boundaries were redrawn.[8] The Twelfth District's boundaries remained in place.

How Congress Is Organized

The limited amount of centralized power that exists in Congress is exercised through party-based mechanisms. Congress is organized by party. When the Democratic Party, for example, wins a majority of seats in either the House or the Senate, Democrats control the official positions of power in that chamber, and every important committee has a Democratic chairperson and a majority of Democratic members. The same process holds when Republicans are in the majority.

In each chamber of Congress, members of each of the two major political parties meet together in *caucuses*. These meetings elect leaders who coordinate party action and negotiate with the other chamber and with the president. Still, much of the actual work of legislating is performed by the committees and subcommittees within Congress.

Thousands of bills are introduced in every session of Congress, and no single member can possibly be adequately informed on all the issues that arise. The committee system is a way to provide for specialization, or a division of the legislative effort. Members of a committee can concentrate on just one area or topic—such as taxation or energy—and develop sufficient expertise to draft appropriate legislation when needed. The flow of legislation through both the House and the Senate is determined largely by the speed with which the members of these committees act on bills and resolutions.

■ **Learning Outcome 4:** Describe the committee structure of the House and the Senate and the key leadership positions in each chamber.

8. *Easley v. Cromartie*, 532 U.S. 234 (2001).

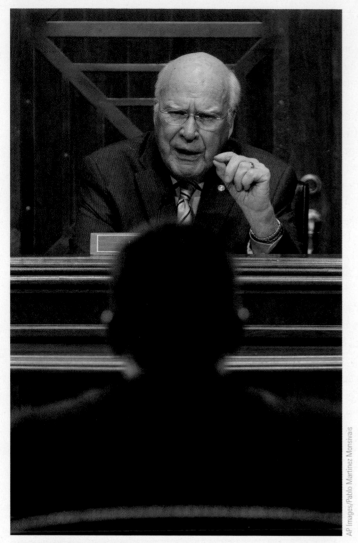

Senator Patrick Leahy (D., Vt.) questions a federal administrator in a committee hearing. Leahy is the most senior Democrat in the Senate and held the honorary post of Senate president pro tem until January 2015, when he was replaced by Orrin Hatch (R., Utah). *What are the benefits of seniority?*

The Power of Committees

Sometimes called "little legislatures," committees usually have the final say on pieces of legislation.[9] Committee actions may be overturned on the floor by the House or Senate, but this rarely happens. Legislators normally defer to the expertise of the chairperson and other members of the committee who speak on the floor in defense of a committee decision. Chairpersons of committees exercise control over the scheduling of hearings and formal actions on bills. They also decide which subcommittee will act on legislation falling within their committee's jurisdiction. Committees normally have the power to kill proposed legislation by refusing to act on it—that is, by never sending it to the entire chamber for a vote.

Committees only very rarely are deprived of control over bills—although this kind of action is provided for in the rules of each chamber. In the House, if a bill has been considered by a standing committee for thirty days, the signatures of a majority (218) of the House membership on a **discharge petition** can pry a bill out of an uncooperative committee's hands. From 1909 to 2014, however, although over nine hundred such petitions were initiated, only slightly more than two dozen resulted in successful discharge efforts. Of those, twenty resulted in bills that passed the House.[10]

Types of Congressional Committees

Over the past two centuries, Congress has created several different types of committees, each of which serves particular needs of the institution.

Standing Committees. By far, the most important committees in Congress are the **standing committees**— permanent bodies that are established by the rules of each chamber and that continue from session to session. A list of the standing committees of the 114th Congress is presented in Table 11–4 that follows. In addition, most of the standing committees have created subcommittees to carry out their work. For example, the 114th Congress has 73 subcommittees in the Senate and 104 in the House. Each standing committee is given a specific area of legislative policy jurisdiction, and almost all legislative measures are considered by the appropriate standing committees.

Because of the importance of their work and the traditional influence of their members in Congress, certain committees are considered to be more prestigious than others. Seats on standing committees that handle spending issues are especially sought after because members can use these positions to benefit their constituents. Committees that control spending include the Appropriations Committee in either chamber and the Ways and Means Committee in the House. Members also normally seek seats on committees that handle matters of special interest to their constituents. A member of the House from an agricultural district, for example, will have an interest in joining the House Agriculture Committee.

Discharge Petition

A procedure by which a bill in the House of Representatives can be forced (discharged) out of a committee that has refused to report it for consideration by the House. The petition must be signed by an absolute majority (218) of representatives and is used only on rare occasions.

Standing Committee

A permanent committee in the House or Senate that considers bills within a certain subject area.

---

9. The term *little legislatures* is from Woodrow Wilson, *Congressional Government* (Mineola, N.Y.: Dover Books, 2006 [first published in 1885]).
10. Congressional Quarterly, Inc., *Guide to Congress,* 7th ed. (Washington, D.C.: CQ Press, 2012) and authors' updates.

committee, influence the allocation of committee assignments for new members or for senators attempting to transfer to a new committee, influence the selection of other party officials, and participate in selecting members of conference committees.

The leaders are expected to mobilize support for partisan legislative or presidential initiatives. They act as liaisons with the White House when the president is of their party, try to obtain the cooperation of committee chairpersons, and seek to facilitate the smooth functioning of the Senate through the senators' unanimous consent. The majority and minority leaders are elected by their respective party caucuses.

Senate party whips, like their House counterparts, maintain communication within the party on platform positions and try to ensure that party colleagues are present for floor debate and important votes. The Senate whip system is far less elaborate than its counterpart in the House, because there are fewer members to track and senators have a greater tradition of independence. A list of the candidates expected to become the formal party leaders of the 114th Congress is presented in Table 11–5 that follows.

did you know?

The Constitution does not require that the Speaker of the House of Representatives be an elected member of the House.

Lawmaking and Budgeting

Each year, Congress and the president propose and approve many laws. Some are budget and appropriations laws that require extensive bargaining but must be passed for the government to continue to function. Other laws are relatively free of controversy and are passed with little dissension. Still other proposed legislation is extremely controversial and reaches to the roots of differences between Republicans and Democrats.

■ **Learning Outcome 5:**
Discuss the process by which a bill becomes law and how the federal government establishes its budget.

Table 11–5 ▶ **Party Leaders in the 114th Congress, 2015–2017**

The named individuals were the leading contenders for the various positions in the 2014 leadership elections. Note that the Republican caucuses are formally known as conferences. *Why might joining the leadership sometimes make a member of Congress less popular in his or her home district?*

Position	Incumbent	Party/State	Leader Since
House			
Speaker	John Boehner	R., Ohio	Jan. 2011
Majority leader	Kevin McCarthy	R., Calif.	June 2014
Majority whip	Steve Scalise	R., La.	June 2014
Chair of the Republican Conference	Cathy McMorris Rogers	R., Wash.	Jan. 2013
Minority leader	Nancy Pelosi	D., Calif.	Jan. 2011
Minority whip	Steny Hoyer	D., Md.	Jan. 2011
Chair of the Democratic Caucus	Xavier Becerra	D., Calif.	Jan. 2013
Senate			
President pro tempore	Orrin Hatch	R., Utah	Jan. 2015
Majority leader	Mitch McConnell	R., Ky.	Jan. 2015
Majority whip	John Cornyn	R., Tex.	Jan. 2015
Chair of the Republican Conference	John Thune	R., S.D.	Jan. 2015
Minority leader	Harry Reid	D., Nev.	Jan. 2015
Minority whip	Dick Durbin	D., Ill.	Jan. 2015
Chair of the Democratic Caucus	Harry Reid	D., Nev.	Jan. 2015

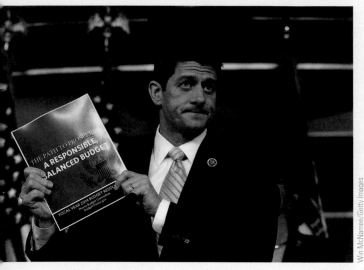

Rep. Paul Ryan (R., Wisc.), chair of the House Budget Committee, presents his proposed 2014 budget plan. *Why does this budget have essentially no chance of being adopted?*

Figure 11–4 that follows shows that each law begins as a bill, which must be introduced in either the House or the Senate. Often, similar bills are introduced in both chambers. A budget bill, however, must start in the House. In each chamber, the bill follows similar steps. It is referred to a committee and its subcommittees for study, discussion, hearings, and markup (rewriting). When the bill is reported out to the full chamber, it must be scheduled for debate (by the Rules Committee in the House and by the leadership in the Senate). After the bill has been passed in each chamber, if it contains different provisions, a conference committee is formed to write a compromise bill, which must be approved by both chambers before it is sent to the president to sign or veto.

How Much Will the Government Spend?

The Constitution is very clear about where the power of the purse lies in the national government: all taxing or spending bills must originate in the House of Representatives. Today, much of the business of Congress is concerned with approving government expenditures through the budget process and with raising the revenues to pay for government programs.

From 1922, when Congress required the president to prepare and present to the legislature an **executive budget,** until 1974, the congressional budget process was so disjointed that it was difficult to visualize the total picture of government finances. The president presented the executive budget to Congress in January. It was broken down into thirteen or more appropriations bills. Some time later, after all of the bills had been debated, amended, and passed, it was more or less possible to estimate total government spending for the next year.

Frustrated by the president's ability to impound, or withhold, funds and dissatisfied with the entire budget process, Congress passed the Budget and Impoundment Control Act of 1974 to regain some control over the nation's spending. The act required the president to spend the funds that Congress had appropriated, ending the president's ability to kill programs by withholding funds. The other major result of the act was to force Congress to examine total national taxing and spending at least twice in each budget cycle. (See Figure 11–5 later for a graphic illustration of the budget cycle.)

Preparing the Budget. The federal government operates on a **fiscal year (FY)** cycle. The fiscal year runs from October through September, so that fiscal year 2016, or FY16, runs from October 1, 2015, through September 30, 2016. Eighteen months before a fiscal year starts, the executive branch begins preparing the budget. The Office of Management and Budget (OMB) receives advice from the Council of Economic Advisers and the Treasury Department. The OMB outlines the budget and then sends it to the various departments and agencies. Bargaining follows, in which—to use only two of many examples—the Department of Health and Human Services argues for more antipoverty spending, and the armed forces argue for more defense spending.

The OMB Reviews the Budget. Even though the OMB has fewer than 550 employees, it is one of the most powerful agencies in Washington. It assembles the budget documents and monitors federal agencies throughout each year. Every year, it begins the budget process with a **spring review,** in which it requires all of the agencies to review their programs, activities, and goals. At the beginning of each summer, the OMB sends

Executive Budget
The budget prepared and submitted by the president to Congress.

Fiscal Year (FY)
A twelve-month period that is used for bookkeeping, or accounting, purposes. Usually, the fiscal year does not coincide with the calendar year. For example, the federal government's fiscal year runs from October 1 through September 30.

Spring Review
The annual process in which the Office of Management and Budget (OMB) requires federal agencies to review their programs, activities, and goals and submit their requests for funding for the next fiscal year.

Figure 11–4 ▶ **How a Bill Becomes Law**

This illustration shows the most typical way in which proposed legislation is enacted into law. Most legislation begins as similar bills introduced into the House and the Senate. The process is illustrated here with two hypothetical bills, House bill No. 100 (HR 100) and Senate bill No. 200 (S 200). The path of HR 100 is shown on the left, and that of S 200 on the right. *Where does the filibuster fit in to this process?*

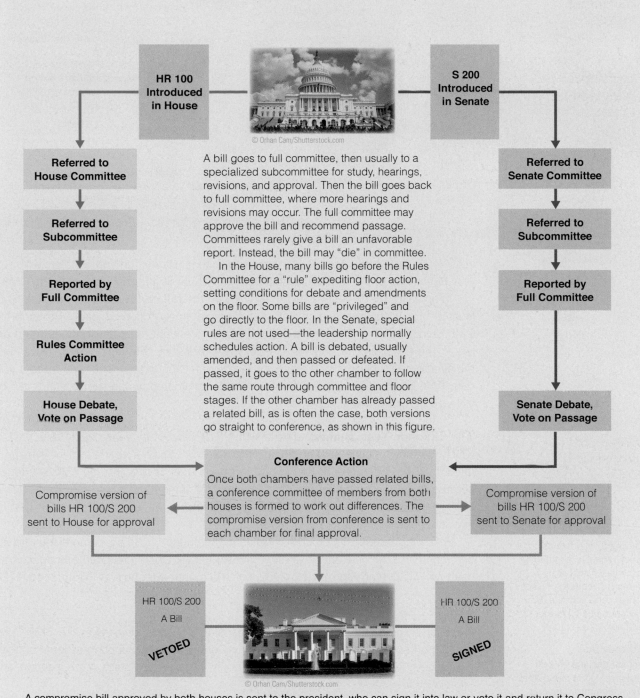

HR 100 Introduced in House

© Orhan Cam/Shutterstock.com

S 200 Introduced in Senate

Referred to House Committee

Referred to Subcommittee

Reported by Full Committee

Rules Committee Action

House Debate, Vote on Passage

A bill goes to full committee, then usually to a specialized subcommittee for study, hearings, revisions, and approval. Then the bill goes back to full committee, where more hearings and revisions may occur. The full committee may approve the bill and recommend passage. Committees rarely give a bill an unfavorable report. Instead, the bill may "die" in committee.

In the House, many bills go before the Rules Committee for a "rule" expediting floor action, setting conditions for debate and amendments on the floor. Some bills are "privileged" and go directly to the floor. In the Senate, special rules are not used—the leadership normally schedules action. A bill is debated, usually amended, and then passed or defeated. If passed, it goes to the other chamber to follow the same route through committee and floor stages. If the other chamber has already passed a related bill, as is often the case, both versions go straight to conference, as shown in this figure.

Referred to Senate Committee

Referred to Subcommittee

Reported by Full Committee

Senate Debate, Vote on Passage

Conference Action

Once both chambers have passed related bills, a conference committee of members from both houses is formed to work out differences. The compromise version from conference is sent to each chamber for final approval.

Compromise version of bills HR 100/S 200 sent to House for approval

Compromise version of bills HR 100/S 200 sent to Senate for approval

HR 100/S 200
A Bill
VETOED

© Orhan Cam/Shutterstock.com

HR 100/S 200
A Bill
SIGNED

A compromise bill approved by both houses is sent to the president, who can sign it into law or veto it and return it to Congress. Congress may override a presidential veto by a two-thirds majority in both chambers. The bill then becomes law without the president's signature.

Figure 11–5 ▶ **The Budget Cycle**

Why does Congress have so much trouble meeting its deadlines?

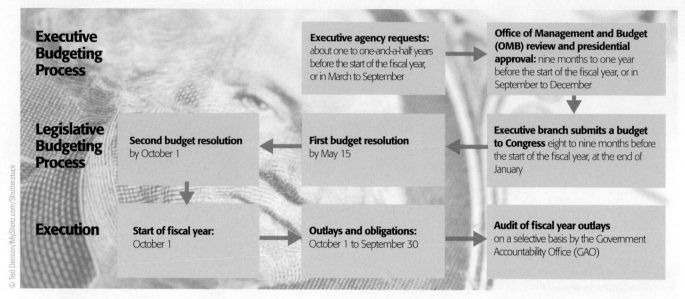

Executive Budgeting Process

Executive agency requests: about one to one-and-a-half years before the start of the fiscal year, or in March to September →

Office of Management and Budget (OMB) review and presidential approval: nine months to one year before the start of the fiscal year, or in September to December

↓

Legislative Budgeting Process

Second budget resolution by October 1 ← **First budget resolution** by May 15 ← **Executive branch submits a budget to Congress** eight to nine months before the start of the fiscal year, at the end of January

↓

Execution

Start of fiscal year: October 1 → **Outlays and obligations:** October 1 to September 30 → **Audit of fiscal year outlays** on a selective basis by the Government Accountability Office (GAO)

out a letter instructing agencies to submit their requests for funding for the next fiscal year. By the end of the summer, each agency must submit a formal request to the OMB.

In actuality, the "budget season" begins with the **fall review.** At this time, the OMB looks at budget requests and, in almost all cases, routinely cuts them back. Although the OMB works within guidelines established by the president, specific decisions often are left to the OMB director and the director's associates. By the beginning of November, the director's review begins. The director meets with cabinet secretaries and budget officers. Time becomes crucial. The budget must be completed by January so that it can be included in the *Economic Report of the President.*

The Election-Year Budget. The schedule just described cannot apply to a year in which the voters elect a new president or to a year in which a new president is inaugurated. In 2008, George W. Bush did not engage in a fall review of the FY 2010 budget, because he would no longer be in office when the budget went into effect in October 2009. Barack Obama could hardly have undertaken the fall review either, given that he was still campaigning for the presidency.

Following the election of a new president, the budget process is compressed into the first months of the new administration. Indeed, Barack Obama released a budget document for FY 2010 on February 26, 2009, barely a month after he was inaugurated.

Congress Faces the Budget

In January, nine months before the fiscal year starts, the president takes the OMB's proposed budget, approves it, and submits it to Congress. Then the congressional budgeting process takes over. The budgeting process involves two steps: authorization and appropriation.

The Authorization Process. First, Congress must authorize funds to be spent. The **authorization** is a formal declaration by the appropriate congressional committee that a certain amount of funding may be available to an agency. Congressional committees and subcommittees look at the proposals from the executive branch and the Congressional Budget Office in making the decision to authorize funds.

Fall Review

The annual process in which the OMB, after receiving formal federal agency requests for funding for the next fiscal year, reviews the requests, makes changes, and submits its recommendations to the president.

Authorization

A formal declaration by a legislative committee that a certain amount of funding may be available to an agency. Some authorizations terminate in a year; others are renewable automatically without further congressional action.

The Appropriation Process. After the funds have been authorized, they must be appropriated by Congress. The appropriations committees of both the House and the Senate forward spending bills to their respective bodies. The **appropriation** of funds occurs when the final bill is passed. In this process, large sums are in play. Representatives and senators who chair key committees have traditionally found it easy to slip additional spending proposals into a variety of bills. These proposals may have nothing to do with the ostensible purpose of the bill. Such *earmarked* appropriations, known as "pork," have their defenders. Many members of Congress believe that they have a better understanding of the needs of their districts than does any executive branch agency.

"After months of partisan bickering, Congress has finally agreed to put a Slinky on an escalator and see if it goes forever."

Evading the Ban on Earmarks. In March 2010, the Republican-controlled House implemented rules designed to eliminate earmarks. The new rules have substantially reduced the amount of pork inserted into appropriations bills, but lawmakers have been creative in attempting to circumvent the ban. In some instances, legislators have simply denied that a particular funding request is actually an earmark. More commonly, members have lobbied the various executive agencies to include projects that benefit their districts. According to the OMB definition, spending requested by executive agencies is not pork. Further, the White House itself frequently inserts special requests into the executive budget, thus making the president the biggest "porkmeister" of all.

Budget Resolutions and Crises

The **first budget resolution** by Congress is due each May. It sets overall revenue goals and spending targets. Spending and tax laws that are drawn up over the summer are supposed to be guided by the first budget resolution. By September, Congress is scheduled to pass its **second budget resolution,** one that will set binding limits on taxes and spending for the fiscal year beginning October 1.

The Continuing Resolution. In actuality, Congress has finished the budget on time in only three years since 1977. The budget is usually broken into a series of appropriations bills. If Congress has not passed one of these bills by October 1, it normally passes a **continuing resolution** that allows the affected agencies to keep on doing whatever they were doing the previous year with the same amount of funding. By the 1980s, continuing resolutions had ballooned into massive measures.

Budget delays reached a climax in 1995 and 1996, when, in a spending dispute with Democratic president Bill Clinton, the Republican Congress refused to pass any continuing resolutions. As a result, some nonessential functions of the federal government were shut down for twenty-seven days. Since 1997, Congress has generally managed to limit continuing resolutions to their original purpose. This forbearance remained in effect even during the successive budget crises that began in 2011.

The Debt Ceiling. After gaining control of the U.S. House in 2011, Republicans sought to use their control of the House to force cuts in federal spending. The result was a series

did you know?

According to Senate rules, flowers are not permitted in the Senate chamber except on the desk of a deceased sitting senator on the day of his or her eulogy.

Appropriation
The passage, by Congress, of a spending bill specifying the amount of authorized funds that actually will be allocated for an agency's use.

First Budget Resolution
A resolution passed by Congress in each May that sets overall revenue and spending goals for the following fiscal year.

Second Budget Resolution
A resolution passed by Congress in each September that sets "binding" limits on taxes and spending for the following fiscal year.

Continuing Resolution
A temporary funding law that Congress passes when an appropriations bill has not been decided by the beginning of the new fiscal year on October 1.

of confrontations between the Republican House and the Democratic president and Senate. Among the most serious of these were the debt ceiling crises of 2011 and 2013.

What Is the Debt Ceiling? If the federal government runs a budget deficit—if it spends more than it takes in—it must issue new debt. The government has, in fact, run a deficit in most recent years. Under current law, the national government is limited in the amount of debt it can issue, and if the federal debt approaches the legal ceiling, Congress must raise the limit to allow additional debt.

Raising the debt ceiling is entirely independent of the tax and spending decisions reached by Congress—the ceiling must be raised to allow the government to fund activities that are already established by law. Many people mistakenly believe that raising the ceiling is a prerequisite for new, future spending, but that is not the case. If the debt ceiling is not raised as needed, the government might be forced to default on its existing obligations.

The Crises of 2011 and 2013. Traditionally, members of Congress often "grandstanded" by voting against the debt ceiling hike, even though passage was never in doubt. In 2011, however, House Republicans, for the first time, sought to use the ceiling as a tool to force Democrats to accept spending cuts. At the last minute, House Republicans and the Democrats under President Obama reached a deal that involved significant cuts.

In 2013, Republicans attempted to use the debt ceiling vote to force additional cuts. Democrats, however, believing that the Republicans had taken advantage of them in 2011, refused to negotiate. Simultaneously, the government was about to run out of funding because no continuing resolution had been passed. On October 1, parts of the federal government were forced to shut down. Following intense pressure from the public and from business interests, the Republicans caved in. On October 16, they accepted legislation to suspend the debt ceiling and to fund the government until early 2014. In February 2014, Congress voted to suspend the debt ceiling again until 2015. That vote marked the end of the tactic of using the debt ceiling to extract concessions.

President Obama attends a meeting with Democratic women lawmakers in 2014. The gathering highlighted new data contending that women earn seventy-seven cents for every dollar earned by a man. *How useful is it for members of Congress to appear with a president of their own party?*

How You Can Make a Difference

To contact a member of Congress, start by going to the Web sites of the U.S. House of Representatives (www.house.gov) and the U.S. Senate (www.senate.gov).

- Although you can communicate easily with your representatives by e-mail, using e-mail has some drawbacks. Representatives and senators are now receiving large volumes of e-mail from constituents, which they rarely read themselves. They have staff members who read and respond to e-mail instead. Many interest groups argue that U.S. mail, or even express mail or a phone call, is more likely to capture the attention of a representative than e-mail.

- You can contact your representatives and senators using one of the following addresses or phone numbers:

United States House of Representatives
Washington, DC 20515
202-224-3121

United States Senate
Washington, DC 20510
202-224-3121

- Interest groups also track the voting records of members of Congress and rate the members on the issues. Project Vote Smart tracks the performance of more than thirteen thousand political leaders, including their campaign finances, issue positions, and voting records. You can locate the Web site of Project Vote Smart at www.votesmart.org.

- Finally, if you want to know how your representatives funded their campaigns, contact the Center for Responsive Politics (CRP), a research group that tracks money in politics, campaign fund-raising, and similar issues. You can see the CRP site by visiting www.opensecrets.org.

Key Terms

agenda setting 315
appropriation 337
authorization 336
bicameralism 312
casework 314
conference committee 329
constituent 312
continuing resolution 337
discharge petition 328
earmarks 313
enumerated power 315

executive budget 334
fall review 336
filibuster 318
first budget resolution 337
fiscal year (FY) 334
gerrymandering 325
Hastert Rule 318
instructed delegate 314
joint committee 329
lawmaking 313
majority leader of the House 331

minority leader of the House 331
ombudsperson 314
oversight 314
president pro tempore 332
reapportionment 324
reconciliation 318
redistricting 324
representation 313
Rules Committee 318
second budget resolution 337

select committee 329
Senate majority leader 332
Senate minority leader 332
seniority system 330
Speaker of the House 330
spring review 334
standing committee 328
trustee 314
whip 332

Chapter Summary

Learning Outcome 1 The authors of the Constitution believed that the bulk of national power should be in the legislature. The Connecticut Compromise established a balanced legislature, with the membership in the House of Representatives based on population and the membership in the Senate based on the equality of states.

The functions of Congress include (a) lawmaking, (b) representation, (c) service to constituents, (d) oversight, (e) public education, and (f) conflict resolution.

The Constitution specifies most of the enumerated, or expressed, powers of Congress, including the right to impose taxes, to borrow funds, to regulate commerce, and to declare war. Congress also enjoys the right to "make all Laws which shall be necessary and proper for carrying into Execution the foregoing Powers, and all other Powers vested by this Constitution in the Government of the United States, or in any Department or Officer thereof." This is called the elastic, or necessary and proper, clause.

Learning Outcome 2 There are 435 voting members in the House of Representatives and 100 members in the Senate. Owing to its larger size, the House has a greater number of formal rules. The Senate tradition of unlimited debate dates back to 1790 and has been used over the years to frustrate the passage of bills.

Members of Congress are not typical American citizens. They are older and wealthier than most Americans, disproportionately white and male, and more likely to be lawyers.

Members of Congress are well paid and enjoy benefits such as free postage. Members have personal and committee staff and enjoy a number of legal privileges and immunities.

Learning Outcome 3 Most candidates for Congress win nomination through a direct primary. Most incumbent representatives and senators who run for reelection are successful. Apportionment is the allocation of legislative seats to constituencies. The Supreme Court's "one person, one vote" rule means that the populations of legislative districts must be effectively equal.

Learning Outcome 4 Most of the work of legislating is performed by committees and subcommittees within Congress. Legislation introduced into the House or Senate is assigned to standing committees for review. Joint committees are formed by the action of both chambers and consist of members from each. Conference committees are joint committees set up to achieve agreement between the House and the Senate on the exact wording of legislative acts that were passed by the chambers in different forms. The seniority rule, which is usually followed, specifies that the longest-serving member of the majority party will be the chairperson of a committee.

The foremost power holder in the House of Representatives is the Speaker of the House. Other leaders are the House majority leader, the House minority leader, and the majority and minority whips. Formally, the vice president is the presiding officer of the Senate. Actual leadership in the Senate rests with the majority leader, the minority leader, and their whips.

Learning Outcome 5 A bill becomes law by progressing through both chambers of Congress and their appropriate standing and joint committees before submission to the president.

The budget process for a fiscal year begins with the preparation of an executive budget by the president. This is reviewed by the Office of Management and Budget and then sent to Congress, which is supposed to pass a final budget by the end of September. Since 1978, Congress generally has not followed its own time rules.

Master the concept of The Congress with MindTap™ for American Government

 REVIEW MindTap™ **for American Government**
Access Key Term Flashcards for Chapter 11.

 TEST YOURSELF MindTap™ **for American Government**
Take the Wrap It Up Quiz for Chapter 11.

 STAY FOCUSED MindTap™ **for American Government**
Complete the Focus Activities for The Congress.

STAY CURRENT MindTap™ **for American Government**
Access the KnowNow blog and customized RSS for updates on current events.

Additional Resources

All senators and representatives have Web sites that you can find simply by keying in their names in a search engine. You can learn the names of your congressional representatives by going to the Web site of the House or the Senate. Once you know their names, you can go to their Web sites to learn more about them. Note that some members of Congress also provide important services to their constituents through their Web sites. Some sites, for example, allow constituents to apply for internships in Washington, D.C.; apply for appointments to military academies; order flags; sign up for tours of the Capitol; and register complaints electronically.

Online Resources

- The Web site of the Senate is at www.senate.gov, and the site of the House is at www.house.gov.
- *RollCall,* the newspaper of the Capitol, is available at www.rollcall.com.
- You can find Politico, a major Web site of political news, at www.politico.com.
- *The Hill,* a newspaper that investigates various activities of Congress, can be found at thehill.com.

Books

Mann, Thomas E., and Norman J. Ornstein. *It's Even Worse Than It Looks: How the American Constitutional System Collided with the New Politics of Extremism.* New York: Basic Books, First Trade Paper Edition, 2013. The authors, political scientists with positions at Washington "think tanks," contend that the political polarization that has tied up Congress endangers the nation. Mann is a Democrat and Ornstein is a Republican, but they agree that extremism among Republicans is the greater threat.

Schaller, Thomas. *The Stronghold: How Republicans Captured Congress but Surrendered the White House.* New Haven, Conn.: Yale University Press, 2013. Schaller is a political science professor at the University of Maryland. He argues that the Republican Party has become more Congress-centered, and that this development goes hand-in-hand with its increased conservatism.

Smith, Steven S. *The Senate Syndrome: The Evolution of Procedural Warfare in the Modern U.S. Senate.* Norman: The University of Oklahoma Press, 2014. Smith, a professor at Washington University in St. Louis, puts the current problems of the Senate into historical context and debunks a variety of myths.

Video

Charlie Wilson's War—One of the best movies of 2007, starring Tom Hanks and Julia Roberts. This hilarious film is based on the true story of how Wilson, a hard-living, hard-drinking representative from Texas, almost single-handedly wins a billion dollars in funding for the Afghans who are fighting a Russian invasion. When equipped with heat-seeking missiles, the Afghans win. The late Philip Seymour Hoffman steals the show portraying a rogue CIA operative.

Gerrymandering—This 2010 documentary by director Jeff Reichert manages to uncover a surprising amount of drama in the process of redrawing district lines, in part by focusing on some of the most outrageous recent examples.

Quiz

Multiple Choice and Fill-Ins

Learning Outcome 1 Describe the various roles played by Congress and the constitutional basis of its powers.

1. The bicameralism of Congress means that:
   a. every district has two members.
   b. every state has two senators.
   c. Congress is divided into two legislative bodies.

2. The process of compromise in which members of Congress support each other's bills is called _____.

Learning Outcome 2 Explain some of the differences between the House and the Senate and some of the privileges enjoyed by members of Congress.

3. The central difference between the House and the Senate is that:
   a. the House is much larger than the Senate.
   b. the Senate is much larger than the House.
   c. the Senate meets only occasionally, but the House meets all of the time.

4. In contrast to the House, only the Senate has the power to accept or reject _____ with foreign nations.

Learning Outcome 3 Examine the implications of apportioning House seats.

5. Congressional redistricting often involves gerrymandering, which means that the redistricting:
   a. results in an equal number of Democratic and Republican districts.
   b. results in strange-shaped districts designed to favor one party.
   c. results in districts that have almost no representation.

6. A high percentage of senators and representatives are reelected, and we describe this as due to the power of _____.

Learning Outcome 4 Describe the committee structure of the House and the Senate and the key leadership positions in each chamber.

7. There are several types of committees in Congress. They include:
   a. standing committees, sitting committees, and joint committees.
   b. sitting committees, joint committees, and select committees.
   c. standing committees, select committees, and joint committees.

8. The representative with the most power in the House is the _____ ___ ___ _____ because he or she is the official leader of the majority party.

Learning Outcome 5 Discuss the process by which a bill becomes law and how the federal government establishes its budget.

9. When an appropriations bill has not been passed on time, Congress may pass a temporary funding law called:
   a. a continuing resolution.
   b. a second budget resolution.
   c. a temporary authorization.

10. In contrast to the calendar year, which starts January 1 and ends on December 31, the federal government's _____ year runs from October 1 through September 30.

Essay Questions

1. The District of Columbia is not represented in the Senate and has a single, nonvoting delegate to the House. Should the District of Columbia be represented in Congress by voting legislators? Why or why not? If it should be represented, how? Would it make sense to admit it as a state? To give it back to Maryland? Explain your reasoning.

2. Identify some advantages to the nation that might follow when one party controls the House, the Senate, and the presidency. Identify some of the disadvantages that might follow from such a state of affairs.

Answers to questions: 1. c, 2. logrolling, 3. a, 4. treaties, 5. b, 6. incumbency, 7. c, 8. Speaker of the House, 9. a, 10. fiscal.

The President

12

President Barack Obama signs a memorandum reducing the burden of student loans in June 2014 as college students look on. *Why has Obama tried to exercise authority without asking for new legislation from Congress?*

Mandel Ngan/Getty Images

The five learning outcomes below are designed to help improve your understanding of this chapter. After reading this chapter, you should be able to:

- **Learning Outcome 1:** Identify the types of people who typically undertake serious campaigns for the presidency.

- **Learning Outcome 2:** Distinguish some of the major roles of the president, including head of state, chief executive, commander in chief, chief diplomat, chief legislator, party chief, and politician.

- **Learning Outcome 3:** Describe some of the special powers of the president, and tell how a president can be removed from office.

- **Learning Outcome 4:** Explain the organization of the executive branch and, in particular, the executive office of the president.

- **Learning Outcome 5:** Evaluate the role of the vice president, and describe what happens if the presidency becomes vacant.

(▶) **WATCH & LEARN** MindTap® for American Government
Watch a brief "What Do You Know?" video summarizing The Presidency.

What If...

We Are Facing a New Cold War?

BACKGROUND

A cold war exists when two nations or alliances are enemies, but there is no actual fighting. History's most famous Cold War was the sustained state of military tension between the United States (and its allies) and the Soviet Union (and its allies) that ended around 1991. Some believe that there is a new cold war in the making, given that Russia's leader, Vladimir Putin, has invaded and taken control of part of Ukraine. Putin has also indicated that Russia has a right to intervene in other countries that were once part of the Soviet empire.

If we are really facing a new cold war, the manner in which the president of the United States addresses this threat becomes crucial.

WHAT IF WE ARE FACING A NEW COLD WAR?

During the "first" Cold War, U.S. presidents firmly resisted aggression by the Soviet Union and its allies. We airlifted supplies to West Berlin when the Soviets blockaded it. We sent troops to Korea and Vietnam to counter Communist advances in those nations. We helped prop up just about any government in Asia, Africa, or Latin America that claimed to be anti-communist.

Presumably, if we are facing a new cold war, the United States would be prepared to fight to defend its allies in the North Atlantic Treaty Organization (NATO), which include the Baltic states and Poland. We can assume the United States would protect other treaty allies, such as South Korea, Japan, and Australia. It is an open question whether President Obama, at least, would be prepared to defend much else. The Obama administration has imposed a limited number of economic sanctions on Russia in response to its aggression. But there has never been any presidential talk about sending arms to support the Ukrainian government, much less U.S. troops.

THERE IS NO IDEOLOGY AT STAKE

In the last Cold War, the Soviet Union and its allies claimed to represent communism, an ideology that gained some support among people in underdeveloped nations. American presidents could rally the nation against an ideology that almost all Americans fiercely rejected.

But today? Putin is throwing Russia's weight around for purely nationalist reasons. Despite some talk in Moscow about a new doctrine of cultural conservatism, Russia does not stand for anything that other nations find attractive. Any new cold war, therefore, would lack the ideological underpinnings of the old one.

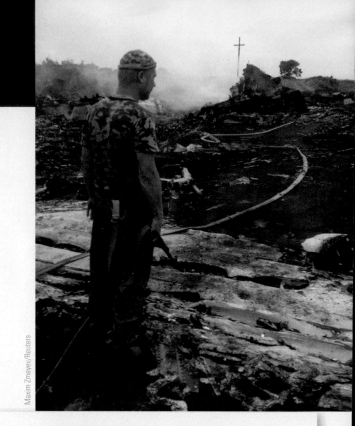

Maxim Zmeyev/Reuters

How much responsibility does Russia share for shooting down Malaysia Airlines flight MH17 over Ukraine in June 2014?

RUSSIA, EUROPE—AND CHINA

A second major difference is that Russia is more economically entangled with the West than the Soviet Union ever was. Much of Russia's prosperity is based on selling oil and gas to western and central Europe. Russia would be in some difficulties if these nations found alternate sources of supply. In contrast, the Soviet Union and its allies were almost entirely self-sufficient.

Perhaps the greatest danger of a new cold war is that it might involve an alliance between Russia and China. Such a bloc would mean real trouble for the United States. Militarily, Russia is relatively weak compared with the United States. But China is about to pass the United States to become the biggest economy in the world. It is already the nation with the world's largest population. If a new cold war were to start, therefore, the United States and its allies could face formidable adversaries.

For Critical Analysis

1. Some argue that Obama's cautious response to Russia's actions in Ukraine will encourage aggressive actions by Iran, North Korea, or China. Do you agree?

2. Can ties of trade and investment ever moderate the actions of a belligerent national leader?

The writers of the Constitution had no models to follow when they created the presidency of the United States. Nowhere else in the world was there an elected head of state. What the founders did not want was a king. The two initial plans considered by the founders—the Virginia and New Jersey plans—both called for an executive elected by Congress. Other delegates, especially those who had witnessed the need for a strong leader in the Revolutionary Army, believed a strong executive would be necessary for the new republic. The delegates, after much debate, created a chief executive who had enough powers granted in the Constitution to balance those of Congress.

In this chapter, after looking at who can become president and at the process involved, we examine closely the nature and extent of the constitutional powers held by the president. These constitutional powers are at their strongest in the area of foreign policy, a topic that we discussed in the chapter-opening *What If. . .* feature.

Who Can Become President?

The president receives a salary of $400,000, plus $169,000 for expenses and a vast array of free services, beginning with residence in the White House. The requirements for becoming president, as outlined in Article II, Section 1, of the Constitution, are not overwhelmingly stringent:

> *No person except a natural born Citizen, or a Citizen of the United States, at the time of the Adoption of this Constitution, shall be eligible to the Office of President; neither shall any Person be eligible to that Office who shall not have attained to the Age of thirty-five Years, and been fourteen Years a Resident within the United States.*

■ **Learning Outcome 1:** Identify the types of people who typically undertake serious campaigns for the presidency.

A "Natural Born Citizen"

The only question that arises about these qualifications relates to the term *natural born Citizen.* Does that mean only citizens born in the United States and its territories? What about a child born to a U.S. citizen visiting or living in another country? Although the question has not been dealt with directly by the Supreme Court, it is reasonable to expect that someone would be eligible if her or his parents were Americans.

These questions were debated when George Romney, who was born in Chihuahua, Mexico, made a serious bid for the Republican presidential nomination in the 1960s.[1] The issue came up again when opponents of President Barack Obama claimed that Obama was not a natural born citizen. In reality, Obama was born in Honolulu, Hawaii, in 1961, two years after Hawaii became a state. Those who disputed Obama's birth claimed that the short-form birth certificate released by the Obama campaign was a forgery—despite the fact that Obama's birth was also recorded by two Honolulu newspapers. Agitation by the "birthers," as they came to be called, subsided somewhat in 2011 after the White House released Obama's long-form birth certificate, which was endorsed as valid by every relevant Hawaiian official, Republican and Democrat.

did you know?

George Washington was a successful liquor distributor—he distilled rye whiskey, apple brandy, and peach brandy at Mount Vernon.

Presidential Characteristics

The American dream is symbolized by the statement that "anybody can become president of this country." It is true that in modern times, presidents have included a haberdasher (Harry Truman—for a short period of time), a peanut farmer (Jimmy Carter),

---

1. George Romney was governor of Michigan from 1963 to 1969. Romney was not nominated for the presidency, and the issue remains unresolved. George Romney was the father of Mitt Romney, the 2012 Republican presidential candidate.

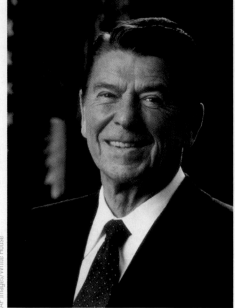

The youngest president ever elected was John F. Kennedy (1961–1963). Despite his youth, Kennedy had serious health problems that he kept secret. *Could a presidential candidate do such a thing today?*

The oldest president ever elected was Ronald Reagan (1981–1989). *Could Reagan's age have helped him with some voters?*

did you know?

Andrew Jackson was allegedly involved in as many as one hundred duels. He was shot in the chest in a duel in 1806 and took a bullet in the arm in a bar fight with Missouri senator Thomas Hart Benton in 1813.

and an actor (Ronald Reagan). But if you examine the list of presidents in Appendix E at the end of this book, you will see that the most common previous occupational field of presidents in this country has been the law. Out of forty-four presidents, twenty-seven have been lawyers, and many have been wealthy.

Although the Constitution states that the minimum-age requirement for the presidency is thirty-five years, most presidents have been much older than that when they assumed office. John F. Kennedy, at the age of forty-three, was the youngest elected president, and the oldest was Ronald Reagan, at age sixty-nine. The average age at inauguration has been fifty-four. There has clearly been a demographic bias in the selection of presidents. All have been male, white, and from the Protestant tradition, except for John F. Kennedy, a Roman Catholic, and Barack Obama, an African American. Should voters care about the religion of a presidential candidate? We discuss that question in this chapter's *Which Side Are You On?* feature that follows.

The Process of Becoming President

Major and minor political parties nominate candidates for president and vice president at national conventions every four years. As discussed in Chapter 9, the nation's voters do not elect a president and vice president directly but rather cast ballots for presidential electors, who then vote for president and vice president in the electoral college.

Because victory goes to the candidate with a majority in the electoral college, it is conceivable that someone could be elected to the office of the presidency without having a plurality of the popular vote cast. Indeed, on four occasions candidates won elections even though their major opponents received more popular votes. One of those elections occurred in 2000, when George W. Bush won the electoral college vote and became president even though his opponent, Al Gore, won the popular vote. In elections in which more than two candidates were running for office, many presidential candidates have

Which Side Are You On?

Should Voters Care about the President's Religion?

The U.S. Constitution in Article VI, Section 3, states, "[N]o religious Test shall ever be required as a Qualification to any Office or public Trust under the United States." In other words, our government cannot bar someone from public office because of her or his religious faith (or lack of any religious faith, for that matter). What the Constitution says and how voters pick candidates, though, are two separate matters. Currently, polls report that two-thirds of Americans want their president to be a person of faith. Under such circumstances, an avowed atheist could not become president of the United States. But what about a candidate's specific religious beliefs? Should voters care about these? Opinions differ.

Religion Should Have No Part in Choosing Candidates

Today, Americans do not accept that those seeking public office must be of a particular gender or ethnic group. Many people would argue that voters should not consider a candidate's church or faith affiliation either. If the framers of the Constitution wanted to make sure that we do not choose our government officials based on their religion, why should we care more than two centuries later? Men and women of faith can govern just as badly as those who have no faith or the "wrong" faith. A candidate's claim, say, to be a practicing Christian guarantees nothing. The religious convictions of our presidential candidates are not good predictors of how they will face real-world problems. Our

votes should be based on character, policies, or party, not on a candidate's religious convictions.

Religion Does, and Should, Matter

Others agree that voters should be willing to vote for candidates of any religion, as long as the candidate takes no orders from religious authorities. Even if voters disregard denomination, however, they should care about how a candidate's religious beliefs affect his or her actions. Many Christians believe, for example, that their religion commands that families and individuals be self-reliant, and that government action in the economic sphere undercuts this obligation. Other Christians, observing how Jesus constantly advocated for the poor, believe their religion calls for social services that benefit the needy. Religious beliefs can affect how people view abortion, gay and lesbian rights, the death penalty, and even matters of war and peace. Voters need to understand the impact of a candidate's beliefs on such issues.

For Critical Analysis

Can you think of examples, either in your own life or in the lives of your friends and relatives, where particular religious beliefs have shaped political ideas? If so, what were these influences?

won with less than 50 percent of the total popular votes cast for all candidates—including Abraham Lincoln, Woodrow Wilson, Harry Truman, John F. Kennedy, Richard Nixon, and, in 1992, Bill Clinton.

Thus far, on two occasions the electoral college has failed to give any candidate a majority. At that point, the House of Representatives takes over, and the president is then chosen from among the three candidates having the most electoral college votes, as noted in Chapter 9. In 1800, Thomas Jefferson and Aaron Burr tied in the electoral college. This happened because the Constitution had not been explicit in indicating which of the two electoral votes was for president and which was for vice president. In 1804, the **Twelfth Amendment** clarified the matter by requiring that the president and vice president be chosen separately. In 1824, the House again had to make a choice, this time among William H. Crawford, Andrew Jackson, and John Quincy Adams. It chose Adams, even though Jackson had more electoral and popular votes.

Twelfth Amendment
An amendment to the Constitution, adopted in 1804, that requires the separate election of the president and the vice president by the electoral college.

The Many Roles of the President

The Constitution speaks briefly about the duties and obligations of the president. Based on this brief list of powers and on the precedents of history, the presidency has grown into a very complicated job that requires balancing at least five constitutional roles. These are (1) head of state, (2) chief executive, (3) commander in chief of the armed forces, (4) chief diplomat, and (5) chief legislator of the United States. In addition to these constitutional roles, the president serves as the leader of his or her political party. Of course, the president is also the nation's most prominent and successful politician. Here we examine each of these significant presidential functions, or roles. It is worth noting that one person plays all these roles simultaneously and that the needs of the roles may at times come into conflict.

Head of State

Head of State
The role of the president as ceremonial head of the government.

Chief Executive
The role of the president as head of the executive branch of the government.

Every nation has at least one person who is the ceremonial head of state. In most democratic nations, the role of **head of state** is given to someone other than the chief executive, who leads the executive branch of government. In Britain, for example, the head of state is the queen. In much of Europe, the head of state is a relatively powerless president. The prime minister is the chief executive. But in the United States, the president is both chief executive and head of state. According to William Howard Taft, as head of state the president symbolizes the "dignity and majesty" of the American people.

The president, as head of state, engages in a number of activities that are largely symbolic or ceremonial. Some students of the American political system believe that having the president serve as both the chief executive and the head of state drastically limits the time available to do "real" work. Not all presidents have agreed with this conclusion, however—particularly those presidents who have skillfully blended these two roles with their role as a politician. Being head of state gives the president tremendous public exposure, which can be an important asset in a campaign for reelection. When that exposure is positive, it helps the president deal with Congress over proposed legislation and increases the chances of being reelected—or getting the candidates of the president's party elected.

Chief Executive

According to the Constitution, "The executive Power shall be vested in a President of the United States of America . . . . [H]e may require the Opinion, in writing, of the principal Officer in each of the executive Departments, upon any Subject relating to the Duties of their respective Offices . . . and he shall nominate, and by and with the Advice and Consent of the Senate, shall appoint . . . . Officers of the United States. . . . [H]e shall take Care that the Laws be faithfully executed." As **chief executive,** the president is constitutionally bound to enforce the acts of Congress, the judgments of federal courts, and treaties signed by the United States. The duty to "faithfully execute" the laws has been a source of constitutional power for presidents.

The Powers of Appointment and Removal. To assist in the various tasks of the chief executive, the president has a federal bureaucracy (see Chapter 13), which currently consists of 2 million federal civilian employees, not counting the U.S. Postal Service (625,000 employees). You might think that the president, as head of the largest bureaucracy in the United States, wields enormous power. The president, however, only nominally runs the executive bureaucracy. Most government positions

American president Harry Truman (1945–1953), right, stands with General Dwight Eisenhower in 1951. A year later, Eisenhower successfully ran for president. *Why might a general make a good president?*

are filled by **civil service** employees, who generally gain government employment through a merit system rather than presidential appointment.[2] Therefore, even though the president has important **appointment power,** it is limited to cabinet and subcabinet jobs, federal judgeships, agency heads, and several thousand lesser jobs—about eight thousand positions in total.

This means that most of the 2.6 million employees of the executive branch owe no political allegiance to the president. They are more likely to owe loyalty to congressional committees or to interest groups representing the sector of the society that they serve. Table 12–1 that follows shows what percentage of the total employment in each executive department is available for political appointment by the president.

The president's power to remove from office those officials who are not doing a good job or who do not agree with the president is not explicitly granted by the Constitution and has been limited. In 1926, however, a Supreme Court decision prevented Congress from interfering with the president's ability to fire those executive-branch officials whom the president had appointed with Senate approval.[3] There are ten agencies whose

Civil Service
A collective term for the body of employees working for the government. Generally, "civil service" is understood to apply to all those who gain government employment through a merit system.

Appointment Power
The authority vested in the president to fill a government office or position. Positions filled by presidential appointment include those in the executive branch and the federal judiciary, commissioned officers in the armed forces, and members of the independent regulatory commissions.

2. See Chapter 13 for a discussion of the Civil Service Reform Act.
3. *Meyers v. United States,* 272 U.S. 52 (1926).

Table 12–1 ▸ Total Civilian Positions in Cabinet Departments Available for Political Appointment by the President

Why might the State Department have a large number of political appointees?

Executive Department	Total Number of Employees	Political Appointments Available	Percentage
Agriculture	87,667	363	0.41
Commerce	45,355	284	0.63
Defense	727,641	598	0.08
Education	4,212	207	4.91
Energy	15,361	558	3.63
Health and Human Services	86,264	536	0.62
Homeland Security	192,582	304	0.16
Housing and Urban Development	8,597	177	2.06
Interior	64,931	302	0.47
Justice	114,233	485	0.42
Labor	16,150	189	1.17
State	12,896	557	4.32
Transportation	54,605	264	0.48
Treasury	100,402	235	0.23
Veterans Affairs	340,926	447	0.13

did you know?
Thomas Jefferson was the first president to be inaugurated in Washington, D.C., where he walked to the Capitol from a boardinghouse, took the oath, made a brief speech in the Senate chamber, and then walked back home.

Sources: *Policy and Supporting Positions* (Washington, D.C.: Government Printing Office, 2012). This text, known as "Plum Book" (see Chapter 13), is published after each presidential election. Also, U.S. Office of Personnel Management. Figures are for December 2013.

President Obama speaks at the Pentagon in January 2012. He is flanked, left to right, by the Army's top general, the chairman of the Joint Chiefs of Staff, and the commandant of the Marine Corps. Obama announced new priorities that will cut the Pentagon budget by hundreds of billions of dollars over the next decade. *How are top members of the military likely to react to budget cuts?*

directors the president can remove at any time. These agencies include the Commission on Civil Rights, the Environmental Protection Agency, the General Services Administration, and the Small Business Administration. In addition, the president can remove all heads of cabinet departments, all individuals in the Executive Office of the President, and all of the political appointees listed in Table 12–1.

Harry Truman spoke candidly of the difficulties a president faces in trying to control the executive bureaucracy. On leaving office, he referred to the problems that Dwight Eisenhower, as a former general of the army, was going to have: "He'll sit here and he'll say do this! do that! and nothing will happen. Poor Ike—it won't be a bit like the Army. He'll find it very frustrating."[4]

The Power to Grant Reprieves and Pardons. Section 2 of Article II of the Constitution gives the president the power to grant **reprieves** and **pardons** for offenses against the United States except in cases of impeachment. All pardons are administered by the Office of the Pardon Attorney in the Department of Justice.

The Supreme Court upheld the president's power to grant reprieves and pardons in a 1925 case concerning a pardon granted by the president to an individual convicted of contempt of court. A federal circuit court had contended that only judges had the authority to convict individuals for contempt of court when court orders were violated and that the courts should be free from interference by the executive branch. The Supreme Court simply stated that the president could grant reprieves or pardons for all offenses "either before trial, during trial, or after trial, by individuals, or by classes, conditionally or absolutely, and this without modification or regulation by Congress."[5]

Reprieve
A formal postponement of the execution of a sentence imposed by a court of law.

Pardon
A release from the punishment for, or legal consequences of, a crime. A pardon can be granted by the president before or after a conviction.

---

4. Quoted in Richard E. Neustadt, *Presidential Power: The Politics of Leadership* (New York: Wiley, 1960), p. 9. Note that Truman may not have considered the amount of politics involved in decision making in the upper ranks of the army.
5. *Ex parte Grossman*, 267 U.S. 87 (1925).

President Andrew Johnson set the record for the largest number of persons ever pardoned in 1868 when he issued a blanket amnesty to all former Confederate soldiers. In 1974, in a controversial decision, President Gerald Ford pardoned former president Richard Nixon for his role in the Watergate affair before any charges were brought in court. In 1977, President Jimmy Carter issued a blanket pardon to Vietnam War–era draft resisters, a group that probably included more than 100,000 persons.

Commander in Chief

The president, according to the Constitution, "shall be Commander in Chief of the Army and Navy of the United States, and of the Militia of the several States, when called into the actual Service of the United States." In other words, the armed forces are under civilian, rather than military, control.

> **Commander in Chief**
> The role of the president as supreme commander of the military forces of the United States and of the state National Guard units when they are called into federal service.

Wartime Powers. Those who wrote the Constitution had George Washington in mind when they made the president the **commander in chief.** Although we do not expect our president to lead the troops into battle, presidents as commanders in chief have wielded dramatic power. Harry Truman made the difficult decision to drop atomic bombs on Hiroshima and Nagasaki in 1945 to force Japan to surrender and thus bring World War II to an end. Lyndon Johnson ordered bombing missions against North Vietnam in the 1960s, and he personally selected some of the targets. Richard Nixon decided to invade Cambodia in 1970. Ronald Reagan sent troops to Lebanon and Grenada in 1983 and ordered U.S. fighter planes to attack Libya in 1986. George H. W. Bush sent troops to Panama in 1989 and to the Middle East in 1990. Bill Clinton sent troops to Haiti in 1994 and to Bosnia in 1995, ordered missile attacks on alleged terrorist bases in 1998, and sent American planes to bomb Serbia in 1999. George W. Bush ordered the invasion of Afghanistan in 2001 and of Iraq in 2003, and most recently, Barack Obama ordered additional troops into Afghanistan in 2009 and authorized air strikes in Libya in 2011.

The president is the ultimate decision maker in military matters. Everywhere the president goes, so too goes the "football"—a briefcase filled with all of the codes necessary to order a nuclear attack. Only the president has the power to order the use of nuclear force.

did you know?

Abraham Lincoln could throw down in the wrestling ring. As a young man, he was only defeated once in approximately three hundred matches.

As commander in chief, the president exercises more authority than in any other role. Constitutionally, Congress has the sole power to declare war, but the president can send the armed forces into situations that are certainly the equivalent of war. Harry Truman dispatched troops to Korea in 1950. Johnson and Nixon waged an undeclared war in Southeast Asia, where more than 58,000 Americans were killed and 300,000 were wounded. In neither of these situations had Congress declared war.

Power over the National Guard. One of the president's powers as commander in chief is the right to assume authority over National Guard units—that is, state militias. Throughout American history, presidents have "nationalized" the Guard to handle domestic problems such as natural disasters or severe social disturbances, including strikes or urban riots. President George W. Bush sent 6,000 members of the National Guard to the Mexican border in 2006–2008 to assist the Border Patrol, and in 2010 President Obama sent 1,200 Guard troops to the border for the same purpose.

The president also has the ability to send National Guard units abroad to supplement the regular armed forces. Both

Why Should You Care about...

The Presidency?

When it comes to caring about the presidency, most people do not need much encouragement. The president is our most important official. The president serves as the public face of the government and, indeed, of the nation as a whole. Many people, however, believe the president is such a remote figure that nothing they can do will affect what he or she does. That is not always true. On many issues, your voice—combined, of course, with the voices of many others—can have an impact. Writing to the president is a traditional way for citizens to express their opinions. Every day, the White House receives several thousand letters and other communications.

War Powers Resolution
A law passed in 1973 spelling out the conditions under which the president can commit troops without congressional approval.

Advice and Consent
Terms in the Constitution describing the U.S. Senate's power to review and approve treaties and presidential appointments.

Chief Diplomat
The role of the president in recognizing foreign governments, making treaties, and effecting executive agreements.

Diplomatic Recognition
The formal acknowledgment of a foreign government as legitimate.

Bush and Obama sent Guard forces abroad on a massive scale. In 2005, National Guard troops comprised a larger percentage of frontline fighting forces than in any war in U.S. history—about 43 percent in Iraq and 55 percent in Afghanistan. Since then, the number of National Guard troops sent abroad has declined substantially.

The War Powers Resolution. In an attempt to gain more control over such military activities, in 1973 Congress passed the **War Powers Resolution**—over President Nixon's veto—requiring that the president consult with Congress when sending American forces into action. Once they are sent, the president must report to Congress within forty-eight hours. Unless Congress approves the use of troops within sixty days or extends the sixty-day time limit, the forces must be withdrawn.

In spite of the War Powers Resolution, the powers of the president as commander in chief are more extensive today than they were in the past. The so-called war on terrorism, which began after the terrorist attacks of September 11, 2001, led to an especially notable increase in presidential powers.

Chief Diplomat

The Constitution gives the president the power to recognize foreign governments, to make treaties with the **advice and consent** of the Senate, and to make special agreements with other heads of state that do not require congressional approval. In addition, the president nominates U.S. ambassadors to other countries. As **chief diplomat,** the president dominates American foreign policy, a role that has been supported many times by the Supreme Court.

Diplomatic Recognition. An important power of the president as chief diplomat is that of **diplomatic recognition,** or the power to recognize—or to refuse to recognize—foreign governments as legitimate. In the role of ceremonial head of state, the president has always received foreign diplomats. In modern times, the simple act of receiving a foreign diplomat has been equivalent to accrediting the diplomat and officially recognizing his or her government. Such recognition of the legitimacy of another country's government is a prerequisite to diplomatic relations or treaties between that country and the United States.

Deciding when to recognize a foreign power is not always simple. The United States, for example, did not recognize the Soviet Union until 1933—sixteen years after the Russian Revolution of 1917. It was only after all attempts to reverse the effects of that revolution—including military invasion of Russia and diplomatic isolation—had proved futile that Franklin D. Roosevelt extended recognition to the Soviet government. In December 1978, long after the Communist victory in China in 1949, President Jimmy Carter granted official recognition to the People's Republic of China.[6]

Proposal and Ratification of Treaties. The president has the sole power to negotiate treaties with other nations. These treaties must be presented to the Senate. A two-thirds vote is required in the Senate for approval, or *ratification.* After ratification, the president can approve the treaty as adopted by the Senate. Approval poses a problem when the Senate has tacked on substantive amendments or reservations to a treaty, particularly when such changes may require reopening negotiations with the other signatory governments. Sometimes, a president may decide to withdraw a treaty if the senatorial changes are too extensive—as Woodrow Wilson did with the Versailles Treaty in 1919, which concluded

---

6. The Nixon administration first encouraged new relations with the People's Republic of China by allowing a cultural exchange of table tennis teams.

World War I. Wilson believed that the senatorial reservations would weaken the treaty so much that it would be ineffective.

Recent Treaty Efforts. Before September 11, 2001, President George W. Bush indicated his intention to steer the United States in a unilateral direction on foreign policy. After the terrorist attacks of September 11, 2001, however, Bush sought cooperation from U.S. allies in the war on terrorism. Bush's return to multilateralism was exemplified in the signing of a nuclear weapons reduction treaty with Russia in 2002. Nonetheless, his attempts to gain international support for a war against Iraq to overthrow that country's government were not as successful as he had hoped.

In April 2010, President Obama and then–Russian president Dmitry Medvedev signed the New START Treaty, a follow-up to earlier arms control treaties. The ten-year pact will cut the number of nuclear warheads allowed to each party by 30 percent, to 1,550 warheads. The number of permitted missile launchers will be cut in half. The treaty includes a verification process. The U.S. Senate ratified the treaty in December 2010.

Executive Agreements. Presidential power in foreign affairs is enhanced greatly by the use of **executive agreements** made between the president and other heads of state. Such agreements do not require Senate approval, although the House and the Senate may refuse to appropriate the funds necessary to implement them. Whereas treaties are binding on all succeeding administrations, executive agreements require each new president's consent to remain in effect.

Among the advantages of executive agreements are speed and secrecy. The former is essential during a crisis. The latter is important when the administration fears that open senatorial debate may be detrimental to the best interests of the United States or to the interests of the president.[7] There have been far more executive agreements (about nine thousand) than treaties (about thirteen hundred). Many executive agreements contain secret provisions calling for American military assistance or other support.

President George H. W. Bush (1989–1993) is the father of President George W. Bush (2001–2009). Here, he is shown meeting with the foreign minister of Saudi Arabia. *Why would a president spend time in such a meeting?*

Chief Legislator

Constitutionally, presidents must recommend to Congress legislation that they judge necessary and expedient. Not all presidents have wielded their powers as **chief legislator** in the same manner. Some presidents have been almost completely unsuccessful in getting their legislative programs implemented by Congress. Presidents Franklin Roosevelt (1933–1945) and Lyndon Johnson (1963–1969), however, saw much of their proposed legislation put into effect.

Creating the Congressional Agenda. In modern times, the president has played a dominant role in creating the congressional agenda. In the president's annual **State of the Union message,** which is required by the Constitution (Article II, Section 3) and is

Executive Agreement
An international agreement made by the president, without senatorial ratification, with the head of a foreign state.

Chief Legislator
The role of the president in influencing the making of laws.

State of the Union Message
An annual message to Congress in which the president proposes a legislative program. The message is addressed not only to Congress but also to the American people and to the world.

7. The Case Act of 1972 requires that all executive agreements be transmitted to Congress within sixty days after the agreement takes effect. Secret agreements are transmitted to the foreign relations committees as classified information.

usually given in late January shortly after Congress reconvenes, the president presents a legislative program. The message gives a broad, comprehensive view of what the president wishes the legislature to accomplish during its session. It is as much a message to the American people and to the world as it is to Congress. Its impact on public opinion can determine the way in which Congress responds to the president's agenda.

Since 1913, the president has delivered the State of the Union message in a formal address to Congress. Today, this address is one of the great ceremonies of American governance, and many customs have grown up around it. For example, one cabinet member, the "designated survivor," stays away to ensure that the country will always have a president, even if someone manages to blow up the Capitol building. Everyone gives the president an initial standing ovation out of respect for the office, but this applause does not necessarily represent support for the individual who holds the office. During the speech, senators and House members either applaud or remain silent to indicate their opinion of the policies that the president announces.

Getting Legislation Passed. The president can propose legislation, but Congress is not required to pass—or even introduce—any of the administration's bills. How, then, does the president get those proposals made into law? One way is by exercising the power of persuasion. The president writes to, telephones, and meets with various congressional leaders. He or she makes public announcements to influence public opinion. Finally, as head of a party, the president exercises leadership over the party's members in Congress. A president whose party holds a majority in both chambers of Congress usually has an easier time getting legislation passed than does a president who faces a hostile Congress.

Saying No to Legislation. The president has the power to say no to legislation through use of the veto,[8] by which the White House returns a bill unsigned to Congress with a **veto message** attached. Because the Constitution requires that every bill passed by the House and the Senate be sent to the president before it becomes law, the president must act on each bill:

1. If the bill is signed, it becomes law.
2. If the bill is not sent back to Congress after ten congressional working days, it becomes law without the president's signature.
3. The president can reject the bill and send it back to Congress with a veto message setting forth objections. Congress then can change the bill, hoping to secure presidential approval, and repass it. Or Congress can simply reject the president's objections by overriding the veto with a two-thirds roll-call vote of the members present in both the House and the Senate.
4. If the president refuses to sign the bill and Congress adjourns within ten working days after the bill has been submitted to the president, the bill is killed for that session of Congress. This is called a **pocket veto.** If Congress wishes the bill to be reconsidered, the bill must be reintroduced during the following session.

Presidents employed the veto power infrequently until after the Civil War, but it has been used with increasing vigor since then (see Table 12–2 that follows). The total number of vetoes from George Washington's administration through the end of Barack Obama's first term in office was 2,564, with about two-thirds of those vetoes being exercised by Grover Cleveland, Franklin Roosevelt, Harry Truman, and Dwight Eisenhower.

Veto Message
The president's formal explanation of a veto when legislation is returned to Congress.

Pocket Veto
A special veto exercised by the chief executive after a legislative body has adjourned. Bills not signed by the chief executive die after a specified period of time. If Congress wishes to reconsider such a bill, it must be reintroduced in the following session of Congress.

---

8. Veto in Latin means "I forbid."

Table 12–2 ▶ **Presidential Vetoes, 1789 to Present**

If the president and Congress are of different parties, what effect might that have on the number of presidential vetoes?

Years	President	Regular Vetoes	Vetoes Overridden	Pocket Vetoes	Total Vetoes
1789–1797	Washington	2	0	0	2
1797–1801	J. Adams	0	0	0	0
1801–1809	Jefferson	0	0	0	0
1809–1817	Madison	5	0	2	7
1817–1825	Monroe	1	0	0	1
1825–1829	J. Q. Adams	0	0	0	0
1829–1837	Jackson	5	0	7	12
1837–1841	Van Buren	0	0	1	1
1841–1841	Harrison	0	0	0	0
1841–1845	Tyler	6	1	4	10
1845–1849	Polk	2	0	1	3
1849–1850	Taylor	0	0	0	0
1850–1853	Fillmore	0	0	0	0
1853–1857	Pierce	9	5	0	9
1857–1861	Buchanan	4	0	3	7
1861–1865	Lincoln	2	0	5	7
1865–1869	A. Johnson	21	15	8	29
1869–1877	Grant	45	4	48	93
1877–1881	Hayes	12	1	1	13
1881–1881	Garfield	0	0	0	0
1881–1885	Arthur	4	1	8	12
1885–1889	Cleveland	304	2	110	414
1889–1893	Harrison	19	1	25	44
1893–1897	Cleveland	42	5	128	170
1897–1901	McKinley	6	0	36	42
1901–1909	T. Roosevelt	42	1	40	82
1909–1913	Taft	30	1	9	39
1913–1921	Wilson	33	6	11	44
1921–1923	Harding	5	0	1	6
1923–1929	Coolidge	20	4	30	50
1929–1933	Hoover	21	3	16	37
1933–1945	F. Roosevelt	372	9	263	635
1945–1953	Truman	180	12	70	250
1953–1961	Eisenhower	73	2	108	181
1961–1963	Kennedy	12	0	9	21
1963–1969	L. Johnson	16	0	14	30
1969–1974	Nixon	26*	7	17	43
1974–1977	Ford	48	12	18	66
1977–1981	Carter	13	2	18	31
1981–1989	Reagan	39	9	39	78
1989–1993	G. H. W. Bush	29	1	15	44
1993–2001	Clinton	36†	2	1	37
2001–2009	G. W. Bush	11	4	1	12
2009–	Obama	2	0	0	2
TOTAL		1,497	110	1,067	2,564

*Two pocket vetoes by President Nixon, overruled in the courts, are counted here as regular vetoes.
†President Clinton's line-item vetoes are not included.
Sources: Office of the Clerk; plus authors' updates through 2014.

President George W. Bush (2001–2009) gives a State of the Union address while Vice President Dick Cheney and Speaker of the House Nancy Pelosi listen. *Where is that address given?*

George W. Bush was the first president since Martin Van Buren (1837–1841) to serve a full term in office without exercising the veto power. Bush, who had the benefit of a Republican Congress, did not veto any legislation during his first term. Only in the summer of 2006 did Bush finally issue a veto, saying "no" to stem-cell research legislation passed by Congress. After the Democrats took control of Congress in January 2007, however, the president issued eleven vetoes, four of which were overridden. President Obama, who for two years also enjoyed a Congress dominated by his own party, issued only two vetoes through mid-2014.

The Line-Item Veto. Ronald Reagan lobbied strenuously for Congress to give another tool to the president—the **line-item veto,** which would allow the president to veto *specific* spending provisions of legislation that was passed by Congress. Reagan saw the line-item veto as the only way that he could control overall congressional spending. In 1996, Congress passed the Line Item Veto Act, which provided for the line-item veto. President Clinton used the line-item veto on several occasions, but the act was challenged in court. In 1998, by a six-to-three vote, the United States Supreme Court agreed with the veto's opponents and overturned the act. The Court stated that "there is no provision in the Constitution that authorizes the president to enact, to amend or to repeal statutes."[9]

Congress's Power to Override Presidential Vetoes. A veto is a clear-cut indication of the president's dissatisfaction with congressional legislation. Congress, however, can override a presidential veto, although it rarely exercises this power. Consider that two-thirds of the members of each chamber who are present must vote to override the president's veto in a roll-call vote. This means that if only one-third plus one of the members voting in one of the chambers of Congress do not agree to override the veto, the veto holds. In American history, only about 7 percent of all vetoes have been overridden.

The President as Party Chief and Superpolitician

Presidents are by no means above political partisanship, and one of their many roles is that of chief of party. Although the Constitution says nothing about the function of the president within a political party (the mere concept of political parties was abhorrent to most of the authors of the Constitution), today presidents are the actual leaders of their parties.

The President as Chief of Party. As party leader, the president chooses the national committee chairperson and can try to discipline party members who fail to support presidential policies. One way of exerting political power within the party is through

Line-Item Veto
The power of an executive to veto individual lines or items within a piece of legislation without vetoing the entire bill.

9. *Clinton v. City of New York,* 524 U.S. 417 (1998).

patronage—appointing individuals to government or public jobs. This power was more extensive in the past, before the establishment of the civil service in 1883 (see Chapter 13), but the president still retains important patronage power. As we noted earlier, the president can appoint several thousand individuals to jobs in the cabinet, the White House, and the federal regulatory agencies.

Perhaps the most important partisan role that the president has played in the 1990s and early 2000s has been that of fund-raiser. The president is able to raise large sums for the party through appearances at dinners, speaking engagements, and other social occasions. President Clinton may have raised more than half a billion dollars for the Democratic Party during his two terms. President George W. Bush was even more successful than Clinton. Barack Obama's spectacular success in raising funds for his presidential campaigns (particularly via the Internet) indicates that he has carried on this fund-raising tradition.

Presidents have a number of other ways of exerting influence as party chief. The president may make it known that a particular congressperson's choice for federal judge will not be appointed unless that member of Congress is more supportive of the president's legislative program.[10] The president may agree to campaign for a particular program or for a particular candidate. Presidents also reward loyal members of Congress with support for the funding of local projects, tax breaks for regional industries, and other forms of "pork."

Presidential Constituencies. Presidents have many constituencies. In principle, they are beholden to the entire electorate—the public of the United States— even those who did not vote. Presidents are certainly beholden to their party, because its members helped to put them in office. The president's constituencies also include members of the opposing party whose cooperation the president needs. Finally, the president must take into consideration a constituency that has come to be called the *Washington community* (also known as those "inside the beltway").[11] This community consists of individuals who—whether in or out of political office—are intimately familiar with the workings of government, thrive on gossip, and measure on a daily basis the political power of the president.

Public Approval. All of these constituencies are impressed by presidents who maintain a high level of public approval, partly because doing so is very difficult to accomplish. Presidential popularity, as measured by national polls, gives the president an extra political resource to use in persuading legislators or bureaucrats to pass legislation.

As you can see from Figure 12–1 that follows, President George W. Bush enjoyed spectacularly high approval ratings immediately after the terrorist attacks of 9/11. Bush's popularity declined steadily after 9/11.

Obama's initial popularity figures were also very high. Much of his support in early 2009, however, came from Republicans, and it was bound to dissipate. From the middle of 2010 to mid-2014, Obama's positive ratings fluctuated between 40 and 50 percent. They were at their lowest during the confrontation with the Republicans over the debt ceiling in 2011, and at the time

---

Patronage
The practice of rewarding faithful party workers and followers with government employment and contracts.

did you know?
Woodrow Wilson was the only president to earn a Ph.D. He was a professor at Princeton before becoming president of that university.

Why Should You Care about...

The Presidency?

The president can influence many issues that directly affect your life. For example, in recent years, many people have raised the question of whether anything could be done soon about reforming the nation's immigration policies. If any change to immigration policies were to succeed, it would need strong support from the president. Immigration might be a topic on which you have strong opinions. If you have opinions on a subject such as this, you may well want to "cast your vote" by adding your e-mail to the many others that the president receives on the issue.

---

10. "Senatorial courtesy" (see Chapter 14) often gives individual senators an important role choosing judicial candidates, however.
11. The *beltway* refers to Interstate 495, which circles the capital, passing through Maryland and Virginia suburbs.

Figure 12–1 ▶ **Public Popularity of Modern Presidents**

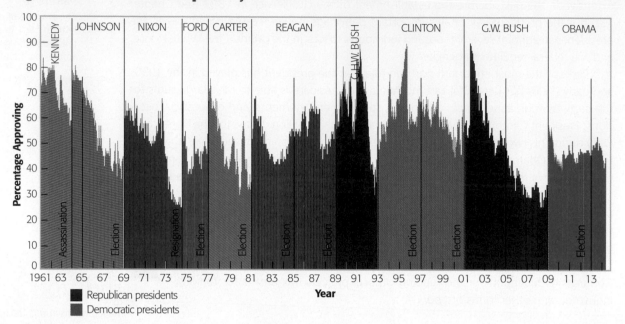

Sources: Adapted from the Roper Center for Public Opinion Research: Gallup and *USA Today*/CNN polls, March 1992 through June 2012 and Real Clear Politics.

of the government shutdown and the troubled Obamacare rollout in 2013. Conveniently, they were at their highest in November and December 2012, right in time for his reelection.

"Going Public." Since the early 1900s, presidents have spoken more to the public and less to Congress. In the 1800s, only 7 percent of presidential speeches were addressed to the public. Since 1900, 50 percent have been addressed to the public. Presidents frequently go over the heads of Congress and the political elites, taking their cases directly to the people.

This strategy, dubbed "going public," gives the president additional power through the ability to persuade and manipulate public opinion. By identifying their own positions so clearly, presidents can weaken the legislators' positions. In times when the major political parties are highly polarized, however, the possibility of compromise with

President Jimmy Carter with his wife Rosalynn in 1980. Carter had just accepted renomination from the Democratic National Convention, but he went on to lose resoundingly to Republican Ronald Reagan. *For what reasons can a sitting president lose popularity?*

the opposition party may actually be reduced if the president openly takes a strong position. If the opposition party dominates Congress, it may argue that its democratic legitimacy trumps that of the president. We examine this issue in the *Beyond Our Borders* feature that follows.

Constitutional Power
A power vested in the president by Article II of the Constitution.

Presidential Powers

Presidents have at their disposal a variety of special powers and privileges not available in the other branches of the U.S. government. The powers of the president discussed earlier in this chapter in the section on the roles of the president are called **constitutional powers,** because their basis lies in the Constitution. In addition, Congress has established by law, or statute, numerous other presidential powers—such as the ability to declare

■ **Learning Outcome 3:**
Describe some of the special powers of the president, and tell how a president can be removed from office.

Beyond Our Borders

Presidents in Latin America

You learned in Chapter 2 about the parliamentary system, a form of democratic government that is an alternative to our system. Many countries do have systems much like ours, however, in which the president and congress are elected separately. Most countries in Latin America have presidential systems. One characteristic of a presidential system is that both the president and the congress can claim democratic legitimacy. Both, after all, were elected by the people.

President versus Congress in Latin America

A presidential system would seem to call for compromise between the president and congress. That, however, does not always happen. In 2009 in Honduras, the military, acting for the Supreme Court and Congress, seized the president and flew him into exile. In 2012 in Paraguay, a Congress dominated by conservatives impeached and convicted a liberal president on purely political grounds. Paraguay's neighbors treated this act as a coup d'état. In contrast, presidents in Argentina and Venezuela have dominated their nations in ways that clearly threaten democracy.

Jose Antonio Chebuib, a political scientist, has calculated that the average parliamentary regime lasts 73 years—and the average presidential regime just 21 years. Political scientist Juan Linz has observed that "the only presidential democracy with a long history of constitutional continuity is the United States."

The U.S. Exception

The United States enjoys the longest-lived political system on earth (with the possible exception of Britain). The weight of constitutional tradition in this country is enormous. We will not end up like Paraguay or Venezuela. Yet there are worrying signs. Linz argued that the ideological diversity of U.S. political parties prevented formation of a congressional leadership that rejects the legitimacy of the president. But we don't have parties like that anymore. Our parties are now ideologically unified.

In recent crises, Republicans in the House have argued that they, not the president, represent the will of the American people. Meanwhile, on issues such as bombing Libya, immigration, and controlling carbon dioxide emissions by power plants, Obama has sought to act unilaterally. A Congress that harasses the executive, and a president who engages in unilateral action whenever he or she can get away with it—in the future, these may be common themes of U.S. politics.

For Critical Analysis

Some people argue that it is a good thing when Congress and the president keep each other in check. When might this checking be an advantage, and when might it be a disadvantage?

Statutory Power
A power created for the president through laws enacted by Congress.

Expressed Power
A power of the president that is expressly written into the Constitution or into statutory law.

Inherent Power
A power of the president derived from the statements in the Constitution that "the executive Power shall be vested in a President" and that the president should "take Care that the Laws be faithfully executed"; defined through practice rather than through law.

Emergency Power
An inherent power exercised by the president during a period of national crisis.

national emergencies. These are called **statutory powers.** Both constitutional and statutory powers have been labeled the **expressed powers** of the president, because they are expressly written into the Constitution or into law.

Presidents also have what have come to be known as **inherent powers.** These depend on the statements in the Constitution that "the executive Power shall be vested in a President" and that the president should "take Care that the Laws be faithfully executed." The most common example of inherent powers is those emergency powers invoked by a president during wartime. Franklin Roosevelt, for example, used his inherent powers to move the Japanese and Japanese Americans living in the United States into internment camps for the duration of World War II. President George W. Bush often justified expanding the powers of his presidency by saying that such powers were necessary to fight the war on terrorism.

Emergency Powers

If you were to read the Constitution, you would find no mention of the additional powers that the executive office may exercise during national emergencies. Indeed, the Supreme Court has stated that an "emergency does not create power."[12] But it is clear that presidents have made strong use of their inherent powers during times of emergency, particularly in the realm of foreign affairs. The **emergency powers** of the president were first enunciated in the Supreme Court's decision in *United States v. Curtiss-Wright Export Corp.*[13] In that case, President Franklin Roosevelt, without authorization by Congress, ordered an embargo on the shipment of weapons to two warring South American countries. The Court recognized that the president may exercise inherent powers in foreign affairs and that the national government has primacy in these affairs.

Examples of emergency powers are abundant, coinciding with crises in domestic and foreign affairs. Abraham Lincoln suspended civil liberties at the beginning of the Civil War (1861–1865) and called the state militias into national service. These actions and his subsequent governance of conquered areas—and even of areas of northern states—were justified by claims that they were essential to preserve the Union. Franklin Roosevelt declared an "unlimited national emergency" following the fall of France in World War II (1939–1945) and mobilized the federal budget and the economy for war.

President Harry Truman authorized the federal seizure of steel plants and their operation by the national government in 1952 during the Korean War. Truman claimed that he was using his inherent emergency power as chief executive and commander in chief to safeguard the nation's security, as an ongoing strike by steelworkers threatened the supply of weapons to the armed forces. The Supreme Court did not agree, holding that the president had no authority under the Constitution to seize private property or to legislate such action.[14] According to legal scholars, this was the first time a limit had been placed on the exercise of the president's emergency powers.

Executive Orders

Congress allows the president (as well as administrative agencies) to issue *executive orders* that have the force of law. These executive orders can do the following: (1) enforce legislative statutes, (2) enforce the Constitution or treaties with foreign nations, and (3) establish or modify rules and practices of executive administrative agencies.

did you know?
Herbert Hoover's son had two pet alligators, which were occasionally permitted to run loose throughout the White House.

12. *Home Building and Loan Association v. Blaisdell,* 290 U.S. 398 (1934).
13. 299 U.S. 304 (1936).
14. *Youngstown Sheet and Tube Co. v. Sawyer,* 343 U.S. 579 (1952).

An executive order, then, represents the president's legislative power. The only apparent requirement is that under the Administrative Procedure Act of 1946, all executive orders must be published in the *Federal Register,* a daily publication of the U.S. government. Executive orders have been used to implement national affirmative action regulations, to restructure the White House bureaucracy, and, under emergency conditions, to ration consumer goods and to administer wage and price controls. They have also been used to classify government information as secret, to regulate the export of restricted items, and to establish military tribunals for suspected terrorists.

President George W. Bush made use of such orders in executing the war on terrorism, and more generally in expanding presidential powers. President Obama's executive orders have covered such matters as regulating the pay and practices of members of the executive branch, raising the fuel efficiency standards of cars and trucks, permitting federal grants to international organizations that support abortion, and lifting restrictions on the federal funding of embryonic stem-cell research.

Executive Privilege

Another inherent executive power that has been claimed by presidents concerns the right of the president and the president's executive officials to withhold information from or refuse to appear before Congress or the courts. This is called **executive privilege,** and it relies on the constitutional separation of powers for its basis.

Invoking Executive Privilege. Presidents have frequently invoked executive privilege to avoid having to disclose information to Congress about actions of the executive branch. Executive privilege rests on the assumption that a certain degree of secrecy is essential to national security. Critics of executive privilege believe that it can be used to shield from public scrutiny actions of the executive branch that should be open to Congress and to the American citizenry.

Limiting Executive Privilege. Limits to executive privilege went untested until the Watergate affair in the early 1970s. Five men had broken into the headquarters of the Democratic National Committee and were caught searching for documents that might damage the candidacy of the Democratic nominee, George McGovern. Later investigation showed that the break-in had been planned by members of Richard Nixon's campaign committee and that Nixon and his closest advisers had devised a strategy for impeding the investigation of the crime. After it became known that all conversations held in the Oval Office had been recorded on a secret system, Nixon was ordered to turn over the tapes to the special prosecutor in charge of the investigation.

Nixon refused to do so, claiming executive privilege. He argued that "no president could function if the private papers of his office, prepared by his personal staff, were open to public scrutiny." In 1974, in one of the Supreme Court's most famous cases, *United States v. Nixon,*[15] the justices unanimously ruled that Nixon had to hand over the tapes. The Court held that executive privilege could not be used to prevent evidence from being heard in criminal proceedings.

AP Images

President Richard Nixon (1969–1974) says goodbye outside the White House after his resignation on August 9, 1974, as he prepares to board a helicopter for a flight to nearby Andrews Air Force Base. *Was Nixon impeached?*

Federal Register
A publication of the U.S. government that prints executive orders, rules, and regulations.

Executive Privilege
The right of executive officials to withhold information from or to refuse to appear before a legislative committee.

---

15. 318 U.S. 683 (1974).

Signing Statement
A written declaration that a president may make when signing a bill into law. Such statements may point out sections of the law that the president deems unconstitutional.

Impeachment
An action by the House of Representatives to accuse the president, vice president, or other civil officers of the United States of committing "Treason, Bribery, or other high Crimes and Misdemeanors."

Signing Statements

Is the president allowed to refuse to enforce certain parts of legislation if he or she believes that they are unconstitutional? This question came to the forefront in recent years because of President George W. Bush's extensive use of signing statements. A **signing statement** is a written declaration that a president may make when signing a bill into law regarding the law's enforcement.

Presidents have been using such statements for decades, but President Bush used 161 statements to invalidate more than one thousand provisions of federal law. No president before Bush used signing statements to make such sweeping claims on behalf of presidential power. Earlier presidents often employed statements to serve notice that parts of bills might be unconstitutional, but they were just as likely to issue statements that were purely rhetorical. Statements might praise Congress and the measure it just passed—or denounce the opposition party. During his campaign, Barack Obama criticized Bush's use of signing statements. As president, Obama's statements have been more in line with tradition. About half of his statements have been entirely rhetorical.

Abuses of Executive Power and Impeachment

Presidents normally leave office either because their first term has expired and they have not sought (or won) reelection or because, having served two full terms, they are not allowed to be elected for a third term (owing to the Twenty-second Amendment, passed in 1951). Eight presidents have died in office. But there is still another way for a president to leave office—by **impeachment** and conviction. Articles I and II of the Constitution authorize the House and Senate to remove the president, the vice president, or other civil officers of the United States for committing "Treason, Bribery, or other high Crimes and Misdemeanors." According to the Constitution, the impeachment process begins in the House, which impeaches (accuses) the federal officer involved. If the House votes to impeach the officer, it draws up articles of impeachment and submits them to the Senate, which conducts the actual trial.

Presidents Andrew Johnson and Richard Nixon. In the history of the United States, no president has ever actually been impeached and also convicted—and thus removed from office—by means of this process. President Andrew Johnson (1865–1869), who succeeded to the office after the assassination of Abraham Lincoln, was impeached by the House but acquitted by the Senate. More than a century later, the House Judiciary Committee approved articles of impeachment against President Richard Nixon for his involvement in the cover-up of the Watergate break-in of 1972. Informed by members of his own party that he had no hope of surviving the trial in the Senate, Nixon resigned on August 9, 1974, before the full House voted on the articles. Nixon is the only president to have resigned from office.

President Bill Clinton. The second president to be impeached by the House but not convicted by the Senate was President Bill Clinton. In September 1998, the Republican House approved two charges against Clinton: lying to a grand jury about his affair with White House intern Monica Lewinsky and obstruction of justice. The articles of impeachment were then sent to the Senate, which acquitted Clinton. The attempt to remove Clinton was very unpopular, although the allegations against him did damage his

---

Why Should You Care about...

The Presidency?

There may also be issues on which the president refuses to consider popular opinion. President George W. Bush refused to be swayed by the public about the war in Iraq, even after the voters turned Congress over to the Democrats, and President Obama did not consult opinion polls when pushing through health-care reform. The determination of these presidents should remind you of the importance of learning about presidential candidates and their positions on important issues, and then making sure to vote. Once a candidate is elected, it is possible that neither public opinion nor Congress will be able to alter presidential policies on certain issues.

popularity as well. Part of the problem for Clinton's Republican opponents was that the charges against the president essentially boiled down to his lying about sex. As one pundit put it, "Everyone lies about sex." Of course, not everyone lies about sex when under oath.

The Executive Organization

Gone are the days when presidents answered their own mail, as George Washington did. It was not until 1857 that Congress authorized a private secretary for the president, to be paid by the federal government. Woodrow Wilson typed most of his correspondence, even though he did have several secretaries. At the beginning of Franklin Roosevelt's long tenure in the White House, the entire staff consisted of thirty-seven employees. With the New Deal and World War II, however, the presidential staff became a sizable organization.

The Cabinet

Although the Constitution does not include the word *cabinet,* it does state that the president "may require the Opinion, in writing, of the principal Officer in each of the executive Departments." Since the time of George Washington, these officers have formed an advisory group, or **cabinet,** to which the president turns for counsel.

On December 19, 1998, the House of Representatives voted to impeach President Bill Clinton (1993–2001), shown here with his vice president, Al Gore. *Why was Clinton not forced to leave office because of this impeachment?*

Members of the Cabinet. Originally, the cabinet consisted of only four officials—the secretaries of State, Treasury, and War and the attorney general. Today, the cabinet numbers fourteen department secretaries and the attorney general. (See Table 12–1 earlier in this chapter for the names of the cabinet departments and Chapter 13 for a detailed discussion of these units.)

The cabinet may include others as well. The president at his or her discretion can, for example, ascribe cabinet rank to the vice president, the head of the Office of Management and Budget, the national security adviser, and additional officials. Under President Barack Obama, the additional members of the cabinet have been the following:

- The vice president.
- The White House chief of staff.
- The administrator of the Environmental Protection Agency.
- The director of the Office of Management and Budget.
- The U.S. trade representative.
- The U.S. ambassador to the United Nations.
- The chair of the Council of Economic Advisers.
- The administrator of the Small Business Administration.

■ **Learning Outcome 4:** Explain the organization of the executive branch and, in particular, the executive office of the president.

Often, a president will use a **kitchen cabinet** to replace the formal cabinet as a major source of advice. The term *kitchen cabinet* originated during the presidency of Andrew Jackson, who relied on the counsel of close friends who allegedly met with him in the kitchen of the White House. A kitchen cabinet is a very informal group of advisers. Usually, they are friends with whom the president worked before being elected.

Presidential Use of Cabinets. Because neither the Constitution nor statutory law requires the president to consult with the cabinet, its use is purely discretionary. Some presidents have relied on the counsel of their cabinets more than others. Dwight Eisenhower was used to the team approach to solving problems from his experience as supreme allied commander during World War II, and therefore he frequently turned to his

Cabinet
An advisory group selected by the president to aid in making decisions. The cabinet includes the heads of fifteen executive departments and others named by the president.

Kitchen Cabinet
The informal advisers to the president.

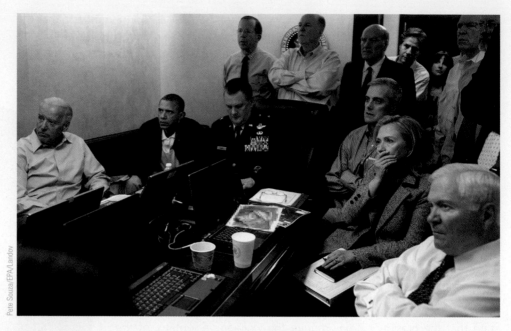

Members of the national security team receive an update on the mission against Osama bin Laden in the Situation Room of the White House on May 1, 2011. Those present included Vice President Joe Biden (left), President Barack Obama (second left), Secretary of State Hillary Clinton (second right), and Secretary of Defense Robert Gates (right). *What happened to bin Laden?*

Pete Souza/EPA/Landov

cabinet for advice on a wide range of issues. More often, presidents have solicited the opinions of their cabinets and then have done what they wanted to do anyway. Lincoln supposedly said—after a cabinet meeting in which a vote was seven nays against his one aye—"Seven nays and one aye, the ayes have it." In general, few presidents have relied heavily on the advice of their cabinet members.

It is not surprising that presidents tend to disregard their cabinet members' advice. Often, the departmental heads are more responsive to the wishes of their own staffs or to their own political ambitions than they are to the president. They may be more concerned with obtaining resources for their departments than with achieving the goals of the president. So there is often a conflict of interest between presidents and their cabinet members.

The Executive Office of the President

When President Franklin Roosevelt appointed a special committee on administrative management, he knew that the committee would conclude that the president needed help. Indeed, the committee proposed a major reorganization of the executive branch. Congress did not approve the entire reorganization, but it did create the **Executive Office of the President (EOP)** to provide staff assistance for the chief executive and to help coordinate the executive bureaucracy. Since that time, a number of agencies have been created within the EOP to supply the president with advice and staff help. Presidents reorganize the EOP and the White House Office constantly, and any table of organization is therefore temporary. As of 2014, the EOP agencies under Barack Obama were the following:

- Council of Economic Advisers.
- Council on Environmental Quality.
- Executive Residence.
- National Security Staff.
- Office of Administration.
- Office of Management and Budget.
- Office of National Drug Control Policy.

- Office of Science and Technology Policy.
- Office of the United States Trade Representative.
- Office of the Vice President.
- White House Office.

Executive Office of the President (EOP)

An organization established by President Franklin Roosevelt to assist the president in carrying out major duties.

Many staff members within the EOP are assigned to specific policy areas, and the number of such individuals grew noticeably during Obama's first term. Popularly referred to as "czars," they have included a cyber security czar, an urban affairs czar, and even an

Asian carp czar, who coordinates efforts to keep Asian carp out of the Great Lakes. Unlike cabinet officers and many other top executive officials, czars are not subject to confirmation by the U.S. Senate. This exemption has been a source of controversy.

The White House Office. The **White House Office** includes most of the key personal and political advisers to the president. Among the jobs held by these aides are those of legal counsel to the president, secretary, press secretary, and appointments secretary. Often, the individuals who hold these positions are recruited from the president's campaign staff. Their duties—mainly protecting the president's political interests—are similar to campaign functions. In 2014, the White House Office was made up of the following units:

- Domestic Policy Council.
- National Security Advisor.
- National Economic Council.
- Office of Cabinet Affairs.
- Office of the Chief of Staff.
- Office of Communications.
- Office of Digital Strategy.
- Office of the First Lady.
- Office of Legislative Affairs.
- Office of Management and Administration.
- Oval Office Operations.
- Office of Presidential Personnel.
- Office of Public Engagement and Intergovernmental Affairs.
- Office of Scheduling and Advance.
- Office of the Staff Secretary.
- Office of the White House Counsel.

In all recent administrations, one member of the White House Office has been named **chief of staff.** This person, who is responsible for coordinating the office, is also one of the president's chief advisers.

The White House Military Office. In addition to civilian advisers, the president is supported by a large number of military personnel, who are organized under the White House Military Office. These members of the military provide communications, transportation, medical care, and food services to the president and the White House staff.

White House Staff Influence. White House staff members are closest to the president and may have considerable influence over the administration's decisions. Often, when presidents are under fire for their decisions, the staff is accused of keeping the chief executive too isolated from criticism or help. Presidents insist that they will not allow the staff to become too powerful, but, given the difficulty of the office, each president eventually turns to staff members for loyal assistance and protection.

The Office of Management and Budget. The **Office of Management and Budget (OMB)** was originally the Bureau of the Budget, which was created in 1921 within the Department of the Treasury. Recognizing the importance of this agency, Franklin Roosevelt moved it into the White House Office in 1939. Richard Nixon reorganized the Bureau of the Budget in 1970 and changed its name to reflect its new managerial function. It is headed by a director, who drafts the annual federal budget that the president presents to Congress each January for approval. In principle, the director of the OMB has broad fiscal powers in planning and estimating various parts of the federal budget, because all agencies must submit their proposed budget to the OMB for approval. In reality, it is not so clear that the OMB truly can affect the greater scope of the federal budget. The OMB may be more important as a clearinghouse for legislative proposals initiated in the executive agencies.

"If I become President, I'm not giving any of my schoolfriends jobs."

### Sidebar

White House Office
The personal office of the president, which tends to presidential political needs and manages the media.

Chief of Staff
The person who is named to direct the White House Office and advise the president.

Office of Management and Budget (OMB)
A division of the Executive Office of the President. The OMB assists the president in preparing the annual budget, clearing and coordinating departmental agency budgets, and supervising the administration of the federal budget.

The National Security Council. The **National Security Council (NSC)** is a link between the president's key foreign and military advisers and the president. Its members consist of the president, the vice president, and the secretaries of State and Defense, plus other informal members. The NSC is managed by the president's assistant for national security affairs, also known as the national security adviser.

The Vice Presidency

■ **Learning Outcome 5:**
Evaluate the role of
the vice president, and
describe what happens
if the presidency
becomes vacant.

The Constitution does not give much power to the vice president. The only formal duty is to preside over the Senate—which is rarely necessary. This obligation is fulfilled when the Senate organizes and adopts its rules and also when the vice president is needed to decide a tie vote. In all other cases, the president pro tem manages parliamentary procedures in the Senate (see "How Congress Is Organized" in Chapter 11). The vice president is expected to participate only informally in senatorial deliberations, if at all.

The Vice President's Job

Vice presidents have traditionally been chosen by presidential nominees to balance the ticket by attracting groups of voters or appeasing party factions. If a presidential nominee is from the North, it is not a bad idea to have a vice-presidential nominee who is from the South. If the presidential nominee is from a rural state, perhaps someone with an urban background would be most suitable as a running mate. Presidential nominees who are strongly conservative or strongly liberal would do well to have vice-presidential nominees whose views lie more in the middle of the political road.

Strengthening the Ticket. In recent presidential elections, however, vice presidents have often been selected for other reasons. Barack Obama picked Joe Biden to be his running mate in 2008 and 2012 to add gravitas (seriousness) and foreign policy experience to the ticket. Republican presidential candidate John McCain's choice of Alaska governor Sarah Palin in 2008 balanced the ticket not only by gender, but also politically. Social conservatives, many of whom were suspicious of McCain, gave enthusiastic support to Palin.

In 2012, Republican presidential candidate Mitt Romney chose Representative Paul Ryan of Wisconsin as his running mate. Ryan, the author of conservative House budget proposals, was greeted with enthusiasm by Republicans who were skeptical of Romney's right-wing credentials.

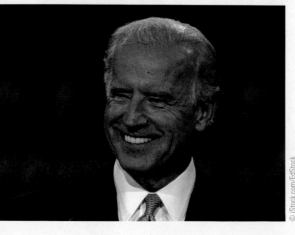

Vice President Joe Biden frequently appears on television talk shows and at conferences. *What are the official duties of the vice president?*

Supporting the President. Traditionally, the job of the vice president has not been very demanding. In recent years, however, presidents have granted their running mates increased responsibilities and power. President Jimmy Carter was the first modern president to rely on his vice president—Walter Mondale—as a major adviser. Under President George W. Bush, Dick Cheney became the most powerful vice president in history. Cheney was able to place his supporters throughout the bureaucracy and exert influence on a wide range of issues. He could exercise this degree of power, however, only because he had the support of the president. In contrast, Vice President Biden's relationship to President Obama has been more conventional.

Vice presidents sometimes have become elected presidents in their own right. John Adams and Thomas Jefferson were the first to do so. Richard Nixon was elected president in 1968 after he had served as Dwight D. Eisenhower's vice president from 1953 to 1961. In 1988, George H. W. Bush was elected to the presidency after eight years as Ronald Reagan's vice president.

Only eight presidents have died in office, after which their vice presidents became president. When John F. Kennedy was assassinated in November 1963, then–Vice President Lyndon B. Johnson was sworn in as president by a federal judge. Standing alongside Johnson (1963–1969) was Kennedy's widow, Jacqueline Kennedy. *Who becomes president if both the president and the vice president are killed?*

Presidential Succession

Eight vice presidents have become president because of the death of the president. John Tyler, the first to do so, took over William Henry Harrison's position in 1841, after only one month. No one knew whether Tyler should simply be a caretaker until a new president could be elected three and a half years later or whether he actually should be president. Tyler assumed that he was supposed to be the chief executive, and he acted as such—although he was commonly referred to as "His Accidency." Since then, vice presidents taking over the position of the presidency because of the incumbent's death have assumed the presidential powers.

But what should a vice president do if a president becomes incapable of carrying out necessary duties while in office? When James Garfield was shot in 1881, he remained alive for two and a half months. What was Vice President Chester Arthur's role?

This question was not addressed in the original Constitution. Article II, Section 1, says only that "[i]n Case of the Removal of the President from Office, or of his Death, Resignation, or Inability to discharge the Powers and Duties of the said Office, the same shall devolve on [the same powers shall be exercised by] the Vice President." There have been many instances of presidential disability. When Dwight Eisenhower became ill a second time in 1958, he entered into a pact with Richard Nixon specifying that the vice president could determine whether the president was incapable of carrying out his duties if the president could not communicate. John F. Kennedy and Lyndon Johnson entered into similar agreements with their vice presidents. Finally, in 1967, the **Twenty-fifth Amendment** was passed, establishing procedures in the event of presidential incapacity, death, or resignation.

When the President Becomes Incapacitated. According to the Twenty-fifth Amendment, when a president believes that he or she is incapable of performing the duties of office, the president must inform Congress in writing. Then the vice president serves as acting president until the president can resume normal duties. When the president is unable

Twenty-fifth Amendment
A 1967 amendment to the Constitution that establishes procedures for filling presidential and vice-presidential vacancies and makes provisions for presidential incapacity.

to communicate, a majority of the cabinet, including the vice president, can declare that fact to Congress. Then the vice president serves as acting president until the president resumes normal duties. If a dispute arises over the return of the president's ability, a two-thirds vote of Congress is required to allow the vice president to remain acting president. Otherwise, the president resumes normal duties.

When the Vice Presidency Becomes Vacant. The Twenty-fifth Amendment also addresses the issue of how the president should fill a vacant vice presidency. Section 2 of the amendment simply states, "Whenever there is a vacancy in the office of the Vice President, the President shall nominate a Vice President who shall take office upon confirmation by a majority vote of both Houses of Congress." This is exactly what occurred when Richard Nixon's first vice president, Spiro Agnew, resigned in 1973 because of his alleged receipt of construction contract kickbacks during his tenure as governor of Maryland. Nixon turned to Gerald Ford as his choice for vice president. After extensive hearings, both chambers of Congress confirmed the appointment.

Then, when Nixon resigned on August 9, 1974, Ford automatically became president and nominated as his vice president Nelson Rockefeller. Congress confirmed Ford's choice. For the first time in the history of the country, neither the president nor the vice president had been elected to their positions.

The Succession Act of 1947. The question of who shall be president if both the president and the vice president die is answered by the Presidential Succession Act of 1947. If the president and vice president die, resign, or are disabled, the Speaker of the House will become president, after resigning from Congress. Next in line is the president pro tem of the Senate, followed by the cabinet officers in the order of the creation of their departments (see Table 12–3 that follows).

Table 12–3 ▶ **Line of Succession to the Presidency of the United States**

How might the public react if the Speaker of the House became president—and was of a different political party than the deceased president?

1. Vice President	10. Secretary of Commerce
2. Speaker of the House of Representatives	11. Secretary of Labor
3. Senate President Pro Tempore	12. Secretary of Health and Human Services
4. Secretary of State	13. Secretary of Housing and Urban Development
5. Secretary of the Treasury	14. Secretary of Transportation
6. Secretary of Defense	15. Secretary of Energy
7. Attorney General (head of the Justice Department)	16. Secretary of Education
8. Secretary of the Interior	17. Secretary of Veterans Affairs
9. Secretary of Agriculture	18. Secretary of Homeland Security

How You Can Make a Difference

The most traditional form of communication with the White House is, of course, by letter.

- Letters to the president should be addressed to

The President of the United States
The White House
1600 Pennsylvania Avenue N.W.
Washington, DC 20500

- Letters may be sent to the First Lady at the same address. Will you get an answer? Almost certainly. The White House mail room is staffed by volunteers and paid employees who sort the mail for the president and tally the public's concerns. You may receive a standard response to your comments or a more personal, detailed response.

- It is possible to call the White House on the telephone and leave a message for the president or First Lady. To call the switchboard, call 202-456-1414. In most circumstances, a better choice is the round-the-clock comment line, which you can reach at 202-456-1111. When you call that number, an operator will take down your comments and forward them to the president's office.

- To find the home page for the White House, go to www .whitehouse.gov. The site is designed to be entertaining and to convey information about the president.

- You can also send your comments and ideas to the White House using e-mail. Send comments to the president at

comments@whitehouse.gov

- Address e-mail to the vice president at

vice_president@whitehouse.gov

Key Terms

advice and consent 352
appointment power 349
cabinet 363
chief diplomat 352
chief executive 348
chief legislator 353
chief of staff 365
civil service 349
commander in chief 351
constitutional power 359
diplomatic recognition 352

emergency power 360
executive agreement 353
Executive Office of the President (EOP) 364
executive privilege 361
expressed power 360
Federal Register 361
head of state 348
impeachment 362
inherent power 360
kitchen cabinet 363

line-item veto 356
National Security Council (NSC) 366
Office of Management and Budget (OMB) 365
pardon 350
patronage 357
pocket veto 354
reprieve 350
signing statement 362
State of the Union message 353

statutory power 360
Twelfth Amendment 347
Twenty-fifth Amendment 367
veto message 354
War Powers Resolution 352
White House Office 365

Chapter Summary

Learning Outcome 1 The office of the presidency in the United States, combining as it does the functions of chief of state and chief executive, was unique at the time of its creation. The framers of the Constitution were divided over whether the president should be a weak or a strong executive.

Learning Outcome 2 The requirements for the office of the presidency are outlined in Article II, Section 1, of the Constitution. The president's roles include both formal and informal duties. The constitutional roles of the president include head of state, chief executive, commander in chief, chief diplomat, and chief legislator. The president also acts as party chief.

As head of state, the president is ceremonial leader of the government. As chief executive, the president is bound to enforce the acts of Congress, the judgments of the federal courts, and treaties. The chief executive has the power of appointment and the power to grant reprieves and pardons.

As commander in chief, the president is the ultimate decision maker in military matters. As chief diplomat, the president recognizes foreign governments, negotiates treaties, signs agreements, and nominates and receives ambassadors.

The role of chief legislator includes recommending legislation to Congress, lobbying for the legislation, approving laws, and exercising the veto power. Presidents are also leaders of their political parties. Presidents rely on their personal popularity to help them fulfill these functions.

Learning Outcome 3 In addition to constitutional and inherent powers, the president has statutory powers written into law by Congress. Presidents also have a variety of special powers not available to the other branches of the government. These include emergency powers and the power to issue executive orders, to invoke executive privilege, and to issue signing statements.

Abuses of executive power are dealt with by Articles I and II of the Constitution, which authorize the House and Senate to impeach and remove the president, vice president, or other officers of the federal government for committing "Treason, Bribery, or other high Crimes and Misdemeanors."

Learning Outcome 4 The president receives assistance from the cabinet and from the Executive Office of the President (including the White House Office).

Learning Outcome 5 The vice president is the constitutional officer assigned to preside over the Senate and to assume the presidency in the event of the death, resignation, removal, or disability of the president. The Twenty-fifth Amendment, passed in 1967, established procedures to be followed in case of presidential incapacity, death, or resignation and when filling a vacant vice presidency.

Master the concept of The Presidency with MindTap™ for American Government

REVIEW MindTap™ **for American Government**
Access Key Term Flashcards for Chapter 12.

STAY CURRENT MindTap™ **for American Government**
Access the KnowNow blog and customized RSS for updates on current events.

TEST YOURSELF MindTap™ **for American Government**
Take the Wrap It Up Quiz for Chapter 12.

STAY FOCUSED MindTap™ **for American Government**
Complete the Focus Activities for The Presidency.

Additional Resources

Today, the Internet has become such a normal part of most Americans' lives that it is almost hard to imagine what life was like without it. Certainly, accessing the latest press releases from the White House was much more difficult twenty years ago than it is today. It was not until the Clinton administration (1993–2001) that access to the White House through the Internet became possible. Correspondence with the president and the First Lady quickly moved from ordinary handwritten letters to e-mail.

Online Resources

- The White House Web site offers extensive information on the White House and the presidency. Locate it at www.whitehouse.gov.
- You can find an excellent collection of data and maps describing all U.S. presidential elections at Dave Leip's Atlas of U.S. Presidential Elections. Go to uselectionatlas.org.
- Inaugural addresses of American presidents from George Washington to Barack Obama are available at www.bartleby.com/124.
- In no field is the president more powerful, relative to the rest of the government, than in foreign policy. If you have an interest in that topic, consider following the Foreign Policy Web site at.www.foreignpolicy.com.

Books

Bohn, Michael K. *Presidents in Crisis: Tough Decisions inside the White House from Truman to Obama.* New York: Arcade Publishing, 2015. Bohn takes us inside the White House during sixteen international crises handled by presidents from Truman to Obama. Now a journalist, Bohn was director of the White House Situation Room under President Reagan.

Clinton, Hillary Rodham. *Hard Choices.* New York: Simon & Schuster, 2014. Clinton's account of her years as secretary of State under President Obama, together with an explanation of how those experiences drive her view of the future. Clinton has a better chance than any other single individual of winning the presidency in 2016, which means that this work will draw close attention.

Goodwin, Doris Kearns. *The Bully Pulpit: Theodore Roosevelt, William Howard Taft, and the Golden Age of Journalism.* New York: Simon & Schuster, 2014 (paperback). This detailed account of the Progressive Era focuses on presidents Roosevelt and Taft, and also on the "muckraking" press of the time. Goodwin's book was one of the most acclaimed works of the year.

Video

American Experience: The Presidents—A box set, released in 2012, that contains eleven presidential biographies produced by PBS. All presidents are from the twentieth century, and they range from Theodore Roosevelt to Bill Clinton. The collection provides one of the most detailed and enjoyable accounts available of U.S. history as seen through the lives of its presidents.

The American President—A 1995 romantic comedy with plenty of ideas about both romance and government. Michael Douglas is the widower president who falls for a lobbyist, played by Annette Bening. Douglas's comedic performance has been called his best.

Quiz

Multiple Choice and Fill-Ins

Learning Outcome 1 Identify the types of people who typically undertake serious campaigns for the presidency.

1. If no presidential candidate has a majority in the electoral college, the question of who should become president is decided by:
   a. the U.S. House.
   b. the U.S. Senate.
   c. the United States Supreme Court.

2. To date, only one president has been a Roman Catholic, and that person was _____ __ _____.

Learning Outcome 2 Distinguish some of the major roles of the president, including head of state, chief executive, commander in chief, chief diplomat, chief legislator, party chief, and politician.

3. Our president is both head of state and chief executive, which means that the president:
   a. engages in ceremonial activities both at home and abroad, as well as faithfully ensuring that the acts of Congress are enforced.
   b. designates the vice president to represent the United States in public ceremonies abroad.
   c. makes sure that treaties are upheld but delegates other actions to the cabinet.

4. When the president issues an executive order, such action represents the president's _____ _____.

Learning Outcome 3 Describe some of the special powers of the president, and tell how a president can be removed from office.

5. Upon impeachment by the House of Representatives, the president:
   a. must leave office immediately.
   b. cannot run for reelection.
   c. is tried by the Senate.

6. A president who disagrees with a part of legislation that he or she has signed into law can make a written declaration regarding the law's enforcement. This declaration is called a _____ _____.

Learning Outcome 4 Explain the organization of the executive branch and, in particular, the executive office of the president.

7. The White House chief of staff, the ambassador to the United Nations, and the head of the Environmental Protection Agency:
   a. have at different times been named members of the president's cabinet.
   b. are all part of the Executive Office of the President.
   c. are not subject to presidential appointment.

8. The president, vice president, secretaries of State and Defense, and national security adviser are part of the

   _____ _____ _____.

Learning Outcome 5 Evaluate the role of the vice president, and describe what happens if the presidency becomes vacant.

9. If the president dies, the vice president takes over. If the vice president is also unavailable, then the following officer becomes president:
   a. the president pro tempore of the Senate.
   b. the Speaker of the House.
   c. the secretary of State.

10. The only formal duty imposed on the vice president by the Constitution is to preside over the _____.

Essay Questions

1. What characteristics do you think voters look for when choosing a president? Might these characteristics change as a result of changes in the political environment and the specific problems facing the nation? If you believe voters almost always look for the same characteristics when selecting a president, why is this? If voters seek somewhat different people as president depending on circumstances, which circumstances favor which kinds of leaders?

2. Many presidents have been lawyers, though George W. Bush was a businessman, Ronald Reagan was an actor, and Jimmy Carter was a naval officer and peanut farmer. What advantages might these three presidents have gained from their career backgrounds? In particular, what benefits might Ronald Reagan have derived from his experience as an actor?

The Bureaucracy

13

An Army Corps of Engineers ranger shows a third grader some tips on water safety before a canoe trip on the Anacostia River in Washington, D.C. *How popular are the government workers who manage our national parks?*
The Washington Post/Getty Images

The five learning outcomes below are designed to help improve your understanding of this chapter. After reading this chapter, you should be able to:

- **Learning Outcome 1:** Discuss the nature of the federal bureaucracy, and identify the largest federal spending programs.
- **Learning Outcome 2:** Describe the various types of agencies and organizations that make up the federal executive branch.
- **Learning Outcome 3:** Explain how government employees are hired and how they are administered.
- **Learning Outcome 4:** Evaluate different methods that have been put into place to reform bureaucracies and make them more efficient.
- **Learning Outcome 5:** Discuss how federal agencies make rules and the role of Congress in this process.

What If...

We Had a Simpler Tax System?

BACKGROUND

In 1913, the Sixteenth Amendment to the Constitution let Congress levy an income tax. In that year, not even 1 percent of Americans paid this tax. Today, the top rate is 39.6 percent. The Tax Code runs about 75,000 pages. Filing consumes vast amounts of time and money. As a result, every few years someone proposes simplifying our tax system.

WHAT IF WE HAD A SIMPLER TAX SYSTEM?

Before discussing a simpler tax system, we have to decide what kind of system we are imagining. Some conservatives have proposed a flat tax in which everyone pays the same rate, say 20 percent. A large standard deduction benefits low earners. Such a plan is a political non-starter. The latest serious tax proposal was released in 2014 by Dave Camp, chair of the House Ways and Means Committee. This "simplification" runs about 1,000 pages.

SOME TAX SIMPLIFICATION IDEAS

Camp's plan does not change the total amount of taxes collected. It is also doesn't change the relative amounts collected from the rich, the middle class, and the poor. It does eliminate a large number of deductions so that it can lower average rates. In doing that, it collapses the current seven income tax rates into three, topping out at 35 percent. Camp keeps the beneficial treatment of capital gains, that is, income from rises in the price of assets such as stocks or property. However, a loophole that lets hedge fund millionaires treat salaries as if they were capital gains is abolished. So is a loophole that lets small businesspersons shield income from the Social Security tax.

WHO WINS AND WHO LOSES?

Camp's plan raises the standard deduction for an individual to $11,000 and for a couple to $22,000. As a result, only 5 percent of taxpayers would benefit from itemizing deductions. The rest would file the simple Form 1040A. Such a reform would dramatically reduce payments to tax preparers, accountants, and lawyers. These are not groups most people want to protect. Many of the deductions that Camp would abolish, however, benefit groups that many people favor:

- Charitable contributions could only be deducted if they exceed 2 percent of income. Yet funding for the entire nonprofit sector is based on soliciting tax-deductible contributions from the middle class and the wealthy. Would people continue to donate if they can't get a tax deduction? Charities, churches, and colleges do not want to find out.
- Deductions for interest on home loans (mortgages) would be limited. This step would reduce the incentive to borrow

to buy a house. Real estate agents, mortgage lenders, and potential home buyers would oppose such a change.
- Current law provides a vast number of education incentives. Camp collapses all of them into just one—a $2,500 American Opportunity Tax Credit. This change would make the system easier to understand, so more people might claim the credit. Total support for education could fall, however.
- Currently, elderly persons can deduct uninsured medical expenses that exceed 7.5 percent of income. Camp would repeal that. Repeal would damage the finances of many people confined to nursing homes, who can now deduct most of what the nursing homes charge.

Advertising a tax preparation service shortly before the April income tax deadline. *Why do some people wait until the last minute to file?*

For Critical Analysis

1. What could the government do to help groups such as charities that might be damaged by the loss of tax deductions?

2. Camp's plan has been called "shockingly bipartisan." Why might both Republicans and Democrats oppose it?

373

LISTEN & LEARN
MindTap® for American Government

Access Read Speaker to listen to Chapter 13.

Bureaucracy
An organization that is structured hierarchically to carry out specific functions.

■ **Learning Outcome 1:**
Discuss the nature of the federal bureaucracy, and identify the largest federal spending programs.

German sociologist Max Weber (1864–1920) created the classic model of the modern bureaucracy. *Does the power in the classic bureaucracy flow upward, downward, or horizontally?*

Faceless bureaucrats—this image provokes a negative reaction from many, if not most, Americans. Polls consistently report that the majority of Americans support "less government." The same polls, however, report that the majority of Americans support almost every specific program that the government undertakes. The conflict between the desire for small government and the desire for the benefits that only a large government can provide has been a constant feature of American politics. For example, the goal of preserving endangered species has widespread support. At the same time, many people believe that restrictions imposed under the Endangered Species Act violate the rights of landowners. Helping the elderly pay their medical bills is a popular objective, but hardly anyone enjoys paying the Medicare tax that supports this effort. (Indeed, politicians and citizens have frequently called for tax reform, as explained in the chapter-opening *What If . . .* feature.)

In this chapter, we describe the size, organization, and staffing of the federal bureaucracy. We review modern attempts at bureaucratic reform and the process by which Congress exerts ultimate control over the bureaucracy. We also discuss the bureaucracy's role in making rules and setting policy.

The Nature and Scope of the Federal Bureaucracy

Bureaucracy is the name given to an organization that is structured hierarchically to carry out specific functions. Generally, bureaucracies are characterized by an organizational chart. The units of the organization are divided according to the specialization and expertise of the employees.

Public and Private Bureaucracies

We should not think of bureaucracy as unique to government. Any large corporation or university can be considered a bureaucratic organization. The fact is that the handling of complex problems requires a division of labor. Individuals must concentrate their skills on specific, well-defined aspects of a problem and depend on others to solve the rest of it.

Public, or government, bureaucracies differ from private organizations in some important ways, however. A private corporation has a single leader—its chief executive officer (CEO). Public bureaucracies do not have a single leader. Although the president is the chief administrator of the federal system, all agencies are subject to the dictates of Congress for their funding, staffing, and, indeed, their continued existence. Public bureaucracies supposedly serve all citizens, while private ones serve private interests.

One other important difference between private corporations and government bureaucracies is that government bureaucracies are not organized to make a profit. Rather, they are supposed to perform their functions as efficiently as possible to conserve taxpayers' dollars. Perhaps it is this ideal that makes citizens hostile toward government bureaucracy when they experience inefficiency and red tape.

Every modern president, at one time or another, has proclaimed that his administration was going to "fix government." All modern presidents also have put forth plans to end government waste and inefficiency. (See Table 13–1 that follows.) Their success has been, in a word, underwhelming. Presidents generally have been powerless to significantly affect the structure and operation of the federal bureaucracy.

Models of Bureaucracy

Several theories have been offered to help us better understand the ways in which bureaucracies function. Each of these theories focuses on specific features of bureaucracies.

Table 13–1 ▸ **Selected Presidential Plans to End Government Inefficiency**

Why does almost every administration need a new plan?

President	Plan
Lyndon Johnson (1963–1969)	Programming, planning, and budgeting systems
Richard Nixon (1969–1974)	Management by Objectives
Jimmy Carter (1977–1981)	Zero-Based Budgeting
Ronald Reagan (1981–1989)	President's Private Sector Survey on Cost Control (the Grace Commission)
George H. W. Bush (1989–1993)	Right-Sizing Government
Bill Clinton (1993–2001)	Reinventing Government
George W. Bush (2001–2009)	Performance-Based Budgeting
Barack Obama (2009–present)	Appointment of a chief performance officer

Weberian Model. The classic model, or **Weberian model,** of the modern bureaucracy was proposed by the German sociologist Max Weber.[1] He argued that the increasingly complex nature of modern life, coupled with the steadily growing demands placed on governments by their citizens, made the formation of bureaucracies inevitable. According to Weber, most bureaucracies—whether in the public or private sector—are organized hierarchically and governed by formal procedures. The power in a bureaucracy flows from the top downward. Decision-making processes in bureaucracies are shaped by detailed technical rules that promote similar decisions in similar situations.

Bureaucrats are specialists who attempt to resolve problems through logical reasoning and data analysis instead of "gut feelings" and guesswork. Individual advancement in bureaucracies is supposed to be based on merit rather than on political connections. Indeed, the modern bureaucracy, according to Weber, should be an apolitical organization.

Acquisitive Model. Other theorists do not view bureaucracies in terms as benign as Weber's. Some believe that bureaucracies are acquisitive in nature. Proponents of the **acquisitive model** argue that top-level bureaucrats will always try to expand, or at least to avoid any reductions in, the size of their budgets. Although government bureaucracies are not-for-profit enterprises, bureaucrats want to maximize the size of their budgets and staffs, which are the most visible trappings of power in the public sector. These efforts are also prompted by the desire of bureaucrats to "sell" their products—such as national defense, public housing, or agricultural subsidies—to both Congress and the public.

Monopolistic Model. Because government bureaucracies seldom have competitors, some theorists have suggested that these bureaucratic organizations may be explained best by a **monopolistic model.** The analysis is similar to that used by economists to examine the behavior of monopolistic firms. Monopolistic bureaucracies—like monopolistic firms—essentially have no competitors and act accordingly. Because monopolistic bureaucracies usually are not penalized for chronic inefficiency, they have little reason to adopt cost-saving measures or to make more productive use of their resources.

Weberian Model
A model of bureaucracy developed by the German sociologist Max Weber, who viewed bureaucracies as rational, hierarchical organizations in which decisions are based on logical reasoning.

Acquisitive Model
A model of bureaucracy that views top-level bureaucrats as seeking to expand the size of their budgets and staffs to gain greater power.

Monopolistic Model
A model of bureaucracy that compares bureaucracies to monopolistic business firms. Lack of competition in either circumstance leads to inefficient and costly operations.

1. Max Weber, *Theory of Social and Economic Organization*, ed. Talcott Parsons (New York: Oxford University Press, 1974).

The Size of the Bureaucracy

In 1789, the new government's bureaucracy was tiny. There were three departments—State (with nine employees), War (with two employees), and Treasury (with thirty-nine employees)—and the Office of the Attorney General (which later became the Department of Justice). The bureaucracy was still small in 1798. At that time, the secretary of state had seven clerks and spent a total of $500 (about $10,000 in 2015 dollars) on stationery and printing. In that same year, an appropriations act allocated $1.4 million (or $28.2 million in 2015 dollars) to the War Department.[2]

Government Employment Today. Times have changed, as we can see in Figure 13–1 that follows, which shows various federal agencies and the number of civilian employees in each. Excluding 1.4 million military service members but including employees of the legislative and judicial branches and the U.S. Postal Service, the federal bureaucracy includes approximately 2.8 million employees. That number has remained relatively stable for the past several decades. It is somewhat deceiving, however, because many other individuals work directly or indirectly for the federal government as subcontractors or consultants.

Conventionally, attempts to measure the size of the federal bureaucracy also leave out the men and women of the Army, Navy, Air Force, and Marines. In 2014, these personnel

did you know?

The total land area occupied by U.S. facilities and military bases is 15,654 square miles—bigger than Washington D.C., Massachusetts, and New Jersey combined.

---

2. Leonard D. White, *The Federalists: A Study in Administrative History, 1789–1801* (New York: Free Press, 1948).

Figure 13–1 ▶ **Federal Agencies and Their Respective Numbers of Civilian Employees**

Why does the Department of Defense need so many civilian employees?

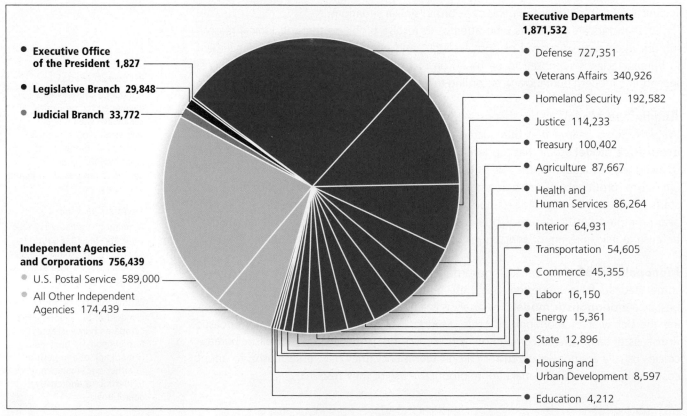

- **Executive Office of the President** 1,827
- **Legislative Branch** 29,848
- **Judicial Branch** 33,772

Independent Agencies and Corporations 756,439
- U.S. Postal Service 589,000
- All Other Independent Agencies 174,439

Executive Departments 1,871,532
- Defense 727,351
- Veterans Affairs 340,926
- Homeland Security 192,582
- Justice 114,233
- Treasury 100,402
- Agriculture 87,667
- Health and Human Services 86,264
- Interior 64,931
- Transportation 54,605
- Commerce 45,355
- Labor 16,150
- Energy 15,361
- State 12,896
- Housing and Urban Development 8,597
- Education 4,212

Sources: U.S. Office of Personnel Management, December 2013; and the Bureau of Labor Statistics.

numbered 1,370,000. Despite their service ethos, it cannot be denied that the armed forces are gigantic bureaucracies with all the characteristics of bureaucracies everywhere.

The figures for federal government employment are only part of the story. Figure 13–2 that follows shows the growth in government employment at the federal, state, and local levels. From 1959 to 2008, this growth was mainly at the state and local levels. If all government employees are included, about 16 percent of all civilian nonfarm employment is accounted for by government.

The Impact of Ronald Reagan. Notice in Figure 13–2 that government employment as a share of the total U.S. population grew rapidly until 1980. In that year, Republican Ronald Reagan was elected president. Under Reagan, government employment actually fell, in large part because of the elimination of revenue sharing, a program through which the federal government transferred large sums to state and local governments. While government employment picked up later in Reagan's administration, it never resumed

Even at $0.49 for the one-ounce first-class rate, postage in the United States is a bargain by international standards. First-class rates are $0.80 in Japan, $0.90 in France, and $1.03 in Britain. *Why has the U.S. Postal Service experienced financial difficulties?*

the constant upward course characteristic of the 1960s and 1970s. In short, Reagan's "conservative revolution" had a genuine impact on the trajectory of government.

The Great Recession and its aftermath also had a major impact on government spending and employment. In 2009, the number of state and local government workers began to fall, because these governments could not collect enough revenue to fund their previous levels of activity. From August 2008 to the beginning of 2013, state and local government employment fell by about 730,000, after which it slowly began rising again.

Federal Employment and Federal Spending. While Figure 13–1 provides a good overview of the number of federal employees, it does not accurately depict federal spending. For example, employees of the U.S. Postal Service (USPS) make up about a quarter of the pie chart. Yet for decades the postal service has been entirely self-supporting and has drawn no funds from the government at all. (Recent financial troubles have raised the question of whether the USPS can remain self-supporting in the future, however.) In contrast, the employees of the Social Security Administration make up only 3 percent of the federal workforce, but they are responsible for 20 percent of what the federal government spends.

Figure 13–2 ▶ **Government Employment**

What kinds of workers might local governments have laid off after 2009?

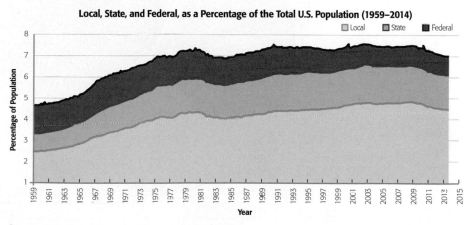

Sources: U.S. Census Bureau and Bureau of Labor Statistics.

The Federal Budget

In 1929, spending by all levels of government was equivalent to only about 11 percent of the nation's gross domestic product. For fiscal year 2015, it was just over 36 percent.

Social Spending. Studies repeatedly show that most Americans have a very inaccurate idea of how the federal budget is spent. Figure 13–3 that follows can help. This pie chart demonstrates that about a third of all federal spending goes to two programs that benefit older Americans—Social Security and Medicare. Additional social programs, many aimed at low-income individuals and families, push the total amount of social spending past the 60 percent mark. In short, the federal government spends much more on the poor than many people realize. Medicaid, a joint federal-state program that provides health-care services, is the largest of these programs. (CHIP is the Children's Health Insurance Program, and SNAP is the Supplementary Nutrition Assistance Program, better known as food stamps.) In contrast, traditional cash welfare—Temporary Assistance for Needy Families (TANF)—accounts for only 0.5 percent of the budget ($17 billion) and is buried in the "Miscellaneous low-income and disability support" slice.

Defense and the Rest. Military defense and veterans' benefits are just over a fifth of the whole. Interest payments on the national debt are about 6 percent. Education and training, transportation, and "everything else" amount to only 12.6 percent of the budget. Foreign aid, which is included in the "everything else" slice, is 1.2 percent, or $48.5 billion. This is a substantial sum, but it is much smaller than many people imagine. Frequently, politicians will claim that they can balance the federal budget by making large cuts to this 12.6 percent slice of federal spending. A quick look at Figure 13–3 reveals that such claims are not based on reality.

Figure 13–3 ▶ **Federal Government Spending, Fiscal Year 2014**

Do you find some of these percentages surprising? If so, which ones?

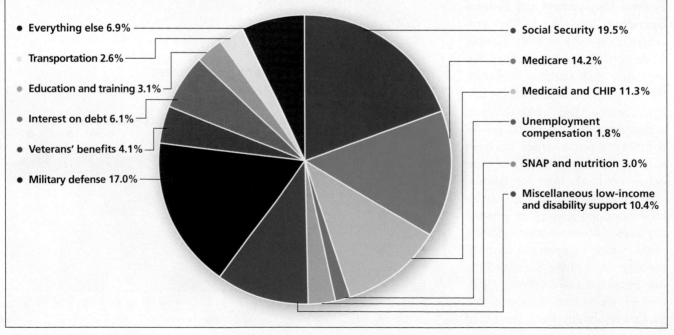

- Everything else 6.9%
- Transportation 2.6%
- Education and training 3.1%
- Interest on debt 6.1%
- Veterans' benefits 4.1%
- Military defense 17.0%

- Social Security 19.5%
- Medicare 14.2%
- Medicaid and CHIP 11.3%
- Unemployment compensation 1.8%
- SNAP and nutrition 3.0%
- Miscellaneous low-income and disability support 10.4%

Source: usgovernmentspending.com.

The Organization of the Federal Bureaucracy

Within the federal bureaucracy are a number of different types of government agencies and organizations. Figure 13–4 that follows outlines the several bodies within the executive branch, as well as the separate organizations that provide services to Congress, to the courts, and directly to the president.

■ **Learning Outcome 2:**
Describe the various types of agencies and organizations that make up the federal executive branch.

Figure 13–4 ▶ **Organizational Chart of the Federal Government**
Consider a few of the independent agencies listed at the bottom of the chart. *Why might each of these agencies have been made independent?*

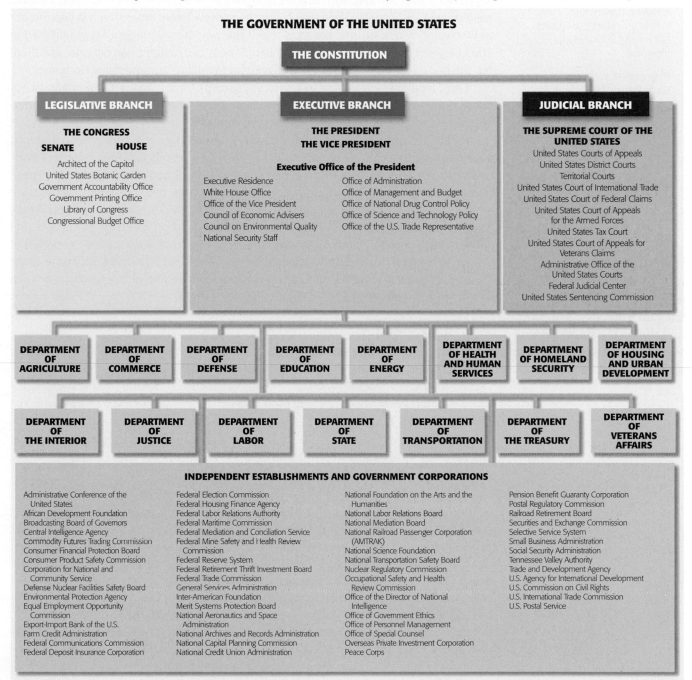

Source: *United States Government Manual* at www.usgovernmentmanual.gov.

Cabinet Department
One of the fifteen major departments of the executive branch.

Line Organization
In the federal government, an administrative unit that is directly accountable to the president.

Independent Executive Agency
A federal agency that is not part of a cabinet department but reports directly to the president.

Independent Regulatory Agency
An agency outside the major executive departments that is charged with making and implementing rules and regulations within a specific area.

The executive branch, which employs most of the government's staff, has four major types of structures. They are (1) cabinet departments, (2) independent executive agencies, (3) independent regulatory agencies, and (4) government corporations. Each has a distinctive relationship to the president, and some have unusual internal structures, overall goals, and grants of power.

Cabinet Departments

The fifteen **cabinet departments** are the major service organizations of the federal government. They can also be described in management terms as **line organizations.** This means that they are directly accountable to the president and are responsible for performing government functions, such as printing money and training troops. These departments were created by Congress when the need for each department arose. The first department to be created was State, and the most recent one was Homeland Security, established in 2003. A president might ask that a new department be created or an old one abolished, but the president has no power to do so without legislative approval from Congress.

Each department is headed by a secretary (except for the Justice Department, which is headed by the attorney general). Each department also has several levels of undersecretaries, assistant secretaries, and other personnel.

Presidents theoretically have considerable control over the cabinet departments, because presidents are able to appoint or fire all of the top officials. Even cabinet departments do not always respond to the president's wishes, though. One reason why presidents are frequently unhappy with their departments is that the entire bureaucratic structure below the top political levels is staffed by permanent employees. Many of these employees are committed to established programs or procedures and resist change. Table 13–2 that follows shows that each cabinet department employs thousands of individuals, only a handful of whom are under the direct control of the president. The table also describes some of the functions of each of the departments.

did you know?

The census is the U.S. government's largest peacetime operation. At its peak during the 2010 census, more than one million census workers counted about 310 million people in some 120 million households.

Independent Executive Agencies

Independent executive agencies are bureaucratic organizations that are not located within a department but report directly to the president, who appoints their chief officials. When a new federal agency is created—the Environmental Protection Agency, for example—Congress decides where it will be located in the bureaucracy. In recent decades, presidents often have asked that a new organization be kept separate or independent rather than added to an existing department, particularly if a department may be hostile to the agency's creation. Table 13–3 that follows describes the functions of selected independent executive agencies.

Independent Regulatory Agencies

Typically, an **independent regulatory agency** is responsible for a specific type of public policy. Its function is to make and implement rules and regulations in a particular sphere of action to protect the public interest. The earliest such agency was the Interstate Commerce Commission (ICC), which was established in 1887 when Americans began to seek some form of government control over the rapidly growing business and industrial sector. This new form of organization, the independent regulatory agency, was supposed to make technical, nonpolitical decisions about rates, profits, and rules that would be for the benefit of all and that did not require congressional legislation. In the years that followed the creation of the ICC, other agencies were formed to regulate such areas as communication (the Federal Communications Commission) and nuclear power (the Nuclear Regulatory Commission). (The ICC was abolished in 1995.)

Table 13–2 ▶ **Executive Departments**

Why do you think the Department of Education might be relatively small?

Department and Year Established	Principal Functions	Selected Subagencies
State (1789) (12,896 employees)	Negotiates treaties, develops foreign policy, protects citizens abroad.	Passport Services Office, Bureau of Diplomatic Security, Foreign Service, Bureau of Human Rights and Humanitarian Affairs, Bureau of Consular Affairs.
Treasury (1789) (100,402 employees)	Pays all federal bills, borrows funds, collects federal taxes, mints coins and prints paper currency, supervises national banks.	Internal Revenue Service, U.S. Mint.
Interior (1849) (64,931 employees)	Supervises federally owned lands and parks, supervises Native American affairs.	U.S. Fish and Wildlife Service, National Park Service, Bureau of Indian Affairs, Bureau of Land Management.
Justice (1870)* (114,233 employees)	Furnishes legal advice to the president, enforces federal criminal laws, supervises federal prisons.	Federal Bureau of Investigation, Drug Enforcement Administration, Bureau of Prisons.
Agriculture (1889) (87,667 employees)	Provides assistance to farmers and ranchers, conducts agricultural research, works to protect forests.	Soil Conservation Service, Agricultural Research Service, Food Safety and Inspection Service, Federal Crop Insurance Corporation, Commodity Credit Corporation, Forest Service.
Commerce (1913)† (45,355 employees)	Grants patents and trademarks, conducts a national census, monitors the weather, protects the interests of businesses.	Bureau of the Census, Bureau of Economic Analysis, Patent and Trademark Office, National Oceanic and Atmospheric Administration.
Labor (1913)† (16,150 employees)	Administers federal labor laws, promotes the interests of workers.	Occupational Safety and Health Administration, Bureau of Labor Statistics, Employment Standards Administration, Employment and Training Administration.
Defense (1947)‡ (727,351 employees)	Manages the armed forces (army, navy, air force, and marines), operates military bases, is responsible for civil defense.	National Security Agency; Joint Chiefs of Staff; Departments of the Air Force, Navy, Army; Defense Advanced Research Projects Agency; Defense Intelligence Agency; the service academies.
Housing and Urban Development (1965) (8,597 employees)	Deals with the nation's housing needs, develops and rehabilitates urban communities, oversees resale of mortgages.	Government National Mortgage Association, Office of Community Planning and Development, Office of Fair Housing and Equal Opportunity.
Transportation (1967) (54,605 employees)	Finances improvements in mass transit; develops and administers programs for highways, railroads, and aviation.	Federal Aviation Administration, Federal Highway Administration, National Highway Traffic Safety Administration, Federal Transit Administration.
Energy (1977) (15,361 employees)	Promotes the conservation of energy and resources, analyzes energy data, conducts research and development.	Federal Energy Regulatory Commission, National Nuclear Security Administration.
Health and Human Services (1979)§ (86,264 employees)	Promotes public health, administers Medicare and Medicaid, enforces pure food and drug laws, conducts and sponsors health-related research.	Food and Drug Administration, Public Health Service, Centers for Disease Control and Prevention, National Institutes of Health, Centers for Medicare and Medicaid Services.
Education (1979)§ (4,212 employees)	Coordinates federal programs and policies for education, administers aid to education, promotes educational research.	Office of Special Education and Rehabilitation Service, Office of Elementary and Secondary Education, Office of Postsecondary Education, Office of Vocational and Adult Education, Office of Federal Student Aid.
Veterans Affairs (1988) (340,926 employees)	Promotes the welfare of veterans of the U.S. armed forces.	Veterans Health Administration, Veterans Benefits Administration, National Cemetery Systems.
Homeland Security (2003) (192,582 employees)	Attempts to prevent terrorist attacks within the United States, control America's borders, and minimize the damage from natural disasters.	U.S. Customs and Border Protection, U.S. Coast Guard, Secret Service, Federal Emergency Management Agency, U.S. Citizenship and Immigration Services, U.S. Immigration Customs Enforcement.

*Formed from the Office of the Attorney General (created in 1789).
†Formed from the Department of Commerce and Labor (created in 1903).
‡Formed from the Department of War (created in 1789) and the Department of the Navy (created in 1798).
§Formed from the Department of Health, Education, and Welfare (created in 1953).

Table 13–3 ▶ **Selected Independent Executive Agencies**

Why might the Small Business Administration have been kept separate from the Commerce Department?

Name	Date Formed	Principal Functions
The Smithsonian Institution (4,807 employees)	1846	Runs the government's museums and the National Zoo.
Central Intelligence Agency (CIA) (number of employees is classified; NSA leaks give the number as 21,575)	1947	Gathers and analyzes political and military information about foreign countries, conducts covert operations outside the United States.
General Services Administration (GSA) (11,677 employees)	1949	Purchases and manages property of the federal government, acts as the business arm of the federal government in overseeing federal government spending projects, discovers overcharges in government programs.
National Science Foundation (NSF) (1,501 employees)	1950	Promotes scientific research, provides grants to all levels of schools for instructional programs in the sciences.
Small Business Administration (SBA) (4,803 employees)	1953	Protects the interests of small businesses, provides low-cost loans and management information to small businesses.
National Aeronautics and Space Administration (NASA) (17,911 employees)	1958	Is responsible for the U.S. space program, including the building, testing, and operating of space vehicles.
Environmental Protection Agency (EPA) (16,833 employees)	1970	Undertakes programs aimed at reducing air and water pollution, works with state and local agencies to help fight environmental hazards.
Social Security Administration (SSA)* (61,957 employees)	1995	Manages the government's Social Security programs, including Retirement and Survivors Insurance, Disability Insurance, Supplemental Security Income, and international programs.

*Separated from the Department of Health and Human Services (created in 1979).

The Purpose and Nature of Regulatory Agencies. In practice, regulatory agencies are administered independently of all three branches of government. They were set up because Congress felt it was unable to handle the complexities and technicalities required to carry out specific laws in the public interest. Regulatory agencies and commissions actually combine some functions of all three branches of government—legislative, executive, and judicial. They are legislative in that they make rules that have the force of law. They are executive in that they provide for the enforcement of those rules. They are judicial in that they decide disputes involving the rules they have made.

Heads of regulatory agencies and members of agency boards or commissions are appointed by the president with the consent of the Senate, although they do not report to the president. When an agency is headed by a board, rather than an individual, the members of the board cannot, by law, all be from the same political party. Presidents can influence regulatory agency behavior by appointing people of their own parties or individuals who share their political views when vacancies occur, in particular when the chair is vacant. Members may be removed by the president only for causes specified in the law creating the agency. Table 13–4 that follows describes the functions of selected independent regulatory agencies.

did you know?

Because the Treasury Department has the right to print platinum coins of any denomination, in 2013 it was proposed that the government meet the debt ceiling crisis by minting a $1 trillion platinum coin and depositing it with the Federal Reserve. The Treasury Department issued a statement saying that it would not do this.

Table 13–4 ▸ **Selected Independent Regulatory Agencies**

Some members of Congress were opposed to the creation of the Consumer Financial Protection Bureau. *What might have been the reasons for the opposition?*

Name	Date Formed	Principal Functions
Federal Reserve System Board of Governors (Fed) (1,369 federal employees; employment in the entire Fed is 20,544)	1913	Determines policy on interest rates, credit availability, and the money supply.
Federal Trade Commission (FTC) (1,171 employees)	1914	Prevents businesses from engaging in unfair trade practices, stops the formation of monopolies in the business sector, protects consumer rights.
Securities and Exchange Commission (SEC) (4,221 employees)	1934	Regulates the nation's stock exchanges, in which shares of stock are bought and sold; requires full disclosure of the financial profiles of companies that wish to sell stocks and bonds to the public.
Federal Communications Commission (FCC) (1,757 employees)	1934	Regulates communications by radio, television, wire, satellite, and cable.
National Labor Relations Board (NLRB) (1,588 employees)	1935	Protects employees' rights to join unions and bargain collectively with employers, attempts to prevent unfair labor practices by both employers and unions.
Equal Employment Opportunity Commission (EEOC) (2,128 employees)	1964	Works to eliminate discrimination based on religion, gender, race, color, national origin, age, or disability; examines claims of discrimination.
Nuclear Regulatory Commission (NRC) (3,869 employees)	1974	Ensures that electricity-generating nuclear reactors in the United States are built and operated safely, regularly inspects the operations of such reactors.
Consumer Financial Protection Bureau (945 employees)	2010	Protects consumers in the financial sector; has jurisdiction over banks, securities firms, payday lenders, mortgage-servicing operations, foreclosure relief services, debt collectors, and others.

Agency Capture. Over the last several decades, some observers have concluded that regulatory agencies, although nominally independent, may in fact not always be so. They contend that many agencies have been **captured** by the very industries and firms that they were supposed to regulate, and therefore make decisions based on the interests of the industry, not the general public. The results have been less competition rather than more competition, higher prices rather than lower prices, and fewer choices rather than more choices for consumers.

Deregulation and Reregulation. During the presidency of Jimmy Carter (1977–1981), significant deregulation (the removal of regulatory restraints—the opposite of regulation) was initiated. For example, Carter appointed a chairperson of the Civil Aeronautics Board (CAB) who gradually eliminated regulation of airline fares and routes. Deregulation continued under President Ronald Reagan (1981–1989). During the administration of George H. W. Bush (1989–1993), calls for reregulation of many businesses increased and several new regulatory acts were passed.

Capture
The act by which an industry being regulated by a government agency gains direct or indirect control over agency personnel and decision makers.

An investigator with the National Transportation Safety Board examines a battery. The device caused a fire aboard a Japan Airlines Boeing 787 Dreamliner at Boston in 2013. The new aircraft was grounded pending results of the investigation. *Why might people be reluctant to turn such an investigation function over to a private corporation?*

Under President Bill Clinton (1993–2001), however, the Interstate Commerce Commission was eliminated, and the banking and telecommunications industries, along with many other sectors of the economy, were deregulated. At the same time, there was extensive regulation to protect the environment, a trend somewhat attenuated by the George W. Bush administration.

<table>
<tr><td>

did you know?

The Pentagon and the Central Intelligence Agency once spent more than $11 million on psychics who were supposed to provide special insights regarding various foreign threats.

</td></tr>
</table>

Regulation Today. After the financial crisis of September 2008, many people saw inadequate regulation of the financial industry as a major cause of the nation's economic difficulties. During President Obama's administration, therefore, reregulation of that industry became a major objective. After intense debate, Congress passed a comprehensive financial industry regulation plan in 2010.

Americans have had conflicting views about the amount of regulation that is appropriate for various industries ever since the government began to undertake serious regulatory activities. Many people find regulation to be contrary to the spirit of free enterprise and the American tradition of individualism. Yet in cases such as BP's Deepwater Horizon oil spill disaster in the Gulf of Mexico in April 2010, citizens of all political stripes were outraged to learn that the relevant regulatory agency at the time, the Minerals Management Service, had failed to do its job.

Government Corporations

Another form of bureaucratic organization in the United States is the **government corporation.** Although the concept is borrowed from the world of business, there are important differences between public and private corporations.

A private corporation has shareholders (stockholders) who elect a board of directors, who in turn choose the corporate officers, such as the CEO. When a private corporation makes a profit, it must pay taxes (unless it avoids them through various legal loopholes). It distributes the after-tax profits to shareholders as dividends or plows the profits back into the corporation to make new investments, or both.

A government corporation has a board of directors and managers, but it does not usually have any stockholders. The public cannot buy shares of stock in a typical government corporation, and if the entity makes a profit, it does not distribute the profit as

Government Corporation
An agency of government that administers a quasi-business enterprise. These corporations are used when government activities are primarily commercial.

dividends. Nor does it have to pay taxes on profits—the profits remain in the corporation. Table 13–5 that follows describes the functions of selected government corporations.

Bankruptcy. The federal government can also take effective control of a private corporation in a number of different circumstances. One is bankruptcy. When a company files for bankruptcy, it asks a federal judge for relief from its creditors. The judge, operating under bankruptcy laws established by Congress (as specified in the Constitution), is ultimately responsible for the fate of the enterprise. When a bank fails, the government has a special interest in protecting customers who have deposited funds with the bank. For that reason, the failing institution is taken over by the Federal Deposit Insurance Corporation (FDIC), which ensures continuity of service to bank customers.

Government Ownership of Private Enterprises. The federal government can also obtain partial or complete ownership of a private corporation by purchasing its stock. Before 2008, such takeovers were rare, although they occasionally happened. When Continental Illinois, then the nation's seventh-largest bank, failed in 1984, the FDIC wound up in control of the institution for ten years before it could find a buyer.

The Bank Bailout. The Continental Illinois rescue provided a blueprint for the massive bank bailout initiated under President George W. Bush in October 2008. The Troubled Asset Relief Program (TARP) gave the Treasury the authority to spend up to $700 billion. Of this sum, about $426 billion was actually disbursed. The government made investments in more than eight hundred businesses, including banks, automobile companies, and the giant insurance company AIG.

The bailout program was tremendously unpopular. Still, by 2011 most banks had paid back the government's investments. By 2014, the government had collected $13 billion

Table 13–5 ▶ **Selected Government Corporations**

Would it be a good idea for the Postal Service to add new services in an attempt to earn more revenue? Why or why not?

Name	Date Formed	Principal Functions
Tennessee Valley Authority (TVA) (12,646 employees)	1933	Operates a Tennessee River control system and generates power for a seven-state region and for the U.S. aeronautics and space programs, promotes the economic development of the Tennessee Valley region, controls floods and promotes the navigability of the Tennessee River.
Federal Deposit Insurance Corporation (FDIC) (7,436 employees)	1933	Insures individuals' bank deposits up to $250,000, oversees the business activities of banks.
Export-Import Bank of the United States (Ex-Im Bank) (426 employees)	1933	Promotes the sale of American-made goods abroad, grants loans to foreign purchasers of American products.
National Railroad Passenger Corporation (AMTRAK) (20,000 employees)	1970	Provides a national and intercity rail passenger service, controls more than 21,000 miles of track and serves 500 communities.
U.S. Postal Service (USPS)* (589,000 employees)	1970	Delivers mail throughout the United States and its territories, is the largest government corporation.

*Formed from the Post Office Department (an executive department).

more than it laid out. This was still a net loss given that a $426 billion investment would normally earn more than $13 billion in interest. Much of the difference was due to the government's decision to sell its stock in General Motors at a loss.

Government-Sponsored Enterprises. An additional type of corporation is the government-sponsored enterprise, a business created by the federal government itself, which then sells part or all of the corporation's stock to private investors. Until 2008, the leading examples of this kind of company were the Federal Home Loan Mortgage Corporation, known as Freddie Mac, and the Federal National Mortgage Association, commonly known as Fannie Mae. Both of these firms buy mortgages from banks and bundle them into securities that can be sold to investors. When the housing market collapsed during the Great Recession, so—eventually—did Freddie Mac and Fannie Mae.

Investors had always assumed that the federal government backed the obligations of the two enterprises, even though the government had never issued an explicit guarantee. In September 2008, the implicit guarantee became real when the Treasury placed the two mortgage giants under a federal "conservatorship" and pumped billions in fresh capital— also provided by the taxpayers—into them. Most financial experts thought these sums would be lost forever. In fact, the corporations eventually became profitable again, and by 2014, the government had retrieved its investment. Because the government now owns Freddie and Fannie outright, all future profits will flow into the Treasury.

■ **Learning Outcome 3:**
Explain how government employees are hired and how they are administered.

Staffing the Bureaucracy

There are two categories of bureaucrats: political appointees and civil servants. As noted earlier, the president can make political appointments to most of the top jobs in the federal bureaucracy. The president also can appoint ambassadors to foreign posts. All of the jobs that are considered "political plums" and that usually go to the politically well connected are listed in *Policy and Supporting Positions,* a book published by the Government Printing Office after each presidential election. Informally (and appropriately), this has been called the "Plum Book." The rest of the national government's employees belong to the civil service and obtain their jobs through a much more formal process.

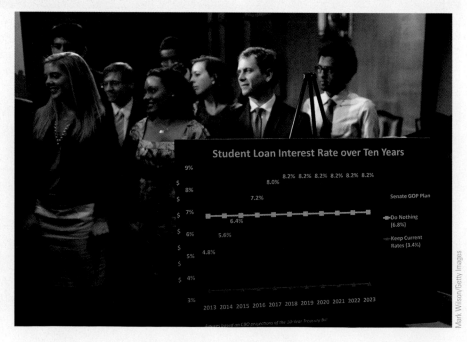

Students lobby against a near-doubling of the interest rates on federally subsidized Stafford loans. The loans are available through the Department of Education. In August 2013, Congress repealed most of the increase. *Is a college degree worth incurring large student loan debts?*

Political Appointees

To fill the positions listed in the "Plum Book,"[3] the president and the president's advisers solicit suggestions from politicians, businesspersons, and other prominent individuals. Appointments to these positions offer the president a way to pay off outstanding political debts. Presidents often use ambassadorships to reward individuals for their campaign contributions. But the president must also take into consideration such things as the candidate's ability to actually do the job.

The Aristocracy of the Federal Government. Political appointees are in some sense the aristocracy of the federal government. But their powers, although they appear formidable on paper, are often exaggerated. Like the president, a political appointee will occupy her or his position for a comparatively brief time. Political appointees often leave office before the president's term actually ends. In fact, the average term of service for political appointees is less than two years. As a result, most appointees have little background for their positions and may be mere figureheads. Often, they only respond to the paperwork that flows up from below. Additionally, the professional civil servants who make up the permanent civil service may not feel compelled to carry out their current chief's directives quickly, because they know that he or she will not be around for very long.

The Difficulty in Firing Civil Servants. This inertia is compounded by the fact that it is very difficult to discharge civil servants. In recent years, fewer than 0.1 percent of federal employees have been fired for incompetence. Because discharged employees may appeal their dismissals, many months or even years can pass before the issue is resolved conclusively. This occupational rigidity helps to ensure that most political appointees, no matter how competent or driven, will not be able to exert much meaningful influence over their subordinates, let alone implement dramatic changes in the bureaucracy itself.

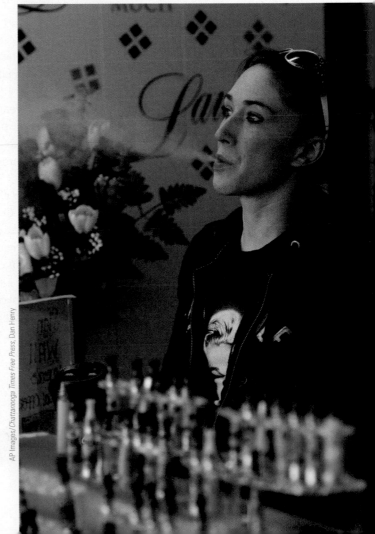

An employee at an e-cigarette shop in Tennessee enjoys her own product. *How tightly should the government regulate e-cigarettes?*

History of the Federal Civil Service

When the federal government was formed in 1789, it had no career public servants but rather consisted of amateurs who were almost all Federalists. When Thomas Jefferson took over as president, few federal administrative jobs were held by members of his party, so he fired more than one hundred officials and replaced them with his own supporters. Then, for the next twenty-five years, a growing body of federal administrators gained experience and expertise, becoming in the process professional public servants. These administrators stayed in office regardless of who was elected president. The bureaucracy had become a self-maintaining, long-term element within government.

To the Victors Belong the Spoils. When Andrew Jackson took over the White House in 1828, he could not believe how many appointed officials (appointed before he became president, that is) were overtly hostile toward him and his Democratic Party. Because the bureaucracy was reluctant to carry out his

AP Images/Chattanooga Times Free Press, Dan Henry

---

3. See Table 12–1 in the Chapter 12 section "The Many Roles of the President" for a list of the number of positions available for presidential appointments in the most recent edition of the "Plum Book."

President James A. Garfield was assassinated in 1881 by a disappointed office seeker, Charles J. Guiteau. One result of this act was the passage of the Pendleton Act in 1883, which created a career civil service. *What kinds of problems would result today if we relied, even in part, on the spoils system?*

programs, Jackson did the obvious: he fired federal officials—more than had been fired by all his predecessors combined. The **spoils system**—an application of the principle that to the victors belong the spoils—became the standard method of filling federal positions. Whenever a new president was elected from a party different from the party of the previous president, there would be an almost complete turnover in the staffing of the federal government.

The Civil Service Reform Act of 1883. Jackson's spoils system survived for a number of years, but it became increasingly corrupt. In addition, the size of the bureaucracy increased by 300 percent between 1851 and 1881. As the bureaucracy grew larger, the cry for civil service reform became louder. Reformers began to look to the example of several European countries—in particular, Germany. That country had established a professional civil service that operated under a **merit system,** in which job appointments were based on competitive examinations.

In 1883, the **Pendleton Act**—or **Civil Service Reform Act**—was passed, placing the first limits on the spoils system. The act established the principle of employment on the basis of open, competitive examinations and created the **Civil Service Commission** to administer the personnel service. Only 10 percent of federal employees were covered by the merit system initially. Later laws, amendments, and executive orders, however, increased the coverage to more than 90 percent of federal employees. The effects of these reforms were felt at all levels of government.

The Supreme Court strengthened the civil service system in 1976 and in 1980.[4] In those two cases, the Court used the First Amendment to forbid government officials from discharging or threatening to discharge public employees solely for not being supporters of the political party in power unless party affiliation is an appropriate requirement for the position. Additional enhancements to the civil service system were added in 1990.[5] The Court's ruling in that year effectively prevented the use of partisan political considerations as the basis for hiring, promoting, or transferring most public employees. An exception was permitted, however, for senior policymaking positions, which usually go to officials who will support the programs of the elected leaders.

The Civil Service Reform Act of 1978. In 1978, the Civil Service Reform Act abolished the Civil Service Commission and created two new federal agencies to perform its duties. To administer the civil service laws, rules, and regulations, the act created the Office of Personnel Management (OPM). The OPM is empowered to recruit, interview, and test potential government workers and determine who should be hired. The OPM makes recommendations to the individual agencies as to which persons meet the standards (typically, the top three applicants for a position), and the agencies then decide whom to hire. To oversee promotions, employees' rights, and other employment matters, the act created the Merit Systems Protection Board (MSPB). The MSPB evaluates charges of wrongdoing, hears employee appeals of agency decisions, and can order corrective action against agencies and employees.

Spoils System
The awarding of government jobs to political supporters and friends.

Merit System
The selection, retention, and promotion of government employees on the basis of competitive examinations.

Pendleton Act (Civil Service Reform Act)
An act that established the principle of employment on the basis of merit and created the Civil Service Commission to administer the personnel service.

Civil Service Commission
The initial central personnel agency of the national government; created in 1883.

---

4. *Elrod v. Burns*, 427 U.S. 347 (1976) and *Branti v. Finkel*, 445 U.S. 507 (1980).
5. *Rutan v. Republican Party of Illinois*, 497 U.S. 62 (1990).

Federal Employees and Political Campaigns. In 1933, when President Franklin D. Roosevelt set up his New Deal, a veritable army of civil servants was hired to staff the many new agencies that were created. Because the individuals who worked in these agencies owed their jobs to the Democratic Party, it seemed natural for them to campaign for Democratic candidates. The Democrats who controlled Congress in the mid-1930s did not object. But in 1938, a coalition of conservative Democrats and Republicans took control of Congress and forced through the Hatch Act—or Political Activities Act—of 1939. The act prohibited federal employees from actively participating in the political management of campaigns. It also forbade the use of federal authority to influence nominations and elections, and it outlawed the use of bureaucratic rank to pressure federal employees to make political contributions.

The Hatch Act created a controversy that lasted for decades. Many contended that the act deprived federal employees of their First Amendment freedoms of speech and association. In 1972, a federal district court declared the act unconstitutional. The United States Supreme Court, however, reaffirmed the challenged portion of the act in 1973, stating that the government's interest in preserving a nonpartisan civil service was so great that the prohibitions should remain.[6] Twenty years later, Congress addressed the criticisms of the Hatch Act by passing the Federal Employees Political Activities Act of 1993. This act, which amended the Hatch Act, lessened the harshness of the 1939 act in several ways. Among other things, the 1993 act allowed federal employees to run for office in non-partisan elections, participate in voter-registration drives, make campaign contributions to political organizations, and campaign for candidates in partisan elections.

> ## did you know?
>
> According to a recent report, federal employees earn an average of $113,000 in total compensation (including benefits) for jobs equivalent to those in the private sector, while the comparable private-sector employees average $61,000.

> ## Why Should You Care about...
>
> ### The Bureaucracy?
>
> Why should you, as an individual, care about the bureaucracy? You might consider that the federal government collects billions of pieces of information on tens of millions of Americans each year. These data are stored in files and sometimes are exchanged among agencies. You are probably the subject of several federal records (for example, in the Social Security Administration, the Internal Revenue Service, and, if you are a male, the Selective Service).

Modern Attempts at Bureaucratic Reform

As long as the federal bureaucracy exists, attempts to make it more open, efficient, and responsive to the needs of U.S. citizens will continue. The most important actual and proposed reforms in the last several decades include sunshine and sunset laws, privatization, incentives for efficiency and productivity, and more protection for so-called whistleblowers.

> ■ **Learning Outcome 4:**
> Evaluate different methods that have been put into place to reform bureaucracies and make them more efficient.

Sunshine Laws before and after 9/11

In 1976, Congress enacted the **Government in the Sunshine Act.** It required for the first time that all multiheaded federal agencies—agencies headed by a committee instead of an individual—hold their meetings regularly in public session. The bill defined meetings as almost any gathering, formal or informal, of agency members, including a conference telephone call. The only exceptions to this rule of openness are discussions of matters such as court proceedings or personnel problems, and these exceptions are specifically listed in the bill. Sunshine laws now exist at all levels of government.

Information Disclosure. In 1966, the federal government passed the Freedom of Information Act (FOIA), which required federal government agencies, with certain exceptions, to disclose to individuals information contained in government files. FOIA requests are helpful not just to individuals. Indeed, the major beneficiaries of the act have been

> **Government in the Sunshine Act**
> A law that requires all committee-directed federal agencies to conduct their business regularly in public session.

---

6. *United States Civil Service Commission v. National Association of Letter Carriers,* 413 U.S. 548 (1973).

Sunset Legislation
Laws requiring that existing programs be reviewed regularly for their effectiveness and be terminated unless specifically extended as a result of these reviews.

Privatization
The replacement of government services with services provided by private firms.

did you know?
In 1964, U.S. Attorney General Robert Kennedy received a complaint that the lyrics to "Louie Louie" by The Kingsmen were obscene. After two years of investigation, the FBI dismissed the complaint on the ground that the lyrics were unintelligible and therefore could not be obscene.

news organizations, which have used it to uncover government waste, scandals, and incompetence.

As one example, in 2012 Fox News obtained documents showing that the General Services Administration (GSA) had wasted large sums in sponsoring lavish and pointless conferences for its employees. Groups opposed to the Obama administration have made much use of the FOIA. For example, a seemingly unending series of FOIA requests have been filed in an unsuccessful attempt to locate information suggesting that Obama is not, in fact, a U.S. citizen.

Curbs on Information Disclosure. Since the terrorist attacks of September 11, 2001, the trend toward open government has been reversed at both the federal and the state levels. Within weeks after September 11, 2001, federal agencies removed hundreds, if not thousands, of documents from Internet sites, public libraries, and the reading rooms found in various federal government departments. Information contained in some of the documents included diagrams of power plants and pipelines, structural details on dams, and safety plans for chemical plants. The military also immediately began restricting information about its current and planned activities, as did the Federal Bureau of Investigation. These agencies were concerned that terrorists could make use of this information to plan attacks.

Sunset Laws

The size and scope of the federal bureaucracy can potentially be controlled through **sunset legislation,** which places government programs on a definite schedule for congressional consideration. Unless Congress specifically reauthorizes a particular federally operated program at the end of a designated period, the program will be terminated automatically—that is, its sun will set.

The idea of sunset legislation was initially suggested by Franklin Roosevelt when he created the host of New Deal agencies in the 1930s. His adviser (and later Supreme Court justice), William O. Douglas, recommended that each agency's charter should include a provision allowing for its termination in ten years. Only an act of Congress could revitalize it. The proposal was never adopted. It was not until 1976 that a state legislature—Colorado's—adopted sunset legislation for state regulatory commissions, giving them a life of six years before their "suns set." Today, most states have some type of sunset law.

National Guard members in 2014 build a sandbag levy against flooding by the North Platte River in Wyoming. *Is the National Guard part of the bureaucracy?*

Privatization, or Contracting Out

Another approach to bureaucratic reform is **privatization,** which occurs when government services are replaced by services from the private sector. For example, the government has contracted with private firms to operate prisons. Supporters of privatization argue that some services can be provided more efficiently by the private sector. A similar scheme involves furnishing vouchers to government "clients" in lieu of services. For example, instead of supplying housing, the government could offer vouchers that recipients could use to "pay" for housing in privately owned buildings.

The privatization, or contracting-out, strategy has been most successful on the local level. Some municipalities have contracted with private companies for such services as trash collection. This approach is not a cure-all, however, because many functions, particularly on the national level, cannot be contracted out in any meaningful way. For example, the federal government could not contract out many of the Defense Department's functions to private firms.

The increase in the amount of government work being contracted out to the private sector has led to significant controversy in recent years. Some have criticized the lack of competitive bidding for many contracts that the government has awarded. Another concern is the perceived lack of government oversight of the work done by private contractors.

> **Whistleblower**
> Someone who brings to public attention gross governmental inefficiency or an illegal action.

Saving Costs through E-Government

Many contend that the communications revolution brought about by the Internet has not only improved the efficiency with which government agencies deliver services to the public but also helped to reduce the cost of government. Agencies can now communicate with members of the public, as well as other agencies, via e-mail. Additionally, every federal agency now has a Web site to which citizens can go to find information about agency services instead of calling or appearing in person at a regional agency office.

Although data-rich high-tech systems have provided new, efficient ways of accomplishing the government's work, privacy concerns have become an issue when the government collects data on individuals. As one example, the American public has never accepted the concept of a national ID card, even though many other nations require their citizens to obtain such ID. Even in the United States, it is difficult to live a normal life without a Social Security number and a state-issued ID such as a driver's license. Lack of adequate ID can also be a tremendous burden to the world's poorest people, as we explain in the *Beyond Our Borders* feature that follows.

did you know?

Thirty-four percent of all land in the United States is owned by the Federal government.

Helping Out the Whistleblowers

A **whistleblower** is someone who blows the whistle on (brings to public attention) a gross governmental inefficiency or an illegal action. Whistleblowers may be clerical workers, managers, or even specialists, such as scientists.

Laws Protecting Whistleblowers. The 1978 Civil Service Reform Act prohibits reprisals against whistleblowers by their superiors, and it set up the Merit Systems Protection Board as part of this protection. Many federal agencies also have toll-free hotlines that employees can use anonymously to report bureaucratic waste and inappropriate behavior. About 35 percent of all calls result in agency action or follow-up.

Further protection for whistleblowers was provided in 1989, when Congress passed the Whistleblower Protection Act. That act established an independent agency, the Office of Special Counsel (OSC), to investigate complaints brought by government employees who have been demoted, fired, or otherwise sanctioned for reporting government fraud or waste.

"It's always cozy in here. We're insulated by layers of bureaucracy."

Frank Cotham/The New Yorker Collection/The Cartoon Bank

Beyond Our Borders

Biometric IDs for More Than One Billion Citizens of India

India has a population of 1.2 billion people. By mid-century, it will have 1.5 billion citizens and surpass China as the world's most populous nation. India's economy is growing, but hundreds of millions of its citizens remain desperately poor. Not surprisingly, the nation is badly governed and famous for corruption and a sluggish bureaucracy. India is also a country with booming high-tech industries, however. Beginning in 2010, the Indian government rolled out a high-tech plan to provide biometric IDs for every one of its citizens. Identifications are based on fingerprints and iris scans, and they are entered into the world's largest online ID database. Why is India undertaking this massive project?

The Anonymous Poor

The primary beneficiaries of the project are expected to be India's poorest citizens. Until now, few poor Indians have had good ways of proving who they are. They had no passport, no driver's license, and no birth certificate. Often, they live in villages where dozens of people share the same name. As a result, they could not open bank accounts or undertake dozens of other activities. The Indian government provides a variety of welfare programs for its poorest citizens, including subsidized grain allotments and make-work schemes. Without proper identification, however, poor Indians have struggled to obtain the services they have been promised. Much of the make-work funding has been stolen by officials who collect the wages of fictitious "ghost workers."

Entering the Modern World

A secure online identity changes a poor person's relationship with the modern world. Banks are more willing to lend to people they can trace. Mobile phone companies can more easily extend credit. It becomes possible to shop online. India's poor are visibly enthusiastic about the project. People continue to line up day after day to obtain their twelve-digit ID numbers. By mid-2014, half of all Indians were enrolled.

Privacy Concerns

The program has its critics. Naturally, these include the corrupt officials who have benefited from the previous situation. More principled critics have raised concerns about India's lack of privacy and data-protection laws. Some claim the scheme could be used to expel illegal immigrants back to Bangladesh, a nation even more impoverished than India. Others point out, however, that people who are destitute have few expectations of privacy.

For Critical Analysis

In what ways could India's biometric ID program be abused?

Some state and federal laws encourage employees to blow the whistle on their employers' wrongful actions by providing monetary incentives to the whistleblowers. At the federal level, the False Claims Act of 1986 allows a whistleblower who has disclosed information about a fraud against the U.S. government to receive a monetary award. If the government chooses to prosecute the case and wins, the whistleblower receives between 15 and 25 percent of the proceeds. If the government declines to intervene, the whistleblower can bring a suit on behalf of the government and, if the suit is successful, will receive between 25 and 30 percent of the proceeds.

The Problem Continues. Despite these efforts to help whistleblowers, there is little evidence that they truly receive much protection. More than 41 percent of the employees who turned to the OSC for assistance in a recent three-year period stated that they were no longer employees of the government agencies on which they had blown the whistle.

Additionally, in 2006 the United States Supreme Court placed restrictions on lawsuits brought by public workers.[7] The case involved an assistant district attorney, Richard Ceballos, who wrote a memo asking if a county sheriff's deputy had lied in a search warrant affidavit. Ceballos claimed that he was subsequently demoted and denied a promotion. The outcome of the case turned on whether an employee has a First Amendment right to criticize an employment-related action. The Court deemed that when he wrote his memo, Ceballos was speaking as an employee, not a citizen, and was thus subject to his employer's disciplinary actions. The ruling will affect millions of governmental employees.

Whistleblowers under Obama. During his 2008 campaign, Obama promised to protect whistleblowers. Many observers believe, however, that in fact the Obama administration's record on whistleblowers is one of the worst ever. This conclusion is based, in large part, on the administration's use of the Espionage Act of 1917 to prosecute persons who leaked national security information to the press. By 2013, the administration had launched seven such prosecutions. The Espionage Act has been used regularly against persons spying for foreign governments. Not since 1984, however, had the government initiated such a case based on leaks to the press. We describe most of these cases in the *Which Side Are You On?* feature that follows.

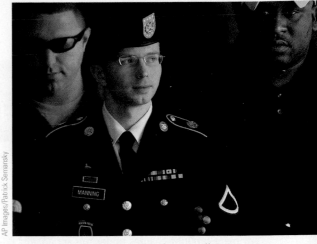

In 2013, Army Private First Class Bradley Manning was sentenced to thirty-five years for giving classified U.S. government information to the anti-secrecy Web site called WikiLeaks. In 2014, Manning sought a name change from Bradley Edward to Chelsea Elizabeth and to live thereafter as a woman. *Is Manning a criminal, a hero—or both?*

The most recent—and most dramatic—case involved Edward Snowden, an employee of a National Security Agency (NSA) contractor. Snowden delivered a vast collection of information on NSA data surveillance to journalists Glenn Greenwald and Laura Poitras. Stories based on the material appeared in the *Guardian* of Britain, in the *Washington Post* and the *New York Times*, and in a variety of other newspapers around the world.

Snowden was aware of how the government had treated Private First Class Chelsea (formerly Bradley) Manning, an earlier leaker. Manning had been held in solitary confinement in ways that some critics saw as abusive. Snowden therefore relocated to Hong Kong, hoping that the Chinese government would grant him asylum. On learning that asylum would not be granted, Snowden then fled to Russia. Both Greenwald and Poitras also now live outside the United States.

Bureaucrats as Politicians and Policymakers

Because Congress is unable to oversee the day-to-day administration of its programs, it must delegate certain powers to administrative agencies. Congress delegates power to agencies through **enabling legislation.** For example, the Federal Trade Commission was created by the Federal Trade Commission Act of 1914, the Equal Employment Opportunity Commission was created by the Civil Rights Act of 1964, and the Occupational Safety and Health Administration was created by the Occupational Safety and Health Act of 1970. The enabling legislation generally specifies the name, purpose, composition, functions, and powers of the agency.

In theory, the agencies should put into effect laws passed by Congress. Laws are often drafted in such vague and general terms, however, that they provide limited guidance to

■ **Learning Outcome 5:** Discuss how federal agencies make rules and the role of Congress in this process.

Enabling Legislation
A statute enacted by Congress that authorizes the creation of an administrative agency and specifies the name, purpose, composition, functions, and powers of the agency being created.

---

7. *Garcetti v. Ceballos,* 547 U.S. 410 (2006).

Which Side Are You On?

National Security Whistleblowers—Heroes or Criminals?

Espionage has always been a crime. In 1917, shortly after the United States entered World War I, Congress passed the Espionage Act to punish citizens who gave aid to our enemies. Since that time, it has been used very rarely. In 2010, however, the government brought charges under the act against Private First Class Chelsea Manning, an Army intelligence analyst who stole thousands of secret documents and passed them to WikiLeaks, a Web site. WikiLeaks then posted much of this material on the Web, causing considerable embarrassment to the United States. From 2010 through 2013, the government brought charges against six other people under the act. These included Edward Snowden, who released material on the National Security Agency's telephone and Internet data collection. (We described the Snowden case in the text.) Are these prosecutions a crackdown on espionage—or an attempt to target legitimate whistleblowers?

The Federal Government Has Become Paranoid

Some argue that most of these Espionage Act cases involve whistleblowing, not espionage. Consider Thomas A. Drake, formerly of the National Security Agency (NSA). He was prosecuted under the Espionage Act and faced thirty-five years in prison. His "crime" was suggesting to a reporter that the NSA should not spend hundreds of millions of dollars on a private-sector digital-data-monitoring program. He thought that an internally developed project would cost less and be more effective. In the end, the government's case against him collapsed, and he pled guilty to one misdemeanor count that carried no jail time.

"The Obama administration has been quite hypocritical about its promises about openness, transparency, and accountability," said Jesselyn Radack, director for national security and human rights at the Government Accountability Project.

"Pursuing whistleblowers as spies is heavy-handed and beyond the scope of the law." The Obama administration has charged more people with leaking government secrets than all previous presidencies combined.

Criminals, Not Heroes

Others believe that it is right to use the Espionage Act to prosecute those who leak critical secrets. There is a difference between a "leaker" and a whistleblower. A leak of classified information may endanger American soldiers and intelligence officers. It can let our enemies know the methods we use to gather information. Consider the case of former CIA officer Jeffrey Sterling. He was charged with giving classified information to a *New York Times* reporter about U.S. attempts to sabotage the Iranian nuclear program. The reporter later published this information in a book. We can assume that the government of Iran was very interested in reading that work. It appears that Sterling sought revenge for the CIA's refusal to let him publish his memoirs or to settle his racial discrimination suit against the agency. Some call former CIA officer John Kiriakou a hero for exposing the agency's use of the waterboarding interrogation technique, widely considered to be a form of torture. Kiriakou also revealed the name of at least one other CIA agent, however. Such leaks can endanger lives, and thus the leakers deserve prosecution.

For Critical Analysis

Under what circumstances is it inappropriate for whistleblowers to take their concerns to the press, even when they believe the government is doing something wrong?

agency administrators as to how they should be implemented. This means that the agencies themselves must decide how best to carry out the wishes of Congress.

The discretion given to administrative agencies is not accidental. Congress has long realized that it lacks the technical expertise and the resources to monitor the implementation of its laws. Hence, administrative agencies are created to fill the gaps. This gap-filling role requires an agency to formulate administrative rules (regulations) to put flesh on the bones of the law. But it also forces the agency itself to become an unelected policymaker.

The Rulemaking Environment

Rulemaking does not occur in a vacuum. Suppose that Congress passes a new air-pollution law. The Environmental Protection Agency (EPA) might decide to implement the new law through a technical regulation on power-plant emissions. This proposed regulation would be published in the *Federal Register*, a daily government publication, so that interested parties would have an opportunity to comment on it. Individuals and companies that opposed parts or all of the rule might then try to convince the EPA to revise or redraft the regulation. Some parties might try to persuade the agency to withdraw the proposed regulation altogether. In any event, the EPA would consider these comments in drafting the final version of the regulation.

Waiting Periods and Court Challenges. Once the final regulation has been published in the *Federal Register*, there is a sixty-day waiting period before the rule can be enforced. During that period, businesses, individuals, and state and local governments can ask Congress to overturn the regulation. After the sixty-day period has lapsed, the regulation can still be challenged in court by a party having a direct interest in the rule, such as a company that expects to incur significant costs in complying with it. The company could argue that the rule misinterprets the applicable law or goes beyond the agency's statutory purview. An allegation by the company that the EPA made a mistake in judgment probably would not be enough to convince the court to throw out the rule. The company instead would have to demonstrate that the rule itself was "arbitrary and capricious."

Controversies. How agencies implement, administer, and enforce legislation has resulted in controversy. For example, decisions made by agencies charged with administering the Endangered Species Act have led to protests from farmers, ranchers, and others whose economic interests have been harmed.

At times, a controversy may arise when an agency *refuses* to issue regulations to implement a particular law. When the EPA during the Bush administration refused to issue regulations designed to curb the emission of carbon dioxide and other greenhouse gases, state and local governments, as well as a number of environmental groups, sued the agency. Those bringing the suit claimed that the EPA was not fulfilling its obligation to implement the provisions of the Clean Air Act. Ultimately, the Supreme Court held that the EPA had the authority to—and should—regulate such gases.[8]

Negotiated Rulemaking

Since the end of World War II in 1945, companies, environmentalists, and other special interest groups have challenged government regulations in court. In the 1980s, however, the sheer wastefulness of attempting to regulate through litigation became increasingly apparent. Today, a growing number of federal agencies encourage businesses and public-interest groups to become directly involved in drafting regulations. Agencies hope that such participation may help to prevent later courtroom battles over the regulations.

Congress formally approved such a process, which is called *negotiated rulemaking*, in the Negotiated Rulemaking Act of 1990. The act authorizes agencies

Piles of coal outside the DTE Energy Company's Monroe Power Plant in Michigan. The Monroe plant is the first coal-fired power plant in Michigan to use "scrubbers," which reduce sulfur dioxide emissions by about ninety-seven percent. *What should be done about carbon dioxide emissions from such plants?*

Bloomberg/Getty Images

---

8. *Massachusetts v. EPA*, 549 U.S. 497 (2007).

Iron Triangle
The three-way alliance among legislators, bureaucrats, and interest groups to make or preserve policies that benefit their respective interests.

to allow those who will be affected by a new rule to participate in the rule-drafting process. If an agency chooses to engage in negotiated rulemaking, it must publish in the *Federal Register* the subject and scope of the rule to be developed, the names of parties that will be affected significantly by the rule, and other information. Representatives of the affected groups and other interested parties then may apply to be members of the negotiating committee. The agency is represented on the committee, but a neutral third party (not the agency) presides over the proceedings. Once the committee members have reached agreement on the terms of the proposed rule, a notice is published in the *Federal Register,* followed by a period for comments by any person or organization interested in the proposed rule. Negotiated rulemaking often is conducted under the condition that the participants promise not to challenge in court the outcome of any agreement to which they were a party.

Bureaucrats as Policymakers

Theories of public administration once assumed that bureaucrats do not make policy decisions but only implement the laws and policies promulgated by the president and legislative bodies. A more realistic view is that the agencies and departments of government play important roles in policymaking. As we have seen, many government rules, regulations, and programs are in fact initiated by the bureaucracy, based on its expertise and scientific studies. How a law passed by Congress eventually is translated into action—from the forms to be filled out to decisions about who gets the benefits—usually is determined within each agency or department. Even the evaluation of whether a policy has achieved its purpose usually is based on studies that are commissioned and interpreted by the agency administering the program.

The bureaucracy's policymaking role has often been depicted as an *iron triangle.* Recently, many political scientists have come to see the concept of an *issue network* as a more accurate description of the typical policymaking process.

did you know?

Each year, federal administrative agencies produce rules that fill an average of 7,500 pages in the *Code of Federal Regulations.* The regulations now contained in this code cover 144,000 pages.

Iron Triangles. In the past, scholars often described the bureaucracy's role in the policymaking process by using the concept of an **iron triangle**—a three-way alliance among legislators in Congress, bureaucrats, and interest groups. Consider as an example the development of agricultural policy. Congress, as one component of the triangle, includes two major committees concerned with agricultural policy, the House Committee on Agriculture and the Senate Committee on Agriculture, Nutrition, and Forestry. The Department of Agriculture, the second component of the triangle, has almost 100,000 employees, plus thousands of contractors and consultants. Agricultural interest groups, the third component of the triangle, include many large and powerful associations, such as the American Farm Bureau Federation, the National Cattlemen's Beef Association, and the National Corn Growers Association. These three components of the iron triangle work together, formally or informally, to create policy.

These farmers—father and son—raise beef cattle on an Iowa farm. *To which part of the iron triangle in agriculture do they belong?*

Gary Fandel/Bloomberg via Getty Images

For example, the various agricultural interest groups lobby Congress to develop policies that benefit their groups' economic welfare. Members of Congress cannot afford to ignore the wishes of interest groups because those groups are potential sources of voter support and campaign contributions. The legislators in Congress also work closely with the Department of Agriculture, which, in implementing a policy, can develop rules that benefit—or at least do not hurt—certain industries or groups. The Department of Agriculture, in turn, supports policies that enhance the department's budget and powers. In this way, according to theory, agricultural policy is created that benefits all three components of the iron triangle.

Issue Networks. With the growth in the complexity of government, policymaking also has become more complicated. The bureaucracy is larger, Congress has more committees and subcommittees, and interest groups are more powerful than ever. Although iron triangles still exist, often they are inadequate as descriptions of how policy is made today. Frequently, different interest groups concerned about a certain area of policy have conflicting demands, making agency decisions difficult. Additionally, during periods of divided government, departments are pressured by the president to take one approach and by Congress to take another.

Many scholars now use the term *issue network* to describe the policymaking process. An **issue network** consists of individuals or organizations that support a particular policy position on the environment, taxation, consumer safety, or some other issue. Typically, an issue network includes legislators and/or their staff members, interest group leaders, bureaucrats, scholars and other experts, and representatives from the media. Members of a particular issue network work together to influence the president, members of Congress, administrative agencies, and the courts to affect public policy on a specific issue. Each policy issue may involve conflicting positions taken by two or more issue networks.

Congressional Control of the Bureaucracy

Many political pundits doubt whether Congress can meaningfully control the federal bureaucracy. These commentators forget that Congress specifies in an agency's "enabling legislation" the powers of the agency and the parameters within which it can operate. Additionally, Congress has the power of the purse and theoretically could refuse to authorize or appropriate funds for a particular agency (see the discussion of the budgeting process in Chapter 11). Whether Congress would actually take such a drastic measure would depend on the circumstances. It is clear, however, that Congress does have the legal authority to decide whether or not to fund administrative agencies.

Congress can also exercise oversight over agencies. Congressional committees conduct investigations and hold hearings to oversee an agency's actions, reviewing them to ensure compliance with congressional intentions. The agency's officers and employees can be ordered to testify before a committee about the details of various actions. Through the questions and comments of members of the House or the Senate during the hearings, Congress indicates its positions on specific programs and issues. The views expressed in any investigations and hearings are taken seriously by agency officials, who often act on those views.

Issue Network
A group of individuals or organizations—which may consist of legislators and legislative staff members, interest group leaders, bureaucrats, scholars and other experts, and media representatives—that supports a particular policy position on a given issue.

CONNECT WITH YOUR CLASSMATES
MindTap for American Government
Access the Bureaucracy Forum: Polling Activity—Bureaucracy at Work

Why Should You Care about...

The Bureaucracy?

Verifying the information that the government has on you can be important. On several occasions, the records of two people with similar names have become confused. Sometimes innocent persons have had the criminal records of other persons erroneously inserted in their files. Such disasters are not always caused by bureaucratic error. One of the most common crimes in today's world is "identity theft," in which one person makes use of another person's personal identifiers (such as a Social Security number) to commit fraud. In some instances, identity thieves have been arrested and even jailed under someone else's name.

How You Can Make a Difference

The 1966 Freedom of Information Act (FOIA) requires that the federal government release, at your request, any identifiable information it has about you or about any other subject. Nine categories of material are exempted, however (classified material, confidential material on trade secrets, internal personnel rules, personal medical files, and the like).

- To request material, write directly to the Freedom of Information Act officer at the agency in question (say, the Department of Education). You must have a relatively specific idea about the document or information you want to obtain.

- A second law, the Privacy Act of 1974, gives you access specifically to information the government may have collected about you. This law allows you to review records on file with federal agencies and to check those records for possible inaccuracies.

- If you want to look at any records or find out if an agency has a record on you, write to the agency head or Privacy Act officer, and address your letter to the specific agency. State that "under the provisions of the Privacy Act of 1974, 5 U.S.C. 522a, I hereby request a copy of (or access to) _____." Then describe the record that you wish to investigate.

- The General Services Administration (GSA) has published a citizen's guide, *Your Right to Federal Records,* that explains both the FOIA and the Privacy Act, and how to go about using them. You can locate this manual by entering its name into your favorite search engine.

Key Terms

acquisitive model 375
bureaucracy 374
cabinet department 380
capture 383
Civil Service Commission 388
enabling legislation 393

government corporation 384
Government in the Sunshine Act 389
independent executive agency 380
independent regulatory agency 380

iron triangle 396
issue network 397
line organization 380
merit system 388
monopolistic model 375
Pendleton Act (Civil Service Reform Act) 388

privatization 390
spoils system 388
sunset legislation 390
Weberian model 375
whistleblower 391

Chapter Summary

Learning Outcome 1 Bureaucracies are hierarchical organizations characterized by a division of labor and extensive procedural rules. In addition to governments, major corporations and universities have bureaucratic organizations.

Several theories have been offered to describe bureaucracies. The Weberian model posits that bureaucracies are rational, hierarchical organizations in which decisions are based on logical reasoning. The acquisitive model views top-level bureaucrats as pressing for ever-larger budgets and staffs to augment their power. The monopolistic model focuses on the environment in which most government bureaucracies operate, stating that bureaucracies are inefficient and excessively costly to operate because they have no competitors.

Since the founding of the United States, the federal bureaucracy has grown from 50 to about 2.8 million employees (including the U.S. Postal Service, but excluding the military). Federal, state, and local employees together make up about 16 percent of the nation's civilian labor force. Social Security, Medicare, Medicaid, and military defense are the largest components of federal spending.

Learning Outcome 2 The federal bureaucracy consists of fifteen cabinet departments, as well as a large number of independent executive agencies, independent regulatory agencies, and government corporations.

Learning Outcome 3 A federal bureaucracy of career civil servants was formed during Thomas Jefferson's presidency. Andrew Jackson implemented a spoils system through which he appointed his own political supporters. A civil service based on professionalism and merit was the goal of the Civil Service Reform Act of 1883. Concerns that the civil service be freed from the pressures of politics prompted the passage of the Hatch Act in 1939. Significant changes in the administration of the civil service were made by the Civil Service Reform Act of 1978.

Learning Outcome 4 There have been many attempts to make the federal bureaucracy more open, efficient, and responsive to the needs of U.S. citizens. The most important reforms have included sunshine and sunset laws, privatization, e-government, and protection for whistleblowers.

Learning Outcome 5 Congress delegates much of its authority to federal agencies when it creates new laws. The bureaucrats who run these agencies may become important policymakers because Congress has neither the time nor the technical expertise to oversee the administration of its laws. In the agency rulemaking process, a proposed regulation is published. A comment period follows, during which interested parties may offer

suggestions for changes. Because companies and other organizations have challenged many regulations in court, federal agencies now are authorized to allow parties that will be affected by new regulations to participate in the rule-drafting process.

Congress exerts ultimate control over all federal agencies because it controls the federal government's purse strings. It also establishes the general guidelines by which regulatory agencies must abide. The appropriations process provides a way to send messages of approval or disapproval to particular agencies, as do congressional hearings and investigations of agency actions.

Master the concept of The Bureaucracy with MindTap™ *for American Government*

 REVIEW MindTap™ **for American Government**
Access Key Term Flashcards for Chapter 13.

 TEST YOURSELF MindTap™ **for American Government**
Take the Wrap It Up Quiz for Chapter 13.

 STAY CURRENT MindTap™ **for American Government**
Access the KnowNow blog and customized RSS for updates on current events.

 STAY FOCUSED MindTap™ **for American Government**
Complete the Focus Activities for The Bureaucracy.

Additional Resources

All federal government agencies (and nearly all state agencies) have Web pages. Citizens can access these Web sites to find information and forms that, in the past, could normally be obtained only by going to a regional or local branch of the agency. For example, if you or a member of your family wants to learn about Social Security benefits available on retirement, you can simply access the Social Security Administration's Web site to find that information.

Online Resources

- Numerous links to federal agencies and information on the federal government can be found at the U.S. government's official Web site at www.usa.gov.
- The *United States Government Manual* describes every federal department and agency. Find it at www.usgovernmentmanual.gov.
- For detailed information on federal spending, visit www.usgovernment spending.com.
- One of the best sites sponsored by a federal agency is that of the Centers for Disease Control. For hilarious advice on what to do in a natural disaster, see the comic book *Preparedness 101: Zombie Pandemic* at www.cdc.gov/phpr/documents/Zombie_GN_Final.pdf.

Books

Goodsell, Charles T. *The New Case for Bureaucracy.* Washington, D.C.: CQ Press, 2014. Goodsell takes on critics of the U.S. federal bureaucracy, arguing that it is one of the best in the world. With Congress largely deadlocked, responsibility falls on the various federal agencies to keep the machinery of government running smoothly. Goodsell is a professor of public administration at Virginia Tech.

Grisinger, Joanna L. *The Unwieldy American State: Administrative Politics since the New Deal.* New York: Cambridge University Press, 2014. Grisinger details the evolution of the U.S. federal bureaucracy in the decades that followed the New Deal of the 1930s. This historical work describes the controversies that resulted in the bureaucracy that exists today. Grisinger is currently on the faculty at Northwestern University.

Morgeson, Forrest. *Citizen Satisfaction: Improving Government Performance, Efficiency, and Citizen Trust.* New York: Palgrave Macmillan, 2014. *Citizen Satisfaction* investigates ways in which agencies can enhance customer satisfaction with their services. Morgeson is the director of research for the American Customer Satisfaction Index, a private-sector research firm.

Video

FBI Takedown—A 2010 documentary by *National Geographic* that provides a straightforward examination of what the FBI really does, without glorification or condemnation. The National Geographic team was granted extraordinary access to make this film.

When the Levees Broke: A Requiem in Four Acts—A strong treatment of Hurricane Katrina's impact on New Orleans by renowned African American director Spike Lee. We learn about the appalling performance of authorities at every level and the suffering that could have been avoided. Lee's anger at what he sees adds spice to this 2006 production.

Quiz

Multiple Choice and Fill-Ins

Learning Outcome 1 Discuss the nature of the federal bureaucracy, and identify the largest federal spending programs.

1. In terms of federal dollars spent, the most important programs are:
   a. social programs, including Social Security and Medicare.
   b. the military and subsidies for corporations.
   c. foreign aid.

2. There are many models of bureaucratic behavior. One argues that top-level bureaucrats always want to expand their bureaucracies. This is called the _____ model.

Learning Outcome 2 Describe the various types of agencies and organizations that make up the federal executive branch.

3. The heads of federal regulatory agencies and members of agency boards and commissions are appointed by:
   a. the president acting alone.
   b. the president with the consent of the Senate.
   c. the Supreme Court.

4. When a federal agency's function is to make and implement rules and regulations to protect the public interest, it is called an _____ _____ _____.

Learning Outcome 3 Explain how government employees are hired and how they are administered.

5. The first significant legislation aimed at making the federal civil service nonpartisan and independent was:
   a. the Civil Service Act of 1978.
   b. the Hatch Act.
   c. the Pendleton Act of 1883.

6. In the early days of this country, when one party won the presidency, government employees were often fired and replaced with those who supported the incoming president's party. This was called the _____ _____.

Learning Outcome 4 Evaluate different methods that have been put into place to reform bureaucracies and make them more efficient.

7. Privatization means that:
   a. the government must provide individuals with the information it has on them.
   b. private companies replace members of the civil service in providing a government service.
   c. bonuses are awarded for efficient work.

8. If it is subject to _____ _____, an agency's existence can be terminated if the legislature does not specifically vote to reauthorize it.

Learning Outcome 5 Discuss how federal agencies make rules and the role of Congress in this process.

9. An issue network consists of individuals or organizations that support a particular policy position. A typical issue network includes:
   a. Congress, the president's cabinet, and the Supreme Court.
   b. federal judges, congressional staff, and the heads of certain private corporations.
   c. legislators (or their staff), interest group leaders, bureaucrats, scholars and other experts, and the media.

10. Because Congress cannot oversee the daily administration of its many programs, it delegates power to agencies through _____ _____.

Essay Questions

1. The U.S. attorney general, head of the Justice Department, is appointed by the president and is frequently the president's close political ally. Should the attorney general and other U.S. attorneys be appointed on a partisan basis? Why or why not?

2. If Congress tried to make civil servants easier to fire, what political forces might stand in the way?

The Courts

14

Six members of the United States Supreme Court applaud as President Barack Obama arrives at the Capitol to deliver his State of the Union speech in 2013. Several of the most conservative members of the Court have avoided the State of the Union event recently. *Why might that be so?*

Chip Somodevilla/Getty Images

The five learning outcomes below are designed to help improve your understanding of this chapter. After reading this chapter, you should be able to:

■ **Learning Outcome 1:** Explain the main sources of American law, including constitutions, statutes and regulations, and the common law tradition.

■ **Learning Outcome 2:** Describe the structure of the federal court system and such basic judicial requirements as jurisdiction and standing to sue.

■ **Learning Outcome 3:** Discuss the procedures used by the United States Supreme Court and the various types of opinions it hands down.

■ **Learning Outcome 4:** Evaluate the manner in which federal judges are selected.

■ **Learning Outcome 5:** Consider the ways in which the Supreme Court makes policy and explain the forces that limit the activism of the courts.

▶ **WATCH & LEARN** MindTap° for American Government
Watch a brief "What Do You Know?" video summarizing The Judiciary.

What If...

Arguments before the Supreme Court Were Televised?

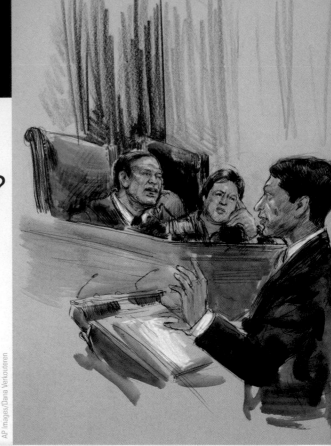

AP Images/Dana Verkouteren

BACKGROUND

Since 1955, the United States Supreme Court has allowed audio recordings of oral arguments before the Court. Also, during every session of the Supreme Court, a court reporter transcribes every word that is spoken, even with indications when there is laughter. You can find written transcripts and audio recordings of each oral argument by going to www.supremecourt.gov /oral_arguments. Scroll down until you see "Argument Transcripts" and "Argument Audio." Today, many states have gone one step further—they allow appellate court sessions to be televised. The federal appellate courts and the Supreme Court have resisted televising their proceedings, however.

WHAT IF ARGUMENTS BEFORE THE SUPREME COURT WERE TELEVISED?

Presumably, coverage of Supreme Court proceedings would be undertaken in the same way that sessions in the Senate and the House of Representatives are televised by C-SPAN. The C-SPAN coverage includes no commentaries about the proceedings in the chambers of Congress. The television coverage is straightforward, word for word, and often quite boring.

In the Supreme Court, similar television coverage would consist of one or two cameras and their operators discreetly positioned in the courtroom where the nine justices hear oral arguments and question the attorneys. Another C-SPAN channel might have to be created to televise Supreme Court proceedings. A low-cost alternative would be Internet video streaming. Available anywhere in the world, Internet video streaming would thereby allow the rest of the world to better understand the American judicial system.

The Supreme Court could follow the states, which have already developed a wide variety of rules governing television coverage of court proceedings.[a] Most states' rules allow the presiding judge to limit or prohibit coverage. Most states also allow the parties to object to television coverage, and some require the parties' consent.

If Supreme Court proceedings were televised, we could expect a media "mini-industry" to follow, particularly on the Internet. There might be new Web sites with portions of Supreme Court proceedings shown in video along with commentary by legal and political experts.

GRANDSTANDING—A POSSIBILITY?

Certain sitting judges and others have argued against televising Supreme Court sessions because of the possibility of

---

a. See the information provided by the Radio Television Digital News Association by visiting www.rtdna.org/content/cameras_in_court.

A lawyer addresses Justices Samuel Alito and Elena Kagan as the Supreme Court hears arguments on the Defense of Marriage Act. *Why does the Court oppose photographing sessions?*

"grandstanding." In other words, they are worried that justices might ask questions and make comments during the proceedings in the hopes that such comments would become sound bites on the evening news. Justice Anthony M. Kennedy has said that televising proceedings would "change our collegial dynamic." Grandstanding by lawyers presenting oral arguments is also a possible danger.

In contrast, Judge Diarmuid O'Scannlain of the U.S. Court of Appeals for the Ninth Circuit believes that the concerns about grandstanding and politicking in the courtroom are "overstated." He argues that televising appellate court proceedings depoliticizes them and improves the public's perception of the legal process.

For Critical Analysis

1. How wide an audience do you believe the television proceedings of the Supreme Court would have?

2. Do you think that televised proceedings of the Supreme Court would significantly increase public awareness of Supreme Court decisions? Why or why not?

As Alexis de Tocqueville, a French commentator on American society in the 1800s, noted, "scarcely any political question arises in the United States that is not resolved, sooner or later, into a judicial question."[1] Our judiciary forms part of our political process. The instant that judges interpret the law, they become actors in the political arena—policymakers working within a political institution.

The most important political force within our judiciary is the United States Supreme Court. The justices of the Supreme Court are not elected but are appointed by the president and confirmed by the Senate. The same is true for all other federal court judges. Because Supreme Court justices are so important in our governmental system, it has been suggested that arguments before the Court should be televised, as this chapter's opening *What If . . .* feature discussed.

How do courts make policy? Why do the federal courts play such an important role in American government? The answers to these questions lie, in part, in our colonial heritage. Most of American law is based on the English system, particularly the English *common law tradition*. In that tradition, the decisions made by judges constitute an important source of law. We open this chapter with an examination of this tradition and of the various other sources of American law. We then look at the federal court system—how it is organized, how its judges are selected, how these judges affect policy, and how they are restrained by our system of checks and balances.

LISTEN & LEARN
MindTap™ for American Government

Access Read Speaker to listen to Chapter 14.

did you know?

When the Supreme Court first convened in 1790, some judges still followed the English custom of wearing wigs. William Cushing was the only justice to appear wearing a wig. He received such mockery that he discarded it. Since then, American justices have not worn wigs—but some English judges still do to this day.

Sources of American Law

The body of American law includes the federal and state constitutions, statutes passed by legislative bodies, administrative law, and case law—the legal principles expressed in court decisions. Case law is based in part on the common law tradition, which dates to the earliest English settlements in North America.

The Common Law Tradition

In 1066, the Normans conquered England, and William the Conqueror and his successors began the process of unifying the country under their rule. One of the ways in which they did this was to establish king's courts. Before the conquest, disputes had been settled according to local custom. The king's courts sought to establish a common, or uniform, set of rules for the whole country. As the number of courts and cases increased, portions of the most important decisions of each year were gathered together and recorded in *Year Books*. Judges who were settling disputes similar to ones that had been decided before used the *Year Books* as the basis for their decisions. If a case was unique, judges had to create new rules, but they based their decisions on the general principles suggested by earlier cases. The body of judge-made law that developed under this system is still used today and is known as the **common law.**

The practice of deciding new cases with reference to former decisions—that is, according to **precedent**—became a cornerstone of the English and American judicial systems and is embodied in the doctrine of ***stare decisis*** (pronounced *ster*-ay dih-*si*-ses), a Latin phrase that means "to stand on decided cases." The doctrine of *stare decisis* obligates judges to follow the precedents set previously by their own courts or by higher courts that have authority over them.

For example, a lower state court in California would be obligated to follow a precedent set by the California Supreme Court. That lower court, however, would not be

■ **Learning Outcome 1:** Explain the main sources of American law, including constitutions, statutes and regulations, and the common law tradition.

Common Law

Judge-made law that originated in England from decisions shaped according to prevailing custom. Decisions were applied to similar situations and gradually became common to the nation.

Precedent

A court rule bearing on subsequent legal decisions in similar cases. Judges rely on precedents in deciding cases.

Stare Decisis

To stand on decided cases; the judicial policy of following precedents established by past decisions.

---

1. Alexis de Tocqueville, *Democracy in America* (New York: Harper & Row, 1966), p. 248.

Case Law
Judicial interpretations of common law principles and doctrines, as well as interpretations of constitutional law, statutory law, and administrative law.

obligated to follow a precedent set by the supreme court of another state, because each state court system is independent. Of course, when the United States Supreme Court decides an issue, all of the nation's other courts are obligated to abide by the Court's decision—because the Supreme Court is the highest court in the land.

Constitutions

The constitutions of the federal government and the states set forth the general organization, powers, and limits of government. The U.S. Constitution is the supreme law of the land. A law in violation of the Constitution, no matter what its source, may be declared unconstitutional and thereafter cannot be enforced. Similarly, the state constitutions are supreme within their respective borders (unless they conflict with the U.S. Constitution or federal laws and treaties made in accordance with it). The Constitution thus defines the political playing field on which state and federal powers are reconciled.

Statutes and Administrative Regulations

Although the English common law provides the basis for both our civil and our criminal legal systems, statutes (laws enacted by legislatures) have become increasingly important in defining the rights and obligations of individuals. Federal statutes may relate to any subject that is a concern of the federal government and may apply to areas ranging from hazardous waste to federal taxation. State statutes include criminal codes, commercial laws, and laws covering a variety of other matters. Cities, counties, and other local political bodies also pass statutes, which are called *ordinances*. These ordinances may deal with such issues as real estate zoning and public safety.

Rules and regulations issued by administrative agencies are another source of law. Today, much of the work of the courts consists of interpreting these laws and regulations and applying them to the specific circumstances of the cases that come before the courts.

Case Law

Because we have a common law tradition, in which the doctrine of *stare decisis* plays an important role, the decisions rendered by the courts also form an important body of law, collectively referred to as **case law.** Case law includes judicial interpretations of common law principles and doctrines, as well as interpretations of constitutional provisions, statutes, and administrative agency regulations. As you learned in previous chapters, it is up to the courts—and ultimately, if necessary, the Supreme Court—to decide what a constitutional provision or a statutory phrase means. In doing so, the courts, in effect, establish law.

Courts in many of the nations formerly governed or settled by Britain—Australia, Canada, Ireland, the United States, and others—exhibit some broad similarities. All make use of the common law, as well as statutes and administrative regulations. All share the basic judicial requirements that you will learn about shortly. In some lands formerly ruled by Britain, such as India, Nigeria, and Pakistan, the common law is supplemented by local traditional law.

Nations that do not share the common law tradition typically rely on a statutory code alone, in what is called the civil law system. Judges under the civil law system are not bound by precedent in the way that judges are under the common law system. Differing

The lawyer holding a microphone seeks a court ruling against the District of Columbia to stop the closing of fifteen public schools in 2013. Activists are concerned that the closures will hurt low-income and minority students. *Why do the activists need an attorney?*

Brendan Hoffman/Getty Images

legal traditions and social customs around the world can have a substantial impact on how various nations address important issues, as you will learn in the *Beyond Our Borders* feature that follows.

The Federal Court System

The United States has a dual court system, with state courts and federal courts. Each of the fifty states, as well as the District of Columbia, has its own independent system of courts. This means that there are fifty-two court systems in total. Here we focus on the federal courts.

Basic Judicial Requirements

Certain requirements must be met before a case can be brought before a court in any court system, state or federal. Two important requirements are *jurisdiction* and *standing to sue.*

■ **Learning Outcome 2:**
Describe the structure of the federal court system and such basic judicial requirements as jurisdiction and standing to sue.

Beyond Our Borders

Gay Rights around the World

Few laws show greater international variation than the ones governing lesbian, gay, bisexual, and transgender (LGBT) individuals. Nations can be divided into three classes. In one group, same-sex unions are wholly or partially recognized. Such nations include Germany, which allows civil unions, and Mexico, where recognition varies by state. A second group does not recognize same-sex unions, but also does not criminalize same-sex behavior. For example, China has a "three nos" policy: "no approval, no disapproval, no promotion." In about seventy countries, however, same-sex intimacy is illegal. (In thirty of these, lesbianism is not outlawed.) In Iran, Saudi Arabia, and a few other nations, same-sex relations are punishable by death.

The French Revolution

Traditional societies have rarely seen same-sex intimacy as a topic for the law to address. In the West, however, following the establishment of Christianity as the official religion, "sodomy laws" outlawed gay relations. Hostile to the church, leaders of the French Revolution (1789–1799) adopted a new legal code that repealed religiously inspired laws—including those against sodomy. French conquests extended the new code to Belgium and the Netherlands.

In the nineteenth century, newly independent Latin American nations adopted the French code, and many of them repealed sodomy laws. Brazil legalized homosexuality in 1830, fifty-eight years before it abolished slavery. When France,

Belgium, and the Netherlands established colonial empires, they did not introduce sodomy laws into these traditional societies. The British, in contrast, imposed such laws on their empire. Today, sodomy laws are common in Muslim lands—and former British colonies. Of course, in many places where gay relations are not officially illegal, LGBT individuals must still fear discrimination and violence.

Same-Sex Marriage Takes the Stage

In the second half of the twentieth century, country by country, same-sex relations were decriminalized across Europe and almost all of the Americas. The most conservative U.S. states were among the last to decriminalize, in 2003. By the twenty-first century, same-sex marriage was on the table in Europe and the Americas. Denmark established "registered partnerships" in 1989. The Netherlands was the first jurisdiction to legalize same-sex marriage in 2001. Belgium, Quebec, and Massachusetts followed in 2003. By 2013, scores of national and sub-national jurisdictions were joining the movement.

For Critical Analysis

Especially in the United States, the courts have taken the lead in establishing same-sex marriage. Why might that be so?

Jurisdiction

The authority of a court to decide certain cases. Not all courts have the authority to decide all cases. Where a case arises and what its subject matter is are two jurisdictional issues.

Federal Question

A question that has to do with the U.S. Constitution, acts of Congress, or treaties. A federal question provides a basis for federal jurisdiction.

Diversity of Citizenship

The condition that exists when the parties to a lawsuit are citizens of different states or when the parties are citizens of a U.S. state and citizens or the government of a foreign country. Diversity of citizenship can provide a basis for federal jurisdiction.

Justiciable Controversy

A controversy that is real and substantial, as opposed to hypothetical or academic.

Litigate

To engage in a legal proceeding or seek relief in a court of law; to carry on a lawsuit.

***Amicus Curiae* Brief**

A brief (a document containing a legal argument supporting a desired outcome in a particular case) filed by a third party, or *amicus curiae* (Latin for "friend of the court"), who is not directly involved in the litigation but who has an interest in the outcome of the case.

Class-Action Suit

A lawsuit filed by an individual seeking damages for "all persons similarly situated."

Jurisdiction. A state court can exercise **jurisdiction** (the authority of the court to hear and decide a case) over the residents of a particular geographic area, such as a county or district. A state's highest court, or supreme court, has jurisdictional authority over all residents within the state.

Because the Constitution established a federal government with limited powers, federal jurisdiction is also limited. Article III, Section 1, of the U.S. Constitution limits the jurisdiction of the federal courts to cases that involve either a federal question or diversity of citizenship. A **federal question** arises when a case is based, at least in part, on the U.S. Constitution, a treaty, or a federal law. A person who claims that her or his rights under the Constitution, such as the right to free speech, have been violated could bring a case in a federal court. **Diversity of citizenship** exists when the parties to a lawsuit are from different states or (more rarely) when the suit involves a U.S. citizen and a government or citizen of a foreign country. The amount in controversy must be at least $75,000 before a federal court can take jurisdiction in a diversity case, however.

Given the significant limits on federal jurisdiction, most lawsuits and criminal cases are heard in state, rather than federal, courts. A defendant or a party to a dispute handled by a state court may file an appeal with a state appeals court, or even the state's supreme court. Appeals cannot be taken to a federal court, however, unless there is a federal question at stake.

Standing to Sue. Another basic judicial requirement is standing to sue, or a sufficient "stake" in a matter to justify bringing suit. The party bringing a lawsuit must have suffered a harm, or have been threatened by a harm, as a result of the action that led to the dispute in question. Standing to sue also requires that the controversy at issue be a justiciable (pronounced jus-*tish*-a-bul) controversy. A **justiciable controversy** is a controversy that is real and substantial, as opposed to hypothetical or academic. In other words, a court will not give advisory opinions on hypothetical questions.

Parties to Lawsuits

In most lawsuits, the parties are the plaintiff (the person or organization that initiates the lawsuit) and the defendant (the person or organization against whom the lawsuit is brought). There may be a number of plaintiffs and defendants in a single lawsuit. In the past several decades, many lawsuits have been brought by interest groups (see Chapter 7). Interest groups play an important role in our judicial system, because they **litigate**—bring to trial—or assist in litigating most cases of racial or gender-based discrimination, almost all civil liberties cases, and more than one-third of the cases involving business matters. Interest groups also file *amicus curiae* (pronounced ah-*mee*-kous *kur*-ee-eye) **briefs,** or "friend of the court" briefs, in more than 50 percent of these kinds of cases.

Sometimes, interest groups or other plaintiffs will bring a **class-action suit,** in which whatever the court decides will affect all members of a class similarly situated (such as users of a particular product manufactured by the defendant in the lawsuit). The strategy of class-action lawsuits was pioneered by such groups as the National Association for the Advancement of Colored People (NAACP), the Legal Defense Fund, and the Sierra Club, whose leaders believed that the courts would offer a more sympathetic forum for their views than would Congress.

Procedural Rules

Both the federal and the state courts have established procedural rules that shape the litigation process. These rules are designed to protect the rights and interests of the parties and to ensure that the litigation proceeds in a fair and orderly manner. The rules also serve to identify the issues that must be decided by the court—thus saving court time and costs. Court decisions may also apply to trial procedures. For example, the Supreme Court has held that the parties' attorneys cannot discriminate against prospective jurors on the basis of race or gender. Some lower courts have also held that people cannot be excluded from juries because of their sexual orientation or religion.

The parties must comply with procedural rules and with any orders given by the judge during the course of the litigation. When a party does not follow a court's order, the court can cite him or her for contempt. A party who commits *civil* contempt (failing to comply with a court's order for the benefit of another party to the proceeding) can be taken into custody, fined, or both, until that party complies with the court's order. A party who commits *criminal* contempt (obstructing the administration of justice or disrespecting the rules of the court) also can be taken into custody and fined but cannot avoid punishment by complying with a previous order.

Types of Federal Courts

As you can see in Figure 14–1 that follows, the federal court system is basically a three-tiered model consisting of (1) U.S. district courts and various specialized courts of limited jurisdiction (not all of the latter are shown in the figure), (2) intermediate U.S. courts of appeals, and (3) the United States Supreme Court.

U.S. District Courts. The U.S. district courts are trial courts. A **trial court** is what the name implies—a court in which trials are held and testimony is taken. The U.S. district courts are courts of **general jurisdiction,** meaning that they can hear cases involving a broad array of issues. Federal cases involving most matters typically are heard in district courts. The other courts on the lower tier of the model shown in Figure 14–1 are courts of **limited jurisdiction,** meaning that they can try cases involving only certain types of claims, such as tax claims or bankruptcy petitions.

There is at least one federal district court in every state. The number of judicial districts varied historically owing to population changes and corresponding caseloads, but no

COMPARE WITH YOUR PEERS
MindTap™ for American Government

Access the Judiciary Forum: Polling Activity—Jury Duty

Trial Court
The court in which most cases begin.

General Jurisdiction
A court's authority to hear cases without significant restriction. A court of general jurisdiction normally can hear a broad range of cases.

Limited Jurisdiction
A court's authority to hear cases with restriction to certain types of claims, such as tax claims or bankruptcy petitions.

Figure 14–1 ▶ The Federal Court System
Why do you think Congress created courts of limited jurisdiction?

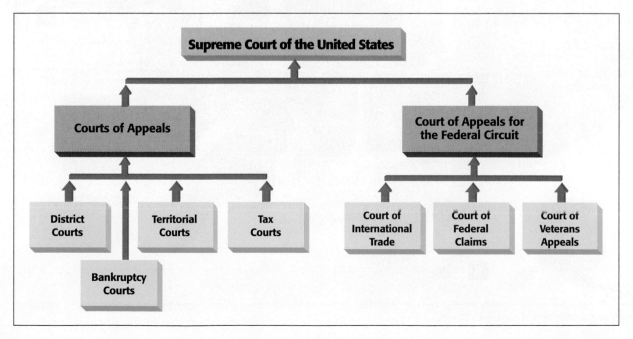

Appellate Court
A court having jurisdiction to review cases and issues that were originally tried in lower courts.

entirely new district has been created since California was redivided in 1966. Today, there are ninety-four federal judicial districts and 678 authorized district court judgeships. The Southern District of New York has the largest number of judges—28. The Central District of California is second with 27.

A party who is dissatisfied with the decision of a district court can appeal the case to the appropriate U.S. court of appeals, or federal **appellate court.** Figure 14–2 that follows shows the jurisdictional boundaries of the district courts (which are state boundaries, unless otherwise indicated by dotted lines within a state) and of the U.S. courts of appeals.

Many federal administrative agencies and most executive departments also employ administrative law judges who resolve disputes arising under the rules governing their agencies. For example, the Social Security Administration might hold a hearing to determine whether a specific class of individuals is entitled to collect a particular benefit. If all internal Social Security appeals processes have been exhausted, a party may have a right to file an appeal in a federal district court. Appeals from the decisions of other agencies may be heard by the district courts, the U.S. courts of appeals, or even a specialized federal court, depending on the agency.

U.S. Courts of Appeals. There are thirteen U.S. courts of appeals—also referred to as U.S. circuit courts of appeals. Twelve of these courts, including the U.S. Court of Appeals for the District of Columbia, hear appeals from the federal district courts located within their respective judicial circuits (geographic areas over which they exercise jurisdiction). The Court of Appeals for the Thirteenth Circuit, called the Federal Circuit, has national

Figure 14–2 ▶ Geographic Boundaries of Federal District Courts and U.S. Courts of Appeals

Why might Congress add more judges to a district instead of creating new districts?

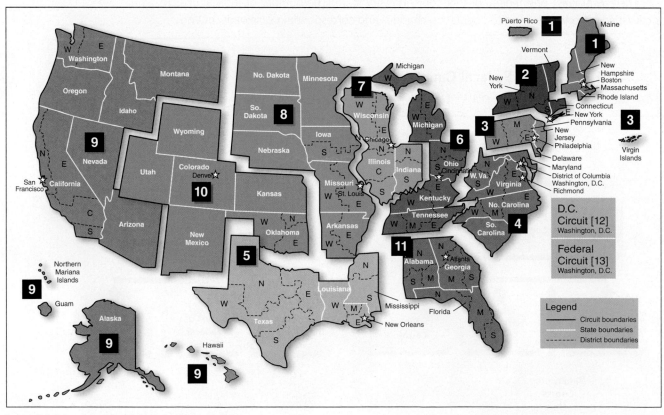

Source: Administrative Office of the United States Courts.

appellate jurisdiction over certain types of cases, such as cases involving patent law and those in which the U.S. government is a defendant.

Note that when an appellate court reviews a case decided in a district court, the appellate court does not conduct another trial. Rather, a panel of three or more judges reviews the record of the case on appeal, which includes a transcript of the trial proceedings. The panel determines whether the trial court committed an error. Usually, appellate courts do not look at questions of *fact* (such as whether a party did, in fact, commit a certain action, such as burning a flag) but at questions of *law* (such as whether the act of burning a flag is a form of speech protected by the First Amendment to the Constitution). An appellate court will challenge a trial court's finding of fact only when the finding is clearly contrary to the evidence presented at trial or when there is no evidence to support the finding.

A party can petition the United States Supreme Court to review an appellate court's decision. The likelihood that the Supreme Court will grant the petition is slim, however, because the Court reviews only a small percentage of the cases decided by the appellate courts. This means that decisions made by appellate courts usually are final.

The United States Supreme Court. The highest level of the three-tiered model of the federal court system is the United States Supreme Court. When the Supreme Court came into existence in 1789, it had six justices. In the following years, more justices were added. Since 1869, there have been nine justices on the Court.

According to the language of Article III of the U.S. Constitution, there is only one national Supreme Court. All other courts in the federal system are considered "inferior." Congress is empowered to create other inferior courts as it deems necessary. The inferior courts that Congress has created include the district courts, the federal courts of appeals, and the federal courts of limited jurisdiction.

Although the Supreme Court can exercise original jurisdiction (that is, act as a trial court) in certain cases, such as those affecting foreign diplomats and those in which a state is a party, most of its work is as an appellate court. The Court hears appeals not only from the federal appellate courts but also from the highest state courts. Note, though, that the United States Supreme Court can review a state supreme court decision only if a federal question is involved. Because of its importance in the federal court system, we look more closely at the Supreme Court later in this chapter.

did you know?
The Supreme Court was not provided with a building of its own until 1935, in the 146th year of its existence.

Federal Courts and the War on Terrorism

As noted, the federal court system includes a variety of trial courts of limited jurisdiction, dealing with matters such as tax claims or international trade. The government's attempts to combat terrorism have drawn attention to certain specialized courts that meet in secret. We look next at these courts, as well as at the role of the federal courts with respect to the detainees accused of terrorism.

The FISA Court. The federal government created the first secret court in 1978. In that year, Congress passed the Foreign Intelligence Surveillance Act (FISA), which established a court to hear requests for warrants for the surveillance of suspected spies. Officials can request a warrant without having to reveal to the suspect or to the public the information used to justify the warrant. The FISA court has approved almost all of the thousands of requests for warrants that officials have submitted. There is no public access to the court's proceedings or records. Hence, when the court authorizes surveillance, suspects normally do not

Chief Justice John Roberts, Jr., speaks at the University of Montana in Missoula. *Do you think there are some subjects that he would avoid in any of his public speeches?*

even know that they are under scrutiny. All FISA court judges are appointed by the chief justice of the Supreme Court without review by any other authority.

In the aftermath of the terrorist attacks on September 11, 2001, the George W. Bush administration expanded the powers of the FISA court. Previously, FISA had allowed secret domestic surveillance only if the "purpose" was to combat intelligence gathering by foreign powers. Amendments to FISA enacted after 9/11 changed this wording to "a significant purpose"—meaning that warrants may now be requested to obtain evidence that can be used in criminal trials.

The FISA Court and the National Security Agency. Some of the National Security Agency (NSA) material that Edward Snowden leaked to the press in 2013 dealt with the FISA court. One of the first stories described a FISA court order that required Verizon to provide a daily, ongoing feed of all cell phone *metadata* to the NSA. That included metadata on domestic calls. Metadata means information about calls, such as time, who called, and who was called. It does not include the content of actual conversations. It soon came out that the FISA court had effectively granted the NSA the right to collect metadata on all phone calls, regardless of carrier.

The FISA court apparently justified the massive data collection through a "special needs" exception to the Fourth Amendment's requirement of a warrant for searches and seizures. It would appear that under this exception the Fourth Amendment does not apply to national security surveillance.

These revelations touched off a massive debate between advocates of civil liberties and those concerned about national security. In March 2014, President Obama proposed legislation to curb the NSA's bulk data collection. The House passed the resulting bill in May. Critics claimed, however, that the proposed law was too weak to seriously alter the NSA's behavior.

Alien "Removal Courts." In 1996, Congress passed the Anti-Terrorism and Effective Death Penalty Act. The new law was a response to the bombing of a federal building in 1995 in Oklahoma City, which killed 168 people. Even though the perpetrators of this crime were white U.S. citizens whose motives were entirely domestic, the new law focused on noncitizens. For example, the act created an alien "removal court" to hear evidence against suspected "alien terrorists." The judges in this court rule on whether there is probable cause for deportation. If so, a public deportation proceeding is held in a U.S. district court. The prosecution does not need to follow procedures that normally apply in criminal cases. In addition, the defendant cannot see the evidence that the prosecution used to secure the hearing.

The Federal Courts and Enemy Combatants. After the 9/11 attacks, the U.S. military took custody of hundreds of suspected terrorists seized in Afghanistan and elsewhere and held them at Guantánamo Bay, Cuba. The detainees were classified as *enemy combatants,* and, according to the Bush administration, they could be held

"And don't go whining to some higher court."

Al Ross/The New Yorker Collection/The Cartoon Bank

indefinitely. The administration also claimed that because the detainees were not prisoners of war, they were not protected under international laws governing the treatment of prisoners of war. The handling of the prisoners at Guantánamo has been a source of ongoing controversy. The United States Supreme Court held, first in 2004 and then in 2006, that the Bush administration's treatment of these detainees violated the U.S. Constitution.[2]

In response to the Court's 2006 decision, Congress passed the Military Commissions Act of 2006. The act eliminated federal court jurisdiction over challenges by noncitizens held as enemy combatants based on *habeas corpus*. (This term refers to the right of a detained person to challenge the legality of his or her detention before a judge.) In June 2008, in *Boumediene v. Bush*, the Court ruled that the provisions restricting the federal courts' jurisdictional authority over detainees' *habeas corpus* challenges were illegal.[3] The decision gave Guantánamo detainees the right to challenge their detention in federal civil courts.

In 2009, the Obama administration abolished the category of *enemy combatant* and promised to close the Guantánamo prison. (As of 2015, though, the prison remained open.) President Obama did not, however, move to try most of the detainees in U.S. civil courts. Under the Military Commissions Act of 2009, a majority of the prisoners were to be tried in a revised system of military commissions. Further, in May 2009, Obama claimed the right to detain certain accused terrorists indefinitely without trial. In May 2010, a federal appeals court ruled that the administration had the right to detain prisoners indefinitely at Bagram Air Base in Afghanistan because the prison is located on foreign soil and within a war zone.[4]

The Supreme Court at Work

■ **Learning Outcome 3:** Discuss the procedures used by the United States Supreme Court and the various types of opinions it hands down.

The Supreme Court begins its regular annual term on the first Monday in October and usually adjourns in late June or early July of the next year. Special sessions may be held after the regular term ends, but only a few cases are decided in this way. More commonly, cases are carried over until the next regular session.

Of the total number of cases that are decided each year in U.S. courts, those reviewed by the Supreme Court represent less than one in four thousand. Included in these, however, are decisions that profoundly affect our lives. In recent years, the United States Supreme Court has decided issues involving freedom of speech, the right to bear arms, healthcare reform, campaign finance, capital punishment, the rights of criminal suspects, affirmative action programs, religious freedom, abortion, states' rights, and many other matters with significant consequences for the nation.

2. *Hamdi v. Rumsfeld*, 542 U.S. 507 (2004); *Hamdan v. Rumsfeld*, 548 U.S. 557 (2006).
3. 553 U.S. 723 (2008).
4. *Maqaleh v. Gates*, 605 F.3d 84 (D.C.Cir. 2010).

United States Supreme Court justice Clarence Thomas stands in his chambers with three of his clerks. *What type of work do clerks do when they assist a Supreme Court justice?*

Because the Supreme Court exercises a great deal of discretion over the types of cases it hears, it can influence the nation's policies by issuing decisions in some types of cases and refusing to hear appeals in others, thereby allowing lower court decisions to stand. Indeed, the fact that George W. Bush assumed the presidency in 2001 instead of Al Gore, his Democratic opponent, was largely due to a Supreme Court decision to review a Florida court's ruling. In *Bush v. Gore*, the Supreme Court reversed the Florida court's order to recount manually the votes in selected Florida counties—a decision that effectively handed the presidency to Bush.[5]

Which Cases Reach the Supreme Court?

Many people are surprised to learn that in a typical case, there is no absolute right of appeal to the United States Supreme Court. The Court's appellate jurisdiction is almost entirely discretionary—the Court chooses which cases it will decide. The justices never explain their reasons for hearing certain cases and not others, so it is difficult to predict which case or type of case the Court might select.

Factors That Bear on the Decision. A number of factors bear on the decision to accept a case. If a legal question has been decided differently by various lower courts, it may need resolution by the highest court. A ruling may be necessary if a lower court's decision conflicts with an existing Supreme Court ruling. In general, the Court considers whether the issue could have significance beyond the parties to the dispute.

Another factor is whether the solicitor general is asking the Court to take a case. The solicitor general, a high-ranking presidential appointee within the Justice Department, represents the national government before the Supreme Court and promotes presidential policies in the federal courts. He or she decides what cases the government should ask the Supreme Court to review and what position the government should take in cases before the Court.

Granting Petitions for Review. If the Court decides to grant a petition for review, it will issue a **writ of *certiorari*** (pronounced sur-shee-uh-*rah*-ree). The writ orders a lower court to send the Supreme Court a record of the case for review. The vast majority of the petitions for review are denied. A denial is not a decision on the merits of a case, nor does it indicate agreement with the lower court's opinion. (The judgment of the lower court remains in force, however.) Therefore, denial of the writ has no value as a precedent. The Court will not issue a writ unless at least four justices approve of it. This is called the **rule of four.**[6]

Court Procedures

Once the Supreme Court grants *certiorari* in a particular case, the justices do extensive research on the legal issues and facts involved in the case. (Of course, some preliminary research is necessary before deciding to grant the petition for review.) Each justice is entitled to four law clerks, who undertake much of the research and preliminary drafting necessary for the justice to form an opinion.

The Court normally does not hear any evidence, as is true with all appeals courts. The Court's consideration of a case is based on the abstracts, the record, and the briefs. The attorneys are permitted to present **oral arguments.** Unlike the practice in most courts, lawyers addressing the Supreme Court can be (and often are) questioned by the justices at any time during oral arguments. All statements and the justices' questions during oral arguments are recorded.

---

5. 531 U.S. 98 (2000).
6. The "rule of four" is modified when seven or fewer justices participate, which occurs from time to time. When that happens, as few as three justices can grant *certiorari*.

The justices meet to discuss and vote on cases in conferences held throughout the term. In these conferences, in addition to deciding cases already before the Court, the justices determine which new petitions for *certiorari* to grant. These conferences take place in the oak-paneled chamber and are strictly private—no stenographers, audio recorders, or video cameras are allowed.

Decisions and Opinions

When the Court has reached a decision, its opinion is written. The **opinion** contains the Court's ruling on the issue or issues presented, the reasons for its decision, the rules of law that apply, and other information. In many cases, the decision of the lower court is **affirmed,** resulting in the enforcement of that court's judgment or decree. If the Supreme Court believes that the lower court made the wrong decision, however, the decision will be **reversed.** Sometimes the case will be **remanded** (sent back to the court that originally heard the case) for a new trial or other proceeding. For example, a lower court might have held that a party was not entitled to bring a lawsuit under a particular law. If the Supreme Court holds to the contrary, it will remand (send back) the case to the trial court with instructions that the trial go forward.

The Court's written opinion sometimes is unsigned; this is called an opinion *per curiam* ("by the court"). Typically, the Court's opinion is signed by all the justices who agree with it. When in the majority, the chief justice decides who writes the opinion and may choose to write it personally. When the chief justice is in the minority, the senior justice on the majority side assigns the opinion.

Types of Opinions. When all justices unanimously agree on an opinion, the opinion is written for the entire Court (all the justices) and can be deemed a **unanimous opinion.** When there is not a unanimous opinion, a **majority opinion** is written, outlining the views of the majority of the justices involved in the case. Often, one or more justices who feel strongly about making or emphasizing a particular point that is not made or emphasized in the majority written opinion will write a **concurring opinion.** That means the justice writing the concurring opinion agrees (concurs) with the conclusion given in the majority written opinion but wants to make or clarify a particular point or to voice disapproval of the grounds on which the decision was made.

Note that it is also possible for a group of justices to issue a **plurality opinion.** Such an opinion does not represent a majority of the Court, but it will still carry the day because one or more concurring opinions agrees with its verdict.

Finally, in other than unanimous opinions, one or more **dissenting opinions** are usually written by those justices who do not agree with the majority. The dissenting opinion is important because it often forms the basis of the arguments used years later if the Court reverses the previous decision and establishes a new precedent.

Publishing Opinions. Shortly after the opinion is written, the Supreme Court announces its decision from the bench. The clerk of the Court also releases the opinion for online publication. Ultimately, the opinion is published in the *United States Reports,* which is the official printed record of the Court's decisions.

The Court's Dwindling Caseload. Some have complained that the Court reviews too few cases each term, thus giving the lower courts insufficient guidance on important issues. Indeed, the number of signed opinions issued by the Court has dwindled notably since the 1980s. For example, in its 1982–1983 term, the Court issued signed opinions in 151 cases. By the early 2000s, this number had dropped to between 70 and 80 per term. In the term ending in June 2014, the number was 77.

Opinion
A statement by a judge or a court of the decision reached in a case. An opinion sets forth the applicable law and details the reasoning on which the ruling was based.

Affirm
To declare that a court ruling is valid and must stand.

Reverse
To annul, or make void, a court ruling on account of some error or irregularity.

Remand
To send a case back to the court that originally heard it.

Unanimous Opinion
A Court opinion or determination on which all judges agree.

Majority Opinion
A court opinion reflecting the views of the majority of the judges.

Concurring Opinion
A separate opinion prepared by a judge who supports the decision of the majority of the court but who wants to make or clarify a particular point or to voice disapproval of the grounds on which the decision was made.

Plurality Opinion
An opinion by a minority of the Court that decides a case because it is supported by one or more concurring opinions.

Dissenting Opinion
A separate opinion in which a judge dissents from (disagrees with) the conclusion reached by the majority of the court and expounds his or her own views about the case.

Sonia Sotomayor is the first Latina justice on the United States Supreme Court.

■ **Learning Outcome 4:**
Evaluate the manner in which federal judges are selected.

Senatorial Courtesy
In federal district court judgeship nominations, a tradition allowing a senator to veto a judicial appointment in his or her state.

The Selection of Federal Judges

All federal judges are appointed. The Constitution, in Article II, Section 2, states that the president is to appoint the justices of the Supreme Court with the advice and consent of the Senate. Congress has established the same procedure for staffing other federal courts. This means that the Senate and the president jointly decide who shall fill every vacant judicial position, no matter what the level.

There are currently 874 federal judicial posts at all levels, although at any given time many of these positions are vacant. Once appointed to a federal judgeship, a person holds that job for life. Judges serve until they resign, retire voluntarily, or die. Federal judges who engage in blatantly illegal conduct may be removed through impeachment, although such action is rare.

In contrast to federal judges, many state judges—including the judges who sit on state supreme courts—are chosen by the voters in elections. Inevitably, judicial candidates must raise campaign funds. What arguments favor the election of judges? What problems can such a system create? We examine such questions in this chapter's *Which Side Are You On?* feature that follows.

Judicial Appointments

Candidates for federal judgeships are suggested to the president by the Department of Justice, senators, other judges, the candidates themselves, and lawyers' associations and other interest groups. In selecting a candidate to nominate for a judgeship, the president considers not only the person's competence but also other factors, including the person's political philosophy (as will be discussed shortly), ethnicity, and gender.

The nomination process—no matter how the nominees are obtained—always works the same way. The president makes the actual nomination, submitting the name to the Senate. To reach a conclusion, the Senate Judiciary Committee (operating through subcommittees) invites testimony, both written and oral, at its various hearings. The Senate then either confirms or rejects the nomination.

Federal District Court Judgeship Nominations. Although the president officially nominates federal judges, in the past the nomination of federal district court judges actually originated with a senator or senators of the president's party from the state in which there was a vacancy (if such a senator existed). In effect, judicial appointments were a form of political patronage. President Jimmy Carter (1977–1981) ended this tradition by establishing independent commissions to oversee the initial nomination process. President Ronald Reagan (1981–1989) abolished Carter's nominating commissions and established complete presidential control of nominations.

A practice used in the Senate, called **senatorial courtesy,** is a constraint on the president's freedom to appoint federal district judges. Senatorial courtesy allows a senator of the president's political party to veto a judicial appointment in her or his state. During much of American history, senators from the "opposition" party (the party to which the president does not belong) have also enjoyed the right of senatorial courtesy, although their veto power has varied over time.

In 2000, Orrin Hatch, Republican chair of the Senate Judiciary Committee, announced that the opposition party (at that point, the Democrats) would no longer be allowed to invoke senatorial courtesy. When the Democrats took over the Senate following the elections of 2006, Senator Patrick J. Leahy (D., Vt.), chair of the Judiciary Committee, let it

Learning Outcome 2 Article III, Section 1, of the U.S. Constitution limits the jurisdiction of the federal courts to cases involving (a) a federal question, which is a question based, at least in part, on the U.S. Constitution, a treaty, or a federal law, or (b) diversity of citizenship—which arises when parties to a lawsuit are from different states or when the lawsuit involves a foreign citizen or foreign government. The federal court system is a three-tiered model consisting of (a) U.S. district (trial) courts and various lower courts of limited jurisdiction, (b) intermediate U.S. courts of appeals, and (c) the United States Supreme Court. Cases may be appealed from the district courts to the appellate courts. In most cases, the decisions of the federal appellate courts are final because the Supreme Court hears relatively few cases.

Learning Outcome 3 The Supreme Court's decision to review a case is influenced by many factors, including the significance of the issues involved and whether the solicitor general is asking the Court to take the case. After a case is accepted, the justices (with the help of their law clerks) undertake research on the issues involved in the case, hear oral arguments from the parties, meet in conference to discuss and vote on the issues, and announce the opinion, which is then released for publication.

Learning Outcome 4 Federal judges are nominated by the president and confirmed by the Senate. Once appointed, they hold office for life, barring gross misconduct. The nomination and confirmation process, particularly for Supreme Court justices, is often extremely politicized. Democrats and Republicans alike realize that justices may occupy seats on the Court for decades and naturally want to have persons appointed who share their basic views. Nearly 20 percent of all Supreme Court appointments have been either rejected or not acted on by the Senate.

Learning Outcome 5 In interpreting and applying the law, judges inevitably become policymakers. The most important policymaking tool of the federal courts is the power of judicial review. This power was not mentioned specifically in the Constitution, but the Supreme Court claimed the power for the federal courts in its 1803 decision in *Marbury v. Madison.*

Judges who take an active role in checking the activities of the other branches of government sometimes are characterized as "activist" judges, and judges who defer to the decisions of the other branches are sometimes regarded as "restraintist" judges. The Warren Court of the 1950s and 1960s was activist in a liberal direction, whereas the Rehnquist and Roberts Courts became increasingly activist in a conservative direction.

Checks on the powers of the federal courts include executive checks, legislative checks, public opinion, and judicial traditions and doctrines.

Master the concept of *The Judiciary* with MindTap™ for American Government

REVIEW MindTap™ **for American Government**
Access Key Term Flashcards for Chapter 14.

TEST YOURSELF MindTap™ **for American Government**
Take the Wrap It Up Quiz for Chapter 14.

STAY CURRENT MindTap™ **for American Government**
Access the KnowNow blog and customized RSS for updates on current events.

STAY FOCUSED MindTap™ **for American Government**
Complete the Focus Activities for The Judiciary.

Additional Resources

Most courts in the United States have sites on the Web. Some courts simply display contact information for court personnel. Others include recent judicial decisions along with court rules and forms.

At the same time, unlike other branches of government, the courts often view social media as an annoyance. Judges don't want jurors to discuss or research their cases, but Twitter, Facebook, and similar tools make these rules hard to enforce. In San Francisco recently, a jury pool of six hundred people was dismissed because all of them had researched a high-profile case.

Online Resources

- The home page of the federal courts is a good starting point for learning about the federal court system. You can locate this page at www.uscourts.gov. Here, you can follow the path of a case as it moves through the federal courts.
- To access the Supreme Court's official Web site, where Supreme Court decisions are made available within hours of their release, go to www.supremecourt.gov.
- Several Web sites offer searchable databases of Supreme Court decisions. You can access Supreme Court cases since 1893 at www.findlaw.com/casecode/supreme.html.
- You can find information on the justices of the Supreme Court, as well as their decisions, at the Oyez Project of the Chicago-Kent College of Law, Illinois Institute of Technology. Visit www.oyez.org.

Books

Coyle, Marcia. *The Roberts Court: The Struggle for the Constitution.* New York: Simon & Schuster (paperback), 2014. This work offers a ringside seat to the struggle to lay down the law of the land. Acclaimed reporter Marcia Coyle is the chief Washington correspondent for the *National Law Journal.* She has covered the Supreme Court for twenty years and regularly appears on PBS's *NewsHour.*

Healy, Thomas. *The Great Dissent: How Oliver Wendell Holmes Changed His Mind—and Changed the History of Free Speech in America.* New York: Metropolitan Books, 2013. In 1919, Justice Holmes wrote a dissenting opinion that would go down in history as a key affirmation of free speech in the United States. But Holmes was not always a First Amendment advocate. This prize-winning account explains how he became one. Healy is a law professor at Seton Hall University.

Stevens, John Paul. *Six Amendments: How and Why We Should Change the Constitution.* New York: Little, Brown and Company, 2014. Justice Stevens retired from the United States Supreme Court in 2010. In this unusual work, Stevens combines an account of how the Supreme Court works with a call to change the Constitution. Among other changes, Stevens would abolish gerrymandering, end the death penalty, allow limits on campaign finance, and limit the scope of the Second Amendment.

Video

Gideon's Trumpet—A 1980 film, starring Henry Fonda as the small-time criminal James Earl Gideon. The film shows the path a case must take to reach the Supreme Court and the importance of cases decided there.

The Supreme Court—A four-part PBS series that won a 2008 Parents' Choice Gold Award. It follows the history of the Supreme Court from the first chief justice, John Marshall, to the earliest days of the Roberts Court. Some of the many topics discussed are the Court's dismal performance in the Civil War era, its conflicts with President Franklin Roosevelt, its role in banning African American segregation, and its place in the abortion controversy.

Quiz

Multiple Choice and Fill-Ins

Learning Outcome 1 Explain the main sources of American law, including constitutions, statutes and regulations, and the common law tradition.

1. One important source of American law is:
   a. the rights and duties of workers as expressed in employment agreements.
   b. case law based in part on the common law tradition.
   c. case law based in part on the federal tradition.

2. The supreme law of the land in the United States is the
   _____ _____ _____.

Learning Outcome 2 *Describe the structure of the federal court system and such basic judicial requirements as jurisdiction and standing to sue.*

3. The distinction between federal district courts and federal appellate courts can be summarized by the following statement:
   a. federal district courts are trial courts that hear evidence, but federal appellate courts do not hear evidence.
   b. federal district courts only hear appeals from federal appellate courts.
   c. federal appellate courts only accept cases involving state constitutions.

4. To bring a lawsuit, a party must show that he or she suffered an actual harm or is threatened by an actual harm as a result of the action that led to the dispute. If so, then that party has
   _____ ___ _____.

Learning Outcome 3 Discuss the procedures used by the United States Supreme Court and the various types of opinions it hands down.

5. "I'll take it all the way to the Supreme Court." A lawyer cannot truthfully promise this because:
   a. the Supreme Court may be too far away from the state in which the controversy occurred.
   b. the Supreme Court only hears a limited number of cases in which a federal question is involved.
   c. the Supreme Court is not in session for a full twelve months each year.

6. When the U.S. Supreme Court issues an opinion that has the support of the entire Court, it is called a unanimous opinion. Otherwise, the Court issues a majority opinion. Those justices in the minority who do not agree with the majority opinion often write a _____ _____.

Learning Outcome 4 Evaluate the manner in which federal judges are selected.

7. The most common occupational position held by a Supreme Court justice before appointment has been:
   a. U.S. senator.
   b. state governor.
   c. federal judgeship.

8. The tradition of _____ _____ gives U.S. senators considerable power over federal judicial appointments in the senators' own state.

Learning Outcome 5 Consider the ways in which the Supreme Court makes policy, and explain the forces that limit the activism of the courts.

9. When a federal court declares that a federal or state law or policy is unconstitutional, that court is engaging in:
   a. judicial review.
   b. congressional condemnation.
   c. administrative oversight.

10. The doctrine of _____ _____ rests on the conviction that the federal judiciary should actively use its powers to check the laws passed by Congress and state legislatures.

Essay Questions

1. What are the benefits of having lifetime appointments to the United States Supreme Court? What problems might such appointments cause? What would be the likely result if Supreme Court justices faced term limits?

2. In the section "Policymaking and the Courts," we described how the Rehnquist Court ruled in favor of states' rights in a gun-control case and against states' rights in a marijuana case. Why do you think the justices might have come to different conclusions in these two cases?

Domestic and Economic Policy 15

Students and parents in Chicago protest funding and staff cuts to their neighborhood schools. The Chicago Public Schools are trying to eliminate a $1 billion budget deficit. Is it possible to spend less on schools without harming education? Why or why not?
Scott Olson/Getty Images News/Getty Images

The six learning outcomes below are designed to help improve your understanding of this chapter. After reading this chapter, you should be able to:

- **Learning Outcome 1:** Describe the five steps of the policymaking process, using the health-care reform legislation as an example.

- **Learning Outcome 2:** Explain why illegal immigration is seen as a problem, and cite some of the steps that have been taken in response to it.

- **Learning Outcome 3:** Discuss recent developments in crime rates and incarceration.

- **Learning Outcome 4:** Evaluate the federal government's responses to high oil prices and the controversy over global warming.

- **Learning Outcome 5:** Define *unemployment, inflation, fiscal policy, net public debt,* and *monetary policy.*

- **Learning Outcome 6:** Describe the various taxes that Americans pay, and discuss some of the controversies surrounding taxation.

▶ WATCH & LEARN MindTap™ for American Government

Watch a brief "What Do You Know?" video summarizing Domestic and Economic Policy.

health care came to be an important issue, and how health-care reform became part of the national agenda, we need to examine the background of the issue.

Health Care's Role in the American Economy. As of 2015, health care was estimated to account for 18 percent of the total U.S. economy. In 1965, about 6 percent of our national income was spent on health care, but that percentage has been increasing ever since, as you can see in Figure 15–1 that follows. Per capita spending on health care is greater in the United States than almost anywhere else in the world. Measured by the percentage of the **gross domestic product (GDP)** devoted to health care, America spends almost twice as much as Britain or Japan. (See Figure 15–2 that follows.)

As of 2010, before the reform legislation was implemented, government spending on health care constituted about 50 percent of total health-care spending. Private insurance accounted for more than 30 percent of payments for health care. The remainder—less than 20 percent—was paid directly by individuals or by charities. The government programs **Medicare** and **Medicaid** have been the main sources of hospital and other medical benefits for about 100 million Americans—one-third of the nation's population. Many of these people are elderly.

Medicare. The Medicare program, which was created in 1965 under President Lyndon Johnson, pays hospital and physician bills for U.S. residents over the age of sixty-five. Since 2006, Medicare has also paid for at least part of the prescription drug expenses of the elderly. In return for paying a tax on their earnings (currently set at 2.9 percent of wages and salaries) while in the workforce, retirees are assured that the majority of their hospital and physician bills will be paid for with public funds.

Medicaid. In recent decades, the joint federal-state taxpayer-funded Medicaid program for the "working poor" has generated one of the biggest expansions of government entitlements ever. In 1990, total Medicaid spending was around $40 billion. By fiscal year 2015, the total cost of Medicaid and the Children's Health Insurance Program (CHIP) was about $540 billion. At the end of the twentieth century, 34 million people were enrolled in the programs. As of March 2014, there were about 65 million enrolled.

In recent years, the federal government has paid about 55 percent of Medicaid's total cost. The states pay the rest. Wealthy states must pick up a greater share of the tab than poor ones. Medicaid costs have imposed major strains on the budgets of many states. As you will learn later in this section, the new health-care reform legislation adopted in 2010 has expanded considerably the share of the population that is eligible for Medicaid. Much of the extra expense due to the new enrollees will be picked up by federal taxpayers.

The Problem of the Uninsured. In 2012, about 48 million Americans—more than 15 percent of the population—did not have health insurance. The uninsured population has been relatively young, in part due to Medicare, which covers almost everyone over the age

> **Gross Domestic Product (GDP)**
> The dollar value of all final goods and services produced in a one-year period.
>
> **Medicare**
> A federal health-insurance program that covers U.S. residents over the age of sixty-five. The costs are met by a tax on wages and salaries.
>
> **Medicaid**
> A joint state-federal program that provides medical care to the poor (including indigent elderly persons in nursing homes). The program is funded out of general government revenues.

Figure 15–1 ▶ **Percentage of Total National Income Spent on Health Care in the United States**

The portion of total national income spent on health care has risen steadily since 1965. *What might people spend more on if health care were less expensive?*

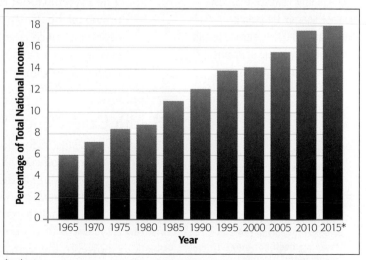

* estimate

Sources: U.S. Department of Commerce; U.S. Department of Health and Human Services; Deloitte and Touche LLP; VHA, Inc.; and Centers for Medicare and Medicaid Services.

Figure 15–2   ▶   Cost of Health Care in
Economically Advanced Nations

Cost is given as a percentage of total gross domestic product (GDP). Figures are for 2010 and 2011. *Is it a problem or an advantage that U.S. physicians are among the world's best paid?*

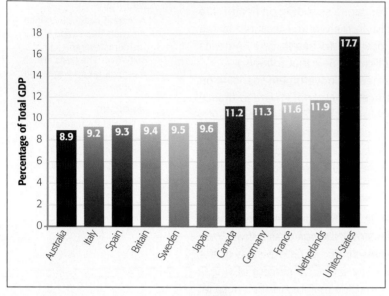

Source: Excerpted and adapted from the Organization for Economic Cooperation and Development, *OECD Health Data*, 2013.

did you know?

The cost of health care for those under fifty isn't that much different in the United States than it is in some of the other high-cost industrialized countries. After age fifty, however, U.S. costs increase sharply. On average, it costs more than $40,000 to provide health care to an 80-year-old in America, and only about $10,000 in Germany.

Universal Health Insurance

Any of several possible programs to provide health insurance to everyone in a country. The central government does not necessarily provide the insurance itself but may subsidize the purchase of insurance from private insurance companies.

of sixty-five. Also, younger workers are more likely to be employed in entry-level jobs without health-insurance benefits.

The traditional system of health care in the United States was based on the assumption that employers would provide health insurance to working-age persons. Many small businesses, however, simply have not been able to afford to offer their workers health insurance. In 2013, employer-provided health insurance cost an average of $5,884 for single coverage and $16,351 for family coverage, according to the Kaiser Family Foundation.

The Problem of High Costs. High medical costs are a problem not only for individuals with inadequate or nonexistent insurance coverage. They are also a problem for the system as a whole. Over the past four decades, per capita spending on health care in the United States grew at an average rate of 4.9 percent per year, even when corrected for inflation. A main driver of the growth in health-care spending was new medical technologies and services.

In addition, people over the age of sixty-five run up health-care bills that are far larger than those incurred by the rest of the population. As a federal problem, therefore, health-care spending growth has been and will remain chiefly a Medicare issue, even after the implementation of the new health-care measures. In 2014, the government's Medicare trustees reported that by 2030 the Medicare trust fund was projected to run out of funds necessary to pay for all of its obligations. Such prospects explain why the issue of health-care cost containment was almost as important as the issue of universal coverage during the 2009 debates.

The International Experience. The Affordable Care Act attempts to provide **universal health insurance** for American citizens. The concept of universal health insurance is not new. Throughout the twentieth century, most economically advanced nations adopted such systems. American progressives considered it unacceptable that the United States could not do what these other nations had done—another argument for placing reform on the agenda.

Health Care: Policy Formulation

During the next step in the policymaking process, various policy proposals are discussed among government officials and the public. Such discussions may take place in the printed media, on television, and in the halls of Congress. Congress holds hearings, the president voices the administration's views, and the topic may even become a campaign issue.

For more than half a century, liberals have sought to establish a universal health-insurance system in this country. All attempts, however, went nowhere. After the 2008 elections, however, the Democrats were in complete control of Congress and the presidency. Universal health insurance now appeared to be politically possible.

Under Democratic plans, universal coverage would result from a mandate that all citizens must obtain health insurance from some source—an employer, Medicare or

Medicaid, or a plan from a private-sector insurance company through a market spon-sored by the federal government or a state government. Low-income families would receive a subsidy to help them pay their insurance premiums. Insurers could not reject applicants.

Health Care: Policy Adoption

The third step in the policymaking process involves choosing a specific policy from among the proposals that have been discussed.

President Obama largely delegated the drafting of a health-care plan to Congress. In contrast, recent presidents had often sought to push presidential proposals through the legislative process without significant alteration. Obama's tactics made it easier to bring Congress on board, but the political cost was high. Congress took a very long time to pass the necessary legislation, and much of the political maneuvering required for passage was highly unpopular with the public.

The Issue of Mandated Coverage.   One key element of the proposed legislation was the **individual mandate,** a penalty on those who do not buy insurance. Congressional Democrats adopted the individual mandate because without it, there was no way that the numbers would add up: universal coverage was impossible unless everyone—healthy and sick alike—chipped in. Unfortunately for the Democrats, the individual mandate allowed the Republicans to accuse the Democrats of "forcing" people to do something, never a popular position in America.

New Taxes.   Funding the legislation required additional taxes. Democrats in the House called for heavier taxes on the rich, while the Senate proposed taxes on drug and insurance companies. In the end, the two chambers compromised on some of each.

Public Reaction.   Initially, popular support for health-care reform, as reported by opinion polls, was relatively high. Support eroded quickly, however, as Congress took up the actual legislation. The process of moving the reform through congressional channels gave the public a close look at how legislatures oper-ate, and many citizens clearly were not happy with what they saw.

Passage.   The House passed its bill in November 2009, and the Senate passed its version in December. Passing the reform legislation became more compli-cated in January 2010, after a Republican won a Massachusetts special election to fill a vacant U.S. Senate seat. The election meant that the Senate Democrats lost their sixtieth vote, which was necessary to end filibusters. If the House and Senate versions of the bill were reconciled in a conference committee—the normal procedure—Senate Democrats would not be able to pass the resulting compromise.

President Obama and then–House Speaker Nancy Pelosi, however, patiently assembled enough Demo-cratic support in the House to pass the Senate bill unaltered, thus eliminating the need for a conference

> **Individual Mandate**
> In health-care reform, the requirement that all citizens obtain health-care insurance coverage from some source, public or private.

did you know?

The Federal Reserve has reported that about 52 percent of collection actions by collection agencies and creditors were due to medical bills.

A physician gives a vaccination to a teenager in Miami, Florida. *When might a patient not have to pay for such services?*

Joe Raedle/Getty Images News/Getty Images

committee. The House then immediately passed a reconciliation act, which was not subject to Senate filibuster. "Obamacare," as it was nicknamed, was the law of the land. Neither the Senate's bill nor the House's reconciliation measure received the vote of even a single Republican.

Details of the Legislation. Most of the major provisions of the new legislation did not go into effect until 2014. Some provisions took effect quickly, however. Young adults were allowed to stay on their parents' health plans until they turned twenty-six, and insurance companies could not drop people when they became sick.

In 2014, most of the program kicked in, including the following:

- State health-insurance exchanges where individuals and small businesses can buy policies from commercial insurance companies.
- Subsidies to help persons with incomes up to four times the federal poverty level purchase coverage on the exchanges.
- Medicaid coverage for individuals with incomes up to 133 percent of the poverty level.

Health Care: Policy Implementation

The fourth step in the policymaking process involves the implementation of the policy alternative chosen by Congress. Government action must be implemented by bureaucrats, the courts, police, and individual citizens.

Congressional Opposition. Implementation would not occur, of course, if Obamacare could be abolished before it was in effect. Complete repeal of the legislation, however, was hard. Repeal would have to pass both chambers of Congress and survive a presidential veto. Republicans, in other words, needed a complete sweep in the 2012 elections, which they did not get.

Also, much of the reform is an entitlement program, like Medicare or Social Security. Funding for entitlement programs does not depend on annual budget votes in Congress for their continued survival. Therefore, even if Republicans in Congress were able to "defund" certain aspects of the reforms, most of the new policies would survive.

Opposition in the Courts. Many conservative state officials challenged the constitutionality of the Affordable Care Act in court. In 2012, however, the Supreme Court ruled that most of the act was constitutional. The one exception: the Court threw out the mechanism by which the federal government could force states to expand their Medicaid programs.

Opposition in the States. Medicaid expansion is fully funded by the federal government for the first six years and funded at 90 percent thereafter. Still, a large number of conservative state governments exercised their option to refuse expansion. As a result, several million low-income persons were not eligible for coverage in 2014. Many state governments also refused to participate in setting up health-insurance exchanges.

Setting Up the Exchanges. On October 1, 2013, the state and federal exchanges were scheduled to open. Many of the state exchange Web sites—such as those in California, Connecticut, New York, and Washington—experienced only a moderate number of initial problems. Two, in Oregon and Maryland, were so badly built that they had to be scrapped altogether. Those buying health-care insurance in those states had to do so without using the Internet. As you learned in the introductory section of Chapter 6, the

**CONNECT
WITH YOUR CLASSMATES**
MindTap™ **for American Government**

Access the Domestic Policy Forum: Discussion—The Public's Impact on Policy Making

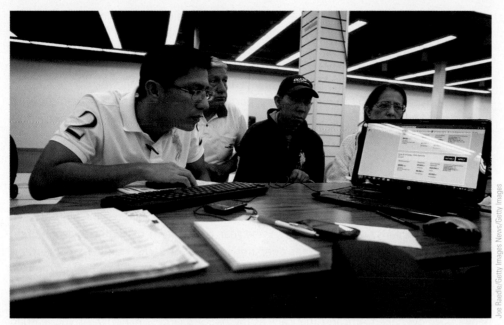

These Miami residents are signing up for health insurance under the Affordable Care Act. An insurance agent is assisting them. Lines were long in the last days before the enrollment period ended on March 31, 2014. *Why did many people wait until the last minute to sign up?*

federal exchanges, set up in states that refused to establish their own, had tremendous difficulties for several months.

Final Sign-Ups. By January 2014, however, the federal exchanges were functioning adequately. A large surge in enrollments in March and extending past the official deadline into April pushed enrollment on the exchanges to 8 million persons. (The Congressional Budget Office had predicted in mid-2013 that first-year enrollment would be about 6 million.) While the percentage of adults without insurance was now 13.4 percent, down from 18 percent before the exchanges opened, millions of people still lacked coverage. Many of them were expected to sign up in later years, however, a common pattern with new benefit programs.

Health Care: Policy Evaluation

After a policy has been implemented, it is evaluated. When a policy has been in place for a given period of time, groups inside and outside the government conduct studies to determine how the program has actually worked. Based on this feedback and the perceived success or failure of the policy, a new round of policymaking initiatives may be undertaken to improve on the effort.

It will take years before the Affordable Care Act can be evaluated adequately. In part, that is because the program is still a work in progress. Will the rates charged by insurance companies remain stable? How many new people will enroll in later years? How many states will continue to hold out against expanding Medicaid? (Many observers expect that in time, the number of holdouts will fall considerably.)

A further reason that evaluation will take time is that Obamacare continues to be caught up in political controversy. Republican members of the House have voted fifty-four times to repeal, defund, or delay the act. None of these bills had a chance to survive the Democrat-controlled Senate or a presidential veto. Still, they reflect the fact that Republicans remain devoted to opposition, not evaluation. Democrats are not ready for impartiality, either.

A majority of the public has had a negative opinion of Obamacare since it was passed, although a majority also supports changing rather than abolishing it. Democrats had assumed that after full implementation, the reforms would gain broad public support. But most people continue to get their insurance through an employer, Medicare, or some other pre-existing system. These people have no actual experience with the reforms and therefore often judge them based on their own partisan preferences. Still, Obamacare is not going away—indeed, many Republican politicians already realize that it is politically impossible to take health-care insurance away from millions of people now that they have it.

■ **Learning Outcome 2:** Explain why illegal immigration is seen as a problem, and cite some of the steps that have been taken in response to it.

Immigration

In recent years, immigration rates in the United States have been among the highest since their peak in the early twentieth century. Every year, more than 1 million people immigrate to this country legally, a figure that does not include the large number of unauthorized immigrants. Those born on foreign soil now constitute about 13 percent of the U.S. population—more than twice the percentage of thirty years ago.

Since 1977, four out of five immigrants have come from Latin America or Asia. Hispanics have overtaken African Americans as the nation's largest minority. As you learned in Chapter 1, if current immigration rates continue, by 2050 minority groups collectively will constitute the "majority" of Americans. If such groups were to form coalitions, they could increase their political power dramatically. The "old guard" white majority would no longer dominate American politics.

Some regard the high rate of immigration as a plus for America because it offsets the low birthrate and aging population, which we also discussed in Chapter 1. Immigrants expand the workforce and help to support, through their taxes, government programs that benefit older Americans, such as Medicare and Social Security. In contrast, nations that do not have high immigration rates, such as Japan, are experiencing serious challenges due to their aging populations.

A significant number of U.S. citizens, however, believe that immigration—both legal and illegal—negatively affects America. They argue, among other things, that the large number of immigrants seeking work results in lower wages for Americans, especially those with few skills. They also worry about the cost of providing immigrants with services such as education and medical care.

The Issue of Unauthorized Immigration

Illegal or unauthorized immigration is a major national issue. We introduced this topic in Chapter 5, both in the *What If . . .* feature and in the section "Experiences of Other Minority Groups." As we noted there, the largest number of unauthorized immigrants are from Latin America, especially Mexico. A current estimate is that there are about 11 million such people. Almost all illegal immigrants come to work, and hiring them

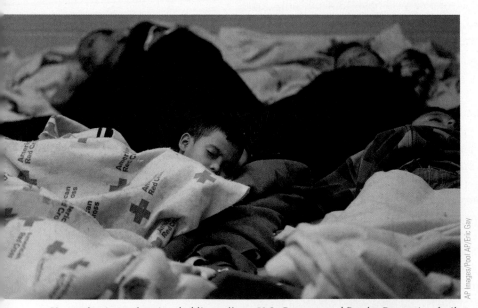

Young detainees sleep in a holding cell at a U.S. Customs and Border Protection facility in Texas in 2014. Many of the young immigrants recently flooding the nation's southern border say they are fleeing violent gangs in Central America. *What would be better: changing the law to deport minors more rapidly, or hiring more immigration judges to speed up legal processing? In either case, why?*

CHAPTER 15 • DOMESTIC AND ECONOMIC POLICY   **439**

was not illegal until 1986. Today, laws designed to prevent the employment of undocumented workers are enforced more strictly than in the past.

In polls by Gallup and other organizations, Americans express opinions about illegal immigration (the term used in the questions) that are highly contradictory. A majority of respondents express sympathy toward the immigrants and believe that a way should be found to normalize their status. Less than a fifth favor immediate, permanent deportation. In the very same polls, however, two-thirds agree that states should be able to set their own immigration laws and that police officers should be able to question anyone about their immigration status. Half believe that illegal immigration to seek work should be a crime.

While a majority of Americans believe that the illegal immigration problem is serious, most do not consider it a priority issue for the government. Those who do consider it a priority, however, have very strong feelings on the topic—and in American politics, a minority with strong feelings can often outweigh a largely indifferent majority.

did you know?

The Associated Press estimates that about 80 percent of agricultural field workers in California are unauthorized immigrants.

The Immigration Debate

The split in the public's attitudes has been reflected in differences among the nation's leaders over how to handle the issue of illegal immigration. Most Republicans in Congress have favored a harder line toward illegal immigrants than have most Democrats. There have been exceptions. Republican president George W. Bush was a strong—if unsuccessful—advocate of immigration reform. By Obama's first term, however, Republicans in Congress were substantially united against reform.

State Immigration Laws. In April 2010, Arizona's governor signed the nation's toughest-ever bill on illegal immigration. The law criminalized the failure to carry immigration documents, and it required police to stop and question anyone suspected of being in the country illegally. The law also penalized anyone transporting, sheltering, or assisting illegal aliens. Opponents contended that the act would lead to harassment of Latinos regardless of their citizenship status. Arizona had earlier passed the nation's toughest law penalizing employers who hired undocumented workers.

In June 2012, the United States Supreme Court ruled that Arizona could not make an immigrant's failure to register under federal law a state crime, could not make it a felony for illegal immigrants to work, and could not arrest people without warrants if they might be deportable under federal law. The Court did not block police from investigating the immigration status of anyone they stop. It left the door open, however, to future challenges to this law based on equal protection principles.[1]

In 2011, Alabama adopted a new law aimed at illegal immigration that was in many respects even tougher than the Arizona legislation. Much of the law is currently blocked as a result of federal court rulings, however, and several provisions were invalidated by the Supreme Court's Arizona ruling. Georgia, Indiana, South Carolina, and Utah have also passed laws that attempt to reduce illegal immigration.

Immigration and the Obama Administration. During his first presidential campaign, Barack Obama supported reforms that would give illegal immigrants a path toward citizenship. Reform was put off to allow Congress to concentrate on health-care issues, however. Obama focused instead on border security and rounding up deportable persons. In fact, in Obama's first term, his administration deported 1.5 million illegal immigrants, an all-time record.

---

1. *Arizona v. United States,* 567 U.S. ___ (2012).

The resulting Latino dissatisfaction with the administration raised the question of whether Hispanics would turn out and vote for Democratic candidates in forthcoming elections. The 2012 Republican presidential candidates, however, took a hard line against illegal immigration. Also, in June 2012, Obama announced a new policy under which immigration authorities would suspend deportations of unauthorized immigrants who were brought into the country as children and who were not otherwise in trouble with the law. In the end, Latinos and Asian Americans turned out for the Democrats in large numbers during the 2012 elections.

The Republican Debate on Immigration. Clearly, the Republicans would be better off in the future if they could increase their support among immigrants, a growing share of the population. Indeed, following the elections, a substantial number of Republicans announced that they were adjusting their position on immigration and were now open to change. It soon became clear, however, that a majority of the Republicans in Congress continued to oppose reform. Also, some Republicans who supported reform immediately after the elections soon opposed it again.

Still, a minority of the Republicans plus almost all of the Democrats would be enough to pass an immigration bill. Republican House Speaker John Boehner, however, refused to allow such a bill to reach the House floor because it did not command the support of a majority of Republicans. (The policy of requiring "a majority of the majority" is the *Hastert Rule*, which we described in Chapter 11 in the section "House–Senate Differences and Congressional Perks.")

■ **Learning Outcome 3:** Discuss recent developments in crime rates and incarceration.

Crime in the Twenty-First Century

Almost all polls taken in the United States in the past several decades have shown that crime remains one of the major concerns of the public. A related issue that has been on the domestic policy agenda for decades is the status of the nation's prisons.

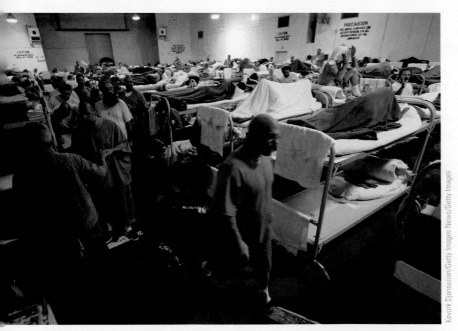

This gymnasium at Chino State Prison in California was modified to house prisoners. A federal judge has ruled that California must release thousands of prisoners due to overcrowding. *Do overcrowded prisons violate prisoners' rights?*

Crime in American History

In every period in the history of this nation, people have voiced apprehension about crime. During the Civil War, mob violence and riots erupted in several cities. After the Civil War, people in San Francisco were told that "no decent man is in safety to walk the streets after dark; while at all hours, both night and day, his property is jeopardized by incendiarism [arson] and burglary."[2] In 1886, *Leslie's Weekly* reported, "Each day we see ghastly records of crime . . . murder seems to have run riot and each citizen asks . . . 'who is safe?'"

In fact, studies by historians have shown that preindustrial agricultural communities had very high levels of interpersonal violence, and that crime rates in the United States and other Western countries fell steadily from the second quarter of the nineteenth century into the twentieth

2. President's Commission on Law Enforcement and Administration of Justice, *Challenge of Crime in a Free Society* (Washington, D.C.: Government Printing Office, 1967), p. 19.

century. Some historians suggest that this century-long decline came about because industrialization, urbanization, and the growth of bureaucratic institutions such as factories and schools socialized the lower classes into patterns of conformity and rule observance. It is notable that newly settled communities in the American West, where such socialization was incomplete, had much higher rates of crime—the "Wild West" was not entirely a myth.

The United States then experienced a substantial crime wave in the 1920s and the first half of the 1930s. This was the period of Prohibition, when the production and sale of alcoholic beverages was illegal. Criminals such as the famous Al Capone organized gangs to provide illicit alcohol to the public. After the end of Prohibition, crime rates dropped until after World War II (1939–1945).

Crime rates in Western countries began to rise in the 1950s. The United States, in particular, experienced an explosive growth in violent crime that began in the 1960s. The murder rate per 100,000 people in 1964 was 4.9, whereas in 1994 it was estimated at 9.3, an increase of almost 100 percent. Since 1995, however, violent crime rates have declined. Some argue that this decline was due to the growing economy the United States had generally enjoyed since about 1993. Others claim that the billions in additional funds that the federal and state governments allotted to curbing crime in the past few years has led to less crime. Still others claim that an increase in the number of persons who are jailed or imprisoned is responsible for the reduction. Some have even argued that legalized abortion has reduced the population that is likely to commit crimes. In any event, the violent crime rate appears to be falling. You can see changes in the rates of homicides, violent crimes, and thefts in Figures 15–3, 15–4, and 15–5, respectively.

The Prison Population Bomb

Many Americans believe that the best solution to the nation's crime problem is to impose stiff prison sentences on offenders. Such sentences, in fact, have become national policy. By 2013, U.S. prisons and jails held 2.2 million people. About two-thirds of the incarcerated population were in state or federal prisons, with the remainder held in local jails. About 60 percent of the persons held in local jails were awaiting court action. The other 40 percent were serving sentences.

Figure 15–3 ▶ **Homicide Rates**

Homicide rates recently declined to levels last seen in the 1960s. (The 2001 rate does not include deaths attributed to the 9/11 terrorist attacks.) *How might advances in medical care affect these numbers?*

Sources: U.S. Department of Justice; and National Center for Health Statistics, *Vital Statistics.*

Figure 15–4 ▶ **Violent Crime Rates**

Violent crime rates began a steep decline in 1995. The crimes included in this chart are rape, robbery, aggravated and simple assault, and domestic violence. *Do you think people today are more or less likely to report crimes than in the past? Why?*

Source: U.S. Department of Justice; rape, robbery, domestic violence, and assault data are from the *National Crime Victimization Survey.*

Figure 15–5 ▶ **Theft Rates**

Theft rates have declined significantly since the 1970s. Theft is defined as completed or attempted theft of property or cash without personal contact. *Have you personally taken steps to avoid becoming a theft victim? If so, what were they?*

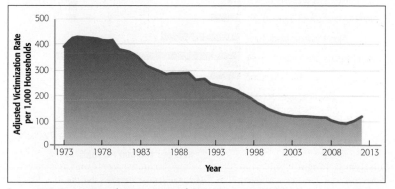

Source: U.S. Department of Justice, *National Crime Victimization Survey.*

Incarceration Rate
The number of persons held in jail or prison for every 100,000 persons in a particular population group.

did you know?

The odds are one in twenty that an American born today will wind up in jail or prison at some point during his or her lifetime.

The number of incarcerated persons has grown rapidly in recent years. In 1990, for example, the total number of persons held in U.S. jails or prisons was still only 1.1 million. From 1995 to 2002, the incarcerated population grew at an average of 3.8 percent annually. The rate of growth slowed after 2002, however, and the number of prisoners has fallen since 2011.

The Incarceration Rate. Some groups of people are much more likely to find themselves behind bars than others. Men are more than ten times more likely to be incarcerated than women. Prisoners are also disproportionately African American. To measure how frequently members of particular groups are imprisoned, the standard statistic is the **incarceration rate.** This rate is the number of people incarcerated for every 100,000 persons in a particular population group. To put it another way, an incarceration rate of 1,000 means that 1 percent of a particular group is in custody. Using this statistic, we can say that U.S. men had an incarceration rate of 1,398 in 2009, compared with a rate of 131 for U.S. women. (The government has not updated these detailed statistics since 2009.)

These figures, close to an all-time high, mean that more than 1 male out of every 100 was in jail or prison in this country. Figure 15–6 that follows shows selected incarceration rates by gender, race, and age. Note the very high incarceration rate for African Americans between the ages of thirty and thirty-four—at any given time, almost 11 percent of this group was in jail or prison. How do American incarceration rates compare with those of other countries? We answer that question in this chapter's *Beyond Our Borders* feature that follows.

Prison Construction and Conditions. To house a growing number of inmates, prison construction and management have become sizable industries in the United States. Ten years ago, prison overcrowding was a major issue. In 1994, for example, state prisons had a rated capacity of about 500,000 inmates but actually held 900,000 people. The prisons were therefore operating at 80 percent above capacity. Today, after a major prison construction program, many state prisons are operating within their capacity, but some state systems are still at 20 percent above capacity or more. The federal prison system is still 37 percent above capacity. Since 1980, Texas has built 120 new prisons, Florida has built 84, and California has built 83. In 1923, there were only 61 prisons in the entire United States.

Effects of Incarceration. When imprisonment keeps truly violent felons behind bars longer, it prevents them from committing additional crimes. The average predatory street criminal commits fifteen or more crimes each year when not behind bars. But most prisoners are in for a relatively short time and are released on parole early, often because of prison overcrowding. Many then find themselves back in prison because they have violated parole, typically by using illegal drugs. Indeed, of the 1.5 million people who are arrested each year, the majority are arrested for drug offenses. Given that from 20 million to 40 million Americans violate one or more drug laws each year, the potential "supply" of prisoners seems almost limitless.

Figure 15–6 ▶ **Incarceration Rates per 100,000 Persons for Selected U.S. Population Groups**

Why do you think the government may have stopped updating incarceration statistics?

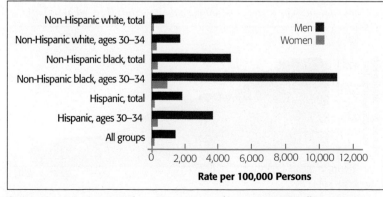

Source: "Prison Inmates at Midyear 2009," *Bureau of Justice Statistics Bulletin*, U.S. Department of Justice (2010).

Beyond Our Borders

How Many People Do Other Countries Send to Prison?

The United States has more people in jail or prison than any other country in the world. That fact is not necessarily surprising, because the United States also has one of the world's largest total populations. More to the point, the United States has the highest reported incarceration *rate* of any country on earth. North Korea almost certainly has a higher incarceration rate than the United States, but that nation does not report its incarceration statistics. (One human rights organization estimates the North Korean rate as 825 prisoners for every 100,000 inhabitants.) Figure 15–7 compares U.S. incarceration rates, measured by the number of prisoners per 100,000 residents, with incarceration rates in other major countries. The figure for China is not the official figure but an estimate by a human rights group.

Figure 15–7 ▶ **Incarceration Rates around the World**

Incarceration rates of major nations, measured by the number of prisoners per 100,000 residents. *Why do you think other advanced nations are so much less likely to send people to prison?*

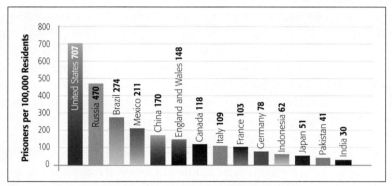

Source: International Centre for Prison Studies, King's College London.

Energy and the Environment

A major part of President Obama's legislative agenda has been directed at energy and environmental issues. Energy policy addresses two major problems: (1) America's reliance on foreign oil, much of which is produced by unfriendly regimes, and (2) global warming (or climate change) purportedly caused by increased emissions of carbon dioxide (CO_2) and other greenhouse gases.

■ **Learning Outcome 4:**
Evaluate the federal government's responses to high oil prices and the controversy over global warming.

Energy Independence—A Strategic Issue

As of 2014, the United States imported about 28 percent of the petroleum it consumes. More than one-third of U.S. imports come from two friendly neighbors, Canada and Mexico, and less than one-quarter from Middle Eastern countries, primarily Saudi Arabia. The world's largest oil exporters include a number of nations that are not friends of the United States. Russia is the world's second-largest oil exporter, after Saudi Arabia. Other major exporters include Venezuela and Iran. Both are openly hostile to American interests, and Venezuela is a major source of U.S. oil imports.

While the United States is far from attaining the goal of energy independence, the nation has taken significant steps in that direction. American reliance on foreign oil is down dramatically from what it was only a few years ago. In 2006, almost 60 percent

Fracking
Short for *hydraulic fracturing*, the injection of a high-pressure solution of water, sand, and chemicals into hydrocarbon-bearing rocks, releasing oil or natural gas.

of our oil came from abroad, compared to the current 28 percent. What changes were responsible for this turnaround?

High Prices and New Production. If the price of a commodity goes up, producers of that commodity have an incentive to produce more of it. The price of gasoline has certainly risen in recent years. In the summer of 2008, before the full impact of the Great Recession, the price of gasoline exceeded $4 for the first time. The price fell during the recession. By the spring of 2011, despite the slow pace of economic recovery, gasoline once again cost more than $4 in many parts of the country. The price has fluctuated since but remains high. Clearly, petroleum producers had an incentive to extract more crude oil, if possible. The question was, could they?

Some experts doubted that enough new oil could be extracted to keep prices from rising indefinitely. They underestimated the impact of increased applications of technology in the form of hydraulic fracturing, or **fracking.** This process involves injecting water, sand, and chemicals under high pressure into hydrocarbon-bearing rocks, releasing oil or natural gas. The high price of oil made fracking profitable.

Fracking has had an even greater impact on the supply of natural gas. A few years ago, it seemed likely that the United States would need to import natural gas. Imports would be expensive, because gas cannot be transported by ship efficiently unless it is converted to liquefied natural gas (LNG). By 2012, however, so much natural gas was available domestically that the nation had run out of storage space. Plans were under way to export LNG from terminals built to import it. Low natural gas prices plus new air-pollution regulations made coal uncompetitive as a source of electricity. As a result, plans for 168 new coal-based power plants were abandoned, and about 100 existing plants were scheduled for retirement. Despite concerns that fracking might harm drinking-water supplies or otherwise damage the environment, use of the process continues to grow rapidly.

did you know?

America burns nearly half of the world's gasoline.

The Politics of Expensive Oil. The high price of gasoline is a political issue, and several presidential candidates claimed that, if elected, they would bring it down. Crude oil prices are set worldwide, however, and the ability of the federal government to affect these prices is very limited. (As noted, natural gas is expensive to transport overseas, so its price has fallen in North America.) Still, the government has taken some steps to encourage increased supplies of gasoline.

President Obama issued higher fuel-efficiency standards for vehicles in 2009 and 2012. The standards followed an agreement negotiated with thirteen automobile manufacturers, the United Automobile Workers, and the state of California. By 2016, new cars should average 39 miles per gallon and light trucks should average 30. By 2025, the nation's combined fleet of new cars and light trucks must have an average fuel efficiency of 54.5 miles per gallon.

A Texas worker unloads a mixture of oil, sediment, and water generated during hydraulic fracturing (fracking). Components of the mixture will be separated and either recycled or eliminated. *Why is fracking controversial?*

Jason Janik/Bloomberg via Getty Images

The federal government also subsidizes the development of alternative fuels. Subsidies to encourage the production of ethanol from corn are controversial. Critics charge that ethanol production is an inefficient method of producing energy. Ethanol also makes food more expensive by driving up the cost of corn. Subsidies for renewable energy sources, such as windmills and solar power panels, have attracted criticisms, too. A problem with wind and especially solar power has been high costs. Prices have fallen rapidly, however, and use of these technologies has risen quickly. Still, they are a small fraction of the nation's power supply.

Disasters in the Energy Industry. For some years, opening new areas for oil and gas drilling has been a major plank in the Republican Party platform. Democrats have been more reluctant, but in March 2010, President Obama announced that major new offshore tracts in the Atlantic would be open to deep-sea drilling. Less than one month later, the BP *Deepwater Horizon* oil spill disaster in the Gulf of Mexico began. The spill, the largest in American history, resulted in a temporary moratorium on new offshore drilling.

Unlike many Democrats, Obama also favored building new energy plants that would use nuclear power. Electric utilities planned several new nuclear plants, but these plans were shelved almost immediately. The major problem was that nuclear power could not compete on cost with natural gas. A second problem was safety. In March 2011, a giant tsunami struck northeast Japan and severely damaged four nuclear reactors located on the coast. The resulting radiation leaks convinced many people that new nuclear power plants would be dangerous.

Climate Change

In the 1990s, many scientists working on climate issues began to conclude that average world temperatures would rise significantly during the twenty-first century. Gases released by human activity, principally carbon dioxide (CO_2), may be producing a "greenhouse effect," trapping the sun's heat and slowing its release into outer space.

The Global Warming Debate. Most scientists who perform research on the world's climate believe that climate change will be significant, but there is considerable disagreement as to how much warming will actually occur. It is generally accepted that world temperatures have already increased by about 0.74 degrees Celsius over the past century. The United Nations' Intergovernmental Panel on Climate Change predicts increases ranging from 1.0 to 4.8 degrees Celsius by 2100. This range of estimates is rather wide and reflects the uncertainties involved in predicting the world's climate.

Global warming has become a major political football to be kicked back and forth by conservatives and liberals. Environmental groups and others have been pressing the federal government to take action now to avert a planet-threatening crisis. Their efforts are complicated by the fact that a major share of the American electorate does not believe that global warming is happening or, if it is happening, that it is caused by human activities. Disbelief in climate change is a partisan phenomenon. According to one poll, skepticism about global warming among Republicans rose by 11 percentage points from 2008 to 2009, and a majority of Republicans now believe that global warming does not exist. The opinions of Democrats have not changed—about four-fifths of them accept that climate change is a problem. If there is no global warming, of course, there would be no reason to limit emissions of CO_2 and other greenhouse gases. By 2014, in the wake of super storms and droughts, skepticism about climate change among Republicans and independents had eased somewhat—but opposition to CO_2 restrictions remained strong.

Recession
Two or more successive quarters in which the economy shrinks instead of grows.

Unemployment
The inability of those who are in the labor force to find a job; also the number of those in the labor force actively looking for a job, but unable to find one.

Inflation
A sustained rise in the general price level of goods and services.

Legislative Stalemate. The centerpiece of the Obama administration's legislative program on energy and the environment was a bill designed to limit greenhouse gas emissions. In June 2009, the House passed a bill, but in the Senate the bill sank without a trace. The Republican takeover of the House in the 2010 elections meant that no action on greenhouse gas emissions was likely in the near future.

Despite the lack of government action, by 2011 CO_2 emissions in the United States were substantially down from 2008. The most important cause was new power plants using natural gas instead of coal. (Gas does release some CO_2, but less than half as much as coal.) More fuel-efficient cars also contributed to the reduction.

Obama and the Environmental Protection Agency. In 2007, in *Massachusetts v. EPA*, the Supreme Court found that the Environmental Protection Agency (EPA) had the authority to regulate the emission of CO_2 and other greenhouse gases under the Clean Air Act.[3] This decision opened up the possibility that the Obama administration might take action against greenhouse gas emissions by electrical power plants without new authority from Congress.

In 2009, the EPA issued a finding that greenhouse gases did in fact threaten the public health and welfare. In 2013, it issued rules covering new power plants. Coal-based power plants were already suffering serious price competition from natural gas, and the EPA's rules made the construction of new coal-based plants almost impossible.

In June 2014, President Obama announced proposed EPA rules covering existing power plants. The rules sought to cut emissions from such plants 30 percent by 2030. States were given a wide menu of options to meet the standards and would not necessarily have to close coal-based plants immediately. The long-term survival of coal-based electricity under the rules, however, appeared bleak. An onslaught of legal and legislative attacks on the proposed rules appeared inevitable.

■ **Learning Outcome 5:**
Define *unemployment, inflation, fiscal policy, net public debt,* and *monetary policy.*

The Politics of Economic Decision Making

Nowhere are the principles of public policymaking more obvious than in the economic decisions made by the federal government. The president and Congress are constantly faced with questions of economic policy. Such issues become especially important when the nation enters a recession.

Good Times, Bad Times

Like any economy that is fundamentally capitalist, the U.S. economy experiences ups and downs. Good times—booms—are followed by lean years. If a slowdown is severe enough, it is called a **recession.** Recessions are characterized by increased **unemployment,** the inability of those who are in the labor force to find a job. The government tries to moderate the effects of such downturns. In contrast, booms are historically associated with another economic problem that the government must address—rising prices, or **inflation.**

Unemployment. Some psychologists say that unemployment is one of the most traumatizing events in a person's life. Certainly, unemployment imposes costs on the entire economy, not just on the unemployed individuals. Since the Great Depression of the 1930s, fighting unemployment has been a major goal of the federal government. The federal government also provides unemployment insurance. Not all unemployed workers are eligible, however. In fact, only about one-third of the unemployed receive benefits.

---

3. 549 U.S. 497 (2007).

Benefits are not available to employees who quit their jobs voluntarily or are fired for cause (for example, constantly showing up late for work). They are also not paid to workers who are entering the labor force for the first time but cannot find a job.

Measuring Unemployment. Estimates of the number of unemployed are prepared by the U.S. Department of Labor. The Bureau of the Census also generates estimates using survey research data. Critics of the published unemployment rate calculated by the federal government believe that it fails to reflect the true numbers of discouraged workers and "hidden unemployed." There is no exact way to measure discouraged workers, however. The Department of Labor defines them as people who have dropped out of the labor force and are no longer looking for a job because they believe that the job market has little to offer them.

High rates of unemployment were one of the most disastrous consequences of the Great Recession, which officially began in December 2007 but entered its most serious stage with the financial crisis of September 2008. In the last months of 2008, the economy was posting net job losses of up to 800,000 each month. The number of job losses peaked in January 2009, at the very start of the Obama administration. Thereafter, the trend line was up, but that was cold comfort for job seekers. Throughout 2009, the employment picture merely got worse ever more slowly. Not until 2010 did the economy actually begin creating jobs again, and even then progress was slow and subject to reversals.

Inflation. Rising prices, or inflation, can also be a serious economic and political problem. Inflation is a sustained upward movement in the average level of prices. Another way of defining inflation is as a decline in the purchasing power of money over time. The government measures inflation using the *consumer price index,* or CPI. The Bureau of Labor Statistics identifies a market basket of goods and services purchased by the typical consumer, and regularly checks the price of that basket. Over a period of many years, inflation can add up. For example, today's dollar is worth (very roughly) about a twentieth of what it was worth a century ago. In effect, today's dollar is a 1915 nickel.

The Business Cycle. Economists refer to the regular succession of economic expansions and contractions as the *business cycle.* An extremely severe recession is called a *depression,* as in the example of the Great Depression of the 1930s. By 1933, actual output was 35 percent below the nation's productive capacity. Unemployment reached 25 percent. Compared with this catastrophe, recessions since 1945 have usually been mild. Nevertheless, the United States has experienced recessions with some regularity. Recession years since 1960 have included 1970, 1974, 1980, 1982, 1990, 2001, and of course 2008 and 2009.

To try to control the ups and downs of the national economy, the government has several policy options. One is to change the level of taxes or government spending. Another possibility involves influencing interest rates and the money side of the economy. We will examine taxing and spending, or **fiscal policy,** first.

> **Fiscal Policy**
> The federal government's use of taxation and spending policies to affect overall business activity.

Job seekers in line for a job fair at a Chicago community college in 2012. When the doors opened, the line was about half a mile long. *Is unemployment still an important issue? Why or why not?*

Scott Olson/Getty Images News/Getty Images

English economist John Maynard Keynes (1883–1946). *What inspired Keynes' theories?*

Fiscal Policy

Fiscal policy is the domain of Congress. A fiscal policy approach to stabilizing the economy is often associated with the twentieth-century British economist John Maynard Keynes (1883–1946). Keynes originated the school of thought that today is called **Keynesian economics,** which supports the use of government spending and taxing to help stabilize the economy. (*Keynesian* is pronounced *kayn*-zee-un.) Keynes believed that there was a need for government intervention in the economy, in part because after falling into a recession or depression, a modern economy may become trapped in an ongoing state of less than full employment.

Government Spending and Borrowing. Keynes developed his fiscal policy theories during the Great Depression of the 1930s. He believed that the forces of supply and demand operated too slowly on their own in such a serious recession. Unemployment meant people had less to spend, and because they could not buy things, more businesses failed, creating additional unemployment. It was a vicious cycle. Keynes's idea was simple: in such circumstances, the *government* should step in and engineer the spending that is needed to return the economy to a more normal state.[4]

The spending promoted by the government could take either of two forms. The government could increase its own spending, or it could cut taxes, allowing the taxpayer to undertake the spending instead. To have the effect Keynes wanted, however, it was essential that the spending be financed by borrowing. In other words, the government should run a **budget deficit**—it should spend more than it receives.

Discretionary Fiscal Policy. Keynes originally developed his fiscal theories as a way of lifting an economy out of a major disaster such as the Great Depression. Beginning with the presidency of John F. Kennedy (1961–1963), however, policymakers have attempted to use Keynesian methods to "fine-tune" the economy. This is discretionary fiscal policy—*discretionary* meaning left to the judgment or discretion of a policymaker.

The Timing Problem. Attempts to fine-tune the economy face a timing problem. It takes a while to collect and assimilate economic data. Therefore, time may go by before an economic problem can be identified. After an economic problem is recognized, a solution must be formulated. There will be an action time lag between the recognition of a problem and the implementation of policy to solve it. Getting Congress to act can easily take a year or two. Finally, after fiscal policy is enacted, it takes time for the policy to act on the economy. Because fiscal policy time lags are long and variable, a policy designed to combat a recession may not produce results until the economy is already out of the recession.

Because of the timing problem, attempts by the government to employ fiscal policy in the past fifty years have typically taken the form of tax cuts or increases. Tax changes can take effect more quickly than government spending. In 2009, therefore, the Obama administration was employing an exceptional approach when it secured from Congress a roughly $900 billion package consisting largely of economic stimulus spending.

Criticisms of Keynes. Following World War II (1939–1945), Keynes's theories were integrated into the mainstream of economic thinking. There have always been economic schools of thought that consider Keynesian economics to be fatally flawed, however.

CONNECT WITH YOUR CLASSMATES
MindTap™ for American Government

Access the Domestic Policy Forum: Discussion—Government Intervention in the Economy

Keynesian Economics

A school of economic thought that tends to favor active federal government policymaking to stabilize economy-wide fluctuations, usually by implementing discretionary fiscal policy.

Budget Deficit

Government expenditures that exceed receipts.

---

4.   Robert Skidelsky, *Keynes: The Return of the Master* (New York: Public Affairs, 2010).

These schools argue that either fiscal policy has no effect or it has negative side effects that outweigh any benefits. Some opponents of fiscal policy believe that the federal government should limit itself to monetary policy, which we will discuss shortly. Others believe that it is best for the government to do nothing at all.

It is worth noting that most voters have neither understood nor accepted Keynesian economics. Despite popular attitudes, politicians of both parties accepted Keynesian ideas for many years. Republican president Richard Nixon (1969–1974) is alleged to have said, "We are all Keynesians now." George W. Bush justified many of his policies using Keynesian language. During the first years of Obama's presidency, however, such thinking among Republicans in Congress vanished almost completely. Instead, Republicans rejected "countercyclical" policies, reflecting the popular belief that during a recession the government should "tighten its belt."

It did not help the Keynesian cause that Obama's 2009 economic stimulus package failed to end high rates of unemployment—Keynesian economists argued that the stimulus was less than half of what was needed to accomplish such a goal. When Obama, in his 2010 State of the Union address, employed the belt-tightening metaphor, Keynesians realized that they had lost control of the political discourse.

The Eclipse of Fiscal Policy. In 2011 and 2012, anti-Keynesian economic proposals dominated the political debate. Both Obama and the Republicans in the House issued competing federal budget plans based on long-term spending cuts. The Republicans also called for immediate cuts in federal and state spending. Yet the unemployment rate remained close to 9 percent, a figure that traditionally would have ruled out short-term efforts to reduce the deficit.

One consequence of the debate was that federal and state spending was, in fact, curbed. Keynesians argued that such steps were prolonging the nation's economic troubles. Conservatives, however, contended that other factors were at work in prolonging unemployment, such as structural changes in the economy and uncertainty resulting from Obama's policies.

Deficit Spending and the Public Debt

The federal government typically borrows by selling U.S. Treasury bills, notes, and bonds, known collectively as *Treasury securities* and informally as **treasuries.** The sale of these federal obligations to corporations, private individuals, pension plans, foreign governments, foreign businesses, and foreign individuals adds to this nation's **public debt, or national debt.** In the past few years, foreign governments, especially those of China and Japan, have come to own about 50 percent of the net U.S. public debt. Thirty years ago, the share of the U.S. public debt held by foreigners was only 15 percent.

The Public Debt. There are two types of public debt—gross and net. The **gross public debt** includes all federal government interagency borrowings, which really do not matter. This is similar to your taking an IOU ("I owe you") out of your left pocket and putting it into your right pocket. Today, federal interagency borrowings account for about $4.8 trillion of the gross public debt. What is important is the **net public debt**—the public debt that does not include interagency borrowing. The best way to examine the relative importance of the public debt is to compare it with the *gross domestic product (GDP),* as is done in Figure 15–8 that follows. (Remember from earlier in this chapter that the gross domestic product is the dollar value of all final goods and services produced in a one-year period.) In the figure, you see that the public debt reached its peak during World War II and fell until 1975. From about 1960 to 2008, the net public debt as a percentage of GDP ranged between 30 and 62 percent.

Treasuries
U.S. Treasury securities—bills, notes, and bonds; debt issued by the federal government.

Public Debt, or National Debt
The total amount of debt carried by the federal government.

Gross Public Debt
The net public debt plus interagency borrowings without the government.

Net Public Debt
The accumulation of all past federal government deficits; the total amount owed by the federal government to individuals, businesses, and foreigners.

Figure 15–8 ▸ **Net Public Debt as a Percentage of Gross Domestic Product**

During World War II, the net public debt as a percentage of GDP grew dramatically. It fell thereafter but rose again from 1980 to 1992, under Republicans Reagan and G. H. W. Bush. The percentage fell under Democrat Clinton. *Why has it risen recently?*

Sources: U.S. Department of the Treasury and Office of Management and Budget.

Note that the net public debt as a percentage of GDP can fall even when the federal government is still running a budget deficit. If the economy is growing faster than the debt, then the debt as a share of the economy will fall even if it is still rising slowly. For example, the government never actually paid off the sums it borrowed to finance World War II. Rather, the economy grew fast enough that over time, the wartime debt ceased to be important.

Are We Always in Debt? From 1960 until the last few years of the twentieth century, the federal government spent more than it received in all but two years. Some observers considered those ongoing budget deficits to be the negative result of Keynesian policies. Others argued that the deficits actually resulted from the abuse of Keynesianism. Politicians have been more than happy to run budget deficits in recessions. They have sometimes refused to implement the other side of Keynes's recommendations—to run a *budget surplus* during boom times, or at least to keep the percentage growth of the debt well below the growth of GDP.

In 1993, however, President Bill Clinton (1993–2001) obtained a tax increase as the nation emerged from a mild recession. Between the tax increase and the "dot-com boom," the United States had a budget surplus each year from 1998 to 2002. Some commentators predicted that we would be running federal government surpluses for years to come.

Back to Deficit Spending. All of those projections went by the wayside because of several events. One event was the "dot-com bust" followed by the 2001–2002 recession, which lowered the rate of growth of not only the economy but also the federal government's tax receipts. Another event was a series of large tax cuts passed by Congress in 2001 and 2003 at the urging of President George W. Bush.

A third event took place on September 11, 2001. As a result of the terrorist attacks, the federal government spent much more than it had planned to spend on security against terrorism. Also, the government had to pay for the war in Iraq in 2003 and the occupation of that country thereafter. Finally, Congress authorized major increases in spending on discretionary programs.

The Great Recession dramatically increased the budget deficit and the level of public debt. Tax revenues collapsed, and spending on such items as unemployment compensation rose automatically. In addition, immediately upon taking office, President Obama obtained legislation from Congress that helped push the public debt to levels not seen since World War II. As noted, such high levels of debt became a major public issue. By 2013, however, due to spending curbs and increased tax collections, the annual federal deficit was falling. From a peak of $1.41 trillion in 2009, the deficit was down to $0.56 trillion in 2015. (As a share of GDP, the drop was from 9.8 percent to 3.1 percent.) As a result of these reductions, the deficit became a less important policy issue.

The Future of Deficit Spending. Can high levels of deficit spending go on forever? Certainly, they can go on for quite a long time for the U.S. government. After all, as long as individuals, businesses, and foreigners (especially foreign governments) are willing to

COMPARE WITH YOUR PEERS
MindTap® for American Government

Access the Economic Policy Forum: Polling Activity—Reforming Social Security purchase Treasury securities, the government can continue to engage in deficit spending. Still, before the onset of the Great Recession, most economists feared that if high levels of deficit spending went on long enough, the rest of the world—which owns about 50 percent of all Treasury securities—might lose faith in our government. Consequently, U.S. government borrowing might become more expensive. A vicious cycle might occur—more deficit spending could lead to higher interest rate costs on the U.S. debt, leading in turn to even larger deficits.

So far, however, there has been little sign that such a problem is imminent. On the contrary, following the financial crisis that struck on September 15, 2008, panicked investors piled into treasuries in the belief that these were the safest instruments in existence. The interest that the U.S. government must pay on its borrowing is also very low. In May 2014, the average interest rate on four-week Treasury bills—the shortest-term Treasury obligations—was 0.025 percent—for all practical purposes, an interest rate of zero. Correcting for inflation, anyone buying short-term treasuries was paying the U.S. government for the privilege of making loans to it. These developments have convinced some economists that as long as the dollar remains the world's dominant currency, "runs" on the dollar are not actually possible.

Monetary Policy

Controlling the rate of growth of the money supply is called **monetary policy.** This policy is the domain of the **Federal Reserve System,** also known simply as the **Fed.** The Fed is the most important regulatory agency in the U.S. monetary system.

The Fed performs a number of important functions. Perhaps the Fed's most important task is regulating the amount of money in circulation, which can be defined loosely as checking account balances and currency. The Fed also provides a system for transferring checks from one bank to another. In addition, it holds reserves deposited by most of the nation's banks, savings and loan associations, savings banks, and credit unions. Finally, it plays a role in supervising the banking industry.

Organization of the Federal Reserve System. A board of governors manages the Fed. This board consists of seven full-time members appointed by the president with the approval of the Senate. There are twelve Federal Reserve district banks. The most important unit within the Fed is the **Federal Open Market Committee.** This is the body that actually determines the future growth of the money supply and other important economy-wide financial variables. This committee is composed of the members of the Board of Governors, the president of the New York Federal Reserve Bank, and presidents of four other Federal Reserve banks, rotated periodically.

The Board of Governors of the Federal Reserve System is independent. The president can attempt to influence the board, and Congress can threaten to merge the Fed into the Treasury Department, but as long as the Fed retains its

Monetary Policy
The use of changes in the amount of money in circulation to alter credit markets, employment, and the rate of inflation.

Federal Reserve System (the Fed)
The agency created by Congress in 1913 to serve as the nation's central banking organization.

Federal Open Market Committee
The most important body within the Federal Reserve System. The Federal Open Market Committee decides how monetary policy should be carried out.

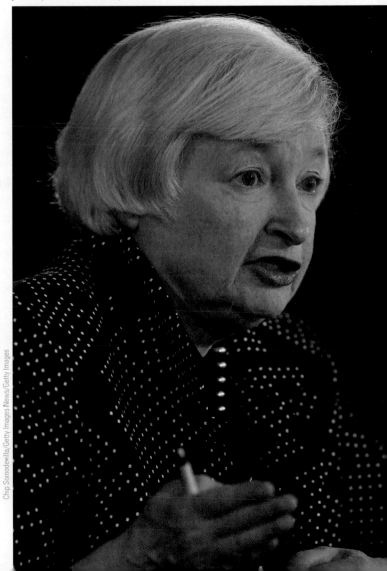

Federal Reserve Chair Janet Yellen at a news conference in 2014. *How powerful is the chair of the Fed?*

Chip Somodevilla/Getty Images News/Getty Images

Loose Monetary Policy
Monetary policy that makes credit inexpensive and abundant, possibly leading to inflation.

Tight Monetary Policy
Monetary policy that makes credit expensive in an effort to slow inflation.

independence, its chairperson and governors can do what they please. Hence, any talk about "the president's monetary policy" or "Congress's monetary policy" is inaccurate. The Fed remains an independent entity.

Loose and Tight Monetary Policies. The Federal Reserve System seeks to stabilize nationwide economic activity by controlling the amount of money in circulation. Changing the amount of money in circulation is a major aspect of monetary policy.

Credit, like any good or service, has a cost. The cost of borrowing—the interest rate—is similar to the cost of any other aspect of doing business. When the cost of borrowing falls, businesspersons undertake more investment projects. When it rises, businesspersons undertake fewer projects. Consumers also react to interest rates when deciding whether to borrow funds to buy houses, cars, or other "big-ticket" items.

If the Fed implements a **loose monetary policy** (often called an "expansionary" policy), the supply of credit increases and its cost falls. If the Fed implements a **tight monetary policy** (often called a "contractionary" policy), the supply of credit falls (or fails to grow) and its cost increases. A loose money policy is often implemented to encourage economic growth. You may be wondering why any nation would want a tight money policy. The answer is to control inflation. If money becomes too plentiful too quickly, prices on average increase, and the purchasing power of the dollar decreases.

Time Lags for Monetary Policy. You learned earlier that policymakers who implement fiscal policy—the manipulation of budget deficits and the tax system—experience problems with time lags. The Fed faces similar problems when it implements monetary policy.

Sometimes, accurate information about the economy is not available for months. Once the state of the economy is known, time may elapse before any policy can be put into effect. Still, the time lag in implementing monetary policy is usually much shorter than the lag in implementing fiscal policy. The Federal Open Market Committee meets eight times a year and can put a policy into effect relatively quickly. A change in the money supply may not have an effect for several months, however.

Monetary Policy during Recessions. A tight monetary policy is effective as a way of taming inflation. (Some would argue that it is the *only* way that inflation can be stopped.) If interest rates go high enough, people *will* stop borrowing. How effective, though, is a loose monetary policy at ending a recession? Under normal conditions, it is very effective. A loose monetary policy will spur an expansion in economic activity.

To combat the Great Recession, however, the Fed reduced its interest rate effectively to zero. It could not go any lower. Yet when consumers had credit, they were still reluctant to make major purchases. Many businesses found that they had little need to borrow to invest in new activities—and no need to hire new staff. Overall demand for goods and services was so low that companies could produce all they needed with their existing capacity and workforce. Monetary policy had run out of steam—using it was like "pushing on a string." The government has little power to force banks to lend, and it certainly has no power to make people borrow and spend. As a result, the Obama administration placed its bets on fiscal policy.

Why Should You Care about...

Domestic Policy?

Your life can be affected by programs such as Medicare, Medicaid, Social Security, unemployment compensation, and several others. These are known as *entitlement programs* because if you meet certain qualifications—of age or income, for example—you are entitled to specified benefits. The federal government can estimate how much it will have to pay out in entitlements but cannot set an exact figure in advance. In this way, entitlement spending differs from other government spending. Along with national defense, entitlements make up by far the greatest share of the federal budget. This fact led a Bush administration staff member to joke: "It helps to think of the government as an insurance company with an army."

Quantitative Easing and Forward Guidance. During 2008 and 2009, the Fed developed a new way to respond to the failure of banks to lend. Relying on its ability to create money, it began to make loans itself, without turning to Congress for appropriations. The Fed bought debt issued by corporations. It bought securities that were based on student loans and credit-card debt. By 2009, the Fed had loaned out close to $2 trillion in fresh credit. In 2010 and 2011, the Fed implemented yet another new policy, called *quantitative easing,* in an attempt to make monetary policy more effective. Quantitative easing essentially means buying quantities of long-term treasuries and mortgage-backed securities to hold down long-term interest rates.

In December 2013, the Fed began a policy of *tapering.* Under this plan, the Fed will slowly reduce the size of its quantitative easing purchases. The Fed has also developed a program of *forward guidance* that will remain in effect even when quantitative easing purchases have been reduced to zero. Under current forward guidance policies, the Fed will not allow an increase in the interest rates that it effectively controls for many years to come.

> ### did you know?
> It costs the U.S. Mint 2.41 cents to make a penny and 11.18 cents to make a nickel.

The Politics of Taxes

■ **Learning Outcome 6:** Describe the various taxes that Americans pay, and discuss some of the controversies surrounding taxation.

Federal taxes are enacted by Congress. Today, the Internal Revenue Code, which is the federal tax code, encompasses thousands of pages, thousands of sections, and thousands of subsections—our tax system is not very simple.

Americans pay a variety of taxes. At the federal level, the income tax is levied on most sources of income. Social Security and Medicare taxes are assessed on wages and salaries. There is an income tax for corporations, which has an indirect effect on many individuals. The estate tax is collected from property left behind by those who have died. State and local governments also assess taxes on income, sales, and land. Altogether, the value of all taxes collected by the federal government and by state and local governments is more than 24 percent of GDP. This is a substantial sum, but it is less than what many other countries collect, as you can see in Figure 15–9.

Federal Income Tax Rates

Individuals and businesses pay income taxes based on tax rates. Not all of your income is taxed at the same rate. The first few dollars of income that you earn are not taxed at all. The highest rate is imposed on the "last" dollar you make. This highest rate is the *marginal* tax rate. Table 15–1 that follows shows the 2014 marginal tax rates for individuals and married couples (which applied to income earned in the previous year, 2013). The higher the tax rate—the action on the part of the government—the greater the public's reaction to that tax rate. If the highest tax rate you pay on the income you make is 15 percent, then any method you can use to reduce your taxable income by one dollar saves you fifteen cents in tax liabilities that you owe to the federal government.

Figure 15–9 ▶ **Total Amount of Taxes Collected as a Percentage of Gross Domestic Product (GDP) in Major Industrialized Nations**

Why might the United States collect less in taxes than many other advanced nations?

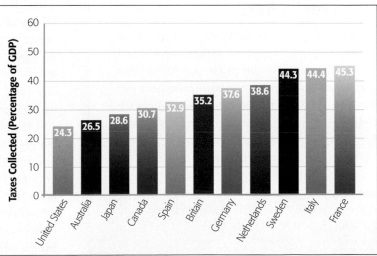

Source: Excerpted and adapted from the Organization for Economic Cooperation and Development.

Table 15–1 ▸ **Marginal Tax Rates for Single Persons and Married Couples (2014)**

How likely is it that people in the 10 percent bracket will actually have to pay income taxes?

Marginal Tax Bracket	Single Persons	Married Filing Jointly
10%	Up to $9,075	Up to $18,150
15%	9,076 to 36,900	18,151 to 73,800
25%	36,901 to 89,350	73,801 to 148,850
28%	89,351 to 186,350	148,851 to 226,850
33%	186,351 to 405,100	226,851 to 405,100
35%	405,101 to 406,750	405,101 to 457,600
39.6%	406,751 or more	457,601 or more

did you know?

In 2014, the difference between the marginal income tax brackets of 35 percent and 39.6 percent was only $1,650 for individuals. This happened because a surcharge to pay for the Affordable Care Act was not coordinated with the IRS's standard tax brackets.

Why Should You Care about...

Domestic Policy?

What happens to entitlements will affect your life in two major ways. Entitlement spending will largely determine how much you pay in taxes throughout your working lifetime. Entitlement policy will also determine how much support you receive from the federal government when you grow old. Also, because entitlements make up such a large share of the federal budget, it is not possible to address the issue of budget deficits without considering entitlement spending. However these programs are changed, you will feel the financial effects throughout your life.

Individuals paying a 15 percent rate have a relatively small incentive to avoid paying taxes, but consider the individuals who faced a marginal tax rate of 94 percent in the 1940s, during and after World War II. They had a tremendous incentive to find legal ways to reduce their taxable incomes. For every dollar of income that was somehow deemed nontaxable, these taxpayers would reduce tax liabilities by ninety-four cents.

Loopholes and Lowered Taxes

Individuals and corporations facing high tax rates will adjust their earning and spending behavior to reduce their taxes. They will also make concerted attempts to get Congress to add **loopholes** to the tax law that allow them to reduce their taxable incomes. When Congress imposed very high tax rates on high incomes, it also provided for more loopholes than it does today. For example, special provisions enabled investors in oil and gas wells to reduce their taxable incomes.

Progressive and Regressive Taxation. As Table 15–1 shows, the greater your taxable income, the higher the marginal tax rate. Persons with large incomes pay a larger share of their income in income tax. A tax system in which rates go up with income is called a **progressive tax** system. The federal income tax is clearly progressive.

The income tax is not the only tax you must pay. For example, the federal Social Security tax is levied on all wage and salary income at a flat rate of 6.2 percent. (Employers pay another 6.2 percent, making the total effective rate 12.4 percent.) In 2014, however, there was no Social Security tax on wages and salaries in excess of $117,000. (This "cap" changes from year to year.) Persons with very high salaries, therefore, pay no Social Security tax on much of their wages. In addition, the tax is not levied on investment income (including capital gains, rents, royalties, interest, dividends, and profits from a business). The wealthy receive a much greater share of their income from these sources than others do. As a result, the wealthy pay a much smaller portion of their income in Social Security taxes than do the working poor.

The Social Security tax is therefore a **regressive tax.** To fund Medicare, a combined employer/employee 2.9 percent tax is also assessed on all wage income. The income of individuals that exceeds $200,000, however, is subject to a rate of 3.8 percent. For married couples filing jointly, the threshold is $250,000. Note that three-quarters of all taxpayers owe more in payroll taxes, such as Social Security and Medicare taxes, than they do in income taxes.

Who Pays? The question of whether the tax system should be progressive—and if so, to what degree—is subject to vigorous political debate. Democrats in general and liberals in particular favor a tax system that is significantly progressive. Republicans and conservatives are more likely to prefer a tax system that is proportional or even regressive.

Overall, what kind of tax system do we have? The various taxes Americans pay pull in different directions. The federal estate tax is extremely progressive, because it is not imposed at all on smaller estates. Sales taxes are regressive because the wealthy spend a relatively smaller portion of their income on items subject to the sales tax. Table 15–2 that follows lists the characteristics of major taxes. Add everything up, and the tax system as a whole is slightly progressive. Given all this, should the rich pay even more in taxes? We look at that question in the *Which Side Are You On?* feature that follows.

> **Regressive Tax**
> A tax that falls in percentage terms as incomes rise.

> **did you know?**
> About 57 percent of all income tax returns are filled in by paid preparers.

Table 15–2 ▶
Progressive versus Regressive Taxes

Progressive Taxes
Federal income tax
State income taxes
Federal corporate income tax
Estate tax
Medicare tax

Regressive Taxes
Social Security tax
State sales taxes
Local real estate taxes

Residents stand in line to file their federal income tax returns on the last legal day. *Why do some taxpayers wait until the last day?*

Which Side Are You On?

Does Our Tax System Promote Excessive Inequality?

The rich have gotten richer—of that we are certain. In 1980, the top-earning 1 percent of U.S. residents collected 9.3 percent of the nation's income. Thirty-five years later, the top 1 percent of income earners received 22.5 percent.

Don't Kill the Geese That Lay the Golden Eggs

It is true that top income earners now receive more of the national income than they did thirty-five years ago. Yet since then, the share of federal income taxes paid by the top 1 percent of earners has increased from 18 percent to 35 percent. The top 1 percent pays more than one-third of all income taxes.

Many Americans pay no federal income tax at all (though this lower-income group does pay Social Security, Medicare, and other taxes). Many actually receive more through the income tax system than they pay. The Earned Income Tax Credit substantially reduces the Social Security and Medicare taxes of working families with children and incomes below about $50,000.

Usually, those with really large incomes have earned them. Today, we live in a global society. Globalization increases the rewards earned by the very best, whether in entertainment or in business. People all over the world are willing to pay J. K. Rowling so they can read about Harry Potter. They vastly outnumber those who were once willing to pay, say, Charles Dickens.

If we use taxes to "soak the rich," we will tax the most productive individuals in the country. High marginal tax rates discourage effort. The higher the rate, the greater the discouragement, and this will reduce the rate of economic growth. More income will be redistributed, but is that the ultimate goal of our society? The American way is to celebrate the best.

Yes, the Rich Should Pay More in Taxes

If in the future we don't slash Social Security, Medicare, and similar programs, eventually we will need to raise taxes. It seems appropriate that those who have benefited the most from America's economic system should pay more. They can afford it, and that's where the money is.

Furthermore, the increasing concentration of wealth into fewer and fewer hands threatens to turn American society into something unrecognizable. The children of today's top earners are on their way to becoming a new aristocracy that gets its wealth from inheritance, not striving.

Economist Thomas Piketty, in his controversial best-seller *Capital in the Twentieth Century*, argues that our economic system naturally generates inequality. Wealth earns new wealth faster than labor can earn it. True, inequality fell in much of the twentieth century because wars and depressions destroyed vast amounts of wealth. After World War II, inequality did not rise again because top marginal federal income tax rates exceeded 90 percent. That didn't stop the economy from growing. Today, these rates are about 40 percent, and inequality is soaring.

When the U.S. income tax was introduced in the early twentieth century, its sponsors didn't see it merely as a way to fund the government. They also saw it as a way to protect the Republic by curbing the growth of vast fortunes. Once, Americans knew that there is a point at which inequality becomes incompatible with democracy. We need to relearn that.

For Critical Analysis

Is it possible that higher taxes—and a lower after-tax income—could actually make some people work more?

How You Can Make a Difference

Should Medicare and Social Security benefits be high, with the understanding that taxes must therefore go up? Should these programs be cut back in the hope of avoiding deficits and tax increases? Do entitlements mean that the old are fleecing the young—or is that argument irrelevant because we will all grow old someday? Progressives and conservatives disagree strongly about these questions. You can develop your own opinions by learning more about entitlement reform. The following organizations take a conservative position on entitlements:

- National Center for Policy Analysis. Find its Web page on entitlement reform at www.ncpa.org/retirement.
- The Heritage Foundation. See what it has to say at www .heritage.org/issues/retirement-security.

The following organizations take a liberal stand on entitlements:

- National Committee to Preserve Social Security and Medicare presents its views at www.ncpssm.org.
- AARP (formerly the American Association of Retired Persons) defends retirement benefits at www.aarp.org/work /social-security.

Key Terms

Affordable Care Act 432
budget deficit 448
domestic policy 432
Federal Open Market Committee 451
Federal Reserve System (the Fed) 451
fiscal policy 447
fracking 444

gross domestic product (GDP) 433
gross public debt 449
incarceration rate 442
individual mandate 435
inflation 446
Keynesian economics 448
loophole 454

loose monetary policy 452
Medicaid 433
Medicare 433
monetary policy 451
net public debt 449
progressive tax 454
public debt, or national debt 449

recession 446
regressive tax 455
tight monetary policy 452
treasuries 449
unemployment 446
universal health insurance 434

Chapter Summary

Learning Outcome 1 Domestic policy consists of all laws, government planning, and government actions that concern internal issues of national importance. Policies are created in response to public problems or public demand for government action. The policymaking process is initiated when policymakers become aware—through the media or from their constituents—of a problem that needs to be addressed by the legislature and the president. The process of policymaking includes five steps: agenda building, policy formulation, policy adoption, policy implementation, and policy evaluation. Policy actions typically result in both costs and benefits for society.

Health-care spending accounts for more than 18 percent of the U.S. economy and is growing. Reasons for this growth

include the increasing number of elderly persons and advancing technology. A major source of funding is Medicare, the federal program that pays health-care expenses of U.S. residents over the age of sixty-five. The federal government has tried to restrain the growth in Medicare spending.

More than 13 percent of the population does not have health insurance—a major political issue. Individual health-insurance policies (not obtained through an employer) are expensive and may be unobtainable at any price. In most wealthy countries, this problem is addressed by a universal health-insurance system under which the government provides basic coverage to all citizens. In 2010, Congress passed a health-care reform package that in time will provide near-universal coverage in the United States. It will require residents not already covered to purchase coverage, which will be subsidized for low-income persons.

Learning Outcome 2 Today, more than 1 million immigrants enter the United States each year, and about 13 percent of the U.S. population consists of foreign-born persons. Illegal immigrants may number about 11 million. The status of these unauthorized immigrants (the Department of Homeland Security term) is a major political issue. Some people wish to give such persons a legally recognized status and allow them to become citizens someday. Others call for tougher laws against illegal immigration and against hiring illegal entrants.

Learning Outcome 3 There is widespread concern in this country about violent crime. The overall rate of violent crime has declined since 1995, however. In response to crime concerns, the United States has incarcerated an unusually large number of persons, compared to other countries.

Learning Outcome 4 Issues concerning energy and the environment are on the nation's agenda today. One problem is our reliance on petroleum imports, given that many petroleum exporters are hostile to American interests. In recent years, however, new production techniques such as fracking have increased the domestic supply of crude oil and especially of natural gas. Global warming, caused by the emission of CO_2 and other greenhouse gases, is a second major problem, although some dispute how serious it actually is.

Learning Outcome 5 Fiscal policy is the use of taxes and spending to affect the overall economy. Time lags in implementing fiscal policy can create serious difficulties. The federal government has run a deficit in most years since 1960. The deficit is met by U.S. Treasury borrowing. This adds to the public debt of the U.S. government. Although the budget was temporarily in surplus from 1998 to 2002, large deficits now seem likely for many years to come.

Monetary policy is controlled by the Federal Reserve System, or the Fed. Monetary policy consists of changing the rate of growth of the money supply in an attempt to either stimulate or cool the economy. A loose monetary policy, in which more money is created, encourages economic growth. A tight monetary policy, in which less money is created, may be the only effective way of ending an inflationary spiral.

Learning Outcome 6 U.S. taxes are about 25 percent of the gross domestic product. Individuals and corporations that pay taxes at the highest rates will try to pressure Congress into creating exemptions and tax loopholes. Loopholes allow high-income earners to reduce their taxable incomes. The federal income tax is progressive—tax rates increase as income increases. Some other taxes, such as the Social Security tax and state sales taxes, are regressive—they take a larger share of the income of poorer people.

Master the concepts of Domestic Policy and Economic Policy with MindTap™ *for American Government*

REVIEW MindTap™ for American Government
Access Key Term Flashcards for Chapter 15.

STAY CURRENT MindTap™ for American Government
Access the KnowNow blog and customized RSS for updates on current events.

TEST YOURSELF MindTap™ for American Government
Take the Wrap It Up Quiz for Chapter 15.

STAY FOCUSED MindTap™ for American Government
Complete the Focus Activities for Domestic Policy and Economic Policy.

Additional Resources

Today, the Internet offers opportunities for you to easily access information about any issue. The *Online Resources* section that follows lists a variety of Web sites where you can learn more about domestic policy issues and how they affect you.

Online Resources

- For data on the 2014 and 2015 budgets of the U.S. government, see the site of the Office of Management and Budget at www.whitehouse.gov/omb.
- You can examine the opinions of two groups with opposing views on immigration. Fwd.us, at www.fwd.us/immigration_reform, is sponsored by high-tech firms that favor immigration. The Federation for American Immigration Reform, at www.fairus.org, opposes any reforms that would allow illegal immigrants to remain in the country.
- The Federal Bureau of Investigation offers uniform information about crime rates at www.fbi.gov/about-us/cjis/ucr.
- Matthew Yglesias offers interesting commentary on economics and society from a liberal, free-market point of view. Follow him at www.vox.com/authors/matthew-yglesias.
- Harvard economics professor Greg Mankiw reviews economic events from a moderate conservative perspective. Find him at gregmankiw.blogspot.com.

Books

Levi, Michael. *The Power Surge: Energy, Opportunity, and the Battle for America's Future.* New York: Oxford University Press, 2013. Levi examines the developments that have dramatically increased U.S. energy production. These include both fracking and other methods of recovering fossil fuels, and also newly affordable renewable technologies.

Levi's highly regarded work attempts to provide a balanced evaluation of both sources. Levi is a senior fellow at the Council on Foreign Relations.

Piketty, Thomas. *Capital in the Twenty-First Century* (Arthur Goldhammer, translator). Cambridge, Mass.: Belknap Press, 2014. This book, the controversial economics blockbuster of 2014, contains vast amounts of information on inequality of wealth and income. Piketty's basic argument, though, is simple: without high taxes on the rich, our capitalist system naturally produces growing inequality. Piketty is a professor at the Paris School of Economics.

Yagoda, Lisa, and Nicole Duritz. *Affordable Care Act for Dummies.* Hoboken, N.J.: For Dummies (Wiley), 2014. The Affordable Care Act, or Obamacare, is an immensely complex set of changes to the health-care system. Who better to explain a complicated topic than the folks at the For Dummies series? The authors are AARP staff members.

Video

An Inconvenient Truth—A 2006 Paramount Classics production of former vice president Al Gore's Oscar-winning documentary on climate change and actions that can be taken in response to this challenge.

The Other Side of Immigration—Based on more than seven hundred interviews, this documentary by Roy Germano asks why so many Mexicans come to the United States, and what happens to the families and communities they leave behind.

Quiz

Multiple Choice and Fill-Ins

Learning Outcome 1 Describe the five steps of the policymaking process, using the health-care reform legislation as an example.

1. The policymaking process includes, but is not limited to:
    a. agenda building, policy formulation, and policy adoption.
    b. agenda building, policy formulation, and judicial approval.
    c. agenda building, policy formulation, and state referendums.

2. The last two phases of the policymaking process involve policy _____ and policy _____.

Learning Outcome 2 Explain why illegal immigration is seen as a problem, and cite some of the steps that have been taken in response to it.

3. Within U.S. borders, illegal immigrants number as many as:
    a. 3 million.
    b. 11 million.
    c. 23 million.

4. Latino citizens have tended to vote for the _____ Party.

Learning Outcome 3 Discuss recent developments in crime rates and incarceration.

5. The incarceration rate is defined as:
    a. the number of people in prison or jail for every 1,000 persons.
    b. the number of people in prison or jail for every 100,000 persons.
    c. the number of people in prison or jail for every 1,000,000 persons.

6. Over the last twenty years, homicide and violent crime rates in America have _____.

Learning Outcome 4 Evaluate the federal government's responses to high oil prices and the controversy over global warming.

7. A major new source of increased energy supplies within the United States comes from:
    a. running existing wells at a faster pace.
    b. nuclear power.
    c. fracking (hydraulic fracturing).

8. Emissions of carbon dioxide (CO_2) have fallen since 2008 in part because of the increased use of _____ in power plants.

Learning Outcome 5 Define *unemployment, inflation, fiscal policy, net public debt,* and *monetary policy.*

9. Fiscal policy involves:
    a. government spending and changes in the money supply in circulation.
    b. government taxation and the changes in the money supply in circulation.
    c. government taxing and spending policies.

10. When an economic slowdown is severe enough, it is officially called a _____, which is characterized by increased _____.

Learning Outcome 6 Describe the various taxes that Americans pay, and discuss some of the controversies surrounding taxation.

11. The federal personal income tax system can be called:
    a. a progressive tax.
    b. a regressive tax.
    c. a degressive tax.

12. Americans who work for a salary typically pay federal income taxes, as well as payroll taxes that fund _____ and _____.

Essay Questions

1. Just how serious an offense should illegal immigration be? Construct arguments in favor of considering it a felony and arguments for viewing it as a mere civil infraction.

2. Until recently, Congress always opposed the establishment of a universal health-insurance system for the United States. What could the reasons for this stance have been? Are the reasons compelling? What political interests might oppose a universal system, and why?

Answers to questions: 1. a, 2. implementation/evaluation, 3. b, 4. Democratic, 5. b, 6. fallen, 7. c, 8. natural gas, 9. c, 10. recession/unemployment, 11. a, 12. Social Security/Medicare.

Foreign Policy

A U.S. paratrooper in 2014 after a military exercise in Lithuania—an American ally. Lithuania borders Russia and feels threatened by Russia's aggression in Ukraine. *How far is Russia likely to go?*

Petras Malukas/AFP/Getty Images

The five learning outcomes below are designed to help improve your understanding of this chapter. After reading this chapter, you should be able to:

■ **Learning Outcome 1:** Define *foreign policy*, and discuss moral idealism versus political realism in foreign policy.

■ **Learning Outcome 2:** Describe recent foreign policy challenges that involve the use of force.

■ **Learning Outcome 3:** Discuss the use of diplomacy in addressing such issues as nuclear proliferation, the rise of China, and the confrontation between Israel and the Palestinians.

■ **Learning Outcome 4:** Explain the role of the president, executive agencies, and Congress in making U.S. foreign policy.

■ **Learning Outcome 5:** Cite the main themes in the history of U.S. foreign policy.

▶ **WATCH & LEARN** MindTap° for American Government
Watch a brief "What Do You Know?" video summarizing Foreign Policy and National Security.

What If...

We Brought Back the Draft?

BACKGROUND

Young people today have no direct memory of the draft—forced military conscription—because military service became voluntary in 1973. From 1948 to 1973, however, all American males were subject to the draft. Required military service provided large forces to confront the Soviet Union during the Cold War (a period you will read about in this chapter). The draft was used during the war in Vietnam (1965–1975), when it became a heated issue. A few years ago, the idea of bringing back the draft reappeared in public debate. In 2006 and 2007, members of Congress and of George W. Bush's administration suggested that the draft be reinstated. In recent years, however, because of high unemployment and the drawdown of forces in Iraq and Afghanistan, the military has had no difficulty in filling its enlistment quotas. As a result, there has been less talk of a draft.

WHAT IF WE BROUGHT BACK THE DRAFT?

If the draft was reinstated, the U.S. Selective Service would once again be a powerful bureaucratic organization. At the height of the Vietnam War, many young men over the age of eighteen focused much of their attention on avoiding the draft. The same might be true if we brought the draft back today.

Today, the pool of draft-eligible men (and women, if they are included) is much larger than required by the U.S. military. Even though the military has recently been stretched thin, "boots on the ground" are becoming less important as the military continues to evolve toward technological warfare. At the peak of the Vietnam War, there were more than 500,000 U.S. troops in Southeast Asia. At the 2010 peak, the United States fielded 112,000 troops in Iraq and 57,000 in Afghanistan, for a total of 169,000. Consequently, the Selective Service might have to create more deferments than were available during the Vietnam War.

BENEFITS OF A DRAFT

At various times during the Iraq and Afghanistan wars, the Department of Defense was forced to extend tours of duty for units that were about to be brought home. A draft would prevent these kinds of troop shortages. In particular, a draft would eliminate the unfairness involved in stationing National Guard troops abroad for long periods of time.

If we brought back the draft, the U.S. military would include children of wealthy families, unlike the situation today. In principle, therefore, service to one's country would become more evenly distributed across social and economic classes. Some argue that a draft would cause Congress and the president to think differently about military operations. If the children of senators and representatives were drafted and sent to dangerous regions, those leaders might be more cautious about going to war.

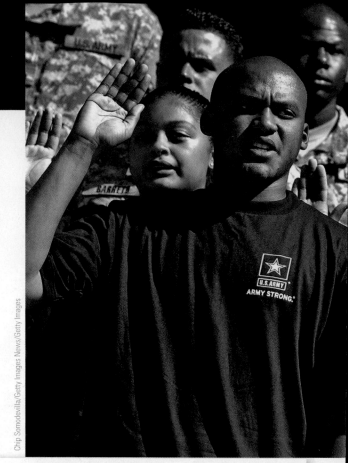

"Future soldiers" take the oath of enlistment as they join the U.S. Army. *What effect might the volunteer army have on the quality of recruits?*

THE DRAFT AS A TAX ON THE YOUNG

Typically, draftees are paid nominal amounts—less than they could earn in the civilian sector. It is not necessary to pay draftees the relatively high salaries and benefits required to induce young Americans to volunteer for military service. As a result, with a draft, federal expenditures for military pay would decline. The financial burden of staging military actions abroad would fall in part on the draftees themselves. They would effectively be paying a tax consisting of the difference between what they could earn outside the U.S. military and what they were paid by the military.

For Critical Analysis

1. Some argue that the volunteer nature of our U.S. military is responsible for the relatively small antiwar movement in this country today. Why might that be so?

2. What alternatives to military service might be possible?

On September 11, 2001, Americans were forced to change their view of national security and of their relations with the rest of the world—literally overnight. No longer could citizens of the United States believe that national security issues involved only threats overseas or that the American homeland could not be attacked.

Within a few days, it became known that the 9/11 attacks on the World Trade Center and on the Pentagon had been planned and carried out by a terrorist network named al Qaeda that was directed by the radical Islamist leader Osama bin Laden. The network was closely linked to the Taliban government of Afghanistan, which had ruled that nation since 1996.

Americans were shocked by the success of the attacks. They wondered how our airport security systems could have failed so drastically. Shouldn't our intelligence community have known about and defended against this terrorist network? How could our foreign policy have been so blind to the anger of Islamist groups throughout the world?

In this chapter, we examine the tools of foreign policy and national security policy in light of the many challenges facing the United States today. One such challenge for U.S. foreign policymakers is how best to respond to the threat of terrorism. A question raised by the resulting U.S. military commitments was whether we needed to bring back the draft, as we discussed in the chapter-opening *What If . . .* feature. We also review the history of American foreign policy.

Facing the World: Foreign and Defense Policies

The United States is only one nation in a world with almost two hundred independent countries, many located in regions where armed conflict is ongoing. What tools does our nation have to deal with the many challenges to its peace and prosperity? One tool is **foreign policy.** By this term, we mean both the goals the government wants to achieve in the world and the techniques and strategies used to achieve them. These techniques and strategies include **diplomacy, economic aid, technical assistance,** and military intervention. Sometimes foreign policies are restricted to statements of goals or ideas, such as the goal of helping to end world poverty. At other times, foreign policies involve comprehensive efforts to achieve particular objectives, such as preventing Iran from obtaining nuclear weapons.

As you will read later in this chapter, in the United States the *foreign policy process* usually originates with the president and those agencies that provide advice on foreign policy matters. Congressional action and national public debate often affect foreign policy formulation as well.

National Security and Defense Policies

As one aspect of overall foreign policy, **national security policy** is designed primarily to protect the independence and the political integrity of the United States. It concerns itself with the defense of the United States against actual or potential future enemies.

U.S. national security policy is based on determinations made by the Department of Defense, the Department of State, and a number of other federal agencies, including the National Security Council (NSC). The NSC acts as an advisory body to the president, but it has often been a rival to the State Department in influencing the foreign policy process.

Defense policy is a subset of national security policy. Generally, defense policy refers to the set of policies that direct the nature and activities of the U.S. armed forces. Defense policy also considers the types of armed forces units we need to have, such as rapid response forces or Marine expeditionary forces, and the types of weaponry that should be

LISTEN & LEARN
MindTap for American Government

Access Read Speaker to listen to Chapter 16.

■ **Learning Outcome 1:**
Define *foreign policy*, and discuss moral idealism versus political realism in foreign policy.

Foreign Policy
A nation's external goals and the techniques and strategies used to achieve them.

Diplomacy
The process by which nations carry on political relations with one another and resolve conflicts by peaceful means.

Economic Aid
Assistance to other nations in the form of grants, loans, or credits to buy the assisting nation's products.

Technical Assistance
The practice of sending experts in such areas as agriculture, engineering, or business to aid other nations.

National Security Policy
Foreign and domestic policy designed to protect the nation's independence and political integrity; policy that is concerned with the safety and defense of the nation.

Defense Policy
A subset of national security policy having to do with the U.S. armed forces.

developed and maintained for the nation's security. Defense policies are proposed by the leaders of the nation's military forces and the secretary of defense, and these policies are greatly influenced by congressional decision makers.

Diplomacy

Diplomacy is another aspect of foreign policy. Diplomacy includes all of a nation's external relationships, from routine diplomatic communications to summit meetings among heads of state. More specifically, diplomacy refers to the settling of disputes and conflicts among nations by peaceful methods. Diplomacy is also the set of negotiating techniques by which a nation attempts to carry out its foreign policy. Of course, diplomacy can be successful only if the parties are willing to negotiate.

Idealism versus Realism in Foreign Policy

Since the earliest years of the republic, Americans have felt that their nation has a special destiny. The American experiment in political and economic liberty, it was thought, would provide the best possible life for its citizens and be a model for other nations. As the United States assumed greater status as a power in world politics, Americans came to believe that the nation's actions on the world stage should be guided by American political and moral principles.

Moral Idealism

A philosophy that sees nations as normally willing to cooperate and agree on moral standards for conduct.

Political Realism

A philosophy that sees each nation acting principally in its own interests.

Moral Idealism. This view of America's mission has led to the adoption of many foreign policy initiatives that are rooted in **moral idealism.** This philosophy views the world as fundamentally benign and assumes that most nations can be persuaded to take moral considerations into account when setting their policies.[1] In this perspective, nations should come together and agree to keep the peace, as President Woodrow Wilson (1913–1921) proposed for the League of Nations. Many foreign policy initiatives taken by the United States have been based on this idealistic view of the world. These include humanitarian relief efforts following great natural disasters. For example, the United States provided aid to Haiti after the earthquake of 2010, and to Japan after the tsunami of 2011.

Political Realism. In opposition to the moral perspective is **political realism.** Realists see the world as a dangerous place in which each nation strives for its own survival and interests, regardless of moral considerations. The United States must therefore base its foreign policy decisions on cold calculations without regard to morality. Realists believe that the United States must be prepared to defend itself militarily, because other nations are, by definition, dangerous. A strong defense will show the world that the United States is willing to protect its interests.

The practice of political realism in foreign policy allows the United States to sell weapons to military dictators who will support its policies, to support American business around the globe, and to repel terrorism through the use of force.

American Foreign Policy—A Mixture of Both. It is important to note that the United States has never been guided by only one of these principles. Instead, both moral idealism and political realism affect foreign policymaking. At times, idealism and realism can pull in different directions, making it difficult to establish a coherent policy. The so-called Arab Spring of 2011 serves as an example of such crosscurrents in American foreign policy.

---

1. Eugene R. Wittkopf, Charles W. Kegley, and James M. Scott, *American Foreign Policy,* 7th ed. (Belmont, Calif.: Wadsworth Publishing, 2007).

The Arab Spring: Egypt and Tunisia. Acting on the basis of political realism, the United States had built long-standing relationships with various dictators in the Arab world, including Hosni Mubarak of Egypt, the Arab world's most populous nation. Close relations with Mubarak helped guarantee the peace between Egypt and Israel. Given such alliances, the United States had to determine whether to support existing governments when they came under attack by popular rebellions. The king of Saudi Arabia, for one, demanded that America support its old allies. President Barack Obama and Secretary of State Hillary Clinton, however, did not believe that realism and idealism were necessarily in conflict. The United States could support democratic movements and remain true to its values.

Initially, this strategy appeared to be realistic because in Egypt and Tunisia, at least, the democratic rebels were winning. In 2013, however, the military seized power in Egypt, ending its experiment with democracy. In 2014, speaking at the graduation ceremony for the U.S. Military Academy, Obama was blunt: American relations with Egypt were again based on political realism.

The Arab Spring: Libya and Syria. In Libya, the rebels were immediately successful in taking power away from dictator Moammar Gadhafi only in the eastern region. The United States and its European allies eventually intervened with air power to assist the rebels. By doing so, these nations were able to demonstrate that their support for Arab popular movements was serious and not just rhetorical. Intervention, however, was possible only because the Libyan rebels had liberated at least part of their country. After the fall of Gadhafi, Libya was torn by disputes among the various rebel militias. As a result, some foreign policy realists accused idealists of supporting an irresponsible intervention.

The rebellion in Syria turned out quite differently. The dictator of that country, Bashar al Assad, was able to retake rebellious cities and neighborhoods by inflicting horrendous casualties on civilians. Short of all-out war against the Syrian regime, foreign governments had little opportunity to affect developments in that country. Western powers did impose sanctions on the Syrian government, but they had little immediate effect. Nevertheless, the rebellion continued into 2012, as previously peaceful rebels began to arm themselves and launch counterattacks.

In 2013, fighting broke out between radical Islamist rebels and more moderate rebel forces. The question for the United States was whether to supply arms to the more moderate rebels. Advocates of moral idealism and political realism came down on both sides of this issue. For his part, President Obama was clearly reluctant to intervene.

An injured Syrian refugee waits for an ambulance after crossing the Syrian border with Turkey in 2014. By mid-2014, civil war in Syria has taken the lives of more than 150,000 people and forced millions to flee their homes. *What, if anything, should the United States do about the fighting in Syria?*

Terrorism and Warfare

The foreign policy of the United States—whether idealist, realist, or both—must be formulated to deal with world conditions. Early in its history, the United States was a weak, new nation facing older nations well equipped for war. In the twenty-first century, the United

■ **Learning Outcome 2:** Describe recent foreign policy challenges that involve the use of force.

Firefighters enter the rubble of the World Trade Center following the terrorist attack on September 11, 2001. *How did 9/11 change U.S. foreign policy?*

States faces different challenges. Now it must devise foreign and defense policies that will enhance its security in a world in which it is the global superpower. In some instances, these policies have involved the use of force.

The Emergence of Terrorism

Terrorism is a systematic attempt to inspire fear to gain political ends. Typically, terrorism involves the indiscriminate use of violence against noncombatants. We often think of terrorists as nongovernmental agents. The term was first coined, however, to refer to the actions of the radicals who were in control of the government at the height of the French Revolution (1789–1799).

In years past, terrorism was a strategy generally employed by radicals who wanted to change the status of a particular nation or province. For example, over many years the Irish Republican Army undertook terrorist attacks in the British province of Northern Ireland with the aim of driving out the British and uniting the province with the Republic of Ireland. In Spain, the ETA organization has employed terrorism with the goal of creating an independent Basque state in Spain's Basque region. In the twenty-first century, however, the United States has confronted a new form of terrorism that is not associated with such clear-cut aims.

September 11. In 2001, terrorism came home to the United States in ways that few Americans could have imagined. In a well-coordinated attack, nineteen terrorists hijacked four airplanes and crashed three of them into buildings—two into the World Trade Center towers in New York City and one into the Pentagon in Washington, D.C. The fourth airplane crashed in a field in Pennsylvania, after the passengers fought the hijackers.

Why did the al Qaeda network plan and launch attacks on the United States? One reason was that the leaders of the network, including Osama bin Laden, were angered by the presence of U.S. troops on the soil of Saudi Arabia, which they regard as sacred. They also saw the United States as the primary defender of Israel against the Palestinians. The attacks were intended to frighten and demoralize America so that it would withdraw troops from the Middle East.

Al Qaeda's Ultimate Aims. Al Qaeda's ultimate goals, however, were not limited to forcing the United States to withdraw from the Middle East. Al Qaeda envisioned worldwide revolutionary change, with all nations brought under the theocratic rule of an Islamicist empire. Governments have successfully negotiated with terrorists who profess

COMPARE WITH YOUR PEERS
MindTap™ for American Government

Access the Foreign Policy and National Security Forum: Polling Activity—U.S. as the World's Superpower.

Terrorism
A systematic attempt to inspire fear to gain political ends, typically involving the indiscriminate use of violence against noncombatants.

limited aims—today, radicals associated with the Irish Republican Army are part of a coalition government in Northern Ireland. In contrast, there is no way to negotiate with an organization such as al Qaeda.

Domestic Terrorism in the United States. Al Qaeda, which by now has been weakened by American attacks, is not the only group ever to launch a terrorist attack on U.S. soil. Radicals opposed to the U.S. war in Vietnam set off bombs in the 1960s and 1970s. Right-wing terrorists were an issue in the 1990s—notably, a bomb set at a federal office building in Oklahoma City killed 168 people.

In more recent years, however, attacks by domestic Islamists have been the major concern. Such individuals are typically "self-radicalized" through the Internet and are not controlled by a foreign organization. As one example, in 2009 a Muslim U.S. Army psychiatrist fatally shot thirteen people at Fort Hood in Texas. The most recent outrage was the bombing at the Boston Marathon in 2013, which killed three people and cost fourteen victims at least one of their legs. The alleged perpetrators were two self-radicalized Muslim brothers, one of them a U.S. citizen.

The War on Terrorism

After 9/11, President George W. Bush implemented stronger security measures to help ensure homeland security and protect U.S. facilities and personnel abroad. The president sought and received congressional support for heightened airport security, new laws allowing greater domestic surveillance of potential terrorists, and increased funding for the military.

A New Kind of War. In September 2002, President Bush enunciated what became known as the "Bush Doctrine," or the doctrine of preemption (forestalling other action). The concept of "preemptive war" as a defense strategy was a new element in U.S. foreign policy. The concept is based on the assumption that in the war on terrorism, self-defense must be *anticipatory*. President Bush stated in March 2003, just before launching the invasion of Iraq, "Responding to such enemies only after they have struck first is not self-defense, it is suicide."

Opposition to the Bush Doctrine. The Bush Doctrine had many critics. Some pointed out that preemptive wars against other nations have traditionally been waged by dictators and rogue states, not democratic nations. By employing such a strategy, the United States would seem to be contradicting its basic values. Others claimed that launching preemptive wars would make it difficult for the United States to pursue world peace in the future. By endorsing such a policy itself, the United States could hardly argue against the decisions of other nations to do likewise when they felt potentially threatened.

Wars in Iraq

In 1990, the Persian Gulf became the setting for a major challenge to the international system set up after World War II (1939–1945). President Saddam Hussein of Iraq sent troops into the neighboring oil sheikdom of Kuwait, occupying that country. This was the most clear-cut case of aggression against an independent nation in half a century. In January 1991, U.S.-led coalition forces launched a massive attack on Iraq. Iraqi troops retreated from Kuwait, and the First Gulf War ended.

As part of the cease-fire that ended the First Gulf War, Iraq agreed to allow UN weapons inspectors to oversee the destruction of its missiles and all chemical and nuclear weapons. In 1999, though, Iraq placed so many obstacles in the path of the UN inspectors that they withdrew from the country.

Members of the Peshmerga, the Kurdish armed forces in Iraq, take aim at forces of the Islamic State of Iraq and Greater Syria (ISIS) in 2014. ISIS, a terrorist organization, has seized extensive territories in Syria and Iraq. *Does the United States have a responsibility to respond to ISIS's advance?*

The Second Gulf War—The Iraq War. In 2002 and early 2003, President Bush began assembling an international coalition that might support further military action in Iraq. Bush was unable to convince the UN Security Council that military force was necessary in Iraq, so the United States took the initiative. In March 2003, U.S. and British forces invaded Iraq and within a month had toppled Hussein's dictatorship. The process of establishing order in Iraq turned out to be very difficult, however.

Occupied Iraq. The people of Iraq are divided into three principal ethnic groups. The Kurdish-speaking people of the north were overjoyed by the invasion. The Arabs adhering to the Shiite branch of Islam live principally in the south and constitute a majority of the population. They were deeply skeptical of U.S. intentions. The Arabs belonging to the Sunni branch of Islam live mainly to the west of Baghdad. Many Sunnis considered the occupation to be a disaster.

In short order, a Sunni guerrilla insurgency arose and launched attacks against the coalition forces. Iraq had begun to be a serious political problem for President Bush. A newly organized al Qaeda in Iraq sponsored suicide bombings and other attacks against coalition troops and the forces of the new Iraqi government. Al Qaeda also issued vitriolic denunciations of the Iraqi Shiites. Rhetoric was followed by violence. While Sunni and Shiite insurgents continued to launch attacks on coalition forces, the major bloodletting in the country now took place between Sunnis and Shiites. By late 2006, polls indicated that about two-thirds of Americans wanted to see an end to the Iraq War—a sentiment expressed in the 2006 elections.

Iraqi Endgame. In January 2007, President Bush announced a major increase, or "surge," in U.S. troop strength. Skeptics doubted that the new troop levels would have much effect on the outcome. In April 2007, however, Sunni tribal leaders rose up against al Qaeda and called in U.S. troops to help them. Al Qaeda, it seems, had badly overplayed its hand by terrorizing the Sunni population.

During subsequent months, the Iraqi government gained substantial control over its own territory. Still, American attitudes toward the war remained negative. In 2008, President Bush and Iraqi prime minister Nouri al-Maliki negotiated a deadline for withdrawing U.S. troops. In fact, U.S. combat forces left Iraq in August 2010. The rest of the American troops were out by the end of 2011.

The Rise of ISIS. You will recall from earlier in this chapter that the rebels in Syria were divided between moderate and radical Islamic factions. The most hard-line Islamic group was the Islamic State in Iraq and Greater Syria (ISIS), also called the Islamic State in Iraq and the Levant (ISIL). This group was in fact a reorganized version of al Qaeda in Iraq. In February 2014, the international al Qaeda movement expelled ISIS due to its "brutal" attacks on other Muslims.

As its name implies, ISIS was active in both Syria and Iraq. In June 2014, ISIS launched a major offensive in Iraq that soon left it in control of Mosul, Iraq's second largest city, and of territory reaching within a few miles of Baghdad. Many Iraqi army units fled without fighting. ISIS was aided in its advance by an alliance with various Sunni groups that had grievances against the Shiite-led government of Iraq. At the end of June, ISIS changed its name to simply the "Islamic State" (IS). It announced that it sought to rule not only the

Middle East, but the entire world. IS soon began driving religious minorities out of the lands it controlled. These included Christians and members of the small Yazidi faith. IS forces also clashed with the *Peshmerga*, the militia of Iraq's autonomous Kurdish region.

By August 2014, it was clear that IS's plans for the Yazidi amounted to genocide. Throughout June and July, President Obama had emphasized that the only solution to the ISIS problem was an Iraqi government that could reconcile with the Sunnis. The United States would not intervene to provide a "Shiite air force." In August, however, Obama authorized ongoing air support for the Kurdish Peshmerga, with the understanding that the Kurds would help protect minority groups in northern Iraq. U.S. advisors and the U.S. Air Force were back in Iraq. Support, initially limited to the Kurds, was later extended to central government forces.

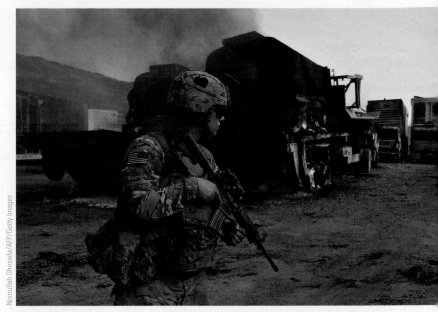

A U.S. soldier investigates the scene of a suicide attack by three Taliban fighters at the Afghan-Pakistan border in 2014. *Why do so many Americans favor pulling our troops out of Afghanistan?*

Afghanistan

The Iraq War was not the only military effort launched by the Bush administration as part of the war on terrorism. The first military effort was directed against al Qaeda camps in Afghanistan and the Taliban regime, which had ruled most of Afghanistan since 1996. In late 2001, after building a coalition of international allies and anti-Taliban rebels within Afghanistan, the United States began an air campaign against the Taliban regime. The anti-Taliban rebels, known as the Northern Alliance, were able to take Kabul, the capital, and oust the Taliban from power.

The Return of the Taliban. The Taliban were defeated, but not destroyed. U.S. forces were unable to locate Osama bin Laden and other top al Qaeda leaders. The Taliban and al Qaeda both retreated to the rugged mountains between Afghanistan and Pakistan, where they were able to establish bases on the Pakistani side of the border. In 2003, the Taliban began to launch attacks against Afghan soldiers, foreign aid workers, and American troops. Through 2008 and 2009, the Taliban were able to take over a number of Pakistani districts, even as the United States began attacking suspected Taliban and al Qaeda targets in Pakistan using small unmanned aircraft.

Obama and Afghanistan. During 2009 and 2010, President Obama almost doubled the number of U.S. troops stationed in Afghanistan. At the same time, he announced that he would begin making troop withdrawals in 2011. The initial drawdown in forces was trivial, but more soldiers were brought home in subsequent years. By the end of 2014, the number of troops was down to about 10,000, and the last of these were scheduled to depart before the end of 2016.

The Death of bin Laden. The CIA and other U.S. intelligence forces were unable to develop information on Osama bin Laden's whereabouts until 2010. In that year and in 2011, the intelligence agencies obtained evidence that bin Laden might be living in a highly secure residential compound in Abbottabad, Pakistan. Pakistan's military academy is located in Abbottabad, which led many observers to surmise that bin Laden was living under the protection of members of Pakistan's military.

did you know?

It is estimated that the U.S. nuclear weapons program will cost $1 trillion over the next thirty years.

On May 1, 2011, U.S. Navy SEALs launched a helicopter raid on the compound. In a brief firefight, the SEALs killed bin Laden and four others. Americans responded to President Obama's announcement of the operation with relief and satisfaction. Reactions in Pakistan itself were mostly negative—the raid was generally seen as a violation of Pakistan's sovereignty.

U.S. Diplomatic Efforts

The United States has dealt with many international problems through diplomacy, rather than the use of armed force. Some of these issues include the proliferation of nuclear weapons, the growing power of China, and the confrontation between Israel and the Palestinians. Economic concerns can also be addressed through diplomacy.

Nuclear Weapons

In 1945, the United States was the only nation to possess nuclear weapons. Several nations quickly joined the "nuclear club," however, including the Soviet Union in 1949, Britain in 1952, France in 1960, and China in 1964. Few nations have made public their nuclear weapons programs since China's successful test of nuclear weapons in 1964. India and Pakistan, however, detonated nuclear devices within a few weeks of each other in 1998, and North Korea conducted an underground nuclear explosive test in October 2006. Several other nations are suspected of possessing nuclear weapons or the capability to produce them in a short time. Israel is known to possess more than one hundred nuclear warheads.

With nuclear weapons, materials, and technology available worldwide, it is conceivable that terrorists could obtain a nuclear device and use it in a terrorist act. In fact, a U.S. federal indictment filed in 1998 charged Osama bin Laden and his associates with trying to buy components for making a nuclear bomb "at various times" since 1992.

Cold War
The ideological, political, and economic confrontation between the United States and the Soviet Union following World War II.

Nuclear Stockpiles. More than twenty-two thousand nuclear warheads are known to be stockpiled worldwide, although the exact number is uncertain because some countries do not reveal the extent of their holdings. The United States and Russia have dismantled many of their nuclear weapons systems since the end of the **Cold War** and the dissolution (breakup) of the Soviet Union in 1991 (discussed later in this chapter). Still, both retain sizable nuclear arsenals. More alarming is the fact that, since the dissolution of the Soviet Union, the security of its nuclear arsenal has declined. There have been reported thefts, smugglings, and illicit sales of nuclear material from the former Soviet Union.

Nuclear Proliferation: Iran. For years, the United States, the European Union, and the UN have tried to prevent Iran from becoming a nuclear power. In spite of these efforts, many observers believe that Iran is now in the process of developing nuclear weapons—although Iran maintains that it is interested in developing nuclear power only for peaceful purposes. The group of nations attempting to talk with Iran includes Britain, China, France, Germany, Russia, and the United States.

By 2009, the UN Security Council had voted three rounds of penalties called *sanctions* against Iran in reaction to its nuclear program. One problem with the attempt to develop meaningful international sanctions was resistance from Russia and China. By 2010, Russia appeared to have lost patience with Iran, but China was able to limit the impact of the new UN sanctions imposed in that year. China is often reluctant to impose sanctions, and Iran is one of China's major trading partners.

By 2012, it was clear that sanctions against Iran were beginning to damage that country's economy. Of special importance was the U.S. campaign to persuade other nations to stop importing Iranian oil, which enjoyed increasing success. The United States was also successful in cutting Iran off from the international banking system.

Some of the U.S. actions against Iran went well beyond sanctions. It was discovered in 2012 that the United States had deployed a computer worm that took down about one thousand of Iran's five thousand uranium enrichment centrifuges, destroying many of them completely. This covert operation may have delayed Iran's nuclear program by as much as a year. Perhaps even more alarming was a series of threats that Israel or the United States might bomb Iran's nuclear sites.

Negotiations with Iran. Before 2013, talks between Iran and the six nations just mentioned went nowhere. In 2013, however, Iran elected a new president, Hassan Rouhani, who initiated a "charm offensive" directed at the West. It appeared that for the first time, Iran was prepared to negotiate seriously. Under an interim deal signed in January 2014, Iran agreed to limit various nuclear activities during the following six months, and in return the six-country team would provide Iran with some sanctions relief. Negotiations continued during 2014.

Nuclear Proliferation: North Korea. North Korea tested a nuclear device in 2006. An agreement reached in February 2007 provided that North Korea would start disabling its nuclear facilities and allow UN inspectors into the country. In return, China, Japan, Russia, South Korea, and the United States—the other members of the six-party negotiations—would provide aid to North Korea. North Korea, however, was allowed to keep its nuclear arsenal, which American intelligence officials believe may include as many as six nuclear bombs or the fuel to make them. In July 2007, North Korea dismantled one of its nuclear reactors and admitted UN inspectors into the country. In October 2008, the United States removed North Korea from its list of states that sponsor terrorism.

By 2009, however, North Korea was pulling back from its treaty obligations. In April, the country tested a long-range missile capable of delivering a nuclear warhead, in violation of a UN Security Council demand that it halt such tests. After the Security Council issued a statement condemning the test, North Korea ordered UN inspectors out of the country, broke off negotiations with the other members of the six-party talks, and conducted a second nuclear test. The United States and other parties have sought to persuade China to take the lead in bringing North Korea back to the negotiating table—China is the one nation that has significant economic leverage over North Korea.

The New Power: China

Since Richard Nixon's visit to China in 1972, American policy has been to engage the Chinese gradually in diplomatic and economic relationships in the hope of turning the nation in a more pro-Western direction. An important factor in U.S.-Chinese relations has been the large and growing trade ties between the two countries. In 1980, China was granted *most-favored-nation status* for tariffs and trade policy on a year-to-year basis. To prevent confusion, in 1998 the status was renamed **normal trade relations (NTR) status.** In 2000, over objections from organized labor and human rights groups, Congress approved a permanent grant of NTR status to China. In 2001, Congress endorsed China's application to join the World Trade Organization (WTO), thereby effectively guaranteeing China's admission to that body.

While officially Communist, China today permits a striking degree of free enterprise. China has become substantially integrated into the world economic system, and it exports considerably more goods and services to the United States than it imports. As a result, its central bank has built up a huge reserve of U.S. federal government treasuries and other American obligations. Ultimately,

Normal Trade Relations (NTR) Status
A status granted through an international treaty by which each member nation must treat other members as well as it treats the country that receives its most favorable treatment. This status was formerly known as *most-favored-nation status.*

did you know?

Every six hours, China exports as much as it did in all of 1978.

North Korean leader Kim Jong-un and his wife Ri Sol-ju attend the opening ceremony of the Rungna People's Pleasure Ground in Pyongyang. *Why is it so difficult to negotiate with North Korea?*

the books must balance, but instead of importing U.S. goods and services, the Chinese have imported U.S. securities. The resulting economic imbalances are good for Chinese exporters, but create financial problems in both countries. The United States has repeatedly asked China to address these imbalances by allowing its currency to rise in value relative to the American dollar. Recently, Chinese authorities have allowed some movement.

China's Explosive Economic Growth. The growth of the Chinese economy during the last thirty-five years is one of the most important developments in world history. For the past several decades, the Chinese economy has grown at a rate of about 10 percent annually, a long-term growth rate previously unknown in human history. Never have so many escaped poverty so quickly.

China now produces more steel than America and Japan combined. It generates more than 40 percent of the world's output of cement. The new electrical generating capacity that China has been adding each year exceeds the entire installed capacity of Britain. (The new plants, which are usually coal fired, may promote global warming and also generate some of the world's worst air pollution.) Skyscrapers fill the skyline of every major Chinese city.

In 2007, for the first time, China manufactured more passenger automobiles than did the United States. China is building a limited-access highway system that, when complete, will be longer than the U.S. interstate highway system. Chinese demand for raw materials, notably petroleum, has led at times to dramatic increases in the price of oil and other commodities. Its people have begun to eat large quantities of meat, which adds to the demand for world food production. By 2020, if not before, the economy of China is expected to be larger than that of the United States. China, in short, will become the world's second superpower.

The Issue of Taiwan. Inevitably, economic power translates into military potential. Is this a problem? It could be if China had territorial ambitions. At this time, China does not appear to have an appetite for non-Chinese territory. China's leaders, however, appear to have a rather expansive concept of what is meant by "Chinese territory." For example, China has always considered the island of Taiwan to be Chinese territory. In principle, Taiwan agrees. Taiwan calls itself the "Republic of China" and officially considers its government to be the legitimate ruler of the entire country—that is, of both Taiwan and mainland China. This diplomatic fiction has remained in effect since 1949, when the Chinese Communist Party won a civil war and drove the anti-Communist forces off the mainland.

China's position is that, sooner or later, Taiwan must rejoin the rest of China. The position of the United States is that this reunification must not come about by force. Is peaceful reunification possible? China holds up Hong Kong as an example. Hong Kong came under Chinese sovereignty peacefully in 1997. The people of Taiwan, however, are far from considering Hong Kong to be an acceptable precedent.

Chinese Nationalism. Growing public expressions of Chinese nationalism have raised concern in some of China's neighbors. The Chinese government has sometimes appeared to support nationalist agitation because it benefits politically. When nationalism has seemed to be getting out of hand, however, the government has cracked down.

did you know?

China's one-child-per-family policy has created a significant gender imbalance due to sex-selective abortions and even female infanticide. China now has 32 million more boys than girls. This means that in the future, millions of men will be unable to find wives.

Chinese workers make final inspections on an automobile production line. The plant is a joint venture between Dongfeng Motor Corporation and the French automobile maker PSA Peugeot Citroen. *If China began exporting cars to the United States, would you consider buying one? Why or why not?*

China has recently engaged in disputes with Japan, Vietnam, the Philippines, and other Asian nations over the ownership of dozens of uninhabited islands in the East China and South China Seas. In November 2011, President Obama visited Australia and promised to establish a new U.S. force of 2,500 Marines at Darwin, on Australia's north coast. In June 2012, U.S. secretary of defense Leon Panetta announced that in the future, America would station 60 percent of its navy in the Pacific area, up from 50 percent. These developments were widely perceived as an attempt to reassure nations in the area that were concerned about potential Chinese pressure. We discuss Chinese nationalism in more depth in the *Which Side Are You On?* feature that follows.

Which Side Are You On?

Is China's Nationalism a Threat to World Peace?

China is the world's third largest country by land area. It is the second largest economy in the world. It is the world's largest international trading power. It also has, with 2.3 million active troops, the largest standing military force in the world.

The leaders of the only permitted political group in the country—the Chinese Communist Party—have long claimed that their country endured a century of humiliation by foreign powers. This "victim nation" narrative goes along with the contention that China is "finally standing up for itself." Recently, China's economic growth has slowed somewhat. It may not be a coincidence that China's leaders have begun placing a much greater emphasis on *nationalism*—an emotional attachment to a nation and its interests. Some people believe that China's nationalism is becoming a threat to world peace.

China Will No Longer Settle for Negotiation

A common tactic in authoritarian countries is to divert attention from domestic difficulties through foreign adventures. Witness the behavior of Russia's authoritarian leader Vladimir Putin, which we first described in Chapter 12. Putin has annexed Ukraine's Crimea Province in the name of protecting ethnic Russians. China appears to be headed down a similar road. Reportedly, the Chinese leadership sees the Great Recession and subsequent sluggish growth as evidence that America is in decline. They seem to have decided that they can now be more assertive. China is laying claim to almost the entire South China Sea. Tensions with neighboring countries such as Vietnam and the Philippines have led to actual clashes.

China has challenged Japan's control of uninhabited islands in the East China Sea. At a 2014 meeting among Asian countries,

Japan's prime minister offered to support the Philippines and Vietnam with coastal patrol boats. Much of the world's economic growth comes from Asia, and if miscalculation led to a war, the results would be disastrous.

China's Nationalism Is Exaggerated

There are those who do not believe China's nationalism is as great as reported in the Western press, or as fierce as you might expect from reading Chinese bloggers. Australian analyst Andrew Chubb has performed surveys in five major Chinese cities. He finds that the average citizen in China would like to see the government compromise on the South China Sea territorial disputes. Those disputes were also less important to respondents than issues such as corruption, income inequality, and food and drug safety. Chubb suggests that China's leaders are exaggerating popular nationalism in an attempt to bluff foreign governments into backing down. And if the Chinese leaders are bluffing, they are unlikely to pursue disputes to the point of war.

Within China, much of the most damaging nationalism takes the form of discrimination against ethnic groups. These include China's Muslim Uighurs and the people of Tibet. Large numbers of China's majority people (the Han Chinese) are moving into Uighur and Tibetan lands. Uighurs and Tibetans are becoming minorities in their own countries. Such developments, while disturbing, have nothing to do with world peace.

For Critical Analysis

Considering Chinese nationalism, does it matter that China is a nuclear power? Why or why not?

In one area—cyberspace—Chinese-American relations are already quite heated. In 2013, the United States accused the Chinese military of sponsoring cyberattacks on U.S. computer networks. Obtaining no satisfactory response from the Chinese government, in 2014 the United States actually indicted five Chinese soldiers on charges of damaging U.S. systems. (The five are unlikely ever to set foot on U.S. soil.) China has responded with its own complaints, many of which are based on information from the Edward Snowden leaks.

Israel and the Palestinians

As a longtime supporter of the state of Israel, the United States has undertaken to persuade the Israelis to negotiate with the Palestinian Arabs who live in the territories occupied by Israel. The conflict between Israel and the Palestinians, which began in 1948, has been extremely hard to resolve. The internationally recognized solution is for Israel to yield the West Bank and the Gaza Strip to the Palestinians in return for effective security commitments and abandonment by the Palestinians of any right of return to Israel proper.

The Palestinians, however, have been unwilling to stop terrorist attacks on Israel, and Israel has been unwilling to dismantle its settlements in the occupied territories. Further, the two parties have been unable to come to an agreement on how much of the West Bank should go to the Palestinians and what compensation (if any) the Palestinians should receive for abandoning all claims to settlement in Israel proper.

In 1991, under pressure from the United States, the Israelis opened talks with the Palestine Liberation Organization (PLO). In 1993, the PLO and Israel agreed to set up Palestinian self-government in the West Bank and the Gaza Strip in 1994. In the months that followed, Israeli troops withdrew from much of the occupied territories, and the new Palestinian Authority assumed police duties.

The Collapse of the Israeli-Palestinian Peace Process. Although negotiations between the Israelis and the Palestinians resulted in more agreements, the agreements were rejected by Palestinian radicals, who began a campaign of suicide bombings in Israeli cities. In 2002, the Israeli government moved tanks and troops into Palestinian towns to kill or capture the terrorists. One result of the Israeli reoccupation was an almost complete—if temporary—collapse of the Palestinian Authority. Groups such as Hamas (the Islamic Resistance Movement), which did not accept peace with Israel even in principle, moved into the power vacuum.

In February 2004, Israeli prime minister Ariel Sharon announced a plan under which Israel would withdraw from the Gaza Strip regardless of whether a deal could be reached with the Palestinians. Sharon's plan met with strong opposition, but ultimately the withdrawal took place.

The Rise of Hamas. In January 2006, the militant group Hamas won a majority of the seats in the Palestinian legislature. American and European politicians refused to talk to Hamas until it agreed to rescind its avowed desire to destroy Israel. In June 2007, the uneasy balance between the Hamas-dominated Palestinian legislature and the PLO president broke down. After open fighting between the two parties, Hamas wound up in complete control of the Gaza Strip, and the PLO retained exclusive power in the West Bank.

Israel sought to pressure the Hamas regime in the Gaza Strip to relinquish power through an economic blockade. Hamas retaliated by firing a series of rockets into Israel. In January 2009, Israel temporarily reoccupied the Gaza Strip.

Israel and the Obama Administration. In February 2009, Israelis elected a new, more conservative government under Prime Minister Benyamin Netanyahu. The tough positions advocated by the new government threatened to create fresh obstacles to the peace process.

In particular, the new government accelerated the growth of Israeli settlements on the West Bank, even though the Obama administration opposed such settlements. As a result, a degree of tension built up between the administration and the new Israeli government.

In 2011, however, the Palestinian Authority appealed to the United Nations to recognize Palestine as an independent state, and Obama opposed such action with some of the strongest pro-Israeli rhetoric in years. This development tended to restore warm Israeli-American relations.

In 2013, the United States attempted to restart negotiations between Israel and the Palestinians. Secretary of State John Kerry took the lead in this effort. By April 2014, however, the talks had collapsed again. One problem was an attempt by the Palestinian Authority and Hamas to resolve their differences, which could result in a Palestinian leadership unacceptable to Israel and the United States. A second problem was Netanyahu's refusal to make any concessions on Israeli settlements policy.

U.S. Secretary of State John Kerry, left, shakes hands with Israeli Prime Minister Benjamin Netanyahu in 2014. Kerry was attempting to negotiate a cease-fire between Israel and Hamas, the Palestinian group that controls the Gaza Strip. *Why have negotiations between Israel and the Palestinians been so difficult?*

Again, Gaza. In June 2014, fighting broke out between Israel and the Hamas regime in the Gaza Strip. Hostilities were triggered by the abduction and murder of three Israeli youths in the West Bank, which Israel blamed on Hamas. Israeli forces arrested several hundred Hamas members, including its entire West Bank leadership. Several Palestinians died in the raids or in attacks by Israeli civilians.

Hamas began firing rockets into Israel, and Israel bombed Hamas targets in response. The exchanges escalated. In July, Israel launched a ground offensive into the Gaza Strip to seize tunnels that Hamas had dug into Israel. Repeated attempts to negotiate a cease-fire finally succeeded in August. By that time, Gaza had suffered massive destruction and almost two thousand fatalities. Israel was largely protected from Hamas rockets by a U.S.-supplied anti-missile system, though it did suffer significant casualties among troops entering Gaza.

Europe's Economic Troubles

U.S. foreign relations are not just a matter of waging wars or trying to prevent them. International economic coordination is another major field of action. One such issue—discussed in a previous section—is our trade relations with China. During 2010, 2011, and 2013, however, an even greater threat was posed by some of our closest international friends, the nations of Europe. We first discussed this crisis in the *Beyond Our Borders* feature in Chapter 3. For other ways in which international economic developments may affect the United States, see this chapter's *Beyond Our Borders* feature that follows.

The Debt Crisis. The eighteen nations that share a common currency—the euro—were hit hard by the worldwide financial panic of 2008. In particular, the nations of the so-called euro periphery faced a debt crisis. In Greece and, to a lesser extent, Portugal, the governments themselves had borrowed irresponsibly. In Ireland and Spain, many real estate loans went sour, threatening the survival of the banks that had made the loans. Ireland and Spain found themselves in danger when their governments assumed the debts of the threatened banks.

did you know?

In 1914, Europe had 25 percent of the world's population. If current demographic trends continue, Europe's share may fall to around 7 percent in 2050.

Beyond Our Borders

The Impact of Population Growth on America's Future Role in the World

After World War II, the United States faced an adversary—the Union of Soviet Socialist Republics (USSR)—which was alleged to have the second-largest economy in the world. Its military was definitely much larger than ours. Many believed that the Soviet army had defeated Hitler during World War II by the sheer force of numbers. By 1990, the Soviet population was 289 million, compared with America's 256 million. A year later, when the Soviet Union disintegrated, Russia was down to fewer than 149 million people.

For a time, Russia's economy didn't even appear on lists of the world's ten largest. The United States was now the world's third most populous nation, with U.S. military spending approaching that of all other nations combined.

Population Changes and World Power Relationships

By 2050, both India and China will have around 1.5 billion residents each, compared with 400 million Americans. Populations in Arab and South Asian Muslim nations are growing. Pakistan's population, for example, will increase from 144 million to almost 300 million by 2050. China's population is stabilizing. Not so the population of Africa. The continent's population was only 224 million in 1950, reached 821 million in 2000, and by 2050 will be almost 2 billion. Africa's economy is growing, albeit slowly. We can predict, therefore, that over time African nations should become more important in world affairs. Russia is another story, as is Japan. By 2050, these two nations won't even be among the top ten nations in the world with respect to population.

And What about the United States?

Currently, the United States is the only major power that is experiencing significant population growth. By 2050, the United States will have an estimated 4.37 percent of the world's population, down somewhat from 4.65 percent in 2000. In contrast, Russia's population is dwindling, sometimes at a shocking rate, because of poor diet, poor health care, and alcoholism.

Many Western European countries are predicted to lose population as well. Russia may dwindle in significance, and Western Europe and Japan could lose clout. The United States should remain one of the world's superpowers for a long time to come, but it is likely to be joined by China and, later on, India as well.

For Critical Analysis

Does it really matter whether the United States remains a superpower? Why or why not?

The nations of the euro periphery began running out of funds to service their debts, and they faced ruinous interest rates if they attempted to borrow in the financial markets. If a nation such as Britain, Japan, or the United States faced such a crisis, it could rely on its central bank—in America, the Fed—to serve as *lender of last resort* and simply "print" the necessary money. In fact, in 2008 Britain did just that, accepting a small amount of inflation. But the periphery nations did not control their own money supplies, and the European Central Bank (ECB) was barred from acting as lender of last resort. Investors began pulling funds out of the troubled nations, reducing their money supplies further. The panic threatened to spread to Italy.

The circumstances faced by the euro periphery were reminiscent of the difficulties confronting nations during the Great Depression of the 1930s. Then, countries were unable to expand their money supplies due to their commitment to the gold standard. (We discussed the gold standard in the *What If* . . . feature in Chapter 14.) In the 1930s, the nations of the world eventually abandoned the gold standard so that they could reflate their economies. Would the euro periphery countries eventually respond by leaving the euro? In 2011, 2012, and 2013 that was the question. Eurozone nations did come up with bailout loans for Greece, Ireland, Portugal, and eventually Spain, however.

The German Question. The response of the ECB to the crisis was to demand that periphery governments follow policies of fiscal austerity, in which they would meet their debts by major reductions in spending and increases in taxes. Such a policy directly contradicted the advice of Keynesian economics, although it had certain similarities to economic measures advocated by some Republicans in the United States. Keynesians argued that austerity could push the periphery further into recession, thus making the debt crisis even harder to resolve.

An alternative would be to strengthen European institutions. Eurozone banks could be backed by a euro-wide support facility, as in the United States. The eurozone could issue joint eurobonds to support troubled governments. Such measures, however, were blocked by Germany and several of its smaller allies within the eurozone. The German government, under Angela Merkel, believed that such joint measures would force the German taxpayer to bail out the rest of Europe.

President Obama was among a number of world leaders calling for a German change of course. Obama's calculation was that a European austerity policy would plunge the continent back into recession, thus damaging the U.S. economy and slowing its recovery. In 2013, advocates of expansionary policies received support from an unexpected source. The new government of Japan, under Prime Minister Shinzō Abe, introduced a series of expansionary monetary and fiscal policies that were meant to boost Japan out of a long period of economic stagnation.

> ## Why Should You Care about...
>
> ### Foreign Policy?
>
> One foreign policy issue worth caring about is human rights. In many countries throughout the world, human rights are not protected. In some nations, people are imprisoned, tortured, or killed because they oppose the current regime. In other nations, certain ethnic or racial groups are oppressed by the majority population. The strongest reason for involving yourself with human rights issues in other countries is simple moral altruism—unselfish regard for the welfare of others. The defense of human rights is unlikely to put a single dollar in your pocket.

Who Makes Foreign Policy?

Given the vast array of challenges in the world, developing a comprehensive U.S. foreign policy is a demanding task. Does this responsibility fall to the president, to Congress, or to both acting jointly? There is no easy answer to this question because, as constitutional authority Edwin S. Corwin once observed, the U.S. Constitution created between the president and Congress an "invitation to struggle" for control over the foreign policy process. Let us look first at the powers given to the president by the Constitution.

Constitutional Powers of the President

The Constitution confers on the president broad powers that are either explicit or implied in key constitutional provisions. Article II vests the executive power of the government in the president. The presidential oath of office given in Article II, Section 1, requires that the president "solemnly swear" to "preserve, protect and defend the Constitution of the United States."

War Powers. In addition, and perhaps more important, Article II, Section 2, designates the president as "Commander in Chief of the Army and Navy of the United States." Starting with Abraham Lincoln, all presidents have interpreted this authority dynamically and broadly. Indeed, since George Washington's administration, the United States has

■ **Learning Outcome 4:** Explain the role of the president, executive agencies, and Congress in making U.S. foreign policy.

COMPARE WITH YOUR PEERS
MindTap™ for American Government

Access the Foreign Policy and National Security Forum: Discussion—Developing Foreign Policy.

Kissinger was Nixon's chief foreign policy adviser not only while he was secretary of state, but also earlier, when he was national security adviser. Earlier, Nixon had developed a strong reputation as an anti-communist. *How might that reputation have actually made it easier for Nixon and Kissinger to open up U.S.–Chinese relations?*

been involved in at least 125 undeclared wars that were conducted under presidential authority. For example, in 1950 Harry Truman ordered U.S. armed forces in the Pacific to counter North Korea's invasion of South Korea. Bill Clinton sent troops to Haiti and Bosnia. George W. Bush initiated wars in Afghanistan and Iraq, and Barack Obama undertook air strikes to support rebels in Libya.

Treaties and Executive Agreements. Article II, Section 2, of the Constitution also gives the president the power to make treaties, provided that the Senate concurs. Presidents usually have been successful in getting treaties through the Senate. In addition to this formal treaty-making power, the president makes use of executive agreements (discussed in Chapter 12). Since World War II executive agreements have accounted for almost 95 percent of the understandings reached between the United States and other nations.

Executive agreements have a long and important history. During World War II, Franklin D. Roosevelt reached several agreements with Britain, the Soviet Union, and other countries. In other important agreements, Presidents Eisenhower, Kennedy, and Johnson all promised support to the government of South Vietnam. In all, since 1946 more than eight thousand executive agreements with foreign countries have been made. There is no way to obtain an accurate count, because perhaps as many as several hundred of these agreements have been made secretly.

Other Constitutional Powers. An additional power conferred on the president in Article II, Section 2, is the right to appoint ambassadors, other public ministers, and consuls. In Section 3 of that article, the president is given the power to recognize foreign governments by receiving their ambassadors.

Other Sources of Foreign Policymaking

There are at least four foreign policymaking sources within the executive branch in addition to the president. These are the (1) Department of State, (2) National Security Council, (3) intelligence community, and (4) Department of Defense.

The Department of State. In principle, the State Department is the executive agency that has primary authority over foreign affairs. It supervises U.S. relations with the nearly two hundred independent nations around the world and with the United Nations and other multinational groups, such as the Organization of American States. It staffs embassies and consulates throughout the world. It does this with one of the smallest budgets of the cabinet departments.

Newly elected presidents usually tell the American public that the new secretary of state is the nation's chief foreign policy adviser. In the Obama administration, this statement was a true description of the role of Secretaries of State Hillary Clinton and John Kerry. Under most presidents since World War II, however, the preeminence of the State Department in foreign policy has been limited. The State Department's image within the White House Executive Office and Congress (and even with foreign governments) has been poor—It has often been seen as a slow, plodding, bureaucratic maze of inefficient, indecisive individuals.

It is not surprising that the State Department has been overshadowed in foreign policy. It has no natural domestic constituency as does, for example, the Department of Defense, which can call on defense contractors for support. Instead, the State Department has what might be called **negative constituents**—U.S. citizens who openly oppose the government's policies.

The National Security Council. The job of the National Security Council (NSC), created by the National Security Act of 1947, is to advise the president on the integration of "domestic, foreign, and military policies relating to the national security." As it has turned out, the NSC—consisting of the president, the vice president, the secretaries of state and defense, the director of emergency planning, and often the chairperson of the joint chiefs of staff and the director of the CIA—is used in just about any way the president wants to use it.

The role of national security adviser to the president seems to adjust to fit the player. Some advisers have come into conflict with heads of the State Department. Henry A. Kissinger, President Richard Nixon's flamboyant and aggressive national security adviser, rapidly gained ascendancy over William Rogers, the secretary of state. More recently, Condoleezza Rice played an important role as national security adviser during George W. Bush's first term. Like Kissinger, Rice eventually became secretary of state.

Under President Obama, however, the national security adviser has ceased to be the most important foreign policy adviser. Obama's national security advisers have been minor figures, and in contrast to previous administrations, they have not been part of the president's cabinet.

The Intelligence Community. No discussion of foreign policy would be complete without some mention of the **intelligence community.** This consists of the forty or more government agencies and bureaus that are involved in intelligence activities. The CIA, created as part of the National Security Act of 1947, is the key official member of the intelligence community.

Covert Actions. Intelligence activities consist mostly of overt information gathering, but covert actions also are undertaken. Covert actions, as the name implies, are carried out in secret, and the American public rarely finds out about them. The CIA covertly aided in the overthrow of the Mossadegh regime in Iran in 1953 and was instrumental in destabilizing the Allende government in Chile from 1970 to 1973.

Negative Constituents
Citizens who openly oppose the government's policies.

Intelligence Community
The government agencies that gather information about the capabilities and intentions of foreign governments or that engage in covert actions.

AP Images/Doug Mills

President Bush is shown with his National Security Council (NSC) the day after the terrorist attacks on September 11, 2001. At that time, the NSC consisted of the director of the Central Intelligence Agency, the secretary of defense, the secretary of state, the vice president, the chairman of the joint chiefs of staff, and, of course, the national security adviser. *How important is the NSC's role in determining U.S. foreign policy?*

During the mid-1970s, the "dark side" of the CIA was partly uncovered when the Senate undertook an investigation of its activities. One of the major findings of the Senate Select Committee on Intelligence was that the CIA had routinely spied on American citizens domestically, supposedly a prohibited activity. Consequently, the CIA came under the scrutiny of oversight committees within Congress.

By 2001, the agency had come under fire again. Problems included the discovery that one of its agents had been spying on behalf of a foreign power, the inability of the agency to detect the nuclear arsenals of India and Pakistan, and, above all, its failure to obtain advance knowledge about the 9/11 terrorist attacks.

The Intelligence Community and the War on Terrorism. With the rise of terrorism as a threat, the intelligence agencies have received more funding and enhanced surveillance powers, but these moves have also provoked fears of civil liberties violations. Legislation enacted in 2004 established the Office of the Director of National Intelligence to oversee the intelligence community.

A simmering controversy that came to a head in 2009 concerned the CIA's use of a technique called *waterboarding* while interrogating several prisoners in the years immediately following 9/11. Before 9/11, the government had defined waterboarding as a form of torture, but former vice president Dick Cheney, a public advocate of the practice, denied that it was. One concern was whether Bush administration officials would face legal action as a result of the practice. In May 2009, President Obama, even as he denounced waterboarding, assured CIA employees that no member of the agency would be penalized for following Justice Department rulings that had legitimized harsh interrogation methods.

The Department of Defense. The Department of Defense (DOD) was created in 1947 to bring all of the various activities of the American military establishment under the jurisdiction of a single department headed by a civilian secretary of defense. At the same time, the joint chiefs of staff, consisting of the commanders of the various military branches and a chairperson, was created to formulate a unified military strategy.

Although the Department of Defense is larger than any other federal department, it declined in size after the fall of the Soviet Union in 1991. In the subsequent ten years, the total number of civilian employees was reduced by about 400,000, to approximately 665,000. After 9/11, the war on terrorism and combat in Afghanistan and Iraq drove the defense budget up again.

Beginning in 2012, however, the defense budget actually fell slightly in response to attempts to reduce the federal budget deficit. In 2014, secretary of Defense Chuck Hagel released plans to cut the size of the U.S. Army from 522,000 to 450,000 soldiers. That would be the smallest army in any year since World War II.

Congress Balances the Presidency

A new interest in the balance of power between Congress and the president on foreign policy questions developed during the Vietnam War

did you know?

Half of the world's terrain is inaccessible to wheeled vehicles. Therefore, the Defense Advanced Research Projects Agency (the group that brought you the Internet) has commissioned Boston Dynamics to develop a rough-terrain quadruped robot called BigDog for military use.

This aerial view of the five-sided Pentagon building shows where many of the defense personnel work in Arlington, Virginia. The Pentagon covers an area of twenty-nine acres. *When was the Department of Defense created?*

(1965–1975). Sensitive to public frustration over the long and costly war and angry at Richard Nixon for some of his other actions as president, Congress attempted to establish limits on the power of the president in setting foreign and defense policy.

The War Powers Resolution. In 1973, Congress passed the War Powers Resolution over President Nixon's veto. The act limited the president's use of troops in military action without congressional approval (see Chapter 12). Most presidents, however, have not interpreted the "consultation" provisions of the act as meaning that Congress should be consulted before military action is taken. Instead, Presidents Ford, Carter, Reagan, George H. W. Bush, and Clinton ordered troop movements and then informed congressional leaders.

The War Powers Resolution was in the news again in 2011, when President Obama failed to seek congressional support for air strikes to support the rebels in Libya. The House passed a resolution rebuking the president, but the Senate refused to consider it.

The Power of the Purse. One of Congress's most significant constitutional powers is the so-called power of the purse. The president may order that a certain action be taken, but that order cannot be executed unless Congress funds it. When the Democrats took control of Congress in January 2007, many asked whether the new Congress would use its power of the purse to bring an end to the Iraq War, in view of strong public opposition to the war. Congress's decision was to add conditions to a war-funding request submitted by the president. The conditions required the president to establish timelines for the redeployment of American troops in Iraq. Bush immediately threatened to veto any bill that imposed conditions on the funding. His threat carried the day.

In this circumstance, the power of Congress was limited by political considerations. Congress did not even consider the option of refusing to fund the war altogether. For one thing, there was not enough support in Congress for such an approach. For another, the Democrats did not want to be accused of placing the troops in Iraq in danger. Additionally, the threat of a presidential veto significantly limited Congress's power. The Democrats simply did not have a large enough majority to override a veto.

Why Should You Care about...

Foreign Policy?

Concerning the importance of human rights, consider that abuses of these rights are often associated with the kind of dictatorial regimes that are likely to provoke wars. To the extent that the people of the world can create a climate in which human rights abuses are unacceptable, they may also create an atmosphere in which national leaders believe that they must display peaceful conduct generally. This, in turn, might reduce the frequency of wars, some of which could involve the United States. Fewer wars would mean preserving peace and human life, not to mention reducing the financial burden imposed by the military.

The Major Foreign Policy Themes

■ **Learning Outcome 5:**
Cite the main themes in the history of U.S. foreign policy.

Although some observers might suggest that U.S. foreign policy is inconsistent and changes with the current occupant of the White House, the long view of American diplomatic ventures reveals some major themes underlying foreign policy. In the early years of the nation, presidents and the people generally agreed that the United States should avoid foreign entanglements and concentrate instead on its own development. From the beginning of the twentieth century until the present, however, a major theme has been increasing global involvement. The theme of the post–World War II years was the containment of communism. The theme for at least the first part of the twenty-first century is countering terrorism, as we discussed earlier in this chapter.

The Formative Years: Avoiding Entanglements

The founders of the United States had a basic mistrust of European governments. This was a logical position at a time when the United States was so weak militarily that it

Monroe Doctrine

A policy statement by President James Monroe in 1823, which set out three principles: (1) European nations should not establish new colonies in the Western Hemisphere, (2) European nations should not intervene in the affairs of independent nations of the Western Hemisphere, and (3) the United States would not interfere in the affairs of European nations.

Isolationist Foreign Policy

A policy of abstaining from an active role in international affairs or alliances, which characterized U.S. foreign policy toward Europe during most of the 1800s.

Soviet Bloc

The Soviet Union and the Eastern European countries that installed Communist regimes after World War II and were dominated by the Soviet Union.

could not influence European developments directly. Moreover, being protected by oceans that took weeks to cross certainly allowed the nation to avoid entangling alliances. During the 1800s, therefore, the United States generally stayed out of European conflicts and politics. In the Western Hemisphere, however, the United States pursued an active expansionist policy. The nation purchased Louisiana in 1803, annexed Texas in 1845, gained substantial territory from Mexico in 1848, purchased Alaska in 1867, and annexed Hawaii in 1898.

The Monroe Doctrine. President James Monroe, in his message to Congress on December 2, 1823, stated that the United States would not accept any new European intervention in the Western Hemisphere. In return, the United States would not meddle in European affairs. The **Monroe Doctrine** was the underpinning of the U.S. **isolationist foreign policy** toward Europe, which continued throughout the 1800s.

The Spanish-American War and World War I. The end of the isolationist policy started with the Spanish-American War in 1898. Winning the war gave the United States possession of Guam, Puerto Rico, and the Philippines (which gained independence in 1946). On the heels of that war came World War I (1914–1918). The United States declared war on Germany in April 1917, because that country refused to give up its campaign of sinking all ships headed for Britain, including passenger ships from America. (Large passenger ships of that time commonly held over a thousand people, so the sinking of such a ship was a disaster comparable to the attack on the World Trade Center.)

In the 1920s, the United States went "back to normalcy," as President Warren G. Harding urged it to do. U.S. military forces were largely disbanded, defense spending dropped to about 1 percent of the total annual national income, and the nation returned to a period of isolationism.

The Era of Internationalism

Isolationism was permanently shattered by the bombing of the U.S. naval base at Pearl Harbor, Hawaii, on December 7, 1941. The surprise attack by the Japanese caused the deaths of 2,403 American servicemen. President Franklin Roosevelt asked Congress to declare war on Japan immediately, and the United States entered World War II.

At the conclusion of the war, the United States was the only major participating country to emerge with its economy intact, and even strengthened. The United States was also the only country to have control over operational nuclear weapons. President Harry Truman had made the decision to use two atomic bombs in August 1945 to end the war with Japan. (Historians still argue over the necessity of this action, which ultimately killed more than 100,000 Japanese and left an equal number permanently injured.) The United States truly had become the world's superpower.

The Cold War. The United States had become an uncomfortable ally of the Soviet Union after Adolf Hitler's invasion of that country. Soon after World War II ended, relations between the Soviet Union and the West deteriorated. The Soviet Union wanted a weakened Germany, and to achieve this, it insisted that Germany be divided in two, with East Germany becoming a buffer against the West. Little by little, the Soviet Union helped to install Communist governments in Eastern European countries, which began to be referred to collectively as the **Soviet bloc.** In response, the United States encouraged the rearming of Western Europe. The Cold War had begun.[2]

James Monroe, the fifth president. *With what foreign policy doctrine is he most commonly associated?*

AP Images

---

2. See John Lewis Gaddis, *The United Nations and the Origins of the Cold War* (New York: Columbia University Press, 1972).

Containment Policy. In 1947, a remarkable article was published in *Foreign Affairs* magazine, signed by "X." The actual author was George F. Kennan, chief of the policy-planning staff for the State Department. The doctrine of **containment** set forth in the article became—according to many—the bible of Western foreign policy. "X" argued that whenever and wherever the Soviet Union could successfully challenge the West, it would do so. He recommended that our policy toward the Soviet Union be "firm and vigilant containment of Russian expansive tendencies."[3]

The containment theory was expressed clearly in the **Truman Doctrine,** which was enunciated by President Harry Truman in 1947. Truman held that the United States must help countries in which a Communist takeover seemed likely. Later that year, he backed the Marshall Plan, an economic assistance plan for Europe that was intended to prevent the expansion of Communist influence there. In 1949, the United States entered into a military alliance with a number of European nations called the North Atlantic Treaty Organization, or NATO, to offer a credible response to any Soviet military attack. Figure 16–1 that follows shows the face-off between the U.S.-led NATO alliance and the Soviet-led Warsaw Pact—an agreement formed by Soviet-bloc nations to counter the NATO alliance.

> **Containment**
> A U.S. diplomatic policy adopted by the Truman administration to contain Communist power within its existing boundaries.
>
> **Truman Doctrine**
> The policy adopted by President Harry Truman in 1947 to halt Communist expansion in southeastern Europe.

Superpower Relations

During the Cold War, there was never any direct military conflict between the United States and the Soviet Union. Only on occasion did the United States enter a conflict with any Communist-led country. Two such occasions were in Korea and in Vietnam.

3. X, "The Sources of Soviet Conduct," *Foreign Affairs,* July 1947, p. 575.

Figure 16–1 ▶ **Europe during the Cold War**

This map shows the face-off between NATO (led by the United States) and the Soviet bloc (the Warsaw Pact). Note that West Germany did not join NATO until 1955, and Albania suspended participation in the Warsaw Pact in 1960. France was out of NATO from 1966 to 1996, and Spain did not join until 1982. *Why might West Germany have been late to join NATO?*

The Korean War. After the end of World War II, northern Korea was occupied by the Soviet Union, and southern Korea was occupied by the United States. The result was two rival Korean governments. In 1950, North Korea invaded South Korea. Under UN authority, the United States entered the war, which prevented an almost certain South Korean defeat. When U.S. forces were on the brink of conquering North Korea, however, China joined the war on the side of the North, resulting in a stalemate. An armistice signed in 1953 led to the two Koreas that exist today. U.S. forces have remained in South Korea since that time.

The Vietnam War. The Vietnam War (1965–1975) also involved the United States in a civil war between a Communist north and pro-Western south. When the French army in Indochina was defeated by the Communist forces of Ho Chi Minh in 1954, two Vietnams were created. The United States assumed the role of supporting the South Vietnamese government against North Vietnam. American forces in Vietnam at the height of the U.S. involvement totaled more than 500,000 troops. More than 58,000 Americans were killed and 300,000 were wounded in the conflict. A peace agreement in 1973 allowed U.S. troops to leave the country, and in 1975 North Vietnam easily occupied Saigon (the South Vietnamese capital) and unified the nation.

Over the course of the Vietnam War, the debate over U.S. involvement became extremely heated and, as mentioned previously, spurred congressional efforts to limit the ability of the president to commit forces to armed combat. The military draft was also a major source of contention during the Vietnam War. Do recent events justify bringing back the draft? We examined this question in this chapter's opening *What If . . .* feature.

In a famous meeting in Yalta in February 1945, British prime minister Winston Churchill (left), U.S. president Franklin Roosevelt (center), and Soviet leader Joseph Stalin (right) decided on the fate of several nations in Europe, including Germany. *What happened to Germany immediately after World War II?*

The Cuban Missile Crisis. Perhaps the closest the two superpowers came to a nuclear confrontation was the Cuban missile crisis in 1962. The Soviets placed missiles in Cuba, ninety miles off the U.S. coast, in response to Cuban fears of an American invasion and to try to balance an American nuclear advantage. President Kennedy and his advisers rejected the option of invading Cuba, setting up a naval blockade around the island instead. When Soviet vessels appeared near Cuban waters, the tension reached its height.

After intense negotiations between Washington and Moscow, the Soviet ships turned around. On October 28, the Soviet Union announced the withdrawal of its missile operations from Cuba. In exchange, the United States agreed not to invade Cuba in the future. It also agreed to remove some of its own missiles that were located near the Soviet border in Turkey.

A Period of Détente. The French word **détente** means a relaxation of tensions. By the end of the 1960s, it was clear that some efforts had to be made to reduce the threat of nuclear war between the United States and the Soviet Union. The Soviet Union gradually had begun to catch up in the building of strategic nuclear delivery vehicles in the form of bombers and missiles, thus balancing the nuclear scales between the two countries. Each nation had acquired the military capacity to destroy the other with nuclear weapons.

As the result of lengthy negotiations under Secretary of State Henry Kissinger and President Nixon, the United States and the Soviet Union signed the **Strategic Arms Limitation Treaty (SALT I)** in May 1972. That treaty limited the number of offensive missiles each country could deploy.

The policy of détente was not limited to the U.S. relationship with the Soviet Union. Seeing an opportunity to capitalize on increasing friction between the Soviet Union and the People's Republic of China, Kissinger secretly began negotiations to establish a new relationship with China. President Nixon eventually visited that nation in 1972. The visit set the stage for the formal diplomatic recognition of that country, which occurred during the Carter administration (1977–1981).

Nuclear Arms Agreements with the Soviet Union and Russia. President Ronald Reagan (1981–1989) initially took a hard line against the Soviet Union. In 1987, however, after several years of negotiations, the United States and the Soviet Union signed the Intermediate-Range Nuclear Forces Treaty. The result was the dismantling of four thousand intermediate-range missiles.

In 1991, President George H. W. Bush and the Soviet Union signed the Strategic Arms Reduction Treaty (START). Implementation was complicated by the collapse of the Soviet Union in December 1991. In 1992, however, the treaty was re-signed by Russia and other former Soviet republics.

The 1992 START agreement expired in December 2009, and in April 2010 President Obama and Russian president Dmitry Medvedev signed New START, a follow-on treaty. New START reduced the number of permitted warheads to 1,550 for each side, a drop of about 30 percent from previous agreements. After some delays, the Senate ratified the treaty in December 2010.

Détente
A French word meaning a relaxation of tensions. The term characterized U.S.-Soviet relations as they developed under President Richard Nixon and Secretary of State Henry Kissinger.

Strategic Arms Limitation Treaty (SALT I)
A treaty between the United States and the Soviet Union to stabilize the nuclear arms competition between the two countries. SALT I talks began in 1969, and the treaty was signed on May 26, 1972.

Gary Hershorn/Files GMHSV/Reuters

Soviet leader Mikhail Gorbachev (left) stands with U.S. president Ronald Reagan (right) in 1987, shortly after the two men finished negotiations on a major arms-control treaty. *What happened to the Soviet Union in 1991?*

The Dissolution of the Soviet Union. In 1989, the fall of the Berlin Wall that had divided that city into eastern and western sectors marked the first step in the reunification of Germany. By then, it was clear that the Soviet Union had relinquished much of its political and military control over the states of Eastern Europe that formerly had been part of the Soviet bloc. No one expected the Soviet Union to dissolve into separate states as quickly as it did, however. Although Soviet leader Mikhail Gorbachev tried to adjust the Soviet constitution and political system to allow greater autonomy for the republics within the union, demands for political, ethnic, and religious autonomy grew. On the day after Christmas in 1991, the Soviet Union was officially dissolved. Figure 16–2 that follows shows the situation in Europe today.

Russia under Putin. In 2000, Boris Yeltsin, president of the newly independent and democratic Russian Federation, resigned because of poor health. He named Vladimir Putin, architect of the Russian military effort against an independence movement in the province of Chechnya, as acting president. A few months later, Putin won the presidency in a national election. Putin chipped away at Russia's democratic institutions, slowly turning the country into what was, in essence, an elected autocracy. When Putin's second term as president came to an end in 2008, he could not immediately run for reelection. He therefore engineered the election of one of his supporters, Dmitry Medvedev, as president. Medvedev promptly appointed Putin as prime minister. It was clear that Putin retained real power in Russia, and in 2012 Putin again took the presidency.

Figure 16–2 ▶ Europe after the Fall of the Soviet Union

This map shows the growth in European unity as marked by participation in transnational organizations. The United States continues to lead NATO (and would be orange if it were on the map). Note the reunification of Germany and the creation of new states from the former Yugoslavia and the former Soviet Union. *Why would a nation such as Poland want to join NATO?*

In recent years, the United States has become concerned over Russia's aggressive attitude toward its neighbors. In 2008, Russian troops entered Georgia to prevent that nation from retaking an autonomous region that was under Russian protection. On several occasions since 2005, Russia has cut off the transmission of natural gas to Europe as a result of disputes. Russia also reacted angrily to U.S. plans for antimissile defenses in Eastern Europe, aimed at protecting Europe from a possible future Iranian attack. Russia appeared to believe that the defenses were directed against it. Still, the United States needed Russian assistance in matters such as curbing Iran's nuclear program.

In 2009, U.S. secretary of State Hillary Clinton announced a policy of "pressing the reset button" in relations with Russia. In other words, the Obama administration hoped to "start over" after the confrontations between Putin and the George W. Bush team. A series of belligerent gestures by Putin, however, soon made the "reset" policy untenable.

Crisis in Ukraine. The most serious of these was Russian aggression against Ukraine in 2014. The crisis began in November 2013 when Ukraine's pro-Russian president Viktor Yanukovych abruptly broke off economic talks with the European Union, apparently under pressure from Putin. Protestors launched large pro-European demonstrations in Kiev, the capital. Eventually, gunmen attacked the demonstrators, killing between one hundred and two hundred. The resulting tumult was so intense that Yanukovych fled the country in February 2014. Parliament assumed power and began steering the country back toward Europe.

Putin denounced the new government as "fascist." (A small number of demonstrators were in fact ultra-right-wing, but most were not.) Claiming the right to protect Russian-speaking populations in Ukraine, Putin annexed the Crimean Peninsula, which has an ethnic-Russian majority. Pro-Russian activists, with Russian support, took control of two eastern provinces.

A pro-Russia militant in eastern Ukraine at the crash site of Malaysia Airlines flight MH17. The crash, apparently the result of an attack by a Russian-made missile, killed 298 people. A majority of them were from the Netherlands. *When Russia supplies insurgents with weapons, is it responsible for what they do with them? Why or why not?*

President Obama responded with a series of sanctions (penalties) applied largely to Putin's closest allies in Russia. Obama tried to persuade European countries to follow suit, with limited success. A greater blow to Russia was inflicted by the international financial community, which began withdrawing investments from the country. Despite sanctions, Putin appeared to be "doubling down" on support of the eastern rebels. When the Ukrainian government seemed to be winning the war in the east, Putin introduced thousands of Russian troops into Ukraine to support the rebels.

How You Can Make a Difference

What can you do to work for the improvement of human rights in other nations? One way is to join an organization that attempts to keep watch over human rights violations. (Two such organizations are listed at the end of this feature.) By publicizing human rights violations, such organizations try to pressure nations into changing their practices. Sometimes, these organizations are able to apply enough pressure and cause enough embarrassment that victims may be freed from prison or allowed to emigrate.

Another way to work for human rights is to keep informed about the state of affairs in other nations and to write personally to governments that violate human rights or to their embassies, asking them to cease these violations.

If you want to receive general information about the position of the United States on human rights violations, you can contact the State Department:

U.S. Department of State
Bureau of Democracy, Human Rights, and Labor

2201 C St. N.W.
Washington, DC 20520
202-647-4000
www.state.gov./j/drl/hr

The following organizations are well known for their watchdog efforts in countries that violate human rights for political reasons:

Amnesty International U.S.A.
5 Penn Plaza
New York, NY 10001
212-807-8400
www.amnestyusa.org

American Friends Service Committee
1501 Cherry St.
Philadelphia, PA 19102
215-241-7000
afsc.org

Key Terms

Cold War 470
containment 483
defense policy 463
détente 485
diplomacy 463
economic aid 463

foreign policy 463
intelligence community 479
isolationist foreign policy 482
Monroe Doctrine 482
moral idealism 464

national security policy 463
negative constituents 479
normal trade relations (NTR) status 471
political realism 464
Soviet bloc 482

Strategic Arms Limitation Treaty (SALT I) 485
technical assistance 463
terrorism 466
Truman Doctrine 483

Chapter Summary

Learning Outcome 1 Foreign policy includes the nation's external goals and the techniques and strategies used to achieve them. National security policy, which is one aspect of foreign policy, is designed to protect the independence and the political and economic integrity of the United States. Diplomacy involves the nation's external relationships and is an attempt to resolve conflict without resort to arms. U.S. foreign policy is based on both moral idealism and political realism.

Learning Outcome 2 Terrorism is the attempt to create fear to gain political ends, usually by violence against noncombatants. It has become a major challenge facing the United States and other nations. The United States waged war on terrorism after the attacks of September 11, 2001.

In 1991 and again in 2003, the United States sent combat troops to Iraq. The second war in Iraq, begun in 2003, succeeded in toppling that nation's decades-long dictatorship but led to a long, grinding conflict with insurgent forces. The current campaign in Afghanistan, which grew out of the war on terrorism, has proven to be equally difficult.

Learning Outcome 3 Recent diplomatic efforts by the United States include containing the nuclear ambitions of Iran and North Korea. The rise of China as a world power and eventually a superpower introduces a series of issues the United States must address. American efforts to promote the peace process between Israel and the Palestinians have had limited success. World economic issues, such as the European debt crisis and the trade with China, demand U.S. attention.

Learning Outcome 4 The formal power of the president to make foreign policy derives from the U.S. Constitution, which designates the president as commander in chief of the army and navy. Presidents have interpreted this authority broadly. They also have the power to make treaties and executive agreements. In principle, the State Department is the executive agency with primary authority over foreign affairs. The National Security Council also plays a major role. The intelligence community consists of government agencies engaged in activities varying from information gathering to covert operations. In response to presidential actions in the Vietnam War, Congress attempted to establish some limits on the power of the president to intervene abroad by passing the War Powers Resolution in 1973.

Learning Outcome 5 Three major themes have guided U.S. foreign policy. In the early years of the nation, isolationism was the primary strategy. With the start of the twentieth century, isolationism gave way to global involvement. From the end of World War II through the 1980s, the major goal was to contain communism and the influence of the Soviet Union.

During the 1800s, the United States stayed out of European conflicts and politics, so these years have been called the period of isolationism. The end of the policy of isolationism toward Europe started with the Spanish-American War of 1898. U.S. involvement in European politics became more extensive when the United States entered World War I in 1917. World War II marked a lasting change in American foreign policy. The United States was the only major country to emerge from the war with its economy intact and the only country with operating nuclear weapons.

Soon after World War II, the Cold War began. A policy of containment, which assumed an expansionist Soviet Union, was enunciated in the Truman Doctrine. Following the apparent arms equality of the United States and the Soviet Union, the United States adopted a policy of détente, or loosening of tensions.

The United States signed arms control agreements with the Soviet Union under Presidents Nixon, Reagan, and George H. W. Bush. After the fall of the Soviet Union, Russia emerged as a less threatening state. Under President Vladimir Putin, however, Russia has moved away from democracy and in part returned to its old autocratic traditions. Putin has also posed a serious military threat to Russia's neighbors.

Master the concepts of Foreign Policy and National Security with MindTap™ *for American Government*

REVIEW MindTap™ **for American Government**
Access Key Term Flashcards for Chapter 16.

STAY CURRENT MindTap™ **for American Government**
Access the KnowNow blog and customized RSS for updates on current events.

TEST YOURSELF MindTap™ **for American Government**
Take the Wrap It Up Quiz for Chapter 16.

STAY FOCUSED MindTap™ **for American Government**
Complete the Focus Activities for Foreign Policy and National Security.

Additional Resources

International organizations do not only dispense aid, loans, and advice. Several of them also field troops supplied by member nations. The "blue helmets" of the United Nations (UN) take part in missions in the Middle East, Africa, and elsewhere. American forces cooperate with those of other nations through the North Atlantic Treaty Organization (NATO). Major multinational organizations all have Web sites where you can learn about the history and status of current international conflicts.

Online Resources

- In addition to materials on international crises, the UN Web site contains a treasure trove of international statistics. To see these, go to www.un.org/en.
- For news about NATO, visit www.nato.int.
- The European Union is a confederation of twenty-eight nations. You can learn more about it at europa.eu/index_en.htm.
- The Organisation for Economic Co-operation and Development (OECD) provides another major source of international statistics and economic analysis. See its Web site at www.oecd.org.
- Finally, *Foreign Policy* magazine reviews a wide variety of foreign policy topics. Visit it at www.foreignpolicy.com.

Books

Fenby, Jonathan. *Will China Dominate the 21st Century?* Boston: Polity, 2014. China's rise has been one of the most important developments of recent history, and it is continuing. Fenby, however, believes that China faces major challenges that stand in the way of its attaining global domination. Fenby, a journalist, is also the author of *The Penguin History of Modern China.*

Gates, Robert M. *Duty: Memoirs of a Secretary at War.* New York: Knopf, 2014. Gates became secretary of Defense under President George W. Bush and remained at his post until 2011 under President Obama. His description of Congress is scathing. He criticizes Vice President Biden's judgment. He finds Obama himself to be motivated by political considerations (though it is hard to see why anyone would find that unusual in a president). He is surprisingly complimentary, however, toward then-secretary of State Hillary Clinton.

Sacco, Joe. *Journalism.* New York: Metropolitan Books, 2013. Sacco is a war correspondent, but his method of reporting is unusual. He is a highly acclaimed graphic novelist. *Journalism,* then, is a cartoon meditation on almost every major international conflict of the last decade.

Video

The Russian Soul—A 2014 film by Andrew Hamilton. The Russian Federation is a highly advanced nation in many ways, but its government is corrupt and autocratic. This documentary asks why it is that Russians put up with such a system.

United 93—A 2006 documentary about the fourth airplane hijacked on 9/11. When they learned the fate of the other three planes through their cell phones, the passengers decided to fight back, with the result that the plane crashed in a Pennsylvania field, far from its intended target. United 93 takes place in real time and is almost unbearably moving. Several critics named it the best film of the year.

Quiz

Multiple Choice and Fill-Ins

Learning Outcome 1 Define *foreign policy,* and discuss moral idealism versus political realism in foreign policy.

1. As part of foreign policy, national security policy is designed to:
   a. ensure that the fifty states respect each other's borders.
   b. ensure that all other countries respect each other's borders.
   c. protect the independence and political integrity of the United States.

2. U.S. support for foreign dictators is sometimes an example of _____ _____ in foreign policy.

Learning Outcome 2 Describe recent foreign policy challenges that involve the use of force.

3. Acts of terrorism are:
   a. the result of small-country governments' attempts to gain new territory.
   b. systematic attempts to inspire fear to gain political ends.
   c. due to large-country governments that failed in diplomacy.

4. The concept of "preemptive war" as a defense strategy was a new element in U.S. foreign policy in the 2000s. It has been called the _____ _____.

Learning Outcome 3 Discuss the use of diplomacy in addressing such issues as nuclear proliferation, the rise of China, and the confrontation between Israel and the Palestinians.

5. The two countries that today represent the most serious problems with nuclear proliferation are:
   a. Iran and North Korea.
   b. Japan and Germany.
   c. China and Brazil.

6. The Palestinian territories are made up of the _____ _____ and the _____ _____.

Learning Outcome 4 Explain the roles of the president, executive agencies, and Congress in making U.S. foreign policy.

7. The intelligence community is involved in foreign policy and consists of:
   a. the CIA and the Department of Defense.
   b. more than forty government agencies and bureaus involved in intelligence activities.
   c. the CIA and the National Security Council (NSC).

8. As part of foreign policy, the Constitution gives the president the power to make _____ provided that the _____ concurs.

Learning Outcome 5 Cite the main themes in the history of U.S. foreign policy.

9. The Cold War refers to a period during which:
   a. the Soviet Union and the United States faced off throughout the world.
   b. the United States reverted back to isolationist policies.
   c. the United States engaged in economic conflict with many Asian countries.

10. Just after World War II, President Harry Truman vowed that the United States must help countries in which a Communist takeover seemed likely. This became known as the _____ _____.

Essay Questions

1. Some people believe that if no U.S. military personnel were stationed abroad, terrorists would have less desire to harm Americans or the United States. Do you agree? Why or why not?

2. Why do you think that North Korea and Iran might want to possess nuclear weapons, even though they can never hope to match the nuclear arsenals of the original nuclear powers?

Appendix A

The Declaration of Independence

IN CONGRESS, JULY 4, 1776

A Declaration by the Representatives of the United States of America, in General Congress assembled. When in the Course of human Events, it becomes necessary for one People to dissolve the Political Bands which have connected them with another, and to assume among the Powers of the Earth, the separate and equal Station to which the Laws of Nature and of Nature's God entitle them, a decent Respect to the Opinions of Mankind requires that they should declare the causes which impel them to the Separation.

We hold these Truths to be self-evident, that all Men are created equal, that they are endowed by their Creator with certain unalienable Rights, that among these are Life, Liberty, and the Pursuit of Happiness—That to secure these Rights, Governments are instituted among Men, deriving their just Powers from the Consent of the Governed, that whenever any Form of Government becomes destructive of these Ends, it is the Right of the People to alter or to abolish it, and to institute new Government, laying its Foundation on such Principles, and organizing its Powers in such Forms, as to them shall seem most likely to effect their Safety and Happiness. Prudence, indeed, will dictate that Governments long established should not be changed for light and transient Causes; and accordingly all Experience hath shewn, that Mankind are more disposed to suffer, while Evils are sufferable, than to right themselves by abolishing the Forms to which they are accustomed. But when a long Train of Abuses and Usurpations, pursuing invariably the same Object, evinces a Design to reduce them under absolute Despotism, it is their Right, it is their Duty, to throw off such Government, and to provide new Guards for their future Security. Such has been the patient Sufferance of these Colonies; and such is now the Necessity which constrains them to alter their former Systems of Government. The History of the present King of Great-Britain is a History of repeated Injuries and Usurpations, all having in direct Object the Establishment of an absolute Tyranny over these States. To prove this, let Facts be submitted to a candid World.

He has refused his Assent to Laws, the most wholesome and necessary for the public Good.

He has forbidden his Governors to pass Laws of immediate and pressing Importance, unless suspended in their Operation till his Assent should be obtained; and when so suspended, he has utterly neglected to attend to them.

He has refused to pass other Laws for the Accommodation of large Districts of People, unless those People would relinquish the Right of Representation in the Legislature, a Right inestimable to them, and formidable to Tyrants only.

He has called together Legislative Bodies at Places unusual, uncomfortable, and distant from the Depository of their Public Records, for the sole Purpose of fatiguing them into Compliance with his Measures.

He has dissolved Representative Houses repeatedly, for opposing with manly Firmness his Invasions on the Rights of the People.

He has refused for a long Time, after such Dissolutions, to cause others to be elected; whereby the Legislative Powers, incapable of Annihilation, have returned to the People at large for their exercise; the State remaining in the mean time exposed to all the Dangers of Invasion from without, and Convulsions within.

He has endeavoured to prevent the Population of these States; for that Purpose obstructing the Laws for Naturalization of Foreigners; refusing to pass others to encourage their Migrations hither, and raising the Conditions of new Appropriations of Lands.

He has obstructed the Administration of Justice, by refusing his Assent to Laws for establishing Judiciary Powers.

He has made Judges dependent on his Will alone, for the Tenure of their offices, and the Amount and payment of their Salaries.

He has erected a Multitude of new Offices, and sent hither Swarms of Officers to harass our People, and eat out their Substance.

He has kept among us, in Times of Peace, Standing Armies, without the consent of our Legislatures.

He has affected to render the Military independent of, and superior to the Civil Power.

He has combined with others to subject us to a Jurisdiction foreign to our Constitution, and unacknowledged by our Laws; giving his Assent to their Acts of pretended Legislation:

For quartering large Bodies of Armed Troops among us:

For protecting them, by a mock Trial, from Punishment for any Murders which they should commit on the Inhabitants of these States:

For cutting off our Trade with all Parts of the World:

For imposing Taxes on us without our Consent:

For depriving us, in many cases, of the Benefits of Trial by Jury:

For transporting us beyond Seas to be tried for pretended Offences:

For abolishing the free System of English Laws in a neighbouring Province, establishing therein an arbitrary Government, and enlarging its Boundaries, so as to render it at once an Example and fit Instrument for introducing the same absolute Rule into these Colonies:

For taking away our Charters, abolishing our most valuable Laws, and altering fundamentally the Forms of our Governments:

For suspending our own Legislatures, and declaring themselves invested with Power to legislate for us in all Cases whatsoever.

He has abdicated Government here, by declaring us out of his Protection and waging War against us.

He has plundered our Seas, ravaged our Coasts, burnt our towns, and destroyed the Lives of our People.

He is, at this Time, transporting large Armies of foreign Mercenaries to compleat the works of Death, Desolation, and Tyranny, already begun with circumstances of Cruelty and Perfidy, scarcely paralleled in the most barbarous Ages, and totally unworthy the Head of a civilized Nation.

He has constrained our fellow Citizens taken Captive on the high Seas to bear Arms against their Country, to become the Executioners of their Friends and Brethren, or to fall themselves by their Hands.

He has excited domestic Insurrections amongst us, and has endeavoured to bring on the Inhabitants of our Frontiers, the merciless Indian Savages, whose known Rule of Warfare, is an undistinguished Destruction, of all Ages, Sexes and Conditions.

In every state of these Oppressions we have Petitioned for Redress in the most humble Terms: Our repeated Petitions have been answered only by repeated Injury. A Prince, whose Character is thus marked by every act which may define a Tyrant, is unfit to be the Ruler of a free People.

Nor have we been wanting in Attentions to our British Brethren. We have warned them from Time to Time of Attempts by their Legislature to extend an unwarrantable Jurisdiction over us. We have reminded them of the Circumstances of our Emigration and Settlement here. We have appealed to their native Justice and Magnanimity, and we have conjured them by the Ties of our common Kindred to disavow these Usurpations, which, would inevitably interrupt our Connections and Correspondence. They too have been deaf to the Voice of Justice and of Consanguinity. We must, therefore, acquiesce in the Necessity, which denounces our Separation, and hold them, as we hold the rest of Mankind, Enemies in War, in Peace, Friends.

We, therefore, the Representatives of the UNITED STATES OF AMERICA, in General Congress Assembled, appealing to the Supreme Judge of the World for the Rectitude of our Intentions, do, in the Name, and by the Authority of the good People of these Colonies, solemnly Publish and Declare, That these United Colonies are, and of Right ought to be, Free and Independent States; that they are absolved from all Allegiance to the British Crown, and that all political Connection between them and the State of Great-Britain, is and ought to be totally dissolved; and that as Free and Independent States, they have full Power to levy War, conclude Peace, contract Alliances, establish Commerce, and to do all other Acts and Things which Independent States may of right do. And for the support of this declaration, with a firm Reliance on the Protection of divine Providence, we mutually pledge to each other our lives, our Fortunes, and our sacred Honor.

Appendix B

Federalist Papers Nos. 10, 51, and 78

In 1787, after the newly drafted U.S. Constitution was submitted to the thirteen states for ratification, a major political debate ensued between the Federalists (who favored ratification) and the Anti-Federalists (who opposed ratification). Anti-Federalists in New York were particularly critical of the Constitution, and in response to their objections, Federalists Alexander Hamilton, James Madison, and John Jay wrote a series of eighty-five essays in defense of the Constitution. The essays were published in New York newspapers and reprinted in other newspapers throughout the country.

For students of American government, the essays, collectively known as the Federalist Papers, are particularly important because they provide a glimpse of the founders' political philosophy and intentions in designing the Constitution—and, consequently, in shaping the American philosophy of government.

We have included in this appendix three of these essays: Federalist Papers Nos. 10, 51, and 78. Each essay has been annotated by the authors to indicate its importance in American political thought and to clarify the meaning of particular passages.

FEDERALIST PAPER NO. 10

Federalist Paper No. 10, penned by James Madison, has often been singled out as a key document in American political thought. In this essay, Madison attacks the Anti-Federalists' fear that a republican form of government will inevitably give rise to "factions"—small political parties or groups united by a common interest—that will control the government. Factions will be harmful to the country because they will implement policies beneficial to their own interests but adverse to other people's rights and to the public good. In this essay, Madison attempts to lay to rest this fear by explaining how, in a large republic such as the United States, there will be so many different factions, held together by regional or local interests, that no single one of them will dominate national politics.

Madison opens his essay with a paragraph discussing how important it is to devise a plan of government that can control the "instability, injustice, and confusion" brought about by factions.

Among the numerous advantages promised by a well-constructed Union, none deserves to be more accurately developed than its tendency to break and control the violence of faction. The friend of popular governments never finds himself so much alarmed for their character and fate as when he contemplates their propensity to this dangerous vice. He will not fail, therefore, to set a due value on any plan which, without violating the principles to which he is attached, provides a proper cure for it. The instability, injustice, and confusion introduced into the public councils have, in truth, been the mortal diseases under which popular governments have everywhere perished, as they continue to be the favorite and fruitful topics from which the adversaries to liberty derive their most specious declamations. The valuable improvements made by the American constitutions on the popular models, both ancient and modern, cannot certainly be too much admired; but it would be an unwarrantable partiality to contend that they have as effectually obviated the danger on this side, as was wished and expected. Complaints are everywhere heard from our most considerate and virtuous citizens, equally the friends of public and private faith and of public and personal liberty, that our governments are too unstable, that the public good is disregarded in the conflicts of rival parties, and that measures are too often decided, not according to the rules of justice and the rights of the minor party, but by the superior force of an interested and overbearing majority. However anxiously we may wish that these complaints had no foundation, the evidence of known facts will not permit us to deny that they are in some degree true. It will be found, indeed, on a candid review of our situation, that some of the distresses under which we labor have been erroneously charged on the operation of our governments; but it will be found, at the same time, that other causes will not alone account for many of our heaviest misfortunes; and, particularly, for that prevailing and increasing distrust of public engagements and alarm for private rights which are echoed from one end of the continent to the other. These must be chiefly, if not wholly, effects of the unsteadiness and injustice with which a factious spirit has tainted our public administration.

Madison now defines what he means by the term faction.

By a faction I understand a number of citizens, whether amounting to a majority or minority of the whole, who are united and actuated by some common impulse of passion, or of interest, adverse to the rights of other citizens, or the permanent and aggregate interests of the community.

Madison next contends that there are two methods by which the "mischiefs of faction" can be cured: by removing the causes of faction or by controlling their effects. In the following paragraphs, Madison explains how liberty itself nourishes factions. Therefore, to abolish factions would involve abolishing liberty—a cure "worse than the disease."

There are two methods of curing the mischiefs of faction: the one, by removing its causes; the other, by controlling its effects.

There are again two methods of removing the causes of faction: the one, by destroying the liberty which is essential to its existence; the other, by giving to every citizen the same opinions, the same passions, and the same interests.

It could never be more truly said than of the first remedy that it was worse than the disease. Liberty is to faction what air is to fire, an aliment without which it instantly expires. But it could not be a less folly to abolish liberty, which is essential to political life, because it nourishes faction than it would be to wish the annihilation of air, which is essential to animal life, because it imparts to fire its destructive agency.

The second expedient is as impracticable as the first would be unwise. As long as the reason of man continues fallible, and he is at liberty to exercise it, different opinions will be formed. As long as the connection subsists between his reason and his self-love, his opinions and his passions will have a reciprocal influence on each other; and the former will be objects to which the latter will attach themselves. The diversity in the faculties of men, from which the rights of property originate, is not less an insuperable obstacle to a uniformity of interests. The protection of these faculties is the first object of government. From the protection of different and unequal faculties of acquiring property, the possession of different degrees and kinds of property immediately results; and from the influence of these on the sentiments and views of the respective proprietors ensues a division of the society into different interests and parties.

The latent causes of faction are thus sown in the nature of man; and we see them everywhere brought into different degrees of activity, according to the different circumstances of civil society. A zeal for different opinions concerning religion, concerning government, and many other points, as well of speculation as of practice; an attachment to different leaders ambitiously contending for pre-eminence and power; or to persons of other descriptions whose fortunes have been interesting to the human passions, have, in turn, divided mankind into parties, inflamed them with mutual animosity, and rendered them much more disposed to vex and oppress each other than to co-operate for their common good. So strong is this propensity of mankind to fall into mutual animosities that where no substantial occasion presents itself the most frivolous and fanciful distinctions have been sufficient to kindle their unfriendly passions and excite their most violent conflicts. But the most common and durable source of factions has been the various and unequal distribution of property. Those who hold and those who are without property have ever formed distinct interests in society. Those who are creditors, and those who are debtors, fall under a like discrimination. A landed interest, a manufacturing interest, a mercantile interest, a moneyed interest, with many lesser interests, grow up of necessity in civilized nations, and divide them into different classes, actuated by different sentiments and views. The regulation of these various and interfering interests forms the principal task of modern legislation and involves the spirit of party and faction in the necessary and ordinary operations of government.

No man is allowed to be a judge in his own cause, because his interest would certainly bias his judgment, and, not improbably, corrupt his integrity. With equal, nay with greater reason, a body of men are unfit to be both judges and parties at the same time; yet what are many of the most important acts of legislation but so many judicial determinations, not indeed concerning the rights of single persons, but concerning the rights of large bodies of citizens? And what are the different classes of legislators but advocates and parties to the causes which they determine? Is a law proposed concerning private debts? It is a question to which the creditors are parties on one side and the debtors on the other. Justice ought to hold the balance between them. Yet the parties are, and must be, themselves the judges; and the most numerous party, or in other words, the most powerful faction must be expected to prevail. Shall domestic manufacturers be encouraged, and in what degree, by restrictions on foreign manufacturers? [These] are questions which would be differently decided by the landed and the manufacturing classes, and probably by neither with a sole regard to justice and the public good. The apportionment of taxes on the various descriptions of property is an act which seems to require the most exact impartiality; yet there is, perhaps, no legislative act in which greater opportunity and temptation are given to a predominant party to trample on the rules of justice. Every shilling with which they overburden the inferior number is a shilling saved to their own pockets.

It is in vain to say that enlightened statesmen will be able to adjust these clashing interests and render them all subservient to the public good. Enlightened statesmen will not always be at the helm. Nor, in many cases, can such an adjustment be made at all without taking into view indirect and remote considerations, which will rarely prevail over the immediate interest which one party may find in disregarding the rights of another or the good of the whole.

The inference to which we are brought is that the causes of faction cannot be removed and that relief is only to be sought in the means of controlling its effects.

Having concluded that "the causes of faction cannot be removed," Madison now looks in some detail at the other method by which factions can be cured—by controlling their effects. This is the heart of his essay. He begins by positing a significant question: How can you have self-government without risking the possibility that a ruling faction, particularly a majority faction, might tyrannize over the rights of others?

If a faction consists of less than a majority, relief is supplied by the republican principle, which enables the majority to defeat its sinister views by regular vote. It may clog the administration, it may convulse the society; but it will be unable to execute and mask its violence under the forms of the Constitution. When a majority is included in a faction, the form of popular government, on the other hand, enables it to sacrifice to its ruling passion or interest both the public good and the rights of other citizens. To secure the public good and private rights against the danger of such a faction, and at the same time to preserve the spirit and the form of popular government, is then the great object to which our inquiries are directed. Let me add that it is the great desideratum by which alone this form of government can be rescued from the opprobrium under which it has so long labored and be recommended to the esteem and adoption of mankind.

Madison now sets forth the idea that one way to control the effects of factions is to ensure that the majority is rendered incapable of acting in concert in order to "carry into effect schemes of oppression." He goes on to state that in a democracy, in which all citizens participate personally in government decision making, there is no way to prevent the majority from communicating with each other and, as a result, acting in concert.

By what means is this object attainable? Evidently by one of two only. Either the existence of the same passion or interest in a majority at the same time must be prevented, or the majority, having such coexistent passion or interest, must be rendered, by their number and local situation, unable to concert and carry into effect schemes of oppression. If the impulse and the opportunity be suffered to coincide, we well know that neither moral nor religious motives can be relied on as an adequate control. They are not found to be such on the injustice and violence of individuals, and lose their efficacy in proportion to the number combined together, that is, in proportion as their efficacy becomes needful.

From this view of the subject it may be concluded that a pure democracy, by which I mean a society consisting of a small number of citizens, who assemble and administer the government in person, can admit of no cure for the mischiefs of faction. A common passion or interest will, in almost every case, be felt by a majority of the whole; a communication and concert results from the form of government itself; and there is nothing to check the inducements to sacrifice the weaker party or an obnoxious individual. Hence it is that such democracies have ever been spectacles of turbulence and contention; have ever been found incompatible with personal security or the rights of property; and have in general been as short in their lives as they have been violent in their deaths. Theoretic politicians, who have patronized this species of government, have erroneously supposed that by reducing mankind to a perfect equality in their political rights, they would at the same time be perfectly equalized and assimilated in their possessions, their opinions, and their passions.

Madison now moves on to discuss the benefits of a republic with respect to controlling the effects of factions. He begins by defining a republic and then pointing out the "two great points of difference" between a republic and a democracy: a republic is governed by a small body of elected representatives, not by the people directly; and a republic can extend over a much larger territory and embrace more citizens than a democracy can.

A republic, by which I mean a government in which the scheme of representation takes place, opens a different prospect and promises the cure for which we are seeking. Let us examine the points in which it varies from pure democracy, and we shall comprehend both the nature of the cure and the efficacy which it must derive from the Union.

The two great points of difference between a democracy and a republic are: first, the delegation of the government, in the latter, to a small number of citizens elected by the rest; secondly, the greater number of citizens and greater sphere of country over which the latter may be extended.

In the following four paragraphs, Madison explains how in a republic, particularly a large republic, the delegation of authority to elected representatives will increase the likelihood that those who govern will be "fit" for their positions and that a proper balance will be achieved between local (factional) interests and national interests. Note how he stresses that the new federal Constitution, by dividing powers between state governments and the national government, provides a "happy combination in this respect."

The effect of the first difference is, on the one hand, to refine and enlarge the public views by passing them through the medium of a chosen body of citizens, whose wisdom may best discern the true interest of their country and whose patriotism and love of justice will be least likely to sacrifice it to temporary or partial considerations. Under such a regulation it may well happen that the public voice, pronounced by the representatives of the people, will be more consonant to the public good than if pronounced by the people themselves, convened for the purpose. On the other hand, the effect may be inverted. Men of factious tempers, of local prejudices, or of sinister designs, may, by intrigue, by corruption, or by other means, first obtain the suffrages, and then betray the interests of the people. The question resulting is, whether small or extensive republics are most favorable to the election of proper guardians of the public weal; and it is clearly decided in favor of the latter by two obvious considerations.

In the first place, it is to be remarked that however small the republic may be the representatives must be raised to a certain number in order to guard against the cabals of a few; and that however large it may be, they must be limited to a certain number in order to guard against the confusion of a multitude. Hence, the number of representatives in the two cases not being in proportion to that of the constituents, and being proportionally greater in the small republic, it follows that if the proportion of fit characters be not less in the large than in the small republic, the former will present a greater option, and consequently a greater probability of a fit choice.

In the next place, as each representative will be chosen by a greater number of citizens in the large than in the small republic, it will be more difficult for unworthy candidates to practice with success the vicious arts by which elections are too often carried; and the suffrages of the people being more free, will be more likely to center on men who possess the most attractive merit and the most diffusive and established characters.

It must be confessed that in this, as in most other cases, there is a mean, on both sides of which inconveniencies will be found to lie. By enlarging too much the number of electors, you render the representative too little acquainted with all their local circumstances and lesser interests; as by reducing it too much, you render him unduly attached to these, and too little fit to comprehend and pursue great and national objects. The federal Constitution forms a happy combination in this respect; the great and aggregate interests being referred to the national, the local and particular to the State legislatures.

Madison now looks more closely at the other difference between a republic and a democracy—namely, that a republic can encompass a larger territory and more citizens than a democracy can. In the remaining paragraphs of his essay, Madison concludes that in a large republic, it will be difficult for factions to act in concert. Although a factious group—religious, political, economic, or otherwise—may control a local or regional government, it will have little chance of gathering a national following. This is because in a large republic, there will be numerous factions whose work will offset the work of any one particular faction ("sect"). As Madison phrases it, these numerous factions will "secure the national councils against any danger from that source."

The other point of difference is the greater number of citizens and extent of territory which may be brought within the compass of republican than of democratic government; and it is this circumstance principally which renders factious combinations less to be dreaded in the former than in the latter. The smaller the society, the fewer probably will be the distinct parties and interests composing it; the fewer the distinct parties and interests, the more frequently will a majority be found of the same party; and the smaller the number of individuals composing a majority, and the smaller the compass within which they are placed, the more easily will they concert and execute their plans of oppression. Extend the sphere and you take in a greater variety of parties and interests; you make it less probable that a majority of the whole will have a common motive to invade the rights of other citizens; or if such a common motive exists, it will be more difficult for all who feel it to discover their own strength and to act in unison with each other. Besides other impediments, it may be remarked that, where there is a consciousness of unjust or dishonorable purposes, communication is always checked by distrust in proportion to the number whose concurrence is necessary.

Hence, it clearly appears that the same advantage which a republic has over a democracy in controlling the effects of faction is enjoyed by a large over a small republic—is enjoyed by the Union over the States composing it. Does this advantage consist in the substitution of representatives whose enlightened views and virtuous sentiments render them superior to local prejudices and to schemes of injustice? It will not be denied that the representation of the Union will be most likely to possess these requisite endowments. Does it consist in the greater security afforded by a greater variety of parties, against the event of any one party being able to outnumber and oppress the rest? In an equal degree does the increased variety of parties comprised within the Union increase this security. Does it, in fine, consist in the greater obstacles opposed to the concert and accomplishment of the secret wishes of an unjust and interested majority? Here again the extent of the Union gives it the most palpable advantage.

The influence of factious leaders may kindle a flame within their particular States but will be unable to spread a general conflagration through the other States. A religious sect may degenerate into a political faction in a part of the Confederacy; but the variety of sects dispersed over the entire face of it must secure the national councils against any danger from that source. A rage for paper money, for an abolition of debts, for an equal division of property, or for any other improper or wicked project, will be less apt to pervade the whole body of the Union than a particular member of it, in the same proportion as such a malady is more likely to taint a particular county or district than an entire State.

In the extent and proper structure of the Union, therefore, we behold a republican remedy for the diseases most incident to republican government. And according to the degree of pleasure and pride we feel in being republicans ought to be our zeal in cherishing the spirit and supporting the character of federalists.

Publius
(James Madison)

FEDERALIST PAPER NO. 51

Federalist Paper No. 51, also authored by James Madison, is another classic in American political theory. Although the Federalists wanted a strong national government, they had not abandoned the traditional American view, particularly notable during the revolutionary era, that those holding powerful government positions could not be trusted to put national interests and the common good above their own personal interests. In this essay, Madison explains why the separation of the national government's powers into three branches—executive, legislative, and judicial—and a federal structure of government offer the best protection against tyranny.

To what expedient, then, shall we finally resort, for maintaining in practice the necessary partition of power among the several departments as laid down in the Constitution? The only answer that can be given is that as all these exterior provisions are found to be inadequate the defect must be supplied, by so contriving the interior structure of the government as that its several constituent parts may, by their mutual relations, be the means of keeping each other in their proper places. Without presuming to undertake a full development of this important idea I will hazard a few general observations which may perhaps place it in a clearer light, and enable us to form a more correct judgment of the principles and structure of the government planned by the convention.

In the next two paragraphs, Madison stresses that for the powers of the different branches (departments) of government to be truly separated, the personnel in one branch should not be dependent on another branch for their appointment or for the "emoluments" (compensation) attached to their offices.

In order to lay a due foundation for that separate and distinct exercise of the different powers of government, which to a certain extent is admitted on all hands to be essential to the preservation of liberty, it is evident that each department should have a will of its own; and consequently should be so constituted that the members of each should have as little agency as possible in the appointment of the members of the others. Were this principle rigorously adhered to, it would require that all the appointments for the supreme executive, legislative, and judiciary magistracies should be drawn from the same fountain of authority, the people, through channels having no communication whatever with one another. Perhaps such a plan of constructing the several departments would be less difficult in practice than it may in contemplation appear. Some difficulties, however, and some additional expense would attend the execution of it. Some deviations, therefore, from the principle must be admitted. In the constitution of the judiciary department in particular, it might be inexpedient to insist rigorously on the principle: first, because peculiar qualifications being essential in the members, the primary consideration ought to be to select that mode of choice which best secures these qualifications; second, because the permanent tenure by which the appointments are held in that department must soon destroy all sense of dependence on the authority conferring them.

It is equally evident that the members of each department should be as little dependent as possible on those of the others for the emoluments annexed to their offices. Were the executive magistrate, or the judges, not independent of the legislature in this particular, their independence in every other would be merely nominal.

In the following passages, which are among the most widely quoted of Madison's writings, he explains how the separation of the powers of government into three branches helps to counter the effects of personal ambition on government. The separation of powers allows personal motives to be linked to the constitutional rights of a branch of government. In effect, competing personal interests in each branch will help to keep the powers of the three government branches separate and, in so doing, will help to guard the public interest.

But the great security against a gradual concentration of the several powers in the same department consists in giving to those who administer each department the necessary constitutional means and personal motives to resist encroachments of the others. The provision for defense must in this, as in all other cases, be made commensurate to the danger of attack. Ambition must be made to counteract ambition. The interest of the man must be connected with the constitutional rights of the place. It may be a reflection on human nature that such devices should be necessary to control the abuses of government. But what is government itself but the greatest of all reflections on human nature? If men were angels, no government would be necessary. If angels were to govern men, neither external nor internal controls on government would be necessary. In framing a government which is to be administered by men over men, the great difficulty lies in this: you must first enable the government to control the governed; and in the next place oblige it to con-

trol itself. A dependence on the people is, no doubt, the primary control on the government; but experience has taught mankind the necessity of auxiliary precautions.

This policy of supplying, by opposite and rival interests, the defect of better motives, might be traced through the whole system of human affairs, private as well as public. We see it particularly displayed in all the subordinate distributions of power, where the constant aim is to divide and arrange the several offices in such a manner as that each may be a check on the other—that the private interest of every individual may be a sentinel over the public rights. These inventions of prudence cannot be less requisite in the distribution of the supreme powers of the State.

Madison now addresses the issue of equality between the branches of government. The legislature will necessarily predominate, but if the executive is given an "absolute negative" (absolute veto power) over legislative actions, this also could lead to an abuse of power. Madison concludes that the division of the legislature into two "branches" (parts, or chambers) will act as a check on the legislature's powers.

But it is not possible to give to each department an equal power of self-defense. In republican government, the legislative authority necessarily predominates. The remedy for this inconveniency is to divide the legislature into different branches; and to render them, by different modes of election and different principles of action, as little connected with each other as the nature of their common functions and their common dependence on the society will admit. It may even be necessary to guard against dangerous encroachments by still further precautions. As the weight of the legislative authority requires that it should be thus divided, the weakness of the executive may require, on the other hand, that it should be fortified. An absolute negative on the legislature appears, at first view, to be the natural defense with which the executive magistrate should be armed. But perhaps it would be neither altogether safe nor alone sufficient. On ordinary occasions it might not be exerted with the requisite firmness, and on extraordinary occasions it might be perfidiously abused. May not this defect of an absolute negative be supplied by some qualified connection between this weaker department and the weaker branch of the stronger department, by which the latter may be led to support the constitutional rights of the former, without being too much detached from the rights of its own department?

If the principles on which these observations are founded be just, as I persuade myself they are, and they be applied as a criterion to the several State constitutions, and to the federal Constitution, it will be found that if the latter does not perfectly correspond with them, the former are infinitely less able to bear such a test.

In the remainder of the essay, Madison discusses how a federal system of government, in which powers are divided between the states and the national government, offers "double security" against tyranny.

There are, moreover, two considerations particularly applicable to the federal system of America, which place that system in a very interesting point of view.

First. In a single republic, all the power surrendered by the people is submitted to the administration of a single government; and the usurpations are guarded against by a division of the government into distinct and separate departments. In the compound republic of America, the power surrendered by the people is first divided between two distinct governments, and then the portion allotted to each subdivided among distinct and separate departments. Hence a double security arises to the rights of the people. The different governments will control each other, at the same time that each will be controlled by itself.

Second. It is of great importance in a republic not only to guard the society against the oppression of its rulers, but to guard one part of the society against the injustice of the other part. Different interests necessarily exist in different classes of citizens. If a majority be united by a common interest, the rights of the minority will be insecure. There are but two methods of providing against this evil: the one by creating a will in the community independent of the majority—that is, of the society itself; the other, by comprehending in the society so many separate descriptions of citizens as will render an unjust combination of a majority of the whole very improbable, if not impracticable. The first method prevails in all governments possessing an hereditary or self-appointed authority. This, at best, is but a precarious security; because a power independent of the society may as well espouse the unjust views of the major as the rightful interests of the minor party, and may possibly be turned against both parties. The second method will be exemplified in the federal republic of the United States. Whilst all authority in it will be derived from and dependent on the society, the society itself will be broken into so many parts, interests and classes of citizens, that the rights of individuals, or of the minority, will be in little danger from interested combinations of the majority.

In a free government the security for civil rights must be the same as that for religious rights. It consists in the one case in the multiplicity of interests, and in the other in the multiplicity of sects. The degree of security in both cases will depend on the number of interests and sects; and this may be presumed to depend on the extent of country and number of people comprehended under the same government. This view of the subject must particularly recommend a proper federal system to all the sincere and considerate friends of republican government, since it shows that in exact proportion as the territory of the Union may be formed into more circumscribed Confederacies, or States, oppressive combinations of a majority will be facilitated; the best security, under the republican forms, for the rights of every class of citizen, will be diminished; and consequently the stability and independence of some member of the government, the only other security, must be proportionally increased. Justice is the end of government. It is the end of civil society. It ever has been

and ever will be pursued until it be obtained, or until liberty be lost in the pursuit. In a society under the forms of which the stronger faction can readily unite and oppress the weaker, anarchy may as truly be said to reign as in a state of nature, where the weaker individual is not secured against the violence of the stronger; and as, in the latter state, even the stronger individuals are prompted, by the uncertainty of their condition, to submit to a government which may protect the weak as well as themselves; so, in the former state, will the more powerful factions or parties be gradually induced, by a like motive, to wish for a government which will protect all parties, the weaker as well as the more powerful.

It can be little doubted that if the State of Rhode Island was separated from the Confederacy and left to itself, the insecurity of rights under the popular form of government within such narrow limits would be displayed by such reiterated oppressions of factious majorities that some power altogether independent of the people would soon be called for by the voice of the very factions whose misrule had proved the necessity of it. In the extended republic of the United States, and among the great variety of interests, parties, and sects which it embraces, a coalition of a majority of the whole society could seldom take place on any other principles than those of justice and the general good; whilst there being thus less danger to a minor from the will of a major party, there must be less pretext, also, to provide for the security of the former, by introducing into the government a will not dependent on the latter, or, in other words, a will independent of the society itself. It is no less certain than it is important, notwithstanding the contrary opinions which have been entertained, that the larger the society, provided it lie within a practicable sphere, the more duly capable it will be of self-government. And happily for the republican cause, the practicable sphere may be carried to a very great extent by a judicious modification and mixture of the *federal principle*.

Publius
(James Madison)

FEDERALIST PAPER NO. 78

In this essay, Alexander Hamilton looks at the role of the judicial branch (the courts) in the new government fashioned by the Constitution's framers. The essay is historically significant because, among other things, it provides a basis for the courts' power of judicial review, which was not explicitly set forth in the Constitution (see Chapters 2 and 13).

After some brief introductory remarks, Hamilton explains why the founders decided that federal judges should be appointed and given lifetime tenure. Note how he describes the judiciary as the "weakest" and "least dangerous" branch of government. Because of this, claims Hamilton, "all possible care" is required to enable the judiciary to defend itself against attacks by the other two branches of government. Above all, the independence of the judicial branch should be secured, because if judicial powers were combined with legislative or executive powers, there would be no liberty.

We proceed now to an examination of the judiciary department of the proposed government.

In unfolding the defects of the existing Confederation, the utility and necessity of a federal judicature have been clearly pointed out. It is the less necessary to recapitulate the considerations there urged, as the propriety of the institution in the abstract is not disputed; the only questions which have been raised being relative to the manner of constituting it, and to its extent. To these points, therefore, our observations shall be confined.

The manner of constituting it seems to embrace these several objects: 1st. The mode of appointing the judges. 2d. The tenure by which they are to hold their places. 3d. The partition of the judiciary authority between different courts, and their relations to each other.

First. As to the mode of appointing the judges; this is the same with that of appointing the officers of the Union in general, and has been so fully discussed in the last two numbers, that nothing can be said here which would not be useless repetition.

Second. As to the tenure by which the judges are to hold their places; this chiefly concerns their duration in office; the provisions for their support; the precautions for their responsibility.

According to the plan of the convention, all judges who may be appointed by the United States are to hold their offices during good behavior; which is conformable to the most approved of the State constitutions and among the rest, to that of this State. Its propriety having been drawn into question by the adversaries of that plan, is no light symptom of the rage for objection, which disorders their imaginations and judgments. The standard of good behavior for the continuance in office of the judicial magistracy, is certainly one of the most valuable of the modern improvements in the practice of government. In a monarchy it is an excellent barrier to the despotism of the prince; in a republic it is a no less excellent barrier to the encroachments and oppressions of the representative body. And it is the best expedient which can be devised in any government, to secure a steady, upright, and impartial administration of the laws.

Whoever attentively considers the different departments of power must perceive, that, in a government in which they are separated from each other, the judiciary, from the nature of its functions, will always be the least dangerous to the political rights of the Constitution; because it will be least in a capacity to annoy or injure them. The Executive not only dispenses the honors, but holds the sword of the community. The legislature not only commands the purse, but prescribes the rules by which the duties and rights of every citizen are to be regulated. The judiciary, on the contrary, has no influence over either the sword or the purse; no direction either of the strength or of the wealth of the society; and can take no active resolution whatever. It may truly be said to have neither force nor will, but merely judgment; and must ultimately depend upon the aid of the executive arm even for the efficacy of its judgments.

This simple view of the matter suggests several important consequences. It proves incontestably, that the judiciary is beyond comparison the weakest of the three departments of power; that it can never attack with success either of the other two; and that all possible care is requisite to enable it to defend itself against their attacks. It equally proves, that though individual oppression may now and then proceed from the courts of justice, the general liberty of the people can never be endangered from that quarter; I mean so long as the judiciary remains truly distinct from both the legislature and the Executive. For I agree, that "there is no liberty, if the power of judging is not separated from the legislative and executive powers." And it proves, in the last place, that as liberty can have nothing to fear from the judiciary alone, but would have everything to fear from its union with either of the other departments; that as all the effects of such a union must ensue from a dependence of the former on the latter, notwithstanding a nominal and apparent separation; that as, from the natural feebleness of the judiciary, it is in continual jeopardy of being overpowered, awed, or influenced by its co-ordinate branches; and that as nothing can contribute so much to its firmness and independence as permanency in office, this quality may therefore be justly regarded as an indispensable ingredient in its constitution, and, in a great measure, as the citadel of the public justice and the public security.

Hamilton now stresses that the "complete independence of the courts" is essential in a limited government, because it is up to the courts to interpret the laws. Just as a federal court can decide which of two conflicting statutes should take priority, so can that court decide whether a statute conflicts with the Constitution. Essentially, Hamilton sets forth here the theory of judicial review—the power of the courts to decide whether actions of the other branches of government are (or are not) consistent with the Constitution. Hamilton points out that this "exercise of judicial discretion, in determining between two contradictory laws," does not mean that the judicial branch is superior to the legislative branch. Rather, it "supposes" that the power of the people (as declared in the Constitution) is superior to both the judiciary and the legislature.

The complete independence of the courts of justice is peculiarly essential in a limited Constitution. By a limited Constitution, I understand one which contains certain specified exceptions to the legislative authority; such, for instance, as that it shall pass no bills of attainder, no ex-post-facto laws, and the like. Limitations of this kind can be preserved in practice no other way than through the medium of courts of justice, whose duty it must be to declare all acts contrary to the manifest tenor of the Constitution void. Without this, all the reservations of particular rights or privileges would amount to nothing. Some perplexity respecting the rights of the courts to pronounce legislative acts void, because contrary to the Constitution, has arisen from an imagination that the doctrine would imply a superiority of the judiciary to the legislative power. It is urged that the authority which can declare the acts of another void, must necessarily be superior to the one whose acts may be declared void. As this doctrine is of great importance in all the American constitutions, a brief discussion of the ground on which it rests cannot be unacceptable.

There is no position which depends on clearer principles, than that every act of a delegated authority, contrary to the tenor of the commission under which it is exercised, is void. No legislative act, therefore, contrary to the Constitution, can be valid. To deny this, would be to affirm, that the deputy is greater than his principal; that the servant is above his master; that the representatives of the people are superior to the people themselves; that men acting by virtue of powers, may do not only what their powers do not authorize, but what they forbid.

If it be said that the legislative body are themselves the constitutional judges of their own powers, and that the construction they put upon them is conclusive upon the other departments, it may be answered, that this cannot be the natural presumption, where it is not to be collected from any particular provisions in the Constitution. It is not otherwise to be supposed, that the Constitution could intend to enable the representatives of the people to substitute their will to that of their constituents. It is far more rational to suppose, that the courts were designed to be an intermediate body between the people and the legislature, in order, among other things, to keep the latter within the limits assigned to their authority. The interpretation of the laws is the proper and peculiar province of the courts. A constitution is, in fact, and must be regarded by the judges, as a fundamental law. It therefore belongs to them to ascertain its meaning, as well as the meaning of any particular act proceeding from the legislative body. If there should happen to be an irreconcilable variance between the two, that which has the superior obligation and validity ought, of course, to be preferred; or, in other words, the Constitution ought to be preferred to the statute, the intention of the people to the intention of their agents.

Nor does this conclusion by any means suppose a superiority of the judicial to the legislative power. It only supposes that the power of the people is superior to both; and that where the will of the legislature, declared in its statutes, stands in opposition to that of the people, declared in the Constitution, the judges ought to be governed by the latter rather than the former. They ought to regulate their decisions by the fundamental laws, rather than by those which are not fundamental.

This exercise of judicial discretion, in determining between two contradictory laws, is exemplified in a familiar instance. It not uncommonly happens, that there are two statutes existing at one time, clashing in whole or in part with each other, and neither of them containing any repealing clause or expression. In such a case, it is the province of the courts to liquidate and fix their meaning and operation. So far as they can, by any fair construction, be reconciled to each other, reason and law conspire to dictate that this should be done; where this is impracticable, it becomes a matter of necessity to give effect to one, in exclusion of the other. The rule which has obtained in the courts for determining their relative validity is, that the last in order of time shall be preferred to the first. But this is a mere rule of construction, not derived from any positive law, but from the nature and reason of the thing. It is a rule not enjoined upon the courts by legislative provision, but adopted by themselves, as consonant to truth the propriety, for the direction of their conduct as interpreters of the law. They thought it reasonable, that between the interfering acts of an equal authority, that which was the last indication of its will should have the preference.

But in regard to the interfering acts of a superior and subordinate authority, of an original and derivative power, the nature and reason of the thing indicate the converse of that rule as proper to be followed. They teach us that the prior act of a superior ought to be preferred to the subsequent act of an inferior and subordinate authority; and that accordingly, whenever a particular statute contravenes the Constitution, it will be the duty of the judicial tribunals to adhere to the latter and disregard the former.

It can be of no weight to say that the courts, on the pretense of a repugnancy, may substitute their own pleasure to the constitutional intentions of the legislature. This might as well happen in the case of two contradictory statutes; or it might as well happen in every adjudication upon any single statute. The courts must declare the sense of the law; and if they should be disposed to exercise will instead of judgment, the consequence would equally be the substitution of their pleasure to that of the legislative body. The observation, if it prove anything, would prove that there ought to be no judges distinct from that body.

If, then, the courts of justice are to be considered as the bulwarks of a limited Constitution against legislative encroachments, this consideration will afford a strong argument for the permanent tenure of judicial offices, since nothing will contribute so much as this to that independent spirit in the judges which must be essential to the faithful performance of so arduous a duty.

The independence of the judges is equally requisite to guard the Constitution and the rights of individuals from the effects of those ill humors, which the arts of designing men, or the influence of particular conjunctures, sometimes disseminate among the people themselves, and which, though they speedily give place to better information, and more deliberate reflection, have a tendency, in the meantime, to occasion dangerous innovations in the government, and serious oppressions of the minor party in the community. Though I trust the friends of the proposed Constitution will never concur with its enemies, in questioning that fundamental principle of republican government, which admits the right of the people to alter or abolish the established Constitution, whenever they find it inconsistent with their happiness, yet it is not to be inferred from this principle, that the representatives of the people, whenever a momentary inclination happens to lay hold of a majority of their constituents, incompatible with the provisions of the existing Constitution, would, on that account, be justifiable in a violation of those provisions; or that the courts would be under a greater obligation to connive at infractions in this shape, than when they had proceeded wholly from the cabals of the representative body. Until the people have, by some solemn and authoritative act, annulled or changed the established form, it is binding upon themselves collectively, as well as individually; and no presumption, or even knowledge, of their sentiments, can warrant their representatives in a departure from it, prior to such an act. But it is easy to see, that it would require an uncommon portion of fortitude in the judges to do their duty as faithful guardians of the Constitution, where legislative invasions of it had been instigated by the major voice of the community.

But it is not with a view to infractions of the Constitution only, that the independence of the judges may be an essential safeguard against the effects of occasional ill humors in the society. These sometimes extend no farther than to the injury of the private rights of particular classes of citizens, by unjust and partial laws. Here also the firmness of the judicial magistracy is of vast importance in mitigating the severity and confining the operation of such laws. It not only serves to moderate the immediate mischiefs of those which may have been passed, but it operates as a check upon the legislative body in passing them; who, perceiving that obstacles to the success of iniquitous intention are to be expected from the scruples of the courts, are in a manner compelled, by the very motives of the injustice they meditate, to qualify their attempts. This is a circumstance calculated to have more influence upon the character of our governments, than but few may be aware of. The benefits of the integrity and moderation of the judiciary have already been felt in more States than one; and though they may have displeased those whose sinister expectations they may have disappointed, they must have commanded the esteem and applause of all the virtuous and disinterested. Considerate men, of every description, ought to prize whatever will tend to beget or fortify that temper in the courts; as no man can be sure that he may not be tomorrow the victim of a spirit of injustice, by which he may be a gainer today. And every man must now feel, that the inevitable tendency of such a spirit is to sap the foundations of public and private confidence, and to introduce in its stead universal distrust and distress.

That inflexible and uniform adherence to the rights of the Constitution, and of individuals, which we perceive to be indispensable in the courts of justice, can certainly not be expected from judges who hold their offices by a temporary commission. Periodical appointments, however regulated, or by whomsoever made, would, in some way or other, be fatal to their necessary independence. If the power of making them was committed either to the Executive or legislature, there would be danger of an improper complaisance to the branch which possessed it; if to both, there would be an unwillingness to hazard the displeasure of either; if to the people, or to persons chosen by them for the special purpose, there would be too great a disposition to consult popularity, to justify a reliance that nothing would be consulted but the Constitution and the laws.

Hamilton points to yet another reason why lifetime tenure for federal judges will benefit the public: effective judgments rest on a knowledge of judicial precedents and the law, and such knowledge can only be obtained through experience on the bench. A "temporary duration of office," according to Hamilton, would "discourage individuals [of 'fit character'] from quitting a lucrative practice to serve on the bench" and ultimately would "throw the administration of justice into the hands of the less able, and less well qualified."

There is yet a further and a weightier reason for the permanency of the judicial offices, which is deducible from the nature of the qualifications they require. It has been frequently remarked, with great propriety, that a voluminous code of laws is one of the inconveniences necessarily connected with the advantages of a free government. To avoid an arbitrary discretion in the courts, it is indispensable that they should be bound down by strict rules and precedents, which serve to define and point out their duty in every particular case that comes before them; and it will readily be conceived from the variety of controversies which grow out of the folly and wickedness of mankind, that the records of those precedents must unavoidably swell to a very considerable bulk, and must demand long and laborious study to acquire a competent knowledge of them. Hence it is, that there can be but few men in the society who will have sufficient skill in the laws to qualify them for the stations of judges. And making the proper deductions for the ordinary depravity of human nature, the number must be still smaller of those who unite the requisite integrity with the requisite knowledge. These considerations apprise us, that the government can have no great option between fit character; and that a temporary duration in office, which would naturally discourage such characters from quitting a lucrative line of practice to accept a seat on the bench, would have a tendency to throw the administration of justice into hands less able, and less well qualified, to conduct it with utility and dignity. In the present circumstances of this country, and in those in which it is likely to be for a long time to come, the disadvantages on this score would be greater than they may at first sight appear; but it must be confessed, that they are far inferior to those which present themselves under other aspects of the subject.

Upon the whole, there can be no room to doubt that the convention acted wisely in copying from the models of those constitutions which have established good behavior as the tenure of their judicial offices, in point of duration; and that so far from being blamable on this account, their plan would have been inexcusably defective, if it had wanted this important feature of good government. The experience of Great Britain affords an illustrious comment on the excellence of the institution.

Publius
(Alexander Hamilton)

Appendix C

Justices of the United States Supreme Court since 1900

CHIEF JUSTICES

Name	Years of Service	State App't from	Appointing President	Age at App't	Political Affiliation	Educational Background*
Fuller, Melville Weston	1888–1910	Illinois	Cleveland	55	Democrat	Bowdoin College; studied at Harvard Law School
White, Edward Douglass	1910–1921	Louisiana	Taft	65	Democrat	Mount St. Mary's College; Georgetown College (now University)
Taft, William Howard	1921–1930	Connecticut	Harding	64	Republican	Yale; Cincinnati Law School
Hughes, Charles Evans	1930–1941	New York	Hoover	68	Republican	Colgate University; Brown; Columbia Law School
Stone, Harlan Fiske	1941–1946	New York	Roosevelt, F.	69	Republican	Amherst College; Columbia
Vinson, Frederick Moore	1946–1953	Kentucky	Truman	56	Democrat	Centre College
Warren, Earl	1953–1969	California	Eisenhower	62	Republican	University of California, Berkeley
Burger, Warren Earl	1969–1986	Virginia	Nixon	62	Republican	University of Minnesota; St. Paul College of Law (Mitchell College)
Rehnquist, William Hubbs	1986–2005	Virginia	Reagan	62	Republican	Stanford; Harvard; Stanford University Law School
Roberts, John G., Jr.	2005–present	District of Columbia	Bush, G. W.	50	Republican	Harvard; Harvard Law School

ASSOCIATE JUSTICES

Name	Years of Service	State App't from	Appointing President	Age at App't	Political Affiliation	Educational Background*
Harlan, John Marshall	1877–1911	Kentucky	Hayes	61	Republican	Centre College; studied law at Transylvania University
Gray, Horace	1882–1902	Massachusetts	Arthur	54	Republican	Harvard College; Harvard Law School
Brewer, David Josiah	1890–1910	Kansas	Harrison	53	Republican	Wesleyan University; Yale; Albany Law School
Brown, Henry Billings	1891–1906	Michigan	Harrison	55	Republican	Yale; studied at Yale Law School and Harvard Law School
Shiras, George, Jr.	1892–1903	Pennsylvania	Harrison	61	Republican	Ohio University; Yale; studied law at Yale and privately
White, Edward Douglass	1894–1910	Louisiana	Cleveland	49	Democrat	Mount St. Mary's College; Georgetown College (now University)
Peckham, Rufus Wheeler	1896–1909	New York	Cleveland	58	Democrat	Read law in father's firm
McKenna, Joseph	1898–1925	California	McKinley	55	Republican	Benica Collegiate Institute, Law Department
Holmes, Oliver Wendell, Jr.	1902–1932	Massachusetts	Roosevelt, T.	61	Republican	Harvard College; studied law at Harvard Law School

*Sources: Educational background information derived from Elder Witt, *Guide to the U.S. Supreme Court,* 2d ed. (Washington, D.C.: Congressional Quarterly Press, Inc., 1990). Reprinted with the permission of the publisher. Plus authors' update.

(Continued)

ASSOCIATE JUSTICES (CONTINUED)

Name	Years of Service	State App't from	Appointing President	Age at App't	Political Affiliation	Educational Background
Day, William Rufus	1903–1922	Ohio	Roosevelt, T.	54	Republican	University of Michigan; University of Michigan Law School
Moody, William Henry	1906–1910	Massachusetts	Roosevelt, T.	53	Republican	Harvard; Harvard Law School
Lurton, Horace Harmon	1910–1914	Tennessee	Taft	66	Democrat	University of Chicago; Cumberland Law School
Hughes, Charles Evans	1910–1916	New York	Taft	48	Republican	Colgate University; Brown University; Columbia Law School
Van Devanter, Willis	1911–1937	Wyoming	Taft	52	Republican	Indiana Asbury University; University of Cincinnati Law School
Lamar, Joseph Rucker	1911–1916	Georgia	Taft	54	Democrat	University of Georgia; Bethany College; Washington and Lee University
Pitney, Mahlon	1912–1922	New Jersey	Taft	54	Republican	College of New Jersey (Princeton); read law under father
McReynolds, James Clark	1914–1941	Tennessee	Wilson	52	Democrat	Vanderbilt University; University of Virginia
Brandeis, Louis Dembitz	1916–1939	Massachusetts	Wilson	60	Democrat	Harvard Law School
Clarke, John Hessin	1916–1922	Ohio	Wilson	59	Democrat	Western Reserve University; read law under father
Sutherland, George	1922–1938	Utah	Harding	60	Republican	Brigham Young Academy; one year at University of Michigan Law School
Butler, Pierce	1923–1939	Minnesota	Harding	57	Democrat	Carleton College
Sanford, Edward Terry	1923–1930	Tennessee	Harding	58	Republican	University of Tennessee; Harvard; Harvard Law School
Stone, Harlan Fiske	1925–1941	New York	Coolidge	53	Republican	Amherst College; Columbia University Law School
Roberts, Owen Josephus	1930–1945	Pennsylvania	Hoover	55	Republican	University of Pennsylvania; University of Pennsylvania Law School
Cardozo, Benjamin Nathan	1932–1938	New York	Hoover	62	Democrat	Columbia University; two years at Columbia Law School
Black, Hugo Lafayette	1937–1971	Alabama	Roosevelt, F.	51	Democrat	Birmingham Medical College; University of Alabama Law School
Reed, Stanley Forman	1938–1957	Kentucky	Roosevelt, F.	54	Democrat	Kentucky Wesleyan University; Foreman Yale; studied law at University of Virginia and Columbia University; University of Paris
Frankfurter, Felix	1939–1962	Massachusetts	Roosevelt, F.	57	Independent	College of the City of New York; Harvard Law School
Douglas, William Orville	1939–1975	Connecticut	Roosevelt, F.	41	Democrat	Whitman College; Columbia University Law School
Murphy, Frank	1940–1949	Michigan	Roosevelt, F.	50	Democrat	University of Michigan; Lincoln's Inn, London; Trinity College
Byrnes, James Francis	1941–1942	South Carolina	Roosevelt, F.	62	Democrat	Read law privately
Jackson, Robert Houghwout	1941–1954	New York	Roosevelt, F.	49	Democrat	Albany Law School
Rutledge, Wiley Blount	1943–1949	Iowa	Roosevelt, F.	49	Democrat	University of Wisconsin; University of Colorado

ASSOCIATE JUSTICES (CONTINUED)

Name	Years of Service	State App't from	Appointing President	Age at App't	Political Affiliation	Educational Background
Burton, Harold Hitz	1945–1958	Ohio	Truman	57	Republican	Bowdoin College; Harvard Law School
Clark, Thomas Campbell	1949–1967	Texas	Truman	50	Democrat	University of Texas
Minton, Sherman	1949–1956	Indiana	Truman	59	Democrat	Indiana University College of Law; Yale Law School
Harlan, John Marshall	1955–1971	New York	Eisenhower	56	Republican	Princeton; Oxford University; New York Law School
Brennan, William J., Jr.	1956–1990	New Jersey	Eisenhower	50	Democrat	University of Pennsylvania; Harvard Law School
Whittaker, Charles Evans	1957–1962	Missouri	Eisenhower	56	Republican	University of Kansas City Law School
Stewart, Potter	1958–1981	Ohio	Eisenhower	43	Republican	Yale; Yale Law School
White, Byron Raymond	1962–1993	Colorado	Kennedy	45	Democrat	University of Colorado; Oxford University; Yale Law School
Goldberg, Arthur Joseph	1962–1965	Illinois	Kennedy	54	Democrat	Northwestern University
Fortas, Abe	1965–1969	Tennessee	Johnson, L.	55	Democrat	Southwestern College; Yale Law School
Marshall, Thurgood	1967–1991	New York	Johnson, L.	59	Democrat	Lincoln University; Howard University Law School
Blackmun, Harry A.	1970–1994	Minnesota	Nixon	62	Republican	Harvard; Harvard Law School
Powell, Lewis F., Jr.	1972–1987	Virginia	Nixon	65	Democrat	Washington and Lee University; Washington and Lee University Law School; Harvard Law School
Rehnquist, William H.	1972–1986	Arizona	Nixon	48	Republican	Stanford; Harvard; Stanford University Law School
Stevens, John Paul	1975–2010	Illinois	Ford	55	Republican	University of Colorado; Northwestern University Law School
O'Connor, Sandra Day	1981–2006	Arizona	Reagan	51	Republican	Stanford; Stanford University Law School
Scalia, Antonin	1986–present	Virginia	Reagan	50	Republican	Georgetown University; Harvard Law School
Kennedy, Anthony M.	1988–present	California	Reagan	52	Republican	Stanford; London School of Economics; Harvard Law School
Souter, David Hackett	1990–2009	New Hampshire	Bush, G. H. W.	51	Republican	Harvard; Oxford University
Thomas, Clarence	1991–present	District of Columbia	Bush, G. H. W.	43	Republican	Holy Cross College; Yale Law School
Ginsburg, Ruth Bader	1993–present	District of Columbia	Clinton	60	Democrat	Cornell University; Columbia Law School
Breyer, Stephen G.	1994–present	Massachusetts	Clinton	55	Democrat	Stanford University; Oxford University; Harvard Law School
Alito, Samuel Anthony, Jr.	2006–present	New Jersey	G. W. Bush	55	Republican	Princeton University; Yale Law School
Sotomayor, Sonia Marie	2009–present	New York	Obama	55	Democrat	Princeton University; Yale Law School
Kagan, Elena	2010–present	District of Columbia	Obama	50	Democrat	Princeton and Oxford Universities; Harvard Law School

Appendix D
Party Control of Congress since 1900

Congress	Years	President	Majority Party in House	Majority Party in Senate
57th	1901–1903	McKinley/T. Roosevelt	Republican	Republican
58th	1903–1905	T. Roosevelt	Republican	Republican
59th	1905–1907	T. Roosevelt	Republican	Republican
60th	1907–1909	T. Roosevelt	Republican	Republican
61st	1909–1911	Taft	Republican	Republican
62d	1911–1913	Taft	Democratic	Republican
63d	1913–1915	Wilson	Democratic	Democratic
64th	1915–1917	Wilson	Democratic	Democratic
65th	1917–1919	Wilson	Democratic	Democratic
66th	1919–1921	Wilson	Republican	Republican
67th	1921–1923	Harding	Republican	Republican
68th	1923–1925	Harding/Coolidge	Republican	Republican
69th	1925–1927	Coolidge	Republican	Republican
70th	1927–1929	Coolidge	Republican	Republican
71st	1929–1931	Hoover	Republican	Republican
72d	1931–1933	Hoover	Democratic	Republican
73d	1933–1935	F. Roosevelt	Democratic	Democratic
74th	1935–1937	F. Roosevelt	Democratic	Democratic
75th	1937–1939	F. Roosevelt	Democratic	Democratic
76th	1939–1941	F. Roosevelt	Democratic	Democratic
77th	1941–1943	F. Roosevelt	Democratic	Democratic
78th	1943–1945	F. Roosevelt	Democratic	Democratic
79th	1945–1947	F. Roosevelt/Truman	Democratic	Democratic
80th	1947–1949	Truman	Republican	Democratic
81st	1949–1951	Truman	Democratic	Democratic
82d	1951–1953	Truman	Democratic	Democratic
83d	1953–1955	Eisenhower	Republican	Republican
84th	1955–1957	Eisenhower	Democratic	Democratic
85th	1957–1959	Eisenhower	Democratic	Democratic
86th	1959–1961	Eisenhower	Democratic	Democratic
87th	1961–1963	Kennedy	Democratic	Democratic
88th	1963–1965	Kennedy/Johnson	Democratic	Democratic
89th	1965–1967	Johnson	Democratic	Democratic
90th	1967–1969	Johnson	Democratic	Democratic
91st	1969–1971	Nixon	Democratic	Democratic
92d	1971–1973	Nixon	Democratic	Democratic
93d	1973–1975	Nixon/Ford	Democratic	Democratic
94th	1975–1977	Ford	Democratic	Democratic
95th	1977–1979	Carter	Democratic	Democratic
96th	1979–1981	Carter	Democratic	Democratic
97th	1981–1983	Reagan	Democratic	Republican
98th	1983–1985	Reagan	Democratic	Republican
99th	1985–1987	Reagan	Democratic	Republican
100th	1987–1989	Reagan	Democratic	Democratic
101st	1989–1991	G. H. W. Bush	Democratic	Democratic
102d	1991–1993	G. H. W. Bush	Democratic	Democratic
103d	1993–1995	Clinton	Democratic	Democratic
104th	1995–1997	Clinton	Republican	Republican
105th	1997–1999	Clinton	Republican	Republican
106th	1999–2001	Clinton	Republican	Republican
107th	2001–2003	G. W. Bush	Republican	Democratic
108th	2003–2005	G. W. Bush	Republican	Republican
109th	2005–2007	G. W. Bush	Republican	Republican
110th	2007–2009	G. W. Bush	Democratic	Democratic
111th	2009–2011	Obama	Democratic	Democratic
112th	2011–2013	Obama	Republican	Democratic
113th	2013–2015	Obama	Republican	Democratic

Appendix E
Presidents of the United States

	Term of Service	Age at Inauguration	Political Party	College or University	Occupation or Profession
1. George Washington	1789–1797	57	None		Planter
2. John Adams	1797–1801	61	Federalist	Harvard	Lawyer
3. Thomas Jefferson	1801–1809	57	Jeffersonian Republican	William and Mary	Planter, Lawyer
4. James Madison	1809–1817	57	Jeffersonian Republican	Princeton	Lawyer
5. James Monroe	1817–1825	58	Jeffersonian Republican	William and Mary	Lawyer
6. John Quincy Adams	1825–1829	57	Jeffersonian Republican	Harvard	Lawyer
7. Andrew Jackson	1829–1837	61	Democrat		Lawyer
8. Martin Van Buren	1837–1841	54	Democrat		Lawyer
9. William H. Harrison	1841	68	Whig	Hampden-Sydney	Soldier
10. John Tyler	1841–1845	51	Whig	William and Mary	Lawyer
11. James K. Polk	1845–1849	49	Democrat	U. of N. Carolina	Lawyer
12. Zachary Taylor	1849–1850	64	Whig		Soldier
13. Millard Fillmore	1850–1853	50	Whig		Lawyer
14. Franklin Pierce	1853–1857	48	Democrat	Bowdoin	Lawyer
15. James Buchanan	1857–1861	65	Democrat	Dickinson	Lawyer
16. Abraham Lincoln	1861–1865	52	Republican		Lawyer
17. Andrew Johnson	1865–1869	56	National Union†		Tailor
18. Ulysses S. Grant	1869–1877	46	Republican	U.S. Mil. Academy	Soldier
19. Rutherford B. Hayes	1877–1881	54	Republican	Kenyon	Lawyer
20. James A. Garfield	1881	49	Republican	Williams	Lawyer
21. Chester A. Arthur	1881–1885	51	Republican	Union	Lawyer
22. Grover Cleveland	1885–1889	47	Democrat		Lawyer
23. Benjamin Harrison	1889–1893	55	Republican	Miami	Lawyer
24. Grover Cleveland	1893–1897	55	Democrat		Lawyer
25. William McKinley	1897–1901	54	Republican	Allegheny College	Lawyer
26. Theodore Roosevelt	1901–1909	42	Republican	Harvard	Author
27. William H. Taft	1909–1913	51	Republican	Yale	Lawyer
28. Woodrow Wilson	1913–1921	56	Democrat	Princeton	Educator
29. Warren G. Harding	1921–1923	55	Republican		Editor
30. Calvin Coolidge	1923–1929	51	Republican	Amherst	Lawyer
31. Herbert C. Hoover	1929–1933	54	Republican	Stanford	Engineer
32. Franklin D. Roosevelt	1933–1945	51	Democrat	Harvard	Lawyer
33. Harry S. Truman	1945–1953	60	Democrat		Businessman
34. Dwight D. Eisenhower	1953–1961	62	Republican	U.S. Mil. Academy	Soldier
35. John F. Kennedy	1961–1963	43	Democrat	Harvard	Author
36. Lyndon B. Johnson	1963–1969	55	Democrat	Southwest Texas State	Teacher
37. Richard M. Nixon	1969–1974	56	Republican	Whittier	Lawyer
38. Gerald R. Ford‡	1974–1977	61	Republican	Michigan	Lawyer
39. James E. Carter, Jr.	1977–1981	52	Democrat	U.S. Naval Academy	Businessman
40. Ronald W. Reagan	1981–1989	69	Republican	Eureka College	Actor
41. George H. W. Bush	1989–1993	64	Republican	Yale	Businessman
42. Bill Clinton	1993–2001	46	Democrat	Georgetown	Lawyer
43. George W. Bush	2001–2009	54	Republican	Yale	Businessman
44. Barack Obama	2009–	47	Democrat	Columbia	Lawyer

*Church preference; never joined any church.
†The National Union Party consisted of Republicans and War Democrats. Johnson was a Democrat.
**Inaugurated Dec. 6, 1973, to replace Agnew, who resigned Oct. 10, 1973.

	Religion	Born	Died	Age at Death	Vice President	
1.	Episcopalian	Feb. 22, 1732	Dec. 14, 1799	67	John Adams	(1789–1797)
2.	Unitarian	Oct. 30, 1735	July 4, 1826	90	Thomas Jefferson	(1797–1801)
3.	Unitarian*	Apr. 13, 1743	July 4, 1826	83	Aaron Burr	(1801–1805)
					George Clinton	(1805–1809)
4.	Episcopalian	Mar. 16, 1751	June 28, 1836	85	George Clinton	(1809–1812)
					Elbridge Gerry	(1813–1814)
5.	Episcopalian	Apr. 28, 1758	July 4, 1831	73	Daniel D. Tompkins	(1817–1825)
6.	Unitarian	July 11, 1767	Feb. 23, 1848	80	John C. Calhoun	(1825–1829)
7.	Presbyterian	Mar. 15, 1767	June 8, 1845	78	John C. Calhoun	(1829–1832)
					Martin Van Buren	(1833–1837)
8.	Dutch Reformed	Dec. 5, 1782	July 24, 1862	79	Richard M. Johnson	(1837–1841)
9.	Episcopalian	Feb. 9, 1773	Apr. 4, 1841	68	John Tyler	(1841)
10.	Episcopalian	Mar. 29, 1790	Jan. 18, 1862	71		
11.	Methodist	Nov. 2, 1795	June 15, 1849	53	George M. Dallas	(1845–1849)
12.	Episcopalian	Nov. 24, 1784	July 9, 1850	65	Millard Fillmore	(1849–1850)
13.	Unitarian	Jan. 7, 1800	Mar. 8, 1874	74		
14.	Episcopalian	Nov. 23, 1804	Oct. 8, 1869	64	William R. King	(1853)
15.	Presbyterian	Apr. 23, 1791	June 1, 1868	77	John C. Breckinridge	(1857–1861)
16.	Presbyterian*	Feb. 12, 1809	Apr. 15, 1865	56	Hannibal Hamlin	(1861–1865)
					Andrew Johnson	(1865)
17.	Methodist*	Dec. 29, 1808	July 31, 1875	66		
18.	Methodist	Apr. 27, 1822	July 23, 1885	63	Schuyler Colfax	(1869–1873)
					Henry Wilson	(1873–1875)
19.	Methodist*	Oct. 4, 1822	Jan. 17, 1893	70	William A. Wheeler	(1877–1881)
20.	Disciples of Christ	Nov. 19, 1831	Sept. 19, 1881	49	Chester A. Arthur	(1881)
21.	Episcopalian	Oct. 5, 1829	Nov. 18, 1886	57		
22.	Presbyterian	Mar. 18, 1837	June 24, 1908	71	Thomas A. Hendricks	(1885)
23.	Presbyterian	Aug. 20, 1833	Mar. 13, 1901	67	Levi P. Morton	(1889–1893)
24.	Presbyterian	Mar. 18, 1837	June 24, 1908	71	Adlai E. Stevenson	(1893–1897)
25.	Methodist	Jan. 29, 1843	Sept. 14, 1901	58	Garret A. Hobart	(1897–1899)
					Theodore Roosevelt	(1901)
26.	Dutch Reformed	Oct. 27, 1858	Jan. 6, 1919	60	Charles W. Fairbanks	(1905–1909)
27.	Unitarian	Sept. 15, 1857	Mar. 8, 1930	72	James S. Sherman	(1909–1912)
28.	Presbyterian	Dec. 29, 1856	Feb. 3, 1924	67	Thomas R. Marshall	(1913–1921)
29.	Baptist	Nov. 2, 1865	Aug. 2, 1923	57	Calvin Coolidge	(1921–1923)
30.	Congregationalist	July 4, 1872	Jan. 5, 1933	60	Charles G. Dawes	(1925–1929)
31.	Friend (Quaker)	Aug. 10, 1874	Oct. 20, 1964	90	Charles Curtis	(1929–1933)
32.	Episcopalian	Jan. 30, 1882	Apr. 12, 1945	63	John N. Garner	(1933–1941)
					Henry A. Wallace	(1941–1945)
					Harry S. Truman	(1945)
33.	Baptist	May 8, 1884	Dec. 26, 1972	88	Alben W. Barkley	(1949–1953)
34.	Presbyterian	Oct. 14, 1890	Mar. 28, 1969	78	Richard M. Nixon	(1953–1961)
35.	Roman Catholic	May 29, 1917	Nov. 22, 1963	46	Lyndon B. Johnson	(1961–1963)
36.	Disciples of Christ	Aug. 27, 1908	Jan. 22, 1973	64	Hubert H. Humphrey	(1965–1969)
37.	Friend (Quaker)	Jan. 9, 1913	Apr. 22, 1994	81	Spiro T. Agnew	(1969–1973)
					Gerald R. Ford**	(1973–1974)
38.	Episcopalian	July 14, 1913	Dec. 26, 2006	93	Nelson A. Rockefeller§	(1974–1977)
39.	Baptist	Oct. 1, 1924			Walter F. Mondale	(1977–1981)
40.	Disciples of Christ	Feb. 6, 1911	June 5, 2004	93	George H. W. Bush	(1981–1989)
41.	Episcopalian	June 12, 1924			J. Danforth Quayle	(1989–1993)
42.	Baptist	Aug. 19, 1946			Albert A. Gore	(1993–2001)
43.	Methodist	July 6, 1946			Dick Cheney	(2001–2009)
44.	United Church of Christ	Aug. 4, 1961			Joe Biden	(2009–)

‡Inaugurated Aug. 9, 1974, to replace Nixon, who resigned that same day.
§Inaugurated Dec. 19, 1974, to replace Ford, who became president Aug. 9, 1974.

Glossary

A

Acquisitive Model A model of bureaucracy that views top-level bureaucrats as seeking to expand the size of their budgets and staffs to gain greater power.

Actual Malice Either knowledge of a defamatory statement's falsity or a reckless disregard for the truth.

Advice and Consent Terms in the Constitution describing the U.S. Senate's power to review and approve treaties and presidential appointments.

Affirm To declare that a court ruling is valid and must stand.

Affirmative Action A policy in educational admissions and job hiring that gives special attention or compensatory treatment to traditionally disadvantaged groups in an effort to overcome present effects of past discrimination.

Affordable Care Act A law passed in 2010 that seeks, among other things, to ensure health-care insurance for American citizens. The act is supplemented by the Health Care and Education Reconciliation Act and nicknamed "Obamacare" by opponents and journalists.

Agenda Setting Determining which public-policy questions will be debated or considered.

Aggregator A Web site that provides search and aggregation services, but creates little or no original content.

Amicus Curiae Brief A brief (a document containing a legal argument supporting a desired outcome in a particular case) filed by a third party, or *amicus curiae* (Latin for "friend of the court"), who is not directly involved in the litigation but who has an interest in the outcome of the case.

Anarchy The condition of no government.

Anti-Federalist An individual who opposed the ratification of the new Constitution in 1787. The Anti-Federalists were opposed to a strong central government.

Appellate Court A court having jurisdiction to review cases and issues that were originally tried in lower courts.

Appointment Power The authority vested in the president to fill a government office or position. Positions filled by presidential appointment include those in the executive branch and the federal judiciary, commissioned officers in the armed forces, and members of the independent regulatory commissions.

Appropriation The passage, by Congress, of a spending bill specifying the amount of authorized funds that actually will be allocated for an agency's use.

Aristocracy "Rule by the best"; in reality, rule by members of the upper class.

Arraignment The first act in a criminal proceeding, in which the defendant is brought before a court to hear the charges against him or her and enter a plea of guilty or not guilty.

Australian Ballot A secret ballot prepared, distributed, and tabulated by government officials at public expense. Since 1888, all states have used the Australian ballot rather than an open, public ballot.

Authoritarianism A type of regime in which only the government itself is fully controlled by the ruler. Social and economic institutions exist that are not under the government's control.

Authority The right and power of a government or other entity to enforce its decisions.

Authorization A formal declaration by a legislative committee that a certain amount of funding may be available to an agency. Some authorizations terminate in a year; others are renewable automatically without further congressional action.

B

Bias An inclination or preference that interferes with impartial judgment.

Bicameral Legislature A legislature made up of two parts, called chambers. The U.S. Congress, composed of the House of Representatives and the Senate, is a bicameral legislature.

Bicameralism The division of a legislature into two separate assemblies.

Bill of Rights The first ten amendments to the U.S. Constitution.

Block Grant A federal grant that provides funds to a state or local government for a general functional area, such as criminal justice or mental-health programs.

Blog From Web log. A Web site where an individual or group posts regular updates on their ideas or experiences.

Boycott A form of pressure or protest—an organized refusal to purchase a particular product or deal with a particular business.

Broad Construction A judicial philosophy that looks to the context and purpose of a law when making an interpretation.

Budget Deficit Government expenditures that exceed receipts.

Bureaucracy An organization that is structured hierarchically to carry out specific functions.

C

Cabinet An advisory group selected by the president to aid in making decisions. The cabinet includes the heads of fifteen executive departments and others named by the president.

Cabinet Department One of the fifteen major departments of the executive branch.

Capitalism An economic system characterized by the private ownership of wealth-creating assets, free markets, and freedom of contract.

Capture The act by which an industry being regulated by a government agency gains direct or indirect control over agency personnel and decision makers.

Case Law Judicial interpretations of common law principles and doctrines, as well as interpretations of constitutional law, statutory law, and administrative law.

Casework Personal work for constituents by members of Congress.

Categorical Grant A federal grant to a state or local government for a specific program or project.

Caucus A meeting of party members to select candidates and propose policies.

Checks and Balances A major principle of the American system of government whereby each branch of the government can check the actions of the others.

Chief Diplomat The role of the president in recognizing foreign governments, making treaties, and effecting executive agreements.

Chief Executive The role of the president as head of the executive branch of the government.

Chief Legislator The role of the president in influencing the making of laws.

Chief of Staff The person who is named to direct the White House Office and advise the president.

Civil Disobedience A nonviolent, public refusal to obey allegedly unjust laws.

Civil Law The law regulating conduct between private persons over noncriminal matters, including contracts, domestic relations, and business interactions.

Civil Liberties Those personal freedoms, including freedom of religion and freedom of speech, that are protected for all individuals. Civil liberties restrain the government from taking certain actions against individuals.

Civil Rights Generally, all rights rooted in the Fourteenth Amendment's guarantee of equal protection under the law.

Civil Service A collective term for the body of employees working for the government. Generally, "civil service" is understood to apply to all those who gain government employment through a merit system.

Civil Service Commission The initial central personnel agency of the national government; created in 1883.

Class-Action Suit A lawsuit filed by an individual seeking damages for "all persons similarly situated."

Climate Control The use of public relations techniques to create favorable public opinion toward an interest group, industry, or corporation.

Closed Primary A type of primary in which the voter is limited to choosing candidates of the party of which he or she is a member.

Coattail Effect The influence of a popular candidate on the success of other candidates on the same party ticket.

Cold War The ideological, political, and economic confrontation between the United States and the Soviet Union following World War II.

Commander in Chief The role of the president as supreme commander of the military forces of the United States and of the state National Guard units when they are called into federal service.

Commerce Clause The section of the Constitution in which Congress is given the power to regulate trade among the states and with foreign countries.

Commercial Speech Advertising statements, which increasingly have been given First Amendment protection.

Common Law Judge-made law that originated in England from decisions shaped according to prevailing customs. Decisions were applied to similar situations and thus gradually became common to the nation.

Concurrent Powers Powers held jointly by the national and state governments.

Concurring Opinion A separate opinion prepared by a judge who supports the decision of the majority of the court but who wants to make or clarify a particular point or to voice disapproval of the grounds on which the decision was made.

Confederal System A system consisting of a league of independent states, in which the central government created by the league has only limited powers over the states.

Confederation A political system in which states or regional governments retain ultimate authority except for those powers they expressly delegate to a central government; a voluntary association of independent states, in which the member states agree to limited restraints on their freedom of action.

Conference Committee A special joint committee appointed to reconcile differences when bills pass the two chambers of Congress in different forms.

Consensus General agreement among the citizenry on an issue.

Conservatism A set of beliefs that includes a limited role for the national government in helping individuals, support for traditional ideals and life choices, and a cautious response to change.

Conservative Movement An American movement in the 1950s that provided a comprehensive ideological framework for conservative politics.

Constituent A person represented by a legislator or other elected or appointed official.

Constitutional Power A power vested in the president by Article II of the Constitution.

Containment A U.S. diplomatic policy adopted by the Truman administration to contain Communist power within its existing boundaries.

Content Provider On the Internet, an individual or organization that generates original content.

Continuing Resolution A temporary funding law that Congress passes when an appropriations bill has not been decided by the beginning of the new fiscal year on October 1.

Cooperative Federalism A model of federalism in which the states and the national government cooperate in solving problems.

Credentials Committee A committee used by political parties at their national conventions to determine which delegates may participate. The committee inspects the claim of each prospective delegate to be seated as a legitimate representative of his or her state.

Criminal Law The law that defines crimes and provides punishment for violations. In criminal cases, the government is the prosecutor.

D

De Facto Segregation Racial segregation that occurs because of past social and economic conditions and residential racial patterns.

De Jure Segregation Racial segregation that occurs because of laws or administrative decisions by public agencies.

Dealignment A decline in party loyalties that reduces long-term party commitment.

Defamation of Character Wrongfully hurting a person's good reputation. The law imposes a general duty on all persons to refrain from making false, defamatory statements about others.

Defense Policy A subset of national security policy having to do with the U.S. armed forces.

Democracy A system of government in which political authority is vested in the people. The term is derived from the Greek words *demos* ("the people") and *kratos* ("authority").

Democratic Party One of the two major American political parties evolving out of the Republican Party of Thomas Jefferson.

Democratic Republic A republic in which representatives elected by the people make and enforce laws and policies.

Détente A French word meaning a relaxation of tensions. The term characterized U.S.-Soviet relations as they developed under President Richard Nixon and Secretary of State Henry Kissinger.

Devolution The transfer of powers from a national or central government to a state or local government.

Diplomacy The process by which nations carry on political relations with one another and resolve conflicts by peaceful means.

Diplomatic Recognition The formal acknowledgment of a foreign government as legitimate.

Direct Democracy A system of government in which political decisions are made by the people directly, rather than by their elected representatives; probably attained most easily in small political communities.

Direct Primary A primary election in which voters decide party nominations by voting directly for candidates.

Direct Technique An interest group activity that involves personal interaction with government officials to further the group's goals.

Discharge Petition A procedure by which a bill in the House of Representatives can be forced (discharged) out of a committee that has refused to report it for consideration by the House. The petition must be signed by an absolute majority (218) of representatives and is used only on rare occasions.

Dissenting Opinion A separate opinion in which a judge dissents from (disagrees with) the conclusion reached by the majority of the court and expounds his or her own views about the case.

Diversity of Citizenship The condition that exists when the parties to a lawsuit are citizens of different states or when the parties are citizens of a U.S. state and citizens or the government of a foreign country. Diversity of citizenship can provide a basis for federal jurisdiction.

Divided Government A situation in which one major political party controls the presidency and the other controls one or more chambers of Congress, or in which one party controls a state governorship and the other controls part or all of the state legislature.

Divided Opinion Public opinion that is polarized between two quite different positions.

Domestic Policy All laws, government planning, and government actions that concern internal issues of national importance, such as poverty, crime, and the environment.

Dual Federalism A model of federalism in which the states and the national government each remain supreme within their own spheres. The doctrine looks on nation and state as co-equal sovereign powers. Neither the state government nor the national government should interfere in the other's sphere.

E

Earmarks Special provisions in legislation to set aside funds for projects that have not passed an impartial evaluation by agencies of the executive branch. Also known as *pork*.

Economic Aid Assistance to other nations in the form of grants, loans, or credits to buy the assisting nation's products.

Elastic Clause, or Necessary and Proper Clause The clause in Article I, Section 8, that grants Congress the power to do whatever is necessary to execute its specifically delegated powers.

Elector A member of the electoral college, which selects the president and vice president. Each state's electors are chosen in each presidential election year according to state laws.

Electoral College A group of persons, called electors, who are selected by the voters in each state. This group officially elects the president and the vice president of the United States.

Elite Theory A perspective holding that society is ruled by a small number of people who hold the ultimate power to further their self-interests.

Emergency Power An inherent power exercised by the president during a period of national crisis.

Enabling Legislation A statute enacted by Congress that authorizes the creation of an administrative agency and specifies the name, purpose, composition, functions, and powers of the agency being created.

Enumerated Power A power specifically granted to the national government by the Constitution. The first seventeen clauses of Article I, Section 8, specify most of the enumerated powers of Congress.

Equality As a political value, the idea that all people are of equal worth.

Establishment Clause The part of the First Amendment prohibiting the establishment of a church officially supported by the national government. It determines the legality of giving state and local government aid to religious organizations and schools, allowing or requiring school prayers, and teaching evolution versus creationism.

Exclusionary Rule A judicial policy prohibiting the admission at trial of illegally obtained evidence.

Executive Agreement An international agreement made by the president, without senatorial ratification, with the head of a foreign state.

Executive Budget The budget prepared and submitted by the president to Congress.

Executive Office of the President (EOP) An organization established by President Franklin Roosevelt to assist the president in carrying out major duties.

Executive Privilege The right of executive officials to withhold information from or to refuse to appear before a legislative committee.

Expressed Power A power of the president that is expressly written into the Constitution or into statutory law.

F

Fairness Doctrine A Federal Communications Commission rule enforced between 1949 and 1987 that required radio and television to present controversial issues in a manner that was (in the commission's view) honest, equitable, and balanced.

Fall Review The annual process in which the OMB, after receiving formal federal agency requests for funding for the next fiscal year, reviews the requests, makes changes, and submits its recommendations to the president.

Federal Election Commission (FEC) The federal regulatory agency with the task of enforcing federal campaign laws. As a practical matter, the FEC's role is largely limited to collecting data on campaign contributions.

Federal Mandate A requirement in federal legislation that forces states and municipalities to comply with certain rules.

Federal Open Market Committee The most important body within the Federal Reserve System. The Federal Open Market Committee decides how monetary policy should be carried out.

Federal Question A question that has to do with the U.S. Constitution, acts of Congress, or treaties. A federal question provides a basis for federal jurisdiction.

Federal Register A publication of the U.S. government that prints executive orders, rules, and regulations.

Federal Reserve System (the Fed) The agency created by Congress in 1913 to serve as the nation's central banking organization.

Federal System A system of government in which power is divided between a central government and regional, or subdivisional, governments. Each level must have some domain in which its policies are dominant and some genuine political or constitutional guarantee of its authority.

Federalist The name given to one who was in favor of the adoption of the U.S. Constitution and the creation of a federal union with a strong central government.

Felony A serious crime punishable in most jurisdictions by a prison sentence longer than one year.

Feminism The movement that supports political, economic, and social equality for women.

Filibuster The use of the Senate's tradition of unlimited debate as a delaying tactic to block a bill.

First Budget Resolution A resolution passed by Congress each May that sets overall revenue and spending goals for the following fiscal year.

Fiscal Having to do with government revenues and expenditures.

Fiscal Federalism A process by which funds raised through taxation or borrowing by one level of government (usually the national government) are spent by another level (typically state or local governments).

Fiscal Policy The federal government's use of taxation and spending policies to affect overall business activity.

Fiscal Year (FY) A twelve-month period that is used for bookkeeping, or accounting, purposes. Usually, the fiscal year does not coincide with the calendar year. For example, the federal government's fiscal year runs from October 1 through September 30.

Focus Group A small group of individuals who are led in discussion by a professional consultant in order to gather opinions on and responses to candidates and issues.

Foreign Policy A nation's external goals and the techniques and strategies used to achieve them.

Fracking Short for *hydraulic fracturing*, the injection of a high-pressure solution of water, sand, and chemicals into hydrocarbon-bearing rocks, releasing oil or natural gas.

Framing Establishing the context of a polling question or a media report. Framing can mean fitting events into a familiar story or activating preconceived beliefs.

Free Exercise Clause The provision of the First Amendment guaranteeing the free exercise of religion. The provision constrains the national government from prohibiting individuals from practicing the religion of their choice.

Free Rider Problem The difficulty interest groups face in recruiting members when the benefits they achieve can be gained without joining the group.

Front-Loading The practice of moving presidential primary elections to the early part of the campaign to maximize the impact of these primaries on the nomination.

Front-Runner The presidential candidate who appears to be ahead at a given time in the primary season.

G

Gag Order An order issued by a judge restricting the publication of news about a trial or a pretrial hearing to protect the accused's right to a fair trial.

Gender Discrimination Any practice, policy, or procedure that denies equality of treatment to an individual or to a group because of gender.

Gender Gap The difference between the percentage of women who vote for a particular candidate and the percentage of men who vote for the candidate.

General Election An election open to all eligible voters, normally held on the first Tuesday in November, that determines who will fill various elected positions.

General Jurisdiction A court's authority to hear cases without significant restriction. A court of general jurisdiction normally can hear a broad range of cases.

Generational Effect The long-lasting effect of the events of a particular time on the political opinions of those who came of political age at that time.

Gerrymandering The drawing of legislative district boundary lines for the purpose of obtaining partisan advantage. A district is said to be gerrymandered when its shape is manipulated to determine which party will win it.

GOP A nickname for the Republican Party; stands for "grand old party."

Government The preeminent institution within society in which decisions are made that resolve conflicts and allocate benefits and privileges. It is unique because it has the ultimate authority for making these decisions.

Government Corporation An agency of government that administers a quasi-business enterprise. These corporations are used when government activities are primarily commercial.

Government in the Sunshine Act A law that requires all committee-directed federal agencies to conduct their business regularly in public session.

Grandfather Clause A device used by southern states to disenfranchise African Americans. It restricted voting to those whose grandfathers had voted before 1867.

Great Compromise The compromise between the New Jersey and Virginia Plans that created one chamber of the Congress based on population and one chamber representing each state equally; also called the Connecticut Compromise.

Gross Domestic Product (GDP) The dollar value of all final goods and services produced in a one-year period.

Gross Public Debt The net public debt plus interagency borrowings without the government.

H

Hastert Rule A rule adopted by Republicans in the U.S. House, under which a Republican Speaker will not bring a measure to the floor for a vote unless it has the support of a majority of the Republican members.

Hatch Act An act passed in 1939 that restricted the political activities of government employees. It also prohibited a political group from spending more than $3 million in any campaign and limited individual contributions to a campaign committee to $5,000.

Head of State The role of the president as ceremonial head of the government.

Hispanic A term used by the federal government to describe someone who can claim a heritage from a Spanish-speaking country.

House Effect In public opinion polling, an effect in which one polling organization's results consistently differ from those reported by other poll takers.

I

Ideology A comprehensive set of beliefs about the nature of people and about the role of an institution or government.

Imminent Lawless Action Test The current standard established by the Supreme Court for evaluating the legality of advocacy speech. Such speech can be forbidden only when it is "directed to inciting... imminent lawless action."

Impeachment An action by the House of Representatives to accuse the president, vice president, or other civil officers of the United States of committing "Treason, Bribery, or other high Crimes and Misdemeanors."

Incarceration Rate The number of persons held in jail or prison for every 100,000 persons in a particular population group.

Incorporation Theory The view that most of the protections of the Bill of Rights apply to state governments through the Fourteenth Amendment's due process clause.

Independent A voter or candidate who does not identify with a political party.

Independent Executive Agency A federal agency that is not part of a cabinet department but reports directly to the president.

Independent Expenditures Nonregulated contributions from PACs, organizations, and individuals. The funds may be spent on advertising or other campaign activities, so long as those expenditures are not coordinated with those of a candidate.

Independent Regulatory Agency An agency outside the major executive departments that is charged with making and implementing rules and regulations within a specific area.

Indirect Primary A primary election in which voters choose convention delegates, and the delegates determine the party's candidate in the general election.

Indirect Technique A strategy employed by interest groups that uses third parties to influence government officials.

Individual Mandate In health-care reform, the requirement that all citizens obtain health-care insurance coverage from some source, public or private.

Inflation A sustained rise in the general price level of goods and services.

Inherent Power A power of the president derived from the statements in the Constitution that "the executive Power shall be vested in a President" and that the president should "take Care that the Laws be faithfully executed"; defined through practice rather than through law.

Initiative A procedure by which voters can propose a law or a constitutional amendment.

Institution An ongoing organization that performs certain functions for society.

Instructed Delegate A legislator who is an agent of the voters who elected him or her and who votes according to the views of constituents regardless of personal beliefs.

Intelligence Community The government agencies that gather information about the capabilities and intentions of foreign governments or that engage in covert actions.

Interest Group An organized group of individuals sharing common objectives who actively attempt to influence policymakers.

Intermediate Scrutiny The standard used by the courts to determine whether a law or government action improperly discriminates against women. Also known as *exacting scrutiny.*

Internet Service Provider (ISP) A company or organization that provides Internet connectivity to end users or to servers.

Interstate Compact An agreement between two or more states. Agreements on minor matters are made without congressional consent, but any compact that tends to increase the power of the contracting states relative to other states or relative to the national government generally requires the consent of Congress.

Invisible Primary The pre-primary campaign to win supporters among elected officials, fund raisers, interest groups, and opinion leaders.

Iron Triangle The three-way alliance among legislators, bureaucrats, and interest groups to make or preserve policies that benefit their respective interests.

Isolationist Foreign Policy A policy of abstaining from an active role in international affairs or alliances, which characterized U.S. foreign policy toward Europe during most of the 1800s.

Issue Advocacy Advertising paid for by interest groups that support or oppose a candidate or a candidate's position on an issue without mentioning voting or elections.

Issue Network A group of individuals or organizations—which may consist of legislators and legislative staff members, interest group leaders, bureaucrats, scholars and other experts, and media representatives—that supports a particular policy position on a given issue.

J

Joint Committee A legislative committee composed of members from both chambers of Congress.

Judicial Activism A doctrine holding that the federal judiciary should take an active role by using its powers to check the activities of governmental bodies when those bodies exceed their authority.

Judicial Implementation The way in which court decisions are translated into policy.

Judicial Restraint A doctrine holding that the courts should defer to the decisions made by the elected representatives of the people in the legislative and executive branches when possible.

Judicial Review The power of the Supreme Court and other courts to examine and possibly declare unconstitutional federal or state laws and other acts of government.

Jurisdiction The authority of a court to decide certain cases. Not all courts have the authority to decide all cases. Where a case arises and what its subject matter is are two jurisdictional issues.

Justiciable Controversy A controversy that is real and substantial, as opposed to hypothetical or academic.

K

Keynesian Economics A school of economic thought that tends to favor active federal government policymaking to stabilize economy-wide fluctuations, usually by implementing discretionary fiscal policy.

Kitchen Cabinet The informal advisers to the president.

L

Labor Movement The economic and political expression of working-class interests.

Latent Interests Public-policy interests that are not recognized or addressed by a group at a particular time.

Latino An alternate word for *Hispanic*, now more widely used. The feminine is *Latina*.

Lawmaking The process of establishing the legal rules that govern society.

Legislature A governmental body primarily responsible for the making of laws.

Legitimacy Popular acceptance of the right and power of a government or other entity to exercise authority.

Libel A written defamation of a person's character, reputation, business, or property rights.

Liberalism A set of beliefs that includes the advocacy of positive government action to improve the welfare of individuals, support for civil rights, and tolerance for political and social change.

Libertarianism A political ideology based on skepticism or opposition toward most government activities.

Liberty The greatest freedom of the individual that is consistent with the freedom of other individuals in the society.

Limited Government A government with powers that are limited either through a written document or through widely shared beliefs.

Limited Jurisdiction A court's authority to hear cases with restriction to certain types of claims, such as tax claims or bankruptcy petitions.

Line Organization In the federal government, an administrative unit that is directly accountable to the president.

Line-Item Veto The power of an executive to veto individual lines or items within a piece of legislation without vetoing the entire bill.

Literacy Test A test administered as a precondition for voting, often used to prevent African Americans from exercising their right to vote.

Litigate To engage in a legal proceeding or seek relief in a court of law; to carry on a lawsuit.

Lobbyist An organization or individual who attempts to influence legislation and the administrative decisions of government.

Loophole A legal method by which individuals and businesses are allowed to reduce the tax liabilities owed to the government.

Loose Monetary Policy Monetary policy that makes credit inexpensive and abundant, possibly leading to inflation.

M

Madisonian Model A structure of government proposed by James Madison in which the powers of the government are separated into three branches: executive, legislative, and judicial.

Majoritarianism A political theory holding that, in a democracy, the government ought to do what the majority of the people want.

Majority The age at which a person is entitled by law to the right to manage her or his own affairs.

Majority Leader of the House The majority leader of the House of Representatives is selected by the majority party in caucus to foster cohesion among party members and to act as spokesperson for the majority party in the House.

Majority Opinion A court opinion reflecting the views of the majority of the judges.

Majority Rule A basic principle of democracy asserting that the greatest number of citizens in any political unit should select officials and determine policies.

Material Incentive A reason or motive based on the desire to enjoy certain economic benefits or opportunities.

Media The channels of mass communication.

Medicaid A joint state-federal program that provides medical care to the poor (including indigent elderly persons in nursing homes). The program is funded out of general government revenues.

Medicare A federal health-insurance program that covers U.S. residents over the age of sixty-five. The costs are met by a tax on wages and salaries.

Merit System The selection, retention, and promotion of government employees on the basis of competitive examinations.

Midterm Elections National elections in which candidates for president are not on the ballot. In midterm elections, voters choose all members of the U.S. House of Representatives and one-third of the members of the U.S. Senate.

Minority Leader of the House The party leader elected by the minority party in the House.

Monetary Policy The use of changes in the amount of money in circulation to alter credit markets, employment, and the rate of inflation.

Monopolistic Model A model of bureaucracy that compares bureaucracies to monopolistic business firms. Lack of competition in either circumstance leads to inefficient and costly operations.

Monroe Doctrine A policy statement by President James Monroe in 1823, which set out three principles: (1) European nations should not establish new colonies in the Western Hemisphere, (2) European nations should not intervene in the affairs of independent nations of the Western Hemisphere, and (3) the United States would not interfere in the affairs of European nations.

Moral Idealism A philosophy that sees nations as normally willing to cooperate and agree on moral standards for conduct.

N

National Committee A standing committee of a national political party established to direct and coordinate party activities between national party conventions.

National Convention The meeting held every four years by each major party to select presidential and vice-presidential candidates, write a platform, choose a national committee, and conduct party business.

National Security Council (NSC) An agency in the Executive Office of the President that advises the president on national security.

National Security Policy Foreign and domestic policy designed to protect the nation's independence and political integrity; policy that is concerned with the safety and defense of the nation.

Natural Rights Rights held to be inherent in natural law, not dependent on governments. John Locke stated that natural law, being superior to human law, specifies certain rights of "life, liberty, and property." These rights, altered to become "life, liberty, and the pursuit of happiness," are asserted in the Declaration of Independence.

Negative Constituents Citizens who openly oppose the government's policies.

Net Public Debt The accumulation of all past federal government deficits; the total amount owed by the federal government to individuals, businesses, and foreigners.

Network Neutrality The principle that an ISP should treat all Internet traffic equally.

Normal Trade Relations (NTR) Status A status granted through an international treaty by which each member nation must treat other members as well as it treats the country that receives its most favorable treatment. This status was formerly known as *most-favored-nation status*.

O

Office of Management and Budget (OMB) A division of the Executive Office of the President. The OMB assists the president in preparing the annual budget, clearing and coordinating departmental agency budgets, and supervising the administration of the federal budget.

Office-Block, or Massachusetts, Ballot A form of general election ballot in which candidates for elective office are grouped together under the title of each office. It emphasizes voting for the office and the individual candidate, rather than for the party.

Oligarchy "Rule by a few."

Ombudsperson A person who hears and investigates complaints by private individuals against public officials or agencies. (From the Swedish word *ombudsman*, meaning "representative.")

Open Primary A primary in which any registered voter can vote (but must vote for candidates of only one party).

Opinion A statement by a judge or a court of the decision reached in a case. An opinion sets forth the applicable law and details the reasoning on which the ruling was based.

Opinion Leader One who is able to influence the opinions of others because of position, expertise, or personality.

Opinion Poll A method of systematically questioning a small, selected sample of respondents who are deemed representative of the total population.

Oral Arguments The arguments presented in person by attorneys to an appellate court. Each attorney presents to the court reasons why the court should rule in her or his client's favor.

Order A state of peace and security. Maintaining order by protecting members of society from violence and criminal activity is one of the oldest purposes of government.

Oversight The process by which Congress follows up on laws it has enacted to ensure that they are being enforced and administered in the way Congress intended.

P

Pardon A release from the punishment for, or legal consequences of, a crime. A pardon can be granted by the president before or after a conviction.

Party Identification Linking oneself to a particular political party.

Party Organization The formal structure and leadership of a political party, including election committees; local, state, and national executives; and paid professional staff.

Party Platform A document drawn up at each national convention, outlining the policies, positions, and principles of the party.

Party-Column, or Indiana, Ballot A form of general election ballot in which all of a party's candidates for elective office are arranged in one column under the party's label and symbol. It emphasizes voting for the party, rather than for the office or individual.

Party-in-Government All of the elected and appointed officials who identify with a political party.

Party-in-the-Electorate Those members of the general public who identify with a political party or who express a preference for one party over another.

Patronage The rewarding of faithful party workers and followers with government employment or contracts.

Peer Group A group whose members share common social characteristics. These groups play an important part in the socialization process, helping to shape attitudes and beliefs.

Pendleton Act (Civil Service Reform Act) An act that established the principle of employment on the basis of merit and created the Civil Service Commission to administer the personnel service.

Pluralism A theory that views politics as a conflict among interest groups. Political decision making is characterized by compromise and accommodation.

Plurality A number of votes cast for a candidate that is greater than the number of votes for any other candidate but not necessarily a majority.

Plurality Opinion An opinion by a minority of the Court that decides a case because it is supported by one or more concurring opinions.

Pocket Veto A special veto exercised by the chief executive after a legislative body has adjourned. Bills not signed by the chief executive die after a specified period of time. If Congress wishes to reconsider such a bill, it must be reintroduced in the following session of Congress.

Podcasting A method of distributing multimedia files, such as audio or video files, for downloading onto mobile devices or personal computers.

Police Power The authority to legislate for the protection of the health, morals, safety, and welfare of the people. In the United States, most police power is reserved to the states.

Policy Demanders Individuals or interest group members who participate in political parties with the intent to see that certain policies are adopted or specific groups favored.

Political Action Committee (PAC) A committee set up by and representing a corporation, labor union, or special interest group. PACs raise and give campaign donations.

Political Consultant A paid professional hired to devise a campaign strategy and manage a campaign.

Political Culture A patterned set of ideas, values, and ways of thinking about government and politics that characterize a people.

Political Party A group of political activists who organize to win elections, operate the government, and determine public policy.

Political Question An issue that a court believes should be decided by the executive or legislative branch—or these two branches acting together.

Political Realism A philosophy that sees each nation acting principally in its own interests.

Political Socialization The process by which people acquire political beliefs and values.

Political Trust The degree to which individuals express trust in the government and political institutions, usually measured through a specific series of survey questions.

Politics The process of resolving conflicts and deciding "who gets what, when, and how." More specifically, politics is the struggle over power or influence within organizations or informal groups that can grant benefits or privileges.

Poll Tax A special tax that had to be paid as a qualification for voting. In 1964, the Twenty-fourth Amendment to the Constitution outlawed the poll tax in national elections, and in 1966 the Supreme Court declared it unconstitutional in state elections as well.

Popular Sovereignty The concept that ultimate political authority is based on the will of the people.

Precedent A court rule bearing on subsequent legal decisions in similar cases. Judges rely on precedents in deciding cases.

President Pro Tempore The temporary presiding officer of the Senate in the absence of the vice president.

Presidential Primary A statewide primary election of delegates to a political party's national convention, held to determine a party's presidential nominee.

Primary Election An election in which political parties choose their candidates for the general election.

Priming A way in which the media can alter public perceptions of an issue—by embedding that issue in particular examples or stories.

Prior Restraint Restraining an activity before it has actually occurred. When expression is involved, this means censorship.

Privatization The replacement of government services with services provided by private firms.

Progressive A popular alternative to the term *liberal*.

Progressive Tax A tax that rises in percentage terms as incomes rise.

Property Anything that is or may be subject to ownership. As conceived by the political philosopher John Locke, the right to property is a natural right superior to human law (laws made by government).

Public Agenda Issues that are perceived by the political community as meriting public attention and governmental action.

Public Debt, or National Debt The total amount of debt carried by the federal government.

Public Figure A public official or any other person, such as a movie star, known to the public because of his or her position or activities.

Public Interest The best interests of the overall community; the national good, rather than the narrow interests of a particular group.

Public Opinion The aggregate of individual attitudes or beliefs shared by some portion of the adult population.

Purposive Incentive A reason for supporting or participating in the activities of a group that is based on agreement with the goals of the group. For example, someone with a strong interest in human rights might have a purposive incentive to join Amnesty International.

R

Ratification Formal approval.

Rational Basis Review The standard used by the courts to determine the constitutionality of a law or government action if neither strict scrutiny nor intermediate scrutiny applies.

Realignment A process in which a substantial group of voters switches party allegiance, producing a long-term change in the political landscape.

Reapportionment The allocation of seats in the House of Representatives to each state after a census.

Recall A procedure allowing the people to vote to dismiss an elected official from state office before his or her term has expired.

Recession Two or more successive quarters in which the economy shrinks instead of grows.

Reconciliation A special rule that can be applied to budget bills sent from the House of Representatives to the Senate. Reconciliation measures cannot be filibustered.

Redistricting The redrawing of the boundaries of the congressional districts within each state.

Referendum An electoral device whereby legislative or constitutional measures are referred by the legislature to the voters for approval or disapproval.

Registration The entry of a person's name onto the list of registered voters for elections. To register, a person must meet certain legal requirements of age, citizenship, and residency.

Regressive Tax A tax that falls in percentage terms as incomes rise.

Remand To send a case back to the court that originally heard it.

Representation The function of members of Congress as elected officials representing the views of their constituents as well as larger national interests.

Representative Assembly A legislature composed of individuals who represent the population.

Representative Democracy A form of government in which representatives elected by the people make and enforce laws and policies; may retain the monarchy in a ceremonial role.

Reprieve A formal postponement of the execution of a sentence imposed by a court of law.

Republic A form of government in which sovereign power rests with the people, rather than with a king or a monarch.

Republican Party One of the two major American political parties. It emerged in the 1850s as an antislavery party and consisted of former northern Whigs and antislavery Democrats.

Reverse Discrimination The situation in which an affirmative action program discriminates against those who do not have minority status.

Reverse To annul, or make void, a court ruling on account of some error or irregularity.

Reverse-Income Effect A tendency for wealthier states or regions to favor the Democrats and for less wealthy states or regions to favor the Republicans. The effect appears paradoxical because it reverses traditional patterns of support.

Rule of Four A United States Supreme Court procedure by which four justices must vote to grant a petition for review if a case is to come before the full court.

Rules Committee A standing committee of the House of Representatives that provides special rules under which specific bills can be debated, amended, and considered by the House.

S

Sampling Error The difference between a sample's results and the true result if the entire population had been interviewed.

Second Budget Resolution A resolution passed by Congress each September that sets "binding" limits on taxes and spending for the following fiscal year.

Select Committee A temporary legislative committee established for a limited time period and for a special purpose.

Senate Majority Leader The chief spokesperson of the majority party in the Senate, who directs the legislative program and party strategy.

Senate Minority Leader The party officer in the Senate who commands the minority party's opposition to the policies of the majority party and directs the legislative program and strategy of his or her party.

Senatorial Courtesy In federal district court judgeship nominations, a tradition allowing a senator to veto a judicial appointment in his or her state.

Seniority System A custom followed in both chambers of Congress specifying that the member of the majority party with the longest term of continuous service will be given preference when a committee chairperson (or a holder of some other significant post) is selected.

Separate-but-Equal Doctrine The doctrine holding that separate-but-equal facilities do not violate the equal protection clause of the Fourteenth Amendment to the U.S. Constitution.

Separation of Powers The principle of dividing governmental powers among different branches of government.

Service Sector The sector of the economy that provides services—such as health care, banking, and education—in contrast to the sector that produces goods.

Sexual Harassment Unwanted physical or verbal conduct or abuse of a sexual nature that interferes with a recipient's job performance, creates a hostile work environment, or carries with it an implicit or explicit threat of adverse employment consequences.

Signing Statement A written declaration that a president may make when signing a bill into law. Such statements may point out sections of the law that the president deems unconstitutional.

Slander The public uttering of a false statement that harms the good reputation of another. The statement must be made to, or within the hearing of, a person other than the defamed party.

Social Contract A voluntary agreement among individuals to secure their rights and welfare by creating a government and abiding by its rules.

Social Movement A movement that represents the demands of a large segment of the public for political, economic, or social change.

Socialism A political ideology based on strong support for economic and social equality. Socialists traditionally envisioned a society in which major businesses were taken over by the government or by employee cooperatives.

Socioeconomic Status The value assigned to a person due to occupation or income. An upper-class person, for example, has high socioeconomic status.

Soft Money Campaign contributions unregulated by federal or state law, usually given to parties and party committees to help fund general party activities.

Solidary Incentive A reason or motive that follows from the desire to associate with others and to share with others a particular interest or hobby.

Sound Bite A brief, memorable comment that easily fits into news broadcasts.

Soviet Bloc The Soviet Union and the Eastern European countries that installed Communist regimes after World War II and were dominated by the Soviet Union.

Speaker of the House The presiding officer in the House of Representatives. The Speaker is always a member of the majority party and is the most powerful and influential member of the House.

Spin An interpretation of campaign events or election results that is favorable to the candidate's campaign strategy.

Spin Doctor A political campaign adviser who tries to convince journalists of the truth of a particular interpretation of events.

Splinter Party A new party formed by a dissident faction within a major political party. Often, splinter parties have emerged when a particular personality was at odds with the major party.

Split-Ticket Voting Voting for candidates of two or more parties for different offices, such as voting for a Republican presidential candidate and a Democratic congressional candidate.

Spoils System The awarding of government jobs to political supporters and friends.

Spring Review The annual process in which the Office of Management and Budget (OMB) requires federal agencies to review their programs, activities, and goals and submit their requests for funding for the next fiscal year.

Standing Committee A permanent committee in the House or Senate that considers bills within a certain subject area.

Stare Decisis To stand on decided cases; the judicial policy of following precedents established by past decisions.

State A group of people occupying a specific area and organized under one government. It may either be a nation or a subunit of a nation.

State Central Committee The principal organized structure of each political party within each state. This committee is responsible for carrying out policy decisions of the party's state convention.

State of the Union Message An annual message to Congress in which the president proposes a legislative program. The message is addressed not only to Congress but also to the American people and to the world.

Statutory Power A power created for the president through laws enacted by Congress.

Straight-Ticket Voting Voting exclusively for the candidates of one party.

Strategic Arms Limitation Treaty (SALT I) A treaty between the United States and the Soviet Union to stabilize the nuclear arms competition between the two countries. SALT I talks began in 1969, and the treaty was signed on May 26, 1972.

Strict Construction A judicial philosophy that looks to the "letter of the law" when interpreting the Constitution or a particular statute.

Strict Scrutiny A judicial standard for assessing the constitutionality of a law or government action when the law or action threatens to interfere with a fundamental right or potentially discriminates against members of a suspect classification.

Suffrage The right to vote; the franchise.

Sunset Legislation Laws requiring that existing programs be reviewed regularly for their effectiveness and be terminated unless specifically extended as a result of these reviews.

Super PAC A political organization that aggregates unlimited contributions by individuals and organizations to be spent independently of candidate committees.

Superdelegate A party leader or elected official who is given the right to vote at the party's national convention. Superdelegates are not selected at the state level.

Supremacy Clause The constitutional provision that makes the Constitution and federal laws superior to all conflicting state and local laws.

Supremacy Doctrine A doctrine that asserts the priority of national law over state laws. This principle is stated in Article VI of the Constitution, which provides that the Constitution, the laws passed by the national government under its constitutional powers, and all treaties constitute the supreme law of the land.

Suspect Classification A classification, such as race, religion, or national origin, that triggers strict scrutiny by the courts when a law or government action potentially discriminates against members of the class.

Swing Voters Voters who frequently swing their support from one party to another.

Symbolic Speech Expression made through articles of clothing, gestures, movements, and other forms of nonverbal conduct. Symbolic speech is given substantial protection by the courts.

T

Technical Assistance The practice of sending experts in such areas as agriculture, engineering, or business to aid other nations.

Terrorism A systematic attempt to inspire fear to gain political ends, typically involving the indiscriminate use of violence against noncombatants.

Theocracy "Rule by God," or the gods; in practice, rule by religious leaders, typically self-appointed.

Third Party A political party other than the two major political parties (Republican and Democratic).

Tight Monetary Policy Monetary policy that makes credit expensive in an effort to slow inflation.

Tipping A phenomenon that occurs when a group that is becoming more numerous over time grows large enough to change the political balance in a district, state, or country.

Total Fertility Rate A statistic that measures the average number of children that women in a given group are expected to have over the course of a lifetime.

Totalitarian Regime A form of government that controls all aspects of the political, social, and economic life of a nation.

Treasuries U.S. Treasury securities—bills, notes, and bonds; debt issued by the federal government.

Trial Court The court in which most cases begin.

Truman Doctrine The policy adopted by President Harry Truman in 1947 to halt Communist expansion in southeastern Europe.

Trustee A legislator who acts according to her or his conscience and the broad interests of the entire society.

Twelfth Amendment An amendment to the Constitution, adopted in 1804, that requires the separate election of the president and the vice president by the electoral college.

Twenty-fifth Amendment A 1967 amendment to the Constitution that establishes procedures for filling presidential and vice-presidential vacancies and makes provisions for presidential incapacity.

Two-Party System A political system in which only two parties have a reasonable chance of winning.

U

Unanimous Opinion A Court opinion or determination on which all judges agree.

Unemployment The inability of those who are in the labor force to find a job; also the number of those in the labor force actively looking for a job, but unable to find one.

Unicameral Legislature A legislature with only one legislative chamber, as opposed to a bicameral (two-chamber) legislature, such as the U.S. Congress. Today, Nebraska is the only state in the Union with a unicameral legislature.

Unitary System A centralized governmental system in which ultimate governmental authority rests in the hands of the national, or central, government.

Universal Health Insurance Any of several possible programs to provide health insurance to everyone in a country. The central government does not necessarily provide the insurance itself but may subsidize the purchase of insurance from private insurance companies.

Universal Suffrage The right of all adults to vote for their government representatives.

V

Veto Message The president's formal explanation of a veto when legislation is returned to Congress.

Vote-Eligible Population The number of people who, at a given time, enjoy the right to vote in national elections.

Voter Turnout The percentage of citizens taking part in the election process; the number of eligible voters that actually "turn out" on election day to cast their ballots.

Voting-Age Population The number of people of voting age living in the country at a given time, regardless of whether they have the right to vote.

W

War Powers Resolution A law passed in 1973 spelling out the conditions under which the president can commit troops without congressional approval.

Weberian Model A model of bureaucracy developed by the German sociologist Max Weber, who viewed bureaucracies as rational, hierarchical organizations in which decisions are based on logical reasoning.

Whig Party A major party in the United States during the first half of the nineteenth century, formally established in 1836. The Whig Party was anti-Jackson and represented a variety of regional interests.

Whip A member of Congress who aids the majority or minority leader of the House or the Senate.

Whistleblower Someone who brings to public attention gross governmental inefficiency or an illegal action.

White House Office The personal office of the president, which tends to presidential political needs and manages the media.

White Primary A state primary election that restricted voting to whites only. It was outlawed by the Supreme Court in 1944.

Writ of *Certiorari* An order issued by a higher court to a lower court to send up the record of a case for review.

Writ of *Habeas Corpus* *Habeas corpus* means, literally, "you have the body." A writ of *habeas corpus* is an order that requires jailers to bring a prisoner before a court or a judge and explain why the person is being held.

Index

American Federation of State, County, and Municipal Employees (AFSCME), 207
American Federation of Teachers, 210
American Hospital Association, 207
American Independent, 249
American Indians
  demographic collapse of, 150–151
  lingering social and economic disparities, 152–153
  in nineteenth and twentieth centuries, 151
American Israel Public Affairs Committee (AIPAC), 207, 213, 215
American Legion, 207
American Medical Association (AMA), 207
American Opportunity Tax Credit, 373
American Petroleum Institute, 222–223
American Revolution, 8, 34–37
  economic depression after, 58
Americans for Democratic Action, 219
Americans for Prosperity, 269
Americans for Tax Reform, 213, 218
American Society for the Prevention of Cruelty to Animals (ASPCA), 207
American Woman Suffrage Association, 154
America's Health Insurance Plans, 207
Amicus curiae brief, 406
Amnesty International USA, 207
Anarchy, 7
Anderson, John, 248, 249
Anthony, Susan B., 154
Anti-Federalists, 236
  ratification of Constitution, 46–47
Anti-Ku Klux Klan Act (Civil Rights Act of 1872), 137
Antiterrorism and Effective Death Penalty Act, 124, 129, 410
Appellate court, 408–409, 415
Appointment power, 349
Apportionment, 50
Appropriation, 337
Arab Spring, 464–465
Argentina, 359
Aristocracy, 7
Arizona, immigration reform, 96, 439
Armitage, David, 35
ARPAnet, 302
Arraignment, 125
Arthur, Chester, 367

Articles of Confederation, 77, 78
  accomplishments under, 37–38
  drafting, 37
  government under, 37
  Shays' Rebellion and need for revision, 39
  weaknesses of, 38
Asian Americans
  Chinese Exclusion Act, 151–152
  college admission and, 152
  Japanese Americans and internment camps, 13, 145, 152
  lingering social and economic disparities, 152–153
  voter turnout and, 281
  voting behavior and political party identification, 181
Assad, Bashar al, 5, 293, 465
Assault-style weapons, 106
Assembly, freedom of, 105, 116
Association of General Contractors of America, 210
Astroturf lobbying, 221
Australia
  agricultural subsidies in, 208
  common law and, 404
  federal system of government in, 78
  health care spending and, 434
  taxes collected as percentage of GDP, 453
Australian ballot, 277
Authoritarianism, 7
Authority, 6
Authorization, 336
Auto industry
  Great Recession and bailout, 15
  higher fuel efficiency standards, 444

B

Bad tendency rule, 113
Bakke, Allan, 147
Ballots
  absentee, 278
  Australian, 277
  Indiana, 278
  Massachusetts, 277
  office-block, 277
  party-column, 278
Banking industry
  bank bailout, 15, 385–386
  banking crisis of 2008, 385–386
  government ownership of, 385
  national bank, 86
Bankruptcy, government control of private corporations and, 385

Barron v. Baltimore, 104
Battered women's shelters, 155
Bear arms, right to, 2, 421
Beard, Charles, 48
Becerra, Xavier, 333
Beck, Glenn, 304–305
Belgium, gay rights in, 405
Benton v. Maryland, 105
Bias, in media, 305–306
Bicameralism, 312–313
Bicameral legislature, 41, 312–313
Biden, Joe, 366
Big government, 14–16
  entitlement programs, 17
  Great Recession and, 15
  health-care reform and, 240
  Obama and, 15, 16
  political parties and, 15–16, 242
Bill, becomes a law, 333–335
Bill of Rights, 2. *See also individual amendments*
  adoption of, 50
  as bill of limits, 49
  defined, 12
  extending to state government, 104–105
  freedom of expression (*See* Press, freedom of; Speech, freedom of)
  incorporating Fourteenth Amendment into, 105–106
  incorporation theory, 105–106
  in main body of Constitution, 50
  writing, 50
Bills of attainder, 50
Bin Laden, Osama, 463, 466, 470
  death of, 469–470
Biometric IDs, 392
Bipartisan Campaign Reform Act, 266
Birth control, Supreme Court decisions, 423
Blackmun, Harry A., 112
Black Power, 141
Blanket primary, 274
Block grants, 92
  Nixon and Reagan, 95
Blogosphere politics, 299
Blogs, 176
  campaigns and, 298–300
  comments on, 300
  vs. magazines, 299
  selected sites, 299
Blue Dog caucus, 235
Boehner, John, 240, 244, 331, 333
Border Patrol, 351
Bork, Robert, 418

Bosnia, 478
Boston Tea Party, 33, 222
Bowers v. Hardwick, 159
Boycott, 222
BP oil spill, 445
Bradford, William, 30
Branch Ministries, Inc., 110–111
Brandeis, Louis, 80
Brandenburg v. Ohio, 113
Brazil
  federal system of government in, 78
  gay rights in, 405
  incarceration rate in, 443
Breyer, Stephen, 55, 418, 422
Broad construction, 420
Brooks, Rebekah, 301
Brown, Linda Carol, 139
Brown, Oliver, 139
Browne, William P., 206
Brown v. Board of Education of Topeka,
  139, 146, 163
Bryan, William Jennings, 239
  election of 1896 and, 237
Buckley v. Valeo, 265
Budget. *See* Federal budget
Budget and Impoundment Control
  Act, 334
Budget deficit
  deficit spending and, 450–451
  defined, 448
  public debt and, 450–451
  public opinion on, 171
Budget surplus, 450
Bull Moose Progressive Party, 251
Bureaucracy, 373–397
  congressional control of, 397
  defined, 374
  e-government and, 391
  federal spending on, 377
  government employment today,
    376–377
  history of civil service, 387–389
  iron triangles, 396–397
  issue network, 397
  merit system, 388
  models of, 374–375
  nature of, 374–375
  organization of federal, 379–386
    cabinet departments, 380
    chart of, 379
    government corporations, 384–386
    independent executive
      agencies, 380
    independent regulatory agencies,
      380, 382–384

policymaking and, 396–397
political appointees, 387
president as head of executive
  bureaucracy, 348–350
private, 374
privatization and, 390–391
public, 374
reform, modern attempts at,
  389–393
response to terrorism, 390
size of, 376–377
spoils system, 388
staffing, 386–389
sunset legislation, 390
sunshine laws and, 389–390
whistleblowers and, 391–393
Bureaucrats
  as policymakers, 396–397
  as politicians, 393–395
Bureau of the Budget, 365
Burger, Warren, 113
Burr, Aaron, 347
Burton, Bill, 268
Bush, George H. W., 353, 366
  armed forces ordered by
    into combat without
      congressional approval, 481
    into Middle East, 351
    into Panama, 351
  election of 1988, gender gap, 182
  election of 1992, 251
    gender gap, 182
  Flag Protection Act, 111
  foreign policy and, 485
  judicial appointment and, 417
  plan to end governmental
    inefficiency, 375
  political trust and, 191
  public opinion of, 358
  reregulation and, 383
  Soviet Union and, 485
Bush, George W., 356
  Afghanistan and, 469
  antiterrorism policies, 353
  appointments, federal district court
    judges, 415
  armed forces ordered by, to
    Afghanistan and Iraq,
    351, 478
  bank bailout, 385–386
  Cheney as vice president, 366
  draft, 462
  election of 2000, 239
    electoral college, 277, 346
    gender gap, 182

    Muslim Americans voting for, 181
    Supreme Court decision
      and, 412
    votes by groups, 178
    without majority of vote, 346
  election of 2004, 239
    gender gap, 182
    Hispanic vote and, 181
    votes by groups, 178
  election-year budget, 336
  enemy combatant detainees,
    410–411
  executive orders, 361
  expansion of presidential powers
    under, 360
  federal government's reach
    expanded by, 95
  federalization of National
    Guard, 85
  FISA court and, 410
  foreign nations' opinion of U.S.
    and, 194
  as fund-raiser, 357
  government spending during, 242
  Great Recession and, 15
  immigration reform, 439
  Iraq War and, 468, 481
  judicial appointment, 417, 418
  Keynesian economics and, 449
  lobbying reform, 223
  media bias, 306
  No Child Left Behind Act, 95
  nuclear weapon reduction with
    Russia, 353
  partial-birth abortions, 120
  plan to end governmental
    inefficiency, 375
  political trust and, 191
  public approval of, 357, 358
  sent National Guard to Mexican
    border, 351
  service in National Guard, 259
  signing statements and, 362
  veto power and, 356
  war on terrorism, 360, 410, 467
  warrantless wiretaps, 122
  waterboarding and, 480
Bush, Jeb, 121
Bush Doctrine, 467
Bush v. Gore, 417–418
Business cycle, 447
Business interest groups, 206–207
Business Roundtable, 207
Busing, 140
Byrd, Harry, 249

C

Cabinet
  defined, 363
  kitchen, 363
  members of, 363
  presidential use of, 363–364
Cabinet departments
  defined, 380
  listed, 381–382
  president and, 380
Cain, Herman, 297
Camp, Dave, 373
Campaign financing
  Bipartisan Campaign Reform Act, 266
  Buckley v. Valeo, 265
  Citizens United, 220–221, 266–267, 268, 421
  congressional elections and, 323
  corporations and, 267
  current environment of, 266–270
  evolution of, 264–266
  Federal Election Campaign Act (FECA), 265
  501(c)4 organizations, 268–269
  527 organizations, 267–268
  Hatch Act, 264–265
  independent expenditures, 267
  Internet and, 298
  issue advocacy advertising, 265–266
  political action committees (PACs), 264, 265
  president as fund-raiser, 357
  presidential candidate committees, 270
  public financing for primaries, 270
  rise and fall of McCain-Feingold Act, 266
  soft money, 266
  super PAC, 267, 268
  top committees contributing in 2014 elections, 269
  unions and nonprofits, 267
Campaigns
  advertising, 295–296
  blogging and, 298–300
  campaign lies, 259
  candidate-centered, 262–263
  changes in, from those earlier, 262–263
  coattail effect and, 323
  congressional, 322–324
  federal employees and, 389
  financing (*See* Campaign financing)
  focus groups and, 264
  interest groups and assistance with, 220–221

Internet and, 298–300
managing news coverage, 296–297
media and, 295–300
negative advertising, 295–296
opinion polls and, 263–264
podcasting, 300
political consultants and, 263
political parties' role in, 263
power of incumbency, 323–324
presidential debates, 297–298
professional, 263
twenty-first century, 260–264
winning strategy of, 263–264
Canada
  agricultural subsidies in, 208
  common law and, 404
  federal system of government in, 78
  health care spending and, 434
  incarceration rate in, 443
  lobbying by, 214
  primary system, 272
  Senate and House of Commons, 316
  taxes collected as percentage of GDP, 453
  U.S. oil imports from, 443
Candidate(s), 260–262
  African Americans as, 261, 262
  candidate-centered campaigns, 262–263
  coattail effect and, 278, 323
  for congressional elections, 322–324
  front-runner, 275
  motivations to seek office, 261–262
  power of incumbency, 323–324
  professionals as, 261–262
  recruiting, by political parties, 230
  requirements for, 260–261
  visibility and appeal of, 263
  women as, 261
Candidate committees, 270
Cantwell v. Connecticut, 105
Capitalism
  defined, 14
  laissez-faire capitalism, 19
  property rights and, 14
Capital punishment. *See* Death penalty
Capone, Al, 441
Capture, 383
Caribbean, lobbying by, 214
Carter, Jimmy, 181, 345
  armed forces ordered by into combat without congressional approval, 481
  China and, 485
  deregulation, 383

election of 1980, 186
  gender gap, 182
judicial appointment and, 414
losing invisible primary in 1976, 273
Mondale and, 366
pardon of draft resisters, 351
People's Republic of China recognized by, 352
plan to end governmental inefficiency, 375
political mood and government success during, 177
public opinion of, 358
Case law, 404
Casework, 314
Castro, Joaquin, 230
Categorical grants, 90–91
  Nixon and Reagan, 95
Catholics, 180, 191, 195, 237
Caucus, 271, 274
CBS, 187, 306
Ceballos, Richard, 393
Cell phone, opinion polls and, 189
Census Bureau, measuring unemployment, 447
Central Intelligence Agency (CIA)
  communication with FBI, 122
  creation of, 479
  criticism of, 480
  failure to detect nuclear arsenals of India and Pakistan, 480
  formation and function of, 382
  USA Patriot Act, 122
Certiorari, writ of, 412
Chamber of Commerce, U.S., 207, 214–215, 216, 217, 218, 244, 269
Change to Win Coalition, 207, 209
Charitable contributions, 373
Chebuib, Jose Antonio, 359
Chechnya, 486
Checks and balances, 44–45
  judicial review and, 419
Cheney, Dick, 356, 366, 480
Chief diplomat, 352–353
Chief executive, 348–351
Chief legislator, 353–356
Chief of staff, 365
Child labor, 89
Children
  child-custody laws, 164
  civil rights of, 163–165
  political socialization of, 174–175
  pornography and, 114
Children's Health Insurance Program (CHIP), 378, 433

Hussein, Saddam, 467
    First Gulf War and, 467
    Iraq War and, 468

I

Identity groups, 213–214
Ideological groups, 213
Ideology, 16
Immigrants/immigration
    Arizona immigration reform, 96, 439
    benefits of, 438
    change in U.S. ethnic distribution,
        22–23
    characteristics of undocumented,
        149–150
    Chinese Exclusion Act, 151–152
    civil rights of, 149–150
    deportation and limits of rights, 124
    domestic policy and, 438–440
    effect of mass deportation of illegal
        immigrants, 135
    Hispanics as largest minority
        group, 438
    immigration reform attempts,
        439–440
    national security and civil liberties
        of, 123–124
    political socialization and media,
        291–292
    rates of, 438
    Republican debate on, 440
    unauthorized immigration issue,
        149, 438–439
Immigration Reform and Control
    Act, 149
Imminent lawless action test, 113
Impeachment, 362–363
Implied power, 86
Incarceration rate, 442, 443
Income
    income inequality, 14
    lingering social and economic
        disparities for minorities,
        152–153
    minimum wage, 202
    voter turnout and, 281
Income tax
    congressional power to impose, 316
    imposed during Civil War, 88
    as progressive tax, 454–455
    rates of, 453–454
    simplification idea, 373
Incorporation theory, 105–106
Independent Democrat, 249
Independent executive agencies, 380

Independent expenditures, 267
    super PAC, 267
Independent Party, 249
Independent regulatory agencies,
        380–384
    agency capture, 383
    deregulation and reregulation,
        383–384
    purpose and nature of, 382
Independents
    defined, 229
    importance of, 253
    midterm elections of 2010, 240
    not-so-independent voters, 253–254
    as swing voters, 254
India
    biometric IDs, 392
    common and traditional law in, 404
    federal system of government in, 78
    nuclear weapons and, 470, 480
    population growth and importance
        in world affairs, 476
Indiana ballot, 278
Indirect primary, 273
Indirect techniques of interest groups,
        218, 221–222
Individual mandate, 435
Inflation
    defined, 446
    gold standard and, 431
    measuring, 447
    monetary policy and, 452
Information disclosure, 389–390
Inherent powers, 360
    of national government, 83
Initiative, 8
Institute for Justice, 213
Institute of Electrical and Electronic
    Engineers, 210
Institution, defined, 3
Instructed delegate, 314
Intelligence community
    covert actions, 479–480
    defined, 479
    foreign policymaking and, 479–480
    war on terrorism and, 480
Intelligent design, 109–110
Interest groups, 202–223. See also
    Lobbying; Lobbyists; Political
    action committees (PACs)
    concentrated benefits and dispersed
        costs, 217
    defined, 203
    527 organizations, 267–268
    free rider problem and, 205

    influence of, 217
    iron triangles, 396–397
    issue network, 397
    lack of, for poor Americans, 210
    lawsuits brought by, 406
    list of most effective, 207
    as natural phenomenon, 203–204
    political parties and, 217–218
    power of
        cohesiveness, 216
        leadership, 215–216
        size and resources of, 214–215
    reasons for joining
        material incentives, 205–206
        purposive incentives, 206
        solidary incentives, 205
    representative democracy and,
        216–217
    social movements and, 204
    strategies of, 218–222
        boycott, 222
        building alliances, 220
        campaign assistance by, 220–221
        climate control, 221
        constituents as lobbyists, 221
        direct techniques, 218–221
        indirect techniques, 218, 221–222
        lobbying techniques, 218–219
        public pressure generated
            by, 221
        ratings game, 219
    types of, 206–214
        agricultural, 207–208
        business, 206–207
        economic, 206–211
        environmental, 212
        foreign governments, 214
        identity groups, 213–214
        ideological groups, 213
        labor, 208–211
        other, 213–214
        professionals, 210
        public employee, 209–211
        public-interest, 212–213
Interior Department, 349
    functions of, 381
    subagencies of, 381
Intermediate-Range Nuclear Force
    (INF) Treaty, 485
Intermediate scrutiny, 146, 161–162
Internal Revenue Code, 453
International Brotherhood of
    Teamsters, 207
International Telecommunication
    Union (ITU), 304

Normal trade relations (NTR)
status, 471
Norquist, Grover, 213
North American Free Trade
Agreement, 220
North Atlantic Treaty Organization
(NATO), 344, 483
Northern Alliance, 469
Northern Ireland, 466, 467
North Korea
government power, 6
Korean war and, 484
nuclear weapons and, 470, 471
South Korea invaded by, 484
Northwest Ordinance, 38
Norway, agricultural subsidies in, 208
Nuclear energy, 445
Nuclear option, 319–320
Nuclear Regulatory Commission,
381, 383
Nuclear weapons, 470–471
arms agreement with Russia, 485
arms agreement with Soviet
Union, 485
Iran and nuclear proliferation,
470–471
North Korea and nuclear
proliferation, 471
stockpiles, 470

O

Obama, Barack, 13, 261
Afghanistan and, 469
African American support of, 181
appointments, to Supreme
Court, 157
Arab Spring, 465
armed forces ordered by
additional troops to
Afghanistan, 351
air strikes in Libya, 351, 478, 481
Biden as vice president, 366
big government and, 15, 16
birth certificate of, 345
contraception insurance, 195–196
corporations and campaign
financing, 221
curbing NSA data collection, 410
death of bin Laden, 469–470
debt-ceiling crisis, 240, 338
deficit spending and, 450
election of 2008, 15, 143
cultural divisions within
Democratic Party and, 244
economy and, 240

gender gap, 182
Hispanic vote and, 181, 254
online fund-raising, 298
popular vote margin, 240
public financing, 270
votes by groups, 178
election of 2012, 16
debates, 298
gender gap, 182
online fund-raising, 298
popular vote for, 240–241
predicted margin of victory, 187
socioeconomic status and cultural
politics, 243
urban-rural split and geographic
region, 181
votes by groups, 178
election-year budget, 336
enemy combatants, 411
energy policies, 444–445
on entitlement programs, 17
European debt crisis, 477
Executive Office of the
President, 364
executive orders, 361
false beliefs about, 246
federalism and, 95
foreign nations' opinion of U.S.
and, 194
as fund-raiser, 357
gay men and lesbians in military, 160
health care reform, 15, 16, 435–437
higher fuel efficiency standards, 444
immigration reform, 439–440
ISIS and, 469
Israeli-Palestinian negotiations
attempted by, 474–475
judicial appointment, 417, 418
Keynesian economics and, 449
Libya and War Powers
Resolution, 481
limiting greenhouse gas
emissions, 446
lobbyists in administration, 223
minimum wage, 202
monetary policy and, 452
national security adviser, 479
New START Treaty, 353
plan to end governmental
inefficiency, 375
public opinion and, 357–358
reregulation, 384
Russia and New START Treaty, 485
sent National Guard to Mexican
border, 351

signing statements and, 362
stimulus plan, 15, 449
waterboarding and, 480
whistleblowers, 393
younger voters to Democratic
Party, 177
Obamacare. *See* Affordable Care Act
Obscenity, 113–114
definitional problem, 113–114
pornography on Internet, 114
protecting children, 114
Occupational Safety and Health
Act, 393
Occupational Safety and Health
Administration, 393
O'Connor, Sandra Day, 157, 417,
420–421
Office-block ballot, 277
Office of Management and Budget
(OMB), 334, 364, 365
Office of National Drug Control
Policy, 364
Office of Personnel Management
(OPM), 388
Office of Science and
Technology, 364
Office of Special Counsel (OSC), 391
Office of the Attorney General, 376
Office of the Director of National
Intelligence, 480
Office of the President, 364
Office of the United States Trade
Representative, 364
Office of the Vice President, 364
Ogden, Aaron, 86
Oil industry
BP oil spill, 384, 445
China's demand for, 472
fracking, 444
high prices and new
production, 444
natural gas supplies
domestically, 444
politics of expensive oil, 444–445
U.S. dependency on foreign
oil, 443
Oklahoma City bombing, 410
Oligarchy, 7
Oliver, In re, 105
Olson, Mancur, 204–205
Ombudsperson, 314
Open primaries, 274
Opinion leaders
influence of, 175
radio talk show hosts, 231

INDEX **I-21**